A Remarkable Medicine Has Been Overlooked
WITH A LETTER TO PRESIDENT REAGAN

A Remarkable Medicine Has Been Overlooked

WITH

A LETTER TO PRESIDENT REAGAN

by Jack Dreyfus

SIMON AND SCHUSTER   NEW YORK

Copyright © 1970, 1975, 1981 by Dreyfus Medical Foundation
All rights reserved
including the right of reproduction, in whole or in part in any form
Published by Simon and Schuster, A Division of Gulf & Western Corporation
Simon & Schuster Building
Rockefeller Center, 1230 Avenue of the Americas
New York, New York 10020
SIMON and SCHUSTER and colophon are trademarks of Simon & Schuster
Manufactured in the United States of America
Printed and bound by R. R. Donnelley & Sons
1 3 5 7 9 10 8 6 4 2

Library of Congress Cataloging in Publication Data

Dreyfus, Jack, 1913–
A remarkable medicine has been overlooked.

Bibliography: p.
Includes index.
1. Phenytoin.   2. Dreyfus, Jack 1913–
3. Depression, Mental —Biography.   4. Philanthropists
—United States—Biography.   I. Title.   [DNLM:
1. Phenytoin. QV 85 D778r]
RM666.P58D73   615′.784   81-9275
AACR2

ISBN 0-671-49052-4

*This book is dedicated to
Mark Twain, to Helen Raudonat, and to Johnny.*

I express deep appreciation, for their friendship and help, to:

DR. J. ANTONIO ALDRETE

DR. WALTER C. ALVAREZ

DR. NATASHA P. BECHTEREVA

DR. LAWRENCE G. BODKIN

DR. SAMUEL BOGOCH

JAMES H. CAVANAUGH

DR. JONATHAN O. COLE

DR. THEODORE COOPER

DR. STUART W. COSGRIFF

DR. JOSE M. R. DELGADO

DR. CHARLES EDWARDS

DR. JOEL ELKES

HON. JOHN W. GARDNER

DR. ELI GOLDENSOHN

DR. PAUL GORDON

DR. LIONEL R. C. HAWARD

DR. RICHARD H. HELFANT

DR. A. D. JONAS

DR. PAUL L. KORNBLITH

DR. HERBERT L. LEY

STUART W. LITTLE

DAVID B. LOVELAND

ALBERT Q. MAISEL

VIVIAN J. McDERMOTT

PROF. RODOLFO PAOLETTI

DR. TRACY J. PUTNAM

DR. OSCAR RESNICK

HON. ELLIOT L. RICHARDSON

HON. NELSON A. ROCKEFELLER

ALBERT ROSENFELD

DR. LAWRENCE C. SCHINE

DR. ALEXANDER M. SCHMIDT

DR. MAXIMILIAN SILBERMANN

HOWARD STEIN

DR. ALFRED STEINER

DR. JOSEPH H. STEPHENS

DR. PETER SUCKLING

DR. WILLIAM H. SWEET

DR. WALTER R. TKACH

DR. WILLIAM J. TURNER

HON. CASPAR W. WEINBERGER

CONTENTS

* Originally published in 1970 in somewhat different form.
† Originally published in 1975 in somewhat different form.

Terminology

The drug that is the subject of this book is known by two generic names, diphenylhydantoin and phenytoin. Diphenylhydantoin (DPH) is used in this book.

DPH's best known trade name in the United States is Dilantin. Other trade names, outside the United States, are Epanutin, Epamin, Eplin, Idantoin, Aleviatan.

Medical Contents of This Book

The medical information in the second part of this book, condensed from the literature by the Dreyfus Medical Foundation, is published here as a service to physicians and other health professionals.

Prescription Medicine

DPH is a prescription medicine, which means it should be obtained through a physician. Nothing in this book should be mistaken to suggest that it be obtained in any other way.

TO THE READER

DEAR READER:

In 1963 a great piece of luck led me to try a medicine that was not supposed to be useful for symptoms I had. It took me out of a miserable condition. When I saw others have similar benefits, I had the responsibility of getting the facts to the medical profession. This was not as easy to do as I thought. A medical foundation was established. Soon it became apparent that the medicine had been overlooked for a wide variety of disorders.

This book begins with a letter to President Reagan in which this matter is outlined, and his help is sought. The rest of the book is divided into two parts. The first part, a narrative, describes my personal experiences with this medicine. The second part, medical and scientific, contains two bibliographies, *The Broad Range of Use of Diphenylhydantoin,* published in 1970, and *DPH, 1975,* prepared by the Dreyfus Medical Foundation and sent to physicians in the United States. In addition there is a review of recent studies.

For eight years, from 1966 through 1973, I did all I could to awaken the Federal government to its obvious responsibilities in this matter—with little success. When the second bibliography had been sent to the physicians, it seemed that all a private foundation could do had been done. And there was progress, but it was slow. Something was wrong.

It's a national pastime to look for culprits. I looked for culprits but I didn't find individual ones. It took me a long time to realize that the culprit was a flaw in our system of bringing prescription medicines to the public.

The only option left was for me to write about my experiences and explain the flaw in our system—for the public, the physician, and health officials, all at the same time. That might get something done.

The letter to President Reagan is a genuine letter to him,

not just my notion of how to start a book. When a matter of great import comes up that cannot be taken care of by government routine it must go to the President. His office has the flexibility, and the authority to get things done, that no other office has.

Nowadays, when you start to read a book, a hand reaches out of the TV set and takes it off your lap. Since this book is about health, you might consider cracking the hand across the knuckles and keep on reading.

Good luck,

JACK DREYFUS

DREYFUS MEDICAL FOUNDATION
767 FIFTH AVENUE
NEW YORK, NEW YORK 10022

The President
The White House
Washington, D. C.

DEAR MR. PRESIDENT:

I write you about a matter of such urgency and importance that it requires the attention of your office.

The properties of a remarkable and versatile medicine are being overlooked because of a flaw in our system of bringing medicines to the public. This is to the great detriment of the health of the American public, and millions of people suffer because of it. This tragic condition can be remedied—almost overnight.

This letter is meant as a briefing, Mr. President. Material outlined in it will be expanded on elsewhere.

The medicine is a prescription medicine. Its best known trade name is Dilantin; generic, diphenylhydantoin (DPH). The first disorder for which it was found useful was epilepsy. This was in 1938. In those days it was customary to think of a single drug for a single disorder, and DPH promptly got the tag "anti-convulsant."

Since this early discovery, over a thousand medical studies have demonstrated DPH to be one of the most widely useful drugs in our pharmacopoeia. Yet today, forty-one years later, DPH's only listed indication-of-use with the Food and Drug Administration is as an anticonvulsant. This description is accurate but tragically inadequate—and plays a major role in the misunderstanding of DPH by the medical profession.

It should be emphasized that this is not the fault of the FDA.

Two lists have been placed in the Appendix (p. 137) for your convenience. If you will glance at them now, it will give you an idea of the breadth of use of DPH. One list is comprised of over fifty symptoms and disorders for which DPH has been reported effective.* The other list shows the names of over 150 medical journals, published throughout the world, in which these studies have appeared.

When we see the number of symptoms and disorders for which DPH has been found therapeutic, our credulity is strained. Nothing could be that good, we say. But then we look closer, and we reevaluate. In number the studies are overwhelming—and not having been sponsored by a drug company they were spontaneous and independent, the authors' only motivation being scientific interest and a desire to help others.

A brief discussion of the basic mechanisms of action of diphenylhydantoin will be helpful here. A general property of DPH is that it stabilizes inappropriate electrical activity in the body, even at the level of the single cell. When we consider that all our body functions are electrically regulated, our messages of pain are electrically referred, and our thinking processes are electrically conducted, it makes it easier to understand DPH's breadth of use.

Although DPH corrects inappropriate electrical activity, in therapeutic amounts it does not affect normal function. Thus it can calm without sedation and effect a return of energy without artificial stimulation. DPH is not habit-forming, and its parameters of safety have been established over a forty-year period.

You may ask, Mr. President, why I haven't brought this matter to the Department of Health or the Food and Drug Administration. Well that was the first thing I thought of years ago.

* New uses continue to be reported.

And for eight years I spent an eternity with officials in government, being shuffled back and forth from one to another with encouragement and even compliments. During this period I saw three secretaries of HEW, two assistant secretaries of HEW, two commissioners of the FDA, members of the staff of the FDA, a surgeon general, and other officials.

It took me a long time to realize this was the wrong approach. Although everyone agreed that something should be done, no official seemed to think he had the authority or responsibility to get it done. (See Travels with the Government, Chapter 9.)

About the flaw in our system for bringing prescription medicines to the public:

Years ago doctors concocted their own remedies, but that's in the past. Today the origination of new drugs is left to the drug companies—motivated by that reliable incentive, the desire to make profits. Between the public and the drug company is the FDA.

The FDA was set up to do for many individuals what they could not do for themselves. Although its broad purpose was to protect and improve the health of our citizens, it was set up as a defensive agency, to protect against ineffective drugs and those more dangerous than therapeutic.

Since 1938 drug companies have been required to seek approval from the FDA as to the safety of new drugs and, since 1962, approval of both safety and effectiveness. When an FDA listing is granted it entitles a company to advertise and promote a drug for the purposes for which it has been approved. If the drug sells well the company has a good thing. Patent protection gives up to seventeen years of exclusive use. During this period profit margins are high. When patents expire, competition comes in and drives the price down. Thus financial incentive to look for a new drug is far greater than it is to look for new uses of an old drug.

Patents on DPH expired in 1963—and much of the incentive to do research on the drug expired at the same time. It should be noted that Parke-Davis, the company that had the patents on DPH, did not synthesize the drug and physicians outside the company discovered it to be therapeutic. There is reason to believe that Parke-Davis never understood their own product. In addition to no patent incentive, this could be a reason they have not applied to the FDA for new uses.*

The public's access to a prescription medicine is through the physician. Physicians get their information about prescription medicines from the drug companies, through advertisements and salesmen, and from the *Physicians' Desk Reference,* which carries only those uses for a drug that are listed with the FDA.

One can see how an FDA listing may carry more weight than is intended. In fact some people think of the lack of FDA approval as the equivalent of FDA disapproval. This is clearly wrong. How could the FDA disapprove a use for a drug if it hasn't even had an application for it?

Let's look at the overall picture. Doctors were taught that DPH is an anticonvulsant. The usual sources that the doctors rely on for prescription medicines only indicate that DPH is an anticonvulsant. Is it any wonder that doctors have DPH out of perspective, and that as far as the public is concerned many of the benefits of DPH might as well not exist?

It is apparent that no drug company is going to apply for new uses of DPH. The clock has run down on that probability. Perhaps the FDA does not have a specific means to reach out for this medicine. But since the FDA's broad purpose is to protect the health of the American public, the neglect of a remarkable drug should be in its province, and a means should be found.

A simple solution would be to put the matter in the hands of those qualified—the 350,000 physicians in this country. The FDA could address itself to the basic mechanisms of action of DPH and list it as a substance effective in the stabilization of

* One exception, see Chapter 11, p. 112.

bioelectrical activity, and refer the physicians to the literature of their colleagues. There are other solutions. The fact is any official nod from the FDA to the physician would let the light from under the bushel, and DPH would find its own level, pragmatically, by its use vis-à-vis other medicines.

Mr. President, this letter is a public one because it is also meant for government officials in health as well as for physicians and the public. The information in this book, for all to see at the same time, should be helpful if you decide to use the influence of your office in this matter. I hope you will. I think you will.

Respectfully,

Jack Dreyfus

Dreyfus Medical Foundation

Part One: Narrative

Experiences with a Remarkable Drug

1.
FROM INSIDE
A DEPRESSION

Until I was in my forties, I never really thought about my nerves—a sure symptom of a person with good nerves. I was president of the Dreyfus Fund and a partner in Dreyfus & Co., with responsibilities in research, in sales, and in management. People would ask, "How do you do all the things you do?" "How do you stand the strain?" I hardly understood the question because at the time I felt no strain.

Sometime in my forty-third year I became aware of a change in myself. At partners' meetings, which I'd used to enjoy, I began to notice that my patience was shorter and I was anxious for the meetings to end. Occasionally I felt a trembling inside me that I didn't understand. On weekend trips to the country it had been my habit to read or take a nap in the car. These trips had been relaxing, but they weren't anymore. My mind would become occupied with pessimistic and aggravating thoughts, thoughts I couldn't turn off.

In 1957 I had spent a few trying weeks with a problem in the stock market. It was resolved successfully, but I had been under a good deal of pressure and needed a vacation. I went to Miami and stayed at the Roney Plaza, a nice old-fashioned hotel that I had visited many times before. Usually after a day or two, with the sun and salt water, I would unwind and relax. But this time I didn't relax.

Some premonition made me invite a good friend, Howard Stein, to come down and join me. Howard accepted, and the next day he was at the Roney. Two days later my depression started.

• • •

I awoke at six o'clock in the morning in a state bordering on terror. The early sun was shining, and the birds were singing. In my room at the Roney I was in the safest of surroundings. Yet I was overwhelmed with fear. The fear couldn't have been greater if a tiger had been clawing at the door. I knew there wasn't any tiger, and common sense told me I was safe. But common sense wasn't in charge—fear was. The fear was so great I was afraid to be alone. I called Howard, at that early hour, and asked if he would come to my room. When he got there I told him I knew it didn't make any sense but I was afraid to be alone.

Howard arranged for me to see a doctor, and a few hours later we were in his office. The doctor said, "Miami is the right place for you. Get some sun, go swimming, play a little golf or tennis, and relax." Normally this would have sounded great. But now this advice didn't seem right, and at two o'clock that afternoon I was on a plane back to New York. Although it was a Saturday and I wouldn't see my doctor until Monday, I hoped more familiar surroundings would make me feel better.

I still remember that trip. The plane was half-filled and I had a seat in a row by myself. Even with a dozen or more people in the plane I felt alone, and was afraid. I wanted to ask one of the stewardesses to sit next to me and keep me company, but I didn't because I thought it would be misunderstood. I couldn't tell a stewardess that I was afraid to sit by myself.

My former wife, Joan Personette, one of my closest friends, met me at the plane, and I spent the weekend at her home in Harrison, New York. It was difficult to explain to Joan how frightened I was. My brain was filled with fearful thoughts I couldn't turn off. Saturday night I slept little. Sunday we went out in the cold weather and roasted hot dogs over a fire—something I'd always enjoyed. But this didn't help. The intense fear never left.

On Monday morning I saw Alfred Steiner, my family physician. He sent me to a neuropsychiatrist, Dr. Maximilian Silbermann. The first question I asked was, "Have I gone crazy?" I'd never had an experience like this—intense fear without apparent cause. And my mood was so pessimistic that the worst seemed plausible. Dr. Silbermann assured me that I was sane but said he thought I was depressed. I remember that he said, "When people are insane, they may think others are a little off, but they rarely question their own sanity."

That first day Dr. Silbermann asked me what I liked to do, what I really enjoyed. I told him that going to the racetrack was something I enjoyed a lot. He said, "Well, why don't you go to the races tomorrow? Don't worry about business." He suggested that I not be alone and have someone spend the night with me in my apartment.

The next day I intended to go to the races. But I didn't. They had no appeal for me, and even seemed a problem. That day, when I saw him for the second time, Dr. Silbermann diagnosed my condition as an endogenous depression. He explained that endogenous meant "coming from within," and he differentiated it from a reactive depression, one with an outside cause. He assured me that this condition was temporary and that I would come out of the depression. He said he didn't know how long it would take; it could be gradual or it could happen suddenly. Being told this was important to me intellectually, but emotionally I had a hard time believing it.

That was the beginning of a long and close relationship with Dr. Silbermann. For the next few years I was to see him five or six times a week. From the start Dr. Silbermann told me that good sleep was important for my condition and prescribed sleeping medication. With the help of this medicine I slept soundly, and the benefits of sleep carried over. In the morning I was at my best. As the day wore on my mind became busier and busier with worries and fears, and occasional angry thoughts. Frequently around dusk a little depressive cloud would descend upon me; I would tremble and my hands and feet would get cold.

Seeing Dr. Silbermann almost every day was important to

me. In his warm office, with his friendliness and willingness to listen, I would unburden my brain of the thoughts that were tormenting me. But intense fear persisted for almost a year. During that period I was afraid to be alone, and I arranged for my housekeeper to spend the night at my apartment.

Of course I had my business responsibilities, and I asked Dr. Silbermann what to do about them. He told me that people misunderstood depressions, and it might be best not to tell any-one about it. He suggested that I leave it vague and say I would be away from the office for a period of time. But this was in conflict with my sense of responsibility, and I didn't feel right about it. Mark Twain advised, "When in doubt, tell the truth." So I told the truth to my partners and asked them to run things without me for a while. Although I was not aware of feeling better, a realistic source of worry was removed.

Dr. Silbermann advised me to try to get out of the house and keep myself occupied, as long as I could do things that were not abrasive to me. I visited museums. One of my main haunts was the Museum of Modern Art and I had many lunches in the cafeteria there. I became friends with the paintings and with the sculptures in the backyard. The attention I gave these pleasing objects was helpful in taking attention off myself. I had similar benefits from the Central Park Zoo where I spent time with the seals, polar bears, and other nice creatures.

I tried to avoid things that would upset me. I found that my mind would magnify the slightest unpleasantness by some large multiple. Newscasts were anathema to me and I couldn't listen to them. If a busload of children overturned in Nevada the news would be dragged fresh and gory to our attention in New York. I quickly learned that the news, with its disaster du jour, made things worse. One piece of news I couldn't avoid was the dog in the Sputnik space capsule. I couldn't get it out of my mind, and I suffered with thoughts of that dog for many weeks.

I gave up watching movies on television. There'd be some sad theme or violent incident that would upset me, and the image of it would stick in my head. I had a similar problem with most books. One author I could always read was Mark Twain. I'm sure I missed many of his subtleties but he never dragged me through unpleasantness.

When I'd been in the depression for about six months Dr. Silbermann asked me if I thought it might make me feel better to be in a hospital. I said I didn't know but I was willing to try it. So he got me a room at the Harkness Pavilion of Presbyterian Hospital. In the room I noticed that the windows were discreetly barred, and I asked the nurse about this. She explained that sometimes deeply depressed persons had to be protected from themselves.

Fortunately I was not classified as deeply depressed. I had outpatient privileges and walked in the neighborhood a few hours each day. It was cold and I would have a bowl of hot soup in a nice little corner restaurant. During the walks I had plenty of time to think. The conversation with the nurse reminded me that Dr. Silbermann had once tactfully brought up the subject of suicide. Now I gave it honest thought and realized I'd never considered it. Not that life seemed that desirable. At that time everyone was talking about the next rocket to the moon, the first to carry men. In my mood I thought chances for success were almost nil. But I remember thinking if a high authority told me it was for the good of the country I might be willing to make the trip.

After three days in the hospital, not feeling better or worse, I returned home. Each day Dr. Silbermann and I talked over my, mostly imagined, problems. Part of me knew that some of the worries were not logical, but the rest of me couldn't feel it. Max cautioned me not to make any major business decisions while I was depressed because my perspective would be out of kilter. This was good advice. The Dreyfus Fund was small at the time, but quite successful, and the only problems it had were the healthy ones connected with growth. Yet on more than one occasion I wished I could give the Fund away.

My apartment was just a few blocks from Dr. Silbermann's office. Often I would leave for my appointment as much as an hour early and kill time by walking. I usually felt cold, and would seek the sunny side of the street. After the appointment, if it was daylight, I would walk in Central Park. I would still try to stay in the sun. As the shadows moved across the park I would walk faster to keep ahead of them.

During these walks I used to think about my condition. I was aware of daily headaches, frequent stomach irregularity, chronic neck pain, and lack of energy. But my dominant symptom was a turned-on mind that never gave me rest and was always occupied with negative thoughts related to anger and fear. And the fear was the worst.

When you have fear in you, you'll find something to be afraid of or to worry about, even if you have to make it up. This happened to me all the time. I'll give two illustrations.

One day, on Madison Avenue, I saw a woman looking at a dress in a small shop. She seemed to be looking at it longingly, as though she wanted it but couldn't afford it. I felt unhappy for her. The dress looked so old-fashioned and unattractive it made me feel even sadder. Now this woman was a complete stranger. For all I knew she might have been able to buy that block of Madison Avenue. But my mood made me decide she couldn't afford the dress. This unhappy picture stuck in my brain and bothered me for days.

Another incident occurred at a cocktail party. One of the guests, a young girl of seventeen, was introduced as the daughter of a well-known movie actress. She mentioned that she would have to leave in a little while because she was taking dancing lessons. The girl seemed plain-looking and I felt sad for her. I knew she didn't have a chance to be successful, and was trying to follow in her mother's footsteps because it was the thing to do. When she left, she kissed us all good-bye. She'd even adopted Hollywood ways, and this made me feel even sadder. I worried about this poor girl for many days. It wasn't really necessary— the "poor girl" was Liza Minnelli.

It is almost impossible to convey to a person who has not had a depression what one is like. It's not obvious like a broken arm, or a fever, or a cough; it's beneath the surface. A depressed person suffers a type of anguish which in its own way can be as painful as anything that can happen to a human being. He has varying degrees of fear throughout the day, and a brain that permits him no rest and races with agitated and frightening thoughts. His mood is low, he has little energy, and he can hardly remember what pleasure means. He's in another country, using a different language. When he uses words such as "worry" and "afraid" he may be expressing deep distress. But these words seem mild to the person whose mood is all right.

• • •

The deepest part of my depression lasted for about a year. Then it lessened gradually and there were periods of improvement. These better periods alternated with periods of mild depression for the next few years. "Mild" depression is plenty unpleasant, but I use the term to distinguish it from severe depression.

It began to look as if chronic depressive periods might be with me for life. Then I had an incredible piece of luck.

2.
AN INCREDIBLE
PIECE OF LUCK

Dr. Silbermann and I had numerous discussions about why I was depressed, without reaching any conclusions. There was a theory, proffered by relatives of mine in Boston, that I was neurotic and needed to be psychoanalyzed. Dr. Silbermann didn't agree that psychoanalysis was what I needed, and as a practical matter felt that it would be too arduous while I was depressed.

On my own, as objectively as I could, I considered my relatives' suggestion. I didn't question that I was neurotic. But I didn't see how that could be the answer. Presumably I'd been neurotic before the depression, yet my nerves had been fine.

I began to notice that changes in my mood frequently occurred without apparent environmental or psychological cause. And the same stimulus didn't always evoke the same response. Sometimes, while driving in the country, I would see a dead woodchuck on the side of the road. The sight would hit me like a blow and I couldn't get it out of my mind. But on other occasions I'd see a dead woodchuck and react in what seemed a normal way. The difference in reactions couldn't be caused by my being neurotic; my childhood from one to five hadn't changed. It seemed plausible that these disparate reactions were due to changes in my body.

I discussed this with Dr. Silbermann, and he was inclined to go along with the idea that there might be something wrong in my body "chemistry." But Max said that he didn't really know, and emphasized that when he said "chemistry," he was using the word in quotes.

· · ·

One night, a seemingly insignificant incident started a chain of events that changed my life. A young woman took my hand and massaged my fingers. I was full of tension at the time. As she pressed my fingertips I felt the tension slip away, and I had the feeling that electricity was going out of my body. This didn't make sense to me. I'd never heard of electricity in the body—but the impression was strong. The next day, a Sunday, the impression of electricity was still with me.

It's a misconception, I believe, that we originate ideas. I used to think we did, but I don't anymore. Too often I find my brain does what it wants—it's on automatic pilot most of the time. That was the case this particular Sunday because, without instruction from me, my brain went into its files and came up with three experiences I'd had with electricity. The first went back almost forty years.

One. When I was a little boy I saw a brass plate with a hole in it, in the baseboard. It aroused my curiosity. I stuck my finger in the hole—and my curiosity was satisfied. The electric shock I got, and the sudden, intense fear that came with it, were indelibly impressed on my memory. I remember that after the shock I had a flat, metallic taste in my mouth.

Two. I had gone into the garage with my former wife to get the car. I picked up an old vacuum cleaner, to get it out of the way, and received an electrical jolt. I said to Joan, "This damn thing shocked me."

"It always does that," she said quietly.

At this calm appraisal I exploded. "What do you mean, 'It always does that!' " and I took Joan by the shoulders and shook her. This was so unlike me that I felt my explosion of anger had been caused by the electricity.

Three. On two successive nights I'd had the same frightening dream, or was it a dream? Each of these nights, before going to sleep, I had intense feelings of fear. The "dreams" occurred early in the morning. I felt that I was awake and couldn't open my eyes. I tried to reach for the table light but couldn't move—in the dream I felt I was frozen with electricity.

Each of these experiences with electricity was associated with a symptom of my depression. As I reviewed them, side by side so to speak, they seemed to be related. Numbers one and three made a connection between electricity and fear. Number two connected electricity with anger. And number one also made a connection with the metallic taste in my mouth which I associated with fear.

The logic of these connections was not clear then. But the pieces held together well enough for me to say to myself, When I see Max on Monday I am going to bring up the subject of electricity.

That Monday my appointment with Dr. Silbermann was after dinner, around ten o'clock. I had some "problems" that I wanted to talk out. It wasn't until late in the hour that I brought up the subject of electricity. I said to Max, "You know, I think my problem is electricity, and electricity causes some people to get depressed, others to bump themselves off, and others to go crazy." I said this as though I meant it, but actually I had little conviction.

At that moment my brain jumped back twenty years to a bridge tournament. My partner and I had got the best of two hands, and one of our opponents, a famous player, P. Hal Sims, made some pointed remarks to his partner. I noticed the partner's neck getting red. As we moved to the next table there was a commotion, and I turned and saw the man on the floor, having convulsions. Someone said he was having an epileptic attack. Now, as I thought back to the attack, the convulsions looked like they had been caused by a series of electrical shocks.

I continued with my hypothesis and said, "And some people have an electrical explosion which we call epilepsy." Max said, "It's curious that you mention epilepsy. We know from brain wave tests that the epileptic has a problem with his body electricity." This was the first time I'd heard that there was such a thing as body electricity. Also, connecting the epileptic to an electrical problem was a direct hit. When I'd started the discussion I thought the odds were 10,000-to-1 against me. But now the odds dropped sharply, and they were realistic enough to make the subject worth pursuing.

I knew a girl who'd had an epileptic attack when she was six. She was now fifteen and seemed to be leading a normal and happy life. She had been given a medicine for her epilepsy and I asked Dr. Silbermann what it was. He told me it was Dilantin.

"Well, why don't I try that?" I asked.

I didn't realize then how crucial Max's answer would be for me. He could easily have said no—and that might have been the end of it. But he said, "You can try it if you like. I don't think it will do you any good, but it won't do you any harm."

That night Max gave me a prescription for Dilantin and told me of an all-night drugstore where I could fill it. He suggested that I take 100 mg before going to bed and skip my sleeping pill. He thought the Dilantin might put me to sleep.

I followed instructions. Around midnight I took 100 mg of Dilantin, and no sleeping pill. Apparently I was dependent on the sleeping medication because when I went to bed I promptly fell awake. Before I finally got to sleep at four in the morning, I thought, this medicine is a flop. Not until years later did it occur to me that I would not have lain quietly in bed for four hours if I'd had my usual fears. I'd have gotten up and taken the sleeping medicine.

I awoke at eight the next morning and, as Dr. Silbermann had instructed me, took another 100 mg of Dilantin. I had missed half a night's sleep. Sleep was so important that when I saw Max that afternoon, I started to tell him the Dilantin didn't work. Max said, "But you look better than you did yesterday." Then I looked at myself and realized that in spite of the loss of sleep I felt much better. We agreed that I should continue the Dilantin.

The following morning, according to routine, I called Dr. Silbermann. I couldn't make an appointment to see him because I was going to be too busy that day. The next day I was too busy again. The third day, when I was going to make the same excuse,

I realized that I wasn't too busy. I was ducking the appointment. It was the first time in five years that I didn't feel a need to see Max.

I saw Dr. Silbermann only three more times in his office. My need for psychotherapy was gone, and we just talked as friends. Max told me he had never heard of DPH being used for the purposes I was using it. And he was a close friend of Dr. Houston Merritt, of Putnam and Merritt, who, twenty years earlier, had discovered the first clinical use for Dilantin. So for a while we were waiting for the phenomenon to go away. At least I'm pretty sure Max was. Intellectually I was too. But my feelings told me things were all right.

On my last visit Max gave me a renewable prescription for DPH. I haven't seen him as a patient since. We've stayed the closest of friends, and frequently have dinner together to swap lies and trade psychotherapy.

From the day I took Dilantin my major symptoms of distress disappeared. I noticed fundamental differences. My brain, which had been overactive and filled with negative thoughts, was calmer and functioned as it did before the depression. The headaches, the stomach distress, the neck pain all disappeared. And my patience returned. I enjoyed partners' meetings again and could sit back and observe someone else getting impatient, which was a switch.

Before taking Dilantin I'd been so tired and worn out I just dragged myself around. Although DPH had a calming effect on me, to my surprise it didn't slow me down. On the contrary my energy returned full force. It was as though the energy that had been wasted in my overactive brain was made available for healthier purposes.

I didn't realize it right away, but my good health had returned. I was neither tranquil nor ecstatic. I was just all right. For the first time in my life I realized how good you feel when you feel "all right."

3.
NEW EVIDENCE
AND A BROADENING
PERSPECTIVE

What had happened to me doesn't happen in real life. You just don't ask your doctor to let you try one drug, out of a pharmacopoeia of tens of thousands, and find that it works. But this did happen. And it happened so casually, in such a matter-of-fact way, that the vast improbability of it didn't occur to me at the time.

Being of the human race, I naturally returned to routine. Much of my new energy went back into the Dreyfus Fund and Dreyfus & Co., as though I were trying to make up for lost time. Still, much of my thinking was on DPH and the intriguing puzzle it presented. There were many questions to be answered.

The first question was whether DPH had been the cause of my return to health. My body might have been due for a recovery and a coincidence could have occurred. But this question was soon answered in the affirmative because I was able to observe benefits from DPH an hour after taking it. A second question, about the safety of the medicine, was answered by Dr. Silbermann. He told me it had side effects but they were rarely serious, and it had been tested by time, millions of people having taken it daily for many years. A question that could not be answered right away was whether the benefits of DPH would last. But as months went by, and I continued to feel well, I gained confidence they would last.

The most important question was a broader question. Could

DPH help others as it had helped me? It seemed highly improbable. How could important uses for a medicine be overlooked for twenty years? It didn't make sense, it seemed almost impossible. But if it were so, I clearly had an obligation to do something about it. I needed more facts.

In the course of the next year I was to get more facts. During this period I saw six people in succession benefit from DPH. I wasn't looking for these cases. They just happened in front of my eyes, so to speak. Each of the six cases was impressive. But the first two, because they were the first two, had the most significance and will be described in some detail.

• • •

The first person I saw benefit from Dilantin was my housekeeper Kathleen Fenyvessy. A month after I had started taking DPH I noticed that Kathleen was not her usual self and seemed depressed. Normally she was energetic but now she seemed worn out. Kathleen, who had recently come from Hungary, spoke imperfect English, and I was in the habit of talking slowly to her. Now she would interrupt before I could finish a sentence, saying, "I understand, I understand"—and most of the time she didn't. Obviously she was extremely impatient.

I asked her what was wrong. She told me her mind was busy with miserable thoughts and she couldn't stop them. She'd seen several physicians and they'd told her she was having a nervous breakdown. She'd tried a variety of medicines that hadn't helped. I thought of DPH. There seemed little to be lost, and much to be gained, by her trying it—if Dr. Silbermann agreed. At my suggestion Kathleen visited him. After considering her condition he prescribed 100 mg a day for her.

Since I saw Kathleen at least a few hours every day, I was in a good position to observe the effects of DPH. Within a day or two it was apparent that her good disposition had returned. And she was full of energy again. As for patience, she no longer interrupted me in mid-sentence. I could even tell her the same thing twice.

Kathleen found her recovery hard to believe. In a letter to her sister describing it, she said, "It was due to a medicine used for an entirely different disorder. If someone else had told me they'd had an experience like this I would not have believed it."

About a month after Kathleen had started taking DPH, she and I participated in an unplanned experiment. Without consulting each other, we both stopped taking DPH for three days. We had gone to Hobeau Farm in Ocala, Florida, a thoroughbred breeding farm managed by Elmer Heubeck, my good friend and partner in the farm. It was pure vacation for Kathleen. Except for the horse business it was vacation for me too.

At that time I thought Dilantin only helped me with stress and problems. By problems I really meant areas of interest. They were not always problems; when they went well they could be pleasures. But the negative mood that I had been in made me think of them as problems. I had five such interests, some of a business nature, some personal. I went over them; they were all in good shape. So it seemed to me that in the nice relaxed atmosphere of the farm, I wouldn't need DPH. I stopped taking it.

The third day off DPH I felt a certain tingling in my nerves. I remember a funny expression entering my mind, that I had "worry gnats." I thought maybe I'd feel better if I went to Miami, played some tennis and swam in the salt water. So I made arrangements to take a plane to Miami at eleven o'clock that night.

That afternoon I said something to Kathleen. It might not have been as tactful as it should have been, but it couldn't possibly have called for the response that it got. Kathleen burst out crying. I was astonished. Then something occurred to me, and I asked, "Kathleen, have you stopped taking DPH?" She said she had; she'd thought it would be so nice on the farm she didn't bring any. "Why didn't you take some of mine?" I asked. She said she hadn't because she'd noticed I had only a few capsules left. Before I left for Miami, Elmer told me he would arrange for Kathleen to get DPH.

At 11 P.M. I got on the plane to Miami. Now I was quite

conscious of the "worry gnats," and I thought of DPH. I figured it wouldn't help since I didn't have any stress or problems. But something inside me said, Well, you're research-minded. Why don't you take some anyway and see if anything happens. My bags were accessible on the plane and I went forward and got a capsule of Dilantin. I took it and looked at my watch. In a little while I thought I felt better, but I wasn't sure. I checked the time; it was twenty-eight minutes since I'd taken the medicine. When the plane arrived in Miami it was an hour since I'd taken the Dilantin. The "worry gnats" were gone. As I walked through the airport I had the nicest feeling that peace had descended on me.

The next morning I called Kathleen. Even before I could ask how she felt, her cheerful voice gave the answer.

Kathleen's experience and my own, in stopping DPH and recontinuing it, confirmed our need for the medicine, and seemed to indicate this need was not based on realistic problems, but on something in our nervous systems at the time.

Now I was in Miami again. I had gone there for the last few years on doctor's orders. These trips were meant to be vacations, but there had been no fun in them. When a vacation is not in you, you don't have one. But now I was on vacation and in a frame of mind to enjoy it. I still stayed at the lovely, dilapidated old Roney Plaza. Everything was beautiful—the air, the sea, just walking to breakfast. I was happy. And I know why. As Mark Twain said in "Captain Stormfield's Visit to Heaven," "Happiness ain't a thing in itself—it's only a *contrast* with something that ain't pleasant." I had the contrast.

Tennis was a pleasure again. I had taken up tennis about eight years earlier, mostly for the exercise. Golf had been my game since childhood and I'd loved it. I'd been almost a fine golfer, won lots of club championships, and at my best had a one handicap. But in recent years golf had started to bore me. Maybe it was my perfectionism. More likely it was the long walks between shots when all that was going on was the windmills of my mind.

I had started playing tennis with the local pros at the Roney

Plaza. At this time Marse Fink was pro of record. Sol Goldman was pro emeritus. I didn't play with the pros to get lessons. I'd had barrels of lessons in golf and I looked forward to doing everything wrong in tennis.

We got up all sorts of games and bet on them all. They gave me large handicaps. Sometimes Marse and Sol played doubles against me and some bum they got as my partner. Sol and Marse were good friends, but if the match got close, they were not loath to comment on each other's play. They called each other names their mothers hadn't taught them. I'd get so interested in their descriptions of each other that I would lose my concentration— and they'd usually win. On the rare occasions they lost, Marse would go to his desk in the tennis shop and mutter to himself, so we could all hear, "I'll never play with that son-of-a-bitch [Sol] again." And he never did—until three o'clock the next afternoon.

Sol and Marse never beat me badly—just consistently. One day they paid me a fine tribute. They told me I was ranked third on the International Sucker List (behind a Frenchman in Monte Carlo and a Greek in Philadelphia). I didn't let this go to my head.

Sol, a remarkable character (the world's leading authority on everything), was the second person I saw benefit from DPH. In his youth Sol was a great athlete, acknowledged to be the best one-wall handball player in the world. When he was thirty he took up tennis and became an outstanding player. In a different field, Sol had ambitions to be an opera singer. He had a fine singing voice and might have made it to the Met if he hadn't damaged a vocal cord.

One morning Sol and I had breakfast at Wolfie's on Collins Avenue. The waitress brought mushroom omelettes and Sol ignored his. He seemed in a fog and was staring into the distance. I'd heard that you could pass your hand in front of someone's face and they wouldn't notice, but I'd never believed this. I passed my hand a few inches in front of Sol's face and didn't get any reaction at all.

I asked Sol what was bothering him. He said that a couple

of weeks ago a wealthy friend of his, whom I knew well, had bought six pairs of tennis shoes from Marse. Sol thought it terrible that Marse had charged his friend retail prices for the shoes. This was of such monumental inconsequence that I had a hard time believing the thought was stuck in Sol's brain. But after listening to him I realized that it was almost an obsession. Then it occurred to me that Sol's tennis game had been off, and he'd been uncharacteristically quiet on the court.

I asked Sol how he'd been feeling. He told me he had constant headaches, that he slept badly and was having nightmares. His worst complaint was that he would wake up at four o'clock in the morning hearing himself shouting. His only relief was to get in his car and drive around for an hour or so. He told me he'd seen a doctor. But the medicines he'd been given hadn't helped and made him feel dopey. It seemed that DPH might be worth trying. I telephoned Dr. Silbermann about it, and he arranged for Sol to get a prescription.

The next day we were at Wolfie's again. Sol had eaten earlier and was keeping me company at breakfast. He had his Dilantin with him and took the first 100 mg at that time. I had found DPH effective in myself within an hour, and this was a chance to observe its effects in someone else. I wanted an objective reading but didn't know how to go about it. By chance I asked Sol, "What about Fink and Russell this afternoon?" We had a doubles game with them for fifty dollars a team. Sol said, "They're awful tough." This answer startled me—it was so unlike Sol, a fierce competitor. I thought, "Fink and Russell" will be a good test question. I looked at my watch.

We left Wolfie's and walked to the beach at the Roney Plaza, a couple of blocks away, and I went in swimming. When I came back it was thirty-five minutes since Sol had taken his DPH. I said, "Sol, do you think we've got a chance with Fink and Russell this afternoon?" Sol said, "We've *always* got a chance." With emphasis on the always. That was more like him.

Twenty-five minutes later, an hour after Sol had taken the DPH, I asked again, "What about Fink and Russell?" Sol said,

"We'll knock the crap out of them." Sol was back to normal.

That night Sol slept soundly and straight through. He started taking Dilantin daily and continued to sleep well—no more waking up at four in the morning. His daily headaches disappeared. The monumental matter of the retail shoes shrunk back to size. And once again Sol became his usual objectionable self on the tennis court.

• • •

In that first year I saw four more people benefit from DPH. Each was depressed and each had symptoms of an overbusy brain occupied with emotions related to fear and anger. Because the cases were so important to me summaries of them are included in the Appendix (p. 139).

Each additional one of these cases had a parlaying effect on the probability factor. A year earlier it had seemed almost impossible that important uses for DPH could have been overlooked. Now it seemed highly probable that they had been overlooked.

Which brings up the subject of probabilities.

4.
THE SUBJECT
OF PROBABILITIES

As I look back, I realize that it was a good instinct for prob-abilities that pulled me through that early period of my pursuit of DPH. Without this instinct I could never have survived the negative inferences drawn from the fact that the medicine had been around for over twenty years. I used to think that everyone had a pretty good sense of probabilities. But I don't now, and I've heard some strange comments about probabilities in the medical field.

Probabilities are an important underlying theme of this book and, partly to qualify myself on the subject, I will depart from the narrative and discuss them.

In some fields a sense of probabilities is much more impor-tant than in others. An insurance actuary would feel naked with-out a sense of probabilities. A painter, on the other hand, might swap his sense of probabilities for a two-percent improvement in color sense. In medicine a sense of probabilities is more impor-tant than generally realized. Sometimes weighing the probabili-ties—the use of a potentially dangerous procedure against the dangerous condition a patient is in—is the whole medical ques-tion. In the FDA the weighing of risk vs. gain looms large in the question of whether a drug should be approved for listing.

I've always had a good sense of probabilities—born with it I believe—and I used to think of it as a form of intelligence. But as I began to assess some of my other "forms of intelligence" and found them lacking, I decided I'd better think of them all as aptitudes.

The word aptitude itself suggests wide variances. It seems that aptitudes come with the baby. We're not all born with a good sense of direction, and a good sense of probabilities is not standard equipment either. On the way to the subject of probabilities, let's discuss aptitudes. If the reader doesn't have a good sense of probability this should make him feel better.

Some of the genetic blanks I drew when aptitudes were being handed out were in mechanics, in remembering names, and in sense of direction.

Things mechanical are a mystery to me. In World War II, I took an exam to qualify for Officers Training School in the U.S. Coast Guard. My aptitude for mechanics helped me get a grade of 29 out of a possible 100. After looking at this score the Coast Guard decided it had enough officers, and awarded me the post of apprentice seaman.

I can't remember people's names no matter how hard I try. I seem to have a scrambling device in my head. If two strangers come into the office, my secretary discreetly writes their names on the side of a paper coffee cup—and I have to refer to it constantly.

My most conspicuous aptitude—in absentia—is my sense of direction. For that reason, and because there is evidence of genetic origin, I will discuss it more fully.

My sense of direction is fine—but it's in backwards. This is not easy to explain to a person with a good sense of direction. I believe such a person has a tug he's not conscious of that pulls him in the right direction. I have such a tug, but it pulls me in the wrong direction. For example, when I leave a washroom in a strange airport, without hesitation I turn the wrong way.

Apparently my aptitude for going the wrong way is not only lateral but vertical. For fifteen years my office was on the twenty-ninth floor of 2 Broadway and our boardroom was on the thirtieth. When I was in a hurry to get to the thirtieth floor I would invariably walk down to the twenty-eighth.

I don't have to climb the family tree very high to see where I got my sense of direction. It was bequeathed me by my father. His sense of direction was in backwards too—and was even stronger than mine. He got lost all the time but it never occurred to him to blame his sense of direction, he just thought it was bad luck. It's a good thing Dad didn't have to make his living as a wagon scout in the old days. He'd have set out for California with his train of covered wagons, and if things went well, in a few months he'd have discovered Plymouth Rock.

It's not surprising that the family hero is the homing pigeon. You can put this rascal in a dark bag, take him 500 miles from home, and without consulting a road map or following the railroad tracks he will fly directly to his coop. Scientists may say he takes radar soundings or something. But what of it? Could Shakespeare do it, could Beethoven? The pigeon has quite an aptitude.

Without realizing it, we gravitate in the direction of our aptitudes. We bounce from one field to another, being repelled or attracted, and if we're lucky we come to rest where our aptitudes are at a premium. When I got out of college, I bounced around for a few years and wound up as assistant to a customer's broker in the stock exchange. The stock market appealed to my sense of probabilities and another aptitude, gambling (speculation as it's called in the market).

An aptitude for gambling by itself is a dubious asset; it's fortunate for me that this aptitude came in a package with my sense of probability. This steered me into games of skill and away from casino games, such as dice and roulette, where the odds against you are slight but inexorable.

My first gambling game was marbles for keeps. I remember bankrupting a kid from down the block when I was six. When I gave up marbles, I took up other games—contract bridge, gin rummy, and handicapping the races. In these games a good sense of probabilities is an asset.

There are two kinds of probabilities. There is the mathematical kind that can be arrived at precisely. As a simple example, the chance of calling the toss of a coin correctly (provided it's not weighted) is exactly one in two. The chance of calling it correctly twice in a row is one-half of one-half of a chance, or one in four, and so forth. If you wish to determine the exact probability that a coin tossed a hundred times will come up heads thirty-one times, there's a formula for it. I don't know it.

Another kind of probability cannot be arrived at by mathematical formula. It's an estimate—exact figures can't be placed on it. Let's call it free-form probability. We use it all the time, some of us more consciously than others. For example, when I make a phone call I start to assess the probability that the person I'm calling is at home. With adjustments for the individual, I might figure it's three-to-one against his or her being home after the third ring, eight-to-one after the fourth ring, etc. After the fifth ring I usually hang up. (When I call my former wife, if the phone is answered before the fourth ring, I know I've got the wrong number.)

One who makes a living by the application of free-form probabilities is the racetrack handicapper. After studying the many variables, he comes up with the probable odds for each horse in a particular race—the morning line. Over a period of time the handicapper's "line" should be close to the odds made by the betting public, or as my friend Dingy Weiss says, "He can tell his story walking."

Free-form probability also deals with odds of a larger magnitude. Some examples. The odds against five horses, in a ten-horse race, finishing in a dead heat. The odds against finding a lion in your backyard in Manhattan. The odds against the next person you meet having a red beard and a wooden leg, and offering you a banana. Or, for a pertinent example, the odds against a thousand physicians, working independently, finding a drug useful for over fifty symptoms and disorders, and that drug being useful for only a single disorder.

When the odds are this large, it's easy to be approximately right. Whether you estimate one chance in a million or one chance in a billion, the estimates are almost the same—the difference between these figures is less than one in a million. (If the reader's sense of probability is like my sense of direction, his feelers will tell him this is wrong.)

High authorities have no problem with this concept. Recently at the Cavendish Club, I found Phil and the Little Beast, top-notch bridge players who bet on anything that moves, discussing a bridge hand. I made myself heard over a cacophony of "hearts," "Ira," and "idiots," and said I wanted to ask a serious question. "What's the difference between a million-to-one shot and a billion-to-one shot?" The answers shot back. From Phil, "Nuthin'." From the Little Beast, "Darn little—less than one in a million." I thanked them, and joined the bridge discussion.

A feel for probabilities is essential in two of the card games I've played, bridge and gin rummy. Although I haven't played gin in fifteen years, the *Encyclopedia of Bridge* is still kind enough to say, "Dreyfus . . . is reputed to be the best American player of gin rummy." This compliment, no longer deserved, is based on a system of play I discovered many years ago that relies heavily on probabilities.

Gin rummy deals mostly with exact probabilities. Another game I've played, the stock market, deals largely with inexact probabilities.

• • •

October. This is one of the peculiarly dangerous months to speculate in stocks in. The others are July, January, September, April, November, May, March, June, December, August, and February.
—MARK TWAIN, *Pudd'nhead Wilson*

With this cautionary note the reader will be given instructions on how to buy a stock.

Take the five-year earnings record of a company, its current earnings, its book value, its net quick assets, the prospect for new products, the competitive position of the company in its own industry, the merits of the industry relative to other industries, your opinion of management, your opinion of the stock market as a whole, and the chart position of the individual stock. Put all this where you think your brains are, circulate it through your sense of probabilities, and arrive at your conclusion. Be prepared to take a quick loss; your conclusion may be wrong even though you approached it the right way.

My introduction to Wall Street was in 1941. I got a job as an assistant to a customer's broker in the garment district branch of Cohen, Simondson & Company, at a salary of $25 a week. One of my duties in this job was the posting of hundreds of weekly charts. This early experience with charts influenced my Wall Street career.

Skipping the intervening travail—fascinating as it would be to nobody—I found myself, in the early fifties, responsible for the management of a small mutual fund, The Dreyfus Fund. The fund was so small that the management fees were only $3,000 a year. Perforce, the fund could not afford a large research staff. Actually our staff consisted of a fine young man, Alex Rudnicki, and myself. Alex was a fundamentalist, a student of the Graham Dodd school. I was a student of charts and market technique. We were at the opposite extremes of investment approach, but we worked together as friends.

Alex had a wonderful memory for the earnings of companies and other statistical information; my contribution was 600 large-scale, weekly line charts. From my experience, monthly charts were too "slow" to be of much use, and daily charts were too volatile to be reliable. I split the difference with weekly charts, posted daily. I developed my own theories about the charts, and read no books on the subject. It seemed best to make my own mistakes—at least then I'd know who to blame.

In those early days our statistical information was no more up-to-date than the latest quarterly reports. Alex and I were too chicken to call a company and ask a vice-president how things were going. Of necessity we put more emphasis on the technical side of the market than did most funds.

When you study the technical side of the stock market you deal with two components. One component is major market trends—bull or bear market. The other is the timing of the purchase or sale of individual securities.

In those days, more than now, the market tended to move as a whole—being right about the major trend was more than half the game. We focused a good deal of our attention on this. With three- and four-million-share days, the trading of the speculator was a key factor in market moves. Speculators tended to move in concert. Excessive optimism, with the parlayed purchasing power of their margin accounts, caused the market to get out of hand on the upside; forced selling in these same margin accounts caused the market to get out of hand on the downside.

The more money a speculator had, the healthier the technical side of the market—he had purchasing power. The more stock the speculator had, the weaker the technical side—he had selling power. Human nature being what it is, when a speculator owned stock he talked bullish. When he had cash, or was short of stock, he talked bearish. In estimating whether we were in a major uptrend or downtrend the speculator's chatter was taken into consideration, along with changes in the short interest and the condition of the margin accounts. And of course our charts were helpful.

Objectivity—difficult to come by—is important in any field. It didn't take us long to learn that stubbornness, ego, and wishful thinking could mess up the best of market techniques; so we tried to keep our emotions separate from our decision-making. When we bought a security we didn't pound the table to emphasize how sure we were that we were right. Instead, we tried to prepare ourselves for the possibility that we might be wrong so that when the unexpected happened, which it usually did, we were psychologically in a position to take a loss.

Our sense of probabilities was always in play. We wouldn't buy a high-risk stock, one that could go down fifty to sixty percent, unless we felt we had a chance of at least doubling our money. If we bought a conservative stock, one not likely to go down more than twenty percent, a thirty percent profit was worth shooting for.

Since our methods differed from those of most other funds, it was likely that our performance would vary considerably from the average. Fortunately for our stockholders this variance was in the right direction—it could have been the other way. At the time of my retirement, our ten-year performance was the best of any mutual fund—nearly 100 percentage points better than the second-best fund.*

That was a long time ago. Recently, my good friend Bill Rogers, of two-Cabinet-post renown, said, "Jack, I guess you're doing well in the market as usual." I said, "No, Bill, to tell you the truth I've been in a long stupid streak." It's nice to see a friend have a good laugh.

• • •

Back to medical probabilities. Including my own case, I had seen seven consecutive persons benefit from DPH. If each case had been the flip of a coin, 50-50, the odds against seven in a row would have been 127-to-1. But the response to DPH had been so prompt and the symptoms that responded so similar, each case deserved a weight far exceeding 50-50.

Of course my objectivity could be questioned. But that didn't bother me; it's only other people's objectivity that bothers me. Even at that early date I placed a high probability figure on the chance that DPH was more than an anticonvulsant.

• • •

During the first year of my experience with Dilantin I had gathered some helpful information on the subject of electricity in the body. This will be discussed in the next chapter.

_____

* 326% to 232%, Arthur Wiesenberger, Inc.

5.
BODY ELECTRICITY

For the first few months that I took DPH I gave little thought to how the medicine worked. How it worked was a lot less important to me than that it did work. But one day I noticed that the flat, metallic taste in my mouth, which I'd associated with electricity, was gone. As I thought back about it, I realized that it had been gone since I'd started taking DPH.

A hypothesis about electricity had led me to ask for DPH. Was this a coincidence? It seemed unlikely. When a hypothesis precedes and leads to a finding, the hypothesis is apt to be correct. My thinking went back to electricity in the body.

Recently I found some notes to myself, made in 1963. These notes help me remember what my thoughts were at that time.

[From my notes:] "I noticed figures of speech that described human emotions in electrical terms. Before then I'd thought of these terms as imaginative inventions of writers. But perhaps they weren't. Maybe sensitive people had used them instinctively because they were near the truth. There are enough of these electrical expressions to make a parlor game. Here are some:

state of tension	shocking experience
room charged with tension	state of shock
get a charge out of something	it gave me a jolt
electrifying experience	blow your fuse
the touchdown electrified the crowd	blow your top
dynamic personality	sparks flew
magnetic personality	explosive temper
galvanized into action	explode with anger

"This list, with its references to anger and fear, led to other thoughts. I knew that an electric goad was used in rodeos to frighten animals into rambunctious performances, and that batteries had been used to make race horses run faster. I'd read that an electric jolt causes the hair to stand on end.

"Could electricity be the mechanism that makes the fur on a dog rise when he is angry or when he is frightened? Could it account for the spectacular bristling of a cat in the act of welcoming a dog? How about our own fur? When we're scared the hair on the nape of our neck rises and we have 'hair-raising' experiences. And don't we bristle with anger? Didn't these things seem to connect anger and fear with electricity in the body?" [End of the notes.]

I had gone as far as I could as an amateur. I needed a professional to tell me whether my ideas about electricity in the body made sense. But where could I find such a person?

Whenever I'm stumped as to how to find someone or locate something, I have a simple method. I ask Howard Stein. I don't know how he does it but he never lets me down. I asked Howard, "Do you know how I can meet with somebody who's an expert on electricity in the body?" Howard said he thought so. He went to Yura Arkus-Duntov, head of the Dreyfus Fund's science research. Within a week Yura had made arrangements for me to meet with Dr. Peter Suckling, a neurobiophysicist from Downstate Medical Center.

Dr. Suckling, with his nice Australian accent, had good vibes for me (a modern electrical term?). He was an expert on bioelectrical activity and had been an associate of Sir John Eccles, an authority in the field and a Nobel prize winner.

Dr. Suckling and I had three long meetings in my office at 2 Broadway. It was a nice office, facing New York harbor, and Peter liked it. He said he thought the moving scenery of boats helped with thinking. I hoped so.

The first question I asked Peter was, "Can you weigh the electricity in a cat?" I thought cats had an extra share of electricity, because of their hair-raising act. Peter disappointed me by saying electricity can't be measured that way. It's inside the body, but the whole animal itself is grounded. I didn't know what that meant but I took his word for it.

For the first time, I heard about the excitatory nervous system, the inhibitory nervous system, membranes, axons, synapses, negative potentials, sodium and potassium, and how a disproportionate amount of chemicals inside and outside the cell made for the electrical potential across the membrane.

Peter labored hard to explain the working of bioelectrical activity to me. By using simple illustrations, he got into me, shoehorn fashion, a rudimentary idea of how electricity works in the body. I won't burden the reader with the whole discussion, but I will summarize some of what Peter said.

The cell is a complicated entity in which thousands of activities take place. Peter said most of them were not relevant to our discussion. What was relevant was the electrical potential of the cell. He explained that the body of a cell is enclosed by a membrane, and in a nerve cell the electrical potential is minus 90 millivolts, relative to the outside of the cell. Peter said the reason there is this negative potential is because of a disproportionate amount of substances inside the cell relative to outside the cell —particularly sodium and potassium. Peter spoke of the membrane with obvious admiration: "This very thin membrane can sustain an electrical tension better than most insulators. The insulation strength is high. It has to be strong; it's so very thin." Then, in considerable detail, he explained the electrochemical mechanisms involved in the discharge of electrical activity. I won't go into that here.

Peter said that there are about 10 billion* cells in the brain —each with an electrical potential. He said that even a slight imbalance in individual cells, because of the proliferative possibilities, could cause a problem in a large area of the brain. He told me that cells vary in length in the human. In nerve cells the

---

* This figure was imprecise. The latest census has it between 100 and 250 billion cells.

speed of impulse transmission varies from one hundred meters a second to three meters a second.

All the cells in the human body, although they do not have the same amount of electrical potential, work on the same principle. Peter said this was true in other animals and, for that matter, all living things. Apparently when the Lord came up with a good thing like the cell he used it over and over again.

At the beginning I didn't tell Peter what my interest was. I didn't want to influence him one way or the other. I realized later that this had been a needless precaution because we were dealing with a pretty exact science. In the meantime, Peter had been trying to figure out why the president of a mutual fund and partner of a brokerage firm was asking all these questions. He'd assumed my interest was in business. On the third day, when I told him about DPH, Peter astonished me by saying, "Oh, my goodness, I thought you were considering giving testosterone to the customer's brokers to make them produce better." Perhaps like making hens lay eggs faster (Merrill Lynch—consider).

Then I explained to Peter what my experiences with DPH had been. Apologizing for the unscientific sound of it, and speaking allegorically, I said I felt that the brain of a person who needed Dilantin was like a bunch of dry twigs. It seemed that a thought of fear or anger would light the dry twigs, the fire would spread out of control, and the thoughts couldn't be turned off. Dilantin seemed to act like a gentle rain on the twigs, and the fire (and thoughts) could be kept under control.

I asked Peter if these impressions made sense. Peter said he had not done specific work with DPH, but my impressions were not inconsistent with the known fact that DPH prevented the spread of excessive electrical discharge. That was good news.

• • •

A few weeks after our last meeting, Peter performed an invaluable service. He sent me a copy of Goodman & Gilman's *Pharmacological Basis of Therapeutics,* considered to be the bible of pharmaceuticals by the medical profession, and said he thought I would find it useful.

I hadn't known there was such a book. In the section on DPH I found this:

> Coincident with the decrease in seizures there occurs improvement in intellectual performance. Salutary effects of the drug DPH on personality, memory, mood, cooperativeness, emotional stability, amenability to discipline, etc., are also observed, *sometimes independently of seizure control.* [Italics mine.]

I read and reread this paragraph. I could hardly believe it. Salutary effects in mood, emotional stability, etc. Here it was—in a medical book of high repute. Yet none of the doctors I'd met had ever heard of these uses. How could this be?

6.
A SOFT VOICE
IN A DEAF EAR

The time had come to tell the story to the medical profession. I had seen seven persons benefit from DPH, the electrical thoughts had been checked out and were not implausible, and there was the medical support of the Goodman & Gilman excerpt.

Now that the time had come, I didn't know how to proceed. I had always assumed that if I had enough evidence I would just "turn it over to the medical profession." That would be no problem, I thought. Now, faced with turning it over, I realized there was no "receiving department" in the medical profession—and I didn't know where to go. Dr. Silbermann and I discussed this problem at length and finally came up with what seemed a sensible plan.

Max, an associate professor at Columbia Presbyterian, was a personal friend of Dean H. Houston Merritt. This was the Merritt of Putnam and Merritt who had discovered that DPH was useful for epilepsy. What could be more logical than to bring the story to Dr. Merritt and Presbyterian Hospital?

At Max's suggestion we invited Dr. Merritt to have dinner at my home. Dr. Merritt accepted and brought with him Dr. Lawrence C. Kolb, Chief of Psychiatric Research at Presbyterian.

Since this was the first opportunity I'd had to present the DPH story in some detail, I was anxious to have other physicians present, and I invited my family physician, Dr. Alfred Steiner, and Dr. Ernest Klarch, a psychiatrist, whom Max had consulted in one of the seven cases. Also at dinner was my friend Sol. He had come from Miami so that the physicians could hear about DPH from a person other than myself.

Sol and I related our experiences with DPH. Then I told the physicians about the other five cases, and reported my observations of the medicine's effects on anger, fear, and the turned-on mind. They didn't express skepticism, but I think that the story, coming from a layman, was hard for them to believe. I was glad I could conclude with the quote from the respected medical source, Goodman & Gilman. To repeat:

> Salutary effects of DPH on personality, memory, mood, cooperativeness, emotional stability, amenability to discipline, etc., are also observed, sometimes independently of seizure control.

Dr. Merritt appeared surprised by this excerpt from Goodman & Gilman. He said he hadn't heard of it but hoped it was true. Then he suggested that maybe Presbyterian could do a study. Dr. Kolb agreed and said it could be arranged.

I couldn't let Dr. Merritt get away without asking him about possible side effects of DPH. He said that DPH had been in use for about twenty years, and a good record of safety had been established. There were side effects but they were rarely serious. He said DPH was non-habit-forming, and unlike many other substances it was not sedative in therapeutic doses. This was good news and I thanked Dr. Merritt. At the end of the meeting Dr. Kolb said he would be in touch with me.

Postscript to the dinner. When I'd invited Dr. Steiner and Dr. Klarch, appreciating their time was valuable, I said they could bill me for it. Dr. Steiner didn't send a bill. Dr. Klarch (fictitious name) sent a bill for $500. This seemed high. His only contribution to the meeting had been "Please pass the butter."

A few days after the meeting, Dr. Kolb phoned and told me he had arranged for Dr. Sidney Malitz to conduct the study. Dr. Malitz and I had dinner, and I repeated the DPH story. He said he was surprised to hear such a plausible story from a layman;

he hadn't expected it. Apparently Dr. Kolb hadn't told him much about our discussion.

Dr. Malitz told me that he would set up two studies and I could fund them for $5,000 each. I said the matter was so urgent that I'd prefer to give $10,000 for each study, and this was agreed upon. I told Dr. Malitz I would appreciate it if he would keep me in close touch with how things were going. I didn't ask how the studies would be conducted; it didn't seem proper. But I had the feeling that much of my responsibility to DPH was now in the hands of professionals.

Alas. Week after week went by without my hearing from Dr. Malitz and a head of steam built up in me. When I finally called him after three months, I regret that I said, "Why the hell haven't I heard from you? You know how important this is." I don't think Sidney liked this opening remark and I can't say I blame him. He explained that the patients he had selected for the study were used to getting medicine three times a day, and since I'd only suggested 100 mg of Dilantin (one capsule) he was wondering if Parke-Davis could make it in smaller dosages, so it could be given three times a day. This excuse was so lame it needed crutches. Apparently Sidney had so little faith in DPH that he didn't think it could help unless the patients were psychologically influenced, and he hadn't even tried it. Further, if he'd looked into it, he would have found that Parke-Davis already made it in smaller dosages—a breakable Infatab, a 33⅓ mg capsule, and a liquid. After explaining to Dr. Malitz the different forms Dilantin came in, I expressed the hope that the study would now move forward.

Four more long months went by. I called Dr. Malitz again and this time, in the quietest way, asked him how things were going. He told me the study hadn't gotten started yet because he hadn't been able to get a placebo from Parke-Davis. I thanked him politely, and hung up with a heavy heart. Maybe Dr. Malitz couldn't get a placebo from Parke-Davis in seven months, but in those days most drugstores could supply a placebo in forty-eight hours.

In a last futile attempt I met with Dr. Kolb. He defended Dr. Malitz and said it was better to proceed slowly and carefully than the other way around. I didn't even argue with this platitude—it was such nonsense. Seven months had been wasted and I was discouraged. I'd taken what I thought was my best shot and hadn't got any results at all—not even negative.

Occasionally it may seem to the reader that I'm being critical of others. This is the opposite of my intention; I have too many motes in my own eye. But sometimes things have to be spelled out—otherwise this story would be too hard to believe. Looking back, it's easy to understand the position Dr. Malitz was in. He had been taught to think of DPH as an anticonvulsant. The idea that it had other uses came from an implausible source, a layman, and that didn't make it any easier for him. He undoubtedly had other research projects to which he gave priority—and DPH got on a back burner.

On other fronts things had not stood still. I had continued to send friends and acquaintances to doctors for trials with DPH. The effects were prompt and similar to those of the earlier cases. The numbers were mounting up. By now there were about twenty-five cases. In addition, I had a new source of information.

Dr. A. Lester Stepner, of Miami, had treated one of the first six people I'd seen take DPH. He had been so impressed with the results that he tried DPH with other patients. In a letter of April 1965, he summarized the cases of twelve patients he'd treated with DPH. In eleven of the twelve (he was unable to follow up the twelfth) he found DPH effective in treating anxiety, depression, anger, impulsiveness, temper outbursts, incoherent thinking. Dr. Stepner's summaries are in the Appendix (p. 141).

Coming at this time, Dr. Stepner's observations were a big psychological help to me, but they didn't seem to mean much to Dr. Silbermann and others I spoke to. I was beginning to understand the French phrase *idée fixe*.

The evidence was growing, but my confidence that I could convey it to others was shrinking. For months I had been buttonholing any doctor I ran into and informally talking about DPH. I must have spoken to a dozen of them during this period. None of them had heard of DPH being used for anything other than epilepsy. They were all (with one exception) polite, even kind, but they didn't give me any encouragement. That one doctor looked at me the way a Great Dane looks at a cricket and explained: "Medicine is a complicated matter, and I'd advise you to stick to Wall Street." Bless his heart.

I called a council of peace with my friends who knew of my interest in DPH. These friends were Dr. Max Silbermann, Dr. Peter Suckling, Yura Arkus-Duntov, and Howard Stein. We met in my office in early 1965 to decide the best way to get our information to the medical profession. For the first half of the meeting, we went over many cases in detail. By this time both Howard and Yura had each seen persons benefit from DPH, and we discussed how consistent our observations were with those reported in Goodman & Gilman.

We tape-recorded the meeting. Reading the transcript brings back those days in a lively way—I can still feel the warmth of my frustrations. There wasn't a suggestion I would make that Peter, Max, or Yura couldn't find an objection to. Toward the end I must have worn through my daily supply of DPH because I was hopping up and down with frustration.

The transcript of the meeting remembers better than I do. Here are a few excerpts:

> JACK: The problem before us is to awaken the doctors in the country to the potential of Dilantin. We're not in this for financial reasons, and we're not in it for glory. It's almost a crime not to try to get this information to the doctors. . . . We've got a lot of cases and we could do a thorough job of writing them up. If Dr. Silbermann would be willing . . .
>
> DR. MAX S: Jack, that would not be accepted by any medical journal. You could publish that at your own expense, there's no law against it.
>
> JACK: Why wouldn't this be accepted by a medical journal?
>
> DR. MAX S: Because. You know the old story. There is no blind control, and no medical journal would accept any drug study unless . . .
>
> DR. PETER S: Unless you have had a computer in on it.

JACK: Max, are you serious? This can't be so.

YURA AND DR. MAX S: Oh, yes this is so.

JACK: Yura, we are talking about research, right? Please listen before you say no.

    None of these people who took DPH knew each other. As far as they were concerned the study was blind. I asked them to write me letters that included details of their experiences. The same results from DPH are reported over and over again. This reinforces the evidence.

DR. PETER S: It is not accepted as proof and there's a devastating word that is applied to it, called anecdotal evidence. It doesn't go.

YURA: It's indirect proof.

JACK: Sorry fellows. Nobody in the room is thinking. These individuals wouldn't know which way to lie if they wanted to. They didn't know each other.

DR. PETER S: No, no. It's not that. This is the way . . .

JACK: Please. Let's not move the medical people all the way down to diapers. At least keep them in rompers, okay? I'm saying that if we added the Goodman & Gilman to Dr. Stepner's observations and the evidence of our twenty-five cases, write it up carefully, it's got to be received. We won't say we discovered America or anything like that. You, Dr. Silbermann, have got to make the effort.

DR. MAX S: Well, if we write it up and I publish it under my name and I send it in, no medical journal will accept it.

JACK: All right, Max, then no medical journal will accept it. At least we can send the information to the heads of the hospitals and say, "It would be a sin if we didn't tell you what we've found. Evaluate it on the basis of your own experience and do what you want." Once we've told the heads of fifty hospitals, at least part of it should be off our conscience. Let the non-use of it rest on other people's consciences . . .

    I don't care if machines are not involved. I can get machines that will lie like anybody else. Will that help? [I wouldn't have done that —in those days I was over eighty percent honest.]

YURA: No, Jack. We are talking about the best means to achieve this.

This discussion seems funny now, but it was very real then. I was too near my own suffering and I was impatient to get DPH to others. This impatience stayed with me, but after bumping into enough brick walls and closed minds, I realized it got in the way, and tabled it—with the help of DPH. Without DPH I'd have had an implosion.

For several weeks after the meeting, I thought about what

was said. I had argued with my friends at the top of my lungs. But I knew they had my best interests at heart, and I had to pay attention to them because they had experience where I had none.

In the course of business I saw Howard Stein almost every day. Every once in a while Howard would say, "If you want to get anything done, you've got to do it yourself." I didn't even respond to this remark at first. But about the fourth time I heard it, I said, "Why are you persecuting me with that cliché?" He said, "I'm not using it as a cliché; I mean it." "How can I do this myself?" I asked. "I don't have any medical background, and besides I have other dishes to wash, like the Dreyfus Fund and Dreyfus & Co."

But Howard said, "You'll see."

7.
ESTABLISHING
A MEDICAL FOUNDATION—
AND THE STORY OF MY LIFE
(THE BEST PARTS LEFT OUT)

When I started to do well in business, I established a small foundation, the Dreyfus Charitable Foundation, for the purpose of giving money to what seemed good causes. It was my hope to be generally helpful, and the foundation gave money to numerous organizations and contributed equally to Protestant, Catholic, and Jewish charities. The responsibility of how to spend the money was left to these organizations.

But now I wanted to take over the responsibility of spending this money—I felt it should be spent on DPH research. DPH would need all the money I had been contributing and more, so I had to discontinue my usual contributions. And I could do this with a clear conscience—if the work on DPH was successful there would be many sources of charitable inquiry that would be helped by it. Consistent with this thinking, in 1965 the Dreyfus Charitable Foundation was changed into the Dreyfus Medical Foundation.

A medical foundation needs a medical director—but such a person can be difficult to obtain. Good physicians are fully occupied with their own matters and not easily sidetracked by what might seem a will-o'-the-wisp. After several months of search, Dr. Suckling introduced me to Dr. William J. Turner, a neuropsychiatrist at Central Islip Hospital on Long Island.

At the first meeting with Dr. Turner I got a fine impression of him, and it's never changed. He said he had been anxious to meet with me because he had seen a number of persons, with disorders other than epilepsy, respond to Dilantin. We had several long discussions. After thinking about it for a few weeks Dr. Turner decided to join the Foundation as Medical Director.

At that time I thought that the Foundation would be able to achieve its goals within two or three years. It seemed unwise for Dr. Turner to break his connections with Central Islip Hospital and move to New York City, so he joined us as Director on a part-time basis. Bill took a small office near his home in Huntington, Long Island, hired a secretary and medical assistant, and we were in business. (Jumping ahead a few years—when it became apparent that my timetable was optimistic, I was fortunate in being able to persuade Dr. Samuel Bogoch, a professor at the Boston University School of Medicine and Chairman of the International Institute for the Brain Sciences, to join the Foundation on a full-time basis as General Director; Dr. Turner continued as Director.)

At the outset, Dr. Turner and I had the objective of proving —or disproving—that DPH was more than an anticonvulsant. We were as open to negative possibilities as to positive ones. I had my ideas as to what we would find; but if they were wrong, I didn't want to spend my time trying to prove something that wasn't so—there are pleasanter ways of making a fool of oneself.

Our plan was simple. The Foundation would sponsor a few studies at medical institutions. My guess was that this might take $150,000 to $200,000 a year for the next two or three years. If these studies were successful, the facts about DPH would then be in the hands of professionals. Once this happened I thought the word would spread like wildfire throughout the medical profession, and the job would be done. If I had been told, then, that in the next fifteen years the Foundation was going to spend over $15 million (and the job not completed), I wouldn't have believed it. One reason is that $15 million was three times as much money as I had at that time.

Talking about money in connection with this work is awkward for me. I don't want to sound like I think I'm a boy scout. But there is a point to be made here. If I hadn't been lucky enough to have the money, I wouldn't have gotten to first base.

When I think back to my first job, at $15 a week, I realize what an implausible person I was to have a lot of money. Implausible is too weak a word. I'll tell how it happened. If you believe in fate, or whatever, you're entitled to believe the money was given to me to spend on DPH.

When I was a boy my parents were not poor, nor were they rich. Once, my father, who sold candy wholesale, was out of a job and down to his last two weeks of spending money for the family. But that was his low point, and I wasn't even aware of it at the time.

When I was ten years old, I learned what money was for. The laws of Montgomery, Alabama, permitted me to go to the movies by myself at that age. My parents would give me a dime on Saturday mornings, and the Strand Theater was assured of an early customer. I would see the Pathé News, the "To Be Continued Next Saturday" serial, and a movie—sometimes twice. After the movie, when I had a nickel slipped to me by one of my uncles, I would go to Franco's and buy a long hotdog with sauerkraut and red sauce. They were especially delicious since my dear mother considered them poisonous.

The first time the thought of making a living came up was when I was fifteen. At that time I played golf in Montgomery with a boy of my age, Alan Rice. We were both good golfers; I played a little better than he did but he didn't think so—this miscalculation kept me in quarters. One day, while at the seventh-hole water fountain, Alan, a serious boy, said that someday he was going to make $100,000. When that happened, that was going to be it! He was going to retire and live on the income of $5,000 a year. Alan's father was a storekeeper, and I figured Alan must have heard this from him. I was impressed, or I wouldn't have remembered it to this day. I knew I'd never make that much money. But if a miracle happened and I made $100,000, there'd be two retirees.

When I was sixteen, my father had enough money to send me to college, Lehigh University. I studied the minimum and got a C average—my only A was in music appreciation, and my only distinction was that I was captain of the golf team. At college my brain didn't come to grips with the problem of how I would earn a living; it didn't occur to me to study something practical. It's just as well. Lehigh is a fine engineering school; if I'd fooled with that, I would have flunked out. Even as it was, for a year after graduation I had nightmares that they took my diploma back.

When I got out of college I didn't know what I wanted to do. Well really, I guess I did, but I didn't discuss it with my father. What I wanted to do was to not work. Sometimes I had this nice fantasy. I thought if I had the courage (I wasn't even close) I'd ask John D. Rockefeller for $1 million. My reason was that he was too old to thoroughly enjoy his money, and I wasn't too old to thoroughly enjoy his money. I could play golf, travel, and be happy in every way, and he could enjoy this—secondhand.

If the reader has gotten the impression that I lacked enthusiasm for work he is on the right track. However, I had to get a job. I tried selling insurance and couldn't stand it. Everybody I said hello to was a prospect. I worked on my first potential customer for two months and must have played golf with him a dozen times (he couldn't hit the ball out of his own shadow) and finally got up enough courage to try to sell him an annuity. He turned me down. I went out to the street and cried—and retired from the insurance business. Money earned in insurance: zero.

My next effort was in the candy business. My father thought that maybe I could help him in sales. By then we had moved to New York. He was concentrating on selling candy to just a few large customers, the chain stores—Woolworth's, Kress, Mc-Crory, and others. To help me learn the business, he got me a job in a candy factory, Edgar P. Lewis, of Malden, Massachusetts. I liked making candy, and for six months worked on the marmalade slab, making imitation orange slices, and barely lifting 100-pound bags of sugar into a boiling cauldron. In the late afternoon I'd go back to my boarding house and take a nap before dinner. Those were solid naps. When I woke up I didn't know where I was or what I was.

My salary at Edgar P. Lewis was $15 a week—and I lived on it. No hardship, but not luxurious either. Room and board was $10.50 (lunch excluded). Both breakfast and dinner had the advantage of baked beans. I had one luxury (a necessity in getting to work), an old Buick my father had given me. Garage used up a buck a week. That didn't leave much out of the $15. When I was on double dates with Mat Suvalsky, an old college friend, Mat was encouraged to split the gas with me. A happy period in my life. But I wasn't any closer to my fortune—the Alan Rice $100,000.

After six months my father felt that I had eaten enough candy and I was ready for sales training with him. My specific chores were to drive the car and carry the samples; and I would listen while my father talked to the candy buyers. I remember the first meeting I attended. While candy was being discussed I toyed with a fountain pen on the buyer's desk. When we got to the street my hand went into my pocket and, to my surprise, came out with the fountain pen. My father was not elated.

Well, we struggled along for a few months, but you know how it is with father and son, they don't always work well together. Besides, I guess selling wasn't my racket. My father had always impressed on me how important the other man's time was, and I think he overdid it. So I retired from the candy business and still needed a job.

We hear about those people who, while still playing with their rattles, know exactly what they want to do in life. Well, I was twenty-two and I'd never had any idea what I wanted to do. Naturally I got in the doldrums. My parents were patient—my mother was the sweetest person I've ever known—and they didn't push me. I lay around the apartment on West 88th Street, played bridge in the afternoon and evening, and fell asleep around 3 A.M. listening to Clyde McCoy playing "Sugar Blues." My father, who was tough on me but loved me, thought I should see a psychiatrist. And I did, twice a week.

During this period an uncle got me a job with an industrial designer. Salary, $18 a week. The designer insisted I wear a hat, a Homburg no less; this purchase ate up my excess profits. I accompanied my employer to different stores he represented, with the thought that sooner or later I would catch on to the business. But I wasn't a quick learner. However, before I could get fired the designer offered to raise my salary from $18 a week to $50 a week, if I stopped seeing the psychiatrist, and he proposed we take a trip to Florida together. I was just bright enough to sense an ulterior motive, and resigned.

Insurance, candy, and industrial design—two strikes and a foul tip. Back to bridge, Clyde McCoy, and the psychiatrist. My parents were discouraged but they weren't surprised. My father always expected I'd have trouble making a living. I had no discernible useful aptitude, and my father had a suspicion that I was lazy (which suspicion he didn't keep from me). Privately, I agreed with him.

Anyway, lazy or not, I didn't have a job. One night at the bridge club one of the players, who knew I was indigent, said I might like the brokerage business. Wall Street was the last place I'd have thought of trying, and with reluctance kept an appointment he made. My father went with me to the garment district branch of Cohen, Simondson & Co., members of the New York Stock Exchange. I was interviewed by a customer's broker who needed an assistant to answer his phones and keep his charts. I got the job, $25 a week. I thought I got it on my good looks, but years later I learned that my father had paid the customer's broker twenty weeks' salary in advance.

This time I took an interest in a job. The fluctuating prices and the gamble of the stock market struck one of my aptitudes. And it wasn't hard looking at the pretty models in the garment district. In a week I felt so much better that I tendered my resignation to the psychiatrist. Six months later I passed a stock exchange test, and became a junior customer's broker.

Although I liked the stock market, I was no threat to make a fortune; part of the job was approaching people for business and I didn't like that—it was selling again. After several years with Cohen, Simondson, I applied for a job as a full customer's broker at Bache & Co., and got turned down. Then E. A. Pierce & Co., later Merrill Lynch, Pierce, Fenner & Bean, took a chance and gave me a job at $75 a week—which I didn't quite earn.

While at Merrill Lynch I met a spry, eighty-year-old partner of the firm, Almar Shatford. In those days I got the flu and colds a lot and, being from Alabama, bundled up in cold weather. Mr. Shatford advised me to cut out that nonsense and wear less clothing. The first year I just wore a topcoat and there was improvement. The next year I discarded the topcoat and didn't get a single cold. And there was a serendipitous effect. Till then, when I was late to work, Victor Cook, our managing partner, would give me a friendly unfriendly look. But now I had the edge on Victor. When I arrived late, without a topcoat, Vic couldn't be sure I wasn't returning from the men's room.

I wasn't what you'd call a hard worker. There was usually an hour for lunch at Wilfred's across the street, and when the market closed at three o'clock I was on my way to my real enjoyment, bridge at the Cavendish Club. At my peak I was no more than a mediocre customer's broker. In market judgment I was probably above average—my charts were a big help here—but in commissions for the firm I was a dud. My career high was a salary of $1,000 a month—and this was more than my friend Victor Cook ever expected of me.

Making a thousand a month must have unsettled my brain because, although classified 4-F, I volunteered for the Coast Guard. At Sheepshead Bay I worked my way steadily up through the ranks, to Seaman 2nd Class. The Coast Guard sifted through my talents, and put me in a high position—on top of a garbage wagon where I was third in charge. But enough of my wartime exploits.

From the Coast Guard I returned to Merrill Lynch and my job as a customer's broker. One afternoon, after playing gin at the City Athletic Club, Chester Gaines, a specialist on the floor of the New York Stock Exchange, said that judging by the way I played gin I'd do well trading on the floor, and should buy a seat. It was a good idea but the funds I had were a little short of the purchase price—about ninety-seven percent short.

In those days I used to play golf with a friend, Jerry Ohrbach, at Metropolis Country Club (let me brag and say I won the club championship seven years in a row). One day, when we were in the same foursome, I got a seven on the first hole, an easy par five. I was steaming, and asked Jerry what odds he would give against my getting a thirty-three on that nine. Par was thirty-five, so that meant I would have to be four under for the next eight holes. Jerry said 1,000-to-1. I said I'll take a hundred dollars worth of that if you like, and he said okay. He could afford the hundred thousand and I could afford the hundred dollars. Jerry had the best of the odds and I had a shot at my Alan Rice fortune. I made him sweat to the last hole. I needed a birdie there for the thirty-three, but didn't come close.

When Chester Gaines made the suggestion of the stock exchange seat, I spoke to Jerry about it. He told me that the golf bet had scared him so much he would like to be partners with me. By borrowing from my father, one of my uncles, my wife, and adding my own few dollars, I got up twenty-five percent of the necessary capital. Jerry and his father, Nathan, put up the rest and became limited partners in the small firm, Dreyfus & Co., members of the New York Stock Exchange. And we lived happily ever after. Well, not quite.

Our back office work was done by Bache & Co., the firm that had turned me down as a customer's broker. A friend of mine, John Behrens, handled my accounts in the office, and I went to the floor of the Exchange where I did two-dollar brokerage and traded for the firm's account. I liked the floor. It was a lot of walking—with a little thinking thrown in—and the hours of ten to three fitted well with my lazy bones.

In the first year, 1946, with capital of $100,000, we made $14,000 trading. Not as bad as you'd think—'46 was a bear market. A floor joke describes it, "The market was so bad that not even the liars made money." I don't think Nathan Ohrbach realized how well we did not to have lost our shirts. Nathan, who had the misfortune to walk into a brokerage office for the first time in 1929, had the indestructible opinion that you couldn't beat the market and was restless for Dreyfus & Co. to become a commission firm.

One day Jerry introduced me to one of the partners of the firm of Lewisohn & Sons. The capital partners wanted to retire, and Jerry and Nathan thought we should take over this old firm, stop clearing through Bache, and do our own back-office work. I mildly resisted—it didn't look like that good a deal, and besides it sounded like work. But I was told that three of the Lewisohn partners would remain and run the business, and I could stay on the floor. So I agreed.

We bought this turkey, with trimmings. The Ohrbachs and I got the trimmings. The excuse the capital partners had given for wanting to retire was that they were getting older. Even if they had been getting younger it would have been a good idea.

Without going into the reasons, it wasn't long before I had to leave the floor, where I was reasonably competent, and take on managing a brokerage firm, where I wasn't competent at all. Nathan Ohrbach soon found there were more ways of losing money on Wall Street than trading in the market. Our capital went down rapidly—mine vanished—and it looked like I was going to make my Alan Rice fortune in reverse. We couldn't even go out of business easily, and decided to try to stick it out. The Ohrbachs were good about it and drew no interest on their money. I cut my salary to zero, and we struggled along.

After a while business got so good we broke even. The Ohrbachs and I thought we should advertise, and we set aside $20,000 of hard (unearned) money for the purpose. In those days one agency handled all the Wall Street advertising, and it was dreary. I thought we should try another agency.

At that time the firm of Doyle, Dane, and Bernbach was in swaddling clothes. The partners were friends of the Ohrbachs and agreed to handle our account. But for our budget they couldn't afford to write the copy. So I had to. To my great surprise I loved it; it was an aptitude that had been hidden from me. Our account executive, Freddie Dossenbach, and I used to have lunch at a corner table next to a window at Schwartz's on Broad Street. Inspired by Swiss cheese and liverwurst, with iced tea, I'd write copy to fit Freddie's cartoons. The ads were so different from what was being done on Wall Street that we got a lot of attention for the money spent. Business got better and the firm started to grow. Soon we had enough partners to always have a quorum for an argument.

One day the Dreyfus Fund walked through the front door and we didn't know it. A fine gentleman, John Nesbett, applied for a position. John was the sole proprietor of a $600,000 mutual fund, the Nesbett Fund. He had struggled with it for several years, but with a management fee of $3,000 a year it had become impractical for him to continue. When John joined Dreyfus & Co. the name of his fund was changed to the Dreyfus Fund, and we took over the struggle. In the next five years Dreyfus & Co. lost about a million and a half dollars of its earnings on the Fund. During that period I got looks from some of my partners that at best could be called askance. But one day the fund started to break even. From then on it became a winner.

I made money in the stock market, a great deal of it in Polaroid stock. Did I carefully screen the list to select this stock? No. I wouldn't even have known there was such a company if I hadn't had a brother-in-law who worked there. I bought the stock initially for the wrong reason—Polaroid's 3-D glasses—and made money because of the camera.

It would appear I had some luck. The Ohrbachs pushed me into the commission business, the Dreyfus Fund walked into the office, and I bought the right stock for the wrong reason. As I said earlier I was an implausible person to have made a lot of money.

In the late 1960s I retired from my businesses. Since then I have worked full time with the Dreyfus Medical Foundation.

• • •

The newly established Dreyfus Medical Foundation funded

its first study in 1966—with hope, and $57,000. It was a dud. It could be called a waste of time and money. But that wouldn't be quite right—it was part of education. I was learning how difficult it was to develop anyone's interest in DPH. As to the study, I'll make it brief. And I'll skip names. As explained earlier, complaining is not one of the purposes of this book.

Dr. Turner introduced me to members of the staff of a large hospital in the metropolitan area. They said they were interested in DPH and had a good patient population for conducting a study. I explained what had happened in the previous study—I didn't want to make that sort of mistake again—and said I'd like to be present in the early stages of the work. My experience, unsophisticated as it was, might be useful. They agreed to this and asked for $57,000 for the study.

I'd been given the impression that the study would start without delay, but it wasn't for several months that I was invited to attend the first interview with patients, conducted by Dr. Blank.

Four patients were interviewed in my presence. To my dismay, I was not allowed to say a word to these patients, although I sat just a few feet from them. If I wanted to ask a question, I had to write it on a slip of paper and hand it to Dr. Blank. Using "local mail" didn't improve my ability to communicate with these patients. One case is worth mentioning, a man who said he jackknifed in bed at night. Dr. Blank didn't ask for particulars, but I did—by note—and learned that several times each night, before he fell asleep, the patient's legs would jerk up almost to his head. I was surprised that DPH had not already been tried with him —these involuntary movements seemed a form of convulsion. After the session I expressed the opinion to Dr. Blank that three of the four patients were good candidates for DPH. I was never told whether they were given it—there was an air of mystery about everything—but I don't think they were.

The upshot of this study was that, two years later, the physician in charge of the study made the vapid statement at a medical meeting that "more work was needed in this field." Well, you couldn't argue with that.

It's hard to realize how frustrating this was. Here I was, eager to give money for studies on an established medicine, and couldn't find the right people to give it to.

• • •

One fine day, in 1966, Dr. Turner asked me if I'd like to participate in the conduct of a study. I told him I'd like to, but I didn't know it was possible. Bill said he thought it could be arranged. A few weeks later Bill made arrangements through a friend of his, Dr. Oscar Resnick of the Worcester Foundation, for that foundation and ours to conduct a joint study at the Worcester County Jail.

Bill and I visited Dr. Resnick at his home in Worcester, Massachusetts, the following Sunday. On both sides of a nice lunch we discussed the proposed study. Until Bill had brought up the subject, I'd never thought about a study in a prison. After all a prison is not a hospital and doesn't necessarily have sick people. But now that I thought about it, it seemed that nervous conditions could be a contributing cause in many criminal acts, particularly those of anger and violence. I discussed this with Dr. Resnick, who had done many studies at this jail. He agreed and said he thought we'd find an ample number of people who had problems with their nerves.

When we discussed how the interview with the prisoners should be conducted, Oscar won a lifelong friendship with me when he said, "Look, Jack, you know what you're looking for. It'll be a lot easier if you ask the questions. I'll chime in when I think it's necessary."

This jail study was to be an unusual experience for me—in some ways the most fruitful of my life.

8.
ELEVEN ANGRY MEN

In 1966 Dr. Resnick and I conducted a study on the effects of DPH with prisoners at the Worcester County Jail in Massachusetts. It was done on a double-blind crossover basis. Helping us with the study was Ms. Barbara Homan, medical assistant to Dr. Turner.

The Worcester County Jail was a "short-term" jail. Although some of the inmates had committed serious crimes, no one sentenced to more than eighteen months was sent there.

From the outside the jail looked like an ordinary building. On the inside, except in the cell area, it resembled an old high school. For our work we were assigned a small room with a nice window on the second floor. This room was plainly furnished but comfortable, with a long table and some chairs. Liaison with the prisoners was handled by Lt. William D'Orsay, a kind and well-liked man.

Drug studies were not uncommon at the jail.* It was the custom for these studies to be done with volunteers, paid a dollar a day. We followed custom. Ms. Homan did preliminary screening of forty-two volunteers, and eliminated twenty of the least likely candidates. This left twenty-two volunteers for Dr. Resnick and me to interview.

These twenty-two volunteers were interviewed carefully. This was a study of individuals, not prisoners; we had no intention of giving DPH to anyone just because he was in prison. We

---

* Clearance for the study was given by the warden, Sheriff Joseph Smith, and Dr. Cyrus Paskevitch, the prison physician.

were looking for individuals who had symptoms we thought would respond to DPH. Among the most important of these symptoms were: excessive anger, excessive fear, and an over-busy mind that was difficult to turn off.

After two days of interviews, eleven prisoners were selected. Most of them had participated in other drug studies and didn't expect to get a medicine that would actually help them. They thought we were doing the study for our own purposes and they had volunteered mainly to ease their boredom. When we told them that we wanted only the truth about what the medicine did, they expressed skepticism that it would do anything. This attitude was good—it minimized the possibility of their being psychologically influenced.

In the initial interviews I was glad I was not alone in the room with a few of the prisoners. There was an animalistic bristle about them you could feel. One man had eyes with a yellowish glow that reminded me of an ocelot I'd seen. After a few interviews, whether because of DPH or getting to know them better, I felt comfortable with all the prisoners.

Dr. Resnick left most of the questioning of the prisoners to me. I tried to keep the interviews comfortable and friendly. This seemed to help the subjects relax and they spoke freely. Some of them were more expressive than others, but communication was good with all of them.

Procedure. The eleven prisoners chosen for the study were interviewed for a second time, this time intensively. As specifically as we could, we got an inventory of their symptoms and complaints. Then they were placed on DPH (100 mg in the morning and 50 mg in the afternoon) and were not told what to expect of the medicine. They were interviewed several hours after the initial dose, the next day, and again at the end of a week.

Remarkable improvement in symptoms was observed. To see if similar results would be obtained under the most objective circumstances, we decided to do a double-blind, crossover to single-blind, study.

To do such a study it was desirable to approximate the original conditions. We thought this could be achieved by taking the prisoners off DPH for a week. However, when they were interviewed at the end of the week, their general condition was better than when we had first met them. It was as though the week on DPH had been a vacation from their nerves and the benefits had carried forward. We had to wait a second week before the original conditions were approximated.

Before starting the double-blind study we explained the procedure to the prisoners. Some of them would receive DPH, others an inert substance called a placebo.* The capsules would be identical in appearance—the prisoners wouldn't know what they contained and we wouldn't know, thus "double-blind." Then they would be interviewed as before: a few hours after the first pill, after a night's sleep, and a week later. At that time we would make our decision as to which of them had received DPH, and which placebo.

What we did not tell the prisoners was that when this decision had been made, those subjects we thought had been on placebo would be placed on "single-blind." They would be given DPH without being told it was DPH. In that way, further non-subjective evidence would be obtained.

Summary

We were correct in our assessment of ten of the prisoners on the double-blind. We were incorrect in one. The circumstances in this case were unusual.†

In the study it was observed that the eleven prisoners had many symptoms in common that responded to DPH. Among these symptoms in common were restlessness, irritability, fear,

---

* Six bottles contained DPH, six placebo. The bottles were coded, the code in a sealed envelope given to us by the druggist.

† In the early part of the study, Danny R.'s response to DPH was similar to that of the other prisoners. During the control part of the study, Danny R. got news that made him think his daughter was going blind. He didn't tell us, and we misassessed his realistic nervousness and decided he was on placebo. (For details, see Appendix, p. 134.)

anger, inability to concentrate, poor mood, lack of energy, sleeping problems, and an overactive brain.

Symptoms not common to all prisoners, such as headache, stomach distress, chest pain, muscular pain, skin rash, and dizziness, disappeared while the subjects were on DPH and reappeared when it was withdrawn.

This study was recorded on tape with the prisoners' permission. Transcribed, there are 605 pages covering 130 interviews.*

The best way to get an understanding of the effects of DPH is by reading the prisoners' own words. Brief summaries of the eleven cases are included in this book—eight in the Appendix, three in this chapter. The three summaries included here are not special. Please see the other eight in the Appendix, p. 129.

PHILIP B.

BEFORE DILANTIN:

I am quite nervous now. I've been more or less nervous all my life. And shake a lot, you just feel it, that you're shaking.

If I get nervous my hands break out in a little rash. I get tightness in my chest quite often. It's a pain, it takes your breath away sometimes.

I think a lot, there is too much on my mind. I try to put it out of my mind and it just stays there. The mind wanders and it doesn't focus on what I'm doing. Sometimes it's three o'clock in the morning before I get to sleep.

ON DILANTIN:

I feel good all over now. I seem to relax a lot more. Since I've been taking the pills I haven't been walking around, pacing back and forth so much. These past few nights I've been going right to sleep.

I haven't been so depressed. I've been eating better. And I haven't had those pains in my chest. And I can concentrate better on my work and I'm not making as many mistakes.

DOUBLE-BLIND

OFF DILANTIN (TWO WEEKS):

Well, I feel I'm right back where I was before I started taking the pills. I don't sleep well. I walk around all the time. Nervous all the time —agitated, quick-tempered, get shook up.

I'm always thinking—wandering away—always thinking of different things. I've been very depressed.

---

* An 80-page condensation is available in limited number for those interested. The 605-page transcript is on file at the Dreyfus Medical Foundation.

I feel good, very good, feel a lot better, honestly. And I haven't had those chest pains this week at all. The rash—it cleared right up. I'm more relaxed.

I can just forget about things now. I've been able to do my work better. The last few days I've been goin' to sleep right off. I feel much better than I have for the last three years.

Philip B. was on Dilantin.

CLIFFORD S.

BEFORE DILANTIN:

I'm very highstrung . . . I let everything build up inside . . . Then I just explode. I do a lot of thinking.

I get these wicked headaches . . . I'll take six or seven aspirin . . . and the headache won't go away. I'll have it all day.

I don't sleep well. Between twelve and two in the morning I usually get these nightmares . . . scare a guy right out of his head.

ON DILANTIN:

I just feel wonderful . . . You know how I can feel my nerves are relaxed? I've done four paintings; I don't paint when I'm nervous because I can't concentrate . . . If I can sit down and do a painting a day it makes me happy.

I'm in a good mood. I don't feel angry at anybody . . . I've only really got mad once since the last time I seen you. It went right away.

I've been sleeping a lot. I ain't jumpy all the time. I ain't looking behind me anymore.

DOUBLE-BLIND

OFF DILANTIN (TWO WEEKS):

I'm tense inside, I can't stay in one place too long, I get up and move around . . . I just pick a book up, look at it and throw it back down.

I feel that anger . . . Whenever I get in a fight I can't control myself.

I wake up about five or six times during the night.

UNIDENTIFIED CAPSULE (ONE WEEK):

My nerves are jittery inside . . . I can't sit in one place too long.

This week when I was lifting, I got dizzy three or four times and I was only working out with light weights.

I know my mind's always been going on. Actually, I don't feel these pills have done anything for me.

Clifford S. was on placebo.

SINGLE-BLIND

ON DILANTIN:

I just feel good. I am completely relaxed . . . I ain't nervous, tense or nothing.

There's no anger at all.

Sleep better . . . ain't tired . . . all kinds of energy; washing windows, floors. I can concentrate better.

DAVID H.

BEFORE DILANTIN:

I have a temper that shouldn't be . . . I shake when I'm angry and can't stop. I have stomach trouble . . . I think it's from nerves.

If something happens, I twist and turn it in my mind until I've made a problem out of nothing . . . I can't turn my mind off. I can't go to sleep.

Quite often I'll get depressed and start worrying about home and what's going on outside these lovely walls. I lose all hope and energy.

ON DILANTIN:

Well, I feel I'm a lot calmer . . . I can sit still, without jumping up.

For the past five or six days I've been sure of myself in the things I say and what I do. I get angry just as fast but I can control it . . . it doesn't keep poppin' back into my mind.

I'll read three or four chapters without knowing what I read. Now I can lie there and remember what I've read.

I've been eating my meals and enjoying them.

DOUBLE-BLIND

OFF DILANTIN (TWO WEEKS):

I feel very tired, irritable and grouchy. I'm not getting along well . . . People are getting on my nerves to the extent where I'm ready to assassinate them.

I don't eat hardly anything . . . I'm not sleeping very well . . . I feel just terrible.

I got a few problems and I just can't get them out of my mind. I'm worrying about them all the time . . . I've tried my case a thousand times.

UNIDENTIFIED CAPSULE (ONE WEEK):

I think I'm on the Dilantin right now. I'm not nervous . . . I'm not tense or ready to jump at anyone.

I'm not grouchy . . . I seem to still have a temper, but I go into a situation with a little more confidence. I don't just jump off the handle.

I seem able to push my thoughts aside . . . read a couple of stories and know what I read.

I feel fine as far as my stomach goes . . . My appetite has picked up . . . I been sleeping better . . . able to go right to sleep.

David H. was on Dilantin.

SUGGESTIONS FROM THE PRISONERS
FOR THE USE OF DPH IN PRISONS

When the study was over we met with the inmates as a group for the first time. Each of the prisoners had told us he wanted to continue taking DPH. But I learned this was not going to be permitted, and there was nothing I could do about that. But I could tell the prisoners what I knew about the medicine—it might be useful to them later on.

We had a long, friendly discussion. As we were saying goodbye John G. volunteered:

> JOHN G: If this pill was ever put on the market it would be a godsend to both Walpole and Concord prisons. Judging by this group here, it'd work miracles up there. You have men doing ten, fifteen, twenty, and life. And that's where I'd like to see them back up a whole truckload of the stuff and—
>
> JACK D: You mean Dilantin?
>
> JOHN G: Dilantin is right. Those guys are walkin' on edge all the time. There's where the trouble starts, more so than here. These fellows are all going fairly short. Up there you got a bunch of fellows that got nothing to lose and, well, they're all packed in together.
>
> JACK D: You think that in those prisons—
>
> JOHN G: I think they need it even worse than the fellows do here. You can ask Jim and Spike.
>
> JACK D: Do you agree with that, Spike?
>
> VICTOR M: Oh, yes, I agree with that very much.
>
> JACK D: What would you say, Jim?
>
> JAMES L: The same thing. I was there for a while myself and I know. It would help a lot of them guys. You walk around there and if you say the wrong thing, you're liable to go bouncing off the wall.
>
> JOHN G: Those guys are so on edge they gotta take yellow jackets and bennies once in a while to relieve that. What if they didn't have this tension built up? They wouldn't have the trouble they do now.
>
> JACK D: Well John, thank you for the thought.

The prisoners' suggestion that the use of DPH, on a voluntary basis, be permitted inside a prison should be considered.

Some prisoners are in jail because of problems in their nervous systems, and these problems are exacerbated by their confinement. With too much time to think and brood, it's no wonder that some prisoners live in a sort of hell—and can't help imposing it on those around them. Allowing DPH to be taken on a voluntary basis could make an important difference to those individuals who need it—and to others who are endangered by their potential for violence. When one realizes that DPH is not habit-forming, withholding it from prisoners may not be a protection of their rights.

• • •

As stated earlier, this study was not of prisoners as such but a study of individuals with problems of their nervous systems. The objective was to see if, in a double-blind study, the effects of DPH that had been observed on an uncontrolled basis would be confirmed. They were, and additional effects of DPH were observed.*

I felt the time had come to go to the Federal government.

---

* I participated in two further studies in institutions, one with Dr. Resnick at the Lyman Reformatory for Boys in Lyman, Massachusetts, the other at the Patuxent Institution in Maryland, with Dr. Joel Elkes, head of psychiatry at Johns Hopkins, and Dr. Joseph Stephens and Dr. Lino S. Covi, also of Hopkins. Although not controlled studies, the results were similar to those of the Worcester study. (See p. 136.)

9.
TRAVELS
WITH THE GOVERNMENT

Few of us have a clear picture of the Federal government and how it operates. With millions of people in it, government has to be run by regulations. This leads to routine. Where there's routine, innovation doesn't thrive. I'm not being critical, government means well. But I'll tell you this, if you want the government to do something outside of routine—and expect to see it happen in your lifetime—you'd better arrange for reincarnation.

I didn't know this in 1966, and with the optimism of a boy scout I approached the Federal government. I would have gone to the government sooner but had felt the evidence was too informal. Now, with the jail study done, the time was right. I had two thoughts in mind. The first was that the government might take the matter off my hands. I hoped for this, but wasn't counting on it. My second thought was that I didn't want to do anything contrary to government policy. Their objectives and mine were the same. If I was to proceed on my own, I needed official advice.

There were two logical places to go: the Department of Health, Education and Welfare, and the Food and Drug Administration. Since I was a layman, the Department of Health seemed the appropriate place. At that time John W. Gardner was Secretary of H.E.W. It took me about a month to get an appointment with the Secretary. That seemed like a long time.

When I got to know the government better I realized that a month was instantaneous.

I met with Secretary Gardner in Washington in May 1966. We talked for fifty minutes. That is, I talked for the first forty minutes and he talked for the last ten. In those forty minutes I summarized my experience with Dilantin and my observations of its benefits in others. I told him of my disappointment in the two hospital studies I'd sponsored, of setting up the Dreyfus Medical Foundation, and of the double-blind study at the Worcester County Jail.

Secretary Gardner listened. From the experience I'd had it wouldn't have surprised me if he had been skeptical. But he wasn't. The Secretary seemed to sense that I was on the right track. Although he didn't suggest that the government take a hand, he gave me three helpful suggestions.

The first suggestion had to do with my unmedical terminology. The Secretary laughed when I made my "dry twigs" analogy. He said he liked it but thought more sophisticated language would stand me in good stead in talking with physicians. Of course he was right, and now I talk of "post-tetanic potentiation" and "post-tetanic afterdischarge" as if they were old friends. His second suggestion was that I should tell Parke-Davis about my findings. I followed this suggestion, too, as will be explained later.

The third suggestion came as a surprise, but I welcomed it. The Secretary said I should seek national publicity for the story. He understood my disappointment with the lack of results from the two hospitals. However, he was sure that somewhere in the United States there were hospitals and physicians who would be interested in the story.

I told Secretary Gardner I could try *Life* magazine. A few months earlier *Life* had done a kind article about me by Marshall Smith with the understated title, "Maverick Wizard Behind the Wall Street Lion." Marshall and I had become good friends, and I thought he might introduce me to *Life*'s science department.

The Secretary said that *Life* would be an excellent place for this story, if they would do it.

The meeting with Secretary Gardner was most helpful. His suggestions were good and I followed them all.

• • •

It wasn't easy to get *Life* magazine to do a medical article recommended by a layman. Albert Rosenfeld, *Life*'s science editor, was understandably cautious. He had several sessions with me in which he listened carefully to the evidence. Then Al said he would like to do the story, but *Life* would require a medical event as a peg. He said a medical meeting would serve the purpose. Before making a firm commitment, however, Al wanted to get the reactions of a good friend, Dr. Joel Elkes, Director of Psychiatry at Johns Hopkins.

Before I met Dr. Elkes I thought of him as a hurdle. But after a discussion with him, I found I had a friend. Dr. Elkes said the subject was of particular interest since ten years earlier he had planned to do research on DPH with other physicians. But just at that time an exciting new medicine, thorazine, had appeared, and their interest had been sidetracked. Dr. Elkes was helpful in setting up the meeting that *Life* required, and in 1966 a symposium on DPH was held at the annual meeting of the American College of Neuropsychopharmacology.

In September 1967 *Life* published an article by Albert Rosenfeld—"10,000-to-1 Payoff." The article was a turning point. The response to it, and to the *Reader's Digest* condensation of it printed in thirteen languages, forced us to increase our small staff to keep up with phone calls and to answer letters. Many physicians wrote that they were using DPH for a variety of purposes.

We received thousands of letters from the public. The best side of human nature showed up. The writers expressed deep appreciation for benefits they got from DPH as a result of the articles. Many described their experiences in detail in the hope that by so doing they might help others. We selected a hundred

of these letters and made a booklet for physicians. But reader-
ship was poor; doctors consider letters "anecdotal."

The *Life* and *Reader's Digest* articles opened things up. Now
there were institutions and individual physicians with genuine
interest in doing work on DPH. Soon the Foundation was sponsoring over a dozen studies. We got as far from home base as
Chichester, England. There, Dr. Lionel Haward, in a series of
double-blind studies with normal volunteers, demonstrated that
DPH improved cognitive function. In the United States, perhaps
the most significant of these early studies was by Stephens and
Shaffer at Johns Hopkins. In a double-blind crossover study,
they found DPH to be markedly effective in reducing symptoms
related to fear and anger.

During this period Dr. Turner was searching the medical
literature to see if previous work had been done on DPH. To my
surprise he and his staff found hundreds of studies, published
over the previous twenty years. These studies, in addition to
confirming our observations in thought and mood, reported
DPH to be useful for a variety of other disorders. Among them
were cardiac disorders, trigeminal neuralgia, migraine, diabetes,
pruritus ani, ulcers, and asthma.

• • •

Three years after I had met with Secretary Gardner, I was
ready to go back to the government. When I had seen the Secretary I didn't have a lot of evidence. But now I was loaded for
bear. This was a mistake. I should have brought an elephant
gun. Republicans were in.

In the sequence of events we come to President Richard M.
Nixon. By chance I knew Mr. Nixon before he became President.
I'd seen his interview on "The David Susskind Show," and as a
result, without being asked, had contributed to his presidential
campaign. When Mr. Nixon was defeated I got to know him.
When he lost the race for Governor of California I knew he had

no chance to become President. If you can't win your own state, you can't win the United States.

That's what I thought, but Mr. Nixon was nominated for President in 1968. Again I contributed to his campaign; I also contributed to the campaign of Senator Hubert Humphrey. And I did what I suppose was an unusual thing. I told each I was contributing to the campaign of the other. In this matter of public health, it was important for me to be known by whichever one became President. I was able to talk to both before the election. With Mr. Nixon, I had a long conversation about DPH at Key Biscayne.

My discussion with Senator Humphrey about DPH took place at his headquarters in New York. When we finished he said, "Listen son [that nearly got my vote], whether I win or lose, I want you to get back to me on this." I couldn't have hoped for anything nicer than that. After the election I was anxious to get back to the Senator but it took three months to get an appointment. We had coffee in his suite at the Waldorf-Astoria. He showed up from a bedroom in shirt sleeves, and I had the feeling we were going to get down to work. I started off enthusiastically. Then I noticed there was no response in his face, and his gaze was fixed on a picture on the wall in back of me. In about fifteen minutes my enthusiasm started to run down. When I left soon after, I had the feeling that Senator Humphrey was relieved. I was too, but deeply disappointed.

• • •

After Mr. Nixon became President I waited a few months for him to settle into position, so to speak, and then called Rose Mary Woods, his nice and well-known secretary. I spoke to her for quite a while, explaining what an urgent medical matter this was, and told her I would send her some written information. I asked her to please not talk to the President about it, just give it some thought and advise me on the best way to approach him on the matter. I'm really dumber than the law allows. Of course Rose Mary, as any good secretary would, told President Nixon about it. A few days later she called to tell me the material had been sent to Secretary of Health Finch and I would hear from him shortly. I had hoped to see the President himself, but this was fine. I waited to hear from Secretary Finch.

Days went by without my hearing from the Secretary and I started to get restless. By the time three months had elapsed I was beside myself (not easy). I didn't have sense enough, or guts enough, to pick up the phone and call Secretary Finch, so I spoke to a friend who had a friend who knew the Secretary. This worked. Apparently the material Miss Woods had sent three months earlier hadn't reached Secretary Finch on the conveyor belt that carries things to the desk of a Secretary of Health. I got a call from Secretary Finch's secretary and an appointment was made.

Dr. Bogoch and I met with Secretary Finch in his office in December 1969. The Secretary didn't say whether he had discussed the matter with President Nixon, but he'd had a chance to look at the material I had sent the President, the *Life* and *Reader's Digest* articles, excerpts from letters from physicians, and a condensed version of the Worcester Jail Study. I hadn't wanted to burden the President with medical studies. But for the Secretary of Health I brought, in a bulging briefcase, hundreds of medical studies on the use of DPH for a variety of disorders. The Secretary was impressed.

After we'd been with Secretary Finch a short while, he asked Dr. Jesse L. Steinfeld, who had been appointed Surgeon General the previous day, to join us. Then, with both present, Dr. Bogoch and I briefly summarized the clinical evidence and basic mechanisms of action of DPH.

When we finished I told Secretary Finch about my meeting with Secretary Gardner three years earlier, and the advice he'd given me. Since that time so much new information had come into the possession of the Dreyfus Medical Foundation, facts not generally known, there was no question that this was now a matter for the government. To convey the information to the government, Dr. Bogoch and I proposed that we have a two-day conference with a broadly representative group of government physicians, including members of the FDA. At such a conference we would present the medical information, and the government would be able to take it from there.

After we had made our proposal, Secretary Finch turned to the Surgeon General and said, "Let's get moving on this. How long will it take you to get a group together to meet with the Dreyfus Medical Foundation? How soon can you get a conference set up?"

"Probably in a couple of weeks," Dr. Steinfeld said.

"Well, do it faster if you can, but do it within two weeks," Secretary Finch told him. Apparently my sense of urgency had been picked up by the Secretary. We thanked him, and after exchanging telephone numbers with Dr. Steinfeld, Dr. Bogoch and I left with the feeling that the government would soon play its part.

When we got back to New York, Dr. Bogoch and I started the hard work of getting the data organized for the conference in two weeks. Four days went by before it occurred to me that we hadn't heard from the Surgeon General. Although Secretary Finch had given him explicit instructions to hold this meeting without delay, I thought it possible Dr. Steinfeld might be waiting for a call from me. I phoned him. His secretary said he was in conference and would call back. He didn't call back and I called again the next day. He was still in conference. This was the beginning of my awareness that phoning the Surgeon General and getting to speak to him were not exactly the same thing.

Several days later the Surgeon General called to say that he had been thinking about the conference; he thought we should have a meeting to discuss it and would like to have Dr. Bert Brown, head of the National Institute of Mental Health, with him. We were prepared to meet without delay, but he said he would be tied up for a week and suggested that the four of us meet in Washington on January 14. I could see that things were not going as smoothly as I'd hoped; the meeting to discuss the meeting that was supposed to have taken place in two weeks, wouldn't take place for three weeks.

On the fourteenth we arrived in Washington to have dinner with Dr. Steinfeld and Bert Brown. Dr. Brown was not present. The Surgeon General explained that his secretary had forgotten to invite him. Without Dr. Brown the Surgeon General felt we didn't have a "quorum" and would have to have another meeting. We were taken aback. Still, we felt the time could be put to good use if we enlarged on Dr. Steinfeld's sketchy background on DPH. We did our best, but we didn't seem to have the Surgeon General's full attention because he would frequently interject, "I don't know how my secretary forgot to call Dr. Brown."

Before we left Washington we discussed our next meeting with Dr. Steinfeld. Where we should meet seemed a problem to him. He said maybe we should meet in a motel. I didn't know what that meant, but to get things moving I would have met in the men's room. We left Washington with no definite date. I began to have the feeling that I was looking at the "Finch medical conference" through the wrong end of a telescope.

I was not born with an oversupply of patience. Even with Dilantin I am short of perfection. This is to explain to the reader that the next six months were about as frustrating and exasperating a period of time as one could hope not to enjoy. It was that long before we had another meeting with the Surgeon General, this time with Dr. Brown. Both before and after this meeting, with a skill unequalled in my experience, Jesse ducked and dodged, retreated and sidestepped, and left me so off balance that I felt something was going to happen any day. Each time I managed to catch the Surgeon General on the telephone, a new subject would come up for consideration, such as, what physicians we should bring with us, where the meeting should take place, how many people should attend, what medical disciplines should be represented, and who should chair the meeting. (It was finally decided that Jesse should chair it.) It could have been chaired by Little Orphan Annie because the meeting never took place.

We kept contact with the Surgeon General, and this mirage of a meeting, for well over a year. His superb talent for keeping our interest alive, without doing anything other than that, explains why we did not think of going back to Secretary Finch until it was too late. (He left office six months after we met.)

The end came in the following way. We had gotten the Surgeon General pinned down to a meeting, the date made well in advance and its importance emphasized. Dr. Bogoch and I were going to review the medical data at length, feeling that this would motivate Dr. Steinfeld to set up the conference without further delay. And I was determined at this meeting to lay it on the line—either get results, or not.

A few days before the scheduled meeting I got a telephone call from Dr. Steinfeld's secretary saying she was sorry but we'd have to cancel the meeting for the coming Monday. I said, "But we had things all arranged for a full presentation. Why can't he make it?"

"He has to go out West on Monday to investigate the earthquake," she said. (An earthquake had occurred in California a week earlier.) If Jesse had been going to California to prevent the earthquake, well, good luck. But to cancel a medical meeting of this importance to visit an earthquake that had already happened, and not even propose a new date for the meeting, was too much. I said to myself, The heck with it, and Jesse didn't have any more of my phone calls to dodge.

I never did find out what a Surgeon General was supposed to do. He didn't do surgery, and he didn't command troops. Maybe the government couldn't find out either because when Dr. Steinfeld left, the office was retired.*

At the time Dr. Steinfeld left government, *The New York Times* reported him to have said that Federal health affairs were in a "kind of chaos." He was "frustrated seeing how much good I might have achieved and how much was actually accomplished."

In a nutshell.

• • •

---

* The office of Surgeon General has been resurrected. We wish the new Surgeon General, Dr. Julius Richmond, the best of luck.

I had placed a lot of hope on the government's taking over DPH. I admit that part of this was because I wanted to be relieved of the responsibility and the work. But there was a more important reason. With its medical institutions, and its enormous resources and authority, the government could do a far better job than a single foundation. However, it wasn't long after the Finch conference that I began to get the idea that government lacked enthusiasm about taking over its responsibilities.

Maybe I should sum up my thoughts during this period. At the outset, when I became convinced that DPH had been overlooked, I knew that medical studies would be necessary to persuade others. After the initial unsuccessful attempts, the Foundation had sponsored numerous successful studies on DPH and was continuing in this effort. But by far the most important source of evidence was already in the medical literature. This evidence had been there for the picking, like good apples under a tree.

I don't know exactly when we passed the equator of ample evidence, but at some point our goal changed, and we decided that communicating already existing evidence was more important than finding new evidence. You know that old philosophical question about the tree falling in the forest—if nobody hears it, was there a sound? I'm not sure about that, but here was a practical question. If a great amount of evidence exists for the usefulness of a medicine, and the physician doesn't know about it, does it do any good? The answer is obvious. So communication became our number one objective.

Something other than trying to tell the story to the government had to be done. By this time we had collected so many published studies on DPH they would have filled a barrel. I would like to have Xeroxed the studies and sent each physician a barrelful saying, "You'll find this useful." But it wasn't practical. We had to attack the barrel ourselves, organize the studies, and condense them for the physicians. And that is what we did.

When we finished we had a bibliography and review of DPH, the clinical section arranged chronologically, the contents fairly evenly divided between clinical and basic mechanism of action studies. It was exhausting work for our group, and just the writing of it took over a year and a half. To keep our spirits up we worked on the theory that if a doctor matched a thousand hours of our effort with ten minutes of his own (aye, there's the rub) we'd show a profit—with 350,000 doctors in the U.S.A. The bibliography, *The Broad Range of Use of Diphenylhydantoin,* was the first of two that the Foundation published. About 400,000 copies were sent to physicians and basic scientists in the United States in 1970. The response was excellent, and we had letters of thanks from nearly a thousand physicians. Still, the facts about DPH did not spread as fast as I had hoped.

• • •

One Sunday morning in July 1971, my brain was playing with the communication problem. The Foundation was sponsoring studies of DPH, mostly in new fields, but we had no other immediate plans. The thought that government had the key responsibility for DPH was always in my mind. But I had taken my best shot with the government—President, Secretary of Health, and Surgeon General. Something else had to be done; I couldn't figure out what, and it bugged me.

It's funny how we remember unimportant things if they are associated with something important. That Sunday, my housekeeper Ida Thomas, whom I love and who has a feeling for me, sensed my mood and said, "Let me fix you something for breakfast instead of those old eggs and tomatoes you eat every day." I thanked her, and went back to thinking about the government. Interesting smells started coming out of the kitchen. Soon a delicious-looking pancake arrived, with powdered sugar and hot blueberry sauce. The first bite was on my fork when the phone rang.

A voice said, "This is Walter Tkach at the White House. I'm President Nixon's doctor, and I was just telling the President and Mrs. Nixon what a wonderful piece of work I thought you'd done." If an ancestor had called I couldn't have been more surprised. Just when I was wondering how to get back to the government, here was a spontaneous recommendation to the President, from his own doctor. I steadied my voice and thanked Dr. Tkach. Dr. Tkach went on to say, "The President suggested that I invite you to visit me in Washington and I hope you can make it soon." I said I could. We made a date for the following Tuesday. Then I ate Ida's pancake—and two more.

Tuesday I took a sensible morning plane to Washington that got me there at a quarter-to-ten. Dr. Tkach met me and drove me to the White House in his car. During the drive he told me that after a personal loss he'd benefited from DPH, and had the *Life* article to thank for it. I was glad he had firsthand experience with DPH; there's nothing like it to get an understanding of the medicine.

When we got to the White House, Dr. Tkach walked me past the gendarmes, and for a moment I had the feeling I was infiltrating the place. But when we got to his office Walter made me feel like a dignitary. He put me in a comfortable chair, got me a jug of coffee, and became a voluntary and patient listener for several hours. In that sympathetic atmosphere I did a good job of summarizing the DPH story.

At about twelve-thirty Dr. Tkach suggested lunch would be appropriate. He didn't have to drag me; I've always noticed that mental effort uses more calories than physical effort, and we went to the White House cafeteria. Walter hadn't told me we would have company for lunch, but he had invited Kenneth R. Cole, Jr., and James H. Cavanaugh, two members of the President's staff, to join us. I didn't get to eat as well as I'd hoped because I had to give a forty-five-minute summary of DPH. I emphasized the government's responsibility. Ken and Jim ate well and listened well.

When lunch was over Ken Cole, who outranked Jim Cavanaugh on the President's staff, said they would both try to be helpful in getting the story to the FDA. He said I could call him whenever necessary, but Jim would work with me on a regular basis. In the past I had been treated with courtesy by the government, but I'd felt a little like a salesman, carrying samples in his briefcase. Now I was being offered help without soliciting it and it put me in a different posture. When lunch was over I thanked them all.

Dr. Tkach drove me back to the airport. He said there wasn't any question that the government should do something about the DPH matter. But he cautioned me against being too optimistic. He said the problem wouldn't be with people I would meet but with the nature of bureaucracy. It was so big, and so besieged on all sides by people clamoring for its attention, that it was distracted from important matters—even if it could figure out which they were. A few years earlier I would have argued with Walter. Now I just kept my fingers crossed.

That same week Jim Cavanaugh came to New York and spent a day with Dr. Bogoch and me. It was one of those calorie-consuming days. I spent at least four hours going over clinical evidence, and Sam spent nearly half that time on the basic mechanisms. When he left, Jim had a good grasp of the facts. He said the next move would be for us to talk to Dr. Charles Edwards, Commissioner of the FDA.

Jim Cavanaugh made the appointment with Commissioner Edwards, and Dr. Bogoch and I spent a morning in the offices of the FDA. After a long talk with the Commissioner, he said he'd like us to explain this matter to senior members of his staff. I don't remember their names, I saw them only once, but they were sympathetic and tried to be helpful. After we outlined the story, they told us that the Foundation itself might be able to apply for new listings of DPH. They suggested that Dr. Herbert Ley, the previous head of the FDA, would be a good person to consult about procedure.* I didn't understand why the Foundation should apply to the FDA in a matter of health for the American public when that health was a direct responsibility of the FDA itself.

* We got in touch with Dr. Herbert Ley. Dr. Ley said he would like to review the summaries of the DPH studies in our bibliography; they seemed almost too good to be true. After spot-checking the summaries for a day he was satisfied. Since then Dr. Ley has been a consultant for the Foundation.

Still, I would have considered following the suggestion except for two reasons. One was that DPH appeared to be useful for so many disorders that to get them through the FDA in the routine way, single file so to speak, would have taken forever. The second reason was that if the Foundation did make applications for new uses of DPH, we might be required to be silent on the subject while applications were pending. We couldn't risk that.

Dr. Edwards visited the Foundation a few weeks later. When he had spent most of a day absorbing the medical information, he agreed that a conference with medical officials would be appropriate and said he would help set up such a conference.

Dr. Edwards made the arrangements and a two-day conference was held in our offices in February 1972. Since Dr. Edwards had already spent a day with us on DPH, he attended only the first day of the meeting. Others in attendance were Dr. Theodore Cooper (Director, the National Heart and Lung Institute), Dr. John Jennings, Dr. James Pittman, Dr. Samuel Kaim, James Cavanaugh, Dr. Samuel Bogoch, and myself.

This conference was hard work. There were four two-hour sessions in the two days. Dr. Bogoch and I conducted them and, except during the discussion periods, we did all the talking. I assure you I looked forward to lunch and coffee breaks (see agenda).

DREYFUS MEDICAL FOUNDATION

CONFERENCE ON DPH with FDA

February 22 and 23, 1972

Tuesday, February 22

10:00 A.M.   Background

                   Early evidence

                   Institutional studies (with reference to both crime and problems
                            within the institutions):
                            Worcester County Jail Study (double-blind)
                            Lyman School for Boys (Juvenile Delinquents)
                            Patuxent Institution

1:00 P.M.	Lunch
2:00 P.M.	Basic mechanisms of action of DPH:

        Effect on hyperexcitable nerve cell
        Suppression of post-tetanic potentiation
        Stabilization of membrane
        Regulatory effect on sodium and potassium
        Resistance to anoxia
        Increase of energy compounds in brain (glucose, ATP, and creatine phosphate)
        Stabilizing effects on labile diabetes
        Cerebral and coronary vessel dilatation
        Protection against digitalis toxicity
        Protection against cortisone toxicity
        Other antitoxic effects of interest: DDT, Cyanide, Alloxan, Radiation, etc.

3:15–3:30 P.M.	Coffee and Discussion
3:30–5:00 P.M.	"The Broad Range of Use of DPH"
	Review of thought, mood, and behavior disorders (1938–1971)
	Discussion
7:30 P.M.	Dinner

Wednesday, February 23

9:00 A.M.	Review of "The Broad Range of Use of DPH" *(cont'd)*

        Symptoms and disorders for which DPH effectiveness has been reported
        Discussion of cardiac uses
        Brief review of other somatic disorders
        Alcoholism and drug addiction
        Safety and toxicology

10:15–10:30 A.M.	Coffee
10:30 A.M.	The effects of DPH on overthinking, anger, fear, and related emotions
	The one-hour test
11:30 A.M.	Recent work reporting therapeutic benefits of DPH in glaucoma, steroid myopathy, hostility in chronic psychotics, violence, radiation, shock lung, asthma, digitalis toxicity, and hypertension
12:30 P.M.	Lunch

1:30 P.M.	DPH's value is based on the combination of many factors:
	    Broad range of effectiveness
	    Rapidity of action
	    Beneficial "side effects"
	    Not addictive
	    Not a sedative at therapeutic doses
	    Safety established by long period of use

	How DPH has been overlooked
	Discussion
4:00 P.M.	Conference ends

By the time we got to the last discussion period, on the afternoon of the second day, the clinical effects of DPH and its basic mechanisms of action had been outlined, and we got down to cases—what the government could do. But none of our visitors could think of a handle for the FDA to grab DPH by; nothing like this had happened before. The only suggestion I remember was that perhaps the government could give the Foundation a grant. I appreciated this, but I didn't want us to lose any freedom of action.

As the meeting was breaking up, Dr. Kaim said to me, "Well, the ball is in your court." This struck my unfunny bone. "In my court?" I said. "Where the devil do you think it's been all these years—and when should it get in your court?" As many of us do, I make the mistake of thinking that an individual in the government is the government itself. Dr. Kaim meant no harm by his comment, but I repeat it because it is typical of a thousand I've heard from people in a position to do something about DPH themselves. They seem to clear their consciences by giving me advice as to what I should do. I've got enough of this advice. It's saved up in a hermetically sealed tank and I plan to sell to a utility—when fuel prices rise a bit more.

Although nothing specific came of the meeting, at least some members of the government had a better understanding of DPH. Jim Cavanaugh kept in touch with me regularly. Jim had a way of saying, "I'll get back to you next week." And he always did. I appreciated his efforts so much that I never pressed him as to when he would call. It was usually about a quarter to five —on Friday.

Occasionally I was able to get Commissioner Edwards on the phone. Charlie, who told me he was trying to work out something with members of the department, finally came up with a suggestion. He said that if we could get a political figure to write a letter of inquiry about DPH to Secretary of Health Richardson, the reply—which would be an official statement and could be made public—might shed light on the matter. By that time I was so worn out I would have settled for an old shoe. But Dr. Edwards' idea seemed constructive.

Since the Foundation was located in New York, I asked Dr. Edwards if a letter from Governor Rockefeller would serve the purpose. He said it would. When I asked Governor Rockefeller, to whom I had spoken previously about DPH, he said he would write such a letter. And he did.

Secretary Richardson's response* meant more to me than it would to someone unfamiliar with the background. It showed that the Foundation's efforts had had some effect. The Secretary's comment, "Conversations with health officials in the Department . . ." indicated the letter, at the least, had tacit FDA approval.

• • •

I invaded the U.S. Government only once more. About two months into President Nixon's second term, I made one more

---

*From Secretary Richardson's letter:

"Conversations with health officials within the Department have revealed that diphenylhydantoin (DPH) was introduced in 1938 as the first essentially nonsedating anticonvulsant drug . . .

"A review of the literature reveals that diphenylhydantoin has been reported to be useful in a wide range of disorders. Among its reported therapeutic actions are its stabilizing effect on the nervous system, its antiarrhythmic effect on certain cardiac disorders, and its therapeutic effect on emotional disorders.

"The fact that such broad therapeutic effects have been reported by many independent scientists and physicians over a long period of time would seem to indicate that the therapeutic effects of diphenylhydantoin are more than that of an anticonvulsant.

"The FDA encourages the submission of formal applications. . . ."

(For the full text and Governor Rockefeller's letter, see p. 274.)

try. I called Rose Mary Woods and told her the DPH matter was just too important to hang in limbo any longer. I had done the best I could with government for the last four years and now I needed presidential advice. Rose Mary understood, and a few days later called back to say a date had been set up for lunch with the President—I should come at eleven-thirty so we would have more time to talk about DPH. Perfect.

I couldn't be late for such an appointment and planned to go to Washington the day before. But when I found the chance for rain approached zero, I made a reservation for a flight scheduled to get to Washington at nine-fifteen, which gave me almost two hours leeway. That darn plane ("Doing What We Do Best") managed to be two-and-a-half hours late and I was thirty-five minutes late for my appointment. If that wasn't embarrassing. But no one other than myself appeared ruffled. The President set me at ease and listened closely to my experiences with the government. I told him the situation was incredible. Everyone had tried to be helpful, but they were so busy with problems they didn't have time for a solution. I said I couldn't get it out of my head that if someone with authority had the facts he'd see to it that something got done in this matter so urgent to public health.

The DPH story was not new to the President, having heard it from me on three occasions. He agreed that something should be done and asked for my suggestion. I had anticipated the possibility that he might ask. I told him that political jokes for at least a century suggested that vice-presidents of the United States were not overworked. I said that if this applied to Vice-President Agnew, he might be able to help. This suggestion got a prompt Presidential veto (I lacked the two-thirds majority to overrule).

The President said he thought Secretary of Health Caspar Weinberger would be the man for me to see. I told him I had already seen two Secretaries of HEW and found them pretty busy; on average I'd spent an hour apiece with them. This time I had to have enough time to tell the whole story. He asked how long this would take. I said at least two days, at a quiet place away from the telephone. I thought this was shooting for the moon, but the President saw the sense in it. He said he'd make arrangements, that at the moment the Secretary was up to his elbows in some matter, but I would hear from him within thirty days. I thanked the President and took a plane back to New York. Of course it got there two minutes early.

Back home I waited for Secretary Weinberger's call. After four weeks went by I began to have Finch flashbacks. But, on the twenty-ninth day, Secretary Weinberger called and made a date to spend the following weekend at Hobeau Farm. Mrs. Weinberger came to the farm with the Secretary and Dr. Bogoch was with me. Over the two days we had four long sessions, during which Dr. Bogoch and I poured information about DPH into the Secretary. Mrs. Weinberger was an interested listener.

Late Sunday we went our separate ways, the Weinbergers to Washington, Dr. Bogoch and I to New York. Caspar said he wanted to cogitate on the matter and would get in touch with me soon. Time went by, more than I'd expected, and I was afraid I had struck a black hole (a semi-anachronism—they were around in those days but who knew). But after two months Secretary Weinberger called and invited me to come to Washington to meet the newly appointed Commissioner of the FDA, Dr. Alexander Mackay Schmidt.

Our meeting was in the office of our friend, Charlie Edwards, who had become assistant head of HEW. Secretary Weinberger was present, but I got the feeling that, not being a physician, he was reluctant to make suggestions of a medical nature to the FDA, and he had asked Dr. Edwards, who knew the subject well, to introduce Dr. Bogoch and me to Dr. Schmidt.

After the introductions we all chatted for a few minutes in Dr. Edwards' office about nothing I can remember. Then Dr. Schmidt and Dr. Bogoch and I went off to another room to have a talk. I assumed, of course, that Dr. Edwards or the Secretary had given Dr. Schmidt the bibliography of the Dreyfus Medical Foundation and a thorough briefing on the nature of our interest in DPH. I was totally unprepared for Dr. Schmidt's opening words, "My number one objective in my new position is to see that the FDA is run in an honest and honorable fashion."

Son-of-a-gun!

After all the years of work with the government it was apparent Dr. Schmidt hadn't even been briefed. I was back at the starting line, with a new Commissioner of the FDA, and the baton hadn't even been passed on.

I considered getting up and going home. But I wasn't delighted with the implications of Dr. Schmidt's opening remark, and I wanted to get that straightened out. I told Dr. Schmidt we were a charitable medical foundation, had no private interest of any sort, but a damned important public one, and that trying to be helpful with our government was getting to be a tiresome job.

Dr. Schmidt's response was a lot nicer than I expected. He said, "Take your time and tell me about it." For the umpteenth time I started telling the story of DPH.

After about an hour Dr. Schmidt said he had an appointment that he couldn't get out of, but he saw how important this was and he intended to pursue it personally. He said of course he knew DPH was more than an anticonvulsant. In fact he had been teaching its use in cardiac arrhythmia since 1969. I said that's just one example of what I'm talking about. "As you know, DPH does not have a listed indication-of-use for arrhythmias." Dr. Schmidt said, "You're mistaken. I'm sure DPH has such a listing." I didn't argue, this not being an opinion but a fact that could be checked. But I said I thought I was right.*

Just before we left, Dr. Schmidt mentioned that he was a specialist in communication. I said, "I've come to believe that communication is just a word in the dictionary, but if there is such a thing, you sure have a good spot to use your specialty."

Well, it turned out that Commissioner Schmidt was a gentleman of the old school (an endangered species). Even with the pressures of his new office he kept his promise to look into DPH himself and visited the Foundation twice in the following month.

---

* A week later Dr. Schmidt called to say that it was hard to believe, but DPH did not have a listed indication-of-use for arrhythmias. The head of the Heart and Lung Institute, Dr. Theodore Cooper, had made the same mistake. At our medical conference, he had said, "There is no question of the usefulness of DPH as an antiarrhythmic, and this is an approved indication-of-use in the package insert."

That was years ago. DPH still doesn't have such a listing.

The second time, he spent a full day getting the facts about DPH from Dr. Bogoch and me and even stayed into the evening so we could finish our discussion at dinner. By that time I had a feeling of empathy with Mac, and with the help of a glass of wine, I emptied myself of my feelings on the subject of the great sin of neglect of DPH. Dr. Schmidt understood. Then he said something I'd been hoping to hear from a government official but had given up on. "You've done what you can. Now the ball is in our court."

Well, that was it; there was no more to do. I had been trying to turn the responsibility for DPH over to the U.S. government for ten years. Finally a Commissioner of the FDA had accepted it.

• • •

Epilogue: Of course I should have figured that a man as sensitive as Mac Schmidt wouldn't last long in government. Five months later he was back at the University of Illinois, and there was a new Commissioner of the FDA.

I have not visited the government since and have no ambition to. That's one reason this book is written. It's for members of the staff and government officials in health, all at the same time. I hope it will make it easier for them to do whatever they think is right.

10.
TRAVELS ABROAD
ENGLAND—ITALY—RUSSIA

It's said that the further you get from where they know you the more respect you get. And so it seems.

Before discussing the "flaw in the system," in the next chapter, I would like to tell you of some experiences I've had with DPH abroad, and of an unusual relationship that developed between the Dreyfus Medical Foundation and the Institute for Experimental Medicine in Leningrad.

England

My first trip abroad, on the subject of DPH, was to England in 1965. Soon after Dr. Turner joined the Foundation, he and I went to Chichester, England, to visit a friend of his, Dr. Lionel Haward. At the Graylingwell Hospital in Chichester, Dr. Haward introduced us to a group of his colleagues. We all sat at a large round table and for an hour I described my experiences with DPH. When I finished, to my surprise, they applauded. I know it was just English good manners but it gave me a nice feeling.

As a result of our trip, Dr. Haward did a series of five controlled studies on DPH.* They were excellent studies, three of them unusual in that they were influenced by his background as a pilot. In simulated air control tests, he demonstrated with students and experienced pilots that DPH was significantly effective in delaying fatigue and accompanying errors. Haward made the point that it's an unusual substance that can calm without sedation and also effect a return of energy and improvement in concentration.

* See pp. 161–62, 165–66, and 215–16.

Italy

Dr. Rodolfo Paoletti, scientific director of the Institute of Pharmacology at the University of Milan, a friend of Dr. Bogoch's, frequently visited our office when in New York. On several occasions I talked to him about DPH. One of the times Dr. Paoletti said, "Why don't you come over to Milan and talk about DPH at a meeting of the Giovanni Lorenzini Foundation." He suggested a date four months in the future and I accepted.

A week before the meeting I found out what I had let myself in for. I was not to be one of many speakers, but the only speaker, before a large group of physicians. I had talked at formal medical meetings before, but only as one of the speakers. This was different.

At the meeting in Milan there were about 120 physicians. Dr. Paoletti gave me a kind introduction, put me on the podium with a microphone attached to me, and told me to speak in my normal way—a UN-type device would see that it came out in Italian. I was close to stage fright, but after I got started it was all right. I talked for an hour and twenty minutes, and apparently it went well because I got a letter from Dr. Paoletti saying, "From the comments I heard afterward you certainly caught everyone's attention," and he invited me to come back the next year.

After the meeting a number of physicians came up to say hello, and I learned that DPH was already being used for purposes other than epilepsy. One physician, G. A. Bozza, who seemed an especially kind man, talked to me about his use of DPH with retarded children, a use I was not familiar with. A few months later he sent me his paper, "Normalization of intellectual development in the slightly brain-damaged, retarded child."*

Russia

One day in October 1972, Dr. Bogoch phoned and said he was coming to the office with a Russian doctor he thought I'd

* Presented at the Italian National Conference of Child Neuropsychology, 1971.

like to meet, and that we might have lunch. The doctor was in New York for an International Brain Sciences Conference, of which Dr. Bogoch was chairman. At eleven o'clock that morning Dr. Bogoch arrived in the office with Dr. Natasha Bechtereva. Sam had not overdescribed Dr. Bechtereva when he referred to her as a Russian doctor. Dr. Bechtereva had the most impressive credentials of anyone I've met in the medical profession.

At that time Dr. Bechtereva was Chairman of the Commission on Public Health of the U.S.S.R. She was also Director (and still is) of the Institute for Experimental Medicine, formerly the Pavlov Institute, a group of seven large hospitals in Leningrad. Dr. Bechtereva was the first woman to become Director of the Institute and she was Chief of its neurophysiological branch.

I remember our meeting clearly. Dr. Bechtereva, Dr. Bogoch, and I sat in chairs at a window overlooking New York Harbor. I had intended to talk about DPH for half an hour or so and, if Dr. Bechtereva showed interest, give her a copy of *The Broad Range of Use of Diphenylhydantoin*. When lunch arrived at one o'clock I was surprised to find that I'd been talking for two hours. Dr. Bechtereva hadn't said a thing, but the patience with which she had listened and something in her remarkable eyes had kept me going.

When I had finished Dr. Bechtereva spoke for the first time. She said, "What you say seems too good to be true but it's not illogical, and I can find out to my own satisfaction. In our Institute we have sensitive electrical equipment that can test DPH. Would you be kind enough to send us a supply of your brand of diphenylhydantoin? If our tests should disagree with what you say I wouldn't want you to think it's because our brand is different from yours." That made sense, and I said we would send the Dilantin.

After many difficulties, Dilantin arrived in Leningrad. Several months later I received a letter from Dr. Bechtereva (mail in those days took about a month—now it's not so rapid). Dr. Bechtereva's electrical instruments had not been disappointed. From the letter:

Thank you very much for the prospect of Dilantin and the Dilantin itself. The Dilantin—really a most peculiar medicine.

I am advising it to more and more people. I simply can't resist doing it—you know how one feels. And so, step by step, Dilantin is used for nonepileptic purposes, not only in Leningrad but in Moscow and Kiev as well.

Dr. Bechtereva has a refreshing way of putting things. In a later letter she said, "People use Dilantin much more, though it met the normal prejudice determined by the engram fixed in each doctor's memory: Dilantin → epilepsy." Apparently we don't have a monopoly on this engram.

A few months after Dr. Bechtereva started work with DPH, she invited Dr. Bogoch and me to visit the Institute in Leningrad, at our convenience. We accepted. Having heard too much about the Russian winters we selected June for the visit. Four of us made the trip—Dr. Bogoch and his wife Dr. Elenore Bogoch, and Joan Personette, my former wife, and I.

We stayed in Leningrad for a week at the Hotel Astoria, a very old hotel, like the Ritz in Paris, but otherwise dissimilar. But the people were nice, which is the most important thing. When we had time we saw the sights, the beautiful cathedrals and the extraordinary Hermitage, and we walked around Leningrad as we pleased. The days were long. We were near the land of the midnight sun, and it got dark at 11 P.M. and light at 2 A.M. It seemed strange reading by daylight at 10 P.M. in a park across from the Astoria.

Dr. Bechtereva's hospitality was reminiscent of our best Southern hospitality. We had a delicious dinner at her home with her family, were taken out to dinner by her, and thoughtfully left to ourselves. The food in the restaurants was good, if you like garlic, which I don't. On one occasion, out to dinner with Dr. Bechtereva, I was trying to finesse my way around the meat and Natasha said, "My dear Jack, you suffer so much." A keen observer.

The first day we were in Leningrad, Dr. Bechtereva took the Drs. Bogoch and me to one of the seven hospitals and introduced us to key members of her staff. Later we went through other hospitals, getting to meet many doctors. I was surprised that so many of the doctors were women until I was told that seventy percent of physicians in Russia are women.

The second day we were there, Dr. Bechtereva introduced us to three patients who'd had dramatic benefits from DPH. Each had a different disorder. The patient I remember best was a woman who'd had severe headaches for many years and had to be hospitalized periodically. This time she had taken Dilantin for a few days and was on her way home. She explained, through an interpreter, that the pain in her head would get so bad she'd sit absolutely still and if anyone came near her it would make her furious. While she was explaining this in Russian, she was smiling happily, as though she were talking about someone else.

The next day Dr. Bechtereva called a meeting and Dr. Bogoch and I had the opportunity to talk about DPH to eighty physicians. I talked for about two hours. That was like talking one hour because translation was not simultaneous. Then Dr. Bogoch discussed the basic mechanisms of action. Several of the Institute's physicians also addressed the group. I was told that they had given favorable reports on DPH.

The day before we left, Dr. Bechtereva and I were alone for a few moments and I brought up what I considered a delicate subject. I told her that I was most impressed with the work the Institute had done. I said our Foundation had funded numerous studies on DPH, some outside the U.S.A., and, if proper, we would be happy to do it here. Natasha set me at ease. She said she appreciated my asking but that her Institute was well financed by the government. However, we might consider a "joint cooperative effort." She said such a possibility was provided for in the recent meeting between President Nixon and Premier Brezhnev.

I thought this a fine idea and asked how we should proceed. Dr. Bechtereva said since we had introduced the DPH idea it would be best if we initiated the matter through our Department of Health—to their Ministry of Health. We discussed it. Our thought was that we'd exchange ideas and information by mail, and would periodically visit each other. It was agreed that when

I got back to New York I would introduce the matter to our Department of Health.

My friend Caspar Weinberger was still Secretary of HEW. He was in agreement with the proposal and was most helpful. As a result of Cap's efforts, Dr. Roger Egeberg, Co-Chairman, US–USSR Joint Committee for Health Cooperation, wrote to the Russian Deputy Minister of Health making the request and "encouraging the establishment of cooperation between Dr. Bechtereva's Institute and the Dreyfus Medical Foundation."

But the mills of government grind slowly all over the world. A long time went by and we heard nothing back. Meanwhile we kept in touch by phone and by mail.

Several years after my trip to Leningrad I learned that Dr. Bechtereva was going to be in London for a few days, and I made arrangements to meet with her there so we could exchange information on DPH. We had an interesting and fruitful discussion. During it I said I didn't know what had happened to our "joint cooperative effort"; certainly our Department of Health had encouraged it. Dr. Bechtereva said she was going to see Deputy Minister Venedictov in a few weeks and would discuss it with him; she thought this might be a good time to reintroduce the idea.

Back in New York I spoke to Dr. Theodore Cooper, then Assistant Secretary of Health. Dr. Cooper knew our Foundation well, having been a participant in the conference we'd held for the FDA. He said he was going to Russia shortly and would bring up the subject with Deputy Minister Venedictov.

This time we had success, and a formal "joint cooperative effort" between the Institute for Experimental Medicine and the Dreyfus Medical Foundation was approved. I've been told that this is the only cooperative medical effort (not sponsored by the two governments) between a Russian and an American institution.

Before closing I'd like to say that Natasha Bechtereva is one of the most unusual persons I've ever met. I thank her for her help.

11.
A FLAW
IN THE SYSTEM
PARKE-DAVIS—THE PHYSICIAN—THE FDA

A medicine can get overlooked for a million years—if no one discovers it. But can the benefits of a discovered medicine get overlooked for decades when thousands of studies have demonstrated its usefulness? The answer is it can.

We have a flaw in our system of bringing prescription medicines to the public. That there's a flaw is no surprise. We're human and all our systems have flaws. But this particular flaw should be explained. It has acted like a barrier between the American public and a great medicine.

• • •

From drug company, through FDA, to physician—that's the route a prescription medicine takes to get to the public. That's our system. It was not set up by anyone, it just evolved. But we're used to it; it has become custom. And as you know, custom can be like iron.

Years ago doctors concocted their own medicines—and leeches outsold aspirins. But for the last century the business of pharmaceuticals has been in the hands of the drug companies. Drug companies, formed for the purpose of making money for shareholders, are not charged with a responsibility to the public that is not consistent with making money. That is not to suggest that drug companies are not interested in public welfare—but they are not charged with a responsibility for it.

In 1938 the FDA was empowered to protect us against medical substances more dangerous than therapeutic. Since that time drug companies have been required to get approval as to the safety of a new chemical entity and, since 1962, approval as to its effectiveness. Although the neglect of a great drug can be more deadly than the use of a bad one, correcting such neglect does not appear to be a function of the FDA.

When a drug company synthesizes a compound which it believes to be therapeutic, it's brought to the FDA. If the drug satisfies that agency's requirements, the company is awarded a "listed indication-of-use," which permits it to market the drug. Getting FDA approval is time-consuming and expensive; it has been estimated, on average, to take seven years and to cost $11 million.

Drug companies patent their new compounds. Patents give the company exclusive rights for seventeen years. If the FDA approves a drug and it becomes popular, the drug company has a winner since the drug will sell at a high price for the life of the patent.* However, when the patent expires, competition enters the picture and the price of the drug drops dramatically. At that point there is more financial incentive for the drug company to look for a *new drug* to patent than to look for new uses of an old drug.

FDA approval is the second of the three steps in our system. The third step is the introduction of the drug to the physician. This is a function of the drug company and is done through advertisements in trade journals and by visits of their salesmen to physicians.

That is the system—and physicians have come to depend on it. If a doctor doesn't hear from a drug company about new uses

* This is not unreasonable; a drug that is a winner has to pay for the research that went into it, the expense of getting FDA approval, and for money spent on the many drugs that are not successful.

for an old medicine, the doctor infers there aren't such uses. This is a reasonable inference. But in the case of DPH it's wrong.

So this is the flaw in the system. When a drug company doesn't do what is expected of it, and the FDA can't or doesn't do anything about it, the physician doesn't get vital information. And, as in this case, a great drug can get overlooked.

Parke-Davis

Parke-Davis's research did not discover DPH. The company bought the compound from a chemist in 1909. For twenty-nine years this remarkable drug sat on the shelf doing nobody any good. Then Putnam and Merritt, two physicians outside the company, discovered its first therapeutic use. Parke-Davis paid almost nothing in money for DPH. They paid less in brains for DPH.

Still, were it not for Parke-Davis we might not have DPH today. Someone in the company did buy the compound, and someone else in the company did give it to Putnam and Merritt for trial. It should also be said, to their credit, that Parke-Davis has been consistent in manufacturing a good product.

• • •

It is not easy to understand how a drug company can overlook its own product. An outline of my own experience with Parke-Davis may help.

In 1966, as Secretary Gardner had recommended, I made contact with Parke-Davis. I phoned the company and spoke to the president, Mr. H. W. Burrows. I told him of Secretary Gardner's recommendation that I speak to Parke-Davis, and supposed that would arouse his interest. But as I talked I didn't hear the noises one expects from an interested listener. To get his attention I said, "Look, I've spent $400,000 on your medicine and I don't want anything for myself, I just want to tell Parke-Davis about it." That got Mr. Burrows's attention. He said, "I wouldn't know anything about this, I'm just a bookkeeper."

That startling statement was my introduction to Parke-Davis. President Burrows said he would have someone get in touch with me. Two months later I got a call from Dr. Leon Sweet of Parke-Davis's research department. He was calling at Mr. Burrows's suggestion and made a date to meet with me in New York.

We met at my home. Dr. Sweet brought Dr. E. C. Vonder Heide with him. Dr. Turner was with me. Dr. Sweet said that Parke-Davis's recent head of research, Dr. Alain Sanseigne, had left the company a few months earlier to go to Squibb, and Dr. Vonder Heide, a former head of research now retired, had come along to be helpful.

Dr. Turner and I talked at length about the overlooked uses of DPH. Dr. Vonder Heide said it didn't surprise him that DPH was more than an anticonvulsant. In fact Parke-Davis had had numerous reports that Dilantin helped with alcohol and drug addiction. He said that he had tried to get doctors to conduct studies in this field without success. He was rather critical of the doctors. I remember thinking, What's going on here? The doctors depend on Parke-Davis to do something, and Parke-Davis depends on the doctors to do something. This is an interesting game of tag, and the public is "it."

I didn't realize till years later what a poor excuse Dr. Vonder Heide had given. Many research-minded doctors had already done a great deal, and at that time, 1966, Parke-Davis's files were stocked with a variety of clinical studies on DPH. Yet apparently neither Dr. Vonder Heide nor Dr. Sweet had heard of them. It seemed Parke-Davis's research department and its filing department were not acquainted with each other.

Our only further contact with Parke-Davis came a few weeks later when we had a visit from a friendly gentleman, Dr. Charles F. Weiss. Dr. Weiss explained that he was a pediatrician and didn't know anything about DPH, but had come to see us because he'd been asked to. He offered the opinion that Parke-

Davis was a little disorganized. He said he wished some company would take them over. Well, he got his wish—but not for six years. Today the company is a subsidiary of Warner Lambert.

When Warner Lambert took over in 1971, Mr. J. D. Williams became President of the Parke-Davis division. I felt I should bring the matter of DPH to the attention of the new management, and had several discussions on the telephone with Mr. Williams. The talks were friendly but not useful in furthering the DPH cause. On one occasion Mr. Williams expressed a thought I'd heard from Parke-Davis before, that since we were working on their product, it might be better if we stayed apart —some notion that the FDA might like it better. I couldn't understand this—I was sure the FDA would want a drug company to know all it could about its own product.

But such is life. An item in the *Arizona Republic* (at the time I retired from Wall Street in 1970) will give the picture. The paper reported Dr. Joseph Sadusk, Vice-President for Medical and Scientific Research of Parke-Davis, to have said that the Dreyfus Medical Foundation is doing "an excellent job" in investigating DPH. As a result he said Parke-Davis has made only "a minimal effort" in this area of research. "Results from an unbiased third party like Dreyfus," he said, "would mean more to the Food and Drug Administration."

I appreciate compliments. But the division of labor seemed uneven. The Dreyfus Medical Foundation should do the research, influence the FDA—and Parke-Davis should make the profits.

There appears to have been only one person who, while passing through Parke-Davis, got a good grasp of DPH. That was Dr. Alain Sanseigne, head of research before Dr. Sweet. Dr. Turner brought DPH to Dr. Sanseigne's attention. Dr. Sanseigne graciously acknowledged this in a letter to Dr. Turner in which he said, "Your very thorough knowledge of Dilantin put me to shame."

Once his attention had been directed to DPH, Dr. Sanseigne, in 1965, reviewed its pharmacology, site of activity, and therapeutic activity.* It's an impressive review, and it refers only to information on DPH available fifteen years ago. There are no signs that this review stirred Parke-Davis.

When Dr. Joseph Sadusk said Parke-Davis's efforts had been "minimal" he selected the right word. I know this from firsthand experience. A few years ago Mr. Williams changed his mind about Parke-Davis staying apart from our Foundation and graciously arranged for three members of the research staff to meet with us on the subject of Parke-Davis's Dilantin package insert. (This package insert will be discussed later.)

At this meeting I met the senior research officer of Parke-Davis. When we finished our discussion he mentioned that the FDA had not approved Parke-Davis's application for the use of DPH in cardiac arrhythmias. The reason, he said, was that the company did not supply cardiograms requested by an individual in the FDA. The research officer said, "We could get them for $100,000 but why spend the money, all the cardiologists are using DPH anyway." I won't take sides in this hassle between the FDA and Parke-Davis. There was foolishness to spare.† But you'd think Parke-Davis would have considered it a privilege to spend the $100,000.

---

* From Dr. Sanseigne's review:
The Parke-Davis Medical Brochure includes as indications of Dilantin the following:

Epilepsy	Migraine
Chorea	Trigeminal neuralgia
Parkinson syndrome	Psychosis

The following indications . . . have been studied and seem to show considerable therapeutic response to treatment with DPH:

Cardiac arrhythmia	Wound-healing acceleration
Neurosis	Polyneuritis of pregnancy
Behavioral disorders in adolescents	Tabetic lancinating pain
Myotonia	Pruritus ani
Diabetes insipidus	Asthma

The following are indications on which the possibility of favorable response to DPH should be investigated:

Prophylaxis and treatment of cerebral anoxia (carbon monoxide poisoning and other asphyxiation, precardiac and pulmonary surgery)	Wilson's disease
	Poorly controlled diabetes
	Cicatrization of oral surgery
	Osteogenesis imperfecta
	Conditions related to hypothalamus

† DPH is so widely used for cardiac arrhythmias that AMA Drug Evaluations has it in the category of antiarrhythmic agents.

A few weeks after this, a physician applied to our Foundation for a modest grant ($6,000). He had done interesting preliminary work on the use of DPH as a protection against brain damage after cardiac arrest. We intended to make the grant, but it occurred to me that the new Parke-Davis management might appreciate the opportunity. I called my new acquaintance, the research officer, and asked him about it. It didn't surprise me that I was told no. It did surprise me how quickly I got the answer, on the phone, without consideration of the matter. The senior officer explained that Parke-Davis was spending its research moneys on a new medicine the company hoped to patent. I thought there will be snow on the Devil's roof before they came up with as good a medicine as Dilantin. But I got the point—patents on DPH had expired.

Well, to sum up, Parke-Davis got Dilantin by luck. They didn't understand their own product, have done little to try to understand it, and haven't spent a bean in furthering its understanding. This has contributed to the overlooking of DPH.

But let's see Parke-Davis in perspective. There's no Mr. Parke, no Mr. Davis—just an entity with those names. Since Parke-Davis did not get DPH by the sweat of its research there was none of the interest in the drug that would be found in a company that developed its own product. As a result, new uses for DPH was a job never assigned to anyone—and no one took it upon himself. It has been easy to cuss Parke-Davis, the entity, but not the people. In fact I've never met anyone at the company I didn't like.

• • •

About Parke-Davis's Dilantin package insert.

I was weaned on the Securities and Exchange Commission. The S.E.C. is a fiend for full disclosure—the positive as well as the negative. If Parke-Davis operated under S.E.C. regulations the S.E.C. would have the company in court for the rest of the century because of the great amount of positive data that's not disclosed in their package insert.

But Parke-Davis operates under FDA regulations. Apparently full disclosure is required on the negative side, but no disclosure is permitted when the evidence is positive, unless it has an FDA listed indication-of-use. No matter how ridiculously flimsy the evidence for the negative, it must be disclosed. No matter how extensive the positive evidence, it may not be mentioned. It seems a poor way to run a railroad.

An example of inexplicable illogic. For some years prior to 1972, Parke-Davis's package insert made reference to a number of the uses of DPH other than epilepsy. In 1971 the insert stated: "Dilantin is also useful in the treatment of conditions such as chorea and Parkinson's syndrome and is employed in the treatment of migraine, trigeminal neuralgia and certain psychoses." In 1972 reference to these uses was deleted, although the evidence for their use had been substantially increased.

Unfathomable. I don't know whether this was the fault of Parke-Davis or the FDA. But an innocent public has suffered.

The Physician

A physician's remedy of the eighteenth century. (Believed to be non-habit-forming.)

> **Aqua Limacum.** Take a great Peck of Garden-snails, and wash them in a great deal of Beer, and make your Chimney very clean, and set a Bushel of Charcoal on Fire; and when they are thoroughly kindled, make a Hole in the Middle of the Fire, and put the Snails in, and scatter more Fire amongst them, and let them roast till they make a Noise; then take them out, and, with a Knife and coarse Cloth, pick and wipe away all the green froth: Then break them, Shells and all, in a Stone Mortar. Take also a Quart of Earthworms, and scour them with Salt, divers times over. Then take two Handfuls of Angelica and lay them in the Bottom of the Still; next lay two Handfuls of Celandine; next a Quart of Rosemary-flowers; then two Handfuls of Bearsfoot and Agrimony; then Fenugreek, then Turmeric; of each one Ounce: Red Dock-root, Bark of Barberry-trees, the Snails and Worms on top of the Herbs; and then two Handfuls of Goose Dung, and two Handfuls of Sheep Dung. Then put in three Gallons of Strong Ale, and place the pot where you mean to set Fire under it: Let it stand all Night, or longer; in the Morning put in three ounces of Cloves well beaten, and a small Quantity

of Saffron, dry'd to Powder; the six Ounces of Shavings of Hartshorn, which must be uppermost. Fix on the Head and Refrigeratory, and distill according to Art.

—From Dr. James's *Dictionary of Medicine,* London, 1740.

I had taken DPH for about a year when I started talking to doctors about it. These were informal talks and occurred when chance brought me together with physicians, as at a dinner or in a locker room. I must have spoken to more than twenty doctors during that early period. None of them had heard of DPH being used for anything other than epilepsy. The discussions were friendly, but it was almost impossible to get a physician interested in the subject of DPH. I thought this was because, as a Wall Street man, I was an improbable source of medical fact.

But my lack of credentials was the smallest part of the communication problem. In the physicians' minds there was the fixed notion that DPH was just an anticonvulsant. They had been taught this in school, the "knowledge" had been in their heads for a long time, and had calcified. Don't pick on the physician. Calcification of ideas is a human trait not special to him.

There was an even bigger obstacle—the sure knowledge the physician had that if Dilantin had as many uses as I said it had, they would have heard about them from Parke-Davis. After all, Dilantin was their product, wasn't it? And they wanted to make money, didn't they? This "irrefutable logic" always defeated me. If I tried to explain, time would run out before we could get back to DPH.

There's been a recent trend to knock the doctor. I think it's a reaction to the pedestal position we had him in a decade ago. We learned from "Dr. Kildare" and "Marcus Welby, M.D." that there are two physicians to every patient. In real life this isn't so. Doctors rarely make house calls anymore. They can see three patients in the office for one in the home—and still it's hard to get an appointment. Don't blame the doctor. It's the ecologists' fault—they've allowed the spread of *Homo sapiens* to get out of hand.

When you are giving a member of the medical profession a

hard time (in your head of course—who would dare do it in person), consider that the doctor's day never ends. Sick people don't care what time it is, and the doctor has to go around with a beeper attached to him or be in constant touch with his telephone service. This means twenty-four hours' tension. We complain about what the doctor doesn't do. But do we appreciate the things he does that we wouldn't do?

• • •

We come to an important subject: medical literature. Medical studies are called literature (Shakespeare might demur) when they're published in a medical journal or as part of the record of a medical conference.

There is a good deal of this literature. You could wallpaper the world with it and have enough left over to do your kitchen. The notion that physicians know what's contained in the literature is bizarre. But some of them sound like they half believe they do. If you ask a physician a question he can't answer, don't be surprised if he responds, "Nobody knows." Which seems to suggest he has read all the literature and has total recall.

It's estimated that there are 3,300 established medical journals. A poll in seventeen counties of upstate New York (not exactly the boondocks) showed that the average physician subscribed to 4.1 of these journals. Double this figure if you like. Even if he read the 8.2 journals cover to cover, he would still be 3,291.8 journals short. You can see it's impossible to expect the physician to read the medical literature to determine which drugs he should use. That's why, in this day of specialization, this is left to the drug companies and the FDA.

However, when a physician gets a new idea about an established drug, he may apply it.* But the opportunity doesn't come up often. Usually new uses of a drug are well explored by the drug company that introduced it. DPH has been a marked ex-

* FDA Commissioner Charles C. Edwards states: "Once the new drug is in a local pharmacy, the physician may, as part of the practice of medicine . . . vary the conditions of use from those approved in the package insert, without informing or obtaining the approval of the Food and Drug Administration." *The Federal Register, Vol. 37, No. 158, Aug. 15, 1972.*

ception, and a rare opportunity was presented to the physicians.

The medical profession did not fail us. The work of thousands of physicians has given us a rich literature on DPH. This literature, international in scope, covers a wide variety of medical disciplines. Published in many languages over a period of years, it is spread far and wide. But intermingled with millions of other studies, this literature is almost lost unless someone seeks it out.

The science fiction writer Robert Heinlein calls it the Crisis of the Librarian. He says:

> The greatest crisis facing us is not Russia, not the Atom Bomb . . . It is a crisis in the *organization* and *accessibility* of human knowledge. We own an enormous "encyclopedia"—which isn't even arranged alphabetically. Our "file cards" are spilled on the floor, nor were they ever in order. The answers we want may be buried somewhere in the heap. . . .

Let me give you an example of how difficult it would be, even in a single field, for a physician to be acquainted with the literature on DPH. Disorders in the field have many names. A general description of the field is uncontrolled muscle movement, or continuous muscle fiber activity.

To illustrate the point, we made up a table of twenty-one published studies on this subject in 1975.* These studies show dramatic recovery by patients given DPH. In many of the cases myogram readings (electrical muscle recordings) confirmed the clinical observations. The difficulty an individual physician would have in becoming acquainted with this work is shown by the following:

The studies were published in eight countries and in sixteen different journals—*Journal of Neurology, Neurosurgery and Psychiatry, Lancet, The Practitioner, South African Medical Journal, Klinische Wochenschrift, Arquivos de Neuro-Psiquiatria, Acta Neurologica, Proceedings of the Australian Association of Neurologists, Ceskolovenska Neurologie, Connecticut Medicine, Neurology, Archives of Neurology, New York State Journal of Medicine, California Medicine,* and *New England Journal of Medicine.*

* Since then more studies have been published. See "Review of Recent Work," p. 280.

In only two of the twenty-one studies was the word diphenylhydantoin in the title. The other studies were published under such dissimilar titles that Scotland Yard couldn't have found them, without the key word diphenylhydantoin.

One other example of the communication problem, a simpler one. Dr. Laurence G. Bodkin, who in 1945 and 1947 published two excellent studies on the usefulness of DPH for pruritus ani (see pp. 177–78), visited our office a few years ago. I took the opportunity to congratulate him on his brilliant work and said, "It must have been gratifying to you when Goodwin confirmed your results in reporting twenty successful cases out of twenty treated with DPH." Dr. Bodkin said, "Who's Goodwin?" Bodkin's and Goodwin's studies are side by side in our first bibliography and I'd always assumed they knew each other well. Not only were they strangers, but Goodwin's study, which confirmed Bodkin's own work, hadn't even come to Bodkin's attention.

Some members of the medical profession have prescribed DPH for a variety of purposes for many years. The breadth of its use is more than might be imagined. IMS America surveys the use of thousands of drugs. For their estimate of the many clinical conditions that physicians are using DPH for, see pp. 275–76.

One might draw the conclusion from the IMS America survey that the medical profession knows all about DPH. But this is not the case. Many physicians know of one or several uses of DPH. Few have an overall picture of the drug. Thus we have a strange situation. Dr. Jones prescribes DPH for depression. Dr. Smith uses it for migraine. Dr. Hemplewaith for trigeminal neuralgia. But, if a patient asks Dr. Snodgrass if he could try DPH for any of these purposes, he may get ushered from the office with the admonishment that DPH is only for epilepsy.

The right of a physician to prescribe whatever drug he wants is fundamental. But in making his decision he should have a reasonable amount of evidence on which to base his judgment.

A reasonable amount of information has not been available to the physician, at least not from the expected source, the drug company. The information has been there, but it's been hidden in millions of medical papers, like trees in a forest.

When physicians know more about DPH they may feel they have been imposed on by the system—and deprived of a remarkable therapeutic tool. If that's so, they will do something about it.

The FDA

This is not going to be a treatise on the Food and Drug Administration. I haven't the facts or the desire to write such a treatise. The FDA is in this book because of its relation to DPH.

The FDA was established, in the best tradition of good government, to help American citizens in matters of health, in ways they can't help themselves. But it was conceived as a defensive unit. If it were a football team it would have six tackles and five guards, and no one to carry the ball. All that was expected of the FDA was defense—to protect us from dangerous substances and unwarranted claims of effectiveness.

Understandably the founding fathers of the FDA presumed that the drug companies, with their profit incentives, would furnish the offense. It could hardly have entered their minds that a drug company would leave a great medicine "lying around." Nor would they have been able to figure out how to equip the FDA against such an eventuality unless the FDA were put into the drug business, which is a far cry from the original premise—and is not being recommended here.

The FDA has done nothing about DPH. That is to be expected when a drug company doesn't play its role. Unfortunately this does not leave the FDA in a neutral position. Through no fault of the FDA's, DPH's narrow listing has a negative effect. Absence of FDA approval is thought of by many as FDA disapproval—or at the least that something is lacking. The system of drug company through FDA to physician has become such a routine that the physician, with other things on his mind, waits for the system to bring him DPH. It's been a long wait.

The real purpose in establishing the FDA was to improve the health and well-being of the citizens of the United States. The neglect of a great drug certainly falls into that category. If a man were drowning and a doctor was prepared to throw him a life preserver that had more lead than cork, the FDA would say, "Hold it! That thing might hit him and kill him, and even if it doesn't it can't help him." Nice work, FDA. But suppose the FDA knew there was a good life preserver under a tree, which the doctor didn't see. Shouldn't they say, "Try that one, Doc." Of course they should.

It is not suggested that the FDA go into the drug business. It is more than suggested, in this extraordinary case, where thousands of physicians have furnished us with many times the evidence required to get approval of a *new* drug (keep in mind this drug has been approved for comparative safety and has stood the test of forty years of use), that the FDA should no longer take a hands-off policy. It's a sure thing our public shouldn't suffer any longer because Parke-Davis stayed in bed after Rip Van Winkle got up.

Let us understand the magnitude of what we're talking about. The non-use of DPH has been a catastrophe. We are not accustomed to thinking of the non-use of a medicine as a catastrophe. We think of a catastrophe as a flood, a famine, or an earthquake. Something tangible, overt, something in the positive tense. But something passive, such as the non-use of a great medicine that can prevent suffering and prolong lives, is also a catastrophe.

Something *must* be done. How it is done is for the government to decide. But here is a suggestion. It would seem a waste of time, and thus to the disadvantage of the American public, for the FDA to attempt to approve the many clinical uses of DPH separately. That could take forever. It would be far simpler for the FDA to address itself to the basic mechanisms of action and give DPH a listed indication-of-use as a stabilizer of electrical activity, or as a membrane stabilizer. Certainly the published evidence for this is overwhelming. Such a listing would stimulate the physician to think of clinical applications of DPH and to refer to the existing medical literature.

Even a nod from the FDA to the physician would help. It could take the form of a letter to the physician, calling attention to the literature of his colleagues, and reminding him that since DPH has been approved for safety he is permitted to use it for whatever purposes his judgment suggests. Certainly the FDA would never try to tell the doctor how he should use DPH. That's always the doctor's decision. But such a letter would lift the cloud of negativism, and the physician would get an unobstructed view of DPH and the work of his colleagues.

I'm sure the problem raisers will say that if the FDA takes any action in this matter it will set a precedent. Fine. Good. If this happens again, if another established drug is found useful for fifty or more disorders by thousands of physicians, then the FDA *should* take this as a precedent.

Every once in a while, routine or no routine, a little common sense should be permitted. This is an extraordinary matter, vital to our health. If the FDA was set up to help the American public, here's a chance to do something great for them—with no one's feelings hurt except routine's.

12.
OBSERVATIONS ON DPH—
EXPLORATION OF
POSSIBLE NEW USES

It used to be that the word drug had a solid respectable meaning. But in recent years drug and abuse have been put together in the same sentence so often, without discrimination, that the word drug has come into disrepute. It's confusing, and a shame. Today people brag, just before they ascend, "I never took a drug in my life." As if St. Peter cared.

Good drugs are a cheerful feature of our society. We should stop tarring them with the same brush we use on the bad ones —and be grateful for them. With this general comment off my chest I would like to make some observations about DPH.

• • •

DPH would appear to be the most broadly useful drug in our pharmacopoeia (unless another is hidden in the literature). Paradoxically, this valuable feature, this versatility, has interfered with our understanding of the drug. The idea that one substance can have as many uses as DPH has been difficult to accept. And this is understandable. Not too long ago the thinking was a single drug for a single disorder.

A discussion of the basic mechanisms of action of DPH will help us understand how one drug can have so many uses.

A basic mechanism of action study was the first study to demonstrate that DPH might be a therapeutic substance. In 1938 Putnam and Merritt tested DPH on cats in which convulsions were induced by electricity. Of a large group of substances, including the best-known anticonvulsants, it was the most effective in controlling the convulsions.* Putnam and Merritt said, Eureka! Maybe we have a superior antiepileptic drug.

They did. And not only was DPH the most effective anticonvulsant but it was found to have another remarkable property. Unlike previously used substances it achieved its therapy without sedation.

Let's go back to Putnam and Merritt's original study—and apply hindsight. Suppose, instead of inferring that DPH would help the epileptic, Putnam and Merritt had drawn a broader inference from their data. Suppose they had inferred that DPH worked against inappropriate electrical activity. That also would have been a correct inference—but with far broader implications. And the properties of DPH would not have been obscured by the label "anticonvulsant." Today basic mechanism scientists use broad terminology for DPH. They refer to it as a membrane stabilizer.

From the early basic mechanisms study of Toman, in 1949, DPH has been found to correct inappropriate electrical activity in groups of cells, and in individual cells. This includes nerve cells, brain cells, muscle cells, in fact, all types of cells that exhibit marked electrical activity. Whether a cell is made hyperexcitable by electrical impulse, calcium withdrawal, oxygen withdrawal, or by poisons, DPH has been shown to counteract this excitability. Further, it has been demonstrated that, in amounts that correct abnormal cell function, DPH does not affect normal function.†

When we understand that DPH is a substance that stabilizes the hyperactive cell without affecting normal cell function, we see its therapeutic potential in the human body, a machine that runs on electrical impulse. It is estimated that there are a trillion cells in the body, 200 billion in the brain alone. Thinking is an electrical process, the rhythms of the heart are electrically regulated, the rhythms of the gut are electrically regulated, muscle

* See p. 245.

† See Stabilization of Bioelectrical Activity, pp. 245–50.

movement is electrically regulated, messages of pain are electrically referred, and more.

It's important to know that after a cell has been stimulated to fire a few times it becomes potentiated, easier to fire than a normal cell. This is called post-tetanic potentiation. If the stimulation is continued, the cell starts to fire on its own, and continues to fire until its energy is depleted—post-tetanic afterdischarge. DPH has a modifying effect on post-tetanic potentiation and a correcting effect on post-tetanic afterdischarge. This may account for DPH's therapeutic effect on persistent and repetitive thinking and on unnecessary repetitive messages of pain.

· · ·

DPH has a number of properties which set it apart from most substances. For nine distinctive characteristics see p. 206–7. For purposes here we should consider several of these properties.

DPH is a non-habit-forming substance.* The desirability of a non-habit-forming drug that can calm and also relieve pain is apparent—it may be particularly useful during withdrawal from habit-forming substances.

DPH, in therapeutic amounts, has a calming effect without being a sedative. This characteristic is unusual, and clinical observations, supported by basic mechanisms studies, show that DPH does not affect normal function. Not only does DPH not sedate but it has been shown to improve concentration and effect a return of energy. This can be attributed, at least in part, to the fact that an overactive brain (hyperexcitable cells) wastes energy compounds.† One can conjecture that when thoughts with negative emotions are diminished, the effect of these "down" emotions is eliminated, and "psychic" energy may return.

Now that preventative medicine is being given more and more consideration, DPH may be of special interest because of its general properties and its versatility.

---

* This is not to be confused with the well-known fact that a person with epilepsy should *not* abruptly discontinue DPH.

† DPH has been shown to increase energy compounds in the brain. See pp. 253–54.

• • •

DPH, as do other drugs, has side effects. Safety and Toxicology of DPH is reviewed in *The Broad Range of Use of Diphenylhydantoin* (pp. 184–86). This review was done in 1970, thirty years after the drug had been introduced. References to recent reviews on this subject are given on pp. 243 and 277. A replication of Parke-Davis's package insert is included in the *Physicians' Desk Reference.* It should be noted that DPH is not on the FDA's list of controlled drugs.

DPH can be used on a regular basis or on an occasional basis by the nonepileptic—depending on need. In the nonepileptic, effective doses tend to be lower than those used for epilepsy. The reader is reminded that DPH is a prescription drug and should be obtained from a physician.

• • •

When the Dreyfus Medical Foundation was preparing *The Broad Range of Use of Diphenylhydantoin,* there were many published studies to draw on—1,900 by the time of publication. Seven hundred fifty references were selected and over 300 of them were summarized. These summaries were presented chronologically in order to show in sequence how the information about DPH developed.

Five years later when *DPH, 1975* was published, there were more than twice the number of studies to review, and the interrelationship between the clinical effects and basic mechanisms of action of DPH was in better perspective. In this bibliography the medical material was arranged according to subject matter for the convenience of the reader. Examples of this are found under such headings as Stabilization of Bioelectrical Activity, Antianoxic Effects, Antitoxic Effects, Treatment of Pain, and others.

As an instance, under Antianoxic Effects of DPH, ten studies are grouped. They were published in nine different journals, over a span of twenty years. Each of them is interesting but, by itself, would not carry much weight. But when these studies are reviewed together, the evidence that DPH has an offsetting effect against oxygen lack in animals is highly significant. These studies furnish rationale for the clinical findings made by Shulman in 1942, *New England Journal of Medicine,* that DPH was effective in asthma.* They also furnish rationale for exploration of new uses.

• • •

Exploration of Possible New Uses

Since Putnam and Merritt's discovery in 1938 that diphenylhydantoin was a therapeutic substance, a steadily increasing number of uses for it have been found. The probabilities are high that there are more to come. Evidence from existing clinical and basic mechanism of action studies furnishes clues for further exploration.

DPH has been reported effective in a wide variety of severely painful conditions.† Its usefulness as a non-habit-forming analgesic in milder forms of pain, and also in rheumatic conditions and arthritis needs investigation.

The antianoxic effects of DPH point to its possible usefulness in stroke, emphysema, shock, in fact in any condition where oxygen lack is a problem.

There are a number of references in the literature to beneficial effects of DPH on hypertension. Recently, in a study of mildly hypertensive patients, treatment with DPH was reported effective.‡ Further study of DPH in hypertension, both by itself and in combination with hypertensive drugs, seems indicated.

A use of DPH that has received little attention, and that may have great potential, is its use topically, for the treatment of pain and for the promotion of healing.

* And other studies in asthma, by Sayer and Polvan, *Lancet* (1968), and Shah, Vora, Karkhanis and Talwalkar, *Indian Journal of Chest Diseases* (1970). The latter authors give another rationale, DPH's potential usefulness against the paroxysmal outbursts of asthma by its ability to stop post-tetanic afterdischarge.

† See Treatment of Pain, pp. 166–69, 227–30 and 279–80.
‡ See de la Torre, Murgia-Suarez and Aldrete, p. 282.

Systemic DPH has been reported useful in healing in a variety of disorders—in leg ulcers, stomach ulcers, scleroderma, pruritus ani, and epidermolysis bullosa.*

The first report of a topical use of DPH was in 1972. Savini, Poitevin and Poitevin, *Revue Francaise d'Odonto-Stomatologie,* found topical DPH effective against pain and in the promotion of healing in periodontal disease. These findings were confirmed by three other studies in 1972 and by a double-blind study in 1977.

No study has been done by me but I have an obligation to report that I've seen DPH used topically many times on cuts, burns, bruises, and other surface conditions. From these informal observations it is apparent that DPH, used topically, is rapidly effective in the elimination of pain, and it would appear to shorten the time of healing. (Since this was written a recent controlled study of forty severely burned patients found that patients treated with topical DPH were able to receive skin grafts in less than half the time of patients conventionally treated.)†

Other areas of investigation will suggest themselves to physicians.

• • •

Except for a personal note, this concludes the first part of this book. The second part is medical and scientific, more for the physician than for the layman. But it is not classified information and the layman may find it of interest.

---

* See pp. 177, 178, 237, 241, 281, 282 and 283.

† Chappa-Alvarez, Mendiola, Espejo-Pascencia and Rodriguez-Noriega, Guadalajara Civil Hospital *(In press.)*

A further controlled study by these authors reports topical DPH effective in the promotion of healing of chronic vascular leg ulcers. *(In press.)*

13.
CONCLUSION
AND PERSONAL NOTE

"Truth is a precious thing and should be used sparingly."—
Mark Twain. I have squandered a good deal of this precious
commodity in writing this book—my supply is low—and it is
time to conclude.

With the completion of this book I will have done what I can
to communicate the facts about DPH. The Dreyfus Medical
Foundation is going out of the communications business. It is
not that we have lost interest, but to continue to argue the case
for DPH could be counterproductive. This is a matter for others
now.

Duplicates of the Foundation's extensive files on DPH are
herewith offered to the Federal government. Access to these files
will continue to be available to physicians. The Foundation in-
tends to stay in the field of DPH and hopes, selectively, to sponsor research in new areas.

Thank you if you have read some of this book. And the best
of everything to you. As for me, I am going to get in a rowboat
and float upstream.

14.
APPENDIX

Transcripts of 8 Cases—Worcester County Jail Study

JOHN G.

Before DPH:

I'm nervous, irritable, and I brood a lot over things that are already over and done with. I make more of them inside which keeps me in quite a state of nervousness, anger, tension, what have you.

I magnify everything to the extent where I make myself uncomfortable . . . I'm never relaxed enough to take time to try to figure out what makes me move—I can't control myself and I just don't seem to give a damn one way or the other.

On DPH:

I'm quite relaxed. I feel good.

I slept real good . . . I'm not as worked up so I stay awake . . . When it's bedtime, I'm ready to go.

I'm more easygoing . . . I'm not as short with the fellas as I usually am . . . I've only blown my top once . . . It just lasted a few seconds . . . I didn't brood about it afterwards.

After Being Off DPH for Two Weeks:

Before I took the medicine, I felt the same way as I do now . . . More or less quick to jump. In fact, a lot of times I might jump before I think it over.

I've had two good arguments since I've been off the medication.

I've had a few headaches in the morning . . . A lot of times I have a headache during the day when I get worked up over something.

I'm not sleeping. I wouldn't say I'm sleeping sound at all . . . I'm having some dreams . . . they are very unpleasant . . . and uncomfortable, tiring.

On (Double-Blind) DPH:

I think I'm improved all over . . . An hour after I took the pill I could have told you it wasn't sugar . . . You could feel the engine just slowing right down.

I'm very relaxed and I'm not uncomfortable in any way . . . I can sort of think ahead.

I been sleeping soundly, no trouble, no lying awake thinking about things. That's more or less what kept me awake; the brain was overactive . . . but now I just drop right off.

I still have anger but I don't blow up . . . Quite a bit of restraint which I never had . . . The anger doesn't hang on like it did before.

VICTOR M.

Before DPH:

Well, I am nervous. I bite my fingernails. I got a nervous disorder . . . my hands shake . . . I have a lot of headaches and a pain in the stomach all the time.

I don't go to sleep till about one or two o'clock in the morning . . . I toss around a lot . . . I could put the blanket over me and sometimes find the blanket on the floor.

My mind must be busy . . . I can't turn it off.

On DPH:

I'm sleeping better . . . I sleep right through and don't get up any more like I used to.

I feel better than I did . . . I don't feel that nervous now . . . About the pain in my stomach, I don't get it as often as I used to . . . I don't get headaches as much.

I'm not as grouchy as I used to be . . . Now very often I don't get mad.

After Being Off DPH for Two Weeks:

When I was taking the pills I felt better and now, after I came off the pills, I don't feel so good . . . I'm restless.

I can't sleep.

I get in my cell and I won't even come out.

On (Double-Blind) DPH:

I'm in a good mood . . . I wasn't angry all week long . . . I didn't have any arguments with anyone.

Right now I've been sleeping more than before . . . Every afternoon, pretty near, I take a nap.

The pain in my stomach went away . . . I haven't had a headache all week . . . I haven't been biting the nails.

JAMES L.

Before DPH:

I feel miserable, a bunch of nerves.

I have a grudge on me I can't get rid of . . . I take it out on everyone. It's so bad that sometimes I have myself locked in so I won't cause any trouble.

I can't work or nothing. When you're down-and-out there isn't much you can do.

I can't digest my food right . . . I don't feel like eating nothing.

My thinking is bad, there are quite a few thoughts in my mind, I can't concentrate at all. It takes me a day and a half to write one letter.

I get them phantom limb pains [he had a wooden leg] quite a bit, at least three times a week. The pain, I can just take so much of it. I can't sleep and I can't sit still or nothing.

Sometimes I have them headaches in the afternoon and at night I get them right back again.

On DPH:

I feel a lot better. All the guys down there say I ain't the same guy . . . because I let them all out of their cells. [James L. was a trusty.] I didn't lock nobody up.

Now I'm eating like a fool, before I couldn't eat.

I get them headaches once in a while but not too often. That's why I stopped taking those aspirins.

After Being Off DPH for Two Weeks:

I never get to sleep . . . I sleep about an hour, that's all.

I get weak but I can't seem to hold my weight. The guys put me on the bed and I come out of it after a while.

I get them headaches quite often now. I've been getting phantom limb pains back . . . I had it again yesterday. I couldn't even lay down on the bed. I kept twisting and turning.

I'll read a story and, as a matter of fact, I won't even know what I read.

On (Double-Blind) Placebo:

I'm down and out right now. My mind's all bunched up now. I passed out Wednesday. I get headaches.

Anger, about the same as it was before the pills.

I had those phantom limb pains Wednesday.

On (Single-Blind) DPH:

I feel good right now . . . I feel altogether different . . . I feel much better since I got them pills.

I've been kidding around with everybody . . . For the last two days the fellows have been saying I'm not the same guy. No headaches. No phantom limb pains.

ALTON B.

Before DPH:

I'm pretty nervous . . . I feel a little shaky all over.

My stomach is all tied up . . . It feels like it's all twisted up. Bothered me quite a lot lately.

I've been having headaches.

At the end of the day I get worn out.

On DPH:

I feel pretty good for a change . . . I don't feel shaky . . . I feel more relaxed.

I don't think too much . . . it seems like I have more patience . . . I sit down and watch television for one program. I never could do that before.

I guess I been sleepin' better . . . When I wake up in the morning my head feels clearer than it did before.

My stomach don't feel like it's all tied up . . . I can eat good.

I haven't had any headaches and I'm not so tired.

After Being Off DPH for Two Weeks:

I have been feeling nervous . . . I feel like I'm going right back where . . . like a nervous stomach and like I was before.

Right now I'm rundown and I'm tired . . . no pep, no nothing.

On (Double-Blind) Placebo:

I feel miserable, lousy, tired, rundown . . . I feel shaky.

On (Single-Blind) DPH:

I don't know what the pill was, but I'm pretty sure it helped me.

I feel pretty good . . . I feel cheerful . . . I feel good all over, I guess.

ALBERT M.

Before DPH:

I get depressed very easily . . . Nothing seems good to me . . . I don't care what happens . . . I don't care if they put me in the hole, put me in solitary confinement.

I'm quick-tempered . . . I hold back sometimes . . . the thought keeps harping, keeps harping . . . it stays longer than I like.

If I get excited . . . if I get mad . . . I'll start shakin' . . . my whole body is goin'.

On DPH:

I feel more relaxed . . . I don't feel as much tension as I had.

I haven't got angry . . . don't wake up grouchy like I used to.

As far as headaches, I haven't had a headache now for about three days.

After Being Off DPH for Two Weeks:

When I come off the pills I got depressed, very depressed. Headaches, anger, not eating well, not sleeping well . . . Nervous, very nervous.

On (Double-Blind) Placebo:

I didn't get to sleep till about three o'clock this morning and I was up about five-thirty.

I'm worried . . . I don't know what's going to happen, but I don't think I can do any more time. It's really got me down. It's really got me depressed.

Everything galls me. I just don't care for anything.

On (Single-Blind) DPH:

I'm pretty steady, sleepin' good, my appetite has come back . . . I'm not angry, not a bit. I was down-and-out. Since I been back on the medicine I feel pretty good.

WILFRED S.

Before DPH:

Once in a while I just feel scared . . . I have a bad habit of biting my fingernails and biting my lip.

I'm quick-tempered. I always want to keep on the move. I pace the floor, it seems to make me feel better if I just keep moving.

I seem to think all the time. I have a hard time sleeping. I toss and turn for about an hour and wake up sometimes in the middle of the night from nightmares.

On DPH:

I feel fine . . . I haven't been nervous. I don't find myself thinking like I used to . . . I don't think as heavy.

I haven't been scared, and I don't get in so many fights and arguments . . . I get along with the other fellas.

I've been sleeping good . . . haven't had nightmares like I did before . . . feel more awake . . . I'm just not so tired.

After Being Off DPH for Two Weeks:

Well, since I've been off the pills, I've seemed to tire more easily, I don't sleep too well at night and I'm more nervous now. And I notice myself quick-tempered.

I do a lot more thinking now.

I've noticed the last couple of days I've slacked down on my eating. I don't have too much of an appetite.

On (Double-Blind) Placebo:

I'm nervous all the time, very quick-tempered, feel depressed, feel tired.

I think constantly. I try to stop but I can't . . . I sort of keep thinking of different things all at the same time . . . I tend to think of other things at the same time I'm reading . . . I have a hard time remembering what I read.

On (Single-Blind) DPH:

Well, it seems like all of a sudden I'm coming back to life . . .

My mood is much better. I don't get in so many arguments . . . I'm not so hot-tempered.

I can understand things better and concentrate on things. I don't have that continuous thinking. I'm not so tired because my mind isn't running all over the place.

ROBERT B.

Before DPH:

I would say I'm nervous . . . I have my fears. I get mad fast . . .

My mind is turned on . . . I go in my cell, I sit down and I start thinking. Many things go through my mind . . . and I work myself up and this can go on for a whole day . . . The only way I could probably turn it off is if somebody started talking to me . . . As soon as I stopped talking . . . it would just start up again.

I have a lot of trouble with sleeping . . . I wake up frequently.

I think I get very easily depressed . . . Many times a day. When anything doesn't go my way I get very depressed . . . I sulk. I don't talk to anybody and nobody can talk to me.

On DPH:

I'm in a very good frame of mind . . . I just feel relaxed and comfortable . . . The feeling that I got now is that I can sit here and listen to you talk rather than me talk to you.

I'm much calmer . . . And I noticed that the days go quicker. I didn't have any run-ins with anybody. Nothing bothered me.

I seem to have a clear outlook and everything seems to be sharper for me. I seem to be able to concentrate better . . . My mind just doesn't seem to be wandering as much.

After Being Off DPH for Two Weeks:

I feel lousy . . . very edgy, constant depression most of the time . . . I'm just not interested in anything . . . I have no desire to do anything.

I tried sleeping all morning, laying down, reading a book, but I just couldn't sleep. And I'm not getting that good a night's sleep.

I go from one subject to another . . . I have a lot of trouble writing a letter. I guess my mind wanders so much that as I'm writing a sentence out I completely forget what I'm writing about.

On (Double-Blind) DPH:

I have no nervousness, no depression, no trouble with sleep. I just feel great.

I'm in a good frame of mind . . . I've been pretty calm, cool and collected. Happy.

I feel pretty lively . . . I have the feeling I want to do something . . . I don't have that tired, dragged-out feeling.

DANNY R.—ASSESSMENT OF DOUBLE-BLIND

In ten of the eleven cases, the investigators, and the subjects themselves, correctly assessed who was on DPH. The assessment of the eleventh case was complicated by a realistic problem that developed during the study which the subject did not tell us about, and the effects of DPH were masked by a realistic reaction. This was the case of Danny R. Before the problem arose, Danny R.'s response to DPH was similar to that of the other subjects. Danny R.'s realistic response to his problem, even with DPH, lends support to the description of DPH as a normalizer.

At the beginning of the study, on DPH, Danny R. reported that he slept sounder, that nervousness and excessive anger disappeared, energy returned, muscular pains in his shoulders went away and his mood improved. He illustrated improvement in concentration:

DANNY R: I started a book yesterday. It's five hundred and some pages. I read about three hundred and fifty of them. I got locked in the bakery. Everybody left and I was still reading. I'm usually the first one out, see? I can concentrate now.

Then a serious question of his daughter's eyesight arose and Danny R. wrote home five times asking about his daughter and received no reply. He explains:

DANNY R: Well, you mail a letter and you don't hear nothin'. Then you mail another one. You can't find out nothin'. You get in your cell at night, you start wonderin' is the baby going to lose an eye . . . You toss around half the night.

JACK D: When we saw you Monday morning, you were nervous.

DANNY R: Right.

JACK D: We noticed it and we assumed that you were on placebo. Then we put you on a pill. You didn't know what it was, but we knew it was Dilantin. After we saw you, you received a letter from home. Well, you explain about the letter.

DANNY R: The head runner give me a letter from my sister. She told me that my wife had said that the baby was all right and they were both doing fine. I felt good about it.

JACK D: Dan, you've had two experiences with the pill. The first one was for about a week. Do you think it helped you then?

DANNY R: It helped me. I know it did. You see, when I went into that first week, my nerves about normal for me . . . That week I was sleeping good, as I told you before. My hands were steadier. And I stayed out of trouble.

JACK D: Your anger was down?

DANNY R: Right.

JACK D: But this week, seemingly, the realistic problems overburdened the medicine. We don't know how you would have reacted without the pills.

DANNY R: Maybe they were helping . . . If I wasn't taking them, truthfully, I think I would be in the state hospital right now. That's how bad I was, to tell you the truth.

JACK D: Okay, Dan. Thanks. Perhaps for the sake of this study it is just as well we had one miss, because nobody would believe it if we got everything right.

Lyman and Patuxent Studies

LYMAN

The study at the Lyman Reformatory School was done with six boys aged eleven to thirteen, and the results were similar to those seen at the Worcester Jail. Five of the boys were moody and belligerent. After DPH they became friendly and smiling, and their fights decreased from five or six a day to one or two. The sixth boy was obviously depressed when we first saw him. We had a hard time even getting a *yes* or *no* from him. He never got into fights and stayed apart from the other boys. After he had taken DPH, he became loquacious and started having the "normal" one or two fights a day. The disparate effects of DPH, the calming effect on the boys that needed calming, and the return of energy to the depressed boy were interesting to observe.

PATUXENT

The Patuxent Institution was different from the Worcester County Jail. Unlike the inmates at Worcester, the prisoners at Patuxent had been convicted of the most serious crimes. But DPH made no distinction and the effects on the nervous systems of the five prisoners studied were similar to those observed at Worcester.

As a result of observations made during this study, Dr. Joseph Stephens conducted two double-blind studies with outpatients at Johns Hopkins and found DPH effective in reducing symptoms relating to fear and anger.*

---

* See Stephens and **Shaffer**, *Psychopharmacologia*, 1970,[700] and Stephens and Shaffer, *J. Clin. Pharmacol.*, 1973,[1592] pp. **163** and 213.

Partial List of Symptoms and Disorders (For Which DPH Has Been Reported Useful)

Anger (impatience, irritability)
Angina pectoris
Asthma
Cardiac arrhythmias
Cardiac conduction
Choreoathetosis
Cognitive function (ruminative thinking, concentration, learning disability)
Compulsive eating (including anorexia nervosa)
Concussion
Continuous muscle fiber activity (myokymia, myotonia, etc.)
Depression
Diabetic neuropathy
Drug and alcohol withdrawal
Dysesthesia
Epidermolysis bullosa
Familial Mediterranean fever
Fear (anxiety, tension)
Gilles de la Tourette syndrome
Glaucomatous field loss
Healing (ulcers, periodontal disease)

Hyperkinesia
Hypertension
Hypoglycemia
Hypokalemia
Intractable hiccups
Ischemic heart disease
Labile diabetes
Migraine and other headaches
Muscle spasms
Myocardial infarction
Narcolepsy
Obsessive-compulsive behavior
Pain of Fabry's disease
Parkinson's syndrome
Phantom limb pain
Pruritus ani
Scleroderma
Sleep disorders
Stuttering
Surgery (pre- and postoperative)
Thalamic pain
Toxic effects of other drugs
Trigeminal neuralgia and other neuralgias
Violent behavior

Partial List of Medical Journals (In Which DPH's Usefulness, Other Than in Epilepsy, Has Been Reported)

Acta Endocrinologica
Acta Medica Venezolana
Acta Neurologica
Acta Neurologica Scandinavica
Actualites Odonto-Stomatologiques
American Heart Journal
American Journal of Cardiology
American Journal of Diseases of Children
American Journal of Digestive Diseases
American Journal of the Medical Sciences

American Journal of Physiology
American Journal of Psychiatry
American Journal of Surgery
Anales de Medicina de Barcelona
Anesthesia & Analgesia
Angiology
Annales de Cardiologie et d'Angeiologie
Annales de Dermatologie et de Syphiligraphie
Annali di Medicina Navale
Annals of Internal Medicine

Annals of Neurology
Antiseptic
Archiv Fur Ohren-, Nasen- und Kehlkopfheilkunde
Archives of General Psychiatry
Archives of Internal Medicine
Archives des Maladies du Coeur et des Vaisseaux
Archives of Neurology
Archives of Neurology and Psychiatry
Archives of Otolaryngology
Archives of Pediatrics
Archives of Surgery
Archivos del Instituto de Cardiologia de Mexico
Arquivos de Neuro-Psiquiatria
Arztliche Wochenschrift
Australian Journal of Dermatology
Brain
British Heart Journal
British Journal of Addiction
British Medical Journal
Bulletin of the Los Angeles Neurological Societies
Bulletin of the New York Academy of Medicine
California Medicine
Canadian Medical Association Journal
Canadian Psychiatric Association Journal
Chest
Child's Brain
Circulation
Clinical Medicine
Clinical Neurology
Clinical Research
Clinical Science and Molecular Medicine
Clinical Therapeutics
Comprehensive Psychiatry
Criminal Psychopathology
Critical Care Medicine
Current Medical Digest
Cutis
Delaware Medical Journal
Deutsche Medizinische Wochenschrift
Deutsche Stomatologie
Diabetes
Diseases of the Chest
Diseases of the Nervous System
Electroencephalography and Clinical Neurophysiology

Epilepsia
European Journal of Clinical Pharmacology
European Neurology
Fertility and Sterility
Folia Psychiatrica et Neurologica Japonica
Gaceta Medica Espanola
Gastroenterology
Geriatrics
Giornale de Psichiatria e di Neuropatologia
Headache
Indian Journal of Chest Diseases
International Drug Therapy Newsletter
International Journal of Neuropsychiatry
International Surgery
Johns Hopkins Medical Journal
Journal of the American Geriatrics Society
Journal of the American Medical Association
Journal of the American Osteopathic Association
Journal of the Association of Physicians in India
Journal of Cardiovascular Surgery
Journal of Clinical Endocrinology and Metabolism
Journal of Clinical Investigation
Journal of Clinical Pharmacology
Journal of Diabetic Association of India
Journal of the Egyptian Medical Association
Journal of the Florida Medical Association
Journal of Formosan Medical Association
Journal of the Indian Medical Association
Journal of Laboratory and Clinical Medicine
Journal of the Kansas Medical Society
Journal of Laryngology and Otology
Journal of Mental Science
Journal of the Michigan State Medical Society
Journal of the National Proctologic Association
Journal of Nervous and Mental Disease
Journal of Neurology, Neurosurgery and Psychiatry
Journal of Neurosurgery
Journal of Oral Surgery
Journal of Pediatrics
Journal of Reproductive Medicine
Journal of Urology
Klinische Wochenschrift
Lancet
Maryland Medical Journal

Medical Clinics of North America
Medical Times
Medical World News
Medicina Experimentalis
Medizinische Monatsschrift
Metabolism
Michigan Medicine
Modern Medicine
Modern Treatment
Mount Sinai Medical Journal
Munchener Medizinische Wochenschrift
Nervenarzt
Neurologia i Neurochirurgia Polska
Neurology
Neuropadiatrie
New England Journal of Medicine
New York State Journal of Medicine
Pediatrics
Physician's Drug Manual
Pittsburgh Medical Bulletin
Polish Medical Journal
Portsmouth Journal of Psychology
Postgraduate Medical Journal
Postgraduate Medicine
Practitioner
Problemy Endokrinologii
Proceedings of the Australian Association of Neurologists

Proceedings of the International Strabismological Association
Proceedings of the Symposium on Aggressive Behavior
Psychopharmacologia
Psychosomatic Medicine
Revista Brasileira de Anestesiologia
Revista Clinica Espanola
Revista Espanola de Pediatria
Revista Iberica de Endocrinologia
Revue de Laryngologie
Revue de Medecine Aeronautique et Spatiale
Revue Neurologique
Revue d'Odonto-Stomatologie
Revue d'Oto-Neuro-Ophtalmologie
Schweizerische Medizinische Wochenschrift
Southern Medical Journal
Stomatologie der DDR
Svensk Larkartidn
Therapeutische Umschau
Therapiewoche
Transactions of the American Neurological Association
Virginia Medical Monthly
Vnitrni Lekarstvi
Western Medicine
Zhurnal Nevropatologii i Psikhiatrii Korsakova

Early Cases

The cases of the third, fourth, fifth, and sixth persons I saw take Dilantin are summarized. The names have been changed.

Third Case. **Elizabeth Brown.** Came from Miami to New York for diagnosis. She couldn't turn off her thoughts and was depressed, agitated, and filled with fear. Was diagnosed in New York by a colleague of Dr. Silbermann's as a schizoid type. DPH was tried. It had been thought she would need a companion to take her back to Miami, but her improvement on DPH was such that the physicians felt it was not necessary. In Miami she was treated by Dr. A. Lester Stepner. A letter from Dr. Stepner stated: "She had suffered from a depression and had suicidal thoughts. She had not been able to function in any constructive manner. She is now taking Dilantin regularly and feels that this has controlled the impulsive acts which have made it difficult for her to keep a job. She is not depressed, has passed the intensive courses of the airline stewardess, and is now working for National Airlines."

Fourth Case. George Lewis. George, a business associate of mine, came to see me about an office procedure. I didn't agree with the procedure he liked, but when I saw how important it was to him I agreed to do it his way. He continued to argue his point, and I realized he hadn't even heard me. I asked him how he felt. He said he was depressed and worried all the time, and for the last few weeks had only slept a couple of hours a night. I sent him to Dr. Silbermann who put him on DPH, on a Friday. When I saw him on Monday he was in a good mood and had slept soundly Saturday and Sunday. He stopped taking DPH on his own, and in a few days his mood deteriorated. He took DPH again and an hour later volunteered, "I've got my strength back! I've got my strength." He continued the medicine with good effect.

In the next two cases, which I couldn't follow closely, I asked the subjects to write me their experiences.

Fifth Case. Mary Jones. Excerpts from her letter:

I was in a state of uneasiness and an undefinable morbid fear accompanied me. A good night's sleep seemed the most elusive of luxuries.

After taking Dilantin for two or three days, I started to feel much better. A calm came over me and I was free from that inner disturbance. What a relief from that nervous jerky feeling I had when I endeavored to do the simplest things. What is really marvelous is that I sleep at night. No longer do I stay awake manufacturing problems.

Then I stopped taking DPH. What a change came over me! Saturday I was depressed and by Saturday evening I was in rare form. Listening to *Tosca,* I started on a crying jag that lasted throughout the night.

After three days of that nonsense, I started taking Dilantin again on Tuesday. I started feeling much better. By the way, I'm now making a test—*Tosca* is on and I feel great!

Sixth Case. Evelyn Smith. Excerpts from her letter:

I want to express my feelings as much as possible before I started taking DPH.

I had become a really sick person. I had got so disgusted with life that I hated people. I started staying by myself, not going anywhere, not doing anything. I couldn't even stand going shopping. I wanted to sleep to escape, but I couldn't sleep. Then I started taking sleeping pills, and

I stopped eating and lost weight. I would have periods of deep depression.

Then I started taking DPH. I remember no reactions as far as a sleeping pill or anything similar makes you feel, but I started taking an interest in life again. After two or three days I noticed that I could drive my car and traffic didn't upset me anymore. Matter of fact I was relaxed, enjoying listening to the car radio. Then I noticed that waiters and people around me didn't bother me anymore.

I have no trouble sleeping now, and I've stopped taking sleeping pills. Now I can talk to someone or read a book without a million thoughts creeping up and crushing what I am thinking about.

I have gained eight pounds and weigh 106. I am happier than I have ever been that I can remember. And my friends have noticed the change in me, for many have mentioned it.

Dr. Stepner's Letter—Summaries of 12 Patients

H. S. is a forty-six-year-old woman who was depressed. She has a son who, at the time she started on the Dilantin, was a patient in a mental hospital in New York City. She was very pessimistic about his future. She was impulsive, not only in her actions, but in her speech as well. In my opinion, the drug has exerted a calming influence on this woman. Her speech is more coherent, and she is able to continue on a topic without going into unrelated channels of thought. She is able to think more clearly about her son's illness and his future. She is continuing on this medication and will keep me informed on her progress while she is away for the summer.

R. W. is a sixteen-year-old boy, who has been a behavior problem in his school and home. He knows he is an adopted child, which, at times, has made him feel very insecure. He was very impulsive and demanding, and very restless. Since he has been on Dilantin, his social behavior has improved. He is still on this medication and continues to maintain this improvement. Other medications which had been tried resulted in a great deal of drowsiness without as great effect.

M. F. B. is a thirty-seven-year-old woman who suffered from a schizo-effective disorder (depressive type). She exhibited a great deal of rage toward her husband, which resulted in their being temporarily separated. She has been on Dilantin for approximately two-and-one-half months. During this time, her rage has almost disappeared. Relations with her husband and children are very much better. She is continuing on this medication, taking two tablets daily.

J. S. is a forty-eight-year-old married male who was depressed and obviously had a great deal of repressed hostility. His outbursts of rage were directed, principally, toward his wife and children. He resorted to barbiturates to control his anxiety; antidepressant medication was only partially successful. At the present time, he is taking two Dilantin capsules, 0.1 mg. daily. His behavior has improved; he is not taking any barbiturates. He is functioning much better on his job, and his relationship with his family has improved.

H. H. is a thirty-six-year-old male who has a reactive depression, caused by his relationship with his wife, a dominating father, and an older brother. His expressions of anger toward the above-mentioned individuals were expressed verbally, but without any emotional accompaniment. He is being seen in group therapy. With the introduction of Dilantin into his treatment, his behavior toward his wife has improved. He is now able to make plans, without undue anxiety, leading toward a severance of his business relations with his father and brother.

G. B. is a forty-two-year-old married female, mother of three children, who was depressed over her marital situation, with her rage vented against her children. She felt hopeless and resorted to barbiturates, Dexamyl, and alcohol. At the present time, she is not drinking, does not use any barbiturates or pep-up pills. She takes one Dilantin daily. Her relationships with her husband are markedly improved.

A. D. was a very unreliable young woman whose statements could not be verified. She seemed to be less depressed and less self-destructive (rage directed inwardly). I have not heard from her for several months.

B. P. is a fifty-year-old depressed male who feels inadequate and unable to function on any job. His hostility is kept under rigid control, although there are times when he does have some "temper outbursts." He has improved tremendously since he has been taking one Dilantin daily.

J. N. is a twenty-one-year-old young woman suffering from a reactive depression and repressed rage toward her parents, which prompted her to do acts which were self-destructive. Since she has been on Dilantin, her behavior has been much improved.

L. K. is a twenty-one-year-old female who was depressed and unable to function following a divorce from a man much older than herself. Rage was manifested by very bizarre behavior. She was started on Dilantin approximately two months ago. She is now living in Washington, D. C. Last report was that she is not depressed; she is functioning very well, maintaining a position in the House of Representatives. She is still taking the medication, although she has cut the dose to one a day.

M. S. is a fifty-three-year-old married female who, in attempting to overcome a depression, began taking excessively large doses of stimulants, resulting in an acute brain syndrome because of the toxic reaction of the medicine. She was hospitalized in January. Following treatment for the drug intoxication, her depression manifested itself. She was put on Dilantin because of her temper outbursts, which accompanied the depression.

E. B. was the first of this series. She suffered from a depressive reaction. She was suicidal and, during the hospitalization, the electroencephalogram showed a focal lesion. She expressed strong feelings of inadequacy and was not able to function in any constructive manner. She is taking Dilantin regularly. At the present time, she is not depressed; she was able to successfully pass the short but intensive courses of the airline stewardess and has maintained a position as a stewardess with an airline for approximately six months. She still continues to take the Dilantin regularly and feels that this has controlled the impulsive acts, which in the past had made it impossible for her to continue in any one position for any length of time.

Part Two

Clinical and Basic Science Information

Vol. I   THE BROAD RANGE OF USE OF
         DIPHENYLHYDANTOIN

Vol. II   DPH, 1975

         Review of Recent Work

EXPLANATORY NOTE

In 1970 a bibliography and review, entitled *The Broad Range of Use of Diphenylhydantoin,* was published by the Dreyfus Medical Foundation and sent to physicians. By 1973 so much new work had been done on DPH that it seemed necessary to issue a supplement. By the time the supplement, *DPH, 1975,* was completed it was larger than the original bibliography. *DPH, 1975* and *The Broad Range of Use* . . . were both sent to physicians in 1975. The two books, together, represented a complete bibliography as of that time.

For the purposes of this book, the bibliographies have been slightly condensed and an authors index has been omitted.

Since 1975 over two thousand additional studies on DPH have been published. A brief review of this new material under the title "Review of Recent Work" will be found starting on p. 277.

VOLUME I
THE BROAD RANGE OF USE OF DIPHENYLHYDANTOIN

CONTENTS

CLINICAL USES OF

VOLUME II
DPH, 1975

CONTENTS

DIPHENYLHYDANTOIN

VOLUME I
THE BROAD RANGE OF USE OF DIPHENYLHYDANTOIN

CONTENTS (continued)

BASIC MECHANISMS

CONTENTS

OF ACTION OF DPH

VOL. I
1970

The Broad Range of Use
of Diphenylhydantoin

BIBLIOGRAPHY AND REVIEW

Samuel Bogoch, M.D., PH.D.
Jack Dreyfus

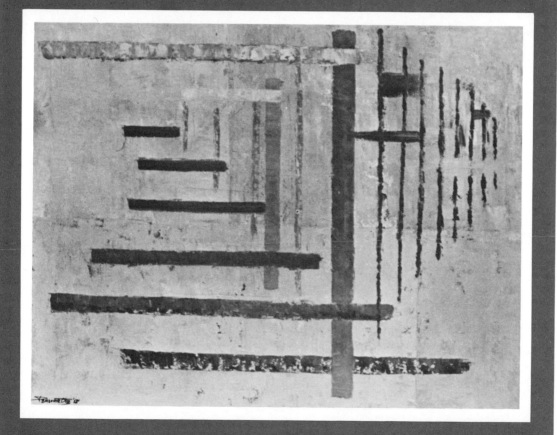

THE DREYFUS MEDICAL FOUNDATION

(WRITTEN IN 1970)

PERSPECTIVE

Diphenylhydantoin (DPH) has been a well known medicine for over thirty years.[1] During most of this time it has been classified as an anticonvulsant. This classification has been unfortunate, not because it is inaccurate but because it has implied that DPH is limited to its anticonvulsant properties.

We now know that DPH is a substance with broad therapeutic effectiveness. For a perspective we suggest that the reader turn to page 137 and look at the list of symptoms and disorders for which DPH effectiveness has been reported.

If one wonders how the general use of DPH could have been overlooked for so long, a review of its history may help. The first benefits of DPH were discovered by Putnam and Merritt in 1937. They were looking for a medicine to help the epileptic and they found one. It is a rare feat to find what one seeks in medical research. We now know that the discovery was even more remarkable than that which was sought. Putnam and Merritt in their earliest paper pointed towards broader implications when they observed "... it was frequently noted by the parents of children (that took DPH) that they were much better behaved, more amenable to discipline and did better work in school."

Since Putnam and Merritt were looking specifically for an anticonvulsant, it is understandable that DPH was quickly labeled an anticonvulsant or antiepileptic. As has been mentioned earlier, this limiting classification tended to obscure the general value of DPH.

In 1885 Gowers observed that "Of all the immediate causes of epilepsy the most potent are psychical—fright, excitement, anxiety." This brings into focus the fact that the medicines that preceded DPH in the treatment of epilepsy, first the bromides and second phenobarbital, were not specifics for epilepsy but were medicines with broad use in the nervous system. It is therefore not surprising that DPH also has broad use in the nervous system—and it should be noted that unlike its predecessors DPH is not a sedative and it is not addictive.

Putnam and Merritt established the effectiveness of DPH by giving it to cats in which convulsions were electrically induced. DPH modified or controlled these convulsions. It also modified or controlled the convulsions of the epileptic. It could have been deduced at that time that DPH had a modifying or regulating effect on electrical activity.[2] External electrical activity caused the convulsions in the cats. Internal (bio) electrical activity is involved in the convulsions of the epileptic.

When DPH is viewed as a substance that has a regulating effect on bioelectrical activity, the breadth of its potential becomes apparent. Bioelectrical activity is a property common to all live cells. In fact, one definition of a dead cell is a cell that has no bioelectrical activity. The rhythms of the heart

---

[1] A number of companies manufacture diphenylhydantoin. Since patents expired some years ago its manufacture is not restricted.

[2] This deduction would have proved correct. See studies on regulation of post-tetanic potentiation and stabilization of excitable membranes under Basic Mechanisms of Action.

are electrically regulated, and the rhythms of the digestive tract are electrically influenced. Messages of pain are electrically transmitted and stimuli for anger and fear are electrically relayed. With an estimated ten billion interconnected nerve cells there is a high concentration of bioelectrical activity in the brain. Therefore it is easy to understand that a medicine which regulates or modifies bioelectrical activity can be effective in a wide variety of medical disorders.

The purpose of this bibliography is to put together in one place much of the work that has been done on the clinical uses of DPH, and on its basic mechanisms of action. When the many facets of this medicine are viewed as a whole, a new perspective of DPH emerges.

SUMMARY OF BASIC MECHANISMS

Diphenylhydantoin (DPH) has a stabilizing effect on the excitability of individual nerve cells and nerve tissue. This effect is reported in peripheral nerve, in spinal cord, in neuromuscular junction and in brain. In addition, DPH is reported to stabilize excitable membrane in skeletal muscle, smooth muscle and cardiac muscle. DPH counteracts hyperexcitability in nerve induced by lowered calcium concentration. DPH decreases or eliminates post-tetanic potentiation, an increase in neuronal excitability following rapid repetitive electrical presynaptic stimulation. DPH in proper amounts does not impair the ability of nerve fibers to carry impulses at high frequency; nor does it notably alter normal excitation and response properties of neurons. DPH has been studied in both vertebrates and invertebrates.

When intracellular sodium is abnormally high or intracellular potassium is abnormally low, DPH is reported to act in the direction of correcting this imbalance; and when sodium or potassium are in the normal range, DPH either leaves these concentrations essentially unchanged or effects minimal decreases in intracellular sodium. DPH acts to stabilize blood sugar levels in labile diabetes.

It is reported to combat anoxia and to increase energy reserve compounds in brain, namely, glucose, glycogen, ATP, and creatine phosphate. Taken together these basic mechanism findings are consistent with clinical findings that have caused DPH to be referred to as a stabilizer, a regularizer, or a normalizer.

Although DPH is observed to have a beneficial effect on pain and sleep disturbances, it is reported not to diminish impulse transmission through the ascending reticular formation. DPH is reported to counteract the toxic effects of digitalis without impairing inotropic benefits. Individuals who have taken DPH for more than three months were found to have significantly lower blood levels of DDE, the principal metabolite of DDT. DPH has been reported to reduce the incidence and severity of convulsive activity due to acute radiation exposure.

Other reported effects of DPH include increase in the flow of blood in coronary and cerebral blood vessels, regulatory effects on ACTH and cortisone secretion, decrease of dermal lipids, decrease of brain acetylcholine, and increase in brain gamma aminobutyric acid (GABA).

SUMMARY OF CLINICAL USES

DPH has been found useful in the treatment and prevention of a wide range of disorders. Among them are cardiac arrhythmias, neuromuscular disorders, sleep disturbances, migraine and other headaches, and neuralgias.

In this summary only one area of the therapeutic use of DPH will be discussed—that is the important and key use of DPH in thought, mood and behavior disorders.

DPH has a therapeutic effect on the overactive brain. Symptoms of this condition are preoccupation, multiple thinking, and flashes and fragments of thoughts coming and going. DPH reduces this uncontrolled activity enabling more normal thinking processes to be restored. This effect is usually achieved within an hour. The therapeutic effect that DPH has on the overactive brain is consistent with basic mechanism findings that DPH decreases hyperexcitability in brain cells.

Anger and fear and related emotions are usually found in combination with the overactive brain. Emotional states related to anger for which DPH is therapeutic are impatience, impulsiveness, irritability, aggression, hostility, rage and violence. Emotional states related to fear for which DPH is therapeutic are worry, anxiety, guilt, pessimism and depression. Although excessive anger and excessive fear are decreased or eliminated by DPH, realistic reactions of anger and fear are not interfered with.

Sleep disturbances found in combination with the overactive brain fall into two general categories. The first and most frequent category is symptomatized by difficulty in falling asleep because of overthinking, light sleep accompanied by unpleasant dreams and frequent nightmares, and insufficient sleep. A second category is symptomatized by excessive sleep, so-called avoidance sleep. Relief from both types of sleep disturbance is usually prompt with DPH.

DPH is effective with extremes of mood ranging from depression to the hyperexcitable state. These apparently disparate effects are observed in the overactive irritable individual who is calmed by DPH and the tired energyless individual who has a return to normal energy levels.[1]

Somatic symptoms associated with thought, mood and behavior disorders are usually relieved by DPH. Among those most frequently observed are headaches, gastrointestinal disorders, pain in back of neck and other pain, shortness of breath, trembling, muscle spasms, skin disorders, and problems with weight. DPH has been found effective in the treatment of acute alcoholism and in the prevention of alcoholism.

DPH is not reported to conflict with commonly used sedatives, tranquilizers or energizers. Alcohol and DPH are not incompatible.[2] It is well recognized that DPH is not a sedative and it is not habit-forming.

The range of safety of DPH has been established by over thirty years of extensive use.

[1] This clinical effect is supported by basic mechanism studies that indicate that DPH tends to increase brain levels of glucose, glycogen, ATP and creatine phosphate, and that it combats anoxia.
[2] This compatibility with alcohol should not be confused with the fact that in epilepsy alcohol is contraindicated.

DISCUSSION

The clinical observations of the use of DPH are consistent with the basic mechanisms of action of DPH which demonstrate that it has a regulatory effect on bioelectrical activity and stabilizes excitable nerve cell and nerve tissue. It is recognized that problems of the nervous system are associated with a wide variety of medical disorders. If one thinks of the common denominator of these disorders as a problem of bioelectrical activity, then grand mal epilepsy can be viewed as an extreme manifestation of this type of problem. There are many stages and conditions of above-normal excitability of nerve cells which do not result in grand mal epilepsy. Some of these are reflected in abnormal electroencephalograms, but many more are not and are seen as behavioral indications of hyperexcitability such as impatience, irritability, impulsiveness and excessive anger, as well as worry, anxiety, fear and depression.

Perhaps thirty-three years ago when the first benefits of DPH were discovered, the thought that bioelectrical activity in the nervous system would have a basic relationship to anger and fear would not have been met with wide acceptance. Today, because of the work of Hess, Penfield, Delgado and others a relationship between electrical stimulation and anger and fear has been demonstrated. Thus, it is far easier today to understand that excessive bioelectrical activity can be the source of excessive anger and fear; and that a substance that tends to stabilize bioelectrical activity can have a beneficial effect against anger and fear. Regardless of mechanism, clinical studies clearly demonstrate that DPH has a therapeutic effect on excessive anger and fear.[1]

If, as it appears, DPH's clinical effectiveness is related to the regulation of bioelectrical mechanisms, since every living cell is invested with bioelectrical activity, then all of the therapeutic uses of DPH have not yet been explored.

---

[1] When one considers the role that excessive anger and fear play in violence and addiction one realizes that one of the important uses of DPH may be as a preventive against addiction and violent behavior. In addition to the sociological problems involved, violence and addiction are disorders that need medical attention. Because DPH is non-addictive, is not a sedative, and has a wide range of safety, it is particularly well suited for this purpose. (See DPH as a Preventive, pp.182–84, and Surgery, pp. 181–82.)

CLINICAL USES OF DIPHENYLHYDANTOIN

TREATMENT OF DISORDERS OF THE NERVOUS SYSTEM

From the outset, in its use with epileptics, side benefits of DPH were noted. Improvements in thought, mood and behavior were observed, sometimes *without* seizure control. As . . .

"Salutary effects of DPH on personality, memory, mood, cooperativeness, emotional stability, amenability to discipline, etc., are also observed, sometimes independently of seizure control."
—GOODMAN AND GILMAN,
The Pharmacological Basis of Therapeutics.[703]

Thought, Mood and Behavior Disorders

EARLY OBSERVATIONS— SIDE BENEFITS IN THE EPILEPTIC

MERRITT and PUTNAM, *Journal of the American Medical Association* (1938),[557] in their early clinical report on DPH observed: "In addition to a relief or a great reduction in the frequency of attacks, it was frequently noted by the parents of children that they were much better behaved, more amenable to discipline and did better work in school."

McCARTAN and CARSON, *Journal of Mental Science* (1939),[556] while reporting on the efficacy of DPH in controlling seizures in a group of twenty patients, noted: "Irritability and violent episodes are markedly diminished in frequency and severity. The patients are bright and alert, and there is a subjective feeling of well-being."

"The undeteriorated patients comment on their increased efficiency, and particularly on the absence of drowsiness which they experienced on bromide and phenobarbital treatment."

KIMBALL and HORAN, *Annals of Internal Medicine* (1939),[535] in a study of 220 children treated with DPH, reported that apart from the influence on convulsions, there are other benefits from the use of DPH.

The authors noted that there is a marked change in mental state and personality evidenced by a definite improvement in memory and concentration, a sense of composure and sureness, with a return of social interest. They also found that if there is no brain injury or mental deficiency, there is a tendency for the child to return to normal in every way.

Ross and JACKSON, *Annals of Internal Medicine* (1940),[313] noted that in consonance with the alleviation of seizures almost all reports on DPH remark on the improvement in behavior, well-being, cooperation, alertness, general attitude, irritability, temperament, and personality of many patients.

The authors were particularly interested in the effects of DPH on conduct, as well as any change in intelligence and performance.

In this study with epileptics the authors reported that in almost half of the patients there was an improvement in conduct. DPH seemed to have a greater beneficial effect on performance than on intelligence.

FRANKEL, *Journal of the American Medical Association* (1940),[106] in a study involving forty-eight patients, reported that besides being an effective anticonvulsant, DPH has the advantage of not producing the sedative effect of the other anticonvulsants.

The author noted that the personality of the epileptic patient treated with DPH is remarkably improved. As an example of this he cited a case where, while taking phenobarbital, the patient "was one of our meanest patients; he would cause fights, refuse to work and destroy property. Now he works steadily, is one of our best behaved patients and helps the attendants to quell fights."

FETTERMAN and SHALLENBERGER, *Diseases of the Nervous System* (1941),[95] observed that an outstanding feature of the benefit of DPH is an amazing improvement in personality.

They observed that in several striking instances individuals who had been dull, fearful and disinterested, emerged bright, confident and capable individuals.

THOUGHT, MOOD AND BEHAVIOR— BENEFITS IN NON-EPILEPTICS

LINDSLEY and HENRY, *Psychosomatic Medicine* (1942),[225] in an early study using DPH where no epilepsy was involved, observed that problem children given DPH showed behavioral improvement.

BROWN and SOLOMON, *American Journal of Psychiatry* (1942),[38] in another early study, reported that delinquent boys committed to a state training school showed important behavioral improvement on DPH therapy.

Improvement was seen in a reduction in extreme hyperactivity, excitability and temper "flare-ups" and in attention span and more efficient work patterns.

SILVERMAN, *Criminal Psychopathology* (1944),[716] in what appears to be the first reported study on the use of DPH in prisoners, found DPH to be superior to all other agents tested.

In addition to EEG changes, improvements were noted in sleep, sense of well-being and cooperativeness. These observations were made in a double-blind crossover study with placebo.

The author found DPH more effective than benzedrine sulphate, phenobarbital and a combination of amytal and benzedrine. The study was done with sixty-four "criminal psychopaths" at the Medical Center for Federal Prisoners, Springfield, Missouri, United States Health Service.

The author stated that management of the psychopathic personality should include a trial of DPH.

BRILL and WALKER, *Journal of Nervous and Mental Diseases* (1945),[35] reported prompt and dramatic improvement in behavior coincident with the administration of DPH in a case of psychopathic behavior with latent epilepsy with a history of theft and assault.

After receiving DPH, this irritable, surly and demanding patient became more cooperative and more friendly and showed for the first time a definite interest in occupational therapy.

BODKIN, *American Journal of Digestive Diseases* (1945),[25] while finding DPH highly effective in treating forty-two cases of pruritus ani (later verified in an expanded study involving 111 cases),[26] noted that one outstanding observation made during his ten years of treating this disorder was that every one of the patients seen had one thing in common —they were all highly nervous.

The author stated that "The new factor that was finally able to change the entire picture was diphenylhydantoin."

GOODWIN, *Journal of the National Proctologic Association* (1946),[127] reported the successful treatment of twenty persons with pruritus ani with DPH. He agreed with BODKIN[25] that nervousness is the one factor common to the vast majority of these patients.

The author described DPH as "superior to any therapy previously employed" in the treatment of pruritus ani.

WALKER and KIRKPATRICK, *American Journal of Psychiatry* (1947),[373] treated ten behavior problem children with abnormal EEG findings with DPH. None of the children had clinical evidence of epilepsy and physical and neurological examinations were all negative.

All of these children were treated on an outpatient basis and showed definite clinical improvement under DPH treatment.

FABRYKANT and PACELLA, *Annals of Internal Medicine* (1948),[92] in discussing the effects of DPH and other drugs on seven labile diabetics, noted that in addition to stabilizing diabetes DPH alleviated anxiety, nervous tension and irritability. In addition, the ability to concentrate and to work increased and the patients exhibited a general feeling of well-being.

BAKWIN and BAKWIN, *Journal of Pediatrics* (1951),[539] found DPH beneficial for irritability, hypermotility and variability of behavior in epileptic children, even when seizures were not the major problem.

PASAMANICK, *Archives of Neurology and Psychiatry* (1951),[560] found that diphenylhydantoin, methylphenylethlhydantoin, trimethadione and phenobarbital caused no significant improvement in behavior in children with EEG abnormalities.

ZIMMERMAN, *New York State Journal of Medicine* (1956),[395] gave DPH to a group of two hundred children having severe behavior disorders. Improvement was seen in 70% of the cases.

These children had a matrix of generally bad behavior. Common characteristics were periodic, paroxysmal outbursts of impulsive behavior and there were abnormal EEGs and organic Rorshach. The use of DPH resulted in reduced excitability, less severe and less frequent temper tantrums, reduced hyperactivity and distractibility, fewer fears, and less tendency to go out of contact.

PUTNAM and HOOD, *Western Medicine* (1964),[287] studied twenty-four delinquents, ranging from six years of age to fourteen, with histories of fire-setting patterns, disruptive behavior, absconding and sexual problems. In an attempt to control explosive behavior, the patients were treated with a group of anticonvulsants including DPH, and some with ataractics. Of the twenty-three who completed the study, the prognosis for fifteen was good, two had a fair response and six did not respond to the therapy.

The degree of success was gratifying to the authors. The number of patients who received DPH was not stated.

CHAO, SEXTON and DAVIS, *Journal of Pediatrics* (1964),[51] conducted an extensive study of 535 children classified as having convulsive equivalent syndrome characterized by autonomic disturbances and dysfunction in behavior and communication. 79% of these patients had 14 and 6 EEG patterns. DPH was used alone with 296 of these children and in combination with other drugs in 117 children. Other drugs included acetazolamide and barbiturates.

The symptoms benefited included headache, abdominal pain, vasomotor disturbances, nausea, dizziness or syncope, altered consciousness, fever and/or chills, dyspnea, eye pain, photophobia, sweating, weakness or limpness, pain in extremities and chest pain.

Behavioral and emotional problems, retardation, school problems in non-retarded, sleep disturbances, speech problems and neurological deficits also responded to treatment. The response to the medication was rapid and often striking.

Based on this extensive experience the authors found DPH the drug of choice.

JONAS (1965),[432] in his book "Ictal and Subictal Neurosis," based on observations of 162 patients over a twelve-year period, found

DPH of benefit in a wide range of nonconvulsive disorders.

Among the specific symptoms which the
author noted were helped by DPH were
anxiety, depression, agitation, irritability, violence, headache, abdominal symptoms,
sexual disturbances and hypochondria. In
some of these cases visual and auditory phenomena and body image distortion were
elicited.

LYNK and AMIDON, *Michigan Medicine*
(1965),[576] studied the effect of medication
with severely disturbed delinquents under
court jurisdiction. The number of patients
who received DPH (out of a total of 125) was
not given.

The authors found that some of the children with borderline EEGs but no definite
epileptic symptoms had markedly aggressive
behavior. These children responded to DPH
when no other drug seemed to help.

DREYFUS (1966)[707] reported on "The Beneficial Effects of Diphenylhydantoin on the
Nervous System of Nonepileptics—As Experienced and Observed in Others by a Layman."

The author observed that multiple simultaneous thoughts as well as obsessive and
preoccupied thinking were relieved by DPH.
Coincident with this relief, marked improvements were noted in symptoms of anger and
the related conditions of impatience, irritability, agitation and impulsiveness. Also coincident with the relief was marked
improvement in fear and the related conditions of worry, pessimism, anxiety, appre-
hensiveness and depression.

He noted that the ability to fall asleep more
promptly, and to sleep more soundly, without nightmares, occurred in the majority of
cases. However, with a minority who slept excessively (so-called avoidance sleep) duration
of sleep tended to be beneficially reduced.

Based on his own experience and observations of others he formed the impression that
excessive bioelectrical activity in the nervous
system causes unfavorable emotional responses, anger and fear being chief among
them. DPH modified this excessive bioelectrical activity, causing excessive anger and
fear to be eliminated.

ROSSI, *New York State Journal of Medicine*
(1967),[314] stated that DPH is clinically effective in impulsivity and behavior control in hyperactive children and particularly effective
in controlling nightmares.

RESNICK, *International Journal of Neuropsychiatry* (1967),[297] reported a double-blind
controlled study with crossover and placebo
involving eleven inmates at a prison, selected
from a group of forty-two volunteers. The
entire study (RESNICK and DREYFUS, 1966)[704]
was recorded on tape. The beneficial effects of DPH were reported in connection
with overthinking, anger and fear, tension,
impatience, impulsiveness, irritability and
hostility. In addition, improvements were observed in relation to symptoms such as sleep
difficulties, headaches, gastrointestinal disturbances and, in one case, phantom limb
pain.

Subsequently observations were made at a
reformatory of the effects of DPH on six juvenile delinquents ranging in age from
twelve to fifteen. After the administration of
100 mg DPH daily, prompt relief in anger
and fear was noted and clearly expressed in
marked diminution in fighting by five of the
boys. The sixth boy who was withdrawn, passive and uncommunicative to the point where
on the initial interview he little more than
said "yes" or "no" became far more outgoing,
talkative and had an occasional fight. General improvements in overthinking, tension,
impatience, impulsiveness, irritability, anger,
fear, sleep difficulties and headaches were
also observed.

TURNER, *International Journal of Neuropsychiatry* (1967),[364] studied the effect of DPH on

patients seen in psychiatric practice during an eighteen-month period, who suffered from a wide variety of emotional and behavioral disorders. Forty-six of fifty-six neurotic patients improved. Improvement was observed in relation to anger, irritability, tension, sleep disturbances, ruminations, anxiety, depression, feelings of guilt and withdrawal, regardless of diagnostic category or EEG findings.

Because of the lack of a sense of intoxication, sedation or stimulation, the author suggested that DPH might be called a normalizer.

JONAS, *International Journal of Neuropsychiatry* (1967),[181] found that over half of 211 patients seen in general psychiatric practice had a therapeutic response to DPH, ranging from easing of dysphoria to a complete reversal of symptoms in the following conditions: anxiety and tension states, reactive depressions, certain cognitive disturbances, obsessive-compulsive manifestations, hypochondria, psychopathy, obesity, and addiction to alcohol and to cigarette smoking. Many patients reported favorable reactions within one hour after intake of DPH.

The author suggested that the action of DPH placed it in a category separate from the tranquilizers, antidepressants or stimulants and agreed with TURNER[364] that the term normalizer seemed appropriate to describe its psychological effects.

HAWARD, *International Journal of Neuropsychiatry* (1967),[527] noted that DPH improved concentration difficulties that seemed to stem from ruminative preoccupation with an irrelevant or nonessential thought content.

These conclusions were based on a study involving twenty neurotic outpatients who had previously responded favorably to DPH and then had been taken off DPH. By separating the sample into two groups based on the psychophysiological method of Ax, matched for degree of maladjustment, statistically significant improvement in terms of elevation of stress threshold appeared in each of the variables according to the psychophysiological type concerned.

AYD, *International Drug Therapy Newsletter* (1967),[538] in a summary of the clinical psychopharmacological value of DPH entitled "New Uses for an Old Drug," pointed out the effectiveness of DPH for psychic overactivity, distractibility, short attention span, irritability, impulsiveness, insomnia and behavioral disorders in children. The author noted that EEG abnormality is not a prerequisite for therapeutic response to DPH.

ITIL, RIZZO and SHAPIRO, *Diseases of the Nervous System* (1967),[178] studied the effect of DPH combined with thioridazine on twenty behaviorally disturbed children and adolescents. These patients showed low frustration tolerance, hyperactivity and restlessness, aggressive destructive behavior, impulsiveness, poor school or work performance, antisocial acts, sexual acting out, irritability and stubbornness.

After three months of treatment, fifteen of the twenty patients showed moderate to marked improvement and fourteen of them were discharged.

The patients were characterized by EEG abnormalities such as paroxysmal activity, dysrhythmic patterns, spikes, sharp waves and focal disturbances. The group included eleven having personality disorders, five with schizophrenic reactions, two with chronic brain syndrome with convulsions, and two with chronic brain syndrome without convulsions.

HAWARD, *Portsmouth Journal of Psychology* (1968),[585] found DPH effective in the improvement of concentration. This was demonstrated in a performance test designed to simulate air traffic control tower conditions.

Twelve students, nineteen to twenty-one years of age, were introduced to an air traffic control task requiring a high degree of concentration. The test was done with placebo, on a double-blind basis, and the essential variable was number of errors made. On this basis, improved efficiency was demonstrated by DPH at the significant level of p 0.01.

Although performance was markedly improved, no individual felt a drug effect of any sort. The author stated that this subtlety of action was consistent with what frequently had been observed in the clinical use of DPH.

The author concludes that because of its high level of safety and its nonaddictive character, DPH has none of the negative qualities of the amphetamines, which have in the past been used for similar purposes.

A report of a study by KANZLER, MALITZ and HIGGINS, *Journal of the American Medical Association* (1968),[651] states that, "A double-blind evaluation of six commonly-prescribed antidepressants (diphenylhydantoin, dextro-amphetamine hydrochloride, amitriptyline-perphenazine, amitriptyline-diazepam, nortriptyline HCL, and amitriptyline HCL) failed to reveal any significant differences between the 128 moderately to severely depressed patients receiving any of the drugs and the twenty receiving a placebo."

TEC, *American Journal of Psychiatry* (1968),[355] reviewed his fifteen years experience with DPH in the treatment of behavior disorders in children.

The author reported that DPH improved disruptive behavior in the large majority of the children seen during that period and emphasized that DPH often helped when the phenothiazines and amphetamines failed.

ALVAREZ, *Modern Medicine* (1968),[4] refers to his repeated recommendations on the use of DPH in treating a variety of nonconvulsive disorders in adults and children.

In this report he discusses the effectiveness of DPH in treating behavioral disorders in children in whom head pains, spells of abdominal pain, nightmares, temper tantrums and erratic behavior are present. The author refers to these symptoms as epileptic equivalents.

BOELHOUWER, HENRY and GLUECK, *American Journal of Psychiatry* (1968),[27] in a double-blind study with crossover features and placebo, reported that DPH alone or in combination with thioridazine (Mellaril) was effective at a statistically significant level in a group of seventy-eight patients, ranging in age from fourteen to thirty. Forty-seven of these patients showed 14 and 6 per second positive spiking, whereas no such abnormality was present in thirty-one.

The thirty-one patients without abnormality responded best to DPH by itself. The positive spike group responded better to DPH in combination with thioridazine than to either drug alone.

The patients had been hospitalized because of uncontrollable, impulsive, self-destructive, aggressive behavior, reaching the extremes of self-mutilation, rape and murder.

Significant changes were observed for the following factors with DPH alone: disturbance of affect, lack of social conformity, lack of insight, hostile aggressive behavior, dissociative tendency, thinking disorder, self-destructive tendency, and guilty self-concept. In addition to the above, significant changes were observed for the following factors with DPH and Mellaril combined: overt anxiety symptoms, dissociative concern, paranoid thinking, and depression.

LEFKOWITZ, *Archives of General Psychiatry* (1969),[218] in a double-blind study with a DPH group and a placebo group found "marked diminution in disruptive behavior in both groups, from the beginning of the treatment period to 30 days after its termination." Placebo results were even better than those with DPH.

BALDWIN, *Maryland Medical Journal* (1969),[706] reported on the treatment with

DPH of behavior disorders in children (see also BALDWIN and KENNY, 1966).[8] The most consistent complaint was hyperactivity. Other important problems were temper tantrums or rage reactions, impulsive behavior and social adaptation. Attention span was short and concentration poor.

On reviewing the records of 300 cases treated during a six-month period, it was found that 109 had improved so markedly that they were able to return to school after being on suspension or about to be suspended for bad behavior. On examining what medications these 109 who showed marked improvement had received, it was found that 78 had received DPH—48 of them had behavior problems not associated with seizures. The other 30 had seizures and behavioral problems.

CASE, RICKELS and BAZILIAN, *American Journal of Psychiatry* (1969),[46] reported that anxious-neurotic psychiatric clinic outpatients were treated over a four-week period with DPH (100 mg twice daily). While some improvement was observed in this patient group, no significant difference was noted between the DPH and a comparable placebo group.

However, the authors reported an interesting finding, namely, "a paucity of side effects in the DPH-treated group (only one patient reported mild dizziness), while our placebo control group had the usual variety of side effects . . . in 12 of the 20 patients." If the only variable in these two groups was that one took DPH and one took placebo, then the probability that DPH was effective in preventing the placebo "side effects" in these anxious-neurotic patients was at the level of significance of p less than 0.001.

STEPHENS and SHAFFER, *Psychopharmacologia* (1970),[700] in a double-blind study with thirty adult outpatients, found DPH to be markedly effective in reducing symptoms relating to anger, irritability, impatience and anxiety.

The therapeutic effectiveness of DPH was demonstrated at statistically high levels by both self-ratings and physician ratings of change. This double-blind study was done on a crossover basis with placebo. The dosage of DPH was 100 mg t.i.d.

When compared to placebo, such standard scale factors as "anger," "furious," and "impatience" improved with DPH at p levels between 0.01 and 0.001. Standard scale factors of "worried," and "angry" improved at p levels less than 0.01. Factors of "tension," "grouchy," "ready for a fight," "nervous," "nervousness and shakiness," "trembling," and "quarrelsomeness" improved at levels of p less than 0.05.

In the crossover analysis, DPH improved "anger," "tension," "worried," "uncertain about things," "bad tempered," "resentful," "angry," "impatience," and global change rated by patient all at the level of p less than 0.01; DPH improved "bewildered," "nervous," "ready for a fight," "confused," "anxious," "irritability," "quarrelsomeness," "heart pounding," "temper outbursts," "trembling," "nervousness and shakiness," all at p levels less than 0.05; and the factors of "furious," "grouchy," and global change rated by physician all were improved by DPH at levels of p less than 0.001.

The patients' feelings of tranquility, composure, relaxation, optimism and cheerfulness also showed statistically significant improvement with DPH.

No undesirable side effects were encountered.

The authors did this double-blind study because of favorable experience they had had in an uncontrolled study with fifty-six outpatients.

GOLDBERG and KURLAND, *Journal of Nervous and Mental Diseases* (1970),[713] in a double-blind study, reported the effectiveness of DPH on the emotional, cognitive and social behavior of forty-seven hospitalized retardates, ages nine to fourteen. These children were retarded and classified as "cultural-familial" because there was no discernible evidence of brain damage. The study was double-blind with placebo control and extended over eight weeks, with assessments before and after treatment.

Patients treated with DPH showed strong improvement in ability to maintain attention, in self-control, and in improved interpersonal relationships with adults.

There was marked improvement in logical thinking, and trends toward decreased temper outbursts, impulsivity and aggression. There were also trends toward increased ability to concentrate and better visual-motor organization.

The effective dose of DPH was 100 mg twice daily. Neither toxicity nor side effects were observed.

Alcoholism and Drug Addiction

WALSH, *American Journal of Psychiatry* (1962),[375] stated that for the last eight years as a routine part of his regimen he had used DPH (100 mg three times a day) along with phenobarbitone and B vitamins in treating convulsions in the withdrawal period of acute alcoholism.

WILHOIT, *Journal of the Florida Medical Association* (1965),[383] reported that one of the most important steps taken in the treatment of acute alcoholism and delirium tremens is the prophylactic use of DPH. With DPH patients tended to have a much easier and quicker recovery from acute alcoholism.

The author also noted that with DPH treatment, by the fourth to the seventh day, there was a marked improvement in sense of well-being, sleep pattern, appetite and motivation.

FOX, *Modern Treatment* (1966),[105] recommended DPH (100 mg four times a day) for five to ten days for prevention of convulsions due to alcohol withdrawal. The author stated that frequently the convulsions due to withdrawal from alcohol are mistaken for epilepsy and the patient is sent home on DPH and phenobarbital. The author stated that DPH offers no problem. However, in the case of phenobarbital, the danger exists that the patient may gradually increase it to the point of addiction.

RAMIREZ, *Personal Communication* (1967),[290] described the effective use of DPH during withdrawal of patients with various forms of addiction including heroin.

During a three-year period of clinical study it was found that after physical detoxification most patients went through a stormy period of behavioral difficulties which lasted from seven to ten days on the average. Patients were irritable, intolerant, upset and angry, and frequently showed temper tantrums. In addition, they were insomniac and depressed. On DPH there was a rapid change in the over-all behavior patterns of the patients. Acting out behavior was much less frequent. Sleeplessness, which is a very difficult problem with addicts, was also modified favorably.

After a preliminary study with thirty patients, the author used DPH routinely. 100 mg three times a day usually resulted in symptomatic and behavioral improvement.

CHAFETZ, *Journal of the American Medical Association* (1967),[571] stated that DPH is most effective in aborting convulsions associated with alcoholic withdrawal. He pointed out that DPH is a desirable medication because it lacks the hypotensive effect sometimes found with the phenothiazines.

Stuttering

BENTE, SCHÖNHÄRL and KRUMP-ERLANGEN, *Archiv für Ohren-, Nasen- und Kehlkopfheilkunde* (1956),[13] reported the beneficial use of hydantoins in thirty-seven patients with stuttering disorders. Used alone, hydantoins helped three of six patients. Used in combination with a phenothiazine, hydantoins were found of benefit in twenty-six of thirty-one patients. The authors did not specify which hydantoin was used.

SCHÖNHÄRL, *Medicina Experimentalis* (1960),[331] reported that hydantoin therapy was helpful in an expanded series of one hundred and forty patients treated for speech and voice disorders. The author did not specify which hydantoin was used.

SACK, *University of California, Doctoral Thesis* (1968),[320] conducted a double-blind study with DPH in twenty-four boys between the ages of eight and twelve. These boys were confirmed as stutterers by competent speech pathologists.

Statistically significant reduction of stuttering intensity was found with DPH (100 mg) when compared with placebo. The intensity of the stuttering was significantly reduced although the frequency of stuttering was not changed.

Psychoses

KALINOWSKY and PUTNAM, *Archives of Neurology and Psychiatry* (1943),[186] reported on the treatment with DPH of sixty psychotic patients. These patients were chosen as representing clear and typical instances of the more important major psychoses. Improvement occurred in over half of the patients during the period of treatment and usually consisted of diminution of excitement and irritability, almost irrespective of the type of the psychosis.

Although DPH did not change the basic psychosis, the patients' mood, behavior and emotions were improved and there was benefit to others because they were more cooperative.

The authors noted that "The psychotic patient with dangerous tendencies becomes pleasant and cooperative."

FREYHAN, *Archives of Neurology and Psychiatry* (1945),[110] reported that forty non-epileptic psychiatric patients were given DPH therapy resulting in positive behavioral changes in certain excited patients.

KUBANEK and ROWELL, *Diseases of the Nervous System* (1946),[201] studied the use of DPH in the treatment of prolonged chronic disturbed behavior in 73 psychotic patients unresponsive to other treatment and found DPH unquestionably a valuable drug for some types of disturbed patients with such conditions as catatonic excitement, manic excitement, and the excitement of organic disorders.

In their conclusion the authors state, "The therapeutic effect of the drug is primarily that of decreasing significantly the extent and severity of persistent disturbed behavior with a consequent better adjustment for the patient."

KLEIN and GREENBERG, *American Journal of Psychiatry* (1967),[196] conducted a pilot study of the effectiveness of DPH on thirteen psychotic patients with character disorders or psychoses severe enough to require hospitalization, and found no general beneficial effect of DPH. However, in one case, a 24-year-old male who was apparently a paranoid schizophrenic, with previous diagnosis of psychomotor epilepsy, appeared to have complete remission with DPH.

HAWARD, *Proceedings of the Symposium on Aggressive Behavior* (1969),[697] reported that DPH was effective in reducing aggressive behavior in a double-blind study involving twenty chronic psychotic patients. While the basic psychoses were not changed, important benefits in mood were noted.

Ratings in wards of aggressive behavior were recorded and verbal aggression was independently tested. While there was individual variability in patients, both verbal aggressive behavior and assaultive behavior were reduced by DPH.

Pain

NEURALGIAS AND OTHER PAIN

BERGOUIGNAN, *Revue de Laryngologie* (1942),[15] appears to be the first to have reported the usefulness of DPH in treating neuralgia. He reported complete cure of essential facial neuralgia in three patients treated with DPH.

DATTNER, in the course of a discussion of a paper by CAVENESS, ADAMS, POPE and WEGNER, *Transactions of the American Neurological Association* (1949),[48] suggested that anticonvulsants might control lightning pains in tabetics. Some patients showed a favorable response to DPH or Tridione.

ALVAREZ, *Gastroenterology* (1950),[3] recommended the use of DPH in the treatment of cases of continued hunger pain (pseudo-ulcer).

BERGOUIGNAN and D'AULNAY, *Revue d'Oto-Neuro-Ophtalmologie* (1951),[16] again reported positive effects in treating essential trigeminal neuralgia with DPH. Of seventeen patients on DPH therapy, sixteen were benefited. Of these, ten had complete cessation of attacks.

The rapidity of the drug's action was noted. The effects usually were felt within twenty-four hours, and seemed to increase over three to four days.

JENSEN, *Arztliche Wochenschrift* (1954),[180] reported on the use of DPH in treating forty-five cases of trigeminal neuralgia. Sixteen patients showed complete cessation of pain, which lasted after discontinuance of DPH. Nineteen patients experienced distinct improvement which did not last after DPH withdrawal. Four patients showed slight im-

provement and five patients did not improve.

The author pointed out the desirability of DPH to relieve pain, as opposed to the potent pain relievers and opiates which all too easily lead to addiction.

JENSEN, *Therapiewoche* (1955),[518] again reported on fifty-nine typical cases of trigeminal neuralgia treated with DPH. Fifty-seven were completely freed of difficulties. Twenty remained so after medication was discontinued; but with thirty-seven pain returned when DPH was withdrawn. Only two cases showed no improvement.

WINIKER–BLANCK, *Deutsche Stomatologie* (1955),[384] reported that of twenty-seven cases of genuine trigeminal neuralgia treated with DPH, fifteen remained completely free of pain and seven showed lasting improvement making the condition entirely bearable for the patient.

Because of its safety, DPH therapy was recommended as the treatment of choice, particularly in patients with poor general condition or of advanced age.

ENDE, *Virginia Medical Monthly* (1957),[605] reported that over a period of two years he had successfully treated nine out of nine cases of trigeminal neuralgia with DPH.

The author found that not only was DPH effective, but frequently with the first capsule relief was begun. The relief was so prompt and the procedure so simple that the author had difficulty in believing it. However, since these patients had been subjected previously to nearly every form of therapy recommended, it seemed most unlikely that it was a placebo effect.

BERGOUIGNAN, *Revue Neurologique* (1958),[14] reported that twenty-six of thirty patients who had been treated for trigeminal neuralgia were relieved of their attacks during the first three days of treatment with DPH. Ten of these patients had previously had peripheral or deep alcohol injections with transient or incomplete results and two had had neurotomy.

Immediate results of DPH therapy were particularly favorable. The longer term results were less striking, although ten of these patients who continued DPH maintained their remission for two years or more.

IANNONE, BAKER and MORRELL, *Neurology* (1958),[175] reported that with DPH definite relief of pain was obtained and the paroxysms of pain controlled in all of four patients with trigeminal neuralgia and one with glossopharyngeal neuralgia.

LAMBERTS, *Journal of the Michigan State Medical Society* (1959),[214] reported on thirty patients with trigeminal neuralgia treated with DPH. In almost every instance relief from pain was complete within forty-eight hours, but usually not before twenty-four hours after treatment commenced. The dosage had to be increased in two of the patients before the pain disappeared, and in only one patient was it ineffective initially.

KUGELBERG and LINDBLOM, *Journal of Neurology, Neurosurgery and Psychiatry* (1959),[202] in a study of fifty patients with trigeminal neuralgia, investigated the relationship between stimuli applied to the trigger zone and the pain paroxysm. DPH was found to raise the attack threshold as well as to shorten the duration of the attack.

DORSEY, HAYSLIP and ANDERSON, *Clinical Medicine* (1959),[81] reported the therapeutic effectiveness of DPH in the treatment of tic douloureux. Of eleven patients treated with DPH, five were completely relieved; two did not get complete relief but the pain was so diminished that they did not require any further therapy; four were afforded no relief.

KELLAWAY, CRAWLEY and KAGAWA, *Epilepsia* (1959–1960),[551] in a review of experience with a group of 459 children who had consistent 14 and 6 per second spike patterns on the EEG and whose primary complaints were headache and abdominal pain, found the most effective treatments were DPH and diamox, alone or in combination.

BRAHAM and SAIA, *Lancet* (1960),[31] used DPH in twenty cases of trigeminal neuralgia. Relief of pain was complete in eight and partial in six. The treatment was not effective in the other six. The abolition of symptoms was striking when successful.

The patients helped by DPH therapy, either by arrest or mitigation of their attacks, noted improvement within twenty-four to forty-eight hours and occasionally after the first dose. The change in their appearance provided strong evidence of the effectiveness of DPH.

The authors also reported DPH effective in treatment of lightning pains in two cases of tabes.

REEVE, *Lancet* (1961),[611] reported that DPH was effective in nine cases of trigeminal neuralgia and four cases of post-herpetic neuralgia, and recommended that a trial of DPH precede more radical treatment.

LINDBLOM, *Svensk Lakartidn* (1961),[224] reported that of thirty cases of trigeminal neuralgia treated with DPH, complete relief or considerable reduction of the symptoms occurred in seventeen cases. Improvement lasted as long as the drug was administered. Some improvement, although not satisfactory, was also seen in most of the remaining thirteen cases.

BAXI, *Antiseptic* (1961),[9] reported that eleven of fifteen patients with trigeminal neuralgia, treated with DPH, obtained relief within a week.

The author stated that DPH is the only drug therapy which gives any lasting relief and the only drug which takes away the apprehension of an impending attack.

GREEN, *Neurology* (1961),[129] reported that

DPH was administered to two patients with severe lightning pains due to tabes dorsalis. Remarkable relief was obtained in both cases.

GABKA, *Medizinische Monatsschrift* (1963),[113] reported that DPH is considered the best medication by far in the conservative therapy of genuine trigeminal neuralgia. The author suggests that persistent head and facial pains from diverse causes may also be favorably influenced by DPH.

SCHÖN, *Giornale Di Psichiatria E Di Neuropatologia* (1964),[330] gave DPH to forty-two patients with trigeminal neuralgia and to thirteen patients with facial spasm. Patients with trigeminal pain improved very well, while those with facial spasm had less improvement.

CRUE, TODD and LOEW, *Bulletin of the Los Angeles Neurological Society* (1965),[68] reported on a group of patients suffering with trigeminal neuralgia who were treated with a combination of DPH and mephenesin carbamate (Tolseram). Fifty-six of these patients were followed up. After one to three years, thirty-nine continued to have relief and three had partial relief.

CHINITZ, SEELINGER and GREENHOUSE, *American Journal of the Medical Sciences* (1966),[54] reported that among diseases characterized by severe pain, trigeminal neuralgia (tic douloureux) presents one of the greatest therapeutic challenges.

In 1957 and 1958, the use of DPH in trigeminal neuralgia was first reported in this country. Good results were obtained. This medication had previously been employed with success by European investigators. Considerable evidence has accumulated since then to support the efficacy of DPH in tic douloureux.

ELLENBERG, *New York State Journal of Medicine* (1968),[431] reported that DPH was effective in the treatment of pain and paresthesias associated with neuropathy in a study of sixty diabetic patients. Good to excellent results were observed in forty-one, fair results in ten, and none were worse (see p. 177).

MIGRAINE AND OTHER HEADACHES

SHAPERA, *Pittsburgh Medical Bulletin* (1940),[338] at this early date, reported that two of four cases of migraine were improved with DPH.

ROWNTREE and WAGGONER, *Diseases of the Nervous System* (1950),[315] cited the value of DPH in the prevention of migraine attacks.

McCULLAGH and INGRAM, *Diseases of the Nervous System* (1956),[235] in their paper "Headaches and Hot Tempers," reported that their experience showed that DPH was by far the most adequate medication in the successful treatment of a syndrome in which migraine headaches were related to familial cerebral dysrhythmias. In a few cases DPH was combined with Thorazine with excellent results.

BURKE and PETERS, *American Journal of Diseases of Children* (1956),[40] reported a study at Mayo Clinic from 1950 to 1955 in which DPH was one of a group of medications suggested in the treatment of migraine in children.

KELLAWAY, CRAWLEY and KAGAWA, *Epilepsia* (1959-1960),[551] in a report on 459 children, found DPH one of the drugs of choice in the treatment of headache accompanied by 14 and 6 per second positive spike patterns.

LIVINGSTON and WHITEHOUSE, *Modern Treatment* (1964),[227] reported that EEG examinations frequently provide significant information relative to the treatment of recurrent paroxysmal headaches. For prophylactic treatment of these headaches the authors stated that DPH is the drug of choice.

HIRSCHMANN, *Therapeutische Umschau* (1964),[161] reported on a study of forty-four patients with migraine not relieved by ergot preparations alone. Of these, thirty-two remained in treatment. When they were treated with a combination of 100 mg DPH, 50 mg caffeine and 1 mg Dihydergot (DCH 151), nineteen were either completely relieved or had less frequent or milder attacks.

ROBERTS, *Southern Medical Journal* (1966),[304] found DPH helpful in the treatment of patients with dysrhythmias whose episodic headaches, severe anxiety, leg cramps, and other neurologic or psychiatric features did not abate sufficiently after they had adhered to the basic treatment program which the author had previously used.

WIEDEMANN, *Medizinische Monatsschrift* (1966),[380] in a series of studies on migraine, found preparations containing DPH and caffeine useful in the treatment of a variety of neuralgias and cephalalgias. This treatment was particularly suitable for patients who had true migraines and trigeminal neuralgias.

JONAS, *Headache* (1967),[693] administered DPH to eighteen migraine sufferers. Nine patients afflicted with paroxysmal migraine experienced complete relief. Of six non-paroxysmal patients, four benefited by the use of DPH.

DIMSDALE, *Practitioner* (1967),[78] in a review of the etiology, clinical features, diagnosis, management and treatment of migraine, stated that DPH was useful in patients with dysrhythmias.

FRIEDMAN, *Bulletin of the New York Academy of Medicine* (1968),[111] in a review of headache classification, symptomatology and treatment, suggested the usefulness of DPH combined with caffeine for temporary relief of cluster migraine in those individuals with family histories of migraine or epilepsy or where evidence exists of EEG abnormality.

Concussion

THE CZECHOSLOVAKIA HEALTH MINISTRY, *Medical World News* (1968),[70] issued a directive requiring doctors to give DPH and phenobarbital to every trauma victim who remains unconscious for more than three hours. After six months, if no signs of epilepsy have appeared, the drugs are phased out over the next nine to eighteen months.

This directive was based upon work by DR. KAREL POPEK, chief neurologist at the Neurological Clinic of the University Medical Faculty in Brno, Czechoslovakia. DR. POPEK conducted a controlled clinical study of DPH and phenobarbital in patients with cerebral concussion or other serious head injuries.

He considered the results of the study persuasive enough to warrant routine use of the drugs as preventive therapy.

Neuromuscular Disorders

CHOREAS

SHAPERA, *Pittsburgh Medical Bulletin* (1940),[338] discussed the narrowness with which new drugs are frequently viewed and suggested that DPH might have broader uses than just that of an anticonvulsant. He decided to study the efficacy of DPH in conditions of involuntary movements such as tremors, rigidity and spasticity.

The author found DPH effective in treating involuntary movements in ten of fifteen patients with Sydenham's chorea.

GINABREDA, *Revista Espanola De Pediatria* (1945),[421] reported on the effectiveness of DPH in six cases of chorea minor in children between the ages of five and twelve years. Improvement occurred in all of the cases in an average of fifteen to sixteen days.

GALINDO and GINABREDA, *Anales De Medicina De Barcelona* (1947),[114] reported four cases of chorea minor in children successfully treated with DPH.

DE LA VEGA, *Revista Clinica Espanola* (1947),[75] reported on an epidemic of chorea minor or Sydenham's chorea. DPH was used in thirty-four cases with excellent results. In twenty-six cases there was complete elimination of symptoms in three weeks of treatment. There were four relapses when DPH was discontinued, which were corrected with the renewal of treatment.

Not only did DPH shorten the duration of the disease, but there was a marked reduction of complications—even those of cardiac lesions, a very frequent and serious sequel to chorea minor.

SERRATE, *Gaceta Medica Espanola* (1947),[334] in a carefully detailed study of a single case of chorea minor, also reported that DPH shortened the duration of the disorder.

SCHWARTZMAN, McDONALD and PERILLO, *Archives of Pediatrics* (1948),[591] in a study of Sydenham's chorea in which many medications were tried, reported that of eight patients given DPH six were improved and two were cured.

STEVENS, *Archives of Neurology* (1966),[351] reported that DPH treatment was usually promptly effective in the relief of symptoms of paroxysmal choreo-athetosis.

HUDGINS and CORBIN, *Brain* (1966),[549] treated a mother, son and daughter suffering from familial paroxysmal choreo-athetosis with DPH and mephobarbital. The results were excellent. The relief was prompt and lasting with continued treatment.

KERTESZ, *Neurology* (1967),[191] reported on ten patients with paroxysmal kinesigenic choreo-athetosis as an entity within the paroxysmal choreo-athetosis syndrome. The attacks consist of athetoid movements or tonic posturing of limbs, trunk and face. They occur on one or both sides and are often associated with dysarthria and grimacing. Consciousness is never lost. Duration is usually fifteen to thirty seconds, never more than two minutes. The paroxysms are precipitated by sudden movements, often associated with surprise or haste.

The author reported that the majority of patients respond well to DPH.

PARKINSON'S SYNDROME

SHAPERA, *Pittsburgh Medical Bulletin* (1940),[338] reported on the treatment with DPH of twenty-two patients with Parkinson's syndrome. These patients had previously received other medication with little or no beneficial effect. Results from the standpoint of anti-spasmodic properties of DPH were noted in improvement in involuntary movements.

The author noted that there was a psychic improvement in some of these patients and that this alone made DPH therapy worthwhile.

KABAT, *Annals of Internal Medicine* (1959),[184] in a discussion of drug therapy for cerebellar ataxia, reported the therapeutic effectiveness of DPH in seven cases of Parkinson's syndrome.

Three of these patients, who had been taking the maximal tolerable dose of anti-Parkinson drugs, still showed rigidity, tremor and poor isotonic function. DPH was added to the regular regimen of medication. With the addition of DPH, isotonic function and isometric function improved. Rigidity disappeared in one case and was reduced in the other two cases. Pill-rolling tremor was moderately reduced in one case and unaffected in the other two cases. More facial expression, and definite improvement in ambulation and in use of the upper extremities were noted on addition of DPH.

The other four patients, who had not previously taken any anti-Parkinson drugs, were treated with DPH alone. In every case, prompt improvement in isotonic contraction of the muscles resulted. Rigidity disappeared in one case and was significantly reduced in the others. Tremor was moderately improved. Voluntary motion of the affected extremities was improved significantly in these four cases.

CONTINUOUS MUSCLE FIBER ACTIVITY SYNDROME

ISAACS, *Journal of Neurology, Neurosurgery and Psychiatry* (1961),[176] presented two cases of continuous muscle fiber activity treated with DPH. One case was a child, the other an adult. With DPH normal mobility was virtually restored.

The barbiturates and their derivatives had been used and failed. DPH produced a dramatic recovery within three days: the muscles relaxed, fasciculation diminished, and signs of hypermetabolism disappeared. The bizarre uncontrolled discharge was restored to normal by the use of DPH.

Both cases were controlled by DPH gr 1½ t.d.s. permitting each to live apparently normal lives at school and work respectively. DPH was effective in both cases as confirmed by a four-year follow-up.[177]

MERTENS and ZSCHOCKE, *Klinische Wochenschrift* (1965),[251] reported on three patients in a state of continuous muscular activity, which they termed neuromyotony, showing incessant involuntary muscular tension. Following an insidious onset of the illness and a chronic generalizing course, a considerable curtailment of movement, respiratory discomfort and contractures, partly irreversible, developed.

After the failure of drugs which were effective in myogenic myotonies, carboanhydrase inhibitors, DPH and carbamyldibenzoazepine proved effective in the described neuromyotonic syndrome.

DPH injected intravenously led to marked relief of symptoms two to four hours later. DPH orally was also quite effective.

MUNSAT, *Neurology* (1967),[262] in a randomized, double-blind and crossover study found DPH to be as effective as procaine amide in relieving myotonia, both subjectively and objectively.

The author stated that DPH was better tolerated by patients than procaine amide and, in addition, unlike procaine amide, it did not increase pre-existing cardiac conductive defects.

GARDNER-MEDWIN and WALTON, *Lancet* (1969),[633] referred to twelve previous reports in the literature of the type of case described by ISAACS[176] and, in presenting a further case of this type which they preferred to designate myokymia, confirmed the beneficial effect of 100 mg DPH three times daily combined with 5 mg diazepam twice daily.

The authors suggested that in addition to its known ability to stabilize nerve membrane, DPH might in a similar way stabilize muscle fiber membrane.

TREATMENT OF CARDIAC DISORDERS

In 1950 HARRIS and KOKERNOT, *American Journal of Physiology*,[141] in what is believed to be the first report on the therapeutic effectiveness of DPH in cardiac disorders, found that DPH prevented ectopic contractions in dogs subject to acute operative coronary occlusion.

The authors reasoned that the disturbances in cardiac electrical excitability that resulted in arrhythmias might have something in common with the disturbances in electrical excitability of brain cells. Accordingly, since DPH was well known to be effective in these brain disturbances, it was decided to try it in cardiac arrhythmias.

By using a method of gradual coronary occlusion, cardiac ischemia was produced causing ventricular arrhythmias. DPH was found to suppress the ectopic discharges in these hearts. Confidence in the interpretation of the results was gained by the observation of quick diminution of frequency of ectopic complexes almost immediately after injection of DPH. When DPH was not present these ectopic complexes returned.

Slow intravenous administration of DPH produced little or no change in blood pressure or respiration. The authors found in their experiments that it was possible to control all ventricular tachycardias by adequate amounts of DPH.

In 1954 MOSEY and TYLER, *Circulation*,[260] showed that DPH reversed ouabain-induced ventricular tachycardia in twelve dogs. DPH was given intravenously during the tachycardia and in a short time, in all cases, normal sinus rhythm was restored and heart rate improved with cessation of ectopic activity.

LEONARD, *Archives of Internal Medicine* (1958),[221] demonstrated the beneficial effect of DPH in controlling ventricular hyperirritability complicating myocardial infarction in a patient.

This appears to be the first recorded experience of the use of DPH in the treatment of cardiac disorders in humans. For this reason it is presented in some detail.

The patient was seen in consultation and found gravely ill with cardiographic findings of typical ventricular tachycardia. In spite of the previous history of complete heart block, it was felt that intravenous procaine amide, if carefully controlled, was the treatment of choice. The patient was in profound shock, although the blood pressure was 110/70. Procaine amide was given intravenously. During a period of approximately two hours, 2300 mg of procaine amide was given, in spite of several episodes of marked hypotension, but finally discontinued because of disturbing widening of the QRS complex without reversion to a normal sinus mechanism.

The patient's condition remained disturbingly critical, and it was considered advisable to investigate the therapeutic potential of intravenous DPH. DPH was administered slowly intravenously in a dose of 250 mg. A cardiogram recorded approximately two minutes later revealed a normal sinus mechanism coupled with premature auricular contractions. In twenty minutes ventricular tachycardia had recurred. An immediate additional dose of 250 mg of DPH was given and within moments a normal sinus mechanism appeared.

Four hours later ventricular tachycardia returned and was again successfully reverted to a normal sinus rhythm with 250 mg of intravenous DPH. Because the duration of effectiveness of DPH was unknown, a constant, slow intravenous infusion of 250 mg of DPH was started. The normal sinus mechanism was maintained in this fashion for successive periods of six and four hours. At these intervals ventricular tachycardia returned but was promptly reverted with additional intravenous doses of 250 mg of DPH.

At this time it was considered advisable to supplement the intravenous therapy with 3 grains of DPH and 500 mg of procaine amide every four hours orally. Eighteen hours after its initiation the intravenous DPH was discontinued. An electrocardiogram at this time showed the posterior myocardial infarction with a normal sinus mechanism.

On the following day procaine amide was discontinued, and the patient was maintained with 3 grains of DPH orally every six hours. There was no recurrence of signs of ventricular irritability.

The patient made an uneventful recovery.

The author states that DPH administered intravenously may represent a drug with a wide margin of safety to effectively control serious ventricular hyperirritability. He also states that the use of DPH orally deserves consideration.

DREIFUS, RABBINO and WATANABE, *Medical Clinics of North America* (1964),[82] reviewing newer agents in the treatment of cardiac arrhythmias, stated that DPH appeared to be effective in both supraventricular and ventricular mechanisms and possessed properties which make it effective against digitalis-induced arrhythmias. It has been found successful in preventing paroxysmal atrial tachycardia when the usual antiarrhythmic agents had failed.

The authors pointed out that DPH exerted its activity in the nervous system without general depression. They noted that the action of DPH on peripheral nerves was such as to stabilize the neuronal membrane and that it was possible that the mechanism of action of DPH on heart muscle and nervous tissue was basically similar.

BERNSTEIN, GOLD, LANG, PAPPELBAUM, BAZIKA and CORDAY, *Journal of the American Medical Association* (1965),[18] used oral DPH prophylactically in the prevention of recurring cardiac arrhythmias in a group of 60 patients and defined the over-all response as excellent. They found it of particular significance that the entire group consisted of patients who were proved refractory to or intolerant of conventional modes of prophylactic antiarrhythmic therapy.

CONN, *New England Journal of Medicine* (1965),[61] found that DPH administered intravenously to twenty-four patients with a variety of cardiac arrhythmias, was particularly effective in supraventricular and ventricular arrhythmias resulting from digitalis excess. It was also of benefit in controlling paroxysmal atrial and ventricular arrhythmias. In three cases of atrial fibrillation and two with atrial flutter no therapeutic effect was noted. Toxicity consisted of transient bradycardia and hypotension in one patient and short-term atrioventricular block with bradycardia in another.

The author stated that DPH appears to be a significant addition to the drug therapy of cardiac arrhythmias.

RUTHEN, *American Heart Journal* (1965),[318] reviewed some examples of the effectiveness of DPH in cardiac arrhythmias and drew attention to the electrophysiologic evidence that DPH stabilizes cell membranes.

LANG, BERNSTEIN, BARBIERI, GOLD and CORDAY, *Archives of Internal Medicine* (1965),[215] in a review, concluded that DPH is a most effective agent for the correction of digitalis-induced arrhythmias. They noted that not only had it been successfully applied in the treatment of humans with digitalis toxicity but that it lowered the mortality in digitalis-intoxicated dogs from 60% to 5%.

LUGO and SANABRIA, *Acta Medica Venezolana* (1966),[517] reported the therapeutic effectiveness of oral DPH in chronic cardiac disease of Chagasic origin, with multifocal extrasystolic ventricular arrhythmia. DPH was used in eleven cases of this type in the dose of 100 mg four times a day. In six cases excellent results were obtained with suppression of the arrhythmia. In two cases the results were moderately successful. In two other cases reduction of the dose to 300 mg per day was required. The authors state that the use of DPH is a contribution to the treatment of this particular arrhythmia.

HELFANT, SCHERLAG and DAMATO, *Clinical Research* (1967),[149] discussed the electrophysiological effects of both DPH and procaine amide in the digitalis-intoxicated and nondigitalized heart.

The authors indicated that the stabilizing effects of DPH on ventricular automaticity, IV conduction and AV conduction could account for its mechanism of action in controlling digitoxic arrhythmias.

HELFANT, LAU, COHEN and DAMATO, *Circulation* (1967),[158] studied the effects of intravenous DPH on atrioventricular conduction in man at constant heart rates in the digitalized and undigitalized state. It was suggested that when digitalis excess is manifested by both ectopia and incomplete AV block, DPH would have special utility since, in contrast to the commonly used antiarrhythmic agents, DPH enhances AV conduction in addition to suppressing ectopia.

CONN, *Postgraduate Medicine* (1967),[62] in a review, refers to DPH as one of the new antiarrhythmic agents, along with propanolol and lidocaine. He discusses the efficacy of these agents and their toxicology.

The author states that DPH has been found to have predictable antiarrhythmic effects and that it has been used in the treatment of a great many patients with cardiac arrhythmias. It is suggested that the antiarrhythmic effects are consistent with the evidence from studies of the basic mechanisms of action; these indicate that DPH is a stabilizing agent against repetitive stimuli, the result of which is an "antispreading effect" from an area of abnormal discharge.

LIEBERSON, SCHUMACHER, CHILDRESS, BOYD and WILLIAMS, *Circulation* (1967),[223] pointed out that two of the most commonly used antiarrhythmic agents, quinidine and procaine amide, often produce undesirable hemodynamic effects. One that is reported is depressed myocardial function, the other, well known, is significant systemic hypotension during intravenous administration.

Based on their observations of the effects of DPH used intravenously on left ventricular function, the authors formed the opinion that DPH is a safer medication for cardiac arrhythmias when given intravenously than quinidine or procaine amide.

KARLINER, *Diseases of the Chest* (1967),[187] described fifty-four patients who received intravenous DPH on fifty-seven occasions for abnormal cardiac rhythm. Nineteen of twenty-three who had digitalis-induced arrhythmias responded with abolition or marked suppression of a ventricular ectopic focus, or with conversion of supraventricular arrhythmias to a regular sinus mechanism. Of twenty-eight patients whose arrhythmias were unrelated to digitalis, seven responded favorably; in three patients, the relationship to digitalis was unclear, and one of these responded.

As a result of this study the author confirmed the usefulness of DPH in a variety of cardiac arrhythmias, especially those which appear to be related to digitalis excess. Rapidity of action and relative paucity of side effects, when it is used properly, make DPH an effective antiarrhythmic agent. The author suggests that intravenous application of DPH should be slow.

HOLECKOVA, *Vnitrni Lekarstvi* (1967),[166] reported that in a group of thirty patients showing various forms of cardiac arrhythmias an improvement in nineteen was achieved using DPH.

MERCER and OSBORNE, *Annals of Internal Medicine* (1967),[248] reviewed the literature including safety and toxicology and basic mechanisms of action, and reported on their own six years experience in the treatment, with DPH, of 774 cases of cardiac arrhythmias.

The authors state that intravenous DPH is highly efficacious in the treatment of ventricular arrhythmias associated with anesthesia, cardioversion, cardiac catheterization, and cardiac surgery. On the basis of their experience they consider DPH to be superior to quinidine and procaine amide in these arrhythmias.

DPH also had a good effect against digitalis-induced ventricular arrhythmias and an even better effect against digitalis-induced atrial tachycardia. Thus, it is a valuable addition to the therapy of digitalis-induced arrhythmias and may be tried first because of its rapid action and relative safety.

Ventricular arrhythmias associated with arteriosclerotic heart disease responded to DPH in over one-quarter of cases, suggesting that this drug contributes significantly to existing therapy.

Intravenous DPH was not effective in the treatment of chronic atrial fibrillation or atrial flutter and not very effective in the termination of paroxysmal atrial tachycardia.

The authors reviewed other reports in the literature and their own series in the use of oral DPH. There were reported successes in twenty out of twenty-four cases of supraventricular arrhythmias, twenty-six out of thirty-eight cases of ventricular arrhythmias and five out of eight cases of unclassified paroxysmal tachycardia.

SCHERLAG, HELFANT and DAMATO, *American Heart Journal* (1968),[327] in a laboratory study, compared the effects of DPH and procaine amide on AV conduction in digitalis-intoxicated and normal heart. DPH consistently converted more acetylstrophanthidin-induced ventricular tachycardia to sinus rhythm than did procaine amide and completely restored AV conduction to control values. In contrast, procaine amide, in doses necessary to counteract digitalis-induced ventricular tachycardia, invariably exacerbated the AV conduction prolongation produced by the glycoside.

The selective effects of DPH are in contrast to agents such as procaine amide which depress both ventricular ectopia and AV transmission in the digitoxic heart.

The authors stated that the effect of DPH on AV conduction makes this a unique drug since it abolishes both the ventricular ectopia and AV conduction abnormalities produced by the glycoside.

VOIGT, *Johns Hopkins Medical Journal* (1968),[566] discussed safety and toxicology in the use of DPH intravenously.

In this review Voigt, while reporting on a case of his own, stated that in 1000 patients given DPH intravenously for the treatment of cardiac arrhythmias there were only seven deaths.

The author stated that all seven of these patients were elderly and at least six were known to be in severe heart failure.

DORPH, *Delaware Medical Journal* (1968),[80] reported that at a meeting of physicians representing coronary care units, DPH was discussed as an antiarrhythmic drug. DPH was stated to be useful in arrhythmias due to digitalis intoxication; a dilute solution of 100 mg given slowly intravenously had been used with very good success.

BASHOUR, EDMONSON, GUPTA and PRATI, *Diseases of the Chest* (1968),[418] reported on twelve patients who were treated with DPH, all of whom had clinical evidence of digitalis toxicity. Most patients had more than one type of arrhythmia.

During administration of DPH continuous electrocardiographic monitoring was usually performed, and after conversion to sinus rhythm or subsidence of the arrhythmia, monitoring of the cardiac rhythm was continued for a period of ten minutes.

In five of the cases atrial fibrillation was present with other arrhythmias. Two of these arrhythmias were of recent origin and were restored to normal sinus rhythm by DPH. Three cases of chronic atrial fibrillation did not respond to treatment.

Four of the patients were uremic. The successful termination of their cardiac arrhythmia, especially ventricular tachycardia with DPH was of special interest. In uremic patients with arrhythmias the usual therapeutic measures are both less effective and more hazardous. It would appear that in such circumstances DPH is the drug of choice.

The authors state that the dramatic response of the arrhythmias to intravenously administered DPH is noteworthy and that patients were maintained on oral DPH for a few days following termination of the arrhythmia.

WEHRMACHER, *Current Medical Digest* (1969),[407] stated that in the jeopardy brought about by certain cardiac arrhythmias, DPH offers protection that physicians should be prepared to use.

Although most physicians recognize DPH's capacity to suppress some cerebral dysrhythmias responsible for epileptic attacks, few take advantage of its capacity to suppress serious cardiac arrhythmias. In these circumstances intravenous DPH acts rapidly and usually a response is seen within four minutes. The author also recommends the oral administration of DPH (100 mg) every six to eight hours. Oral maintenance can be carried on for months or years.

TREATMENT OF OTHER DISORDERS

Diabetes

FABRYKANT and PACELLA, *Annals of Internal Medicine* (1948),[92] detailed the use of DPH in the treatment of three cases of labile diabetes. In all three cases DPH was successful in stabilizing the diabetes.

With DPH therapy all three patients studied showed remarkable psychological improvement. Anxiety, nervous tension and irritability were alleviated, the ability to concentrate and to work increased and the patients exhibited a general feeling of well-being.

The authors stated that the term labile diabetes referred to that group of diabetics who exhibited a very narrow time-margin between excessively high and critically low blood sugar values and who in consequence showed rapid transitions from hypoglycemia and aglycosuria to massive glycosuria and acidosis.

It was shown that reactions usually associated with insulin hypoglycemia may occur in labile diabetes at a time of exceedingly high blood sugar readings. Such reactions were found to be refractory to carbohydrate therapy but were favorably influenced by DPH therapy.

Very favorable results were obtained with DPH in the three patients who had been selected for this study on the basis of two borderline and one abnormal EEG.

DPH was discontinued for periods of from five to thirty-three days to serve as a control. While off DPH, all patients reverted to frequent reactions and nervousness. Two of the patients also had favorable results with Mesantoin.

The authors found that DPH had a favorable effect on (a) reactions, (b) hypoglycemia and glycosuria, (c) insulin requirements and (d) behavior disorders.

WILSON, *Canadian Medical Association Journal* (1951),[382] described three cases of labile diabetes whose control was entirely unsatisfactory and not compatible with a normal life outside hospital. In all instances abnormal electroencephalograms were found. Prior to the institution of DPH therapy these patients presented extremely labile diabetes, characterized by frequent reactions, uncontrollable glycosuria, and evidence of personality changes.

The institution of DPH therapy resulted in a marked improvement in diabetic control and enabled these individuals to lead a relatively normal life, not necessitating a return to the hospital to control the labile status of their diabetes.

FABRYKANT, *Annals of Internal Medicine* (1953),[91] again confirmed the effectiveness of DPH therapy in the management of labile diabetes associated with electrocerebral dysfunction. In this study of seven patients, five showed an appreciable diminution in the frequency and severity of insulin reactions along with a decrease in insulin requirement which led to better control of diabetes and to psychologic rehabilitation. The other two patients did not adhere to therapy, although the author noted that in one case there was a marked improvement while on DPH.

FABRYKANT, *Journal of the American Geriatrics Society* (1964),[430] in a report on the etiology, laboratory aids and therapy in treating labile diabetes, again cited the value of DPH in treating those diabetics with frequent and unpredictable insulin reactions accompanied by cerebral dysrhythmias.

ROBERTS, *Journal of the American Geriatrics Society* (1964),[429] reported an extensive study entitled, "The Syndrome of Narcolepsy and Diabetogenic ("Functional") Hyperinsulinism, with Special Reference to Obesity, Diabetes, Idiopathic Edema, Cerebral Dysrhythmias and Multiple Sclerosis (200 patients)."

Although the use of DPH was not the major focus of his work, the author stated that DPH was given successfully to sixteen patients with EEG dysrhythmias when their headaches, severe anxiety and other neurologic and psychiatric features did not respond to the treatment being used. Treatment with DPH resulted in both EEG and clinical improvement.

The author stated that with regard to the symptoms of labile diabetes his experiences with DPH confirm those of others who have observed clinical and electroencephalographic improvement following its administration.

ELLENBERG, *New York State Journal of Medicine* (1968),[431] recognized the urgent need for a beneficial therapeutic agent in diabetic neuropathy and stated that this need was underscored by the frequent indication for narcotics to control the severe pain, with the ever-present threat of addiction. The author noted that DPH has little or no hypnotic action and, on the assumption that the symptoms of diabetic neuropathy might have a similar background to tic douloureux in which DPH was used with considerable success, a therapeutic trial was undertaken.

DPH was used to treat painful diabetic peripheral neuropathy in sixty patients. Based on symptomatic relief of pain and paresthesias, excellent results were obtained in forty-one patients and fair response in ten patients. Improvement was noted in from twenty-four to ninety-six hours. Recurrence of symptoms frequently occurred when the drug was discontinued. On reinstitution of the medication a salutary response was uniformly repeated.

In two of the sixty cases skin rash occurred, one associated with fever. These reactions disappeared upon withdrawal of the medicine.

In addition to its effect on neuropathy, five patients reported that DPH improved control of their diabetes and also increased their feeling of general well-being.

Pruritus Ani

BODKIN, *American Journal of Digestive Diseases* (1945),[25] described the successful treatment of forty-one of forty-two cases of pruritus ani upon the addition of DPH to oral therapy.

In this series of forty-two cases, only one showed no improvement and another recovered rather slowly. Almost all of the others responded in a surprisingly short time.

The author stated that, "Pruritus ani has always been a difficult and baffling problem to the proctologist . . . It is notable for its chronicity and resistance to treatment. No one form of therapy has been effective, as is evidenced by the lengthy list of measures employed. It is therefore most interesting to come upon a method of treatment, mainly oral, that gives prompt symptomatic relief and which produces clearly visible results in the skin. It is aimed at the most likely site of origin of the condition—the nervous system. . . . The one definite and positive finding that stood out in all the cases that I have carefully studied for the past ten years or more was this: every one of them was highly nervous."

The duration of the symptoms in the group studied was from one to thirty years and included three cases that also had pruritus vulvae. The author had previously used takadiastase, novatropin and phenobarbital. When DPH was added, the results were rather striking. Even long standing cases obtained marked symptomatic relief within a few days.

The author stated that a review of the literature on the subject of pruritus ani failed to disclose any previous treatment of this type.

GOODWIN, *Journal of the National Proctologic Association* (1946),[127] described the successful treatment of twenty cases of pruritus ani treated with DPH and a starch digestant. The results obtained were superior to any therapy previously employed. The author stated that this study confirmed the work of BODKIN.[25]

Length of treatment varied. Usually the physical signs of bleeding, maceration, leathery appearance, moist skin, fissures, cracked skin and itching began to disappear from one to three weeks after institution of therapy. The patients usually volunteered before they were examined that they were much better after two or three weeks' treatment.

One severe case of pruritus was observed in which there was extensive maceration and bleeding of the anus, scrotum and groin. So intense was the pruritus that nothing seemed of value in bringing even temporary relief. With DPH and a starch digestant the patient showed marked improvement rapidly to the point that treatment was discontinued at the end of six weeks.

Recurrence was observed in only one patient. Reestablishing treatment effected prompt relief in this case.

In the author's experience such rapid relief of symptoms as had been obtained with DPH had not been obtained with the use of any local treatment.

BODKIN, *American Journal of Digestive Diseases* (1947),[26] in an expanded series of 111 cases of pruritus ani, again reported excellent results with DPH. Of the 111 cases treated, only six failed to respond; five discontinued medication and their outcome was unknown; and twelve were still under treatment at the time the report was written.

The author stated that it was a pleasant surprise to find that recurrences were not too numerous and that they were rather easily controlled as soon as they appeared. Patients were ordinarily advised to decrease medication and to gradually stop it one month after all symptoms had been relieved. They were also told to take their capsules again promptly at the first sign of any recurrence.

Ulcers

SIMPSON, KUNZ and SLAFTA, *New York State Journal of Medicine* (1965),[344] reported that DPH promoted the healing of leg ulcers. The study contained double-blind and crossover controls.

Thirty hospitalized psychiatric patients (age range forty to seventy-seven years) were chosen for the project. The sole criterion for the patient selection was that all had chronic leg ulceration. The ulcers had been present for from two to fifteen years. Occasional healing had taken place but this was minimal and most of the patients had an area of ulceration present at all times despite the fact that they received standard topical treatment and occasional bed rest.

Repeated measurements were carried out under double-blind conditions. Measurements were made by means of a planimeter reading of the ulcer area as well as the actual scaling area around the ulcer. A clinical rating was also given.

All three indices measured showed improvement in the DPH group compared with the placebo group. Statistical analysis of the actual ulcer areas demonstrated a difference at better than the 0.05 level of significance between the two groups.

Small doses such as 200 mg a day were found to be associated with better healing than were large doses of 400 to 600 mg a day.

STREAN, *Chemical Abstracts* (1966),[669] reported DPH effective in promoting the complete healing of an antecubital ulcer, a diabetic ulcer and two peptic ulcers, all of long duration. It was found that DPH provided for the regeneration of healthy and complete tissue in the denuded zone.

TAYLOR, *Personal Communication* (1969),[730] reported on a twenty-four year old female patient with Behcet's syndrome. There was involvement of temporomandibular joints, or true Costen's syndrome—non-use of jaw and also clenching it produced pain typical of the syndrome, in addition to conjunctivitis, urethritis and vaginitis. She was tried on 100 mg DPH daily. The patient reported a worsening of the symptoms for the first three days and on the fourth and fifth days the ulcerated areas became intensely itchy. She reported that by the sixth day the ulcerated areas had healed and the other symptoms had disappeared.

Asthma

SHULMAN, *New England Journal of Medicine* (1942),[341] selected seven cases of severe bronchial asthma, which were considered intractable because they had not responded to routine and accepted treatment. These cases were treated with DPH. In a detailed study the author reported marked relief of asthma in six of seven cases and partial relief in the seventh.

In this study DPH was used exclusively and was not begun until all other medications were eliminated. With the application of DPH six of the patients were consistently free of attacks of bronchial asthma and the seventh showed some improvement. The efficacy of DPH was further evidenced by the fact that the patients were able to successfully engage in situations and environments which formerly precipitated attacks of bronchial asthma.

Two of the patients had seasonal allergies, such as sneezing, which did not respond to DPH. Two others had cases of stubborn eczema that had persisted since infancy and these cleared to a remarkable degree with DPH.

BLATMAN and METCALF, *American Journal of Diseases of Children* (1961),[23] studied a group of severely asthmatic children who had been generally unresponsive to previous hospitalization and treatment. Their asthma was associated with poor pulmonary function and the onset of asthmatic attacks seemed strikingly related to the child's emotional needs. These children were aggressive, destructive, disobedient, uncooperative, and represented severe management problems in the ward.

Three children with 6 and 14 per second spiking were selected for treatment with phenobarbital and DPH. With this treatment they showed appreciable improvement in their behavior concurrent with a decrease in frequency and severity of wheezing.

SAYER and POLVAN, *Lancet* (1968),[401] described sixteen patients with bronchial asthma, with frequent asthmatic crises, in which fourteen had abnormal EEGs and two had EEGs within normal limits.

All patients were taken off other medications and given DPH for an average of forty-five days. Ten patients were closely followed up during this period. Seven had neither asthmatic crises nor wheezing. One patient had occasional wheezing and in the other two cases the frequency of crises was greatly diminished.

Hypertension

JOURNAL OF AMERICAN MEDICAL ASSOCIATION (1954).[414] A physician sought advice for his twenty-nine year old son who had been suffering with essential hypertension for four years. He wanted a medicine that would lower blood pressure without retarding mental activities. The reply in a column, "Queries and Minor Notes," was . . .

"A safe sedative which calms without creating dullness and/or depression is diphenylhydantoin sodium, ½ grain three times daily."

Enuresis

CAMPBELL and YOUNG, *Journal of Urology* (1966),[43] reported that twenty-nine patients having enuresis and evidencing EEG abnormalities were treated with DPH alone or in combination with other anticonvulsant medication.

Only twenty-two of these patients could be followed up. Eleven were reported to be cured or improved and eleven showed no change.

BALDWIN, *Maryland Medical Journal* (1969),[706] noted that among the symptoms observed in behavior problem children, toilet training may be late with enuresis until late school age.

Although the number of cases with enuresis was not given, DPH was found of value in the group of behavior problem children reported (see pp. 162–63).

DDT in Man

DAVIES, EDMUNDSON, CARTER and BARQUET, *Lancet* (1969),[701] studied the levels of DDT storage in man in the Florida Community Studies Pesticides Project. This study was done under contract with the Department of Health, Education and Welfare.

Individuals who had been taking diphenylhydantoin for more than three months were found to have strikingly lower blood levels of DDE (the principal metabolite of DDT) than those found in the general population.

The levels of DDE in blood of 77 outpatients taking diphenylhydantoin and/or phenobarbitone for more than three months were compared with DDE levels of 199 healthy controls. Those patients taking these two drugs had significantly lower DDE (p less than 0.001). 82% of the patients on therapy had DDE values less than two parts per billion, whereas only 1% of the controls had DDE concentrations of less than two parts per billion.

78% of the patients taking diphenylhydantoin alone had less than two parts per billion. 32% of the patients taking phenobarbitone had levels less than two parts per billion of DDE in blood. With the two drugs combined, 87% of the patients had less than two parts per billion.

The authors did further studies of DDE in adipose tissue. These studies further confirmed the finding that diphenylhydantoin significantly reduced DDE levels in man.

The effect of DDT, which is deadly in some other species, has not been proven in man. There is increasing concern about this as evidenced by the fact that Sweden and several states in the U.S.A. have decided to ban the use of DDT for a trial period.

Accommodative Esotropia

GALIN, KWITKO and RESTREPO, *Proceedings of the International Strabismological Association* (1969),[746] found DPH useful in the treatment of accommodative esotropia.

A study with thirty-five children was completed. Their ages ranged from two-and-a-half to fourteen years. Children less than six years of age were given 30 mg DPH twice daily, then increased to three times daily if after two days it was well tolerated. Standard orthoptic studies were performed before and after DPH.

Of twenty-five patients with abnormal near point of accommodation, twenty improved with a decrease of three diopters and ten of these had a concomitant decrease in esotropia. Because they were too young, the near point of accommodation was not obtained in ten patients.

Nine out of twenty-one patients responded to DPH in the combined accommodative groups (including thirteen accommodative and eight partial accommodative).

Accommodative convergence/accommodation (AC/A) ratios were most favorably influenced by DPH in those patients having high ratios. DPH had little effect on normals. Phospholine iodide, which had a greater effect on AC/A ratios than DPH, was not selective and had an effect on normals as well as abnormals.

SURGERY—PREOPERATIVE AND POSTOPERATIVE

JAFFE, *Personal Communication* (1966),[747] found DPH useful in the preoperative and postoperative periods and during the course of cataract surgery.

DPH replaced large doses of barbiturates previously used preoperatively to combat apprehension. DPH replaced demerol and opiates preoperatively and was especially useful in cases where unpredictable or aggressive behavior was anticipated.

During the course of surgery where intravenous demerol had previously been required to control violent outbursts in the operating room, intravenous DPH was successfully substituted.

In the postoperative period if delirium occurred, DPH was found to be useful in clearing this complication.

CHAMBERLAIN, *Personal Communication* (1970),[744] reported on the therapeutic value of DPH in a series of 200 surgical cases.

The ages of the patients varied from six months to ninety years.

Dosage of DPH: 25 mg to 600 mg depending on age of patient and severity of symptoms and surgical procedure used.

DPH was successfully employed as follows:

1. In preparation for a planned surgical procedure—for apprehension, etc.
2. As a preoperative medication.
3. As a postoperative medication for pain.
4. As a postoperative medication for anxiety and as a substitute for narcotics.
5. In the patient with advanced malignancy with inoperability of tumor.
6. In the long-term treatment of both the operative and inoperative patients with malignant disease.
7. In the elderly surgical patient (all types).
8. In the agitated, depressed and alcoholic surgical patient.

Certain trends presented themselves with the use of DPH, some of which briefly follow:

(a) In children, from six months to twelve years old, on dosages of DPH varying from 25 mg four times daily to 100 mg three times daily—the use of preoperative and postoperative narcotics could be reduced or discontinued.

(b) As a preoperative medication in adults a dose of 200 mg of DPH prior to surgery alleviated the use of preoperative narcotics such as demerol, morphine and so forth.

(c) Postoperative use of DPH in adults, up to 500 and 600 mg daily made it possible to do away with practically all postoperative narcotics, decreased anxiety and promoted a generalized feeling of well-being in most of the cases.

(d) In the inoperative malignant cases, doses up to 600 mg of DPH daily, made it possible to greatly cut down on the amount of narcotics used and definitely promoted and improved the mental outlook of these patients.

(e) The elderly agitated and difficult patients became much calmer.

(f) In postoperative malignant cases undergoing radiation, cobalt and other forms of treatment, the use of DPH in dosages of 400 to 600 mg daily caused a marked decrease in the use of narcotics and in some cases no other form of medication other than DPH was needed.

The improvement of mental attitude and outlook in these patients was remarkable.

BARASCH, BARAS and GALIN, *Personal Communication* (1970),[732] found that DPH replaced all preoperative and postoperative medication in cataract surgery other than the local anesthetic. The authors previously had used barbiturates, demerol, compazine, codeine and aspirin.

Because DPH does not impair normal function, its use instead of narcotics and sedatives permitted the prompt ambulation of the patient. For the same reason the use of DPH enabled the discharge of patients within twenty-four hours, in a series of 100 consecutive uncomplicated cases of cataract surgery.

The authors state that since this study, they now use DPH routinely in cataract surgery.

SEUFFERT, HELFANT, DANA and URBACH, *Anesthesia and Analgesia* (1968),[409] in a group of twenty patients, found that DPH protects against the development of arrhythmias during cyclopropane anesthesia. Of eleven patients pretreated with DPH only one developed an arrhythmia. Eight out of nine patients who were not pretreated with DPH developed arrhythmias. Even though the groups were small, the difference between the two groups is such that the results are highly significant.

DPH AS A PREVENTIVE

DPH, in its first application, the treatment of epilepsy, was used primarily as a preventive. There are indications that some of DPH's most important uses will be that of a preventive. A few studies which particularly point in this direction are included below. These studies are in animals and man.

Cardiac

DREIFUS, RABBINO and WATANABE, *Medical Clinics of North America* (1964),[82] stated that DPH orally can be used as a prophylaxis against recurrent paroxysmal tachycardia.

BERNSTEIN, GOLD, LANG, PAPPELBAUM, BAZIKA and CORDAY, *Journal of the American Medical Association* (1965),[18] used oral DPH prophylactically in the prevention of recurring cardiac arrhythmias. The authors found the over-all response excellent and particularly impressive because the sixty patients treated had proved resistant to conventional antiarrhythmic therapy.

MERCER and OSBORNE, *Annals of Internal Medicine* (1967),[248] stated that "oral DPH was highly efficacious in the prevention of recurrent arrhythmias, both supraventricular and ventricular."

HELFANT, SCHERLAG and DAMATO, *Circulation* (1967)[155] and *Clinical Research* (1967),[685] used DPH prophylactically in dogs as a protection against cardiac arrhythmias induced by digitalis toxicity. The amount of digitalis necessary to produce arrhythmias was significantly increased in the animals in which DPH was used prophylactically. DPH did not impair the therapeutic effect of digitalis on cardiac contractility.

The authors state that if the combined use of DPH and digitalis is shown to operate similarly in humans, then patients may be protected against arrhythmias while deriving inotropic benefits of digitalis.

GUPTA, UNAL, BASHOUR and WEBB, *Diseases of the Chest* (1967),[496] demonstrated that DPH increases coronary blood flow in dogs.

LÜLLMANN and WEBER, *Arztliche Forschung* (1968)[233] and *Naunyn-Schmiedebergs Archiv fur Pharmakologie* (1968),[403] in a study in which DPH was used prophylactically, showed that it significantly protected against the lethal effects of digoxin in guinea pigs.

SEUFFERT, HELFANT, DANA and URBACH, *Anesthesia and Analgesia* (1968),[409] in a group of twenty patients, found that DPH protects against the development of arrhythmias during cyclopropane anesthesia. (See p. 182.)

ZEFT, WHALEN, RATLIFF, DAVENPORT and McINTOSH, *Journal of Pharmacology and Experimental Therapeutics* (1968),[392] conducted a controlled study to evaluate the hypothesis that DPH given prophylactically would be effective in preventing death from ventricular arrhythmias resulting from experimental myocardial infarction in forty farm pigs.

Farm pigs were chosen because their coronary artery pattern is relatively constant and similar to that of man.

70% of the DPH treated animals survived the infarction, whereas only 45% of the controls survived. Almost twice as many control animals (eleven of twenty) expired as DPH treated animals (six of twenty).

The authors state that these findings are not conclusive but suggest that consideration should be given to the use of DPH on a regular basis as a preventive of fatalities originating from coronary artery disorders.

NAYLER, McINNES, SWANN, RACE, CARSON and LOWE, *American Heart Journal* (1968),[402] demonstrated, in dogs, that DPH increases the coronary blood flow and that DPH reduces myocardial oxygen consumption.

DDT in Man

DAVIES, EDMUNDSON, CARTER and BARQUET, *Lancet* (1969),[701] found in humans that DPH strikingly reduced storage of DDT residues in both blood and fat. (See p. 180.)

Acute Radiation Exposure

LAIRD and FONNER, *U. S. Army Medical Research Lab, Fort Knox, Ky.* (1957),[213] demonstrated, in mice, that DPH offered protection against the incidence and severity of convulsive activity due to acute radiation exposure. (See p. 189.)

Thought, Mood and Behavior

It is implicit in the studies in this review that the use of DPH in mood and behavior disorders is primarily preventive. By stabilizing hyperexcitable cells, DPH prevents overthinking and unrealistic anger and fear. Because of the role that anger and fear play in addiction and violent behavior, one of the important uses of DPH may be as a preventive against addiction and violent behavior. When it is taken into consideration that DPH is non-addictive, and is not a sedative, one recognizes that DPH is particularly suited for use against addiction and violent behavior.

Other

DPH has been reported to be useful in the prevention of migraine, trigeminal neuralgia, complications following head injury, and of convulsions of alcoholism.

SAFETY AND TOXICOLOGY

Background

Diphenylhydantoin has been in wide use for over thirty years. It is estimated that more than twenty billion doses have been taken, by several million people.[1] Most of these individuals have taken it on a daily basis for many years. Thus this medicine has been subjected to the tests of (1) time, (2) volume of use, (3) number of individuals who have used it, and (4) continuous use over long periods.

Reviews

For comprehensive reviews of the safety and toxicology of DPH the reader is referred to TOMAN (in GOODMAN and GILMAN, *The Pharmacological Basis of Therapeutics* 1965),[359] and MAGEE and DeJONG, *Modern Treatment* (1964).[238] (See also KUTT, WINTERS, KOKENGE and McDOWELL, *Archives of Neurology* 1964).[555]

Note

Most of the reports on safety and toxicology are based on experience with dosage levels of from 200 to 600 mg daily (epileptic dosages). In nonepileptics effective doses are lower (100 to 300 mg daily) and at these levels the margin of safety is even greater. ("Un-

toward responses are more frequently observed if the dose is above 500 mg daily."
—TOMAN, *The Pharmacological Basis of Therapeutics* 1965)[359]

Safety

MAGEE and DeJONG, *Modern Treatment* (1964),[238] state that DPH "is one of the safest anticonvulsants, so proved by the tests of widespread use and time."

In a review of DPH, *AMA Drug Evaluations* (1968)[712] states: "Diphenylhydantoin is considered the drug of first choice among the hydantoins; it is safer than mephenytoin and more effective than ethotoin."

HANS-PETER JENSEN, *Arztliche Wochenschrift* (1954),[180] states: "This method (diphenylhydantoin) is especially recommended because of its safety."

KUTT, WINTERS, KOKENGE and McDOWELL, *Archives of Neurology* (1964),[555] discussed the relatively low incidence of serious side reactions and related these to blood level of DPH.

SHAPIRO, *Experimental Medicine and Surgery* (1958),[339] states: "The systemic toxic reactions associated with the administration of the drug (DPH) are few and minor."

ROSENBLUM and SHAFER, *Current Therapeutic Research* (1970),[708] felt it important to determine if there were adverse effects on sudden withdrawal from DPH.

Forty-nine nonepileptic patients were given DPH, 200 to 600 mg daily, from one to eight months (average four and one-half months). When the medication was abruptly withdrawn, the patients experienced no adverse effects, seizures, or other withdrawal symptoms.[2]

"Doses totaling many grams have occasionally been ingested by accident or taken with

---

[1] These estimates seem conservative based on the information that in 1966 alone one billion four hundred sixty million doses (100 mg) were used.

[2] It is well known that with the epileptic sudden withdrawal is not recommended.

suicidal intent . . . deaths are rare. Fortunately, diphenylhydantoin is a very poor drug with which to commit suicide." TOMAN in GOODMAN and GILMAN, *The Pharmacological Basis of Therapeutics* (1965).[359]

Toxicology

"Toxic reactions to diphenylhydantoin are usually mild, rarely interfere with therapy, and may often be relieved by proper adjustment of the dosage. Tolerable effects include those referable to the CNS, gastrointestinal tract, skin, and gums.

"Reactions referable to the CNS from therapeutic doses include giddiness, ataxia, nervousness, tremors, nystagmus, head nodding, diplopia, blurring of vision, ptosis, ocular pain, and slurring of speech . . . Untoward responses are more frequently observed if the dose is above 0.5 g daily." TOMAN in GOODMAN and GILMAN, *The Pharmacological Basis of Therapeutics* (1965).[359]

SVENSMARK and BUCHTHAL, *American Journal of Diseases of Children* (1964),[666] discussed the rarity of toxic reactions. In eighty-eight children with serum levels below 25 micrograms/ml they observed no untoward reactions. However, with higher serum levels toxic reactions appeared.

SKIN RASH—Used at anticonvulsant dose levels, 200 to 600 mg daily, morbilliform rash occurs in about 2 to 5% of patients. "It is wise to discontinue diphenylhydantoin . . . after the appearance of a rash, reinstituting medication cautiously after the cutaneous reaction has cleared." (TOMAN, 1965)[359] It should be noted that in non-epileptic doses, usually 100 to 300 mg daily, the incidence of rash is lower. Occasionally a rash may appear years after the institution of treatment.

MELCHIOR and SVENSMARK, *Acta Paediatrica Scandinavica* (1963),[247] state: "Previously, various forms of allergic dermatitis were observed in about 5% of patients treated (with DPH), but this is rare nowadays. As a rule, the symptoms rapidly subside, not to return when the medication is resumed."

OTHER—There is evidence that gingival hyperplasia, a well known side reaction, has been connected with poor oral hygiene and that it can be minimized or prevented with good oral hygiene (FILKOVA, *Deutsche Stomatologie,* 1968[547] and GERTENRICH, FRY and HART, *American Journal of Mental Deficiency,* 1969).[607] The possibility of areflexia has been studied.[232] Gastric distress has been reported and may be avoided by taking DPH with meals.[359]

The occurrence of megaloblastic anemia, which is reversed by folic acid, may be related to the action of folate deconjugase or to the diet of the patient (see for example references 300, 636, 638, 640, 641, 649, 654, 657). "Administration of folic acid has caused complete hematologic remission in each case studied. The dosage necessary is quite small, as little as 25 micrograms being effective." (SPARBERG, *Annals of Internal Medicine,* 1963)[349]

Previous liver disease resulting in impaired metabolic capacity may increase the chance of intoxication since normal doses of DPH may have the effect of an overdose (see for example references 207, 554 and 698).

In the great majority of cases DPH is given orally. With reference to the intravenous use of DPH, VOIGT, *Johns Hopkins Medical Journal* (1968),[566] states that there are over 1000 patients reported in whom this drug (DPH) has been used intravenously for the treatment of cardiac arrhythmias. The incidence of serious untoward cardiovascular reactions (to intravenous DPH) would appear to be low from the paucity of clinical reports documenting this . . . Including the patient presented here, there have been only seven reported deaths following intravenous DPH given for a cardiac arrhythmia. All of these patients were elderly and at least six were in severe heart failure.

Surveys of the incidence of abnormalities in infants born to mothers treated with DPH show the same incidence as in the general population (JANZ and FUCHS, *German Medical Monthly,* 1964[536] and GOTTWALD, *Fortschritte der Neurologie, Psychiatrie und Ihrer Grenzgebiete,* 1969).[705] Approximately ten times the therapeutic dose in man (on a body weight basis) has been reported to be pathologic to mouse fetuses.[558,595,635]

Idiosyncratic Reactions

Severe idiosyncratic reactions to DPH are rare (SPARBERG, *Annals of Internal Medicine,* 1963).[349] The difficulty of assigning with certainty the relationship of DPH to the idiosyncrasy reported, when other drugs and other variables cannot be excluded, limits even further the number of such reactions which can be confirmed.

BIANCHINE, MACARAEG, LASAGNA, AZARNOFF, BRUNK, HVIDBERG and OWEN, *American Journal of Medicine* (1968),[711] in a review of 426 cases recorded in the literature of Stevens-Johnson syndrome for which drugs, infections, etc. were possibly relevant, listed seven cases where DPH was considered a possible etiologic factor.

In 1959 SALTZSTEIN and ACKERMAN, *Cancer,*[322] summarized the reported incidence of lymphadenopathy and lymphoma-like lesions in patients receiving anticonvulsant drugs over a twenty-year period. Seven such cases were reported in patients who used DPH alone, and five more in patients who used DPH in combination with another drug. Of these, one death occurred in the patients treated with DPH alone, and two where DPH was used in combination with another drug.

The occurrence of severe blood dyscrasias coincident with the use of DPH is so rare that the relationship has not been established. SPARBERG, *Annals of Internal Medicine* (1963),[349] reported that severe blood dyscrasias are extremely uncommon since leukopenia without anemia has been reported in only nine cases, with one death; pancytopenia in two, with one death; and thrombocytopenia in two.

Liver disorders have rarely been reported as one part of generalized idiosyncratic reactions to DPH.[49,65,86,133,140]

Editor's Note

The foregoing was written in 1970. For more recent studies on safety and toxicology see Haruda,[1884] Keith,[1923] Heinonen, Slone and Shapiro,[1891] Friis,[1836] Reynolds,[2403] and Kutt and Solomon.[1940]

For possible interactions with other drugs see *Physicians' Desk Reference.*

BASIC MECHANISMS OF ACTION

NEUROPHYSIOLOGICAL MECHANISMS

The most frequently reported neurophysiological effect of DPH is that, in therapeutic concentrations, it stablizes nerve cells against hyperexcitability. This stabilizing effect of DPH is observed in peripheral nerve, in spinal cord, in neuromuscular junction and in brain. It is observed in both vertebrates and invertebrates. DPH reduces hyperexcitability whether induced electrically or chemically. This effect can be quantitated, and it has been demonstrated that in proper concentrations DPH stabilizes nerve cells without causing sedation.

Peripheral Nerve

The stabilization by DPH of nerve thresholds against hyperexcitability was demonstrated in frog nerve by TOMAN (1949),[458] in squid sciatic nerve by KOREY (1951)[472] and in mammalian peripheral nerve by MORRELL, BRADLEY and PTASHNE (1958).[257]

In the squid sciatic nerve studies, hyperexcitability was decreased by DPH in the isolated axon in which the calcium had been reduced by treatment with sodium oxalate. Hyperexcitability of frog nerve, induced the same way, was also decreased by DPH. In mammalian peripheral nerve, posterior tibial of the rabbit, DPH increased the threshold, decreased spike amplitude in A fibers, abolished "nerve repetition" and, again, reversed the enhanced excitability of oxalated nerve.

OROZCO and SABELLI, *Pharmacologist* (1968),[471] also found the low-calcium induced hyperexcitability of earthworm ventral cords and lateral giant axons to be reduced by DPH without an effect on conduction.

ROSENBERG and BARTELS, *Journal of Pharmacology and Experimental Therapeutics* (1967),[311] studying the effects of DPH on the spontaneous electrical activity of squid giant axon, found that at concentrations of DPH which do not affect the action potential response to stimulation, unevoked spontaneous activity is decreased. Resting potential was unaltered.

HOPF, *Deutsche Zeitschrift fur Nervenheilkunde* (1968)[168] and *Electroencephalography and Clinical Neurophysiology* (1968),[470] found that DPH tended to slow the conduction velocity of the ulnar nerve, mainly in the slow conducting fibers. BRUMLIK and MORETTI, *Neurology* (1966),[469] found no effect by DPH on conduction velocities in median and ulnar nerve.

Spinal Cord (Post-Tetanic Potentiation)

ESPLIN, *Journal of Pharmacology and Experimental Therapeutics* (1957),[90] studied the effect of DPH on synaptic transmission in cats. DPH markedly reduced and in some instances almost completely suppressed post-tetanic potentiation (PTP). The results were qualitatively the same for both spinal cord and stellate ganglion.

TUTTLE and PRESTON, *Journal of Pharmacology and Experimental Therapeutics* (1963),[365] confirmed and amplified the findings by ESPLIN of the effects of DPH on PTP. The effect of DPH was observed on segmental and suprasegmental facilitation and inhibition of segmental motor neurons in the cat. Repetitive discharge was reduced as was the response to repetitive stimulation.

RAINES, *Pharmacologist* (1965),[468] and RAINES and STANDAERT, *Journal of Pharmacology and Experimental Therapeutics* (1967),[467] also showed that DPH abolishes PTP originating in the central terminals of dorsal root fibers of spinal cats.

Neuromuscular Junction and Smooth Muscle

RAINES and STANDAERT, *Journal of Pharmacology and Experimental Therapeutics* (1966),[289] found that the principal effect of DPH on the muscle response to indirect stimulation is a reduction of post-tetanic potentiation (PTP). This study in muscle parallels the findings of the effect of DPH in nerve.

DPH affected both pre- and post-junctional elements of the neuromuscular junction. DPH abolished neural repetitive after-discharges originating in the nerve terminals of soleus motor axons of the cat. The suppression of these after-discharges markedly reduced PTP of the soleus muscle.

SCHAAF and PAYNE, *New England Journal of Medicine* (1966),[326] studied the effect of DPH and phenobarbital in ten patients with overt and latent tetany. Phenobarbital was relatively ineffective alone. DPH eliminated tetany, tetanic equivalents and a strongly positive Trousseau test in six of these patients with hypocalcemia due to hypoparathyroidism or pseudohypoparathyroidism, and in one patient with hypocalcemia and hypomagnesemia due to malabsorption. Chvos-

tek's sign also became negative in five of these patients. However, the authors noted that serum calcium, phosphorus and magnesium were unchanged by treatment. DPH was not effective in three patients with idiopathic latent tetany.

The authors cited extensive studies that have confirmed that calcium is a critical "stabilizer" of neuromuscular membranes. In their study they found that DPH in doses therapeutic in man can counteract the increased nervous excitability and can eliminate overt tetany, tetanic equivalents and signs of latent tetany in hypocalcemic patients.

KHAN and McEWEN, *Proceedings of the Canadian Federation of Biological Societies* (1967),[192] studied the effect of DPH and 5,5-diphenyl-2-thiohydantoin (DTH) on the activity of isolated uterine tissue from the albino rat. DPH and DTH decreased the rate and amplitude of contractions. To attain complete relaxation DPH was required in a concentration of 33 micrograms/ml and for DTH 17 micrograms/ml was required.

Cerebral Cortex and Nuclei

TOMAN, *The Pharmacological Basis of Therapeutics* (1965),[359] noted that DPH modifies the pattern of maximal tonic-clonic electroshock seizures elicited by supramaximal current. The characteristic tonic phase, representing maximal interneuronal facilitation in the brain, can be abolished completely by DPH.

MORRELL, BRADLEY and PTASHNE, *Neurology* (1959),[258] showed that DPH was superior to phenobarbital in blocking cortical spread of seizure activity from an induced focus, while trimethadione was inactive in this respect.

HERMAN and BIGNALL, *Electroencephalography and Clinical Neurophysiology* (1967),[159] studied the effects of DPH in single doses of 10–85 mg/kg (approximately two to seventeen times the therapeutic dose in man) on spontaneous and evoked activity in cats anesthetized with alpha chloralose. Spontaneous spikes induced by chloralose were markedly decreased for periods of thirty minutes to three hours by DPH in doses of 35–50 mg/kg. The nonspecific thalamo-cortical projection system was similarly affected, as revealed by decrease of cortical responses to single or repetitive stimulation of nucleus centrum medianum of the thalamus. DPH (40 mg/kg) abolished responses to click throughout the central auditory pathway without blocking responsiveness of the ascending pathway to electrical stimulation of the cochlear nucleus. Auditory nerve response to click similarly was not blocked. Responses evoked in both primary and polysensory cortical areas by photic and somesthetic stimuli were minimally or not depressed by DPH.

NAKAMURA and KUREBE, *Japanese Journal of Pharmacology* (1962),[264] demonstrated that DPH elevated hippocampal seizure threshold and suppressed propagation, with no effect on after-discharge pattern. At doses sufficient to suppress hippocampal seizure DPH did not suppress reticular arousal thresholds.

ASTON and DOMINO, *Psychopharmacologia* (1961),[6] found, in the rhesus monkey, that the effective elevation of motor cortical thresholds could be accomplished by DPH without markedly altering the reactivity of the reticular core to electrical stimulation and without significant anesthetic effect.

STILLE, *Nervenarzt* (1960),[352] in a study of the basis for the beneficial effect of DPH on pain, found that DPH reduces the cortical response to electrical single stimuli or low frequency series stimulation of the reticular formation in rabbits. However, DPH differs from the barbiturates and chlorpromazine in that it does not change the arousal reaction

produced by frequent electrical stimulation of the mesencephalic reticular formation, nor the EEG arousal reaction to sensory stimulation.

RIEHL and MCINTYRE, *Neurology* (1968),[461] found that EEG discharges from abnormal sites were decreased by DPH. No changes occurred in EEGs of normal controls.

Acute Radiation Exposure

LAIRD and FONNER, *U.S. Army Medical Research Lab, Fort Knox, Ky.* (1957),[213] found that administration of DPH to CF_1 mice, prior to exposure to x-rays, controlled convulsive activity and increased median survival time several fold (between 55,000 and 150,000 roentgen). Control by DPH was measured by (1) decrease in the incidence and severity of convulsions and (2) delay in onset of the convulsive phase.

Sleep

ZUNG, *Personal Communication* (1967),[397] studied the effect of DPH on sleep in man. Ten adults, between the ages of twenty and forty-six, were studied with all night EEG and EOG (electrooculogram) recordings. Comparison between control and drug nights indicated that with DPH the time spent in REM sleep was significantly decreased. Time spent in sleep stages A and D were decreased. There was no change in stage C, and there was an increase in time spent in sleep stages B and E.

COHEN, DUNCAN and DEMENT, *Electroencephalography and Clinical Neurophysiology* (1968),[58] studied the effect of DPH on the sleep patterns of cats. DPH decreased REM sleep time significantly. REM periods were both shorter and less frequent. There was no consistent change in any non-REM sleep time.

The decrease of REM sleep time with DPH was not followed by the usual compensatory rebound. The authors found this to be the first clear-cut instance of a prolonged pharmacological REM decrease not followed by a compensatory rise in REM sleep.

Other Animal Studies

FINK and SWINYARD, *Journal of Pharmaceutical Sciences* (1962),[99] compared a group of pharmacological agents in an effort to detect possible tranquilizing effects. One of the tests showed that DPH markedly reduced amphetamine toxicity in aggregated mice. From their studies the authors concluded that DPH possessed tranquilizing properties and should be more fully studied in patients.

TEDESCHI, TEDESCHI, MUCHA, COOK, MATTIS and FELLOWS, *Journal of Pharmacology and Experimental Therapeutics* (1959),[749] and CHEN, BOHNER and BRATTON, *Archives Internationales de Pharmacodynamie et de Therapie* (1963),[419] found that DPH suppressed fighting behavior in mice. CHEN and BOHNER (1960)[740] found that DPH significantly inhibited the self-inflicting scratching induced by mescaline.

COHEN and BARONDES, *Science* (1967),[59] found that DPH significantly improved retention of learned behavior in mice given puromycin. Puromycin is a protein synthesis inhibitor, which interferes with the retention of learned behavior.

GORDON, *Recent Advances in Biological Psychiatry* (1968),[126] found that DPH improved the deteriorated performance of older rats in both habituation and conditioned avoidance paradigms, but did not affect normal behavior in young rats.

The author noted that these findings had possible application to aging in humans. He noted that the decrease in memory function and slowing of task performance in aged humans had been postulated to be caused by an abnormal prolongation of electrophysiological activity in brain, akin to "static" or "noise," and that DPH might exert its therapeutic effects in this regard.

DOTY and DALMAN, *Psychonomic Science* (1969),[702] also found DPH facilitated learning on discrimination and avoidance tasks. The enhancement of performance was more prominent among older rats.

BLOCK and MOORE[670] found that protein-deficient pigs performed worse on learning tasks than did normal pigs. The performance of these protein-deficient pigs was significantly improved with DPH.

MILLICHAP and BOLDREY, *Neurology* (1967),[254] showed that DPH suppressed locomotor activity in mice. An application to hyperkinetic behavior in children was suggested.

PHYSIOLOGY OF DPH ACTION ON THE CARDIOVASCULAR SYSTEM

HARRIS and KOKERNOT, *American Journal of Physiology* (1950),[141] observed that DPH was effective in preventing ectopic contractions in dogs subjected to acute operative coronary occlusion.

MOSEY and TYLER, *Circulation* (1954),[260] showed that DPH reversed ouabain-induced ventricular tachycardia in dogs.

SCHERF, BLUMENFELD, TANER and YILDIZ, *American Heart Journal* (1960),[410] also found that DPH reversed aconitine and delphinine-induced ventricular and atrial arrhythmias in dogs.

COX, PITT, BROWN and MOLARO, *Canadian Medical Association Journal* (1966),[64] studied the effect of DPH on isolated atrial tissue by means of the microelectrode technique of recording transmembrane potentials. DPH promptly abolished acetylcholine-induced arrhythmias.

HOCKMAN, MAUCK and CHU, *American Heart Journal* (1967),[163] employed electrical stimulation of diencephalic and mesencephalic loci in both dogs and cats to induce a spectrum of ventricular arrhythmias which frequently persisted for five minutes or longer after stimulation. The intravenous administration of DPH (10 mg/kg) not only abolished the ectopic ventricular rhythms, but also prevented their induction by a subsequent stimulus for periods varying from thirty minutes to seven hours. A central nervous system action on the heart for DPH was suggested by the authors.

MERCER, ZIEGLER, WICKLAND and DOWER, *Journal of Pharmacology and Experimental Therapeutics* (1967),[249] examined the effect of DPH upon contraction of untreated and digoxin-treated discrete chick embryo heart cells grown *in vitro*. It was proposed that the antiarrhythmic effect of DPH might be due to a direct effect on heart cells.

ROSATI, ALEXANDER, SCHAAL and WALLACE, *Circulation Research* (1967),[308] studied the effects of direct action of DPH (10 mg/kg, I.V.) electrocardiographically in canine hearts via intraventricularly implanted electrodes. DPH increased the sinus rate, decreased atrioventricular conduction (AVC) time, and slightly increased conduction time in Purkinje tissue and total ventricular activation time. DPH produced no change in ventricular pacemaker activity of transiently increased spontaneous ventricular rate in chronic heart block but, when ventricular tachycardia was induced in these dogs by toxic doses (0.16-0.3 mg/kg) of deslanoside, DPH abolished the ectopic arrhythmia and restored the control rhythm.

ROSATI and WALLACE, *American Journal of Cardiology* (1967),[519] examined the electro-

physiologic effects of DPH on the hearts of awake dogs. Their findings suggested that the major actions of DPH on the heart are to (1) facilitate AVC by a vagolytic action, (2) raise the threshold for excitation of atrial and ventricular muscle, (3) decrease the maximal response rate of the atrium and (4) abolish digitalis-induced pacemaker activity. These actions appeared to the authors to form a reasonable basis for the clinical effectiveness of DPH on the heart.

RAINES, LEVITT and STANDAERT, *Pharmacologist* (1967),[514] studying spinal cats, found DPH effective in reversing arrhythmias induced by ouabain in animals with high initial heart rates and high adrenergic tone, and relatively ineffective in animals with low initial heart rates and depressed adrenergic tone.

RAINES and LEVITT, *Archives Internationales de Pharmacodynamie et de Therapie* (1968),[288] found that the therapeutic effectiveness of DPH was not due to blockade of the beta-adrenergic receptors.

BIGGER, SCHMIDT and KUTT, *Bulletin of the New York Academy of Medicine* (1966),[21] found that DPH abolished ventricular irritability, excluding a parasystolic focus, usually with plasma levels of 10 to 18 microgram/ml. DPH was effective in abolishing atrial tachycardia, but it was ineffective in atrial or nodal arrhythmias.

BIGGER, BASSETT and HOFFMAN, *Circulation Research* (1968),[19] studied the effects of DPH on isolated, perfused Purkinje fibers over a range of concentrations from 10^{-8} to 10^{-4} M. The effects of DPH on Purkinje fibers under *in vitro* conditions seemed to suggest an explanation for its antiarrhythmic effects on ventricular arrhythmias *in vivo*. The authors found these effects were ample to support the view that DPH acts directly on the heart to exert its antiarrhythmic effect.

BIGGER, STRAUSS and HOFFMAN, *Federation Proceedings* (1968),[22] studied the effects of DPH in anesthetized dogs with electrodes chronically implanted at selected sites on the conducting system, and in isolated rabbit hearts by means of intracellular microelectrodes. In dogs, DPH (5-10 mg/kg) accelerated atrioventricular conduction (AVC) by 20% under control conditions and also in the presence of incomplete atrioventricular (AV) block and atrial flutter.

In the rabbit heart DPH was found to accelerate AVC by 10-15% under control conditions and more in the presence of partial AV block at low rates. DPH also accelerated the impaired AVC caused by acetylcholine (ACh) without altering the ACh-induced sinus bradycardia.

HELFANT, SCHERLAG and DAMATO, *Circulation* (1967),[155] and *Clinical Research* (1967),[685] demonstrated that DPH given prophylactically to dogs protected against digitalis toxicity. With DPH, 72 to 224% more digitalis was required to produce toxic arrhythmias. The authors state that DPH's effect on the toxic-therapeutic ratio of digitalis may have important clinical implications.

HELFANT, SCHERLAG and DAMATO, *Circulation* (1967),[154] in studies on dogs concluded that in the normal and digitoxic heart, DPH consistently reversed the AVC prolongations induced by procaine amide while having little or no effect on intraventricular conduction.

SCHERLAG, HELFANT and DAMATO, *American Heart Journal* (1968),[327] in a laboratory study, compared the effects of DPH and procaine amide on AVC in digitalis-intoxicated and normal heart. DPH consistently converted more acetylstrophanthidin-induced ventricular tachycardia to sinus rhythm than did procaine amide and completely restored AVC to control values. In contrast, procaine amide, in doses necessary to counteract digitalis-induced ventricular tachycardia, exacer-bated the AVC prolongation produced by the glycoside.

The authors stated that the effect of DPH on AVC makes this a unique drug since it abolishes both the ventricular ectopia and AVC abnormalities produced by the glycoside.

HELFANT, RICCIUTTI, SCHERLAG and DAMATO, *American Journal of Physiology* (1968),[157] studied the effects of digitalis and DPH on myocardial ion fluxes in dogs. DPH converted digitalis-induced arrhythmias and this was accompanied by a prompt reversal of the digitalis-induced myocardial potassium loss.

HILMI and REGAN, *American Heart Journal* (1968),[404] compared the effectiveness of procaine amide, lidocaine, propranolol and DPH in digitalis-induced cardiac arrhythmias in dogs. DPH and lidocaine were the most successful in conversion of ventricular tachycardia to normal sinus rhythm.

DPH and lidocaine restored sinus rhythm in all animals and the normal rhythm was maintained in the majority.

LÜLLMANN and WEBER, *Arztliche Forschung* (1968)[233] and *Naunyn-Schmiedebergs Archiv fur Pharmakologie* (1968),[403] found that DPH (20-80 mg/kg) given intravenously to guinea pigs almost doubled the amount of intravenous digoxin necessary to produce death (from 0.9 to 1.7 mg/kg). The normalization of rhythm by DPH occurred without abolishing the positive effect of digitalis.

BIOCHEMICAL MECHANISMS

Glycogen and Creatine Phosphate in Brain, and Anoxia

WOODBURY, TIMIRAS and VERNADAKIS, *Hormones, Brain Function and Behavior* (1957),[483] in a controlled study in rats, observed that there was a significant increase in brain glycogen in response to a single dose of DPH.

BERNSOHN, POSSLEY and CUSTOD, *Pharmacologist* (1960),[17] did a controlled study of some aspects of the energy metabolism of *in vivo* rat brain with Librium, chlorpromazine, and DPH. Determinations were made for inorganic phosphate, adenine nucleotides and creatinine phosphates. The most marked change occurred in creatinine phosphate values. Compared with control values (untreated) of 3.30 micromoles/gm of brain, the creatinine phosphate values were 1.30 for Librium, 4.40 for chlorpromazine, and 7.38 micromoles/gm for DPH.

BRODDLE and NELSON, *Federation Proceedings* (1968),[37] found that DPH (50 mg/kg) can decrease brain metabolic rate 40 to 60% as well as increase the concentrations of brain "energy reserve" compounds measured, *i.e.*, phosphocreatine, serum and brain glucose and glycogen.

HUTCHINS and ROGERS, *British Journal of Pharmacology* (1970),[739] found that a single dose of DPH intraperitoneally (20 mg/kg) increased the concentration of brain glycogen in mouse brain by 7% at 30 minutes and by 11% at 120 minutes.

FORDA and McILWAIN, *British Journal of Pharmacology* (1953),[717] electrically stimulated guinea pig brain slices at 500 and 2,000 cyc./sec., 3.5 V. At the 500 and 2,000 cyc./sec. more oxygen per gm per hour was used. When DPH was added, this increase in oxygen use was reduced.

NAIMAN and WILLIAMS, *Journal of Pharmacology and Experimental Therapeutics* (1964),[263] found that DPH prolonged the duration of respiratory activity in cats and guinea pigs subjected to nitrogen anoxia as well as in the decapitated guinea pig head.

The anti-anoxic effect of DPH was thought to be due in part to a direct effect on the respiratory neurons of the central nervous system.

GAYET-HALLION and BERTRAND, *Comptes Rendus des Seances de la Societe de Biologie* (1959),[118] found that DPH prolonged respiratory activity. Rats were immersed in water at 14–15°C, with the times of immersion varying from trial to trial. DPH given intraperitoneally three hours before the test permitted prolongation of respiratory activity (p less than 0.001). In addition, there was a marked increase in survival of the animals (p = 0.02 in males; 0.01 in females).

HOFF and YAHN, *American Journal of Physiology* (1944),[164] studied the effect of DPH upon tolerance of rats and mice to reduced atmospheric pressures. After subcutaneous injection of DPH, rats withstood a lower pressure than was possible during the control decompression. Under the conditions of these experiments in which decompression was carried out at the rate of 100 mm Hg per minute, rats and mice given single doses of DPH tolerated lower pressures or withstood a given low pressure for a longer time than controls. Animals receiving DPH could be taken to extraordinarily low pressures and survive.

It was proposed that DPH prolongs normal function of nerve cells, in particular of the respiratory and cardiac centers, under conditions of severe lack of oxygen.

Since severe and similar neuronal lesions are found in death from decompression, low oxygen mixtures, carbon monoxide, and nitrous oxide, as well as from hypoglycemia and electric shock, the possibility was raised by the authors that such pathological changes may be prevented, or their incidence effectively reduced, by administration of DPH.

Sodium and Potassium in Cells (Stabilization of Excitable Membranes)

WOODBURY, *Journal of Pharmacology and Experimental Therapeutics* (1955),[387] demonstrated that in normal rats, DPH decreased both the total and the intracellular concentration of brain sodium (Na) and increased the rate of movement of radiosodium into and out of brain cells. The net result was that the ratio of extracellular to intracellular brain Na was increased. DPH also decreased intracellular Na concentrations in skeletal and cardiac muscle, but to a lesser extent than in brain.

Acutely induced low sodium in blood was associated with an increase in intracellular brain sodium and a decrease in intracellular brain potassium. These changes from normal were largely prevented by treatment with DPH.

PINCUS, GROVE, MARINO and GLASER, *Archives of Neurology* (1970),[699] indicate that DPH does not affect intracellular sodium in normally functioning, oxygenated nerves, but that it tends to reduce the abnormal accumulation of intracellular sodium in hypoxic nerves. DPH was also found to limit the rise in intracellular sodium in nerves in which the sodium extrusion mechanism has been destroyed by ouabain, cyanide or both.

The authors state: "Diphenylhydantoin has been shown to have a stabilizing influence on virtually all excitable membranes. These effects have been seen in a wide variety of vertebrate and invertebrate species." (For earlier work see PINCUS and GIARMAN[285] and RAWSON and PINCUS.)[293]

FESTOFF and APPEL, *Journal of Clinical Investigation* (1968),[94] studied rat brain synaptosomes as a source for Na-K-Mg-ATPase. With a ratio of 5-10:1 of sodium to potassium, DPH had no effect. When the ratio of sodium:potassium was raised to 50:1 or higher, DPH exerted an increasingly greater effect on enzyme activity, causing stimulation of synaptosome ATPase. Thus the authors observed a selectivity of action of DPH on ATPase, depending on whether the ratio of sodium to potassium is in the normal or abnormal range.

HELFANT, RICCIUTTI, SCHERLAG and DAMATO, *American Journal of Physiology* (1968),[157] demonstrated that DPH prevented the efflux of potassium from cardiac tissue pretreated with toxic doses of digitalis and reversed digitalis-induced ventricular arrhythmias.

CRANE and SWANSON, *Neurology* (1970),[728] demonstrated the effect of DPH in preventing the loss of potassium and gain in sodium by brain slices, which occur during repeated high frequency electrical stimulation. With repeated depolarization of neuronal membranes, it becomes increasingly likely that the resting balance of ions intra- and extracellularly will not be restored. These "down-hill" movements of sodium and potassium ion balance represent the failure of active transport to restore the resting balance of ions between intracellular and extracellular compartments. DPH was shown both to prevent and to reverse these shifts, and thus it tended to restore the balance toward the normal resting state.

Acetylcholine in Brain and Heart

AGARWAL and BHARGAVA, *Indian Journal of Medical Research* (1964),[1] determined brain acetylcholine (ACh) level in rat using frog rectus abdominis muscle bioassay. DPH 100 mg/kg intraperitoneally, lowered brain ACh levels 38%; methedrine lowered brain ACh by 42% and cardiazol lowered brain ACh by 47%. In contrast, phenobarbital, pentobarbital, morphine, meprobamate and reserpine increased brain ΛCh, and chlorpromazine produced no change.

Bose, Saifi and Sharma, *Archives Internationales de Pharmacodynamie et de Therapie* (1963),[30] found DPH lowered acetylcholine levels in rat heart by 9.6% at 4 mg/kg DPH, and by 18.9% at 8 mg/kg.

Brain Gamma Aminobutyric Acid (GABA)

Vernadakis and Woodbury, *Inhibitions of the Nervous System and Gamma-aminobutyric Acid* (1960),[532] demonstrated that DPH enhanced the conversion of free glutamic acid to glutamine and GABA in brain. This was in contrast to the effect of cortisol which shunted free glutamic acid to the Krebs cycle and away from glutamine and GABA.

Bhattacharya, Kishor, Saxena and Bhargava, *Archives Internationales de Pharmacodynamie et de Therapie* (1964),[522] confirmed the significant increase in brain GABA in several species with DPH.

Verster, Garoutte, Ichinosa and Guerrero-Figueroa, *Federation Proceedings* (1965),[454] observed that the uptake of GABA-C^{14} by brain was increased by 35% with DPH.

Brain 5-Hydroxytryptamine (5HT) and Tryptophane Metabolism

Although 5HT (serotonin) and norepinephrine levels in mouse brain were reported not to be affected by DPH (P'an, Funderburk and Finger, 1961),[510] DPH was found by Bonnycastle, Paasonen and Giarman (1956)[575] and Bonnycastle, Bonnycastle and Anderson (1962)[573] to increase significantly the concentration of 5HT in brain. By fluoroassay, DPH at 50 mg/kg produced a 32.7% elevation of brain 5HT in 30 minutes. This was similar to the effect produced by pentobarbital (31.5%), but less than

that produced by harmaline (58.1%). Francis and Melville (1959)[629] confirmed the increase of brain serotonin by DPH in the ferret.

The inhibition by reserpine of the effect of DPH on 5HT as reported by Chen and Ensor (1954)[463] and confirmed by Gray, Rauh and Shanahan (1963),[545] is apparently not due to brain amine depletion (Rudzik and Mennear, 1965).[448]

Healing Process

Shapiro, *Experimental Medicine and Surgery* (1958)[339] reported that the administration of DPH to patients, and in animal studies, increased the rate of healing of gingival wounds.

Shafer, Beatty and Davis, *Proceedings of the Society of Experimental Biology and Medicine* (1958),[337] demonstrated an increase in the tensile strength of healing wounds by DPH. Kelln and Gorlin, *Dental Progress* (1961),[189] confirmed the wound healing effects of DPH in rats, and also showed that DPH increased tensile strength of the wound and increased fibrous growth. The effectiveness of DPH in corneal wound healing was reported by Kulbert, *American Journal of Ophthalmology* (1968).[504] Shafer, *Journal of Dental Research* (1965),[336] and *Journal of Oral Therapeutics and Pharmacology* (1966),[335] found that DPH stimulated growth of normal fibroblasts in tissue culture.

Evidence was presented by Smith and Robinson, *Proceedings of the Western Pharmacology Society* (1962),[505] and by Shafer, *Journal of Oral Therapeutics and Pharmacology* (1966),[335] that DPH stimulated the regeneration of liver, as measured by increased nucleic acid synthesis.

Sklans, Taylor and Shklar, *Journal of Oral Surgery* (1967),[343] demonstrated that

DPH improved the healing rate of experimentally produced fractures in rabbits.

SIMPSON, KUNZ and SLAFTA, *New York State Journal of Medicine* (1965),[344] reported that DPH improved the healing of leg ulcers in humans.

Carbohydrate Metabolism

HOUCK, JACOB and MAENGWYN-DAVIES, *Journal of Clinical Investigation* (1960),[172] demonstrated that the administration of DPH resulted in the following changes in the chemistry of rat skin: a marked decrease in dermal water and fat, a marked increase in acid-soluble collagen and acid-soluble mucopolysaccharide, a marked increase in insoluble collagen and hexosamine, and the appearance of a previously unrecognized insoluble non-collagenous protein.

HOUCK and JACOB, *Proceedings of the Society of Experimental Biology and Medicine* (1963),[502] showed in rats that DPH diminished the catabolic effect of cortisol which reduces hexosamine, nitrogen and collagen fractions in skin. HOUCK, *Journal of Investigative Dermatology* (1963),[501] also showed the action of DPH to increase skin hexosamine and collagen fractions is diminished by cortisol.

BELTON, ETHERIDGE and MILLICHAP, *Epilepsia* (1965),[12] demonstrated that very high doses of DPH (70 mg/kg) produced a significant increase in blood sugar levels in rabbits. SANBAR, CONWAY, ZWEIFLER and SMET, *Diabetes* (1967),[323] observed a hyperglycemic effect in dogs with large intravenous doses of DPH (25 mg/kg), but no effect was observed with oral doses equivalent to the therapeutic dose in man (5 mg/kg) given daily for one month.

Stabilization by DPH of blood sugar levels in labile diabetes has been reported by FABRYKANT and PACELLA (1948),[92] by WILSON (1951),[382] by FABRYKANT (1953)[91] and (1964)[430] and by ROBERTS (1964).[429]

Lipid Metabolism

CHUNG, *Journal of Atherosclerosis Research* (1967),[56] studied the effect of DPH on aortic lipid concentrations. Daily oral administration of DPH to rabbits for 30 days resulted in a significant reduction of aortic concentrations of cholesterol and phospholipids, and an increase in triglyceride concentration. On the other hand, no significant changes in concentrations of these lipids were noted in the liver and plasma. These effects of DPH were not observed when an atherogenic diet was fed to the rabbits. The study by HOUCK, *et al.*, *Journal of Clinical Investigation* (1960),[172] already cited, also showed decrease in dermal lipids as a result of DPH treatment. NAKAMURA and MASUDA, *Archives Internationales de Pharmacodynamie et de Therapie* (1966),[265] also demonstrated a marked decrease in dermal lipids (triglycerides, cholesterol and phospholipids) and a decrease in the conversion of C^{14}-acetate into these compounds with DPH.

ARIYOSHI and REMMER, *Naunyn-Schmiedeberg Archiv fur Pharmakologie* (1968),[529] found that DPH counteracted the tendency for alcohol together with a choline-deficient diet to produce fatty liver in mice. The liver triglycerides were lowered.

Protein-Bound Iodine (PBI) and Thyroxine

OPPENHEIMER, FISHER, NELSON and JAILER, *Journal of Clinical Endocrinology and Metabolism* (1961),[276] demonstrated in *in vivo* studies that DPH lowered the serum PBI level by some extrathyroidal mechanism. *In vitro* data derived from erythrocyte uptake studies provided further evidence for the extrathyroidal effect of DPH. Unlike dinitrophenol and aspirin, however, DPH does not decrease the thyroidal uptake of I^{131} nor increase the metabolic rate. Chromatographic studies in a paticnt receiving DPH indicated a normal distribution of radio-iodinated amino acids in the plasma. This observation, as well as the absence of goiter in the patients receiving DPH, indicates that there was no intra-thyroidal block in the synthesis of thyroid hormone. (Also see OPPENHEIMER and TAVERNETTI, 1962[490,491] and OPPENHEIMER, 1968.)[492]

LEVY and MARSHALL, *Archives of Internal Medicine* (1964),[488] observed that DPH did not influence PBI or I[131] uptake after 300 mg per day for one week. In a study by CANTU and SCHWAB, *Archives of Neurology* (1966),[44] the administration of DPH (300–400 mg daily) to thirty-nine adult patients for two weeks was associated with a significant reduction in PBI levels and no change in the prior normal thyroid clinical status in all patients. Triiodothyronine (T-3) red blood cells and thyroid I[131] uptakes were unchanged in the five patients in whom these were measured. No further significant reduction in PBI levels was observed at one month as compared with two weeks.

Pituitary-Adrenal Functions

WOODBURY, TIMIRAS and VERNADAKIS, *Hormones, Brain Function, and Behavior* (1957),[483] showed that the DPH elevation of electroshock threshold was antagonized by cortisone.

BONNYCASTLE and BRADLEY, *Endocrinology* (1960),[520] found in rats that DPH blocks the adrenal ascorbate depletion which follows unilateral adrenalectomy. DPH also blocked intravenous vasopressin and subcutaneous epinephrine stimulation of adrenocorticotropic (ACTH) release. They suggested the hypothalamus or pituitary as the possible sites of inhibition of the release of ACTH. KRIEGER, *Journal of Clinical Endocrinology and Metabolism* (1962),[198] also presented evidence

suggesting that short-term administration of DPH affects pituitary-adrenal function by blocking the pituitary release of ACTH.

DILL, *Archives Internationales de Pharmaco-dynamie et de Therapie* (1966),[76] reported the results of an investigation demonstrating a marked adrenal cortical stimulation resulting from the intraperitoneal injection of DPH in both rest and stress conditions. It was shown that while DPH did not inhibit the initial elevation of the plasma level of corticosterone in stressed rats, it did reduce the duration of the effect. The inhibition of the adrenal ascorbic acid depletion response in rats treated with DPH was verified in part. CHRISTY and HOFMANN, *Clinical Research* (1958),[486] observed that thirteen out of fifteen adult patients on DPH showed a normal four hour i.v. ACTH test.

HOUCK and PATEL, *Nature* (1965),[171] discussed the evidence that in normal rat skin and in various collagen diseases cortisol diminishes the collagen content of connective tissues. This effect of cortisol was not observed in young animals pretreated with DPH. Further experiments presented in this report confirmed and extended these observations.

SHOLITON, WERK and MACGEE, *Metabolism* (1964),[451] demonstrated that DPH increased the side-chain reduction of cortisol in male rat liver slices and increased ring-A reduction in female rat liver slices. In addition, DPH decreased 6-hydroxylation reduction in both sexes. If the animals were pretreated with DPH for two to four weeks prior to sacrifice, no DPH effect on the liver slices was found.

WERK, MACGEE and SHOLITON, *Journal of Clinical Investigation* (1964),[377] in studies in man, found DPH caused a net increase in excretion of 6-hydroxycortisol and an unconjugated polar metabolite concomitant with a relative decrease in conjugated tetrahydro derivatives.

NATELSON, WALKER and PINCUS, *Proceedings of the Society of Experimental Biology and Medicine* (1966),[268] showed that DPH does not influence the effect of ACTH to depress calcium levels and elevate citrate levels.

RINNE, *Medicina et Pharmacologia Experimentalis* (1967),[303] also found that patients on DPH excreted 17-hydroxycorticosteroids and 17-ketosteroids at normal levels and their response to synthetic lysine vasopressin and to ACTH was also normal.

WERK, THRASHER, CHOI and SHOLITON, *Journal of Clinical Endocrinology and Metabolism* (1967),[378] presented evidence that DPH prevents effective inhibition of 11-hydroxylation by mepyrapone.

LEE, GRUMER, BRONSKY and WALDSTEIN, *Journal of Laboratory and Clinical Medicine* (1961),[219] noted that inappropriate antidiuretic hormone (ADH) syndrome, diagnosed in hyponatremic patients by acute water loading was reversed in two cases by the administration of intravenous DPH. FICHMAN and BETHUNE, *Annals of Internal Medicine* (1968),[96] found that the defect in acute water load excretion was improved by intravenous DPH in four of five cases tested. There was marked improvement in the percent water excreted, in the minimum urine osmolality found, and in the achievement of positive free water clearance in all four cases, although long-term benefits with oral DPH were not observed in several patients.

TAKAHASHI, KIPNIS and DAUGHADAY, *Journal of Clinical Investigation* (1968),[487] found in humans that growth hormone secretion during sleep was not affected by DPH.

The regulatory effect of DPH on labile diabetes as reported by FABRYKANT and PACELLA (1948),[92] by WILSON (1951),[382] by FABRYKANT (1953)[91] and (1964)[430] is discussed in the Clinical section, pp. 176–77.

CHEMISTRY OF DPH

Chemical Structure of DPH

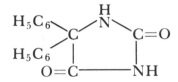

5,5-diphenylhydantoin (DPH) is related in structure to the other hydantoins—ethotoin and mephenytoin, to phenobarbital, and to the acetylureas and the succinimides. These structural relationships, and the effect of different substitutions on pharmacological properties of DPH have been discussed by TOMAN, *The Pharmacological Basis of Therapeutics* (1965).[359]

DPH is usually dispensed in 100 mg capsules. 50 mg tablets are also available, as are oral suspensions and sterile preparations for parenteral use.

Chemical Determination of DPH and its Metabolites

CHANG and GLAZKO, *Clinical Research* (1968),[50] have described analytical procedures for DPH and its p-hydroxyphenyl metabolite based upon solvent extraction, formation of trimethylsilyl derivatives, and gas chromatography of the resulting products.

A second gas-liquid chromatography method, this one employing the methoxy derivative of DPH, has been described by SANDBERG, RESNICK and BACALLAO, *Analytical Chemistry* (1968).[324]

Thin-layer chromatography methods for DPH have been described by HUISMAN (1966),[173] deZEEUW and FEITSMA (1966),[393] KUTT, WINTERS and McDOWELL (1964),[209] and OLESEN (1967),[272] (1967),[275] and (1968).[274] Spectrophotometric methods have been described by SVENSMARK and KRISTENSEN (1963),[437] WALLACE and DAHL (1965),[438] WALLACE, BIGGS and DAHL (1965),[374] and OLESEN (1967).[272] KRISTENSEN, HANSEN, HANSEN and LUND (1967)[200] discussed the substances which interfere with the determination of DPH in their methods.

VINCENT and BLAKE, *Drug Standards* (1958),[372] WESTERINK, *Pharmaceutisch Weekblad* (1962),[379] and LACH, BHANSALI and BLAUG, *Journal of the American Pharmaceutical Association* (1958),[212] described ion-exchange procedures for the separation of DPH and its subsequent determination by titration. The pKa' of DPH was found by AGARWAL and BLAKE, *Journal of Pharmaceutical Science* (1968),[398] to be 8.33 by potentiometric titration and 8.31 by ultraviolet spectrophotometry. It was not possible to adequately determine DPH by titration in a mixture of DPH and phenobarbital. A procedure for the identification of DPH in urine by use of two-dimensional paper chromatography was described by TOMPSETT, *Journal of Pharmacy and Pharmacology* (1964).[360]

ABSORPTION AND EXCRETION OF DPH

NOACH, WOODBURY and GOODMAN, *Journal of Pharmacology and Experimental Therapeutics* (1958),[269] comprehensively studied the absorption and excretion of DPH.

The principal urinary metabolite in dogs and man results from parahydroxylation of a single phenyl group, which is sufficient to destroy the anticonvulsant activity of DPH (TOMAN, 1965).[359] Further hydroxylation of the same site or of the other phenyl group can also occur, and the glucuronide has been described by MAYNERT (1960).[444] More than forty-eight hours are required for excretion of N^{15}-labeled DPH in feces and urine (MAY-

NERT, 1960[444] and LOESER, 1961).[440] About one-half of administered DPH appears in the urine as 5-(p-hydroxyphenyl)-5-phenylhydantoin (HPPH). (BUTLER, 1957)[443]

CHANG, BAUKEMA, DILL, BUCHANAN, GOULET and GLAZKO, *Clinical Research* (1968),[445] reinvestigated the excretion of DPH products in the urine by means of gas chromatography. They found that urinary excretion accounted for almost two-thirds of the dose over a five day period.

The metabolism of DPH is probably under the influence of genetic variability, age and the presence of other drugs. PORTER, *Diseases of the Nervous System* (1966),[521] in a comprehensive review of the genetics of response to several drugs found it likely that DPH metabolism is under polymorphic genetic control.

KUTT, HAYNES and McDOWELL, *Archives of Neurology* (1966),[553] in a study of three patients with unusually rapid DPH metabolism and one with defective absorption of DPH also concluded that the metabolism of DPH may be influenced by genetic factors.

PETTY and KARLER, *Journal of Pharmacology and Experimental Therapeutics* (1965),[284] comparing the anti-convulsant effect of DPH in young and old animals, found a difference in peak time of action for DPH. In young mice the peak time was thirty minutes; however, in old mice, peak time was two hours.

SVENSMARK, SCHILLER and BUCHTHAL, *Acta Pharmacologica et Toxicologica* (1960),[446] noted individual variation in the metabolism of DPH after oral or intravenous administration as reflected in human spinal fluid, saliva and milk levels.

CUCINELL, *Bulletin of the New York Academy of Medicine* (1966),[69] observed, in agreement with JENSEN and GRYNDERUP, *Epilepsia* (1966),[179] that when the same amount of DPH is given, the rate of disappearance of the drug from plasma is variable from individual to individual. However, CUCINELL stated that this rate can vary over a wide range in the same person under different conditions. The rate of decay was found to depend upon prior or concomitant administration of other chemical substances to the individual. Phenobarbital was found capable of increasing the rate of metabolism of DPH (see also BURNS and CONNEY, 1965[442] and BURNS, CUCINELL, KOSTER and CONNEY, 1965).[544] GERBER and ARNOLD, *Journal of Pharmacology and Experimental Therapeutics* (1968),[528] found that hydroxyzine also stimulates DPH metabolism in mice but does not affect the half-life of DPH in man. SOLOMON and SCHROGIE, *Clinical Pharmacology and Therapeutics* (1967),[348] demonstrated that when phenyramidol was given to subjects taking DPH, the mean biologic half-life of DPH increased from twenty-five hours to fifty-five hours.

FREY, KAMPMANN and NIELSEN, *Acta Pharmacologica et Toxicologica* (1968),[109] studying the metabolism of DPH with and without phenobarbital in dogs, found considerable individual variation in the degree of interaction of the two agents.

KUTT, HAYNES and McDOWELL, *Neurology* (1965),[205] also studied the effect of phenobarbital upon DPH metabolism in man and pointed out that it can both increase and decrease the rate of metabolism of DPH. In addition, KUTT, VEREBELY and McDOWELL, *Neurology* (1967)[452] and *Neurology* (1968),[453] studied the competitive inhibition by antitubercular drugs of DPH metabolism in rats and in rat liver microsomes. OLESEN, *Archives of Neurology* (1967),[559] noted that serum DPH was raised by the simultaneous administration of disulfiram (Antabuse) and, in urine, DPH metabolite (HPPH) levels were concurrently reduced.

KUTT, WINTERS, SCHERMAN and McDOWELL, *Archives of Neurology* (1964),[554] observed the metabolism of DPH in fifteen patients with liver disease. At normal daily dosage DPH intoxication was observed in five. They concluded that a lowering of the ability to metabolize DPH may be present in liver disease.

TRIEDMAN, FISHMAN and YAHR, *Transactions of the American Neurological Association* (1960),[361] drew attention to the manner in which the route of administration and dosage schedule of DPH affects the level of DPH in the plasma. To maintain a uniform maximum level, repeated oral doses of DPH at twelve hour intervals were required. The concentration of DPH in the cerebrospinal fluid was found to be equal to the fraction of plasma DPH not bound to plasma protein.

ENTRY AND BINDING OF DPH IN BRAIN

FIREMARK, BARLOW and ROTH, *International Journal of Neuropharmacology* (1963),[101] examined in considerable detail the mechanism of DPH entry into and binding by the brain. DPH penetrated the brain rapidly and concentrations two to three times greater than plasma levels were found in all brain regions for twenty-four hours after injection. DPH was bound in brain and plasma. The drug concentration in cerebrospinal fluid (CSF) was equivalent to the concentration in ultra-filtrates of brain and plasma. They found, consistent with the findings of NOACH, WOODBURY and GOODMAN, *Journal of Pharmacology and Experimental Therapeutics* (1958),[269] that brain and plasma of rats contained predominantly unchanged DPH.

FIREMARK, *et al.*[101] found that circulation was a determining factor in the entry of DPH into gray matter. Cerebral gray matter was penetrated more quickly than cerebral white matter. The concentration of DPH in white matter increased during the first hour following a single injection but rose only slightly thereafter. At three, six and twenty-four hours, the concentration of DPH in white matter exceeded that in cerebral cortex. The concentrations of DPH in all areas of brain at twenty-four hours were only slightly lower than the levels at three hours, illustrating an unusual retention of this drug. Furthermore, between thirty minutes and twenty-four hours following injection, the concentrations of DPH in all brain areas were two to three times greater than the concentrations in plasma. Equilibrium was rapidly achieved between the unbound concentration of DPH in plasma, CSF and brain water.

The authors speculated that the affinity for DPH in brain may be due to binding to protein constituents of brain. The authors expressed the opinion that the exceptionally high binding of DPH in brain correlates with the persistence of the drug in this organ after a single dose and serves to explain its long pharmacological action.

The authors felt it was possible that the interaction of DPH with protein, lipoprotein or other constituents of brain could be a reflection of interaction with neural membranes or with enzymes, which function in maintaining the neuronal ion permeabilities and polarization on which normal neuronal activity depends.

NAKAMURA, MASUDA, NAKATSUJI and HIROKA, *Naunyn-Schmiedelbergs Archiv fur Pharmakologie* (1966),[267] showed that the oral administration of extremely large doses (100 mg/kg/day) of DPH to dogs and cats for more than one year resulted in preferential accumulations of the drug in the superior and inferior colliculus, amygdala and hippocampus, compared to sixteen other cerebral areas examined, without any manifestation of neurotoxicity. DPH was found concentrated in the pituitary and adrenal. (See also NAKAMURA, MASUDA and NAKATSUJI, 1967.)[266]

ROSENBLUM and STEIN, *Biochemical Pharmacology* (1963),[400] demonstrated that DPH localizes preferentially in human primary brain tumors when compared to adjacent normal brain tissue. In experimental subcutaneous mouse ependymomas and adenocarcinomas this preferential localization did not occur.

KEMP and WOODBURY, *Pharmacologist* (1962),[531] studied the intracellular distribution of 4-C^{14} DPH in rat brain at intervals between 15 and 240 minutes. Initial fixation of DPH in the cell nucleus was suggested followed by transfer to microsomes for fixation or metabolism.

[The references that pertain to *The Broad Range of Use of DPH (1970)* are found on pages 287 to 302.]

THE TWO BIBLIOGRAPHIES

DPH, 1975 is a supplement to *The Broad Range of Use of Diphenylhydantoin*, and should be read in combination with it. Neither book is complete without the other.

The Broad Range of Use of Diphenylhydantoin, published in 1970, will be referred to here as Vol. I. It covers the period from 1937 to 1970 and is arranged chronologically. *DPH, 1975* is based mainly on studies published between 1970 and 1975.

The purpose of this work is to bring to the physician much of the published information on the many clinical uses[1] of DPH and its basic mechanisms of action.

---

[1] Clinical uses other than in epilepsy. The reference library of the Foundation is accessible to interested persons.

VOL. II

DPH, 1975

A Supplement to The Broad Range of Use of Diphenylhydantoin

BIBLIOGRAPHY AND REVIEW

Samuel Bogoch, M.D., PH.D.

Jack Dreyfus

The painting on the cover is by Joan Personette.

THE DREYFUS MEDICAL FOUNDATION

DPH, 1975—CONTENTS

Clinical Uses of Diphenylhydantoin

Basic Mechanisms of Action

BACKGROUND AND DISTINCTIVE CHARACTERISTICS OF DPH

Background

In its first clinical trials, in epilepsy, diphenylhydantoin was so effective that it was labeled an anticonvulsant, and the concept that it was a single-purpose medicine persisted for many years. However, from the beginning, other uses were being found for DPH.

Starting in 1938, a series of published works indicated that DPH had salutary effects on personality, memory, mood, cooperativeness and emotional stability. As early as 1944, Silverman, in a double-blind study with prisoners, reported that DPH was more effective than any other substance tried, in improving sleep disturbances, sense of well-being and cooperativeness. Other studies found DPH effective in emotions related to fear and anger, and in depression. It was observed that these improvements in thought, mood and behavior were achieved without sedation.

As early as 1940, Shapera found DPH effective in conditions of involuntary movements and in the treatment of migraine. By 1942, Shulman had reported DPH therapeutic in intractable bronchial asthma and, in the same year, Bergouignan observed DPH useful in trigeminal neuralgia. Bodkin, in 1945, reported DPH successful in the treatment of pruritus ani. In 1948, Fabrykant found DPH effective in stabilizing labile diabetes. In 1950, Harris and Kokernot reported that DPH controlled ventricular tachycardias in dogs. The first clinical report of DPH's usefulness in ventricular tachycardias was by Leonard in 1958. In 1961, Isaacs found DPH effective, when other substances had failed, in the treatment of continuous muscle fiber activity. A series of studies have demonstrated that DPH is useful in a variety of painful conditions—from mild headache to such severe conditions as trigeminal neuralgia and thalamic pain.

Today, DPH is no longer thought of as a single-purpose medicine but is broadly known as a stabilizer of bioelectrical activity, or cell membrane stabilizer. Clinically, it is referred to as a stabilizer or a normalizer.

The recognition of DPH as a multi-purpose medicine has opened new areas for exploration and it is being found useful for an increasingly wide range of disorders.

Because DPH is useful in so many medical disciplines an over-all summary is impractical.[1] However, a review of some of its distinctive characteristics follows.

Distinctive Characteristics

DPH has distinctive characteristics which viewed together set it apart from other substances.

---

[1] Individual summaries will be found in the sections on Thought, Mood and Behavior, Cardiovascular Disorders, Muscle Disorders, Treatment of Pain and Basic Mechanisms of Action.

1. DPH regulates bioelectrical activity at the individual cell level.[1] This action at a level fundamental to all body functions helps explain how DPH achieves its therapeutic effects in a wide range of disorders.

2. DPH is selective in its action in that it corrects inappropriate electrical activity, but does not affect normal function.[1]

3. When cells are overstimulated electrically or chemically a hyperexcitable state develops, referred to as post-tetanic potentiation, which can develop into spontaneous firing, referred to as post-tetanic after-discharge. DPH has a corrective effect on both these conditions.[1] This delineation of a basic action of DPH helps in understanding how repetitive messages of pain are offset or reduced; it may also explain how repetitive and uncontrolled thinking is decreased.

4. DPH has regulatory effects on endocrine and metabolic processes.[2] It has been demonstrated to have anti-anoxic effects,[3] anti-toxic properties,[4] and to promote healing.[7]

5. DPH has been found to be effective in both hyperexcitable and hypoexcitable conditions.[5]

6. In therapeutic doses DPH is not a sedative, nor is it an artificial stimulant.

7. DPH's action is prompt. Taken orally, it is effective within an hour, intravenously within a few minutes.[6]

8. DPH is non-habit forming.

9. DPH's range of safety has been established over a thirty-seven year period.

[1] Stabilization of Bioelectrical Activity, p. 245.
[2] Other Regulatory Effects of DPH, p. 259.
[3] Anti-anoxic Effects of DPH, p. 252.
[4] Anti-toxic Effects of DPH, p. 266.
[5] Related basic mechanism studies—Stabilization of Bioelectrical Activity, p. 245, and Preservation of Energy Compounds in Brain, p. 253.
[6] These clinical observations are confirmed by a variety of quantitative measures.
[7] Healing, pp. 177–79, 195–96, 268–69.

CLINICAL USES OF DIPHENYLHYDANTOIN

THOUGHT, MOOD AND BEHAVIOR DISORDERS

Summary

The growth of understanding of the therapeutic value of diphenylhydantoin in thought, mood and behavior disorders dates back to the first paper, in 1938, of Merritt and Putnam.[1] The progress in this field from 1938 to 1970 is reviewed in Vol. I, pp. 157–165, in which fifty-two studies are arranged chronologically. Here, in Vol. II, recent studies of the last five years are reviewed.

Basic mechanism studies are consistent with and make easier to understand the clinical observations of the effectiveness of DPH.

The reader will find relevant the section, "Stabilization of Bioelectrical Activity,"[2] in which it is demonstrated that DPH corrects hyperexcitability, as in post-tetanic potentiation or post-tetanic repetitive discharge, in single cells or in groups of cells. This corrective action is achieved without affecting initial appropriate single impulse, or without affecting normal transmission of electrical impulse.

Of further interest is the section, "Preservation of Energy Compounds in Brain,"[3] in which it is shown that DPH preserves ATP, creatine phosphate and glucose. Of additional interest is the section, "Anti-anoxic Effects of DPH,"[4] in which DPH is shown to have a protective effect against oxygen lack; also the section, "Other Regulatory Effects of DPH,"[5] in which it is shown that DPH has a regulatory effect on norepinephrine, acetylcholine, GABA, calcium metabolism, serotonin, insulin, glucagon and blood sugar; and the observations that DPH increases cerebral blood flow.[6]

Clinically, DPH has a calming effect on the overactive brain. Symptoms of this condition are preoccupation, multiple thinking, and flashes and fragments of thoughts coming and going. DPH reduces this uncontrolled activity enabling more normal thinking processes to be restored. This effect is usually achieved within an hour, and without sedation.

Anger and fear and related emotions are usually found in combination with the overactive brain. Emotional states related to anger for which DPH is therapeutic are impatience, impulsiveness, irritability, aggression, hostility, rage and violence. Emotional states related to fear for which DPH is therapeutic are worry, anxiety, guilt, pessimism and depression. Although these excessive anger and fear states are decreased or elimi-

[1] Ref. 557, p. 157, Vol. I.
[2] P. 245. Ref. 90, 250, 257, 289, 365, 458, 467, 468, 472, 789, 885, 954, 955, 1197, 1198, 1221, 1291, 1343, 1400, 1467, 1469, 1494, 1580, 1602.
[3] P. 253. Ref. 17, 37, 483, 739, 1071.
[4] P. 252. Ref. 118, 164, 263, 717, 804, 1160, 1216, 1374, 1419, 1576, 1591.
[5] P. 259. Ref. 454, 522, 532, 573, 575, 629, 789, 872, 885, 909, 924, 1015, 1021, 1062, 1092, 1108, 1109, 1131, 1154, 1220, 1222, 1269, 1272, 1273, 1274, 1282, 1327, 1330, 1355, 1404, 1406, 1417, 1454, 1509, 1567, 1608, 1642, 1644.
[6] Ref. 790, 938, 1216, 1560.

nated by DPH, realistic reactions of anger and fear are not interfered with.

Sleep disturbances found in combination with the overactive brain fall into two general categories. The first and most frequent category is symptomatized by difficulty in falling asleep because of over-thinking, light sleep accompanied by unpleasant dreams and frequent nightmares, and insufficient sleep. A second category is symptomatized by excessive sleep, so-called avoidance sleep. Relief from both types of sleep disturbances is usually prompt with DPH.

DPH is effective with extremes of mood ranging from depression to the hyperexcitable state. These apparently disparate effects are observed in the overactive impatient individual who is calmed by DPH, and the tired energyless individual who has a return to normal energy levels. These clinical effects are supported by basic mechanism studies.[1]

Somatic symptoms associated with thought, mood and behavior disorders are usually relieved by DPH. Among those most frequently observed are headaches, gastrointestinal disorders, pain in back of neck and other pain, shortness of breath, trembling, muscle spasms, skin disorders, and problems with weight. DPH has been found useful in the treatment of acute alcoholism and in the prevention of alcoholism, and the treatment of drug abuse.

THOUGHT, MOOD AND BEHAVIOR DISORDERS

Fifty-two studies on thought, mood and behavior (1938-1970) have been reviewed in Vol. I.

Work of the last five years includes studies of the effect of DPH on violence and uncontrolled behavior, its effect on concentration and cognitive function in the young and aged, its effect on patients with hypoglycemia, its effect on cerebral blood flow in the aged, on compulsive eating, and on drug withdrawal.

In the first two studies that follow, the effectiveness of DPH is demonstrated by quantitative laboratory methods. Stambaugh and Tucker used the radioimmunoassay method to demonstrate that DPH regulates plasma insulin levels. In a basic mechanisms study, Delgado, Mora and Sanguinetti, using radiotelemetry, record the ability of DPH to eliminate post-tetanic repetitive after-discharge in the brain of the awake and functioning rhesus monkey.

Hypoglycemia

STAMBAUGH and TUCKER, *Diabetes* (1974),[1583] describe the successful treatment, with diphenylhydantoin, of five patients with functional hypoglycemia previously unresponsive to dietary management.

Among the symptoms, typical of the hypoglycemic patient, were chronic anxiety, extreme lethargy, chills, frequent nausea, sensory deficits and other neurological complaints. These symptoms disappeared during DPH therapy, and clinical reversal of hypoglycemia was observed in all five cases. In addition, laboratory tests confirmed this observation in both six-hour glucose tolerance and insulin level tests, performed before and after DPH therapy.

Detailed data for all five patients in terms of six-hour plasma glucose tests and plasma insulin values[2] are shown in the figures which follow.

---

[1] See "Stabilization of Bioelectrical Activity," p. 245, and "Preservation of Energy Compounds in Brain," p. 253.
[2] This demonstration of DPH's regulatory effect on plasma insulin and plasma glucose levels supports the work of Fabrykant[91,92,430] and Wilson[382] on the clinical improvement with DPH in labile diabetes. See also Ref. 733, 909, 924, 959, 1015, 1092, 1154, 1193, 1222, 1272, 1274, 1275, 1354, 1355, 1404, 1509.

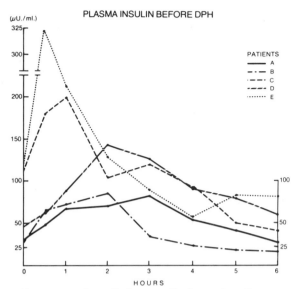

Demonstration of abnormally large insulin response to a glucose load in hypoglycemic patients.

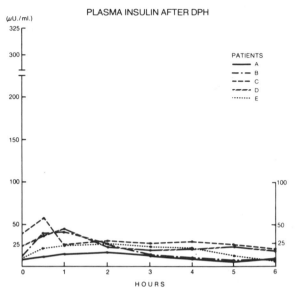

With DPH, the same patients do not have a hyperinsulin response to the glucose load. The response is in the normal range.

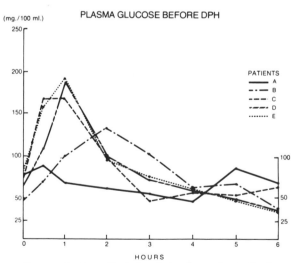

Demonstration that in hypoglycemic patients, blood sugar falls to abnormally low levels in response to a glucose load.

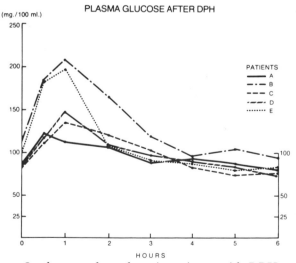

In the same hypoglycemic patients, with DPH, the blood sugar returns to normal levels in response to a glucose load.

DPH demonstrated a regulatory effect on both plasma insulin and plasma glucose in that it brought abnormally high plasma insulin levels down into the normal range and abnormally low plasma glucose levels up into the normal range.

Repetitive After-discharge
(BASIC MECHANISMS STUDY)

DELGADO, MORA and SANGUINETTI, *Personal Communication* (1973),[954] studied the effect of DPH on after-discharge in the amygdala of the brain of awake active rhesus monkeys.

Earlier work[953] had shown that certain forms of abnormal spread of electrical after-discharge could be induced in the monkey by intracerebral electrical stimulation in several areas of the brain, including the thalamus and amygdala. Electrical after-discharge was decreased dramatically in the thalamus by DPH. The strong effect of DPH upon limiting the spread of electrical after-discharge in the cerebral cortex was also noted.

In the present study, with repeated electrical stimulation sufficiently close together, in this case ten minutes apart, repetitive after-discharge could be obtained with 100% reliability. These after-discharges are analogous to the post-tetanic potentiation and post-tetanic after-discharges described in the studies of others. Certain abnormal behavioral sequences accompanied the measurable after-discharges from the amygdala.

Intramuscular or intracerebral injection of DPH was found to completely prevent these electrical after-discharges. (See accompanying Figure.)

The time course of action of DPH in these experiments is of interest. DPH showed some effect in reducing after-discharge fifteen to thirty minutes after injection, and produced

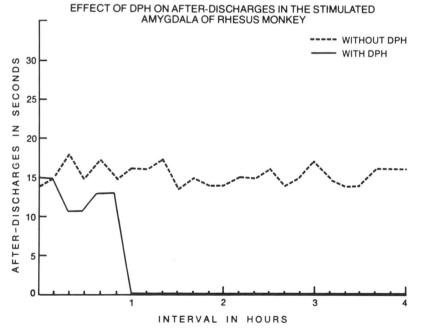

Demonstration of the ability of DPH to eliminate post-tetanic after-discharge, within one hour, in an alert and functioning rhesus monkey.

complete abolition of after-discharges by one hour after injection.

The authors note that in all animals, no changes were recorded in the normal spontaneous electrical activity when DPH was given. However, when the abnormal state of after-discharge was induced, DPH was found to prevent this after-discharge.[1]

General

ALVAREZ, in a book titled *"Nerves in Collision"* (1972),[761] reviews his twenty-five years of experience in the use of diphenylhydantoin for a wide variety of disorders.

In this book, the author reports on the successful use of DPH in the treatment of anxiety, nervousness, tension, fear, nightmares, depression, rage, violent outbursts, confusion, fatigue (extreme), abdominal pain, alcoholism, anorexia nervosa, bed wetting, blackouts, dizzy spells, head pain, involuntary movements, migraine-like headaches and premature ejaculation.

TURNER, *Drugs and Cerebral Function* (1970),[1626] in reporting on the effects of diphenylhydantoin on emotionally disturbed children, states that those of us who prescribe DPH have become so accustomed to finding marked improvement in these children that we almost take it for granted that everyone knows of these effects and prescribes DPH accordingly.

Typical of the problems of these children are hostility, destructiveness, hyperkinesis, inability to get along with others and poor school adjustments. In a recent group of nine emotionally disturbed children, the author reports that treatment with DPH resulted in improvements in seven cases ranging from substantial to complete elimination of symptoms. In one case there was a substantial temporary improvement, and in one case no effect was observed.

BOZZA, in a detailed paper presented at the *Fourth Italian National Congress of Child Neuropsychiatry* (1971),[863] reports on an individual basis on twenty-one slightly brain damaged retarded children who were observed for periods of from twelve to thirty-six months. In most of the cases DPH was tried. The author concluded that DPH and vitamins materially improved the expected intellectual growth rate of these retarded children. (See also Ref. 8, 355, 373 and 1626.)

JONAS, *American Journal of Psychiatry* (1969),[1189] who had reported on twelve years of experience with the use of diphenylhydantoin in his book "Ictal and Subictal Neurosis," comments in a letter to the editor of the American Journal of Psychiatry that investigators who have prescribed DPH over a period of time have found remarkable reversal of symptoms on occasion ranging from the complete disappearance of anxiety to structural changes in the character makeup of the patient.

LOOKER and CONNERS, *Archives of General Psychiatry* (1970),[1304] report on three children in whom diphenylhydantoin was effective to a marked degree in the treatment of severe temper tantrums. In each case the response to DPH was prompt. The children had been previously treated with dextroamphetamine sulfate, to which none of them had any beneficial response.

The children, a seven-year-old girl, a nine-year-old boy and a twelve-year-old girl, were followed-up six months later and the marked improvement had persisted. In two of the cases, when the parents had forgotten to give DPH, deterioration was noted within twenty-four to forty-eight hours. This deterioration was promptly corrected with the reinstitution of DPH.

The authors conducted a double-blind

---

[1] This study demonstrates, in an awake and functioning animal, the corrective action of DPH on hyperexcitability. The time course of this effect, correction within one hour, is consistent with therapeutic effects seen in man.

study with placebo on seventeen subjects, ranging in age from five-and-a-half to four-teen years, who had periodic episodes of mis-behavior.

It was the impression of the authors that among the patients "there were *some* who re-sponded rather dramatically, as in the case histories presented earlier." However, "no statistically significant group changes were at-tributable to drug effect."

STEPHENS and SHAFFER, *The Journal of Clinical Pharmacology* (1973).[1592] In an earlier paper[700] the authors had reported on the suc-cessful treatment with diphenylhydantoin of thirty private psychiatric outpatients. This study had been done on a double-blind cross-over basis and there had been significantly favorable response in symptoms such as anx-iety, irritability, impatience and explosive temper.

About two years later, ten of this group of patients agreed to participate in a double-blind study of DPH for four consecutive two-week periods.

Consistent with the previous study, 100 mg t.i.d. of DPH proved significantly more effec-tive than a 5 mg placebo dosage in relieving symptoms of anxiety, anger and irritability as assessed both by self-ratings and physicians' ratings of change.

DANIEL, *Geriatrics* (1970),[938] states that symptoms of confusion which are so common in the aged often are caused by underlying physical illness, frequently cardiac and respi-ratory disorders resulting in cerebral anoxia. He states that diphenylhydantoin is thera-peutically useful in this group, yet it is often overlooked.

Among the symptoms of confusion so com-mon in the aged are: 1) disorientation, often not of person but in particular of time, place and space; 2) lack of attention and concentra-tion; 3) fluctuation in state of consciousness; 4) memory loss, particularly of current events; 5) poor performance when tested on

immediate retention and recall; and 6) im-pairment of conventional judgment.

The author states that although problems of insufficient cerebral blood flow are well known in the aged, direct measurement of cerebral blood flow is at best difficult.[1] How-ever, the author states that symptoms of in-sufficient cerebral blood flow are identifiable clinically. Among these symptoms are irrita-bility, restlessness, mental confusion and sometimes severe depression. The author notes that after cerebrovascular accident the patient often has paresthesias and tingling. He states that DPH not only frequently gives relief from the paresthesias, but that mental symptoms also improve.

The author states experience has shown that the improving mental state of the patient on DPH is a reasonable guide to over-all im-provement in cerebral function.[2]

Violent Behavior

MALETSKY, *Medical Times* (1972),[1329] states that it is currently fashionable to ascribe the roots of violence to social ills. The role of brain dysfunction has been relatively ne-glected until recently.

The author reports on a study of twenty-two patients with the syndrome referred to as episodic dyscontrol. In describing this syn-drome he states that the subjects usually have a history of hyperactivity and poor school performance as children, aggression towards other children and animals and fire-setting. Truancy and petty stealing frequently lead them to grand larceny, assault and battery and even murder. Other typical symptoms are traffic violations and recklessness. The author states that central to this dyscontrol syndrome is the "storm of violence." Upon

[1] For other work on the effect of DPH in Cerebral Blood Flow, see Ref. 790, 1216, 1560.
[2] This discussion of DPH by Daniel is part of a larger study of other substances entitled, "Psychiatric drug use and abuse in the aged."

minimal or even no provocation these patients lose control, wrecking property and directing violence against anyone in their way. These "storms" are directed against close members of the family as well as society. Frequently following such "storms of violence" these persons have extreme feelings of remorse.

Twenty-two patients with episodic dyscontrol were treated with diphenylhydantoin. Tabulation of the results of this treatment was based on the author's observations and, in addition, was based on reports of relatives and friends of the patient. It seemed implausible to the author that a bias would exist in these reports since the patients had all been through futile drug trials in the past.

The results with DPH were so good that the author calls attention to the fact that this was not a "controlled" study. (Later these effects were confirmed in a controlled study. See below.)

The tabulation of results indicated that nineteen of twenty-two subjects, or 86%, achieved a result equal to or better than "good response." Fifteen of these achieved an excellent response with virtually complete absence of attacks. This response usually occurred within the first two weeks and persisted thereafter. Data collected at twelve months showed that all cases responding to DPH remained free of violent outbreaks.

The author finds it interesting to note that none of the patients claimed to have lost the ability to *feel* anger, but that they were better able to prevent its escalation.

MALETSKY and KLOTTER, *Diseases of the Nervous System* (1974),[1328] in a controlled study, found diphenylhydantoin significantly effective (p less than .01) in twenty-two patients with episodic dyscontrol syndrome.

The authors state that this study, with placebo, confirms the earlier work of Maletsky in which he found DPH highly effective in the treatment of this syndrome. As a result of these studies, the authors conclude that DPH should be tried in patients with episodic dyscontrol syndrome.

DIAMOND and YARYURA-TOBIAS, *Paper presented at the Fifth World Congress of Psychiatry* (1971),[961] found diphenylhydantoin effective in the treatment of violent and aggressive behavior in schizophrenics without epilepsy. Twenty-two patients were studied.

The authors state that DPH has been reported to be therapeutic not only for epilepsy but for disorders of the central and peripheral nervous system, cardiac arrhythmias, diabetes, arterial hypertension, asthma and some skin diseases. They state that from the neuropsychiatric viewpoint it is interesting to know that DPH exerts a regularizing effect on human behavior, irritability and anxiety and that it also has an antidepressant action. Aggressive attitude and violent behavior have also been improved by DPH.

The authors state that as early as 1943, Kalinowsky and Putnam[186] observed an improvement of the excitability and excitation of psychotic patients. Some benefits were seen by Freyhan[110] in 1945, by Kubanek and Rowell[201] in 1946 and by Haward[697] in 1969 and negative results were reported by Klein and Greenberg[196] in 1967.

The purpose of the present investigation was to study the action of DPH on psychotics without epilepsy who had symptoms of violent, impulsive, destructive and aggressive behavior. Patients with severe depression and obsessive-compulsive personalities were also included in the study. Some of the patients had EEG disturbances but they were not epileptics and nine of the patients had functional hypoglycemia curves.

With DPH, in doses up to 300 mg a day, violent behavior was well controlled in all cases of schizophrenia, eleven with excellent results and seven with moderate results. A slight improvement in their depression was noticed in five schizophrenic patients. In the cases with neurotic depression and obsessive-compulsive neurosis, the results were negative. The beneficial effects of DPH were observed not only by the investigator and patient, but also by the patient's family.

The authors state that it is necessary to underline that all therapeutic methods used by the patients prior to DPH administration were ineffective. DPH was the variable that changed their behavioral symptoms.

BACH-Y-RITA, LION, CLIMENT and ERVIN, *American Journal of Psychiatry* (1971),[787] reported that in the course of two years they had seen 130 patients with a wide range of complaints pertaining to assaultive and destructive acts. Diphenylhydantoin was found useful whether or not EEG abnormalities were displayed by the patients. Phenothiazines were also found useful. As a result, many patients were maintained on a regimen of DPH and phenothiazines for long periods. Psychotherapy, group or individual, was also found useful.

SOLOMON and KLEEMAN, *California Medicine* (1971),[1569] in reporting seven cases of episodic dyscontrol syndrome, comment separately on the only two in which diphenylhydantoin was given. In both cases the patient's behavior was markedly improved.

In the case detailed, a 39-year-old woman entered the hospital because of repeated attacks of wild uncontrolled behavior. Without warning, she would be assailed by intense feelings of either rage or sexual excitement. In rage, she usually attacked her husband. In sexual excitement, she sought partners wherever she could find them and her demands were insatiable. Prolonged psychotherapy and tranquilizing medication had proved ineffective. DPH caused a remarkable improvement in this patient's behavior and she returned to reasonable conduct.

PINTO, SIMOPOULOS, McGEE, UHLENHUTH and DeROSA, *Comprehensive Psychiatry* (1974),[1415] in a study of thirty-two severely regressed chronic schizophrenic patients,

found that diphenylhydantoin in doses of 250–350 mg per day, when added to phenothiazine, was more effective than the phenothiazine by itself in reducing irritability, aggression and negative behavior. (See also Simopoulos, Pinto, Uhlenhuth, McGee and DeRosa.)[1551]

Cognitive Function

HAWARD, *Drugs and Cerebral Function* (1970),[1139] studied the effect of diphenylhydantoin upon performance in a complex task, subject to fatigue, in twelve college students who had concentration difficulties. A double-blind cross-over procedure was followed. The students were given a task in which each subject received two hours of training in an air traffic control simulator. On two subsequent two-hour trials, each subject received either 150 mg of DPH or placebo.

DPH was found to be significantly effective in delaying the onset of fatigue and accompanying errors. The author notes that although many substances have been used to improve concentration over the past pentade, these substances are usually stimulants. Although DPH improved concentration significantly, it produced none of the effects of a stimulant.

The author notes that these findings are in accord with the observations of Dreyfus[707] that poor concentration can result from forced ruminative thinking, or the "turned-on mind," and that this can be corrected by DPH.

SMITH and LOWREY, *Drugs, Development and Cerebral Function* (1972),[1564] suggest that improvement in cognitive performance can be due to improved ability to concentrate. Using standard IQ tests to measure ability to perform the authors compared the effects of diphenylhydantoin and placebo on twenty general hospital employee volunteers with no evidence of CNS disorders.

The test was done on a double-blind crossover basis against placebo, and two retests were made. DPH, 100 mg three times daily, improved Verbal Scale and Full Scale scores at highly significant levels (.0005) and the Performance Scale improvement was significant (.01). The authors suggest that the validity of this latter result should be tempered by the possibility of the influence of practice effects.

The authors note that although they used an entirely different method, their findings are consistent with those obtained by Haward[1139] by means of perceptual and vigilance tests.

HAWARD, *Revue de Medicine Aeronautique et Spatiale* (1973),[1140] found that diphenylhydantoin significantly improved the performance of three separate groups of pilots in simulated flying and radar target-fixing tasks.

The author introduces the subject by saying that previous experiments[585,1139] have shown that single doses of DPH are able to counteract the onset of mental fatigue in an Air Traffic Control task. Smith and Lowrey[1564] have also shown that DPH can improve performance on IQ tests. These findings suggest that DPH may also have some value in pilots suffering from operational fatigue, or other conditions in which intellectual processes or work performance is temporarily impaired.

In the present study three groups of pilots were included, twenty-two commercial pilots, eighteen military pilots and nineteen private pilots. Two absorbing tasks were required of the pilots in an attempt to reach full channel capacity. The first was a standard flight simulation procedure. The second task consisted of monitoring and responding to a new type of forward-looking radar.

The pilots were scored on their ability to bring the simulated aircraft into position to correctly intercept a moving target. The time of performing the task as well as the number of correct responses were measured. Sixty minutes before each task 150 mg of DPH was given.

With DPH the test results showed significant improvement in performance both in terms of lessened time spent and the increased number of correct responses made when compared to the tests without DPH. In all three groups the improvement was significant.

The author states that he chose DPH for this test not only because of its already established efficacy in improving cognitive processes, but because other substances which have been tried for this purpose, such as amphetamine, pemoline and prolintane, have undesirable side or after effects. In the dosage used for this purpose, DPH has proved to be free of any side reactions. In an earlier paper Haward[1139] mentioned that, "Unlike other substances DPH has a stabilizing effect on the nervous system, acting neither as a stimulant nor as a depressant, but as what has been called a normalizer."

The author concludes that DPH may have a useful role in the maintaining of efficiency of critical aircraft personnel.

SMITH and LOWREY, *Journal of the American Geriatrics Society* (1975),[1565] observed the beneficial effect of diphenylhydantoin upon cognitive function in a group of elderly normal subjects.

The authors note that a growing amount of evidence has accumulated over the past decade demonstrating the beneficial use of DPH on a variety of physical conditions. They also note that several studies have appeared in the last few years which demonstrate that DPH not only assists concentration when impairment in cognitive function is caused by irrelevant ruminative preoccupation, but that it also improves concentration when efficiency is impaired by fatigue.

The authors state that the purpose of the present study was to examine the effect of DPH upon ability to concentrate in a group of elderly people. Standard intelligence tests were used to compare the subjects' abilities to perform with and without DPH. Intelligence improvement was not expected, but it was thought that improved ability to concentrate would show up in better scores on the intelligence tests.

In the present study ten volunteers, four male and six female, average age 69 years, were studied in a double-blind cross-over test with placebo control. This cross-over design was used to eliminate possible practice effects on performance.

With DPH significant improvement in scores occurred in information, comprehension, digit symbol and full scale IQ. The authors conclude that these significant improvements illustrate the effectiveness of DPH in improving generalized mental functions.

The authors note that in addition to Haward's findings, these observations are consistent with the findings of the beneficial effects of DPH on the "turned-on mind" (Worcester County Jail double-blind study, Resnick and Dreyfus).[704]

Other Disorders

Compulsive Eating

GREEN and RAU, *American Journal of Psychiatry* (1974),[1097] found diphenylhydantoin highly effective in treating ten patients who had three distinct types of symptoms of compulsive eating.

One group was extremely underweight. Sometimes they ate nothing, yet they constantly thought about food. Frequently they would overeat and then would overcorrect this condition by forcing themselves to vomit. Thus they stayed underweight. These patients were considered by the author to come under the category of primary anorexia nervosa.

The second group consisted of persons of normal weight. They were also preoccupied with food and they had a compulsive wish to eat. Their entire lives were structured to avoid exposure to food through various and complicated maneuvers. They occasionally went on eating binges that lasted for hours or days. They would then diet back to normal, unlike group one, who always dieted back to below normal.

Group three consisted of patients who gave in to their strong compulsion to eat. They became overweight over a period of years, some rapidly, some slowly. They were from 150 to 250 pounds above normal weight.

Of the ten patients, nine had abnormal EEGs but none was epileptic. DPH was highly effective in nine of these patients, including the one with normal EEG. The authors give particulars of the successful use of DPH in three remarkable cases, one from each of the groups mentioned. It is apparent that compulsive eating is one of a group of undesirable symptoms, and improvement with DPH in the compulsive eating syndrome coincided with improvement in other symptoms, including depression. In two of the three cases DPH was withdrawn and symptoms returned. When DPH was reinstated, the symptoms disappeared.

LSD Flashbacks

THURLOW and GIRVIN, *Canadian Medical Association Journal* (1971),[1616] reported the successful treatment with diphenylhydantoin of two cases of flashbacks (recurrent visual hallucinations after LSD). In one of the cases DPH was given intravenously, and it terminated the flashback while in progress. In the other case DPH was used orally, and within forty-eight hours marked improvement was noted.

In one of the cases the patient had been suffering from flashbacks five months after the discontinuance of all hallucinogenic drugs. She was given chlorpromazine, 25 mg t.i.d., with moderate diminution in the intensity, frequency and affective component of her flashbacks. Big hallucinations continued to occur, but were less terrifying. Chlorpromazine was discontinued and the previous level of flashbacks returned within twenty-four hours.

Two days after discontinuance of chlorpromazine, DPH was instituted, 100 mg t.i.d. The patient was not informed of the nature of the medicine or of its possible effects. Within forty-eight hours she noted a very marked reduction in all types of flashbacks, a complete disappearance of big ones and a reduction of the little ones to a barely discernible level. DPH was discontinued after four months and the patient was followed for eight months with no return of flashback symptoms.

In the other case 100 mg of DPH intravenously terminated a flashback while in progress. Before injecting DPH, saline solution was injected, as a control, with no effect.

Addiction

FISHER and DiMINO, *British Journal of Addiction* (1975),[1033] in discussing their clinical experience, report that they found diphenylhydantoin to be useful in their over-all therapeutic approach to withdrawal from addictive agents, including heroin, amphetamines, and alcohol.[1]

Gilles de la Tourette

BARSKY, *Journal of Pediatrics* (1967),[796] reports on the unusual symptom complex known as "Tic Convulsif de Gilles de la Tourette." The author states that the hallmarks of this disorder are involuntary movements beginning in childhood in association with a phenomenon referred to as coprolalia (an irresistible use of obscene language).

In this case of a nine-year-old girl, the par-

---

[1] See Fertziger, et al.[1026,1027] on counteraction by DPH of morphine effects in animals.

ents had observed during the preceding year an alarming increase in sudden, purposeless jerking movements of her body. These would vary from sharp, repetitive head jerks, to arm flexions, eye blinking, or leg kicking. Lately, coprolalia had manifested itself. The child would repeat the same obscene statement over and over again and, although aware of it, could not stop repeating it. Except for these attacks, the girl was pleasant and quite normal. Upon the recommendation of a colleague, Dr. Donald Besant, the patient was treated with diphenylhydantoin, 100 mg t.i.d.

The author states that with DPH there was remarkable improvement within six weeks, and the patient was free of manifestations within six months. DPH was administered for a total of twenty-four months. In a follow-up four years after the discontinuation of DPH, the patient was entirely symptom free.

CARDIOVASCULAR DISORDERS

Summary

The first evidence that diphenylhydantoin would be useful in cardiology was presented by Harris and Kokernot in 1950 when they showed that it reversed cardiac arrhythmias in dogs. The first evidence that DPH was useful in the treatment of cardiac arrhythmias, in man, was presented in a remarkable paper by Leonard in 1958. These studies, and subsequent studies, of the treatment of cardiac arrhythmias are summarized in Vol. I on pp. 171–76. They show the progression of use of DPH as a therapeutic substance for cardiac arrhythmias.

Studies that have been published in the last few years greatly increase the understanding of DPH and point to broader uses in cardiovascular disorders. It has been demonstrated that DPH offsets the toxic effects of digitalis without impairing its inotropic benefits. A recent study suggests that DPH may enhance these inotropic benefits.[1] DPH's ability to offset toxic effects of digitalis enables larger amounts of digitalis to be given before toxic levels are reached.

The use of DPH in conduction defects has been further studied.[2] The preponderance of evidence suggests that DPH does not impair conduction. Recent studies indicate that it may improve conduction.[3]

A group of studies in animals indicates that DPH is useful against hypoxia. One of these studies shows that it protects the Purkinje fibers of the heart against oxygen lack. There is evidence that DPH improves coronary blood flow in animals, and there are indications that DPH increases cerebral blood flow in animals and also in man. One study suggests that DPH is useful in the treatment of hypertension in man and another reports that in animals it decreases cardiac calcification.

Consistent throughout both clinical and basic mechanisms studies is the evidence that DPH is rapidly effective, and that it has a wide margin of safety in comparison with other substances.

In addition to its specific actions, DPH has three general properties relevant to the treatment of cardiovascular disorders. These properties are its effectiveness against hypoxia,[4] its effectiveness against pain of a variety of conditions (without impairment of cognitive and motor functions),[5] and its effectiveness against fear and tension.[6]

Cardiac Arrhythmias

Cardiac arrhythmias have been reviewed in Vol. I (pp. 171–76). Many reviews on this subject have been published recently (see below.)[7]

In addition to recent studies of the use of DPH in cardiac arrhythmias, there are included here recent studies showing the effect

---

[1] Ref. 1085.

[2] Ref. 753, 764, 793, 816, 826, 830, 831, 832, 833, 884, 923, 935, 1114, 1120, 1264, 1339, 1390, 1434, 1450, 1488, 1562, 1590, 1645, 1710.

[3] Ref. 753, 764, 793, 816, 826, 830, 831, 884, 935, 1264, 1434, 1488, 1562, 1645, 1710.

[4] Ref. 164, 699, 717, 804, 1160, 1216, 1373, 1576, 1591.

[5] Ref. 3, 9, 14, 15, 16, 31, 40, 48, 54, 66, 68, 78, 81, 111, 112, 113, 114, 129, 160, 161, 175, 180, 202, 214, 224, 227, 295, 304, 315, 317, 329, 330, 338, 380, 384, 386, 420, 422, 429, 465, 518, 543, 551, 564, 583, 586, 587, 605, 611, 633, 693, 707, 727, 732, 744, 747, 748, 881, 883, 1066, 1116, 1171, 1192, 1242, 1243, 1299, 1342, 1360, 1369, 1444, 1501, 1541, 1611, 1657, 1658, 1676.

[6] See Thought, Mood and Behavior, p. 157, Vol. I and p. 208, Vol. II.

[7] ITALY: Lotto, et al., *Cardiologia Pratica* (1971),[1307] Porciello and Zanini, *Fracastoro* (1971),[1425] Porciello, et al., *Giornale Italiano Cardiologia* (1972).[1426]
SWITZERLAND: Bender, *Schweizerische Medizinische Wochenschrift* (1973),[817] Burckhardt and Sefidpar, *Schweizerische Rundschau Medizinische* (1971),[880] Vaughan Williams, *Schweizerische Medizinische Wochenschrift* (1973).[1946]
NETHERLANDS: Van Dijk, *Folia Medica Neerlandica* (1971).[1638]
GERMANY: Herbinger, *Wiener Medizinische Wochenschrift* (1971).[1148]
ROMANIA: Fica, et al., *Medicina Interna* (1971).[1029]
UNITED STATES: American Medical Association on Drugs, *AMA* (1971),[762] Damato, *Progress in Cardiovascular Diseases* (1969),[936] Danzig, *Nebraska Medical Journal* (1971),[941] Doherty, *Annals of Internal Medicine* (1973),[969] Dreifus, *Cardiovascular Therapy, The Art and The Science* (1971),[975] Dreifus and Watanabe, *American Heart Journal* (1970),[972] Dreifus, et al., *American Heart Journal* (1974),[973] Gettes, *American Journal of Cardiology* (1971),[1067] Goldstein, *American Journal of Pharmacy* (1973),[1084] Huffman and Azarnoff, *Rational Drug Therapy* (1974),[1170] Lawrence, *Topics on Medicinal Chemistry* (1970),[1261] Levitt, et al., *Mt. Sinai Journal of Medicine* (1970),[1277] Lown, et al., *Circulation* (1973),[1311] Lucchesi, *University of Michigan Medical Center Journal* (1971),[1312] Mason, et al., *Drugs, Part I and Part II* (1973),[1336] and [1537] Mason, et al., *The Acute Cardiac Emergency—Diagnosis and Management* (1972),[1335] Mason, et al., *Cardiovascular Therapy, The Art and The Science* (1971),[1338] Moss and Patton, *Antiarrhythmic Agents* (1973),[1372] Preston, et al., *Geriatrics* (1973),[1429] Schick and Scheuer, *American Heart Journal* (1974),[1508] Schwender, *Annual Reports in Medicinal Chemistry* (1970),[1515] Smith, *New England Journal of Medicine* (1973).[1563]

of DPH in cardiac conduction, myocardial infarction, angina pectoris, hypokalemia, cardioversion, hypertension and cerebral blood flow.

Arrhythmias—Digitalis

HANSEN and WAGENER, *Deutsche Medizinische Wochenschrift* (1971),[1121] in a controlled study of 200 patients with DPH and 300 patients without DPH, evaluated the effect of diphenylhydantoin when added to cardiac glycoside administration.

By combining DPH and glycosides, the incidence of arrhythmias was reduced from 21% in the non-DPH group to 2.5% in the DPH-treated group. This significantly enhanced the possibility of achieving adequate digitalization.

The authors state that this clinical experience indicates that DPH administration reduces the toxic effect of glycosides in man without adverse influence on their positive inotropic effect. Thus, the use of DPH improves the chance of effective treatment in heart failure.

GATTENLOHNER and SCHNEIDER, *Munchener Medizinische Wochenschrift* (1969),[1052] reported on the results of their study of cardiac hemodynamics during the intravenous use of diphenylhydantoin. They found that DPH has very good antiarrhythmic efficiency, especially in digitalis-induced arrhythmias where it may be life saving.

The authors state that DPH in the doses which they used (125 and 250 mg per patient) did not change cardiac output or stroke volume.

CHUNG, *Modern Treatment* (1971),[905] in a review of digitalis therapy, states that various clinical investigations have demonstrated that diphenylhydantoin is effective in treating digitalis-induced arrhythmias, including paroxysmal atrial tachycardia, A-V nodal (junctional) rhythm, wandering atrial pacemaker,

ventricular bigeminy and multifocal ventricular tachycardia. Most patients respond within less than a minute to five minutes with intravenous administration of DPH. After conversion to sinus rhythm or the disappearance of the arrhythmia, oral maintenance doses between 300 and 400 mg daily, in divided doses, are sufficient.

The author states that DPH has prophylactic value when given before direct-current shock to the digitalized patient, since DPH is capable of preventing arrhythmias induced by cardioversion. The author states that DPH is probably the safest and most effective drug in the treatment of all types of digitalis-induced tachyarrhythmias.

STAZI and MARASA, *Annali di Medicina Navale* (1972),[1590] in a review, state that during the past few years diphenylhydantoin has become the drug of choice for use against cardiac arrhythmias due to intoxication from digitalis. The authors state that DPH has the following properties: 1) it suppresses atrial and ventricular hyperexcitability; 2) it reduces increased ventricular automatism; 3) at the usual therapeutic dosage (5 mg/kg), it has little effect on the automatism of the sinus and on intraventricular conduction; 4) it facilitates or leaves unaltered A-V conduction; and 5) it shortens the refractory period.

In addition to its therapeutic action, the authors state that DPH also exerts prophylactic effect. Its preventive administration has been shown to permit up to a 224% increase in the usable dose of digitalis, without interfering with its inotropic benefit.

SMITH and HABER, *New England Journal of Medicine* (1973),[1562] in a review of digitalis toxicity, say that toxic manifestations of digitalis persist as one of the most prevalent adverse drug reactions encountered in clinical practice.

In discussing substances therapeutic in digitalis toxic ectopic arrhythmias, the authors state that diphenylhydantoin is a highly useful drug. It has little adverse effect on sino-atrial rate, atrial conduction, atrioventricular conduction or conduction in the His-Purkinje system. Indeed, DPH may improve sinoatrial block and atrioventricular conduction under some circumstances.

RUMACK, WOLFE and GILFRICH, *British Heart Journal* (1974),[1488] detailed the effective treatment with diphenylhydantoin in a seventeen-year-old patient who attempted suicide with a massive digoxin overdose. Fifty tablets of digoxin (0.25 mg) were ingested.[1] Serum digoxin levels reached 35 ng/ml. Pronounced hyperkalemia[2] was noted fourteen hours after ingestion.

The authors state that though several papers suggest that very large doses of DPH are necessary to overcome digitalis intoxication, they did not find this to be the case. The patient responded to seven doses of 25 mg intravenous DPH over a period of thirty-six hours. Repeated doses of DPH are known to improve A-V conduction, resulting in greater atrial input to the ventricle. The patient had complete heart block early in her course and DPH restored this to a first-degree block.

The authors note that low doses of DPH were effective in this case and they suggest that it should be used early in the treatment of acute digoxin overdose.

ADAMSKA-DYNIEWSKA, *Polish Medical Journal* (1970),[753] reported on forty-nine patients with chronic heart failure who received diphenylhydantoin (100–300 mg orally) together with cardiac glycosides (deslanoside 0.4 mg or ouabain 0.25 mg, intravenously).

In patients with chronic heart failure, the author states that combined administration of the average clinical doses of cardiac glycosides plus DPH can be applied in clinical conditions which require counteracting of the chrono- and dromotropic action of digitalis,

but without any interference with its beneficial effect on heart muscle contractility.

REVIEWS (DIGITALIS)

Levitt, Raines, Sohn, Standaert and Hirshfeld,[1277] Ellis and Dimond,[1007] Smith,[1563] Schwender,[1515] Doherty,[969] Burckhardt and Sefidpar,[880] Schick and Scheuer,[1508] Goldstein,[1084] Huffman and Azarnoff,[1170] and Danzig.[941]

Arrhythmias—Other

REIMANN, LEMMEL and THEISEN, *Munchener Medizinische Wochenschrift* (1971),[1450] found that in forty-seven of fifty patients diphenylhydantoin eliminated extrasystoles and tachycardias of both atrial and ventricular origin. They noted that A-V conduction was not delayed.

Intravenous injection of 125 to 375 mg was usually immediately effective.

EDDY and SINGH, *British Medical Journal* (1969),[987] treated thirty-seven patients with cardiac arrhythmias with intravenous diphenylhydantoin. Twenty-one had acute myocardial infarctions and sixteen had other conditions. There was a favorable response in eighteen of the twenty-one cases of myocardial infarction and in six of the other sixteen cases.

The authors make note that in a child with Ebstein's anomaly and recurrent supraventricular tachycardia, the response to oral DPH was very satisfactory, and when the drug was given for a long period as a prophylactic measure it led to significant improvement.

LESBRE, CATHALA, SALVADOR, FLORIO, LESCURE and MERIEL, *Archives des Maladies du Coeur et des Vaisseaux* (1969),[1264] investigated the antiarrhythmic value of diphenylhydantoin, both clinically and experimentally.

In the clinical study, a variety of arrhythmia disturbances were treated with DPH with the following results:

---

[1] Seventeen 400 mg tablets of meprobamate had also been ingested.
[2] For a report of beneficial effects of DPH in hypokalemia, see O'Reilly and MacDonald.[1390]

	PATIENTS	SUCCESSES
Atrial tachysystole	3	2
Atrial extrasystole	3	3
Ventricular extrasystoles	17	16
Bouts of tachycardia	3	3
First degree block	8	5
Second degree block	6	5

In addition, in forty patients with atrial fibrillation, DPH was given before electroconversion was attempted. In a similar group, forty patients were given a beta-blocking agent before cardioversion was attempted. A comparison of these two groups showed to the advantage of DPH.

In a laboratory study, the authors performed atrial pacing with variable rhythm on ten dogs previously intoxicated by digitalis, and observed the effect of DPH. In three of ten cases, they observed a shortening of the P-R interval without modification of rhythm. In another experiment, a ligature was placed on both branches of the left coronary artery, to create a ventricular dysrhythmia. When overdigitalization produced rhythm disturbances, DPH was remarkably efficient, and in nine of ten cases the arrhythmia disappeared during injection.

The authors note that DPH corrects the disturbances of both atrial and ventricular excitability without impairing atrioventricular conduction.

MATHUR, WAHAL, SETH and HAZRA, *Journal of the Indian Medical Association* (1971),[1339] state that diphenylhydantoin, administered orally to eighty-five patients with a variety of cardiac arrhythmias, was effective in the treatment of ventricular ectopics, ventricular tachycardia and in the majority of cases with supraventricular tachycardia. It was not found effective in cases with atrial fibrillation and heart block. Doses of DPH, 100 mg q.i.d. orally, were found to be safe and effective with minimal side effects.

STONE, KLEIN and LOWN, *Circulation*, (1971),[1598] state that the efficacy of diphenylhydantoin in preventing recurrent ventricular tachycardia was studied in ten patients, nine of whom had had myocardial infarction. The authors found DPH ineffective.

KOCH-WESER, *Archives of Internal Medicine* (1972),[1224] found diphenylhydantoin less effective than procainamide for the suppression of ventricular ectopic activity and prevention of serious ventricular arrhythmias in hospitalized patients with acute myocardial infarction. The author suggested that a trial of DPH in ambulatory patients with coronary heart disease appears worthwhile because its long-term administration is tolerated well by most patients.

KEMP, *Journal of the American Geriatrics Society* (1972),[1214] studied the effect of diphenylhydantoin on ventricular ectopic rhythms. These arrhythmias were not caused by digitalis. DPH was given to five patients and five patients were given placebo.

For the first three weeks the dosage of DPH was 100 mg q.i.d. Then for maintenance therapy during the rest of the three-month study the dosage was reduced to 100 mg t.i.d. The numbers of premature ventricular contractions during a five-minute continuous EKG monitoring period were recorded before therapy, after three weeks of therapy, and after three months of therapy.

There was a marked reduction in the number of ventricular ectopic beats in the DPH group compared with the control group, and the beneficial results continued despite reduction in the dosage of DPH.

Conduction

BISSETT, DE SOYZA, KANE and MURPHY, *The American Journal of Cardiology* (1974),[831] directly measured conduction in the His-Purkinje system in fourteen patients and found that diphenylhydantoin improved intraventricular conduction.

The authors state that the purpose of their

study was to determine the effect of DPH on intraventricular conduction in man. Utilizing the introduction of premature atrial beats, the relative refractory period of the His-Purkinje system and the functional refractory period of the atrioventricular (A-V) node were measured in fourteen patients before and after administration of DPH. Before infusion of DPH, His-Purkinje conduction delay occurred with right bundle branch block in nine patients, and with left bundle branch block in five patients. After infusion of DPH (5 mg/kg at a rate of 50 mg/min) the onset or degree of His-Purkinje delay was improved in all patients. In the nine patients, DPH reduced the relative refractory period of the His-Purkinje system to a value less than that of the functional refractory period of the A-V node, so that His-Purkinje conduction delay no longer occurred after DPH.

In the five patients, DPH also reduced the relative refractory period of the His-Purkinje system or altered the degree of aberrant conduction, or both.

The authors note that before the introduction of His-bundle recordings, early reports had suggested that DPH may have no effect on intraventricular conduction in man. The results of the present study significantly demonstrate that DPH does improve intraventricular conduction in man.

ANDERSON, DAVIS, DOVE and GRIGGS, *Neurology* (1973),[764] studied the effect of diphenylhydantoin on cardiac conduction in patients who suffered from myotonic dystrophy. They found that DPH was beneficial, not only for the myotonia, but also for cardiac conduction defects common in this disease.

In five of the eight patients treated with oral DPH the P-R interval was shortened by 5 to 35 msec. This was in marked contrast to quinine and procainamide. Quinine produced P-R interval prolongation in four of ten patients, and procainamide produced P-R interval prolongation in nine of ten patients.

The authors' studies indicate diffuse involvement of the His-Purkinje system in myotonic dystrophy. They note that studies by others in normal subjects have shown a depression of His-Purkinje conduction with procainamide and quinine, but not with DPH.

BENAIM, CHAPELLE and CHICHE, *Annales de Cardiologie et d'Angeiologie* (1972),[816] reported on fifteen patients with arrhythmia who were injected with doses of 5 to 10 mg/kg of diphenylhydantoin. Recordings of the His potential achieved during the therapeutic test showed that 1) the drug does not usually alter the frequency of the sinus node; 2) it definitely improves atrioventricular conduction. In fact, a shortening of the P-H interval was obtained eight times out of eleven in conducted sinus rhythmus; 3) in most cases it did not alter intraventricular conduction: H-V remained constant eleven times out of fifteen. In four cases, a depression in intraventricular conduction was noted with a lengthening of the H-V interval.

In conclusion, the authors emphasize how valuable diphenylhydantoin is in arrhythmias, where these are accompanied by atrioventricular conduction defects.

QUIRET, BENS, DUBOISSET, LESBRE and BERNASCONI, *Archives des Maladies du Coeur et des Vaisseaux* (1974),[1434] studied the cardiovascular effects of diphenylhydantoin in 105 patients. They state that DPH appears to have the following pharmacodynamic properties. It favors or in any case respects atrioventricular conduction as well as intraventricular conduction; it checks manifestations of atrial and/or ventricular hyperexcitability secondary to organic cardiopathy or an excess of digitalis; and it has little or no effect on sinoatrial automatism.

The authors conclude that DPH thus appears to be an effective antiarrhythmic as shown by their clinical trial covering 105 patients.

Damato, Berkowitz, Patton and Lau, *American Heart Journal* (1970),[935] showed that in thirteen patients diphenylhydantoin enhanced atrioventricular conduction (i.e., shortened the P-H interval) over various paced heart rates. Also DPH did not prolong intraventricular conduction as measured by H-Q interval.

These observations were made while studying His bundle activities with an electrode catheter technique. (See also Caracta, et al.)[884]

Myocardial Infarction

Hansen and Wagener, *Munchener Medizinische Wochenschrift* (1969),[1120] reported the effective use of diphenylhydantoin in the treatment of cardiac arrhythmias following myocardial infarction.

In fifty patients who had a fresh myocardial infarction, DPH was slowly injected intravenously with excellent tolerance. There was no evidence of a pronounced hypotensive effect. The duration of action of 125 mg of DPH administered intravenously was eight to ten hours.

The authors state that bradycardiac arrhythmia does not constitute a contraindication to DPH.

Yang, *Journal of the Kansas Medical Society* (1973),[1705] states, "When faced with an intractable ventricular tachycardia and bewildered by the failure of treatment, try diphenylhydantoin (DPH); it could be life saving."

The author reports on a case of intractable ventricular tachycardia following acute myocardial infarction. Procainamide, large doses of lidocaine, repeated DC countershock, and propranolol failed to convert this life threatening cardiac arrhythmia which was dramatically controlled with DPH. DPH abolished the persistent ventricular tachycardia, which was believed to be due to circus re-entry

rather than digitalis intoxication; it also permitted continuous digitalization when digitalis was so critically needed.

Angina Pectoris

Taylor, *Chest* (1974),[1611] reports the effectiveness of diphenylhydantoin in angina pectoris, based on a double-blind crossover study with sixteen patients. The patients had typical symptoms of angina pectoris including chest pain, discomfort and tightness, radiating to arm, neck or jaw, precipitated by exertion, emotion and cold, and accompanied by dyspnea.

No drug therapy, apart from glyceryl trinitrate, was taken in the two-week period prior to the trial. The double-blind study showed that oral DPH used as a prophylactic significantly reduced the frequency of the attacks and the severity of symptoms in patients with angina pectoris.[1]

Bernstein, Gold, Lang, Pappelbaum, Bazika and Corday, *JAMA* (1965),[18] in reporting on the effectiveness of diphenylhydantoin in the treatment of recurrent cardiac arrhythmias, noted that it was also useful in the treatment of angina pectoris in a sixty-seven year old female who had angina pectoris for six years.

When DPH was administered, 100 mg, orally three times a day, there was a marked lessening in the frequency and severity of the episodes of angina, and the patient reported a concurrent decrease in the frequency of palpitations, and a decrease in need for nitroglycerin. Before DPH, she required twelve

---

[1] Significant differences were not noted in initial pain but duration of pain was reduced. *Note:* This is consistent with the basic mechanisms findings that initial pain impulses are not interfered with by DPH, but that repetitive after-discharge impulses are eliminated or decreased by DPH.

Relevant basic mechanism studies are the demonstration of an increase in coronary blood flow by Gupta, et al.,[496] the improvement in coronary blood flow in dogs by Nayler, et al.[402] and by Haft, et al.[1110] and the improved survival, with DPH, of pigs after coronary occlusion by Zeft, et al.[392] and by Kong, et al.[433] See also Davies.[945]

to sixty nitroglycerin tablets per week; with DPH, she required only zero to four tablets per month.

Hypokalemia

O'REILLY and MACDONALD, *British Heart Journal* (1973),[1390] reported on the successful use of diphenylhydantoin in treating two cases of ventricular arrhythmia induced by hypokalemia.

The authors state that the effectiveness of DPH in suppressing a variety of ventricular arrhythmias is well established. Despite this they say little emphasis has appeared in the published reports on the effectiveness of DPH in the presence of hypokalemia. This is the more remarkable as both procainamide and quinidine prolong the Q-T interval and so must aggravate the underlying defect which predisposes to arrhythmias when the serum potassium is low.[1]

The authors state that DPH, which has a different action at the cellular level and does not prolong the Q-T interval, seems an obvious choice in such cases.

The authors emphasize the usefulness of DPH in the management of the notoriously resistant and malignant arrhythmias associated with hypokalemia, where the usual antiarrhythmic agents are at best ineffective and may even be dangerous.

Cardioversion

CUAN-PEREZ and ORTIZ, *Archivos del Instituto de Cardiologia de Mexico* (1971),[923] found diphenylhydantoin effective in preventing recurrence of fibrillation after cardioversion.

The study included 230 cases. DPH was compared with quinidine and propranolol and the authors found DPH the drug of choice.

DPH and the other two drugs acted in similar fashion with regard to percentage of recurrence. However, the authors found DPH the drug of choice because no toxic complications were observed with it and this was not the case with quinidine and propranolol.

LINDE, TURNER and AWA, *Pediatrics* (1972),[1289] in a review, suggest that because of the increased risk in cardioversion following digitalis administration, cardioversion should be preceded by diphenylhydantoin (5 mg/kg) administered intravenously over ten minutes, monitoring the electrocardiogram and blood pressure.

Hypertension

ROSE, WILLIAMS, JAGGER, LAULER and THORN, *Metabolism* (1969),[1480] in a detailed study of two cases, demonstrate that diphenylhydantoin had a regulatory effect on labile hypertension.

When DPH was given to two patients whose blood pressure was abnormally elevated, the blood pressure returned to the normal range and stayed in the normal range as long as DPH was continued. DPH was discontinued in one of the patients, on two occasions, and each time his blood pressure rose to pretreatment abnormal levels. Each time, when DPH was reinstituted, the patient's blood pressure returned to the normal range.

Both of these patients had a paradoxical response to dexamethasone. The authors suggest that in patients of this type the regulation of corticotropin-releasing-factor may be critical in the control of hypertension.[2]

Cerebral Blood Flow

SLOSBERG, *Mount Sinai Medical Journal* (1970),[1560] reports on his eight years of experience with medical therapy for cerebrovas-

---

[1] Hypokalemia results in below normal potassium in nerve and muscle cells. Relevant to the above paper is the fact that DPH has been demonstrated to counteract low potassium levels in cells. (See "downhill movement" of ions, Ref. 387, 728, 731, 843, 1025, 1225, 1379, 1418, 1642, 1662.)

[2] The above study calls attention to the fact that further exploration of the therapeutic effect of DPH on hypertension is indicated. Also see Ref. 414 and 1282.

cular insufficiencies in a series of sixty-one patients.

The author found a simple and effective method for treating cerebrovascular insufficiencies of diverse origins. This method consists of the use of diphenylhydantoin in conjunction with carotid sinus therapy and support stockings. He states that these simple measures avoid the risk of surgical intervention and the hazards of anticoagulants.

In the sixty-one patients, most of whom were in their sixties and seventies, there were a variety of cerebrovascular insufficiencies. Among these were patients with occlusive disease of the neck arteries, occlusive disease of the intracranial arteries, hypoplastic arteries; vascular anomalies of the circle of Willis; patients with reaction to compression of the common carotid arteries or of the carotid sinus areas; and patients with postural hypotension. There were included patients who had been candidates for neck vascular surgery, anticoagulants, vasodilators, or no treatment at all.

The author states that this method has been both applicable and safe in a heterogeneous group of cases of cerebrovascular insufficiency for a period of over eight years; and has been well tolerated in both the acute stages of the illness and the long-term follow-up.

DANIEL, *Geriatrics* (1970),[938] states that symptoms of confusion which are so common in the aged often are caused by underlying physical illness, frequently cardiac and respiratory disorders resulting in cerebral anoxia. He states that diphenylhydantoin is therapeutically useful in this group, yet it is often overlooked.[1]

KENNEDY, ANDERSON and SOKOLOFF, *Neurology* (1958),[1216] studied cerebral blood flow in four epileptic children, before and after DPH for one week, using a modified nitrous oxide test. Although the group was small, the authors found the increase in mean blood flow to be statistically significant (from 85 to 102 cc per 100 gram per minute).[2]

Cardiovascular
Basic Mechanisms Studies

For some relevant basic mechanisms studies the reader is referred to: Bassett, Bigger and Hoffman[804] on the protective effects of DPH against hypoxia in Purkinje fibers of heart; Sperelakis and Henn[1580] on the effects of DPH on membrane potential of chick heart cells; Singh, Sinha, Rastogi, Dua and Kohli[1557] on the antiarrhythmic effects of DPH in dogs, Curtis[927] on the protective effects of DPH against atrial fibrillation in dogs; Gupta, Unal, Bashour and Webb[496] and Zeft, Rembert, Curry and Greenfield[1711] on the increase of coronary blood flow in dogs by DPH; Nayler, McInnes, Swann, Race, Carson and Lowe[402] on the increase of coronary blood flow and reduction of myocardial oxygen consumption by DPH in dogs; Zeft, Whalen, Ratliff, Davenport and McIntosh[392] on the prophylactic effect of DPH in preventing death from ventricular arrhythmias; Baldy-Moulinier[790] on the protective effect of DPH against cerebral ischemia in cats; Wax, Webb and Ecker[1668] on the effect of DPH on the resting potential and the action potential of ventricular heart muscle of the rat; Kleinfeld and Stein[1221] on the effect of DPH on the refractory period in canine Purkinje and ventricular fibers; Bigger, Weinberg, Kova-

---

[1] Occasionally a study is directly relevant in two separate clinical areas. This study also appears under Thought, Mood and Behavior Disorders.
   For fuller summary see p. 213.

[2] The above observations were part of a study in which the authors found that the mean cerebral blood flow in ten epileptics, with no medication, was significantly less than the mean cerebral blood flow of eleven normals, 91.6 vs. 106.3cc/100g./min.

lik, Harris, Cranfield and Hoffman[828] on the effects of DPH on excitability and automaticity in the canine heart; Rettura, Stamford and Seifter[1454] on the effect of DPH in reversal of cardiac calcification in rats; Goldstein, Penzotti, Kuehl, Prindle, Hall, Titus and Epstein[1085] on the protective effect of DPH against digoxin-induced arrhythmias and its enhancement of the inotropic benefits of digoxin; Hansen and Wagener,[1122] Scherlag, Helfant, Ricciutti and Damato,[1507] Baskin, Dutta and Marks,[801] and Watson and Woodbury[1663] on the effect of DPH in protecting against digitalis- and ouabain-induced arrhythmias. For summaries of these papers see Basic Mechanisms of Action, pp. 256–59.

TREATMENT OF PAIN

Summary

The effectiveness of DPH in a variety of painful conditions is reviewed in *The Broad Range of Use of DPH,* pp. 166–69. Among these are the cranial nerve neuralgias including trigeminal neuralgia and glossopharyngeal neuralgia,[1] peripheral nerve neuralgias including polyneuritis, syphilitic and diabetic neuralgias,[2] migraine headache,[3] post-operative pain,[4] phantom limb pain,[5] pain of skeletal muscle spasms and of smooth muscle spasms.[6]

In recent studies, summaries of which follow, DPH is reported to be useful against other painful conditions. These are the pain of Fabry's disease, thalamic pain, angina pectoris, painful touching syndrome (dysesthesia), post-herpetic neuralgia, post-sympathectomy neuralgia and pain of Wallenberg syndrome. Included elsewhere in this volume is found the effect of DPH on the pain of muscle spasms in myokymia[7] and multiple sclerosis.[8]

Initial messages of pain are necessary protective mechanisms. DPH does not interfere with initial electrical impulses.[9] However, when the usefulness of the initial messages of pain has ceased, persisting repetitive electrical impulses can occur (post-tetanic after-discharge). DPH reduces or abolishes post-tetanic after-discharge.[10] This seems to be an important mechanism by which DPH achieves its effect against pain.

DPH has general properties which enhance its usefulness in the treatment of pain.

1. DPH is not a sedative. In therapeutic doses, it does not slow cognitive and motor functions, as do many other substances used for pain.

2. DPH is not habit-forming. If it is necessary to use habit-forming substances for pain, smaller amounts of these substances may be used in conjunction with DPH.

Pain in Fabry's Disease

LOCKMAN, HUNNINGHAKE, KRIVIT and DESNICK, *Neurology* (1973),[1299] based on a double-blind study, report the effectiveness of DPH

---

[1] Ref. 9, 14, 15, 16, 31, 54, 68, 81, 113, 160, 175, 180, 202, 214, 224, 317, 330, 384, 518, 543, 583, 605, 611.

[2] Ref. 48, 129, 386.

[3] Ref. 40, 78, 111, 112, 113, 161, 227, 235, 315, 329, 338, 380, 420, 422, 429, 551, 587, 693, 748.

[4] Ref. 732, 744, 747.

[5] Ref. 704.

[6] Ref. 3, 66, 114, 304, 330, 429, 465, 551, 564, 586, 727.

[7] Ref. 633, 881, 1171, 1501, 1657, 1658, 1676.

[8] Ref. 304, 429, 586, 1192, 1242, 1243, 1342, 1360, 1541.

[9] Lack of interference with initial electrical impulses or other normal transmission, Ref. 90, 257, 289, 365, 458, 472, 954, 955, 1197, 1198, 1291, 1400, 1469, 1494, 1602.

[10] Ref. 90, 257, 264, 289, 359, 365, 458, 462, 467, 468, 472, 480, 580, 582, 789, 953, 954, 955, 1197, 1198, 1291, 1343, 1400, 1435, 1467, 1469, 1494, 1567, 1602, 1696.

in the relief of the pain of Fabry's disease, a rare disorder (see description below).[1]

The authors state that the single most debilitating and morbid aspect of Fabry's disease is the pain; this consists of two types, crises and continuous discomfort. Excruciating crises of abdominal, chest and muscle pain, as well as arthralgias and fever may occur episodically. These acute episodes occur periodically and may last several days. The second type of pain is initially noted in the fingers and toes and is characterized by a burning quality accompanied by paresthesias.

Since DPH has been reported to be useful in relieving pain associated with a variety of disease processes, the authors conducted a double-blind crossover study with eight patients to evaluate possible pain-relieving effects of DPH in Fabry's disease.

The medications compared were DPH, aspirin, and a multi-vitamin used as a placebo. The treatment period consisted of nine weeks with three-week treatment with each substance. Adults received 300 mg of DPH daily; younger patients less. The daily dose of aspirin was 1800 mg per day.

The difference in relief between DPH and both aspirin and multi-vitamins was statistically significant (less than 0.001).

The authors note that the pain in Fabry's disease is unrelieved by salicylates and it is only partially relieved by narcotics at soporific doses.

Thalamic Pain

CANTOR, *British Medical Journal* (1972),[883] reports that in two patients with thalamic pain, both experienced good relief with diphenylhydantoin.

The author states that the treatment of the painful, burning dysesthesias which can occur after thalamic infarction has been a particularly vexing problem, in that a variety of drugs have been tried with variable but generally ineffective results.

The author notes, with references to the literature, that relief of severe persistent pain by DPH has been reported in cases of trigeminal neuralgia, sphenopalatine neuralgia, tabes, and peripheral neuropathy. He also notes that in laboratory studies DPH has been shown to stabilize electrolyte transfer across neuronal membranes and to increase the neuronal threshold to repetitive stimulation.

In light of both the clinical and laboratory findings the author postulated that DPH might be effective in thalamic pain by reducing the spread of abnormally excessive excitatory discharges resulting from the thalamic lesion.

The author reports that in each of the cases, when DPH treatment was stopped, the painful dysesthesia recurred. Reinstitution of DPH again resulted in alleviation of the pain.

Angina Pectoris

TAYLOR, *Chest* (1974),[1611] in a double-blind crossover study with sixteen patients, found that DPH used prophylactically reduced the frequency and severity of the pain of angina pectoris.[2]

Dysesthesia (Painful Touching)

GERZ, *Physicians' Drug Manual* (1972),[1066] reports on an unusual case of "painful touching" (dysesthesia) in which a patient showed

---

[1] An X-linked inborn error of glycosphingolipid metabolism resulting from the deficient activity of ceramide trihexosidase, a specific alpha-galactosidase. The clinical manifestations are the result of the multisystemic accumulation of the glycosphingolipid substrate, trihexosyl ceramide, and include the characteristic cutaneous vascular lesions (angiokeratoma corporis diffusum), severe episodes of excruciating pain, and corneal opacities.

[2] For more detailed summary see Cardiovascular Disorders, p. 224.

dramatic response to diphenylhydantoin.

The patient, a forty-year-old male, reported that a painful intolerable cold stream would run all over his body when being touched by human hand. He had once been married for two weeks, but the marriage was not consummated, since both partners had to sleep in separate bedrooms because of his refusal to be touched. Since being touched caused him frequently to become dangerous and violent, he wanted a certificate from the clinic stating that he suffered from a "mental problem."

The patient presented a considerable diagnostic problem. He refused to have an EEG because of the extreme pain upon being touched. He was tried on a variety of medications without success.

Finally the patient was given DPH, 100 mg t.i.d. Within two weeks he was completely free of disturbing symptoms. Two months after taking DPH he reported that he had a girl friend and was now getting "the best things in life."

Neuralgias

HALLAQ and HARRIS, *Journal of American Osteopathic Association* (1969),[1116] report the successful use of diphenylhydantoin in a case of postherpetic neuralgia, with motor paralysis of an extremity, a rare complication. The patient, a seventy-six-year-old woman, had persistent pain in the right upper extremity, causing the entire limb to assume a semi-flexed and adducted position. Diagnosis after examination was postherpetic right brachial neuralgia and monoparesis.

After the seventh day in the hospital the patient was placed on DPH, 300 mg t.i.d. Within three days she was free of pain and remained free of pain when narcotic analgesics were withdrawn and an extra 100 mg of DPH was added.

With the relief of pain it became possible to institute vigorous rehabilitative and manipulative measures. Thirteen days after institution of DPH, 25% of lost functions were restored. The patient became an outpatient on a regimen of DPH and therapeutic exercises. A month later re-evaluation showed further improvement in function. The patient continued free of pain as long as she took DPH.

RASKIN, LEVINSON, PICKETT, HOFFMAN and FIELDS, *American Journal of Surgery* (1974),[1444] report on fifty-six patients who had had lumbar sympathectomy. Forty-four percent of these patients developed postsympathectomy neuralgia. Leg pain of these patients persisted one to two weeks. Aspirin or codeine were required by almost all patients who experienced this pain.

Eleven of the patients had pain of such great magnitude that they did not respond to meperidine. Carbamazepine was used with good effect in nine of these patients.

In two patients, intravenous diphenylhydantoin was used. Immediate relief from pain was experienced.

The authors conclude that DPH and carbamazepine appear to be useful in the management of the pain of the postsympathectomy syndrome.

Pain in Wallenberg Syndrome

MLADINICH, *JAMA* (1974),[1369] reports success in the use of diphenylhydantoin for relief of facial pain associated with Wallenberg syndrome. The author notes that the Wallenberg or posterior inferior cerebellar artery syndrome is the most common of the recognized brain stem "stroke" syndromes.

A forty-year-old man, who had developed this syndrome two years previously, had been afflicted with ipsilateral burning facial pain around the eye. Ordinary analgesics did not relieve this pain. Because of the value of DPH in other pain syndromes, the author tried DPH, 1 gm in divided doses the first day and then 300 mg daily. Symptoms of facial pain were considerably relieved within several days, and in follow-up he continued to be relatively free of pain.

MUSCLE DISORDERS

Summary

The effectiveness of diphenylhydantoin in continuous muscle fiber activity is observed clinically and demonstrated by quantitative electrophysiology.

In most of the cases which follow, a variety of medication had been used with little or no effect before the use of DPH. Clinical recovery following the use of DPH was usually prompt.

Electromyographic tests demonstrate the electrical abnormality in these disorders before the use of DPH and demonstrate correction of this abnormality with DPH. This provides evidence, in muscle, as in other areas, that DPH corrects inappropriate electrical activity such as post-tetanic after-discharge and dysrhythmias.

There are many symptoms in common in continuous muscle fiber activity disorders, and there are also differences. A wide variety of terminology is used for these disorders. The disorders are the cause of much suffering, are disabling, and frequently incapacitating.

Continuous Muscle Fiber Activity

The following report, by Isaacs, is believed to be the first publication of the successful use of diphenylhydantoin in the treatment of continuous muscle fiber activity syndrome.

ISAACS, *Journal of Neurology, Neurosurgery and Psychiatry* (1961),[176] in a study entitled "Continuous Muscle Fiber Activity" describes this disorder in a twelve-year-old boy.

This twelve-year-old boy walked with extreme difficulty, in a rigid manner. All his muscles showed evidence of fasciculation and were weak. He was constantly covered with a thin film of perspiration, had a persistent tachycardia and slight fever. Electrocardiograms appeared normal. However, electromyography recorded a state of constant rapid dysrhythmic discharge of independent muscle fibers. The spontaneous activity was increased by voluntary contraction, an increase which persisted for $30 \pm$ seconds after the stimulus had ceased.

The author defines the state as myotonic after-discharge and likens it to post-tetanic after-discharge.

The patient showed no improvement following the administration of quinidine, procainamide, cortisone or potassium depletion by exchange resins. Short-lived improvements followed injections of Dimercaprol.

Over the next two years the patient was further investigated whenever possible. His condition appeared static. Splints were made and applied at night to prevent flexion deformities. Growth remained retarded, muscle bulk had diminished, and he had brief attacks of acute respiratory embarrassment due to chest and diaphragmatic stiffness.

By this time, Isaacs had successfully used diphenylhydantoin with another patient. As a result of this success, the twelve-year-old boy was brought back to the hospital and treated with DPH. The author states that his recovery was dramatic.

A second case of continuous muscle fiber activity, a fifty-three-year-old male, was successfully treated with DPH.

The patient had been treated with atropine, quinine, cortisone, artane, adenosine triphosphate, thiamine diphosphate and procainamide without effect.

The patient's condition had been deteriorating for over a year, and he became unable to walk, and developed contractures in the upper and lower limbs, producing flexion deformities at the elbows and wrists and pes cavus. There were several episodes of respiratory distress and dysphagia.

Diphenylhydantoin was used in an attempt to diminish the bizarre uncontrolled discharge in the lower motor neuron which characterizes this condition.

The patient was given 100 mg of DPH every four hours. Marked improvement was noted over the next two days and the dose was reduced to 100 mg q.i.d.

The electromyography was vastly improved both at rest and on voluntary effort. The basic metabolic rate and the oxygen consumption had markedly improved when tested after two weeks of DPH therapy.

In a follow-up of the two patients five years later, Isaacs[1183] reports that both patients were still well, had lost their abnormal stiffness and live fairly normal lives. He also notes that whenever DPH has been stopped, the symptoms have returned.

Isaacs, *Journal of Neurology, Neurosurgery and Psychiatry* (1967),[1183] reports on another patient with continuous muscle fiber activity, a twenty-year-old Indian male. The rapid effectiveness of diphenylhydantoin was apparent. DPH, 100 mg q.i.d., enabled this patient to return to an almost normal state, within three days.

In discussing the basic physiological problem in this disorder, Isaacs notes that normal muscle is virtually electrically silent until contraction is initiated. In myotonia, however, during relaxation, the clinical problem becomes apparent because, as the author points out, this is when the myotonic after-discharge occurs.[1]

---

[1] The stabilization of myotonic after-discharge is a demonstration of the property of DPH to stabilize a hyperexcitable condition as in post-tetanic potentiation and post-tetanic after-discharge. (See Ref. 90, 257, 289, 365, 458, 467, 468, 472, 789, 954, 955, 1197, 1198, 1291, 1343, 1400, 1467, 1469, 1494, 1602.)

Mertens and Zschocke, *Klinische Wochenschrift* (1965),[251] in a paper entitled "Neuromyotonia" report on three cases. Each patient had in common a continuous spastic contraction of the entire skeletal musculature, which did not even diminish while asleep or under anesthesia. Extensive electromyographic, histologic and other laboratory studies confirmed the electrophysiological abnormality. Quinine, quinidine, novocamid, cortical hormones and saldiuretics had little or no effect.

Diphenylhydantoin and Mephenytoin were tried. DPH was far more effective. With two injections of DPH, 250 mg, at sixty-minute intervals it was possible to obtain significant elimination of spastic contractions and inhibition of movement in all muscle groups within two to four hours.

The authors state that with oral DPH they were able to maintain this astonishing effect. A trial of discontinuing the DPH resulted in recurrence or rapid increase of the abnormal contraction. Later carbamezapine was used with similar effectiveness on these patients.

Levy, Wittig and Ferraz, *Arquivo de Neuro-Psiquiat* (1965),[1280] in a paper entitled "Scleroderma Associated with Continuous Muscular Electrical Activity" described a case, difficult to diagnose, in which clinical examination and laboratory tests indicated probable scleroderma. However, there was a definite condition of continuous muscle fiber activity at rest, revealed by electromyography. The condition showed some clinical improvement with corticosteroids, although this improvement was not reflected on the electromyogram.

The authors expressed surprise at the results of the use of 300 mg of DPH daily because of its speed in markedly improving both the clinical picture and the abnormal electrical tracing in a few days.

Hughes and Matthews, *Journal of Neurology, Neurosurgery and Psychiatry* (1969),[1171] in a paper entitled "Pseudo-Myotonia and Myo-kymia" report on a man whose symptoms had gradually worsened from the age of twenty-two. When seen he was fifty-five. Electromyography demonstrated the patient's electrical abnormality. He had been tried on a variety of substances without benefit.

Thirty-two years after the first symptoms had been noted he was treated with 100 mg of diphenylhydantoin q.i.d. This produced immediate and continuing benefits. The patient found that he could control the stiffness adequately with 200 to 300 mg of DPH daily, although fasciculation continued and delayed relaxation of grip could still be detected. The patient noticed that if he stopped taking DPH for as short a period as twenty-four hours the symptoms would return.

Five years after the institution of DPH, carbamezapine was also tried and found effective. The patient seemed to prefer carbamezapine, but the authors stated that they failed to find any convincing difference in the response to the two medications.

GARDNER-MEDWIN and WALTON, *Lancet* (1969),[633] in a paper entitled "Myokymia with Impaired Muscular Relaxation," describe a twenty-one-year-old female who had suffered with this disorder for about four-and-a-half years. This patient had characteristic clinical and electromyographic evidence of myokymia, and had had operations on her tendons with only temporary relief.

The patient was treated with diphenylhydantoin, 100 mg t.i.d., and diazepam, 5 mg twice daily. On this treatment the patient improved considerably and was able to lead a relatively normal life.

WALLIS, VAN POZNAK, and PLUM, *Archives of Neurology* (1970),[1658] in a paper entitled "Generalized Muscular Stiffness, Fasciculations and Myokymia of Peripheral Nerve Origin" report on two cases with this disorder. Electromyographic and other laboratory findings were consistent with the clinical diagnosis.

In one case the authors state diphenylhydantoin, 100 mg t.i.d., provided dramatic relief. In the other case a three-day trial with DPH was not found effective. In the successful case, after one month of treatment, the DPH was discontinued, and three days later all pretreatment symptoms and findings had returned. With the reinstitution of DPH prompt relief recurred, and this has lasted for eight months to the present writing. This patient had been severely incapacitated and has returned almost to normal.

BUSCAINO, CARUSO, DE GIACOMO, LABIANCA and FERRANNINI, *Acta Neurologica* (1970),[881] in a paper entitled "Unusual Neuromuscular Pathology" describe a case of continuous muscle fiber activity syndrome (neuromyotonia).

The man, age forty-five, had suffered for twenty years from stiffness of all muscles, wide-spread fasciculations, myokymia and excessive sweating. The muscular stiffness was present even during sleep. The nature of the electrical abnormality in this disorder was observed on the electromyogram.

This condition, present for twenty years, had been treated with a variety of substances without success. The authors state that the condition was dramatically resolved by the use of diphenylhydantoin or carbamezapine.

WELCH, APPENZELLER and BICKNELL, *Neurology* (1972),[1676] in a study entitled "Peripheral Neuropathy with Myokymia, Sustained Muscular Contraction and Continuous Motor Unit Activity" describe a twenty-two-year-old female who over the years had had gradually increasing symptoms of this disorder. The patient's symptoms included stiffness and weakness of the upper arms and shoulders and proximal lower extremities, dysarthric speech and occasional labored respiration because of tightness of the chest wall.

The patient was tried with quinine regularly for one month but no change in symptoms was noted. Then the patient was given diphenylhydantoin, 100 mg before noon and 200 mg at bedtime, with almost immediate remission of the symptoms. This remission continued with daily DPH.

KOSTOV, TACHEV and NASTEV, *Zhurnal Nevropatologii i Psikhiatrii imeni S.S. Korsakova* (1973),[1231] in a paper entitled "Pseudo-Myotonia (Isaacs' Syndrome)" report on a case with a form of this syndrome characterized by muscular hypertonia mainly expressed in the distal regions of the extremities. Diffuse fascicular tics were present. Spontaneous electromyographic activity was present at rest, and typically did not disappear even after novocain blockade of the peripheral nerve.

Diphenylhydantoin and carbamezapine each had favorable therapeutic effect. Withdrawal of the medications resulted in a return of the disorder.

BHATT, VIJAYAN and DREYFUS, *California Medicine* (1971),[825] in a review of clinical and laboratory aspects of myotonia, state that of treatments which have been used successfully for myotonia, including diphenylhydantoin, procainamide, quinine, and adrenocorticotropic hormone, DPH appears to be the most effective, the safest and the best tolerated.

MUNSAT, *Neurology* (1967),[262] in a randomized, double-blind and crossover study, found diphenylhydantoin to be as effective as procainamide in relieving myotonia, both subjectively and objectively.

The author stated that DPH was better tolerated by patients than procainamide and, in addition, unlike procainamide, it did not increase preexisting cardiac conductive defects.

THOMPSON, *New England Journal of Medicine* (1972),[1614] in a letter to the editor wrote:

"Therapy of myotonia with diphenylhydantoin was reported by T. L. Munsat in *Neurology* (17:359, 1967). However, there has been little published in the literature to support or contradict his studies.

In three members of a family in my practice with myotonia congenita, diphenylhydantoin, 100 mg three times a day, was started on April 29, 1971. The patients were 16, 20 and 23 years of age. Their disabilities included inability to dance, difficulty getting up from a sitting position, difficulty relaxing grips, and some falling because of inability to relax the muscles.

On diphenylhydantoin therapy they are all much improved. The 16-year-old girl is particularly delighted because she can now dance. No side effects have occurred and the improvement is dramatic."

The writer says that certainly other patients with myotonia should be given the benefits of diphenylhydantoin.

GIMENEZ-ROLDAN and ESTEBAN, *European Neurology* (1973),[1073] reported a case of myotonia associated with hypothyroidism in which diphenylhydantoin and quinine sulfate was rapidly effective for some but not all of the symptoms.

ANDERSON, DAVIS, DOVE and GRIGGS, *Neurology* (1973),[764] studied the effect of diphenylhydantoin on cardiac conduction in patients who suffered from myotonic dystrophy. They found that DPH was beneficial, not only for the myotonia, but also for cardiac conduction defects common in this disease.

In five of the eight patients treated with oral DPH the P-R interval was shortened by 5 to 35 msec. This was in marked contrast to quinine and procainamide. Quinine produced P-R interval prolongation in four of ten patients, and procainamide produced P-R interval prolongation in nine of ten patients.

The authors' studies indicate diffuse involvement of the His-Purkinje system in myotonic dystrophy. They note that studies by others in normal subjects have shown a depression of His-Purkinje conduction with procainamide and quinine, but not with DPH.

The authors state that since they and others have found that DPH is an effective anti-myotonic agent and since their own findings have shown that it does not have negative effects on conduction abnormalities as do quinine and procainamide, DPH is the treatment of choice in myotonic dystrophy.

Choreoathetosis

TASSINARI and FINE, *Proceedings of the Australian Association of Neurologists* (1969),[1610] give the history of a patient with paroxysmal choreoathetosis, a twenty-three-year-old man, complaining of episodes of uncontrollable involuntary movements since the age of eleven. The writhing, flinging movements in this patient were of such intensity that sometimes the patient was thrown to the floor.

The patient was treated with diphenylhydantoin, 100 mg t.i.d., and Valium, 5 mg t.i.d. With this treatment the frequency and intensity of attacks were reduced to once or twice a week and never severe enough to cause a fall, and the patient resumed a normal social life. On the two occasions that the treatment was interrupted, there followed a reappearance of attacks as frequent and severe as before treatment.

JUNG, CHEN and BRODY, *Neurology* (1973),[1200] report on ten cases of paroxysmal choreoathetosis in two families. They also report on two sporadic cases. The authors state that to their knowledge this is the first report of its occurrence among the Chinese. The authors state that the onset of this disorder usually appears in childhood with sudden brief and intermittent choreoathetoid movements of the extremities and face. Episodes may occur several times daily with varying degrees of bizarre posturing, which can reach

such intensity that the patient is hurled to the floor. Consciousness is not lost. With age these attacks tend to diminish in frequency and severity, and this sometimes makes it more difficult to evaluate the effectiveness of drugs.

The authors state that the therapeutic effect of diphenylhydantoin is so prompt and so dramatic that there is little doubt as to the effectiveness of the treatment. They state that except for one early report, DPH has been the drug of choice for this disorder.

LOONG and ONG, *Journal of Neurology, Neurosurgery and Psychiatry* (1973),[1305] reported a case of a twenty-one-year-old Chinese man whose choreoathetosis was successfully treated with diphenylhydantoin after chlordiazepoxide and amitriptyline produced no improvement. DPH 100 mg t.i.d. was effective in completely freeing the patient of "big" attacks, and "small" ones occurred only a few times a day. L-dopa was also effective in this case. When DPH was withdrawn symptoms returned; when DPH was reinstituted improvement again occurred.

Other Muscle Disorders

Steroid Myopathy

STERN, GRUENER and AMUNDSEN, *JAMA* (1973),[1594] treated a forty-seven-year-old man with steroid myopathy with diphenylhydantoin with favorable results. The myopathy was well documented and the effectiveness of DPH was demonstrated by a double-blind crossover method.

The patient required steroids (prednisolone) for his rheumatoid arthritis. Without changing the regimen of prednisolone, two six-week trial periods of DPH and placebo capsules were instituted with crossover every three weeks. The results of the two trials revealed that while on DPH there was a significant improvement as measured by increase in hip flexor strength as contrasted to placebo. Muscle strength was measured with a dynamometer.

The authors state that although this was only one case, the results are encouraging because they suggest that DPH, when used along with steroids, may decrease the risk of steroid myopathy. (See Gruener and Stern,[1103] DPH protection against steroid myopathy in mice. See Houck, et al.,[172,501,502] DPH protection against side effects of cortisone as observed in the skin of rats.)

Restless Legs

Hogg, *Practitioner* (1972),[1155] in a paper on "Restless Legs or Ekbom's Syndrome" describes the successful treatment of seven cases of "restless legs" with diphenylhydantoin. The author says that interest in this syndrome was renewed by Ekbom twenty-six years ago, but it was first described as far back as 1685. It is still a syndrome of unknown etiology. Vasodilators, iron intravenously and intravenous Dextran have been tried with only partial success.

The syndrome, he states, derives its name "restless legs" from the fact that the majority of these patients are unable to rest in bed at night and take to moving their legs sometimes vigorously because of the gnawing aches in them and the "crawling pains."

The author states that this syndrome can be seen in all age groups, but chiefly in premenopausal women. Frequently these patients suffer from depression or anxiety states.

The author gives brief descriptions of the seven cases.

In each of the seven patients, 100 mg of diphenylhydantoin daily resulted in cessation of symptoms. Since the symptoms occurred at night, and interrupted sleep, the 100 mg was given before going to bed.

Parkinson's Syndrome

Domzal, *Neurologia i Neurochirurgia Polska* (1972),[971] reported on the use of diphenylhydantoin in treating fourteen patients exhibiting a complete clinical picture of Parkinson's syndrome. Eight of these patients had received synthetic anti-cholinergic drugs, and six had not received any previous anti-Parkinsonism medication. The clinical condition of these patients was evaluated according to four parameters, i.e., tremor, sluggishness, muscle tone and the patient's frame of mind.

With DPH, in doses of 300–400 mg per day over a two-week period, eleven patients reported marked improvement in sense of well-being; ten reported improvement in muscle tone; and six exhibited improvement in general tremor (tremor disappeared entirely in three). Steadier mobility, better expression and improved gait were observed in three patients.

The author says that it is apparent that DPH exerts a favorable effect on the clinical condition in some cases of Parkinsonism, appearing to be more effective in the initial stages of the disease. DPH affects the increase of muscle tone most favorably, but immobility, disturbances of posture, gait and speech are less affected.

The author stated that there are few drugs that can withstand the test of time and still continue to stir increasing interest; DPH, in particular, belongs in this category.

Muscle Spasms

Satoyoshi and Yamada, *Archives of Neurology* (1967),[1501] in a paper entitled "Recurrent Muscle Spasms of Central Origin" present two cases of painful intermittent muscle spasms of a slowly progressive nature. Each began in early life. Multiple bony abnormalities with epiphyseal destruction and retarded growth, diarrhea, disturbed carbohydrate metabolism and endocrine disorders were additional features. Numerous drugs were given without effect on the symptoms: potassium chloride, acetazolamide, hydrochlorothiazide, Vitamin D, desoxycorticosterone, dexamethazone, hydrocortisone, prednisolone, diazepoxide, diazepam, neostigmine, mephenesin and phenobarbital.

Diphenylhydantoin (200 to 300 mg daily by mouth) was effective. This effectiveness was further evidenced by the fact that when the medicine was withdrawn the attacks would return. Combination of DPH, quinine sulfate and chlorpromazine was found to be even more effective than DPH by itself. Even with this regimen muscle spasms could not be completely forestalled.

Later in 1967 a third case was presented by Satoyoshi[1502] in which he reports similar results.

MATTHEWS, *Brain* (1958),[1342] reported the effectiveness of diphenylhydantoin in the treatment of tonic seizures in a patient with multiple sclerosis. When DPH, 100 mg t.i.d. was prescribed, the attacks stopped within two days. Treatment was stopped after two months with no return of these symptoms. Other sensory and ataxic symptoms recurred later, characteristic of multiple sclerosis. It was not claimed by the author that DPH had any primary beneficial action on multiple sclerosis itself, but that it was found useful in the treatment of the painful spasms of this disorder.

JOYNT and GREEN, *Archives of Neurology* (1962),[1192] found that diphenylhydantoin had definite suppressing effects on tonic seizures in three patients with multiple sclerosis.

KUROIWA and SHIBASAKI, *Folia Psychiatrica et Neurologica Japonica* (1968),[1243] found that diphenylhydantoin and/or carbamazepine were useful in suppressing the painful tonic spasms in four patients with multiple sclerosis. The authors noted that various other drugs (phenobarbital, diazepam, chlorpromazine, biperiden, procainamide, quinine hydrochloride, calcium gluconate and gamma-hydroxy beta-amino butyric acid) were tried in all four cases, but all without success.

The authors noted that the beneficial effects of DPH might relate to its known regulatory effects on spinal cord and peripheral nerves (see also Shibasaki and Kuroiwa).[1541]

Intractable Hiccups

PETROSKI and PATEL, *Lancet* (1974),[1411] in a letter to the editor, report on a patient with refractory hiccups. On admission to the hospital, the patient, a thirty-seven-year-old man, had a three-year history of hypertension, an old right-hand hemiparesis and hiccups. He was mentally alert, but repetitive attacks of hiccups seriously interfered with his feeding and sleep and left him exhausted. The hiccups did not respond to pharyngeal stimulation by catheter or parenteral prochlorperazine, up to 50 mg per day, nor did the frequency vary with sleep. By the sixth day the frequency of hiccups increased to more than thirty per minute. On the hypothesis that an irritable focus in the area of the inspiratory center of the medulla might be occurring, diphenylhydantoin was started.

Initially 200 mg of DPH intravenously was given over five minutes, completely eliminating hiccuping within an hour. Then 100 mg. q.i.d. orally was continued until the eleventh day without any recurrence of hiccups.

DAVIS, *Lancet* (1974),[946] in a letter to the editor, stated that he was interested to read the report by Petroski and Patel on the use of DPH in treating hiccups. He states: "Unfortunately, in a patient with long-established hiccups with whom I have recently been concerned, this drug (DPH) was ineffective. Nevertheless, it should no doubt be added to the list of preparations to be considered in cases of intractable hiccup."

Respiratory Myoclonus

PHILLIPS and ELDRIDGE, *New England Journal of Medicine* (1973),[1414] in a paper entitled "Respiratory Myoclonus (Leeuwenhoek's Disease)" describe a case of abnormal repetitive diaphragmatic contractions in which treatment with diphenylhydantoin either abolished or markedly reduced the abnormal activity. The authors state that these cases are sometimes called diaphragmatic flutter, and they suggest the term respiratory myoclonus might be appropriate.

The authors note that diphenylhydantoin had escaped previous reported clinical trial for this disorder. Because of its established effect on synapse and membrane stabilization they decided to try it on this patient. A dosage of 300 mg daily was not found effective, but at 400 mg daily the desired effect occurred. Improvement was noted after five or six days of therapy. DPH was discontinued on three separate occasions with return of the disorder.

A diaphragmatic electromyogram taken during DPH therapy, during quiet breathing, showed definite slowing of the respiratory rate. More important was the absence of the alternating electrical bursts of activity and silence during inspiration, and the disappearance of abnormal activity during expiration. Identical desired effects were also demonstrated by electromyography in the scalene and intercostal muscles.

The authors state that a trial of quinidine to a maximum of three grams daily had been ineffective. At the time of the writing the patient had taken DPH daily for about a year with no recurrence of symptoms.

The authors note that in the past the only effective form of therapy for this disorder has been phrenicectomy. They state that therapy with DPH might be effective in some patients with this disorder.

Cases in Which DPH Not Found Useful

Diphenylhydantoin was reported to not be useful in a case of post-stroke palatal myoclonus,[1462] a case of hereditary essential myoclonus,[942] a case of facial contraction in brain stem glioma,[1613] a case of congenital disorder of motor control,[1701] a case of involuntary movements associated with erythrocyte malformations,[922] and one of facial spasm associated with Paget's disease.[952] Twelve patients were reported not significantly helped with "irritable bowel syndrome."[1098]

TREATMENT OF OTHER DISORDERS

Scleroderma

MORGAN, *Cutis* (1971),[1371] reports that patients with scleroderma, treated with DPH, showed marked improvement, in a study comparing them with patients treated by conventional therapy.

The study consisted of sixty-five patients with two general types of scleroderma, morphea and systemic. Twenty-nine were treated with DPH and thirty-six were treated by conventional means.

The author notes that no therapeutic measures advocated in the past have resulted in consistent improvement in scleroderma, although on occasion some symptoms and complications have shown response to a wide variety of substances.

The attention of the author was brought to the use of DPH in scleroderma in an unusual way. A sixty-seven-year-old woman had progressive generalized morphea with associated headaches, arthralgias, dysphagia, and palmar and plantar hyperhidrosis. For over a year numerous medications (including phenylbutazone, methysergide, diazepam, belladonna, alkaloids, proteolytic enzymes, entozyme, DMSO, tocopherol, potassium p-aminobenzoate, ergotamine tartrate, steroids, and tolazoline) had failed to halt progression of the disease.

The patient had a mild stroke and as a result was placed on DPH by attending neurologists. Progressive improvement in scleroderma was evident three weeks after she began DPH therapy. Two years later her skin showed no evidence of scleroderma and has remained clear to date.

Because of the unexpected improvement in this case, the author decided to explore the possibility that DPH might be effective in the treatment of scleroderma. In his study the author used DPH in twenty-nine patients and conventional therapy in thirty-six patients. The results follow:

NUMBER OF PATIENTS	WITH DPH 29	OTHER THERAPY OR NONE 36
Worse	0 (0%)	11 (30.5%)
No change	2 (7%)	10 (28%)
Improved (patient and doctor agree)	12 (41.5%)	9 (25%)
Complete clearing of sclerosis	12 (41.5%)	4 (11%)
Complete clearing of sclerosis plus atrophy and pigment	3 (10%)	2 (5.5%)

The author concludes that in this series of patients with scleroderma, the administration of DPH not only appeared to prevent progression of sclerosis but to aid in its resolution.[1,2]

[1] In a smaller group of patients, the author also investigated the use of DPH in a less serious disorder, lichen sclerosis et atrophicus, and found DPH effective but, in this case, no more than conventional therapy.

[2] Of interest in connection with this study are both clinical and basic mechanisms studies which report other healing effects of DPH. (See Ref. 25, 127, 171, 172, 188, 189, 335, 336, 337, 339, 341, 343, 344, 499, 500, 501, 502, 504, 505, 669, 730, 811, 894, 1080, 1104, 1164, 1403, 1485, 1504.)

Asthma

SHAH, VORA, KARKHANIS and TALWALKAR, *Indian Journal of Chest Diseases* (1970),[1535] conducted a study of the usefulness of DPH in bronchial asthma in twenty-seven patients. Both clinical and laboratory observations were made.

The authors state that the prevention of the spread of electrical discharge is one of the most important, interesting and unexploited pharmacological properties of diphenylhydantoin. Noting that other paroxysmal disorders have responded to DPH, they felt that its use in the paroxysmal spasm of asthma should be explored.

In the study of the twenty-seven patients, careful histories were recorded, the severity of asthma was graded by age at onset, frequency of attacks during past twelve months, absenteeism from work, number of days absent in the last month, and number of sleepless nights in the last month. Effort tolerance tests were performed during attacks and between attacks. Appraisal of previous therapy during the last month was noted by the number of adrenalin and/or aminophylline injections and oral drugs—bronchodilators and/or steroids. Each patient had laboratory investigations, chest x-ray and electrocardiogram to exclude any cardiopulmonary disease simulating bronchial asthma. Ventilation studies, including maximum breathing capacity, were carried out initially and repeated at weekly follow-up examinations. At the end of the treatment period all examinations were repeated.

Before starting patients on DPH therapy all other medicines which were being taken were discontinued. Dosage was 100 mg DPH t.i.d. The trial was for one month. Assessment of subjective and objective results were verified by all participating physicians.

While on DPH, of the total of twenty-seven patients, subjective relief was impressive in twenty-five. These patients found complete or at least partial relief. Fifteen patients showed improved ventilation tests. The group of patients as a whole were generally more relaxed and, although some wheezing persisted in twelve patients, the distress was less evident.

The results of this study led the authors to suggest that DPH would seem to be a useful anti-asthmatic agent.[1]

WINTER, *International Surgery* (1972),[1692] presents a detailed study of surgical techniques in bilateral carotid body resection for asthma and emphysema.

In this study the author says that severe respiratory problems require careful preoperative and postoperative medical treatment. He states that in patients with severe respiratory problems he does not use narcotics and that, in his opinion, they should never be used in such cases. He further says that barbiturates should also be avoided, except in small doses, and that tranquilizers should only be used in small doses.

The author states that he has found DPH of considerable value in severe respiratory problems, both preoperatively and postoperatively. He notes that DPH appears to have special value in patients with bronchospastic problems.[2]

Hyperthyroidism

ROMERO, MARANON and BOBILLO, *Revista Iberica de Endocrinologia* (1970),[1479] review in detail a variety of therapeutic approaches in the treatment of hyperthyroidism. They state that in addition to well-known general measures of rest, healthful diet, food supplements and avoidance of stressful situations, therapeutic measures that are commonly employed are thyroidostatic treatment, surgical resection and radioisotopic treatment. Although each of these methods has therapeutic usefulness, they are not without complications and side effects, and there is no general agreement that any is thoroughly satisfactory.

The authors state that about twenty years ago they started using diphenylhydantoin, 50 mg t.i.d., usually in combination with hydrazides, 50 mg q.i.d. The treatment consisted of alternating DPH one week with hydrazides the next week. Based on this twenty years of experience with DPH in the treatment of three hundred patients with various forms of hyperthyroidism, the authors conclude that the lack of complications in this long experience has indicated that DPH is safe as well as effective.[3] The exacting regulation of dosage frequently required with other substances, to avoid hypothyroidism, has not been a problem with this regimen.

Response to this treatment has been consistently favorable, and 70% of the patients require no change in this regimen. In the other 30% of the patients, the use of DPH every day instead of every other week, and continuing hydrazides every other week, achieved a high percentage of success.

In the last two years, as a result of their eighteen years' favorable clinical experience with DPH, the authors initiated a study on a detailed basis. They state that in this study one hundred patients with hyperthyroidism have been treated with DPH and hydrazides.

---

[1] A number of people with emphysema have reported to the Dreyfus Medical Foundation that since taking DPH for other reasons they had experienced improvement in their breathing. There does not appear to be published work on the use of DPH for emphysema, but it would seem an area for research, particularly in view of DPH's reported anti-anoxic effects. (See Anti-anoxic Effects of DPH, p. 252.)

[2] See Anti-anoxic Effects of DPH, p. 252.

[3] Hansen, Skovsted, Lauridsen, Birk, Kirkegaard and Siersbaek-Nielsen[1125] studied the effect of DPH on serum T_3 and T_4. During the course of this study it was noted that one of two patients with hyperthyroidism, on DPH for four weeks, showed considerable improvement in the clinical picture, both subjectively and objectively. There was also a decrease in thyroid hormone levels.

At the time of their report, full data encompassed nineteen of these patients. Based on this data, the authors state that the clinical effects are as follows: eight showed very favorable improvement, four favorable improvement, four moderate improvement, one slight improvement, and two no improvement. Along with these improvements, marked relief of nervousness characteristic of this disorder was also observed.

The authors state that it is significant, and unlike what is often observed with other thyroidostatic drugs, that neither the size of the goiter nor the exophthalmus increased in any of these patients. Further, in some of the patients, decrease in size of the goiter and of the exophthalmus was very evident.

The authors state that the results have been so encouraging with these nineteen patients of the study of one hundred, that they felt that this interim report should be made.

Glaucomatous Field Loss

BECKER and PODOS, *Symposium on Ocular Therapy* (1973),[812] in earlier studies had found that diphenylhydantoin partly protected the optic nerve *in vitro* when subjected to anoxia, cyanide or ouabain. Because of these findings, the authors decided to explore the possibility that DPH might reverse some of the effects of ischemia on the optic nerve, in humans.

The authors instituted a pilot study to examine the effects of diphenylhydantoin in glaucomatous field loss. This study involved fifty patients who were given 100 mg DPH t.i.d. for two to five months. The effects on visual fields were quantitatively recorded by means of Goldmann perimetry and/or static perimetry.

When treated with DPH, only one of the fifty patients had a worsening of visual fields, twenty-nine showed no worsening, and twenty patients showed improvement in visual fields. This salutary effect in visual fields occurred despite the fact that intraocular pressures, which previously had been deleterious, persisted. In seven of the patients that showed improvement, DPH was discontinued and worsening of visual fields occurred. The authors found of considerable interest the fact that when DPH was reinstituted in five of these seven patients, improvement in visual fields again occurred.

The authors conclude that this pilot study suggests that where the blood supply is decreased, DPH may be able to protect optic nerve function. The authors state that a larger and controlled study has been initiated by them on ischemic neuropathy.[1]

Glycogen Storage Disease

JUBIZ and RALLISON, *Archives of Internal Medicine* (1974),[1193] report on four patients with glycogen storage disease, two with debranching system deficiency, one with phosphorylase deficiency and one with glucose-6-phosphatase deficiency.

The authors state that these patients were treated with diphenylhydantoin for more than two years and there was a good response. This was evidenced by a reduction in liver size and a reduction in hepatic glycogen content. Hyperlacticacidemia improved.

As a result of their findings, the authors state that clinical trials in larger groups of patients with different forms and severity of glycogen storage disease seem indicated.

---

[1] Ellenberger, Burde and Keltner,[1005] in a group of fifteen patients with sharp borders to their visual field defects indicating pathological interruption of nerve fibers, did not find that DPH significantly affected visual acuity. They note that the patients which they studied differed from those with glaucomatous visual field loss. They suggest that examination of the protective effect of DPH in ischemic cerebral disease would be of interest.

Healing[1]—Periodontal

SAVINI, POITEVIN and POITEVIN, *Revue Francaise d'Odontostomatologie* (1972),[1504] presented a study of the use of diphenylhydantoin locally in the treatment of periodontal disease in 118 cases.

The authors examined the effect of DPH in a gingival-paste-type ointment which was applied by the patient with massage to the gingival mucosa inside and outside after normal tooth brushing, morning and evening, and left for about five minutes before rinsing.

The findings were based both on the patient's observations and by physical examination, x-rays and in forty-six cases by histological examination of the gingival biopsies.

Biopsy results showed that in thirty-one cases there was marked improvement characterized by stabilization of inflammatory lesions and appreciable healing of the connective tissue. In fourteen cases a marked healing sclerosis was observed without inflammatory elements.

In the clinical observations the following were noted: regression, and in most cases total resolution, of the painful phenomena associated with the disorder; rapid regression of spontaneous and provoked gingival bleeding; more or less rapid resolution of infectious and inflammatory phenomena; return of normal coloring to gums; and improvement in the signs of dental mobility. There was no periodontal restoration, although lesions were stabilized.

The authors concluded that DPH is an effective aid in the treatment of periodontal disease.

PAYEN, *Revue d'Odontostomatologie du Midi de la France (1972)*, [1403] reported on the topical use of diphenylhydantoin, in seventy-five patients with periodontal disease.

The author noted that with gingival massage, with a diphenylhydantoin preparation, inflammatory nodules tended to diminish in volume, considerably more than would be expected based on his previous experience. He also noted that the repeated inflammatory processes, characteristic of this disorder, subsided with increased production of collagen in the healing process. The seventy-five patients were studied in two groups. In the first group of forty-six patients from private practice there were forty-five improvements with DPH. In the second group of twenty-nine patients in a hospital ward there were twenty improvements with DPH.

The author concludes that local application of DPH in periodontal disease would seem to promote the disappearance of inflammatory lesions and the production of collagenous healing.

CHIKHANI, *Actualites Odontostomatologiques* (1972),[894] reports in a study of fifty-eight patients, the clinical and histological effects of diphenylhydantoin in daily gingival massage in periodontopathies. The author states that the study demonstrates the beneficial effect of DPH, particularly on bleeding gums and on pain; and histological findings confirmed the fibroblastic action of DPH and the healing with sclerosis which accompanied the decrease in inflammatory infiltration.

The author states that beneficial effects become manifest after forty to sixty days of treatment and suggests a minimum trial of at least six weeks should be adopted.

GOEBEL, *Journal of Oral Surgery* (1972),[1080] reported on a controlled clinical study to determine the effect of diphenylhydantoin on wound healing in extraction sockets.

As controls, one group of patients was

---

[1] For studies on the promotion of healing in animals with DPH, see basic mechanisms studies, pp. 195, 268–69.

given chlorpromazine hydrochloride, and another group was untreated. Statistically significant improvement was observed in wound healing in patients who received DPH before and after surgery, as compared with the control groups.

Single Case Reports

Although the following reports are of single cases, they are carefully reported and, since they are in new fields, they are reviewed here.

Narcolepsy

BJERK and HORNISHER, *Electroencephalography and Clinical Neurophysiology* (1958),[835] refer to generalities in the literature that "anti-convulsants" are not effective for narcolepsy.

The authors present a case, which they consider typical narcolepsy, that showed excellent response to treatment with diphenylhydantoin. The patient, a thirty-seven-year-old female, had overpowering attacks of sleep and other typical symptoms of narcolepsy. A thorough examination, skull films, lumbar puncture and visual fields were normal, and electroencephalogram revealed a highly irregular dysrhythmic record. On 100 mg of DPH t.i.d. the patient's symptoms left her on the seventh day. The authors state that the improvement was marked by a complete loss of symptoms. With the loss of symptoms, appetite improved and the patient said that she had never felt so well in a long time. This condition had been maintained for eight months, to the time of the present writing.

The authors point out that the role of DPH was further evidenced by the fact that when the patient stopped taking the medication the symptoms recurred.

Recurrent Fever

BERGER, *Postgraduate Medicine* (1966),[819] reports on an unusual case of recurrent fever, successfully treated with diphenylhydantoin.

A sixteen-year-old boy, who was first seen when he was twelve years old, began to have irregular attacks of fever at the age of eight. These attacks would appear suddenly, last from four to twenty-four hours, and disappear abruptly regardless of treatment. His temperature would rise to 102°F and stay within a degree of this reading until the attack was terminated. Headache, vertigo, weakness, irritability, and sometimes violent rages accompanied the fever.

From 1957 to 1961 the patient missed 260 days of school because of a total of 164 of these attacks of fever. Extensive tests for possible causes of fever proved negative. Penicillin, tetracycline and sulfadimethoxine were tried without effect.

The patient was treated with 400 mg of DPH per day and the attacks stopped. The dose was adjusted downward to 100 mg (25 mg q.i.d.) and with this dose (60 mg per day was found insufficient) he has been free of fever and the symptoms that accompanied it for the past four years. On four separate occasions, as an experiment, DPH was withdrawn. Each time the fever and other symptoms returned within a few days.[1]

Rabies

HATTWICK, WEIS, STECHSCHULTE, BAER and GREGG, *Annals of Internal Medicine* (1972),[1138] give an extensive and detailed report on their successful treatment of a six-

---

[1] This appears to be the only published report of DPH's usefulness in the alleviation of fever, and it is an unusual case but well documented. A number of individuals who have taken DPH for other purposes have reported to the Dreyfus Medical Foundation that their "usual" attacks of "flu," "virus," etc., have been accompanied by little or no fever. Research in this area may be indicated.

year-old boy with clinical rabies, with complete recovery. The authors comment that this is extremely rare, and possibly the first documented case of recovery from rabies in humans.

Many conventional and other measures were used to offset this desperate condition. Special attention was given to the prevention of hypoxia, cardiac arrhythmias and seizure.[1] Approximately forty days after the infection occurred and while the boy had been in a comatose condition for several days, DPH was administered, 150 mg daily. Four days later recovery started and progressed steadily to complete recovery.[2]

---

[1] The role, if any, that DPH played in this recovery is not known. However, since no remedy for clinical rabies is known, this case is of interest. It is well established that DPH is effective against seizures and cardiac arrhythmias, and it is also reported to have anti-anoxic effects. Of possible relevance is the evidence that DPH has antitoxic effects against a wide variety of substances. See pp. 266–67.

[2] See also Pollen,[1424] reporting the use of DPH in the successful treatment in a case of cat-scratch encephalitis.

Edema

MICK, *JAMA* (1973),[1359] reports on the case of a girl who had edema of the legs, fingers and puffiness of the face, accompanied by dizzy spells. These symptoms occurred about ten days before each menstrual cycle.

Diuretics had been tried without success. On 100 mg of DPH, twice daily, the patient became completely free of her episodic edema. Improvement in dizziness was also noted.

SAFETY AND TOXICOLOGY

Safety and Toxicology is reviewed in *The Broad Range of Use of Diphenylhydantoin,* pages 184–86.

For recent general reviews on safety and toxicology, the reader is referred to Glaser,[1075] and Woodbury, Penry and Schmidt.[1700]

BASIC MECHANISMS OF ACTION OF DPH

Summary

Basic mechanism studies demonstrate that DPH has a stabilizing effect on bioelectrical activity in single cells, and groups of cells. This ability to regulate bioelectrical activity has been demonstrated in brain, spinal cord, ganglia, peripheral nerve, neuromuscular junction, muscle endplate, cardiac muscle, Purkinje fibers of heart, and smooth muscle of intestine. The action of DPH is observed in vertebrates and invertebrates and is achieved whether the bioelectrical abnormality is caused by chemical or electrical means.[1]

It has been demonstrated that DPH reduces or eliminates excessive post-tetanic potentiation and repetitive after-discharge[1] and, in therapeutic doses, does not interfere with normal function; it does not affect normal transmission of initial impulses and does not impair normal resting potential.[2]

There are studies that show that DPH preserves energy compounds[3] and decreases the "downhill movement" of ions characteristic of energy depletion in nerve.[4] Additional studies demonstrate that DPH has anti-anoxic properties.[5]

Separate from the studies that have established that DPH has a regulatory effect on bioelectrical activity, and on sodium and potassium transport,[6] are other studies which report that DPH has regulatory effects on insulin and glucagon secretion and blood sugar levels. Other studies report that DPH has regulatory effects on acetylcholine, on cortisol metabolism, on norepinephrine and dopamine uptake, binding and release, on calcium uptake and metabolism, on calcitonin secretion, GABA uptake and concentration, serotonin concentration, antidiuretic hormone secretion, and on oxytocin and vasopressin secretion.[7]

DPH has been reported to diminish or counteract, in animals or in man, the toxic effects of substances as diverse as acetylstrophanthidin, aconitine, alloxan, amitriptyline, amphetamine, bilirubin, brain mucoprotein, bulbocapnine, corticosteroids, cyanide, DDT, delphinine, deslanoside, digitalis, estradiol, gold preparations, imipramine, lithium carbonate, mephenytoin, mephobarbital, methaqualone, methylphenidate, morphine,

---

[1] Ref. 11, 90, 257, 264, 270, 289, 359, 365, 458, 462, 468, 472, 580, 582, 789, 885, 953, 954, 955, 1117, 1197, 1198, 1199, 1221, 1291, 1343, 1400, 1435, 1467, 1469, 1494, 1580, 1602

[2] Ref. 90, 257, 289, 365, 458, 472, 782, 954, 955, 1197, 1198, 1291, 1400, 1467, 1469, 1494, 1602

[3] Ref. 17, 37, 483, 739, 1071

[4] Ref. 94, 293, 387, 728, 731, 782, 834, 1012, 1025, 1144, 1197, 1418, 1662, 1664

[5] Ref. 118, 164, 263, 285, 293, 717, 804, 1160, 1216, 1374, 1419, 1576, 1591

[6] Ref. 94, 96, 144, 157, 219, 285, 287, 293, 387, 480, 481, 483, 530, 618, 645, 699, 714, 717, 728, 731, 782, 800, 834, 955, 958, 1012, 1013, 1014, 1023, 1024, 1025, 1028, 1035, 1070, 1085, 1103, 1144, 1147, 1197, 1221, 1225, 1227, 1283, 1284, 1285, 1291, 1358, 1379, 1385, 1409, 1418, 1419, 1507, 1547, 1548, 1567, 1580, 1622, 1642, 1662, 1664, 1688, 1696, 1699

[7] Ref. 91, 92, 96, 172, 219, 382, 430, 454, 502, 522, 532, 763, 776, 789, 872, 885, 896, 909, 924, 964, 1015, 1021, 1062,

ouabain, phenylisothiocyanate, propoxyphene, reserpine, streptozotocin, strychnine, tetrabenazine, thyroxine and trimethadione, and of radiation.[8]

Other studies demonstrate that DPH enhances healing processes in animals.[9]

STABILIZATION OF BIOELECTRICAL ACTIVITY

From the earliest studies to the latest, the evidence is consistent that diphenylhydantoin corrects hyperexcitability as in post-tetanic potentiation and post-tetanic after-discharge. This normalizing of hyperexcitability is achieved without impairment of normal transmission of nerve impulses and without initial single impulse being affected.

The following studies are in chronological order (1937–1974).

PUTNAM and MERRITT, *Science* (1937),[11] *Archives of Neurology and Psychiatry* (1938),[250] and *JAMA* (1938),[557] were the first to discover that diphenylhydantoin was a therapeutically effective substance when they demonstrated that it counteracted hyperexcitability electrically induced in the cat brain. Others had previously tested DPH and, finding that it was not a sedative, had not investigated its properties further.

In their experiments, Putnam and Merritt electrically induced convulsions in cats. They demonstrated that DPH was much more effective in controlling these convulsions than were the bromides and phenobarbital. They also confirmed the earlier findings that DPH was not a sedative.

The authors applied their laboratory findings to clinical use and with DPH treated a group of 118 patients with chronic grand mal attacks who had not responded to treatment with bromides and phenobarbital. The results were dramatic. Fifty-eight percent of these intractable cases became free of attacks and twenty-seven percent showed marked improvement, without sedation. Although Putnam and Merritt were focusing on epilepsy at the time, they suggested that DPH might be useful for a broad range of cerebral dysrhythmias.

TOMAN, *Electroencephalography and Clinical Neurophysiology* (1949),[458] studied the effect of DPH on isolated frog sciatic nerve. The frog sciatic nerve was electrically stimulated and the action potential with and without DPH was recorded.

DPH was found to have little effect upon the membrane threshold for single shocks. However, DPH increased the membrane stability when repetitive shocks were used. The author noted that these findings might explain DPH's effectiveness in preventing abnormal spread of electrical discharge, without affecting normal function.

The author stressed the fact that the stabilization effects were achieved with low concentrations of DPH—and he noted that this

---

1092, 1103, 1105, 1108, 1109, 1128, 1131, 1154, 1157, 1220, 1222, 1240, 1256, 1269, 1272, 1274, 1282, 1327, 1351, 1355, 1368, 1404, 1406, 1417, 1454, 1480, 1495, 1509, 1567, 1583, 1627, 1642, 1644, 1678, 1679

[8] Ref. 19, 61, 62, 80, 82, 90, 99, 149, 150, 151, 153, 154, 155, 157, 158, 171, 182, 183, 187, 213, 215, 233, 248, 249, 260, 308, 310, 318, 327, 328, 377, 403, 404, 405, 407, 410, 415, 418, 425, 451, 454, 482, 483, 504, 514, 519, 530, 567, 596, 597, 625, 685, 699, 701, 714, 753, 754, 799, 800, 805, 812, 823, 860, 880, 896, 905, 914, 921, 941, 943, 944, 963, 969, 978, 991, 998, 999, 1007, 1015, 1022, 1026, 1027, 1052, 1079, 1084, 1085, 1092, 1103, 1114, 1121, 1122, 1128, 1151, 1170, 1208, 1209, 1214, 1238, 1253, 1264, 1267, 1277, 1289, 1306, 1349, 1354, 1382, 1388, 1402, 1419, 1428, 1430, 1434, 1466, 1488, 1507, 1508, 1509, 1510, 1515, 1525, 1527, 1528, 1529, 1530, 1557, 1562, 1563, 1590, 1622, 1637, 1643, 1663, 1666, 1696, 1705, 1707

[9] Ref. 171, 172, 188, 189, 335, 336, 337, 339, 343, 499, 500, 501, 502, 504, 505, 811, 1104, 1164, 1485. For studies in humans, see Ref. 25, 127, 341, 344, 669, 730, 894, 1080, 1371, 1403, 1504

stabilization was achieved without sedation. He suggested that the protective properties of DPH could have broad applicability when neurons are more sensitive than normal, such as the conditions brought on by injury or ischemia.

KOREY, *Proceedings of the Society of Experimental Biology and Medicine* (1951),[472] studied the effect of DPH on the giant axon of squid. The nerve and its ganglion were dissected and kept in a solution of artificial sea water to maintain ionic equilibrium. The nerve was then exposed to various solutions and electrical recordings were made.

When DPH was added to the 'normal' artificial sea water, no appreciable effect on the electrical activity of the giant axon was observed. When the sea water was changed by reducing calcium and magnesium, but without DPH, a hyperexcitable state of spontaneous firing occurred in the axon. When the sea water was brought back to normal by adding calcium and magnesium, it took ten to fifteen minutes to reverse the spontaneous firing. However, when DPH was added to the solution from which calcium and magnesium had been withdrawn, it took only two or three minutes to correct the excessive firing.

The author concludes that DPH does not seem to affect normal nerve function. However, in an abnormal condition of hyperexcitability, induced by withdrawal of calcium and magnesium, DPH effectively corrected this hyperexcitability. When calcium or magnesium was omitted from the solution, the squid axon became hyperirritable for a brief period and then its fibers lost their ability to fire.[1]

ESPLIN, *Journal of Pharmacology and Experimental Therapeutics* (1957),[90] studied the effect of DPH on post-tetanic potentiation in the spinal cord and stellate ganglion of the cat. Post-tetanic potentiation is a state of hyperexcitability of nerve in which, following unusually intense stimulation, the threshold of the nerve is lowered to subsequent stimuli, that is, the nerve fires more easily with less intense stimuli. In its most hyperexcitable state, the nerve fires spontaneously without stimulus.

The author found that DPH reduced or abolished post-tetanic potentiation. He also demonstrated that DPH counteracted post-tetanic potentiation in other experiments on the C fibers of the cat vagus nerve *in vivo*.

The author noted that DPH had no effect upon isolated single impulses measured in spinal cord transmission, and in stellate ganglion transmission.[2]

The author states that post-tetanic potentiation may be significantly concerned in all functions of the nervous system characterized by repetitive activity.

MORRELL, BRADLEY and PTASHNE, *Neurology* (1958),[257] examined the effects of DPH on the peripheral nerve in the rabbit. Conditions of hyperexcitability were induced by both chemical and electrical methods.

The authors found that DPH raised the resistance of the peripheral nerve to being made hyperexcitable by repetitive electrical stimulation. In a separate experiment they showed that when the nerve was made hyperexcitable chemically by the removal of calcium, DPH corrected this hyperexcitability.

TUTTLE and PRESTON, *Journal of Pharmacology and Experimental Therapeutics* (1963),[365] studied the influence of DPH on neural pathways in the cat. They state that, confirming previous studies, DPH was found to have no apparent effect on single-impulse transmission. The monosynaptic reflex amplitude,

---

[1] This provides an understanding of how DPH by correcting hyperexcitability prevents the sequelae of exhaustion. See later evidence of preservation of energy compounds (Ref. 17, 37, 483, 739, and 1071) and evidence of the offsetting of "downhill movement" of ions (Ref. 387, 728, 731, 834, 1025, 1144, 1225, 1379, 1385, 1418, 1642, and 1662).

[2] Evidence that DPH does not alter the initial transmission of a nerve impulse, in this case a nerve impulse measured in both the stellate ganglion and in the spinal cord.

whether initiated by dorsal root stimulation or by peripheral nerve stimulation, was not influenced by DPH. The authors note that these findings agree with those of Esplin.[90]

However, when post-tetanic potentiation was produced by increased repetitive electrical stimulation, the authors found that DPH counteracted the abnormal state.

The authors conclude that DPH does not change single-volley transmission, but that it corrects post-tetanic potentiation.

PARISI and RAINES, *Federation Proceedings* (1963),[1400] studied the effect of DPH on the soleus nerve of the cat, and on the neuromuscular transmission via this nerve.

In this study the effect that DPH had on neuromuscular transmission was gauged by its effect on twitch response to repeated nerve volleys and also on the twitch response to single impulses. Repeated nerve volleys caused post-tetanic repetitive discharge of the motor nerve terminals which in turn caused a contractile post-tetanic potentiation in the muscle. The authors found that intravenous DPH abolished this abnormal muscle post-tetanic potentiation. When a normal muscle was given a single volley, DPH did not affect the normal twitch. The authors placed emphasis on this selective action of DPH which enabled it to counteract post-tetanic repetitive activity without interfering with normal transmission phenomena.

RAINES and STANDAERT, *Journal of Pharmacology and Experimental Therapeutics* (1966),[289] found that the effect of DPH on the muscle response to indirect stimulation is a reduction of post-tetanic potentiation (PTP). They noted that this study in muscle paralleled their previous findings and the findings of others of the effect of DPH in nerve.

DPH affected both pre- and post-junctional elements of the neuromuscular junction. DPH abolished neural repetitive after-discharges originating in the nerve terminals of soleus motor axons of the cat.

The suppression of these after-discharges markedly reduced PTP of the soleus muscle. (See also Raines.)[468]

KLEINFELD and STEIN, *Circulation* (1968),[1221] electrically stimulated both isolated canine Purkinje and ventricular fibers of the heart and studied the action potentials. They found that DPH decreased the effective refractory period of both fibers with the greater effect being in the Purkinje fibers.

SPERELAKIS and HENN, *American Journal of Physiology* (1970),[1580] studied the effect of DPH on membrane potentials of individual cells of the chick heart growing in tissue culture. This method of separating cells from their nerves has the advantage of showing the direct effect of DPH on single cells, in this case, heart cells.

DPH was found to prevent hyperexcitability caused by both strontium and electrical pulses. Although DPH was protective against these insults, it did not affect the normal function of heart cells with regard to resting potentials, nor the maximum rate of rise or duration of the action potentials (even in high concentrations such as 1.8×10^{-5} M).

JULIEN and HALPERN, *Journal of Pharmacology and Experimental Therapeutics* (1970),[1197] studied the effect of DPH on the electrical responsiveness of isolated rabbit vagus nerve after repetitive electrical stimulation. They found that DPH did not affect the compound action potential produced by a single electrical stimulation, and that conduction velocity of both the myelinated and nonmyelinated fibers were not affected by DPH. The authors noted that the effects of DPH were in contrast to those of barbiturates which depress axonal conduction. Further, they noted that in addition to not depressing axonal impulse transmission resulting from a single stimulus, DPH shortens the duration of post-tetanic depressed excitability of C fibers.

After repetitive electrical stimulation, nonmyelinated C fibers in the vagus nerves of control animals exhibited a period of decreased excitability. DPH, 5-20 mg/kg t.i.d. intraperitoneally for five days was found to markedly shorten the recovery period. This recovery with DPH was accomplished without an accompanying depression of conduction velocity or excitability thresholds.

RIEHL and MCINTYRE, *Electroencephalography and Clinical Neurophysiology* (1970),[1467] studied the effect of intravenous DPH on the electroencephalogram analyzed quantitatively in terms of the over-all ratio of frequency to voltage. The authors note that this frequency/voltage ratio of the EEG has been used previously as an index of over-all "EEG activity."

In seven of eight previously untreated epileptic patients with unilateral EEG abnormalities, DPH (250 mg) was observed to produce a decrease in EEG activity in the range of 20 to 25%. The effect was observed within 10 to 15 minutes in the pathologically affected hemisphere. In the normal unaffected hemisphere of these same patients DPH had no observable effect. Similarly, in three control normal subjects no effect of DPH was observed.[1]

JULIEN and HALPERN, *Life Sciences* (1971),[1198] studied the effect of DPH on firing rates of cerebellar Purkinje cells and their relation to abnormal cortical discharge in cat brain.

Without DPH, cerebellar Purkinje cells were found under normal circumstances to have firing rates varying from 5 to 300 Hz (average 24). With DPH a sustained frequency of discharge of Purkinje cells was maintained (average 140 Hz).

Without DPH, when abnormal maximal and generalized cortical bursts were induced by penicillin foci, the Purkinje cell discharges abruptly ceased. With DPH a sustained frequency of discharge of Purkinje cells at approximately 140 Hz was maintained, and at the same time a reduction in the abnormal discharge from the cerebral cortex occurred.

The authors note that it is of interest that DPH is here seen to produce an increase in discharge of a particular group of cells, in this case the Purkinje cells of the cerebellum, which produce regulatory inhibitory effects upon abnormally discharging cortical cells. (See also Ref. 1199 and 1117.)

RUTLEDGE, SOHN and SARDINAS, *Pharmacologist* (1971),[1494] studied the effect of DPH on the hyperexcitability of a cat soleus nerve-muscle preparation. They found that succinylcholine produced muscle fasciculation and twitch potentiation.

The authors note that DPH counteracted post-tetanic twitch potentiation, but did not impair normal neuromuscular transmission.

BAKER, OKAMOTO and RIKER, *Pharmacologist* (1971),[789] found that in a cat soleus nerve-muscle preparation, pretreatment with DPH counteracts the additional excitation produced by injecting acetylcholine. The authors note that DPH selectively suppresses the post-tetanic potentiation of motor nerve terminals without impairing single-impulse transmission.

AYALA and LIN, *Federation Proceedings* (1971),[782] studied the effect of DPH on the electrical characteristics of the isolated crayfish stretch receptor. They observed that the resting membrane potential of this preparation was essentially unchanged by DPH. However, the authors noted that the long-lasting hyperpolarization which follows a train of action potentials was absent in the presence of DPH.

LIPICKY, GILBERT and STILLMAN, *Proceedings of the National Academy of Sciences* (1972),[1291] studied the effect of DPH on the voltage-dependent currents of the squid

---

[1] Another example of the selective action of DPH on abnormal cells, leaving normal cells unaltered. In this case the different effect was observed in the same brain.

giant axon. The authors noted that DPH does not change the resting membrane potential.

The authors found that DPH decreased the early transient 'sodium currents,' with little or no effect on 'potassium currents.' The authors suggest that this observation may be relevant to DPH's antiarrhythmic action in heart and its stabilizing effects in peripheral nerve.

RIKER, *Japanese Journal of Pharmacology* (1972),[1469] studied the effect of DPH on motor nerve terminals under conditions of normal transmission of impulses and abnormal states of post-tetanic potentiation. He states that extensive studies in his laboratory support the finding that DPH selectively counteracts the post-tetanic potentiation in motor nerve terminals, yet it does not affect normal transmission.

DEN HERTOG, *European Journal of Pharmacology* (1972),[955] studied the effect of DPH on rabbit vagus nerve which had been desheathed. The author found that DPH in both single and repeated doses did not effect normal excitability or membrane permeability.

SU and FELDMAN, *Archives of Neurology* (1973),[1602] discuss the possibility that DPH might have a direct effect on muscle membrane (endplate) as well as the already established effect on motor nerve terminal. The authors note that studies had been done with extracellular recordings, and that their study was done with intracellular recordings.

This study utilized the gracilis anticus muscle of twenty adult rats. The authors state that by using fine capillary microelectrodes they were able to repeatedly pierce the muscle endplates and thus to record miniature endplate potentials, without the resting membrane potential being interfered with. By both electrically and chemically stimulating the motor nerve terminal, the authors were able to determine that DPH had a stabilizing effect on the excitable membrane of the muscle endplate.

The authors note that in three separate tests involving fibers from three different animals the beginning of the effect of intravenous DPH was apparent within ten minutes.

They suggest that the stabilizing effect of DPH on the excitable membrane of the muscle endplate could be a factor in the success of DPH in the treatment of generalized myokymia and myotonia.

DELGADO, MORA and SANGUINETTI, *Personal Communication* (1973),[954] studied the effect of DPH on after-discharge in the amygdala of the brain of awake active rhesus monkeys.

DPH was found to completely prevent electrical after-discharges. The authors state that these after-discharges are analogous to the post-tetanic potentiation and post-tetanic after-discharges described in studies of others. (For more complete summary of this study see p. 211.)

CARNAY and GRUNDFEST, *Neuropharmacology* (1974),[885] studied the effects of DPH and calcium on electrical properties of the pre- and postsynaptic membranes of frog neuromuscular junction. When muscle fibres were bathed in solutions either deficient in calcium or containing germine monoacetate, membrane instability and repetitive firing of the fibers were produced. DPH was effective in preventing this abnormal repetitive firing.

The authors concluded that DPH has a stabilizing effect similar to that of calcium on abnormal membrane states. At concentrations of 10–20 micrograms/ml. in the bathing fluid, DPH did not alter normal muscle fibers in normal media in terms of the resting potential, effective membrane resistance, threshold membrane potential, miniature endplate potential frequency and amplitude.

MATTHEWS and CONNOR, *Pharmacologist* (1974),[1343] studied the effect of DPH on post-tetanic potentiation in the brain of rats. The authors studied the effect of DPH both on single impulse transmission and on post-tetanic potentiation. Post-tetanic potentiation of the hippocampal was induced by stimulating the commissural fibers with rapid repetitive impulses (10 Hz, five seconds duration). DPH counteracted this post-tetanic potentiation without diminishing single impulse transmission.

SODIUM AND POTASSIUM TRANSPORT

WOODBURY, *Journal of Pharmacology and Experimental Therapeutics* (1955),[387] demonstrated that in normal rats, DPH decreased both the total and the intracellular concentration of brain sodium and increased the rate of movement of radiosodium into and out of brain cells. The net result was that the ratio of extracellular to intracellular brain sodium was increased.

DPH also decreased intracellular sodium concentrations in skeletal and cardiac muscle, but to a lesser extent than in brain. Acutely induced low sodium in the blood was associated with an increase in intracellular brain sodium concentration and a decrease in intracellular brain potassium concentration. These changes were largely prevented by treatment with DPH.

KOCH, HIGGINS, SANDE, TIERNEY and TULIN, *Physiologist* (1962),[1225] studied the effect of DPH on the reabsorption of ions by the kidney in dogs, and found that DPH appears to enhance active sodium transport in the kidney.

VAN REES, WOODBURY and NOACH, *Archives Internationales de Pharmacodynamie et de Therapie* (1969),[1642] found that in loops of intestine of intact rats DPH was shown to increase the rate of absorption of both sodium and water from the lumen of the intestine.

CRANE and SWANSON, *Neurology* (1970),[728] demonstrated the effect of DPH in preventing the loss of potassium and the gain in sodium by brain slices, which occur during repeated high frequency electrical stimulation. Repeated depolarization of neuronal membranes makes it increasingly likely that the resting balance of ions intra- and extracellularly will not be restored.

These "downhill movements" of sodium and potassium ion balance represent the failure of active transport to restore the resting balance of ions between intracellular and extracellular compartments. DPH was shown both to prevent and to reverse these shifts, and thus it tended to restore the balance toward the normal resting state.

FERTZIGER, LIUZZI and DUNHAM, *Brain Research* (1971),[1025] studied the effect of DPH on potassium transport in lobster axons using radioactive potassium. The authors observed that DPH stimulated potassium influx. They postulated that this regulatory effect on potassium transport, in addition to the well established regulation of intracellular sodium content of nerve, might relate to the stabilizing effect of DPH on hyperactive neurons.

ESCUETA and APPEL, *Archives of Internal Medicine* (1972),[1012] studied the effect of DPH upon the levels of sodium and potassium in isolated brain synaptosomes. Rat brain rendered hyperexcitable by electrical stimulation resulting in seizure states was found to contain a decreased level of potassium and an increased level of sodium within the synaptic terminals. The authors noted that both these changes reflected the "downhill movement" of ions in the synaptic terminals, and that these were both pathological processes.

DPH was shown to correct both of these pathological processes in membrane function.

NASELLO, MONTINI and ASTRADA, *Pharmacology* (1972),[1379] studied the effect of DPH on the rat dorsal hippocampus when electrically stimulated and when not stimulated. When the hippocampus was constantly electrically stimulated, potassium release was observed. DPH counteracted this release.

PINCUS, *Archives of Neurology* (1972),[1418] found that DPH reduced the sodium influx by 40% in stimulated nerves. Sodium influx was not found to be affected in the resting nerve. DPH had no effect on the rate of sodium efflux in either resting or stimulated lobster nerve.

The author concluded that DPH acts primarily by limiting the increase in sodium permeability which occurs during stimulation. He noted further that DPH appeared to counteract "downhill" sodium movements in stimulated nerves without affecting normal sodium movements.[*1*]

WATSON and WOODBURY, *Chemical Modulation of Brain Function* (1973),[1664] studied the effect of DPH on sodium transport and membrane permeability of the epithelium of frog skin and toad urinary bladder preparations. The authors concluded that DPH increases net sodium transport in both cases by increasing the permeability of the outer membrane to sodium. They noted that their findings would be consistent with the action of DPH in stimulating sodium-potassium-ATPase when the sodium-potassium ratio in the system is high (greater than 25 to 1).

NOACH, VAN REES and DE WOLFF, *Archives Internationales de Pharmacodynamie et de Therapie* (1973),[1385] found that when sodium is lacking from the intestinal lumen DPH causes the sodium to increase in the lumen by active extrusion of sodium from the gut wall.

WOODBURY and KEMP, *Psychiatria, Neurologia, Neurochirurgia* (1971),[1696] reviewed the pharmacology and mechanisms of action of

DPH, and described their new studies on the stabilizing effect of DPH on cardiac muscle and on intestinal smooth muscle.

The authors state that the predominant effect of DPH in the brain is its anti-spreading activity on abnormal discharges. "The anti-spreading effect of DPH appears to be a result of its ability to block post-tetanic potentiation, a process that is related to the known effect of DPH to stabilize membranes, particularly when they are hyperexcitable. . . . Electrolytes are concerned with stabilization of the membrane, a process regulated by DPH."

The authors referred to the previously unpublished experiments of Watson and Woodbury on the protective effect of DPH on the guinea pig heart. They found that DPH counteracted ouabain's lethal and electrolyte-disturbing effects, and that these protective effects could be recorded on the electrocardiogram.

The authors referred to the study of Van Rees, Woodbury and Noach[1642] which demonstrated that DPH increased the rate of absorption of both water and sodium from the lumen of loops of the intestine of intact rats. The authors concluded that in both excitable and nonexcitable tissues, DPH increases the transport of sodium across cell membranes.

The authors found that DPH tended to reduce towards normal levels the amplitude of contraction of the smooth muscle of rat ileum when it had been rendered hyperexcitable by barium ions.

The authors did experiments to determine the exact site of binding of DPH in the cell. They found that DPH had a marked affinity for the microsomal fraction of rat brain and liver.

In separate experiments in which radioactive orotic acid was given to determine its incorporation into nucleic acids of liver and brain, DPH was found to enhance the incorporation of orotic acid into the nucleic acids of both the nuclei and microsomes.

---

1 See also Lipicky, Gilbert and Stillman.[1291]

They refer to their other unpublished results which indicate that DPH makes more energy available to various functions in the body.

ANTIANOXIC EFFECTS OF DPH

Although this is a diverse group of studies, they are consistent in the finding that DPH has a protective effect against oxygen deprivation.

The following studies are in chronological order (1944–1973).

HOFF and YAHN, *American Journal of Physiology* (1944),[164] studied the effect of DPH upon tolerance of rats and mice to reduced atmospheric pressures. After injection of DPH, animals withstood a lower pressure than was possible for animals without DPH. Animals receiving DPH could be taken to extraordinarily low pressures and survive.

The authors propose that under conditions of severe oxygen lack, DPH prolongs normal function of nerve cells, in particular of the respiratory and cardiac centers.

For more detailed summary see page 193, Vol. I.

FORDA and MCILWAIN, *British Journal of Pharmacology* (1953),[717] electrically stimulated guinea pig brain slices at 500 and 2,000 cyc./sec., 3.5 V. At this level more oxygen per gm per hour was used. When DPH was added, this increase in the use of oxygen was reduced.

The increase in oxygen use produced by the less intense stimulation of 50 cyc./sec., 1.3 V or 2 V, was not changed by DPH.

GAYET-HALLION and BERTRAND, *Comptes Rendus des Seances de la Societe de Biologie et de Ses Filiales* (1959),[118] found that DPH prolonged respiratory activity. Rats were immersed in water at 14–15°C, with the times of immersion varying from trial to trial.

DPH given intraperitoneally three hours before the test permitted highly significant prolongation of respiratory activity. There was a marked increase in survival of the animals with DPH.

NAIMAN and WILLIAMS, *Journal of Pharmacology and Experimental Therapeutics* (1964),[263] studied the effects of DPH on anoxia. DPH prolonged the duration of respiratory activity in cats and guinea pigs subjected to nitrogen anoxia.

It also prolonged the duration of respiratory activity in decapitated guinea pig head.

BASSETT, BIGGER and HOFFMAN, *The Journal of Pharmacology and Experimental Therapeutics* (1970),[804] in a study in which thirteen isolated dog hearts were used, found that DPH protected canine Purkinje fibers in heart, during hypoxia.

To determine the effect of DPH, the Purkinje fiber preparation of the isolated heart was stimulated electrically at a constant rate, and the electrical responses were measured until optimal performance was established. Then hypoxia was induced by perfusion with a nitrogen-carbon dioxide mixture. This hypoxia resulted in a sharp reduction in electrical response. The authors found that DPH improved electrical response, as measured by phase zero V_{max}, induced by hypoxia. They also found that DPH improved electrical response, as measured by phase zero V_{max}, when the Purkinje fiber had already been depressed by hypoxia.

The authors observed that DPH protected the normal function of Purkinje fibers against lowered oxygen. They also noted that when the Purkinje fibers had been impaired by hypoxia, DPH transiently improved this condition.[1]

---

[1] For other instances of restoration of electrical activity by DPH (in brain) see Crane and Swanson,[728] and (in skeletal muscle) see Su and Feldman.[1602] In addition, see increase in level of energy compounds (Ref. 17, 37, 483, 739, 1071). These laboratory findings parallel the clinical observations that DPH tends to increase energy levels when they are below normal.

PINCUS, GROVE, MARINO and GLASER, *Presented at the International Society of Neurochemistry* (1969),[1419] observed that DPH tends to reduce the abnormal accumulation of intracellular sodium in hypoxic nerves. But in normally functioning, oxygenated nerves, DPH does not affect intracellular sodium.

The authors state: "Diphenylhydantoin has been shown to have a stabilizing influence on virtually all excitable membranes. These effects have been seen in a wide variety of vertebrate and invertebrate species." (For earlier work see Pincus and Giarman[285] and Rawson and Pincus.)[293]

SPECTOR, *British Journal of Pharmacology* (1972),[1576] demonstrated that DPH reduced the rate of utilization of oxygen by a rat cerebral cortex homogenate preparation.

The homogenates were composed largely of free mitochondria and synaptosomes.

MOSS, *Bulletin of the New York Academy of Medicine* (1973),[1374] found that DPH pretreatment protects against the development of "shock lung" in dogs.

Fourteen dogs were included in the study. Six were used as controls. All fourteen dogs were subjected to the same amount of femoral arterial hemorrhage followed by reinfusion of the shed blood, and all were sacrificed one hour later.

Six dogs (the controls) were not treated with DPH. When sacrificed, all showed pulmonary edema, hemorrhage, congestion and atelectasis typical of shock lung.

Eight dogs were treated with DPH, 5 mg/kg intramuscularly, one hour prior to the hemorrhage regimen. When these eight dogs were sacrificed, none had shock lung. Their lungs appeared normal both grossly and microscopically.

The author states that DPH is known to protect brain metabolism and function under conditions of hypoxia. This study furnishes evidence that DPH provides protection against lung damage under conditions of hypoxia, as induced by a hemorrhagic trauma.

STEIN and MOSS, *Surgical Forum* (1973),[1591] in a controlled study found that pretreatment with DPH afforded statistically significant protection against "shock lung" in rats.

HONDA, PODOS and BECKER, *Investigative Ophthalmology* (1973),[1160] observed the protective effect of DPH against oxygen deprivation in the retina of rabbits as registered on one of the two major peaks of the electroretinogram.

PRESERVATION OF ENERGY COMPOUNDS IN BRAIN

WOODBURY, TIMIRAS and VERNADAKIS, *Hormones, Brain Function, and Behavior* (1957),[483] reported that DPH increased glycogen in rat brain.

BERNSOHN, POSSLEY and CUSTOD, *Pharmacologist* (1960),[17] demonstrated that DPH increased creatinine phosphate in rats. With control values of 3.30 micromoles/gm of brain, creatinine phosphate values were 1.30 micromoles/gm for chlordiazepoxide, 4.40 micromoles/gm for chlorpromazine, and 7.38 micromoles/gm for DPH.

BRODDLE and NELSON, *Federation Proceedings* (1968),[37] found that DPH (50 mg/kg) can decrease brain metabolic rate 40 to 60% as well as increase the concentrations of brain energy compounds measured, i.e., phosphocreatine, serum and brain glucose and glycogen.

HUTCHINS and ROGERS, *British Journal of Pharmacology* (1970),[739] found that a single dose of DPH intraperitoneally (20 mg/kg) increased the concentration of brain glycogen in mouse brain by 7% at 30 minutes and by 11% at 120 minutes.

GILBERT, GRAY and HEATON, *Biochemical Pharmacology* (1971),[1071] demonstrated that brain glucose levels were increased in mice who received DPH. The authors also found that DPH significantly increased the uptake of xylose by brain slices, without glucose utilization by cerebral cortex slices being appreciably changed.

The authors concluded that DPH also may stimulate glucose transport into the brain. They considered the possibility that, with DPH, the extra glucose may play a role independent of its more obvious one as a substrate in oxidative metabolism, such as a stabilization of water molecules in the cell membrane, with a consequent stabilizing effect on neuronal excitability.

MUSCLE BASIC MECHANISMS

Skeletal Muscle

PARISI and RAINES, *Federation Proceedings* (1963),[1400] studied the effect of DPH on the soleus nerve of the cat, and on the neuromuscular transmission via this nerve.

Repeated nerve volleys caused post-tetanic repetitive discharge of the motor nerve terminals which in turn caused a contractile post-tetanic potentiation in the muscle. The authors found that intravenous DPH abolished this abnormal muscle post-tetanic potentiation. When a normal muscle was given a single volley, DPH did not affect the normal twitch. The authors placed emphasis on this selective action of DPH which enabled it to counteract post-tetanic repetitive activity without interfering with normal transmission phenomena.

SU and FELDMAN, *Archives of Neurology* (1973),[1602] utilizing the gracilis anticus muscle of twenty adult rats and fine capillary microelectrodes, were able to repeatedly pierce the muscle endplates and thus to record miniature endplate potentials, without the resting membrane potential being interfered with. By both electrically and chemically stimulating the motor nerve terminal, the authors

were able to determine that DPH had a stabilizing effect on the excitable membrane of the muscle endplate.[1] For fuller summary see p. 249.

RUTLEDGE, SOHN and SARDINAS, *Pharmacologist* (1971),[1494] studied the effect of DPH on the hyperexcitability of a cat soleus nerve muscle preparation. The authors found that succinylcholine produced muscle fasciculation and twitch potentiation. DPH was found to suppress or abolish the muscle fasciculation and twitch potentiation induced by succinylcholine.

The authors note that the doses of DPH used did not impair neuromuscular transmission but did counteract post-tetanic twitch potentiation.

RIKER, *Japanese Journal of Pharmacology* (1972),[1469] studied the effect of DPH on motor nerve terminals under conditions of both normal transmission of impulses and abnormal states of post-tetanic potentiation.

The author states that extensive studies in his laboratory support the finding that DPH selectively counteracts the post-tetanic potentiation in motor nerve terminals, yet it does not affect normal transmission.

GRUENER and STERN, *Nature, New Biology* (1972),[1103] found that DPH protects against steroid myopathy induced by dexamethasone in mice.

Myopathy was induced in twelve mice by intraperitoneal injection of dexamethasone. Then six of these mice received four injections of DPH over a period of two days and were sacrificed. None of these DPH-treated mice had myopathy as measured both histologically and by membrane action potential. In the other six mice not treated with DPH,

---

1 The authors note that DPH did not affect normal resting muscle fiber membrane potential (in agreement with Gruener and Stern[1103] and Woodbury and Kemp[1695]), but when the membrane was depolarized with high potassium solution, DPH had a definite membrane stabilizing effect.

each had myopathy. As further controls, six mice had been given DPH alone without effect on normal muscle membrane properties. (See Stern, Gruener and Amundsen,[1594] for clinical effectiveness of DPH in a patient with steroid myopathy.)

Smooth Muscle

Druckman and Moore, *Proceedings of the Society for Experimental Biology and Medicine* (1955),[465] studied the effect of DPH on isolated rabbit intestine smooth muscle contractions. DPH was found to produce a decrease in the amplitude of contractions.

The authors state that this direct effect of DPH on smooth muscle of intestine is important to note with reference to the use of DPH in the treatment of clinical conditions of intestinal hypermotility and spasticity. The direct smooth muscle relaxing effect of DPH would be in addition to its stabilizing effect on the central nervous system in these intestinal disorders.

Van Rees, Woodbury and Noach, *Archives Internationales de Pharmacodynamie et de Therapie* (1969),[1642] found that small amounts of DPH increased the release of acetylcholine from parasympathetic nerve endings in the wall of the ileum and also from the intramural ganglia and thus had a stimulating effect on the contraction of the ileum. However, demonstrating DPH's selective effect, when the contraction of the ileum was made excessive by the addition of acetylcholine, DPH inhibited the excessive contractions of the ileum. Thus, a "biphasic effect" of DPH in this circumstance was referred to by the authors.[1]

Woodbury and Kemp, *Psychiatria, Neurologia, Neurochirurgia* (1971),[1696] showed that DPH tended to reduce towards more normal levels the amplitude of contraction of the smooth muscle of rat ileum when it had been rendered hyperexcitable by barium ions.

Chou, Kuiper and Hsieh, *Gastroenterology* (1972),[899] noted that DPH has been used in the treatment of spastic colon patients. Their study was designed to see if DPH would alter the phasic motor activity and contractile state of an *in situ* segment of the ascending colon and terminal ileum of dog.

The authors concluded that these studies indicate that DPH decreases the contractile state of both ileum and colon making them more distensible, and also decreases the phasic activity of the colon.

Ferrari and Furlanut, *Archives Internationales de Pharmacodynamie et de Therapie* (1973),[1021] studied the effect of DPH on the mechanical and electrical activity of the isolated guinea pig ileum, and also of the isolated smooth muscle strips of guinea pig ileum. DPH was found to enhance muscular relaxation and to regulate the response of smooth muscle to acetylcholine stimulation. The authors note that these effects are consonant with the previously demonstrated stabilizing activity of DPH on excitable membranes.

Vanasin, Bass, Mendeloff and Schuster, *American Journal of Digestive Diseases* (1973),[1644] studied the direct effect of DPH on isolated strips of smooth muscle of colon from fourteen humans and twenty-four dogs. The effect of DPH on colon smooth muscle was studied by chemical stimulation with acetylcholine and 5-hydroxytryptamine, and also by electrical stimulation. In both conditions when compared to controls, DPH was found to significantly increase relaxation time and decrease contraction time.

The authors conclude that DPH's mode of action can be directly on smooth muscle as well as on neuromuscular junction, and sug-

---

[1] Another example of the two-way action of DPH in its regulatory function, this time on acetylcholine and contraction of smooth muscle of intestine. (See also the controlling effect of DPH on acetylcholine levels in brain, Agarwal and Bhargava[1] and in heart, Bose, Saifi and Sharma,[30] both discussed in Vol. I, pp. 194–95.)

gest that the observed effect of DPH on isolated smooth muscle of the colon suggests a basis for therapeutic use of DPH in the treatment of spastic colon syndrome.

(See also effect of DPH on smooth muscle of bronchi,[1535] on peripheral muscle (muscle endplate)[1602] and on cortisone myopathy of skeletal muscle.)[1103, 1594]

CARDIOVASCULAR BASIC MECHANISMS

Hypoxia in Purkinje Fibers of the Heart[1]

BASSETT, BIGGER and HOFFMAN, *The Journal of Pharmacology and Experimental Therapeutics* (1970),[804] in a study in which thirteen isolated dog hearts were used, found that DPH protected canine Purkinje fibers in heart, during hypoxia.

Background: The authors call attention to recent reports that indicate that ventricular arrhythmias are encountered in a high percentage of cases of ischemia caused by coronary artery occlusion, and that the results of numerous experiments suggest that Purkinje fibers are involved in the genesis of many ventricular arrhythmias. Hypoxia, ischemia and release of potassium and other intracellular substances could disturb cardiac rhythm by altering the sensitivity of Purkinje fibers.

The authors note that DPH has been found effective in abolishing many induced ventricular arrhythmias in dogs, and that DPH has widely been found effective in abolishing many arrhythmias in man. In an earlier study using microelectrode techniques, the authors found that DPH had a protective effect on the electrophysiologic properties of canine Purkinje fibers.

Methods and Conclusions: In the present study with isolated dog hearts, the authors state that they were concerned with the effectiveness of DPH in helping cardiac tissues survive during low oxygen tension. To determine the effect of DPH, the Purkinje fiber preparation of the isolated heart was stimulated electrically at a constant rate, and the electrical responses were measured until optimal performance was established. Then hypoxia was induced by perfusion with a nitrogen-carbon dioxide mixture. This hypoxia resulted in a sharp reduction in electrical response. The authors found that DPH improved electrical response, as measured by phase zero V_{max}, during hypoxia. They also found that DPH improved electrical response, as measured by phase zero V_{max}, when the Purkinje fiber had already been depressed by hypoxia.

The authors conclude that DPH improves the normal function of Purkinje fibers against lowered oxygen. They also note that when the Purkinje fibers had been impaired by hypoxia, DPH transiently improved this condition.

The authors suggest that the protective and therapeutic action of DPH on Purkinje fiber may in part explain the effectiveness of DPH in suppressing arrhythmias caused by myocardial ischemia and hypoxia.[2]

Protection Against Arrhythmias Induced by a Variety of Agents

SPERELAKIS and HENN, *American Journal of Physiology* (1970),[1580] studied the effect of DPH on membrane potentials of individual chick heart cells in tissue culture. This method of separating cells from their nerves has the advantage of showing the direct ef-

---

[1] For other demonstrations of DPH's usefulness in hypoxia, see Anti-anoxic Effects of DPH, p. 252.

[2] This demonstration of the protective effect by DPH in isolated Purkinje fibers, against anoxia, is a separate source of evidence that DPH protects against anoxia at the cell level. See also Pincus,[699] Hadfield,[1109] Becker and Podos,[812] and pp. 252–53.

fect of DPH on single cells, in this case, heart cells.

DPH was found to prevent hyperexcitability caused by both strontium and electrical stimulation. Although DPH was protective against these insults, it did not affect the normal function of heart cells with regard to resting potentials, nor the maximum rate of rise or duration of the action potentials (even in high concentrations such as 1.8×10^{-5} M).

SINGH, SINHA, RASTOGI, DUA and KOHLI, *Japanese Journal of Pharmacology* (1971),[1557] studied the antiarrhythmic effects of DPH, paramethadione and trimethadione in dogs. Arrhythmias were induced by means of aconitine, hydrocarbon-epinephrine and coronary ligation. These arrhythmias were of both central and peripheral origin, and DPH was protective against both.

In addition, the authors state that DPH was effective against all types of arrhythmias, irrespective of the nature and site of their origin, possibly because of its membrane-stabilizing properties.

CURTIS, *University of Michigan Doctoral Thesis* (1971),[927] in a study of experimental atrial fibrillation in dogs, reported that DPH was as effective as quinidine in terminating stable atrial fibrillation which followed hypertonic solution administration.[1]

Coronary Blood Flow

GUPTA, UNAL, BASHOUR and WEBB, *Diseases of the Chest* (1967),[496] were the first to demonstrate that DPH increases coronary blood flow in dogs.

NAYLER, MCINNES, SWANN, RACE, CARSON

and LOWE, *American Heart Journal* (1968),[402] demonstrated, in dogs, that DPH increases the coronary blood flow and that DPH reduces myocardial oxygen consumption.

ZEFT, REMBERT, CURRY and GREENFIELD, *Cardiovascular Research* (1973),[1711] in a study examining coronary blood flow, found that in intact conscious dogs, with the heart rate uncontrolled, DPH (5 mg/kg) produced a mean increase of 61% in coronary blood flow. With the heart rate controlled by ventricular pacing, a similar dose of DPH produced a mean increase in coronary blood flow of 57%. There was no significant change in either aortic blood flow or peripheral vascular resistance.

The authors concluded that to date DPH is the only antiarrhythmic agent which has been shown to improve coronary blood flow.

ZEFT, WHALEN, RATLIFF, DAVENPORT and MCINTOSH, *The Journal of Pharmacology and Experimental Therapeutics* (1968),[392] conducted a study to evaluate the hypothesis that DPH given prophylactically would be effective in preventing death from ventricular arrhythmias resulting from experimental myocardial infarction. The left anterior descending coronary artery of forty farm pigs was gradually occluded with an Ameroid constrictor. The farm pig was chosen because the coronary artery pattern of this animal is relatively constant and similar to that of man.

Almost twice as many control animals (eleven of twenty) expired as DPH treated animals (six of twenty). Although the sample was not large enough to be conclusive, the authors state that there is an indication that DPH used prophylactically increases the chance of survival in experimental myocardial infarction in pigs.

As a result of this experiment the authors suggest that consideration should be given to the use of DPH on a regular basis as a prevention of fatalities originating from coronary artery disorders.

---

[1] The papers of Singh, et al. and Curtis, above, agree on the effectiveness of DPH in atrial fibrillation in animals. However, they point out that in man differences still exist in the literature on the degree of effectiveness of DPH in chronic atrial arrhythmias. Further clinical evidence should make for clarification.

Cerebral Blood Flow

BALDY-MOULINIER, *European Neurology* (1971–2),[790] found that DPH protected against the effects of cerebral ischemia. This anti-anoxic effect of DPH was demonstrated experimentally by clamping the aorta.

The animals treated with DPH could be revived for as long as fifteen minutes after occlusion of the aorta. The animals not treated with DPH could only be revived within seven minutes of occlusion. (Seven and fifteen are mean values.)

Conduction

WAX, WEBB and ECKER, *Surgical Forum* (1969),[1668] in a study titled "Myocardium Stabilization by Diphenylhydantoin," observed the effect of DPH on the resting potential and the action potential of ventricular heart muscle of the rat. With DPH the resting potential plateau phase and the recovery period were both lengthened.

The authors note that these actions of DPH would stabilize the heart and would make the heart less susceptible to early reentry from circus mechanisms or other rapid aberrant stimuli.

KLEINFELD and STEIN, *Circulation* (1968),[1221] electrically stimulated both isolated canine Purkinje and ventricular fibers and studied the action potentials. They found that DPH decreased the effective refractory period of both fibers with the greater effect being in the Purkinje fiber.

BIGGER, WEINBERG, KOVALIK, HARRIS, CRANEFIELD and HOFFMAN, *Circulation Research* (1970),[828] studied the effects of diphenylhydantoin on excitability and automaticity in the canine heart.

The authors report that DPH 1) shortened the refractory period, particularly of ventric-ular muscle; 2) increased the multiple response and fibrillation thresholds in atrium and ventricle; 3) had little effect on diastolic threshold; 4) slightly enhanced the conduction velocity in ventricular muscle that was stimulated either in diastole or in its relative refractory period; and 5) produced slight decreases in automaticity in the ventricular specialized conducting system *in vivo*.

The authors state that their clinical experience suggests that DPH differs from quinidine in its effect on fundamental electrophysiological processes in the human heart. DPH does not prolong the Q-R-S interval and shortens the Q-T interval. These observations indicate that the drug does not prolong intraventricular conduction and suggest that it shortens the refractory period.

Calcification (cardiac)

RETTURA, STAMFORD and SEIFTER, *Paper presented at Northeast Regional Meeting of American Chemical Society* (1973),[1454] conducted a controlled study of the effect of DPH in mice with predisposition to cardiac calcification. This calcification was enhanced by stress.

The authors found that DPH reversed the calcification process as determined grossly, microscopically and by chemical analysis. The authors suggest that this might be one mechanism by which DPH is effective in the prevention of cardiac arrhythmias.

Norepinephrine

LEW, *Proceedings of the Society of Experimental Biology and Medicine* (1975),[1282] found that DPH increased the concentration of norepinephrine in the hypothalamus, cerebellum and brainstem in a strain of naturally hypertensive rats. The author notes that a deficiency in norepinephrine in the hypothalamus has been reported to coincide with hypertension, and that certain treatments effective in reducing high blood pressure produce an increase of norepinephrine in the hypothalamus. The author also notes that as animals get older, there is a decrease of norepinephrine in the hypothalamus.

Since DPH was found to increase the concentration of norepinephrine in the hypothalamus, the author suggests that further study is indicated to see if DPH might be useful against hypertension.

Protection Against Digitalis Toxicity

GOLDSTEIN, PENZOTTI, KUEHL, PRINDLE, HALL, TITUS and EPSTEIN, *Circulation Research* (1973),[1085] state that the efficacy of DPH in treating digoxin toxicity is well established. In reporting the results of an extensive study of isolated dog heart, the authors state that DPH, when added to digoxin enhances the inotropic benefits of digoxin.

The authors found that before digoxin toxic levels are reached, DPH ultimately produces greater increase in contractile force, greater potassium efflux and greater inhibition of sodium-potassium-ATPase activity. The authors suggest that these are mechanisms which enable DPH to enhance the inotropic benefits of digoxin.[1]

HANSEN and WAGENER, *Zeitschrift fur Kardiologie und Angiologie* (1974),[1122] by using both isolated atrium and barbiturate-damaged heart-lung preparations of guinea pigs, showed that the toxic arrhythmic side effects of digoxin are prevented by DPH, without affecting its inotropic benefits. By the addition of DPH, glycoside dosages can be beneficially increased.

The authors conclude that DPH offers new aspects for the treatment of cardiac failure.

SCHERLAG, HELFANT, RICCIUTTI and DAMATO, *American Journal of Physiology* (1968),[1507] demonstrated in dogs that DPH

consistently converted digitalis-induced ventricular tachycardia to sinus rhythm with a corresponding reversal of the digitalis-induced potassium efflux.

At the same time that the toxicity of digitalis was markedly delayed by DPH and the rate of myocardial potassium efflux slowed, the improvement in myocardial contractility with digitalis was not altered by DPH.

BASKIN, DUTTA and MARKS, *British Journal of Pharmacology* (1973),[801] in a study of the guinea pig heart, showed that DPH and potassium significantly prevent ouabain intoxication without preventing the inotropic benefits of ouabain.

WATSON and WOODBURY, *Archives Internationales de Pharmacodynamie et de Therapie* (1973),[1663] studying ouabain intoxication in guinea pigs, observed that DPH prevented ouabain-induced electrolyte changes and prevented the development of ouabain-induced arrhythmias. Under some conditions, pretreatment with DPH reduced the lethality of ouabain from 90% to 34%. The authors concluded that these results are consistent with the concept that the antiarrhythmic effect of DPH is due to an action on active transport of electrolytes across cell membranes, since the plasma potassium was normalized by DPH pretreatment.

In addition, the authors measured the intracellular concentration of sodium, potassium and chloride in cardiac muscle and again observed a normalizing effect of DPH pretreatment.

OTHER REGULATORY EFFECTS OF DPH

Additional regulatory effects of DPH are reported in the following studies. They include the regulatory effect of DPH on calcium metabolism and calcitonin secretion, norepinephrine uptake, binding and release,

---

[1] Although it is well established that DPH does not impair the inotropic benefits of the glycosides, this appears to be the first paper to suggest that it may actually enhance the inotropic benefits of digoxin.

acetylcholine concentration and effect, GABA uptake and concentration, adrenocortical function, oxytocin secretion, antidiuretic hormone secretion, and carbohydrate metabolism.

Calcium Metabolism and Calcitonin Secretion

PINCUS and LEE, *Archives of Neurology* (1973),[1417] found that when DPH was added to rat brain slices the uptake of calcium was decreased and there was a decrease in the release of norepinephrine from the cells. The authors state that it has been demonstrated that in the absence of calcium the electrical stimulation of brain slices does not result in norepinephrine being released from the cell. They also note that when calcium concentration is reduced, norepinephrine release from the cells is also reduced. The present study shows that when DPH decreased calcium uptake by the cells there was a decrease in norepinephrine release from the cells.

The authors note that the effects of DPH upon calcium uptake may be relevant to the regulatory action of DPH in other situations, including the secretion of insulin, and the contractile mechanisms in skeletal and cardiac muscle.

(See also Carnay and Grundfest,[885] p. 249.)

SOHN and FERRENDELLI, *Neurology* (1973),[1567] studied the effect of DPH on calcium uptake by synaptosomes isolated from rat brain. At low concentrations of DPH, 0.2mM or greater, DPH consistently inhibited calcium uptake by synaptosomes which had been depolarized with potassium. In synaptosomes not depolarized, low concentrations of DPH had no significant effect on calcium uptake, but much higher concentrations of DPH, 0.4 mM or greater, had some inhibitory effect on calcium uptake.

These results support the concept that one pharmacological action of DPH is inhibition of calcium transport into stimulated neuronal tissue. The authors suggest that this may be a mechanism by which DPH inhibits neurotransmitter release and in turn suppresses post-tetanic potentiation.

PENTO, GLICK and KAGAN, *Endocrinology* (1973),[1406] state that DPH, which has been used therapeutically for more than thirty years, exhibits a wide spectrum of therapeutic effects which appear to be associated with the stabilizing influence of DPH on excitatory tissues.

The present study demonstrates the effect of DPH on calcitonin secretion in the pig. Normal basal levels of calcitonin secretion were not significantly changed by DPH. When extra calcitonin secretion was stimulated by means of glucagon or calcium administration, DPH tended to reduce the level of elevation in plasma calcitonin produced by these two stimuli.

The authors state that these findings are in accord with other demonstrations that DPH does not alter normal basal function of the pituitary-adrenal hormones, or normal basal function of insulin secretion; but that when unusual stimuli are present DPH exerts a regulatory influence.

RETTURA, STAMFORD and SEIFTER, *Paper presented at Northeast Regional Meeting of the American Chemical Society* (1973),[1454] conducted a controlled study of the effect of DPH in a strain of mice with predisposition to cardiac calcification. This calcification was enhanced by stress.

The authors found that DPH reversed the calcification process as determined grossly, microscopically and by chemical analysis. The authors suggest that this might be one mechanism by which DPH is effective in the prevention of cardiac arrhythmias.

HARRIS, JENKINS and WILLS, *British Journal of Pharmacology* (1974),[1131] found that when calcium release from bone cells growing in tissue culture was induced by the addition of parathyroid hormone, DPH significantly inhibited this release.

Norepinephrine Uptake, Binding and Release

HADFIELD, *Archives of Neurology* (1972),[1109] studied the effect of DPH on the uptake and binding of the catecholamines, norepinephrine and dopamine, in rat brain synaptosomes and in brain slices. Different effects of DPH were observed depending on whether the preparations were anoxic or well oxygenated. In anoxic preparations DPH stimulated the uptake of norepinephrine intracellularly in synaptosomes, whereas in oxygenated preparations DPH reduced the uptake of norepinephrine in synaptosomes.

HADFIELD and BOYKIN, *Research Communication on Chemistry, Pathology and Pharmacology* (1974),[1108] studied the effect of DPH, administered orally and intraperitoneally to rats, on the norepinephrine uptake by the brain synaptosomes isolated from these rats.

The authors observed that DPH stimulated the uptake of norepinephrine when the medium was anoxic. They note that these *in vivo* results are confirmatory of their earlier *in vitro* results in which DPH was added directly to the isolated synaptosomes.[1109]

The authors conclude that this provides further evidence for the regulatory effect of DPH on uptake, storage and release of neurotransmitters in brain.

PINCUS and LEE, *Archives of Neurology* (1973),[1417] found that DPH limits the release of norepinephrine from the cells in rat brain slices.

LEW, *Proceedings of the Society of Experimental Biology and Medicine* (1975),[1282] found that DPH increased the concentration of norepinephrine in the hypothalamus, cerebellum and brain stem in a strain of naturally hypertensive rats.

The author notes that a deficiency of norepinephrine in the hypothalamus has been reported to coincide with hypertension.

Acetylcholine Concentration and Effect

VAN REES, WOODBURY and NOACH, *Archives Internationales de Pharmacodynamie et de Therapie* (1969),[1642] found that small amounts of DPH increased the release of acetylcholine from parasympathetic nerve endings in the wall of the ileum and also from the intramural ganglia and thus had a stimulating effect on the contraction of the ileum. However, when the contraction of the ileum was made excessive by the addition of acetylcholine, DPH inhibited the excessive contractions of the ileum. Thus, a "biphasic effect" of DPH in this circumstance was referred to by the authors. (See the effect of DPH on acetylcholine levels in brain, Agarwal and Bhargava[1] and in heart, Bose, Saifi and Sharma,[30] pp. 194–95, Vol. I.)

BAKER, OKAMOTO and RIKER, *The Pharmacologist* (1971),[789] found that in a cat soleus nerve-muscle preparation, pretreatment with DPH counteracts the additional excitation produced by injecting acetylcholine. The authors note that DPH selectively suppresses the post-tetanic potentiation of motor nerve terminals without impairing single impulse transmission. (See also Rutledge, Sohn and Sardinas.)[1494]

VANASIN, BASS, MENDELOFF and SCHUSTER, *American Journal of Digestive Diseases* (1973),[1644] studied the direct effect of DPH on isolated strips of smooth muscle of colon from fourteen humans and twenty-four dogs. The authors concluded that DPH's mode of action can be directly on smooth muscle as well as on neuromuscular junction.

The effect of DPH on colon smooth muscle was studied by chemical stimulation with acetylcholine and 5-hydroxytryptamine, and also by electrical stimulation. In both conditions when compared to controls, DPH was found to significantly increase relaxation time and decrease contraction time.

The authors suggest that the observed effect of DPH on isolated smooth muscle of the colon suggests a basis for therapeutic use of DPH in the treatment of spastic colon syndrome.

(See also effect of DPH on smooth muscle of bronchi,[1535] on peripheral muscle (muscle endplate)[1602] and on cortisone myopathy of skeletal muscle.)[1103, 1594]

FERRARI and FURLANUT, *Archives Internationales de Pharmacodynamie et de Therapie* (1973),[1021] studied the effect of DPH on the mechanical and electrical activity of the isolated guinea pig ileum, and also of the isolated smooth muscle strips of guinea pig ileum.

DPH was found to enhance muscular relaxation and to regulate the response of smooth muscle to acetylcholine stimulation. The authors note that these effects are consonant with the previously demonstrated stabilizing activity of DPH on all excitable membranes.

GABA Uptake and Concentration

SAAD, EL MASRY and SCOTT, *Communications in Behavioral Biology* (1972),[1495] studied the effect of DPH (in mice) on the GABA content of normal cerebral hemispheres, and of cerebral hemispheres depleted of GABA. DPH was found to increase normal cerebral hemisphere GABA, and also to increase cerebral hemisphere concentrations of GABA previously reduced by isoniazid.

(See also studies indicating DPH enhances the conversion of glutamic acid to glutamine and GABA in brain,[532] increases brain GABA in several species,[522] and increases uptake of radioactive GABA by brain.)[454]

Adrenocortical Function

GRUENER and STERN, *Nature, New Biology* (1972),[1103] found that DPH protects against steroid myopathy induced by dexamethasone in mice.

Myopathy was induced in twelve mice by intraperitoneal injection of dexamethasone. Then six of these mice received four injections of DPH over a period of two days and were sacrificed. None of these DPH-treated mice had myopathy as measured both histologically and by membrane action potential. In the other six mice not treated with DPH, each had myopathy. As further controls, six mice had been given DPH alone without effect on normal muscle membrane properties. (See Stern, Gruener and Amundsen,[1594] for clinical effectiveness of DPH in a patient with steroid myopathy.)

DILL, *Anatomical Record* (1964),[964] studied the effect of DPH on the corticosterone response in surgically-stressed rats. DPH did not affect the normal rise in plasma corticosterone in response to the stress of a standard laparotomy. DPH was found to not affect the normal plasma corticosterone levels in non-stressed rats.

HOLDAWAY, *Proceedings of the Indiana Academy of Science* (1968),[1157] found that chronic administration of DPH to rats produced no change in weight of the adrenal glands when compared to the normal.

KUNTZMAN and SOUTHREN, *Advances in Biochemical Psychopharmacology* (1969),[1240] demonstrated that the metabolism of cortisol in liver microsomes of guinea pigs was increased by pretreatment of the animals with DPH. The authors conclude that these results are in agreement with previous observations that DPH increases the metabolism of cortisol.

CHOI, THRASHER, WERK, SHOLITON and OLINGER, *Journal of Pharmacology and Experi-*

mental Therapeutics (1971),[896] studied the effect of DPH on the metabolism of injected cortisol in man. DPH was found to increase the turnover kinetics of this labelled cortisol. DPH was not found to affect normal plasma cortisol binding.

Werk, Thrasher, Sholiton, Olinger and Choi, *Clinical Pharmacology and Therapeutics* (1971),[1679] studied, for up to twenty-four months, the cortisol production and metabolism in twenty-one patients with convulsive disorders, with and without DPH therapy. Cortisol metabolism was evaluated by the ratio in the urine of 6-hydroxycortisol to 17-hydroxycorticosteroids. During DPH therapy there was a positive correlation between cortisol secretion rates, measured by isotope dilution method, and an increase in the ratio of 6-hydroxycortisol to 17-hydroxycorticosteroids. The cortisol secretion rate was found to increase significantly only when the ratio of the hydroxycortisol to corticosteroids increased more than 0.14.

The authors concluded that this regulatory effect of DPH on cortisol metabolism was achieved with no deleterious effects in the patients.[1]

Tyler, West, Jubiz and Meikle, *Transactions of the American Clinical and Climatological Association* (1970),[1627] found DPH to have a suppressing effect on the artificial stimulation of cortisone secretion in metyrapone tests. The authors found that it was necessary to approximately double the amount of metyrapone to produce the usual artificial stim-

ulation response in patients receiving DPH.[1351]

Haque, Thrasher, Werk, Knowles and Sholiton, *Journal of Clinical Endocrinology and Metabolism* (1972),[1128] found that DPH administration markedly increases the removal rate of dexamethasone from plasma. The authors note that the metabolism of plasma dexamethasone varies considerably among individuals. (See also Ref. 776, 1480 and 1678.)

American Pharmaceutical Association (1973).[763] The authors state that when dexamethasone is used for testing adrenocortical function in patients receiving DPH, these tests should be interpreted carefully. If this test is used in patients regularly receiving DPH, a higher dose of dexamethasone has been recommended.

In spite of this the authors state that there is no clinical evidence that DPH inhibits the therapeutic effect of dexamethasone.

Houck, Jacob and Maengwyn-Davies, *Journal of Clinical Investigation* (1960),[172] found that DPH decreases dermal water and fat and increases collagen in rat skin. Houck and Jacob[502] showed that DPH diminished the catabolic effect of cortisol which reduces hexosamine, nitrogen and collagen fractions in the skin.

Oxytocin Secretion

Mittler and Glick, *Abstracts of the Fourth International Congress on Endocrinology* (1972),[1368] studied the effect of DPH upon the release of oxytocin from isolated rat pituitary gland. Increase of potassium in the medium was found to increase oxytocin release. Pre-incubation with DPH reduced this stimulated release of oxytocin by 35%.

Antidiuretic Hormone Secretion

Landolt, *Acta Endocrinologica* (1974),[1256] found that DPH had a definite therapeutic

---

[1] See also Choi, Thrasher, Werk, Sholiton and Olinger.[896] For further studies of the regulatory effect of DPH on adrenal cortisol function see also Christy and Hofmann,[903] Costa, Glaser and Bonnycastle,[918] Bray, Ely and Kelley,[864] Bray, Kelley, Zapata and Ely,[866] Bray, Ely, Zapata and Kelley,[865] Bonnycastle and Bradley,[520] and Dill.[964] Dill,[76, 964] demonstrated the selective effect of DPH in not inhibiting the initial elevation of plasma corticosterone in stressed rats, and the reduction in the duration of the elevation of corticosterone in chronically stressed rats. See also Ref. 997.

diuretic effect in a patient who postoperatively demonstrated an inappropriate antidiuretic hormone (vasopressin) syndrome. The author noted that this regulatory effect of DPH is remarkable in that it corrects the abnormal condition but does not affect normal water metabolism.

See also Lee, Grumer, Bronsky and Waldstein,[219] and Fichman and Bethune.[96]

GUZEK, RUSSELL and THORN, *Acta Pharmacologica et Toxicologica* (1974),[1105] demonstrated that DPH inhibits the release of vasopressin from isolated rat neurohypophysis. The effect was observed both during release conditions and after electrical stimulation of the hypophysis.

The authors note that their observations are relevant to the other situations in which DPH has been shown to have a regulatory effect upon endocrine secretions such as insulin, glucagon and calcitonin.

Carbohydrate Metabolism

STAMBAUGH and TUCKER, *Diabetes* (1974),[1583] describe the successful treatment, with diphenylhydantoin, of five patients with functional hypoglycemia previously unresponsive to dietary management.

Clinical reversal of hypoglycemia was observed in all five cases. In addition, laboratory tests confirmed this observation in both six-hour glucose tolerance and insulin level tests, performed before and after DPH therapy. For full summary see pp. 209–11.

LEVIN, BOOKER, SMITH and GRODSKY, *Journal of Clinical Endocrinology and Metabolism* (1970),[1269] studied the effect of DPH on insulin secretion by the isolated perfused rat pancreas. When the pancreas was perfused with glucose in the absence of DPH, insulin was secreted which could be measured by an immunoreactive method. With DPH, the amount of insulin released was reduced, illustrating DPH's regulatory effect.

KIZER, VARGAS-CORDON, BRENDEL and BRESSLER, *Journal of Clinical Investigation* (1970),[1220] studied the effect of DPH on the secretion of insulin *in vitro* by isolated islets of Langerhans and pancreatic pieces. DPH was found to reduce the release of insulin in proportion to the dose of DPH employed. The effect was found to be reversible by potassium and ouabain.

KNOPP, SHEININ and FREINKEL, *Archives of Internal Medicine* (1972),[1222] reported that DPH inhibited the "stimulated" insulin release from the islet cell tumor. They noted that their observations indicate that DPH may warrant consideration as a safe therapeutic adjunct in inoperable or poorly controlled islet cell tumors.

HOFELDT, DIPPE, LEVIN, KARAM, BLUM and FORSHAM, *Diabetes* (1974),[1154] reported on the use of DPH in three patients with surgically proven insulinomas, tested with oral and intravenous glucose.

The authors found that DPH had no significant effect on basal glucose or insulin values and is therefore limited in its use in insulinomas. It was useful in reducing insulin secretion after stimuli.

COHEN, BOWER, FIDLER, JOHNSONBAUGH and SODE, *Lancet* (1973),[909] studied the effect of DPH on a patient with a benign insulinoma. The authors found that DPH effectively raised the mean fasting plasma glucose concentration and improved the immunoreactive insulin to glucose ratio.

The authors stated that these studies suggest that DPH has an advantage over diazoxide for the reduction of insulin release. They conclude that DPH appears to be a promising agent in the treatment of certain patients with insulinoma.

BRODOWS and CAMPBELL, *Journal of Clinical Endocrinology and Metabolism* (1974),[872] describe the successful control of refractory hypoglycemia with therapeutic doses of DPH, in a patient with a suspected functional islet cell tumor. The authors state that the adequacy of the control of the hypoglycemia by DPH was evidenced by normal overnight fasting glucose levels and the absence of hypoglycemia during total fasting up to twenty-four hours. They note that it is of interest that there was a high degree of correlation between postabsorptive glucose and serum DPH levels and also a significant lowering of basal insulin levels during DPH therapy.

They conclude that DPH could be tried at therapeutic levels to control the hypoglycemia associated with islet cell adenomas and should be given consideration for the management of such tumors. (See similar recommendation by Knopp, Sheinin and Freinkel).[1222]

LEVIN, REED, CHING, DAVIS and BLUM, *Clinical Research* (1972),[1274] measured the effect of DPH on the total insulin in blood after oral glucose tolerance tests, and after intravenous arginine stimulation. The authors found that diabetics of normal weight and non-diabetics who are overweight demonstrate DPH's regulatory influence on insulin secretion more than do normals.

CUDWORTH and CUNNINGHAM, *Clinical Science and Molecular Medicine* (1974),[924] studied glucose tolerance tests, serum insulin, and growth hormone levels in healthy volunteers before and after receiving DPH, 100 mg every eight hours, for fourteen days. The response of insulin to oral glucose was reduced in different individuals by 11 to 44%. Glucose tolerance remained normal, and no changes in growth hormone levels were observed.

MADSEN, HANSEN and DECKERT, *Acta Neurologica Scandanavica* (1974),[1327] investigated intravenous glucose tolerance in eight patients before and during treatment with DPH. They found that neither glucose tolerance nor insulin secretion was affected after

a glucose load. In eight patients, who had for several years been treated with DPH, the results were comparable to those found in the patients before treatment.

LEVIN, GRODSKY, HAGURA, SMITH, LICKO and FORSHAM, *Clinical Research* (1972),[1272] and *Diabetes* (1972),[1273] studied the kinetics of DPH's regulation of insulin secretion by the isolated perfused pancreas.

By comparison of the results with a computerized model of regulatory control, the authors concluded that DPH exerts its regulatory effect both in terms of the labile compartment of insulin and in terms of the provision of insulin to this compartment prior to secretion. (See also Levin, et al. Ref. 1271 and 1270.)

GERICH, CHARLES, LEVIN, FORSHAM and GRODSKY, *Journal of Clinical Endocrinology* (1972),[1062] studied the effect of DPH on glucagon secretion in the isolated perfused rat pancreas. At 25 micrograms/ml DPH markedly diminished glucagon release and had no effect on insulin release. Higher concentrations of DPH were shown earlier to reduce the release of insulin as well.[1220, 1269]

The authors note that this selective action of DPH in controlling glucagon release presumably reflects the special sensitivity to DPH of the alpha cells of the pancreas as compared with the beta cells. Since glucagon and insulin act in opposite manner in the control of blood sugar, DPH is shown in these experiments to influence the release of both hormones and consequently to have at least two potential regulatory actions on blood sugar.

The authors note the reports in the literature which indicate that DPH stabilizes poorly controlled diabetes mellitus in humans.[91,92,382,430] They conclude that the results of the present study are in accord with the observations that DPH is clinically useful.

GOSSEL and MENNEAR, *Pharmacologist* (1971),[1092] studied the effect of pretreatment with DPH on the development of alloxan diabetes in mice. DPH administered one hour prior to alloxan was found to prevent the development of alloxan diabetes. Administration of DPH after alloxan had no effect. The authors noted the work of others[1220, 1269] indicating that DPH has a regulatory effect on insulin secretion by the isolated pancreas and suggested that the findings of their study are in accord with the notion that DPH binds to and exerts a selective action on these pancreatic cells. The authors concluded that DPH appeared to be protecting the pancreatic beta cell binding sites from alloxan. (See also Mennear and Gossel.)[1354]

ESPOSITO-AVELLA and MENNEAR, *Proceedings of the Society of Experimental Biology and Medicine* (1973),[1015] studied the protective effect of DPH against alloxan diabetes in mice. The authors found that both DPH administered intraperitoneally and D-glucose administered intravenously afforded complete protection against alloxan. The authors concluded that both D-glucose and DPH exerted their protective effects by binding to the pancreatic beta cell.

SCHIMMEL and GRAHAM, *Hormone and Metabolic Research* (1974),[1509] studied the protective effect of DPH on normal male rats against streptozotocin-induced diabetes. Intravenous injection of DPH, 20 mg/kg, nineteen minutes prior to or within sixty minutes after administration of streptozotocin was found to prevent the development of diabetes.

MENNEAR and GOSSEL, *Toxicology and Applied Pharmacology* (1973),[1355] studied the effect of DPH on blood glucose levels in normally fed mice. DPH was found not to alter the resting blood glucose levels. The glucose values were somewhat reduced. In mice, DPH did not interfere with the hypoglycemic effect of injected insulin, but DPH did counteract the hypoglycemic effect of tolbutamide.

ANTITOXIC EFFECTS OF DPH

The toxic effects of the following substances have been reported to be diminished or counteracted by DPH. Some of these substances are poisons; others are therapeutic but can have toxic effects in overdose.

DPH has been reported to have protective effects against:

cardiac arrhythmias and conduction defects due to *acetylstrophanthidin* toxicity, in dogs (Ref. 327);

aconitine induced arrhythmias, in dogs (Ref. 410 and 1557);

alloxan induced diabetes, in mice (Ref. 1015, 1092, 1354);

cardiac arrhythmias induced by *amitriptyline* poisoning, in humans (Ref. 1382, 1428, 1430);

amphetamine toxicity, in mice (Ref. 99);

bilirubin toxicity in that it reduces the incidence of physiological jaundice of the newborn, in humans (Ref. 1388);

bulbocapnine induced catatonia, in rats and cats (Ref. 596);

toxic effects of *corticosteroid* excess, in animals and humans; e.g., steroid myopathy, in mice (Ref. 171, 377, 425, 451, 454, 482, 483, 504, 896, 1103, 1128 and 1238);

toxic effects of *cyanide* on nerve, in animals (Ref. 699 and 812);

delphinine induced arrhythmias, in dogs (Ref. 410);

deslanoside induced ectopic arrhythmias, in animals and humans (Ref. 308, 753 and 754);

DDT in that it reduces storage levels of DDT and DDE, in animals and humans (Ref. 701, 823, 914, 921, 943, 944, 998, 999, 1022, 1253, 1349, 1510 and 1666);

digitalis induced arrhythmias permitting more digitalis to be used before toxic effects occur; and does not interfere with inotropic benefits of digitalis, in animals and humans (Ref. 61, 62, 80, 82, 149, 150, 151, 154, 155, 157, 158, 187, 215, 233, 248, 249, 310, 318, 328, 403, 404, 405, 407, 415, 418, 519, 597, 685, 753, 880, 905, 941, 963, 969, 991, 1007, 1052, 1084, 1085, 1114, 1121, 1122, 1151, 1170, 1209, 1214, 1264, 1277, 1289, 1402, 1434, 1488, 1507, 1508, 1515, 1562, 1563, 1590, 1705 and 1707;

toxic effects of *estradiol* excess, in quail (Ref. 823);

nephropathy induced by *gold,* in rats (Ref. 1525);

arrhythmias induced by toxic doses of *imipramine,* in humans (Ref. 1382 and 1428);

the symptoms of *lithium* toxicity, in humans (Ref. 1637);

the neurotoxicity of *mephenytoin,* in mice (Ref. 567);

the neurotoxicity of *mephobarbital,* in mice (Ref. 567);

methaqualone intoxication, in rats (Ref. 1529);

severe paralysis and mortality induced by toxic combination of *methylphenidate* and *thyroxine,* in rats (Ref. 1530);

symptoms of *morphine* withdrawal, in rats, and morphine induced mania, in cats (Ref. 1026 and 1027);

brain *mucoprotein* induced coma, in mice and rabbits (Ref. 1466);

ouabain induced cardiac arrhythmias, in dogs, and to counteract ouabain induced toxicity in nerve, in animals (Ref. 19, 153, 158, 233, 260, 514, 530, 699, 714, 753, 754, 799, 800, 805, 812, 860, 978, 1079, 1419, 1622, 1663 and 1696);

phenylisothiocyanate toxicity in the liver, in rats (Ref. 1528);

propoxyphene induced dyskinesia, in rats (Ref. 1527);

reserpine induced hyperexcitability and rigidity, in rats, and hypothermia, in mice (Ref. 182, 183, 1306 and 1643);

streptozotocin induced diabetes, in rats (Ref. 1509);

strychnine toxicity, in rats, cats, and humans (Ref. 90, 625 and 1208);

the suppression of locomotion induced by *tetrabenazine,* in mice and rats (Ref. 1306);

the neurotoxicity of *trimethadione,* in mice (Ref. 567).

Other Studies

Behavior

BERNSTEIN and JOHNSON, *Bulletin of Environmental Contamination and Toxicology* (1973),[823] while studying the effects of diphenylhydantoin upon estrogen metabolism in pesticide-treated quail, observed that the pesticide (DDT) caused excitability and aggressive behavior in the quail and that diphenylhydantoin reduced this excitable and aggressive behavior, without any apparent sedative effect.[1]

FERTZIGER, LYNCH and STEIN, *Brain Research* (1974),[1026] found that DPH decreased the withdrawal syndrome in rats who had been made dependent on morphine. The authors state that abrupt withdrawal of morphine is known to increase neuronal excitability in animals as well as in man.

The DPH treated animals contrasted sharply with controls in some aspects of the abstinence syndrome. Hyperexcitability was remarkably reduced and significantly fewer "wet dog" or body shakes occurred in the DPH treated groups.

FERTZIGER, STEIN and LYNCH, *Psychopharmacologia* (1974),[1027] studied the effects of DPH pretreatment on the morphine-mania response in cats.

The authors note that in the cat, morphine has been classically recognized to produce a species-specific excitant or manic response. This response includes extreme excitation and agitation, with explosive impulsivity, jumping abruptly and intermittently vocalizing. When the cats were pretreated with DPH, morphine no longer elicited these hypermanic responses.

The authors say that this study, taken together with their previous study that showed that DPH modifies withdrawal symptoms in rats, suggests that treatment with DPH may prove to be effective in reducing some of the withdrawal symptoms commonly seen in human addicts.

HOUGHTON, LATHAM and RICHENS, *European Journal of Clinical Pharmacology*

---

[1] See also study by Fink and Swinyard[99] showing that diphenylhydantoin markedly reduced amphetamine toxicity in aggregated mice, and Tedeschi, et al.[749] and Chen, et al.[419] demonstrating that diphenylhydantoin suppressed fighting behavior in mice.

(1973),[1168] examined the effect of diphenylhydantoin in six normal volunteers with regard to critical flicker fusion threshold (CFF). No significant change in CFF was observed at 200 mg, 300 mg and 400 mg of diphenylhydantoin given when CFF was tested hourly from one to seven hours after ingestion of DPH.

STEPHENS, SHAFFER and BROWN, *Journal of Clinical Pharmacology* (1974),[1593] investigated effects of DPH compared with placebo on mood and psychomotor functioning in 107 normal volunteers. A double-blind procedure with crossover was employed. Substantial doses of DPH, 100 mg t.i.d. were given for two week periods. Twenty-nine different measures of mood and psychomotor functioning were used. There was essentially no alteration in mood or psychomotor function as determined by the twenty-nine measures in the men and in only one of the measures, mild dysphoria, in the women.

GEHRES, RANDALL, RICCIO and VARDARIS, *Physiology and Behavior* (1973),[1058] found that DPH markedly reduced the retrograde amnesia produced by lowered body temperature in rats. In addition, electrophysiological data indicated that DPH reduced the paroxysmal electrical activity induced in the hippocampus and amygdala by the lowered body temperature.

MOURAVIEFF-LESUISSE and GIURGEA, *Archives Internationales de Pharmacodynamie et de Therapie* (1970),[1376] found that DPH shortened spinal fixation time in normal rats and also in those in which spinal fixation time had been prolonged by electroshock. The authors note that spinal fixation time reflects a form of memory consolidation process within spinal cord reflexes.

GORDON, CALLAGHAN and DOTY, *Pharmacologist* (1968),[1088] reported that DPH did not appear to affect the performance of normal young adult rats, but that DPH enhanced the learning level and stable memory of aged rats for avoidance paradigms.

Cognitive Performance

These studies deal with essentially normal human beings. For more detailed summaries, see Thought, Mood and Behavior section, pp. 215–17.

HAWARD, *Drugs and Cerebral Function* (1970),[1139] found DPH effective to a significant degree in improving concentration in twelve college students.

SMITH and LOWREY, *Drugs, Development and Cerebral Function* (1972),[1564] in a double-blind study, found that DPH improved cognitive performance to a significant level in twenty volunteer hospital employees.

HAWARD, *Revue de Medecine Aeronautique et Spatiale* (1973),[1140] found DPH improved performance to a significant degree in three separate groups of pilots in simulated flying and radar-fixing tasks.

SMITH and LOWREY, *Journal of the American Geriatrics Society* (1975),[1565] in a double-blind study, found improvement in cognitive functions in a group of elderly normal subjects.

Healing

Recent studies on healing follow. For other studies on healing in animals see Ref. 171, 172, 188, 189, 335, 336, 337, 339, 343, 499, 500, 501, 502, 504, 505, 811. For studies in humans, see Ref. 25, 127, 341, 344, 669, 730, 894, 1080, 1371, 1403, 1504.

FRACTURES

GUDMUNDSON and LIDGREN, *Acta Orthopaedica Scandinavica* (1973),[1104] in a controlled study (eighty mice) found that DPH accelerates healing of fractures experimentally induced. The tensile strength of healing unstable fractures and the breaking strength of healing fractures were significantly greater in animals treated with DPH than in controls. In the DPH-treated animals the fractured callus contained a larger amount of extractable collagen.

The authors noted that these results in mice are in agreement with previous findings of improved healing of fractures of the mandible of rabbits treated with DPH (Sklans, et al.)[343] They note that the organic matrix of bone is more than 90% composed of collagen and that DPH has been shown to stimulate the synthesis of collagen in various tissues (Houck, et al.[172] and Shafer, et al.)[506, 507]

The authors concluded that this higher rate of collagen synthesis may contribute to the better rate of healing of fractures with DPH.

SKIN

HOUCK, CHENG and WATERS, *Antiepileptic Drugs* (1972),[1164] reported that DPH increases the amount of insoluble collagen in the connective tissue of rats. In addition, they observed an increase in another protein (insoluble, noncollagenous) which they termed scleroprotein. With this increase of scleroprotein, the authors noted a significant reduction in the amount of triglyceride or neutral fats from the tissue.

The authors note these findings in animals are consistent with those observed of improved wound healing in clinical studies.

CARIES

ROVIN, SABES, EVERSOLE and GORDON, *Journal of Dental Research* (1973),[1485] studied the effect of DPH in preventing caries. The authors state that during the course of a previous study on periodontal disease in rats, there had been an attempt to produce gingival hyperplasia with DPH. Although they were unsuccessful in producing gingival hyperplasia, they noticed that the DPH treated rats did not develop caries as previous studies would have indicated they should.

As a result of this observation, the authors studied the effect of DPH on the prevention of caries in rats, using controls. In this study a ligature of the first mandibular molar was used as the irritant for inducing experimental caries. They found that DPH had a marked effect in retarding caries in these animals. The effect was particularly apparent for five months; at the end of ten months, the effect was less because by this time the ligation process was highly effective in creating caries.

The authors concluded that in their experiments DPH appears to act as a caries retarder, and it was possible that there was a significant clinical application for their findings.

Other

LOTTI, TORCHIANA and PORTER, *Archives Internationales de Pharmacodynamie et de Therapie* (1973),[1306] found in mice that the suppression of movement induced by tetrabenazine, and the lowered body temperature induced by reserpine, were offset by DPH.

The authors state that these actions of DPH were unique in that twelve other substances which were tested did not provide this protection.

LEVO, *Naunyn-Schmiedeberg's Archiv fur Pharmakologie* (1974),[1279] in a controlled study, observed that DPH reduced the incidence of lung adenomas induced by urethane in SWR mice. Fifteen mice were injected with solvent used to suspend DPH, fifteen others were untreated and fourteen were treated with DPH. The animals were sacrificed after twelve weeks.

The fifteen mice treated with solvent had a total of seventy adenomas. The fifteen mice untreated had a total of sixty-eight adenomas. The fourteen mice treated with DPH had a total of forty-one adenomas (forty-four when corrected to fifteen).

DPH METABOLISM

A review of the absorption, transport, metabolism and excretion of DPH is in Vol. I, page 270. These subjects have been extensively reviewed recently by others: Ausman,[781] Gabler and Hubbard,[1044] Garrettson,[1051] Glazko,[1076] Kutt,[1247] Weber-Eggenberger and Kaufmann[1669] and Woodbury and Swinyard.[1697]

The determination of DPH concentration in serum is clearly useful in cases of overdose and in cases where there is uncertainty as to whether the patient is taking DPH. A direct relationship between clinical effectiveness and blood levels has not been established for all patients. The tissue to blood ratios are of interest because of the selective action of DPH in preferential binding in brain, established in animal studies.[1]

Clinically, authors stress the need for DPH dosage to be adjusted to the individual patient and to the condition being treated. On average smaller amounts of DPH are effective in the treatment of disorders other than epilepsy.

Binding to Cell Constituents

The following studies demonstrate an unusual property of DPH, its preferential binding in brain. This selectivity has been demonstrated in brain cortex, in nerve cells in preference to glial cells, and within nerve cells for nuclei and microsomes in preference to other cell constituents.

[1] Ref. 794, 862, 1081, 1082, 1215, 1383, 1471, 1539, 1608, 1636, 1687 and 1704.

RIZZO, MORSELLI and GARATTINI, *Biochemical Pharmacology* (1972),[1471] studied levels of DPH in plasma and brain of rats after short and long term administration of DPH. Plasma levels of DPH were not always found to be a reliable index of brain levels.

SHERWIN, EISEN and SOKOLOWSKI, *Presented at the Annual Meeting of the American Neurological Association and the Canadian Congress of Neurological Sciences* (1973),[1539] studied the ratio of DPH in brain and plasma, in rats, and found that the concentration was 50% greater in brain than in plasma. In a study of a single patient the same ratio was found.

BARLOW, FIREMARK and ROTH, *Journal of Neuropathology and Experimental Neurology* (1965),[794] studied the regional entry and accumulation of radioactive DPH in both adult and immature cat brain. Autoradiography and radioassay were used to observe the accumulation of DPH in brain from two minutes to twenty-four hours after a single intravenous injection. The authors observed that the level of DPH in adult brain exceeded DPH's concentration in plasma two to threefold, from one-half to twenty-four hours after injection. This preferential concentration in brain was not present in immature animals but became prominent at one month of age.

KEMP and WOODBURY, *Journal of Pharmacology and Experimental Therapeutics* (1971),[1215] studied the subcellular distribution of radioactive DPH in rat brain.

The authors concluded that the microsomal fraction is the major binding site for DPH in the cerebral cortex.

WILENSKY and LOWDEN, *Epilepsy Abstracts* (1972),[1687] studied the binding of DPH to subcellular fractions of brain of rats injected with radioactive DPH. The authors noted that twelve hours after injection there was increased concentration in a heavy microsomal fraction which contained mainly small nerve endings.

When subcellular fractions from brains of uninjected rats were dialyzed against solutions containing radioactive DPH, there was a tendency for DPH to bind to fractions containing plasma membranes. The degree of binding was decreased by the presence of calcium; magnesium had no effect. When both calcium and magnesium were present, binding of DPH was the same as when both ions were absent.

The authors concluded that DPH interacts with plasma membranes.

YANAGIHARA, *Antiepileptic Drugs* (1972),[1704] studied the distribution of radioactive DPH into neuronal and glial fractions of rat brain. He found that DPH, at least in particle-bound form, has a high affinity for nerve cells and tends to remain attached to some subcellular structures of nerve cells.

NEILSEN and COTMAN, *European Journal of Pharmacology* (1971),[1383] studied the binding of DPH to brain in the rat. The authors noted that earlier work had shown that brain appears to retain DPH more effectively than plasma and some other tissues. In addition, they cited the experimental evidence that DPH's effects are mediated by its acting on and modulating neural membrane processes.

In these experiments the binding of radioactive DPH to homogenates and subcellular fractions of rat brain was studied both *in vitro* and after *in vivo* administration. The amount of DPH bound to subcellular particles was found to be small, and selective for only certain particles. Synaptosomes bound DPH but myelin membranes did not. Extracted brain lipids exhibited less affinity for DPH than intact subcellular particles.

The authors concluded that DPH's action on membrane components of brain is achieved even at relatively low concentrations, perhaps less than 10^{-8}M. This indicated to the authors that the action of DPH may be quite specific to certain key macromolecular components in brain.[1]

TAPPAZ and PACHECO, *Journal of Pharmacology* (1973),[1608] studied the subcellular binding of DPH by rat brain cortex slices. Binding to nuclei and microsomes was observed with lesser binding to other subcellular particulates. The authors concluded that their results were in accord with those of Woodbury and Kemp[1696] and Nielsen and Cotman.[1383]

BOYKIN, *Neurology* (1974),[862] studied the binding of radioactive DPH to brain subfractions. DPH was found to bind to nuclei and microsomes, and in each case some of the bound DPH was shown to be attached to protein. As an illustration of the selectivity of binding of DPH, it was found not to bind *in vitro* to nucleic acid fractions from yeast, mammalian transfer RNA, mammalian ribosomes, and calf thymus.

GOLDBERG and TODOROFF, *Neurology* (1972),[1082] studied the binding of DPH to subcellular fractions of mouse brain. They concluded that DPH is differentially bound to several brain subcellular constituents, that this binding is not covalent in nature, and that it does not appear to require an active biochemical process. See also Ref. 1081.

Plasma Protein and Red Cell Binding

The plasma protein binding properties of DPH have been studied by Loeser,[440] by Lightfoot and Christian,[1288] by Lunde, Rane, Yaffe, Lund and Sjoqvist,[1316] by Borga,[849] by Rane, Lunde and Jalling,[1442] by Ehrnebo, Agurell, Jalling and Boreus,[1000] by Conard, Haavik and Finger,[916] by Lunde,[1315] by Krasner,[1232] by Lund, Berlin and Lunde,[1314] by Krasner, Giacoia and Yaffe,[1233] by Baggot and Davis,[788] by Odar-Cederlof and Borga,[1393] and red cell binding by Hansotia and Keran.[1126]

---

[1] See also similar conclusion by Firemark, Barlow and Roth[101] reviewed in Vol. I, p. 200.

Chemical Identification and Determination

Methods for the chemical determination of DPH have been reviewed by Glazko,[1077] and by Friedlander.[1039] Methods include infrared studies by Elliott and Natarajan;[1006] spectrophotometric titration and determination by Agarwal and Blake,[755] by Wallace,[1654,1655,1656] by Dill, Baukema, Chang and Glazko,[965] and by Thurkow, Wesseling and Meijer;[1615] utilizing benzophenone as the oxidation product of DPH, in spectrophotometric determination, as by Dill, Chucot, Chang and Glazko,[966] and Chrobok;[904] vapor-phase chromatography as utilized by Van Meter, Buckmaster and Shelley;[1639] gas liquid chromatography as utilized by O'Malley, Denckla and O'Doherty,[1389] by Erdey, Kapler, Takacs and Dessouky,[1010] by Baylis, Fry and Marks,[810] by Kupferberg,[1241] by Evenson, Jones and Darcey,[1017] by Solow and Green,[1570] by Sampson, Harasymiv and Hensley,[1498] by Cooper, Greaves and Owen,[917] by Goudie and Burnett,[1095] by Solow, Metaxas and Summers,[1571] and by Berlin, Agurell, Borga, Lund and Sjoqvist.[821]

Methods utilizing high-speed liquid chromatography have been described by Gauchel, Gauchel and Birkofer.[1054] Thin-layer chromatography methods have been described by Vedso, Rud and Place,[1647] by Simon, Jatlow, Seligson and Seligson,[1550] and by Sabih and Sabih.[1496] A radio-immunoassay method for DPH has been described by Tigelaar, Rapport, Inman and Kupferberg.[1617] A high-speed ion exchange chromatography method has been described by Anders and Latorre.[766] Microassay of DPH in blood and brain has been described by Lee and Bass,[1262] and a method for determining DPH in saliva has been described by Bochner, Hooper, Sutherland, Eadie and Tyrer.[843]

[The references that pertain to *DPH, 1975* are found on pages 302 to 323.]

BACKGROUND—SOCIOMEDICAL INFORMATION

Origin of interest of the Dreyfus Medical Foundation in DPH

The interest of the Dreyfus Medical Foundation in diphenylhydantoin started with the experience of one of the authors who had personal benefits from DPH. This experience led to the formation of the Foundation in 1963. Details have been reported at a medical meeting, and also in the lay press.[1,2]

Cooperation with and from the Federal Health Agencies

The initial objective of the Dreyfus Medical Foundation was to prove or disprove that DPH was useful other than in epilepsy. After a double-blind crossover study at the Worcester County Jail, in 1966, had produced convincing evidence of broad benefits of DPH,[3] the then Secretary of Health, Education and Welfare, John W. Gardner, was consulted. Secretary Gardner made several suggestions. One of these was to have the information communicated to physicians through a national publication. Secretary Gardner predicted such publication would yield much useful information from physicians throughout the country. The Secretary's suggestion was followed (see below).[2]

Since these first discussions with Secretary Gardner, The Department of Health, Education and Welfare and The Food and Drug Administration and members of their staffs have been apprised of the growing evidence of the broad therapeutic benefits of DPH. Secretary Finch, Secretary Richardson and Secretary Weinberger have all been interested and helpful, as have been FDA Commissioners, Dr. Charles C. Edwards and Dr. Alexander M. Schmidt.[4]

FDA approved indication for use of DPH

The only FDA approved indication for use of DPH is for epilepsy. It is a function of the FDA to respond to applications for use of a new drug or for new uses for an old drug. It has not been the function of the FDA to discover new uses for old drugs. If no application for indication of new uses has been submitted to the FDA, the absence of indication for such new uses neither implies that the FDA approves nor disapproves such uses. To the best of our knowledge, the only submission for new use of DPH has been in cardiology, presently being reviewed. (See below.)[5]

DPH now in wide use

DPH is widely used throughout the world for disorders other than epilepsy. This use is based on the extensive published works of physicians and scientists throughout the world, and on physicians' personal experiences. For an indication of the breadth of use in the United States, see independent survey by IMS America, Ltd. (formerly Lea Associates), pp. 275–76.

[1] Dreyfus, J., "The Beneficial Effects of Diphenylhydantoin on the Nervous Systems of Nonepileptics—As Experienced and Observed in Others by a Layman," Am. Coll. Neuropsychopharmacology, 1966, Ref. 707.

[2] "Ten Thousand-to-One Payoff," LIFE, 1967, and "DPH: New Wonders from an Old Drug," Reader's Digest, 1968.

[3] Resnick, O. and Dreyfus, J., Worcester County Jail Study, 1966, Ref. 704.

[4] See exchange of letters, pp. 274–75.

[5] Patents on DPH expired in 1963. No company has exclusive rights to sell it. It is inexpensive. One of the incentives for a drug company to apply to the FDA for approval of indication for a new use for an old drug is the exclusive right to sell it.

Exchange of Letters Between
Former Governor Nelson Rockefeller
and Former Secretary of HEW Elliot Richardson

April 19, 1972

Dear Mr. Secretary:

It has come to my attention that a great many published reports, written over a thirty-year period by physicians and other scientists, have indicated that the substance diphenylhydantoin has a broad range of beneficial uses. Further, it is my understanding that physicians are prescribing diphenylhydantoin for many purposes other than its original indicated use, in 1938, as an anticonvulsant. In spite of the evidence of diphenylhydantoin's broad usefulness, I understand that today, in 1972, its only listed indication is that of an anticonvulsant.

I realize that the Food and Drug Administration is set up essentially to rectify errors of commission. This certainly does not fall into that category. However, I believe a public clarification of the status of diphenylhydantoin by the FDA would be most valuable, and timely.

I enclose with this letter a publication, "The Broad Range of Use of Diphenylhydantoin —Bibliography and Review," that extensively deals with this subject.

I hope you will give this your consideration.

With warm regard,

Sincerely,
/s/ Nelson A. Rockefeller

• • •

June 22, 1972

Dear Governor Rockefeller:

Please forgive the delay of this response to your April 19 letter concerning the current status of the drug, diphenylhydantoin.

Conversations with health officials within the Department have revealed that diphenylhydantoin (DPH) was introduced in 1938 as the first essentially nonsedating anticonvulsant drug. The dramatic effect of DPH and its widespread acceptance in the treatment of convulsive disorders may have tended to obscure a broader range of therapeutic uses.

A review of the literature reveals that diphenylhydantoin has been reported to be useful in a wide range of disorders. Among its reported therapeutic actions are its stabilizing effect on the nervous system, its antiarrhythmic effect on certain cardiac disorders, and its therapeutic effect on emotional disorders.

The fact that such broad therapeutic effects have been reported by many independent scientists and physicians over a long period of time would seem to indicate that the therapeutic effects of diphenylhydantoin are more than that of an anticonvulsant.

The FDA encourages the submission of formal applications which, of course, would include the necessary supporting evidence for the consideration of approval for a wider range of therapeutic uses.

Your interest in encouraging the Department to provide a public clarification of the status of diphenylhydantoin is very welcome and I hope that this information is responsive to your concerns.

With warm regard,

Sincerely,
/s/ Elliot L. Richardson

•　•　•

Survey of Use of Diphenylhydantoin

There follows a survey by IMS America, Ltd.[1] (year ending March, 1975) of the number of prescriptions of DPH[2] and diagnosis and desired action.

Description of Method of Data Collection—The survey by IMS America, Ltd. is a continuing study of private medical practice in the United States; the study began in 1956. Data are obtained from a representative panel of physicians who report case history information on private patients seen over a given period of time.

Fifteen hundred physicians report four times a year on a forty-eight-hour period of their practice. Each physician fills out a case record form for every private patient treated. Case histories are returned to IMS America, Ltd. for processing. The books are coded and edited by pharmacists. All information is recorded on computer tapes, from which the monthly and quarterly reports are compiled.

Physicians in private practice are selected at random and include representatives of all specialties.

DESIRED ACTION	No. of Prescriptions in Thousands
Anticonvulsant	3057
Prophylaxis	255
Curb Cardiac Arrhythmia	124
Anticoagulant	121
Symptomatic	64
Pain Relief	62
Sedative-Unspecific	46
Control Heart Rate	27
Relieve Headache	24
Withdrawal Symptoms	19
Analgesic	17
Psychotherapeutic	17
Control Dizziness	17
Antineuritic	16
Reduce Tension	15
Relieve Migraine	12
Anticonvulsant and Prophylaxis	12
Sedative Night and Promote Sleep	12
Stimulant	11

DESIRED ACTION	No. of Prescriptions in Thousands
Calming Effect and Tranquilizer	11
Antinauseant	10
Uterine Sedative	9
Antidepressant	7
Prophylaxis and Sedative-Unspecific	6
Antispasmodic	5
Mood Elevation	5
Antiallergic and Anticonvulsant	4
Prevent Migraine	4
Control Vertigo	4
GI Antispasmodic	4
Antihemorrhagic	3
Relieve Headache and Anticonvulsant	3
Cardiotonic	3
No Reason Given	1820
Total	5827

---

[1] Formerly Lea Associates.
[2] This survey is of the prescriptions for the best known trade name of DPH.

DIAGNOSIS	No. of Prescriptions in Thousands	DIAGNOSIS	No. of Prescriptions in Thousands
Diseases of CNS and Sensory Organs	2,534	Circulatory Disorders	452
Epilepsy—not otherwise specified	1,052	Disorders of Heart Rhythm	107
Grand Mal	452	Myocardial Infarct	49
Cerebral Hemorrhage	178	Arteriosclerotic Heart Disease	43
Cerebral Arteriosclerotic Congestion	177	Essential Benign Hypertension	35
Other Diseases of the Brain	176	Other Hypertensive Arteriosclerotic Heart Disease	33
Petit Mal	99	Angina Pectoris	27
Trigeminal Neuralgia	89	Myocardial Occlusion	26
Cerebral Embolism/ Thrombosis	80	Coronary Artery Disease with Selected Complications	26
Cerebral Paralysis/Seizure	48	Arteriosclerosis without Gangrene	23
Stroke—not otherwise specified	38	Myocardial Occlusions with Complications	17
Other Cerebral Paralysis	28	Arteriosclerotic Coronary Artery Disease	17
Migraine	20	Heart Block	9
Facial Paralysis	20	Specific Conditions without Sickness	386
Late Effects of Intracranial Abscess	16	Surgical Aftercare	361
Subarachnoid Hemorrhage	10	Medical Aftercare	25
Intracranial Spinal Abscess	10	Neoplasms	306
Other Neuralgia or Neuritis	9	Malignant Neoplasms—Other Unspecified Sites	103
Symptoms and Senility	1,354	Unspecified Neoplasms Brain/ Nervous System	60
Convulsions	1,145	Malignant Neoplasms of the Brain	41
Syncope or Collapse	44	Malignant Neoplasms of the Nervous System— Unspecified	24
Encephalopathy	27		
Jacksonian Epilepsy	26	Benign Neoplasms of the Brain or Other Parts of the Nervous System	22
Headache—not otherwise specified	22	Malignant Neoplasms of the Lung—Unspecified	19
Vertigo	13	Malignant Neoplasms of Thoracic Organs	15
Tension Headache	12	Accidents and Poisoning	228
Other Ill Defined Conditions	12	Head Injuries	129
Mental Disorders	656	Other Accidents—Poisoning	35
Unspecified Alcoholism	118	Effects of Poisons	28
Chronic Alcoholism	113	Injury of Nerves of Spinal Cord	21
Other Drug Addiction	74	Fractures	16
Acute Alcoholism	45	All Others	212
Depressive Reaction	44	Total[1]	6127
Other Mental Deficiency	41		
Primary Childhood Behavior Disorders	37		
Other Schizophrenia	24		
Alcoholic Psychosis	23		
Presenile Psychosis	21		
Hysteria—not otherwise specified	21		
Psychosis with Organic Brain Disorder	18		
Neurotic Depressive Reaction	16		
Other Pathological Personality	15		
Epileptic Psychosis	13		

[1] Since occasionally more than one diagnosis is given per prescription, the total for diagnosis is not exactly the same as the total for desired action.

Review of
Recent Work

Since 1975 over two thousand studies have been published on clinical uses of DPH and on its basic mechanisms of action. Some of this work is briefly reviewed, and over 400 references are included. No attempt has been made at a complete bibliography.

Safety and toxicology of DPH has been reviewed periodically over its 43 years of use—in 1970 by the Dreyfus Medical Foundation. For other reviews and recent reviews the reader is referred to Haruda,[1884] Keith,[1923] Heinonen, Slone and Shapiro,[1891] Friis,[1836] Reynolds,[2043] Kutt and Solomon,[1940] Staples,[1586] and Woodbury, Penry and Schmidt.[1700]

CONTENTS

CLINICAL USES OF DIPHENYLHYDANTOIN

Thought, Mood and Behavior[1]

The usefulness of DPH has been reported in the treatment of frightening visual and auditory hallucinations, persecutory delusions, ambivalence and bizarre behavior (MOHAN, SALO and NAGASWAMI, *Diseases of the Nervous System,* 1975);[1988] in the treatment of drug-induced psychosis including cocaine, LSD, hashish and mescaline (IFABUMUYI AND JEFFRIES, *Canadian Psychiatric Association Journal,* 1976);[1904] in the treatment of paroxysmal nightmares and frightening hallucinations, a sequel of stroke (BOLLER, WRIGHT, CAVALIERI and MITSUMOTO, *Neurology,* 1975);[1752] in the treatment of unusual sleepwalking episodes characterized by screaming and violent automatisms (PEDLEY AND GUILLEMINAULT, *Annals of Neurology,* 1977);[2014] in the treatment of recurrent psychotic episodes accompanied by bizarre and catatonic behavior (KRAMER, *American Journal of Diseases of Children,* 1977);[1936] and in the treatment of neurological dysfunction manifested by tingling, numbness, weakness and pain in the limbs, and dysarthria (CAPLAN, WEINER, WEINTRAUB AND AUSTEN, *Headache,* 1976).[1763]

RAU AND GREEN, *Comprehensive Psychiatry,* 1975,[2037] report further evidence of the usefulness of DPH in the treatment of patients with the syndrome of compulsive eating (see also Green and Rau[1097] and Rau and Green.)[2038] WEREMUTH, DAVIS, HOLLISTER AND STUNKARD, *American Journal of Psychiatry,* (1977),[2117] with reference to the work of Rau and Green, conducted a double-blind cross-

over study and found DPH useful in the syndrome of binge eating.

Pain[2]

Additional reports of DPH's effectiveness for a variety of painful disorders—frequently when other substances have failed—suggest its possible use as a general non-sedative and non-addictive analgesic.

KANNAN, DASH and RASTOGI, *Journal of Diabetic Association of India* (1978),[1920] in a double-blind crossover study of sixteen patients with diabetic neuropathy, found that thirteen had significant relief of pain and/or paresthesia on 100 mg DPH t.i.d.

CHADDA and MATHUR, *Journal of the Association of Physicians in India* (1978),[1767] in a double-blind study with DPH found significant improvement in pain and paresthesia in 28 of 38 patients with diabetic neuropathy. The authors concluded that DPH is an effective and well tolerated drug for the relief of pain in diabetic neuropathy, and is preferred to narcotics.

ELLENBERG, *JAMA* (1977),[1819] recommended the use of DPH in the treatment of painful diabetic neuropathy, thus eliminating the use of narcotics (see also Ellenberg, Ref. 431).

VON ALBERT, *Munschener Medizinische Wochenschrift* (1978),[2109] in the treatment of 18 patients with typical trigeminal or glossopharyngeal neuralgia for whom previous

---

[1] See Vol. I, pp. 157–66 and Vol. II, pp. 208–18.

[2] See Vol. I, pp. 166–69 and Vol. II, pp. 227–30.

treatment was no longer possible or was not effective, tried DPH. DPH was reported successful in 14 of the 18 cases.

Lee, Lee and Tsai, *Journal of Formosan Medical Association* (1975),[1949] reported the successful use of DPH in treating a case of glossopharyngeal neuralgia. The paroxysms of pain, about 30 a day, were so unbearable that the patient was in fear of swallowing or talking. On 400 mg DPH a day the patient became symptom-free.

Swerdlow, *Postgraduate Medical Journal* (1980),[2097] reported DPH useful in the treatment of the lancinating and shooting pain components in 33 of 36 patients with a variety of painful disorders.

Hatangdi, Boas and Richards, *Advances in Pain Research and Therapy* (1976),[1886] reported DPH useful in the treatment of pain in five cases of postherpetic neuralgia.

Duperrat, Puissant, Saurat, Delanoe, Doyard and Grunfels, *Annales de Dermatologie et de Syphiligraphie* (1975),[1813] described a 23-year-old male patient who from birth had suffered from angiokeratomas and Fabry's disease. Pain progressed in intensity over the years. 200 mg DPH a day resulted in complete disappearance of pain in less than a week.

Peppercorn, Herzog, Dichter and Mayman, *JAMA* (1978),[2018] found DPH useful in the treatment of three patients with paroxysmal abdominal pain. When two of the patients stopped their medication the symptoms returned and with the resumption of the medication the symptoms disappeared.

Swanson and Vick, *Neurology* (1978),[2096] treated three cases of basilar artery migraine with DPH, 300 mg daily. In two cases the attacks were completely relieved; in the third case the frequency and severity were reduced.

Millichap, *Child's Brain* (1978),[1987] found DPH effective in relieving severe recurrent headaches associated with other symptoms, including nausea, vomiting, dizziness and vertigo, in 47 of 70 children.

Agnew and Goldberg, *Bulletin of the Los Angeles Neurological Societies* (1976),[1715] tried DPH in a group of 10 patients with chronic, severe, intractable thalamic pain, unresponsive to previous treatment. Three patients were markedly improved and two were slightly improved.

Muscle Disorders[1]

Zenteno Vacheron, Carrasco Zanini and Ramos Ramirez, *Epilepsy Abstracts* (1977),[2137] describe the successful use of DPH in treating two patients with paroxysmal dystonic choreoathetosis symptomatized by tonic dystonic movements of limbs, trunk and head.

Waller, *American Journal of Psychiatry* (1977),[2111] describes a case of paroxysmal kinesgenic choreoathetosis in a 22-year-old female whose condition was markedly improved by DPH. The author states the condition was characterized by recurrent, brief attacks of involuntary bizarre posturing and writhing, that were sometimes so violent that the patient was hurled to the floor.

Fukuyama, Ochiai, Hayakawa and Miyagawa, *Neuropadiatrie* (1979),[1841] reported the complete elimination of choreoathetoid attacks in an eight-year-old boy with DPH. Marked improvement in sleep was also observed.

Biryukov, *Zh Nervopatol Psikhiatr* (1976),[1752] compared the effects of DPH and Novacainamid in the treatment of sixteen patients, nine with Thomsen's myotonia and seven with atrophic myotonia, and found

[1] See Vol. I, pp. 169–71 and Vol. II, pp. 230–37.

DPH more effective and safer than Novacainamid.

KURIHARA, TAWARA, ARAKI, OKAMOTO and SHIRABE, *Clinical Neurology (Tokyo)* (1976),[1939] reported the successful treatment with DPH of a sixteen-year-old-boy with Thomsen's disease (myotonia congenta).

BROSER, DITZEN and FRIEDRICH, *Nervenarzt* (1975),[1758] report the successful use of DPH in the treatment of a case of neuromytonia. With DPH the symptoms disappeared quickly and almost completely.

LEVINSON, CANALIS and KAPLAN, *Archives of Otolaryngology* (1976),[1954] reported an unusual case of continuous muscle activity complicated by airway obstruction secondary to laryngeal spasm. With DPH the patient returned to near normal motor function.

IRANI, PUROHIT and WADIA, *Acta Neurologica Scandinavica* (1977),[1907] reported prompt and remarkable improvement upon administration of DPH in three of four patients with continuous muscle fiber activity.

GOODENOUGH, FARIELLO, ANNIS and CHUN, *Archives of Neurology* (1978),[1866] reported the complete cessation of symptoms of from two to eight years duration in three cases of familial kinesigenic dyskinesia treated with DPH.

LUTSCHG, JERUSALEM, LUDIN, VASSELLA and MUMENTHALER, *Archives of Neurology* (1978),[1970] reported the successful treatment with DPH of a seven-year-old boy who had suffered for two years with the syndrome of continuous muscle fiber activity.

LUBLIN, TSAIRIS, STRELETZ, CHAMBERS, RIKER, VAN POZNAK and DUCKETT, *Journal of Neurology, Neurosurgery and Psychiatry* (1979),[1967] detailed two cases of myokymia and impaired muscular relaxation with continuous motor unit activity. Both patients improved markedly with DPH.

COHAN, RAINES, PANAGAKOS and ARMITAGE, *Archives of Neurology* (1980),[1778] evaluated the efficacy of DPH and chlorpromazine, in combination, in the treatment of spasticity of various etiologies in open and controlled studies. Reduction of spasticity in muscles, as well as improvement in functional status, was observed.

Localized Linear Scleroderma

NELDNER, *Cutis* (1978),[1994] reported significant reversal of localized linear scleroderma in five patients treated with 100–300 mg DPH daily.

The duration of the disease prior to DPH treatment was one to sixteen years. Morbidity included arthralgia and joint stiffness, decreased range of motion, gait disturbances, inability to grasp or throw, alopecia, headache, neuralgias, and neuroses. The most distressing complication was that of deep atrophy beyond the area of linear sclerosis, which produced facial hemiatrophy or atrophy of an entire limb with varying degrees of permanent joint fixation and deep sclerotic bands underlying cutaneous hyperpigmentation.

The author states that the response to DPH treatment, and the recurrence of the condition when DPH was prematurely discontinued, point towards the true pharmacologic effect of DPH in the treatment of this disorder. (See also Vol. II, p. 237.)

Familial Mediterranean Fever

HAMED, ABDEL-AAL, ABDEL-AZIZ, NASSAR, SWEIFY, ATTA, EL-AWADY, EL-AREF and EL-GARF, *Journal of the Egyptian Medical Association* (1975),[1879] state that since 1966 they have treated 47 children for a periodic disease of unknown etiology, which has many names and which they refer to as familial Mediterranean fever. Thirty-one of the children were available for follow-up. Twenty-two had improvement in the severity and frequency of attacks, six were unimproved and three became worse. The authors concluded that DPH significantly reduces the frequency and severity attacks of familial Mediterranean fever. (See also Vol. II, p. 242.)

Periodontal Disease

OTTO, LUDEWIG and KOTZSCHKE, *Stomatologie der DDR* (1977),[2009] in a double-bind study, treated eighty patients with complex periodontal disease with a local application of DPH gel. The authors report that there was marked subjective and objective improvement in the group treated with DPH as compared with the control group. (See also Vol. II, p. 241.)

Head Injuries

WOHNS and WYLER, *Journal of Neurosurgery* (1979),[2122] reported on 62 patients whose head injuries were sufficiently severe to cause high probability of post-traumatic seizure. Of 50 patients treated with DPH, 10% developed seizure of late onset. Twelve patients not treated with DPH but who had head injuries of equal magnitude had a 50% incidence of seizure.

YOUNG, RAPP, BROOKS, MADAUSS and NORTON, *Epilepsia* (1979), in a study involving 84 patients with head injuries reported the beneficial use of DPH for post-traumatic seizure prophylaxis. The authors selected DPH because it has minimal effects upon sensorium, enabling unimpaired evaluation of patients with cerebral injuries.

With DPH only 5 of 84 individuals had seizures within a year after severe head injury, and only one of these patients had more than one seizure. The authors concluded that the greatly reduced incidence of post-traumatic seizures in these patients (6%) suggests a prophylactic effect of DPH. (See also Vol. I, p. 169.)

Cushing's Syndrome

STARKOVA, MAROVA, LEMESCHEVA, GONCHAROVA, ATAMANOVA and SEDYKH, *Problemy Endokrinologii* (1972),[2090] in a study of fifteen patients with Cushing's syndrome (hyperodrenocorticism), found that DPH, 300 mg per day, for a period of three weeks, led to normalization of the urinary excretion of ketosteroids and of aldosterone and pregnanediol, and to a normalization of the content of 17-hydroxyketosteroids in blood. There was also an increase in the potassium content in blood. The rate of secretion of cortisol decreased for all patients.

The authors noted that all the patients displayed a reduction or normalization of blood pressure and body weight, and a decrease in headaches and in weakness. (See also Werk, Sholiton and Olinger, Ref. 427, and DPH regulatory effect on cortisol, Vol. I, pp. 197–98 and Vol. II, pp. 262–63.)

Hypertension

DE LA TORRE, MURGIA-SUAREZ and ALDRETE, *Clinical Therapeutics* (1980),[1797] compared DPH with conventional therapy in two groups of 40 adult mildly hypertensive patients and found DPH useful in the reduction of both systolic and diastolic blood pressure. The authors also found DPH more effective in relieving symptoms such as anxiety, headaches, tinnitus, palpitations, chest pain, and dyspnea than the conventional therapy. The authors suggest that DPH would seem to provide an alternative hypertensive therapy that is simple compared with most conventional therapies, and has fewer side effects. (See also Ref. 414, 1282, 1480, 1717, 1789, 1892, and 2090.)

Cardiac Conduction Disorders

COCHRAN, LINNEBUR, WRIGHT and MATSUMOTO, *Clinical Research* (1977),[1776] did electrophysiologic studies of three patients with hereditary long Q-T interval syndrome. When admitted to the hospital these patients had ventricular tachyarrhythmias unresponsive to maximum doses of i.v. lidocaine. DC countershock terminated ventricular tachyarrhythmias in two patients and intravenous DPH abruptly terminated the tachyarrhythmia in the third patient.

Intravenous DPH shortened the Q-T interval in all patients.

DHATT, AKHTAR, REDDY, GOMES, LAU, CARACTA and DAMATO, *Circulation* (1977),[1804] studied the effect of i.v. DPH on the modification and abolition of macro-reentry within the His-Purkinje system in ten patients.

DPH shortened the critical V_1V_2 and critical V_2H_2 intervals in seven patients, and abolished reentry in three patients by precluding attainment of critical V_2H_2 intervals. DPH significantly shortened functional and effective refractory periods of the His-Purkinje system without significantly affecting the effective refractory period of the ventricular muscle. DPH either abolished or significantly shortened the retrograde gap zones in the His-Purkinje system.

(See also Vol. I, pp. 173–75 and Vol. II, pp. 222–24.)

Epidermolysis Bullosa

EISENBERG, STEVENS and SCHOFIELD, *Australian Journal of Dermatology* (1978),[1817] studied the effects of DPH on the collagenolytic system in tissue samples from patients with epidermolysis bullosa. The collagenolytic system is known to be excessive in epidermolysis bullosa. DPH was found to inhibit the excessive activity. As a result of these findings, two children with epidermolysis bullosa were given DPH and marked improvement in skin fragility resulted. The authors concluded that the clinical effects of DPH on both blister formation and on collagenase activity may mirror the protective effect observed *in vitro* and suggested that DPH may be useful in the management of this disease.

BAUER, COOPER, TUCKER and ESTERLY, *The New England Journal of Medicine* (1980),[1738] with reference to the work of Eisenberg, Stevens and Schofield, studied the effect of DPH on the collagenolytic system *in vitro* and clinically in 17 patients with recessive dystrophic epidermolysis bullosa. There was a significant decrease in blistering in all patients and in 12 patients the reduction was from 46% to 90%.

The authors stated that the correlation of the clinical responsiveness and *in vitro* inhibition of collagenase indicates that DPH represents a therapeutic option of relatively low risk in a disease for which there has been no rational method of therapy. (See also regulatory effect of DPH on collagen synthesis and hydrolysis, Ref. 172, 501, 502, 811, 1867, 1882 and 2107.)

BASIC MECHANISMS OF ACTION

Cerebral Ischemia

ALDRETE, ROMO-SALAS, JANKOVSKY and FRANATOVIC, *Critical Care Medicine* (1979),[1718] studied the effects of pretreatment with DPH and thiopental on postischemic brain damage in rabbits. The authors concluded that pretreatment with DPH appeared to protect against ischemic cerebral lesions, as evidenced by both neurological recovery and microscopic findings.

Lung Ischemia

DAS, AYROMLOOI, TOBIAS, DESIDERIO and STEINBERG, *Pediatric Research* (1980),[1791] studied the effects of DPH on fetal rabbit lung ischemia *in vivo*. Normal levels of CoA, Acetyl CoA, and long chain Acetyl CoA were restored after treatment with DPH. NADH/NAD ratio was increased in hypoxic untreated lung and restored to normal after treatment with DPH.

Pulmonary Vasodilation

MENTZER, ALEGRE and NOLAN, *Surgical Forum* (1975),[1981] studied the effects of DPH on pulmonary vascular resistance and pulmonary vascular caliber in dogs.

The authors concluded that DPH is a pulmonary vasodilator, that its effects are independent of myocardial performance or changes in systemic resistance, and that its mechanism of action is not mediated through adrenergic receptor sites. The authors suggested that DPH may have a beneficial effect in patients with alveolar hypoxia and pulmonary hypertension by reducing pulmonary vascular resistance.

Cardiovascular Regulation

NIKKILA, KASTE, EHNHOLM and VIIKARI, *Acta Medica Scandinavica* (1978),[2002] measured the serum high-density lipoproteins (HDL) and other lipoprotein and apolipoprotein A levels in 28 epileptic patients who received DPH as the only medication and in 44 healthy male and 49 female controls. The patients treated with DPH had significantly higher HDL levels than the controls.

The authors state that since serum HDL shows an inverse correlation with the risk of coronary heart disease, one might expect that epileptic patients using DPH through the years are protected from this disease. The authors say that they are not aware of a systematic study having been done on this subject, but that two recent independent reports have mentioned that some clinicians taking care of epileptic patients have been impressed by the low incidence of myocardial infarction among them. The authors state that this observation, if confirmed, may be an example of a beneficial side-effect of DPH.

EL-SHERIF and LAZZARA, *Circulation* (1978),[1822] studied the mechanism of action of DPH on re-entrant ventricular arrhythmias in dogs, utilizing direct recordings of the re-entrant pathway from the epicardial surface of the infarction zone.

DPH, in therapeutic doses, consistently prolonged refractoriness of potentially re-entrant pathways in the infarction zone. On the other hand, DPH had no significant effect on conduction in the normal adjacent zone.

RAINES and NINER, *Neuropharmacology* (1975),[2032] studied the response to bilateral carotid occlusion in cats before and after administration of DPH. Occlusion produced the expected increases in diastolic blood pressure, heart rate and occasional cardiac arrhythmias. DPH, 5 mg/kg reduced the reflex-induced tachycardia. Higher doses reduced the hypertensive responses as well as the tachycardia.

Membrane Stabilization

ROSES, BUTTERFIELD, APPEL and CHESTNUT, *Archives of Neurology* (1975),[2057] using electron spin resonance spectroscopy, substantiated the presence of membrane defects, increased membrane fluidity and decreased polarity, in red blood cells from patients with myotonic dystrophy. DPH caused the local increased fluidity near the surface of myotonic red blood cells to decrease to essentially the same level as normal controls. DPH did not significantly change parameters of the normal red blood cell membranes.

HANSOTIA, MAZZA and GATLIN, *American Journal of Clinical Pathology* (1975),[1881] studied the effects of DPH on membrane function and fragility of red blood cells in normal subjects and in patients with hereditary spherocytic anemia.

Red blood cells from five normal individuals and from three patients with congenital spherocytic hemolytic anemia were incubated with DPH and osmotic fragility was measured. It was shown that DPH reduces the osmotic fragility of normal and spherocytic erythrocytes. In the presence of ouabain, which may induce hemolysis, DPH still had a protective effect on red blood cells.

ROSEN, DANILO, ALONSO and PIPPENGER, *The Journal of Pharmacology and Experimental Therapies* (1976),[2055] using intracellular microelectrode techniques, studied the effects of therapeutic concentrations of DPH on transmembrane potentials of normal and depressed canine Purkinje fibers. The authors state that their findings show that the electrophysiologic effects of DPH are determined by the condition of the cardiac fiber. Depending on the condition of the cardiac fiber, DPH either enhances or depresses conduction, in the direction of the normal.

Regulation of Neurotransmitters

FERRENDELLI and KINSCHERF, *Epilepsia* (1977),[1830] demonstrated that in mouse brain slices DPH reduced elevations of cyclic GMP and cyclic AMP produced by ouabain or veratridine. (See also Ferrendelli and Kinscherf[1829,1831] and Ferrendelli.[1828])

FRY and CIARLONE, *Pharmacologist* (1979),[1839] found that norepinephrine and serotonin levels were significantly increased in mice pretreated with DPH as compared with controls. The authors state that these results suggest that DPH's therapeutic effects may be the result of increased levels of norepinephrine and serotonin, known to have neuronal inhibitory effects on excitatory pathways in brain.

DRETCHEN, STANDAERT and RAINES, *Epilepsia* (1977),[1811] evaluated the effects of DPH on the motor nerve terminal of the *in vivo* cat soleus nerve muscle preparation. DPH, 10 mg/kg, reduced the repetitive aftercharges in motor nerve endings due to tetanic conditioning. It also reduced the repetitive activity due to adenylate cyclase activation with sodium fluoride, or to exogenous dibutyryl cyclic AMP.

HADFIELD and WEBER, *Biochemical Pharmacology* (1975),[1875] say that others have observed that DPH abolishes fighting in animals and reduces aggressive behavior in humans. In a study of fighting mice and non-fighting mice the authors found that the uptake of norepinephrine at nerve terminals was increased by fighting. DPH significantly decreased this uptake. The authors state that inhibition of norepinephrine may account for decreased aggressive behavior in animals and humans.

HADFIELD and RIGBY, *Biochemical Pharmacology* (1976),[1874] measured dopamine uptake in striatal synaptosomes in the brain of fighting mice and tested the effects of DPH on dopamine uptake. They found that intense fighting produced virtually instantaneous changes in dopamine uptake and that DPH inhibited this dopamine uptake.

Regulation of Calcium and Potassium

GOLDBERG, *Neurology* (1977),[1860] states that DPH, which acts on many levels of the nervous system, must affect some general membrane property, and only when the membrane is unstable.

In a study of the binding of DPH in rabbit and human brain fractions, the authors found that binding of DPH to phospholipids was related to fatty acid composition and phospholipid binding of $^{45}Ca+++$ could be increased up to five times by the addition of DPH.

HERZBERG, CHALLBERG, HESS and HOWLAND, *Biochemical and Biophysical Research Communications* (1975),[1897] reported that potassium efflux from diaphragm of dystrophic mice is substantially elevated when compared to efflux observed with normal tissue. When dystrophic mice were treated with a combination of DPH and lithium chloride, potassium efflux returned to normal limits. The requirement for the combination of the two drugs may be due to the fact that each drug is performing a quite different function, with DPH acting as a general membrane stabilizer and lithium chloride inhibiting $K+$ transport directly.

Other Studies

COOKSON and MANN, *Neuroscience Abstracts* (1978),[1781] reported that DPH reversed morphine-induced catalepsy in rats and that pretreatment with DPH prevented morphine-induced catalepsy.

GIBBS and NG, *Brain Research Bulletin* (1976),[1851] found that DPH counteracted amnesia, induced by ouabain and cycloheximide, in one-day-old chicks.

[The references that pertain to *Recent Work* are found on pages 323 to 332.]

REFERENCES

The Broad Range of Use of DPH
(Ref. 1-750)

1. Agarwal, S. L. and Bhargava, V., Effect of drugs on brain acetylcholine levels in rats, *Indian J. Med. Res.*, 52: 1179-1182, 1964.

2. Alarcon-Segovia, D., Wakim, K. G., Worthington, J. W., and Ward, L. E., Clinical and experimental studies on the hydralazine syndrome and its relationship to systemic lupus erythematosus, *Medicine*, 46: 1-33, 1967.

3. Alvarez, W. C., Pseudo-ulcer, *Gastroenterology*, 14: 321-323, 1950.

4. Alvarez, W. C., "Why, that's our Jimmy," *Mod. Med.*, 75-76, 1968.

5. Aring, C. D., Management of fits in adults, *Ohio Med. J.*, 37: 225-230, 1941.

6. Aston, R. and Domino, E. F., Differential effects of phenobarbital, pentobarbital and diphenylhydantoin on motor cortical and reticular thresholds in the rhesus monkey, *Psychopharmacologia*, 2: 304-317, 1961.

7. Baer, P. N., Davis, R. K., and Merrit, A. D., Studies on Dilantin hyperplastic gingivitis: the role of magnesium, *J. Dent. Res.*, 44: 1055, 1965.

8. Baldwin, R. W. and Kenny, T. J., Medical treatment of behavior disorders, *Learning Disabilities*, J. Hellmuth, Ed., 2: 313-327, Special Child Publications of The Seattle Seguin School, Inc., Seattle, 1966.

9. Baxi, S. M., Trigeminal neuralgia: treatment with diphenylhydantoin, *Antiseptic*, 58: 329-330, 1961.

10. Becker, R. and Balshüsemann, T., Treatment of facial pain, *Deutsch Med. Wschr.*, 90: 2014-2020, 1965.

11. Putnam, T. J. and Merritt, H. H., Experimental determination of the anticonvulsant properties of some phenyl derivatives, *Science*, 85: 525-526, 1937.

12. Belton, N. R., Etheridge, J. E., Jr., and Millichap, J. G., Effects of convulsions and anticonvulsants on blood sugar in rabbits, *Epilepsia*, 6: 243-249, 1965.

13. Bente, D., Schönhärl, E., and Krump-Erlangen, J., Electroencephalographic findings in stutterers and their application to medical therapy, *Archiv für Ohren-, Nasen- und Kehlkopfheilkunde*, 169: 513-519, 1956.

14. Bergouignan, M., Fifteen years of therapeutic trials in essential trigeminal neuralgia: the place of diphenylhydantoin and its derivatives, *Rev. Neurol.* (Paris), 98: 414-416, 1958.

15. Bergouignan, M., Successful cures of essential facial neuralgias by sodium diphenylhydantoinate, *Rev. Laryng.* (Bordeaux), 63: 34-41, 1942.

16. Bergouignan, M. and d'Aulnay, N., Effects of sodium diphenylhydantoin in essential trigeminal neuralgia, *Rev. Otoneuroopthal.* (Paris), 23: 427-431, 1951.

17. Bernsohn, L., Possley, L., and Custod, J. T., Alterations in brain adenine nucleotides and creatinine phosphate *in vivo* after the administration of chlorpromazine, JB-516, Dilantin and RO 5-0650 (Librium), *Pharmacologist*, 2: 67, 1960.

18. Bernstein, H., Gold, H., Lang, T. W., Pappelbaum, S.,

Bazika, V., and Corday, E., Sodium diphenylhydantoin in the treatment of recurrent cardiac arrhythmias, *JAMA*, 191: 695-697, 1965.

19. Bigger, J. T., Jr., Bassett, A. L., and Hoffman, B. F., Electrophysiological effects of diphenylhydantoin on canine Purkinje fibers, *Circ. Res.*, 22: 221-236, 1968.

20. Bigger, J. T., Jr., Harris, P. D., and Weinberg, D. I., Effects of diphenylhydantoin on cardiac conduction and repolarization, *Amer. J. Cardiol.*, 19: 119-120, 1967.

21. Bigger, J. T., Jr., Schmidt, D. H., and Kutt, H., The relationship between the antiarrhythmic effect and the plasma level of diphenylhydantoin sodium (Dilantin), *Bull. N.Y. Acad. Med.*, 42: 1039, 1966.

22. Bigger, J. T., Jr., Strauss, H. C., and Hoffmann, B. F., Effects of diphenylhydantoin on atrioventricular conduction, *Fed. Proc.*, 27: 406, 1968.

23. Blatman, S. and Metcalf, D. R., Abnormal electroencephalograms in asthmatic children, *Amer. J. Dis. Child.*, 102: 531, 1961.

24. Blaw, M. E. and Torres, F., Treatment of pseudoretardation associated with epilepsy, *Mod. Treatm.*, 4: 799-816, 1967.

25. Bodkin, L. G., Oral therapy for pruritus ani, *Amer. J. Dig. Dis.*, 12: 255-257, 1945.

26. Bodkin, L. G., Pruritus ani: a review of oral therapy, *Amer. J. Dig. Dis.*, 14: 109-113, 1947.

27. Boelhouwer, C., Henry, C. E., and Glueck, B. C., Positive spiking: a double blind control study on its significance in behavior disorders, both diagnostically and therapeutically, *Amer. J. Psychiat.*, 125: 473-481, 1968.

28. Bogoch, S., Diphenylhydantoin: therapeutic uses and mechanisms of action, *Dreyfus Medical Foundation*, 1968.

29. Booker, H. E., Matthews, C. G., and Slaby, A., Effects of diphenylhydantoin on physiological and psychological measures in normal adults, *Neurology*, 17: 949-951, 1967.

30. Bose, B. C., Saifi, A. Q., and Sharma, S. K., Studies on anticonvulsant and antifibrillatory drugs, *Arch. Int. Pharmacodyn.*, 146: 106-113, 1963.

31. Braham, J. and Saia, A., Phenytoin in the treatment of trigeminal and other neuralgias, *Lancet*, 2: 892-893, 1960.

32. Braverman, I. M., and Levin, J., Dilantin-induced serum sickness: case report and inquiry into its mechanism, *Amer. J. Med.*, 35: 418-422, 1963.

33. Bray, P. F., Diphenylhydantoin (Dilantin) after 20 years: a review with re-emphasis by treatment of 84 patients, *Pediatrics*, 23: 151-161, 1959.

34. Brennan, R. W., Dehejia, M., Kutt, H., and McDowell, F., Diphenylhydantoin intoxication attendant to slow inactivation of isoniazid, *Neurology*, 18: 183, 1968.

35. Brill, N. Q., and Walker, E. F., Psychopathic behavior with latent epilepsy, *J. Nerv. Ment. Dis.*, 101: 545-549, 1945.

36. Brittingham, T. E., Lutcher, C. L., and Murphy, D. L., Reversible erythroid aplasia induced by diphenylhydantoin, *Arch. Intern. Med.*, 113: 764-768, 1964.

37. Broddle, W. D. and Nelson, S. R., The effect of diphenylhydantoin on energy reserve levels in brain, *Fed. Proc.*, 27: 751, 1968.

38. Brown, W. T. and Solomon, C. I., Delinquency and the electroencephalograph, *Amer. J. Psychiat.*, 98: 499-503, 1942.

39. Buchthal, F. and Svensmark, O., Aspects of the pharmacology of Phenytoin (Dilantin) and phenobarbital relevant to their dosage in the treatment of epilepsy, *Epilepsia,* 1: 373-384, 1959-1960.

40. Burke, E. C. and Peters, G. A., Migraine in childhood: a preliminary report, *A.M.A. J. Dis. Child.,* 92: 330-336, 1956.

41. Byrne, J. E. and Dresel, P. E., A model for evaluating drugs which prolong post-countershock periods of normal sinus rhythm (NSR), *Pharmacologist,* 10: 220, 1968.

42. Cameron, A. J., Baron, J. H., and Priestley, B. L., Erythema multiforme, drugs, and ulcerative colitis, *Brit. Med. J.,* 2: 1174-1178, 1966.

43. Campbell, E. W., Jr., and Young, J. D., Jr., Enuresis and its relationship to electroencephalographic disturbances, *J. Urol.,* 96: 947-949, 1966.

44. Cantu, R. C. and Schwab, R. S., Ceruloplasmin rise and PBI fall in serum due to diphenylhydantoin, *Arch. Neurol.,* 15: 393-396, 1966.

45. Cantu, R. C., Schwab, R. S., and Timberlake, W. H., Comparison of blood levels with oral and intramuscular diphenylhydantoin, *Neurology,* 18: 782-784, 1968.

46. Case, W. G., Rickels, K., and Bazilian, S., Diphenylhydantoin in neurotic anxiety, *Amer. J. Psychiat.,* 126: 254-255, 1969.

47. Caspers, H. and Wehmeyer, H., The action of diphenylhydantoin on the seizure threshold of the brain, *Z. Ges. Exp. Med.,* 129: 77-86, 1957.

48. Caveness, W., Adams, R. D., Pope, A., and Wegner, W. R., The role of the dorsal root ganglia in the production of the lancinating pains of central nervous system syphilis, *Trans. Amer. Neurol. Assn.,* 60-64, 1949.

49. Chaiken, B. H., Goldberg, B. I., and Segal, J. P., Dilantin sensitivity: report of a case of hepatitis with jaundice, pyrexia and exfoliative dermatitis, *New Eng. J. Med.,* 242: 897-898, 1950.

50. Chang, T. and Glazko, A. J., Quantitative assay of 5,5'-diphenylhydantoin (Dilantin) and 5-(4-hydroxyphenyl)-5'-phenylhydantoin by gas-liquid chromatography, *Clin. Res.,* 16: 339, 1968.

51. Chao, D., Sexton, J. A., and Davis, S. D., Convulsive equivalent syndrome of childhood, *J. Pediat,* 64: 499-508, 1964.

52. Chenoweth, M. B., Clinical uses of metal binding drugs, *Clin. Pharmacol. Ther.,* 9: 365-387, 1968.

53. Childress, R. H., Higgs, L. M., Boyd, D. L., and Williams, J. F., Jr., Effect of diphenylhydantoin on left ventricular function in patients with heart disease, *Circulation,* 33-34: 73, 1966.

54. Chinitz, A., Seelinger, D. F., and Greenhouse, A. H., Anticonvulsant therapy in trigeminal neuralgia, *Amer. J. Med. Sci.,* 252: 62-67, 1966.

55. Christensen, K., On the preparation and stability of Phenytoin solutions for injection, *Dansk Tidsskr. Farm.,* 34: 97-109, 1960.

56. Chung, A. C., The influence of diphenylhydantoin (Dilantin) on the development of atherosclerosis in rabbits, *J. Atheroscler. Res.,* 7: 373-379, 1967.

57. Chung, A. C., Duren, B. Y., and Houck, J. C., Effect of diphenylhydantoin administration upon concentration of liver and aortic lipids, *Proc. Soc. Exp. Biol. Med.,* 110: 788-789, 1962.

58. Cohen, H. B., Duncan, R. F., II, and Dement, W. C., The effect of diphenylhydantoin on sleep in the cat, *Electroenceph. Clin. Neurophysiol.,* 24: 401-408, 1968.

59. Cohen, H. D. and Barondes, S. H., Puromycin effect on memory may be due to occult seizures, *Science,* 157: 333-334, 1967.

60. Cole, J. O. and Davis, J. M., Brief report of papers on diphenylhydantoin in plenary session, American College of Neuropsychopharmacology, fifth annual meeting, *Psychopharm. Bull.* 4: 28-31, 1967.

61. Conn, R. D., Diphenylhydantoin sodium in cardiac arrhythmias, *New Eng. J. Med.,* 272: 277-282, 1965.

62. Conn., R. D., New drugs for old hearts: newer antiarrhythmic and diuretic agents, *Postgrad. Med.* 42: 71-79, 1967.

63. Corday, E., Lang, T. W., Bazika, V., and Pappelbaum, S., Antiarrhythmic acts directly on myocardium, *JAMA,* 193: 28, 1965.

64. Cox, A. R., Pitt, W., Brown, T. C. K., and Molaro, A., Antiarrhythmic action of diphenylhydantoin (Dilantin) studied in isolated cardiac tissue, *Canad. Med. Assn. J.,* 94: 661, 1966.

65. Crawford, S. E. and Jones. C. K., Fatal liver necrosis and diphenylhydantoin sensitivity, *Pediatrics,* 30: 595-600, 1962.

66. Crue, B. L., Jr., Alvarez-Carregal, E., and Todd, E. M., Neuralgia: consideration of central mechanisms, *Bull. Los Angeles Neurol. Soc.,* 29: 107-132, 1964.

67. Crue, B. L., Jr., Todd, E. M., and Duemler, L. P., Pain as sensory epilepsy, *Bull. Los Angeles Neurol. Soc.,* 32: 53, 1967.

68. Crue, B. L., Jr., Todd, E. M., and Loew, A. G., Clinical use of mephenesin carbamate (Tolseram) in trigeminal neuralgia, *Bull. Los Angeles Neurol. Soc.,* 30: 212-215, 1965.

69. Cucinell, S. A., Factors affecting drug metabolism, *Bull. N.Y. Acad. Med.,* 42: 324, 1966.

70. Popek, K., Czechs make anticonvulsants a must for coma victims, *Med. World News,* 33, March 8, 1968.

71. Dahl, J. R., Diphenylhydantoin toxic psychosis with associated hyperglycemia, *Calif. Med.,* 107: 345-347, 1967.

72. Dam, M., Organic changes in Phenytoin intoxicated pigs, *Acta Neurol. Scand.,* 42: 491-494, 1966.

73. Dam, M. and Olesen, V., Intramuscular administration of Phenytoin, *Neurology,* 16: 288-292, 1966.

74. Dayton, P. G., Cucinell, S. A., Weiss, M., and Perel, J. M., Dose dependence of drug plasma level decline in dogs, *J. Pharm. Exp. Ther.,* 158: 305-316, 1967.

75. de la Vega, P., Clinical results of the treatment of Sydenham's chorea with sodium diphenylhydantoin, *Rev. Clin. Esp.* 24: 113-115, 1947.

76. Dill, R. E., Discrepancy of adrenal responses in diphenylhydantoin treated rats, *Arch. Int. Pharmacodyn.,* 160: 363-372, 1966.

77. Dill, W. A., Kazenko, A., Wolf, L. M., and Glazko, A. J., Studies on 5,5'-diphenylhydantoin (Dilantin) in animals and man, *J. Pharm. Exp. Ther.,* 118: 270-279, 1956.

78. Dimsdale, H., Migraine, *Practitioner,* 198: 490-494, 1967.

79. Dixon, R. L., The interaction between various drugs and methotrexate, *Toxic. Appl. Pharmacol.,* 12: 308, 1968.

80. Dorph, M., Coronary care units and the aggressive management of acute myocardial infarction, *Delaware Med. J.* 44-48, February, 1968.

81. Dorsey, J. F., Hayslip, G. W., and Anderson, K., Tic douloureux: treatment with diphenylhydantoin, *Clin. Med.,* 6: 1395-1397, 1959.

82. Dreifus, L. S., Rabbino, M. D., and Watanabe, Y., Newer agents in the treatment of cardiac arrythmias, *Med. Clin. N. Amer.,* 48: 371-387, 1964.

83. Druskin, M. S., Anticonvulsants and anemia, *Clin. Med.,* 71: 1911-1916, 1964.

84. Druskin, M. S., Wallen, M. H., and Bonagura, L., Anticonvulsant associated megaloblastic anemia: response to 25 microgm. of folic acid administered by mouth daily, *New Eng. J. Med.,* 267: 483-485, 1962.

85. Dubois, E. L., Toxic hepatic necrosis associated with taking Dilantin, Tridione and phenobarbital, *Amer. J. Clin. Path.,* 20: 153-158, 1950.

86. Duma, R. J., Hendry, C. N., and Donahoo, J. S., Hypersensitivity to diphenylhydantoin (Dilantin): a case report with toxic hepatitis, *Southern Med. J.,* 59: 168-170, 1966.

87. Dutton, P., Phenytoin toxicity with associated meningeal reaction, *J. Ment. Sci.,* 104: 1165-1166, 1958.

88. Eissner, H., Diphenylhydantoin exanthema in the form of infectious mononucleosis, *Arch. Toxik.,* 18: 282-295, 1960.

89. Endröczi, E. and Fekete, T., Amino acid composition of the Ammon's horn and the effect of anticonvulsant drugs, *Acta Physiol. Acad. Sci. Hung.,* 32: 389-398, 1967.

90. Esplin, D. W., Effects of diphenylhydantoin on synaptic

transmission in cat spinal cord and stellate ganglion, *J. Pharm. Exp. Ther.*, 120: 301-323, 1957.

91. Fabrykant, M., Further studies on electrocerebral dysfunction and the use of anticonvulsants in labile diabetes, *Ann. Intern. Med.*, 38: 814-823, 1953.

92. Fabrykant, M. and Pacella, B. L., Labile diabetes: electroencephalographic status and effect of anticonvulsive therapy, *Ann. Intern. Med.*, 29: 860-877, 1948.

93. Ferngren, H. and Paalzow, L., Studies on electrically induced seizures and their antagonism by anticonvulsants during neonatal development in the mouse, *Acta Pharmacol. Toxicol.*, 25: 60, 1967.

94. Festoff, B. W. and Appel, S. H., Effect of diphenylhydantoin on synaptosome sodium-potassium-ATPase, *J. Clin. Invest.*, 47: 2752-2758, 1968.

95. Fetterman, J. L. and Shallenberger, W. D., Further studies in Dilantin sodium therapy of epilepsy, *Dis. Nerv. System*, 2: 383-389, 1941.

96. Fichman, M. P. and Bethune, J. E., The role of adrenocorticoids in the inappropriate antidiuretic hormone syndrome, *Ann. Intern. Med.*, 68: 806-820, 1968.

97. Fichman, M. P., Bethune, J. E., and Kleeman, C. R., Inhibition of antidiuretic hormone by diphenylhydantoin, *Clin. Res.*, 15: 141, 1967.

98. Finch, E. and Lorber, J., Methaemoglobinaemia in the newborn: probably due to Phenytoin excreted in human milk, *J. Obstet. Gynaec. Brit. Emp.*, 61: 833-834, 1954.

99. Fink, G. B. and Swinyard, E. A., Comparison of anticonvulsant and psychopharmacologic drugs, *J. Pharm. Sci.*, 51: 548-551, 1962.

100. Finkelman, I. and Arieff, A. J., Untoward effects of Phenytoin sodium in epilepsy, *JAMA*, 118: 1209-1212, 1942.

101. Firemark, H., Barlow, C. F., and Roth, L. J., The entry, accumulation and binding of diphenylhydantoin-2-C^{14} in brain: studies on adult, immature and hypercapnic cats, *Int. J. Neuropharmacol.*, 2: 25-38, 1963.

102. Fishbeck, R. and Zucker, G., Phenytoin (5,5-diphenylhydantoin) hypersensitivity presenting a clinical picture of scarlatiniform erythroderma, *Deutsch. Gesundh.*, 21: 1273-1277, 1966.

103. Floyd, F. W., The toxic effects of diphenylhydantoin: a report of 23 cases, *Clin. Proc. Child Hosp., D. C.*, 17: 195-201, 1961.

104. Forshaw, J. W. B., Megaloblastic anemia associated with anticonvulsant therapy, *Postgrad. Med. J.* (London), 33: 242-243, 1957.

105. Fox, V., Treatment of the non-neurologic complications of alcoholism, *Mod. Treatm.*, 3: 502-508, 1966.

106. Frankel, S. I,. Dilantin sodium in the treatment of epilepsy, *JAMA*, 114: 1320-1321, 1940.

107. Frantzen, E., Hansen, J. M., Hansen, O. E., and Kristensen, M., Phenytoin (Dilantin) intoxication, *Acta Neurol. Scand.*, 43: 440-446, 1967.

108. Freed, L. F., The psychopath: a social challenge, *Med. Proc.*, 13: 408-414, 1967.

109. Frey, H. H., Kampmann, E., and Nielsen, C. K., Study on combined treatment with phenobarbital and diphenylhydantoin, *Acta Pharmacol. Toxic.*, 26: 284-292, 1968.

110. Freyhan, F. A., Effectiveness of diphenylhydantoin in management of nonepileptic psychomotor excitement states, *Arch. Neurol. Psychiat.*, 53: 370-374, 1945.

111. Friedman, A. P., The migraine syndrome, *Bull. N.Y. Acad. Med.*, 44: 45-62, 1968.

112. Friedman, A. P. and Merritt, H. H., Treatment of headache, *JAMA*, 163: 1111-1117, 1957.

113. Gabka, J., On the therapy of idiopathic and symptomatic head and facial pains, *Med. Mschr.*, 17: 430-443, 1963.

114. Galindo, A. M. and Ginabreda, J. M. S., Treatment of chorea minor with diphenylhydantoin sodium, *Ann. Med.* (Barcelona), 34: 165-168, 1947.

115. Garouette, J. V., A suggested mechanism of action for

the anticonvulsant properties of diphenylhydantoin, *Tulane U. Med. Fac. Bull.*, 24: 319-328, 1965.

116. Gatenby, P. B. B., Anticonvulsants as a factor in megaloblastic anemia in pregnancy, *Lancet*, 2: 1004-1005, 1960.

117. Gautray, J. P. and Natter, S., The significance of EEG and of neuro-sedative therapies in the gynecology clinic, *Ann. Endocr.*, 22: 173-185, 1961.

118. Gayet-Hallion, T. and Bertrand, I., Favorable action of diphenylhydantoin on the resistance of rats to drowning, *Compt. Rend. Soc. Biol.*, 153: 757-759, 1959.

119. Gellerman, G. L. and Martinez, C., Fatal ventricular fibrillation following intravenous sodium diphenylhydantoin therapy, *JAMA*, 200: 337-338, 1967.

120. Gellman, V., A case of diphenylhydantoin (Dilantin) intoxication, *Manitoba Med. Rev.*, 46: 388-390, 1966.

121. Gershbein, L. L., Effect of drugs and catecholamines on rat diaphragm carbohydrate metabolism, *J. Pharm. Sci.*, 55: 846-848, 1966.

122. Gilbert, J. C., Ortiz, W. R., and Millichap, J. G., The effects of anticonvulsant drugs on the permeability of brain cells to D-xylose, *J. Neurochem.*, 13: 247-255, 1966.

123. Golbert, T. M., Sanz, C. J., Rose, H. D., and Leitschuh, T. H., Comparative evaluation of treatments of alcohol withdrawal syndromes, *JAMA*, 201: 99-102, 1967.

124. Goldschlager, A. W. and Karliner, J. S., Ventricular standstill after intravenous diphenylhydantoin, *Amer. Heart J.*, 74: 410-412, 1967.

125. Goldstein, N., Leider, M., and Baer, R. L., Drug eruptions from anticonvulsant drugs, *Arch. Derm.*, 87: 612-617, 1963.

126. Gordon, P., Diphenylhydantoin and procainamide normalization of suboptimal learning behavior, *Recent Advances Biol. Psychiat.*, 10: 121-133, 1968.

127. Goodwin, F. B., Oral therapy in anogenital pruritus, *J. Nat. Proct. Assn.*, 18: 84-87, 1946.

128. Granick, S., The induction *in vitro* of the synthesis of δ-aminolevulinic acid synthetase in chemical porphyria: a response to certain drugs, sex hormones, and foreign chemicals, *J. Biol. Chem.*, 241: 1359-1375, 1966.

129. Green, J. B., Dilantin in the treatment of lightning pains, *Neurology*, 11: 257-258, 1961.

130. Green, J. B., Electroencephalographic findings in a case of acute reaction to Dilantin, *Electroenceph. Clin. Neurophysiol.*, 20: 201-202, 1966.

131. Gretter, T. E., Danner, P. K., Nibbelink, D. W., Green, D., and Sahs, A. L., The effect of diphenylhydantoin (Dilantin) on acute intermittent porphyria, *Trans. Amer. Neurol. Assn.*, 88: 170-178, 1963.

132. Grissom, J. H., Sy, B. G., Duffy, J. P., and Dunea, G., Dangerous consequence from use of Phenytoin in atrial flutter, *Brit. Med. J.*, 4: 34, 1967.

133. Gropper, A. L., Diphenylhydantoin sensitivity: report of fatal case with hepatitis and exfoliative dermatitis, *New Eng. J. Med.*, 254: 522-523, 1956.

134. Grosz, H. J., Dilantin intoxication—with a report of one case, *Amer. Pract. Dig. Treatm.*, 7: 1633-1636, 1956.

135. Gupta, R. C. and Kofoed, J., Toxicological statistics for barbiturates, other sedatives, and tranquilizers in Ontario: a 10-year survey, *Canad. Med. Assn. J.*, 94: 863-865, 1966.

136. Gydell, K., Megaloblastic anemia in patients treated with diphenylhydantoin and primidone, *Acta Haemat.*, 17: 1-15, 1957.

137. Hamfelt, A., Killander, A., Malers, E., and de Verdier, C., Megaloblastic anemia associated with anticonvulsant drugs, *Acta Med. Scand.*, 177: 549-555, 1965.

138. Hansen, J. M., Kristensen, M., Skovsted, L., and Christensen, L. K., Dicoumarol-induced diphenylhydantoin intoxication, *Lancet*, 2: 265-266, 1966.

139. Hansen, H. A., Nordqvist, P., and Sourander, P., Megaloblastic anemia and neurologic disturbances combined with folic acid deficiency: observations on an epileptic patient treated with anticonvulsants, *Acta Med. Scand.*, 176: 243-251, 1964.

140. Harinasuta, U. and Zimmerman, H. J., Diphenylhydantoin sodium hepatitis, *JAMA*, 203: 1015-1018, 1968.

141. Harris, A. S. and Kokernot, R. H., Effects of diphenylhydantoin sodium (Dilantin sodium) and phenobarbital sodium upon ectopic ventricular tachycardia in acute myocardial infarction, *Amer. J. Physiol.*, 163: 505-516, 1950.

142. Harris, J. and Ritchie, K., Anticonvulsant effects on copper uptake by neural tissue, *Fed. Proc.*, 25: 2091, 1966.

143. Harris, P. D., Bigger, J. T., Jr., Weinberg, D., and Malm, J. R., Use of diphenylhydantoin in ventricular arrhythmias following open heart surgery, *Surg. Forum*, 17: 185-188, 1966.

144. Hartmann, J. F., High sodium content of cortical astrocytes: electron microscope evidence, *Arch. Neurol.*, 15: 633-642, 1966.

145. Hatzmann, I., Neuhold, R., and von Rittner, W., Exfoliative dermatitis after hydantoin therapy, *Ann. Pediat.* (Basel), 179: 305-316, 1952.

146. Hausser, E., Bergoz, R. and Croci, D., Megaloblastic anemia provoked by antiepileptic medications, *Nouv. Rev. Franc. Hemat.*, 4: 221-232, 1964.

147. Hawkins, C. F. and Meynell, M. J., Macrocytosis and macrocytic anemia caused by anticonvulsant drugs, *Quart. J. Med.*, 27: 45-63, 1958.

148. Hawkins, C. F. and Meynell, M. J., Megaloblastic anemia due to Phenytoin sodium, *Lancet*, 2: 737-738, 1954.

149. Helfant, R. H., Scherlag, B. J., and Damato, A. N., The comparative electrophysiological effects of diphenylhydantoin and procaine amide in the digitalis intoxicated and nondigitalized heart, *Clin. Res.*, 15: 206, 1967.

150. Helfant, R. H., Scherlag, B. J., and Damato, A. N., The use of diphenylhydantoin in ventricular arrhythmias unresponsive to procaine amide: a dissociation of procaine amide's actions on automaticity and conduction, *Circulation*, 36: 139, 1967.

151. Helfant, R. H., Scherlag, B. J., and Damato, A. N., Diphenylhydantoin prevention of arrhythmias in the digitalis-sensitized dog after direct-current cardioversion, *Circulation*, 37: 424-428, 1968.

152. Helfant, R. H., Scherlag, B. J., and Damato, A. N., Diphenylhydantoin toxicity, *JAMA*, 201: 894, 1967.

153. Helfant, R. H., Scherlag, B. J., and Damato, A. N., Electrophysiological effects of direct current countershock before and after ouabain sensitization and after diphenylhydantoin desensitization in the dog, *Circ. Res.*, 22: 615-623, 1968.

154. Helfant, R. H., Scherlag, B. J., and Damato, A. N., The electrophysiological properties of diphenylhydantoin sodium as compared to procaine amide in the normal and digitalis intoxicated heart, *Circulation*, 36: 108-118, 1967.

155. Helfant, R. H., Scherlag, B. J., and Damato, A. N., Protection from digitalis toxicity with the prophylactic use of diphenylhydantoin sodium: an arrhythmic-inotropic dissociation, *Circulation*, 36: 119-124, 1967.

156. Helfant, R. H., Scherlag, B. J., and Damato, A. N., Use of diphenylhydantoin sodium to dissociate the effects of procaine amide on automaticity and conduction in the normal and arrhythmic heart, *Amer. J. Cardiol.*, 20: 820-825, 1967.

157. Helfant, R. H., Ricciutti, M. A., Scherlag, B. J., and Damato, A. N., Effect of diphenylhydantoin sodium (Dilantin) on myocardial A-V potassium difference, *Amer. J. Physiol.*, 214: 880-884, 1968.

158. Helfant, R. H., Lau, S. H., Cohen, S. I., and Damato, A. N., Effects of diphenylhydantoin on atrioventricular conduction in man, *Circulation*, 36: 686-691, 1967.

159. Herman, C. J. and Bignall, K. E., Effects of diphenylhydantoin on spontaneous and evoked activity in the cat under chloralose anesthesia, *Electroenceph. Clin. Neurophysiol.*, 23: 351-359, 1967.

160. de la Herran, J., Martinez-Lage, J. M., and Molina, P., Treatment of trigeminal neuralgia with diphenylhydantoin and disulphur of pyridoxine, *Medicina Clinica*, 38: 375-378, 1962.

161. Hirschmann, J., On the interval treatment of migraine, *Ther. Umsch.*, 21: 48-51, 1964.

162. Hoaken, P. C. S., and Kane, F. J., Jr., Unusual brain syndrome seen with diphenylhydantoin and pentobarbital, *Amer. J. Psychiat.*, 120: 282-283, 1963.

163. Hockman, C. H., Mauck, H. P., Jr., and Chu, N., ECG changes resulting from cerebral stimulation. III. Action of diphenylhydantoin on arrhythmias, *Amer. Heart J.*, 74: 256-260, 1967.

164. Hoff, E. C. and Yahn, C., The effect of sodium 5,5-diphenylhydantoinate (Dilantin sodium) upon the tolerance of rats and mice to decompression. *Amer. J. Physiol.*, 141: 7-16, 1944.

165. Hofmann, W. W., Cerebellar lesions after parenteral Dilantin administration, *Neurology*, 8: 210-214, 1958.

166. Holecková, R., Some experiences in treatment of cardiac arrhythmias using diphenylhydantoin, *Vnitrni. Lek.*, 13: 1195-1196, 1967.

167. Holland, P. and Mauer, A. M., Diphenylhydantoin-induced hypersensitivity reaction, *J. Pediat.*, 66: 322-332, 1965.

168. Hopf, H. C., On the alteration of transmission function of peripheral motor nerve fibers through diphenylhydantoin, *Deutsch Z. Nervenheilk*, 193: 41-56, 1968.

169. Horsfield, G. I. and Chalmers, J. N. M., Megaloblastic anemia associated with anticonvulsant therapy, *Practitioner*, 191: 316-321, 1963.

170. Horwitz, S. J., Klipstein, F. A., and Lovelace, R. E., Relation of abnormal folate metabolism to neuropathy developing during anticonvulsant drug therapy, *Lancet*, 1: 563-565, 1968.

171. Houck, J. C. and Patel, Y. M., Proposed mode of action of corticosteroids on the connective tissue, *Nature*, 206: 158-160, 1965.

172. Houck, J. C., Jacob, R. A., and Maengwyn-Davies, G. D., The effect of sodium Dilantin administration upon the chemistry of the skin, *J. Clin. Invest.*, 39: 1758-1762, 1960.

173. Huisman, J. W., The estimation of some important anticonvulsant drugs in serum, *Clin. Chim. Acta*, 13: 323-328, 1966.

174. Husby, J., Delayed toxicity and serum concentrations of Phenytoin, *Danish Med., Bull.*, 10: 236-239, 1963.

175. Iannone, A., Baker, A. B., and Morrell, F., Dilantin in the treatment of trigeminal neuralgia, *Neurology*, 8: 126-128, 1958.

176. Isaacs, H., A syndrome of continuous muscle-fibre activity. *J. Neurol. Neuro-surg. Psychiat.*, 24: 319-325, 1961.

177. Isaacs, H., Quantal squander, *S. A. J. Lab. Clin. Med.*, 10: 93-95, 1964.

178. Itil, T. M., Rizzo, A. E., and Shapiro, D. M., Study of behavior and EEG correlation during treatment of disturbed children, *Dis. Nerv. Syst.*, 28: 731-736, 1967.

179. Jensen, B. N. and Grynderup, V., Studies on the metabolism of Phenytoin, *Epilepsia*, 7: 238-245, 1966.

180. Jensen, H. P., The treatment of trigeminal neuralgia with diphenylhydantoin, *Arztl. Wochschr.*, 9: 105-108, 1954.

181. Jonas, A. D., The diagnostic and therapeutic use of diphenylhydantoin in the subictal state and non-epileptic dysphoria, *Int. J. Neuropsychiat.*, 3: S21-S29, 1967.

182. Jurna, I., Depression by antiparkinson drugs of reserpine rigidity, *Naunyn-Schmiedeberg Arch. Pharm.*, 260: 80-88, 1968.

183. Jurna, I. and Regélhy, B., The antagonism between reserpine and some antiparkinson drugs in electroseizure, *Naunyn-Schmiedeberg Arch. Pharm.*, 259: 442-459, 1968.

184. Kabat, H., Drug therapy of cerebellar ataxia and disorders of the basal ganglia, based on cerebellar-striatal antagonism, *Ann. Intern. Med.*, 50: 1438-1448, 1959.

185. Kabat, H. and McLeod, M., Neuromuscular dysfunction and treatment in athetosis, *Conn. Med.*, 23: 710-714, 1959.

186. Kalinowsky, L. B. and Putnam, T. J., Attempts at treatment of schizophrenia and other nonepileptic psychoses with Dilantin, *Arch. Neurol. Psychiat.*, 49: 414-420, 1943.

187. Karliner, J. S., Intravenous diphenylhydantoin sodium (Dilantin) in cardiac arrhythmias, *Dis. Chest*, 51: 256-269, 1967.

188. Kelln, E. E., Further studies of an epilepsy drug, *Dental Prog.*, 3: 271-273, 1963.

189. Kelln, E. E. and Gorlin, R. J., Healing qualities of an epilepsy drug, *Dental Prog.*, 1: 126-129, 1961.

190. Kemp, J. W. and Swinyard, E. A., Diphenylhydantoin inhibition of hexobarbital metabolism by liver microsomes in mice and rats, *Fed. Proc.*, 27: 350, 1968.

191. Kertesz, A., Paroxysmal kinesigenic choreoathetosis: an entity within the paroxysmal choreoathetosis syndrome, *Neurology*, 17: 680-690, 1967.

192. Khan, M. T. and McEwen, H. D., Effect of diphenylhydantoins on rat uterus *in vitro*, *Proc. Can. Fed. Biol. Soc.*, 10: 161, 1967.

193. Kidd, P. and Mollin, D. L., Megaloblastic anemia and vitamin-B_{12} deficiency after anticonvulsant therapy: report of two cases, *Brit. Med. J.*, 2: 974-976, 1957.

194. Kiørboe, E., Phenytoin intoxication during treatment with antabuse (Disulfiram), *Epilepsia*, 7: 246-249, 1966.

195. Kiørboe, E. and Plum, C. M., Megaloblastic anemia developing during treatment of epilepsy, *Acta Med. Scand.*, 179: suppl. 445, 349-357, 1966.

196. Klein, D. F. and Greenberg, I. M., Behavioral effects of diphenylhydantoin in severe psychiatric disorders, *Amer. J. Psychiat.*, 124: 847-849, 1967.

197. Klipstein, F. A., Subnormal serum folate and macrocytosis associated with anticonvulsant drug therapy, *Blood*, 23: 68-86, 1964.

198. Krieger, D. T., Effect of diphenylhydantoin on pituitary-adrenal interrelations, *J. Clin. Endocrinol. Metab.*, 22: 490-493, 1962.

199. Krieger, D. T. and Krieger, H. P., The effect of short-term administration of CNS-acting drugs on the circadian variation of the plasma 17-OHCS in normal subjects, *Neuroendocrinology*, 2: 232-246, 1967.

200. Kristensen, M., Hansen, J. M., Hansen, O. E., and Lund, V., Sources of error in the determination of Phenytoin (Dilantin) by Svensmark and Kristensen's method, *Acta Neurol. Scand.*, 43: 447-450, 1967.

201. Kubanek, J. L. and Rowell, R. C., The use of Dilantin in the treatment of psychotic patients unresponsive to other treatment, *Dis. Nerv. Syst.*, 7: 1-4, 1946.

202. Kugelberg, E. and Lindblom, U., The mechanism of the pain in trigeminal neuralgia. *J. Neurol. Neurosurg. Psychiat.*, 22: 36-43, 1959.

203. Kurtzke, J. F., Leukopenia with diphenylhydantoin, *J. Nerv. Ment. Dis.*, 132: 339-343, 1961.

204. Kutt, H., Intravenous use of diphenylhydantoin sodium, *JAMA*, 201: 210, 1967.

205. Kutt, H., Haynes, J., and McDowell, F., The effect of phenobarbital upon diphenylhydantoin metabolism in man, *Neurology*, 15: 274-275, 1965.

206. Kutt, H., Louis, S., and McDowell, F., Intravenous diphenylhydantoin in experimental seizures: I. Correlation of dose, blood, and tissue level in cats, *Arch. Neurol.*, 18: 465-471, 1968.

207. Kutt, H. and McDowell, F., Management of epilepsy with diphenylhydantoin sodium: dosage regulation for problem patients, *JAMA*, 203: 969-972, 1968.

208. Kutt, H., Winters, W., and McDowell, F., Depression of parahydroxylation of diphenylhydantoin by antituberculosis chemotherapy, *Neurology*, 16: 594-602, 1966.

209. Kutt, H., Winters, W., and McDowell, F., Determination of diphenylhydantoin and phenobarbital metabolites, *Fed. Proc.*, 23: 2346, 1964.

210. Kutt, H., Wolk, M., Scherman, R., and McDowell, F., Insufficient parahydroxylation as cause of Dilantin toxicity, *Neurology*, 13: 356, 1963.

211. Kutt, H., Wolk, M., Scherman, R., and McDowell, F., Insufficient parahydroxylation as a cause of diphenylhydantoin toxicity, *Neurology*, 14: 542-548, 1964.

212. Lach, J. L., Bhansali, K., and Blaug, S. M., The chromatographic separation and determination of diphenylhydantoin and phenobarbital, *J. Amer. Pharm. Assn.*, 47: 48-49, 1958.

213. Laird, R. D. and Fonner, R. L., The protective effect of sodium diphenylhydantoin in the hyperacute radiation syndrome, *U.S. Army Med. Res. Lab., Fort Knox, Kentucky, Report No. 262*, 1957.

214. Lamberts, A. E., Tic douloureux, *J. Mich. State Med. Soc.*, 58: 95-96, 1959.

215. Lang, T. W., Bernstein, H., Barbieri, F. F., Gold, H. and Corday, E., Digitalis toxicity: treatment with diphenylhydantoin, *Arch. Intern. Med.*, 116: 573-580, 1965.

216. Laubscher, F. A., Fatal diphenylhydantoin poisoning: a case report, *JAMA*, 198: 1120-1121, 1966.

217. Lauriault, C. D. and Jim, R. T. S., Diphenylhydantoin toxicity; lymphadenopathy and low platelet count, *Pediatrics*, 37: 341-342, 1966.

218. Lefkowitz, M. M., Effects of diphenylhydantoin on disruptive behavior: study of male delinquents, *Arch. Gen. Psychiat.*, 20: 643-651, 1969.

219. Lee, W. Y., Grummer, H. A., Bronsky, D., and Waldstein, S. S., Acute water loading as a diagnostic test for the inappropriate ADH syndrome, *J. Lab. Clin. Med.*, 58: 937, 1961.

220. Lees, F., Radioactive vitamin B_{12} absorption in the megaloblastic anemia caused by anticonvulsant drugs, *Quart. J. Med.*, 30: 231-248, 1961.

221. Leonard, W. A., Jr., The use of diphenylhydantoin (Dilantin) sodium in the treatment of ventricular tachycardia, *A.M.A. Arch. Intern. Med.*, 101: 714-717, 1958.

222. Levitt, J. M. and Blonstein, M., Toxic amblyopia resulting from sodium diphenyl hydantoinate, *New York J. Med.*, 40: 1538-1539, 1940.

223. Lieberson, A. D., Schumacher, R. R., Childress, R. H., Boyd, D. L., and Williams, J. F., Jr., Effect of diphenylhydantoin on left ventricular function in patients with heart disease, *Circulation*, 36: 692-699, 1967.

224. Lindblom, U., Diphenylhydantoin for trigeminal neuralgia, *Svensk Lakartidn*, 58: 3186-3191, 1961.

225. Lindsley, D. B. and Henry, C. E., The effect of drugs on behavior and the electroencephalograms of children with behavior disorders, *Psychosom. Med.*, 4: 140-149, 1942.

226. Livingston, S., Petersen, D., and Boks, L. L., Hypertrichosis occurring in association with Dilantin therapy, *J. Pediat.*, 47: 351-352, 1955.

227. Livingston, S. and Whitehouse, D., Treatment of headaches in children, *Mod. Treatm.*, 1: 1391-1398, 1964.

228. Livingston, S., Whitehouse, D., and Pauli, L. L., Study of the effects of diphenylhydantoin sodium on the lungs, *New Eng. J. Med.*, 264: 648-651, 1961.

229. Long, M. T., Childress, R. H., and Bond, W. H., Megaloblastic anemia associated with the use of anticonvulsant drugs: report of a case and review of the literature, *Neurology*, 13: 697-702, 1963.

230. Louis, S., Kutt, H., and McDowell, F., The cardiocirculatory changes caused by intravenous Dilantin and its solvent, *Amer. Heart J.*, 74: 523-529, 1967.

231. Louis, S., Kutt, H., and McDowell, F., Intravenous diphenylhydantoin in experimental seizures: II. Effect on penicillin-induced seizures in the cat, *Arch. Neurol.*, 18: 472-477, 1968.

232. Lovelace, R. E. and Horwitz, S. J., Peripheral neuropathy in long-term diphenylhydantoin therapy, *Arch. Neurol.*, 18: 69-77, 1968.

233. Lüllmann, H. and Weber, R., On the action of Phenytoin on digitalis-induced arrhythmia, *Arztliche Forschung*, 22: 49-55, 1968.

234. Lustberg, A., Goldman, D., and Dreskin, O. H., Megaloblastic anemia due to Dilantin therapy, *Ann. Intern. Med.*, 54: 153-158, 1961.

235. McCullagh, W. H. and Ingram, W., Jr., Headaches and hot tempers, *Dis. Nerv. Syst.*, 17: 279-281, 1956.

236. McDonald, D. B., Diphenylhydantoin and multiple system disease, *Grace Hosp. Bull.*, 44: 40-44, 1966.

237. MacIntosh, P. C. and Hutchison, J. L., Megaloblastic anemia due to anticonvulsant therapy: report of a case responding to vitamin B_{12}, *Canad. Med. Assn. J.*, 82: 365-368, 1960.

238. Magee, K. R. and DeJong, R. N., Complications of treatment and side reactions to anticonvulsant drugs, *Mod. Treatm.*, I: 1138-1149, 1964.

239. Malygina, E. H., Effect of phenobarbital, diphenylhydantoin and trimethadione on the blood sugar level (rabbit), *Farmakol. Toksik.*, 28: 725-727, 1965.

240. Mandelbaum, H. and Kane, L. J., Dilantin sodium poisoning; report of a case with dermatitis exfoliativa, pyrexia and hepatic and splenic enlargement, *Arch. Neurol. Psychiat.*, 45: 769-771, 1941.

241. Manlapaz, J. S., Abducens nerve palsy in Dilantin intoxication, *J. Pediat.*, 55: 73-77, 1959.

242. Mark, V. H., Sweet, W. R., Ervin, F. R., Solomon, P., and Geschwind, N., Brain disease and violent behavior, *Neuroophthalmology*, Chap. 20, 4: 282-287, J. L. Smith, ed., C. V. Mosby, St. Louis, 1968.

243. Marriott, H. J. L., Management of cardiac dysrhythmias complicating acute myocardial infarction, *Geriatrics*, 147-156, Sept., 1968.

244. Martin, C. M., Rubin, M., O'Malley, W. E., Garagusi, V. F., and McCauley, C. E., Comparative physiological availability of brand and generic drugs in man: chloramphenicol, sulfisoxazole, and diphenylhydantoin, *Pharmacologist*, 10: 167, 1968.

245. Massey, K. M., Teratogenic effects of diphenylhydantoin sodium, *J. Oral Ther. Pharmacol.*, 2: 380-385, 1966.

246. Meeuwisse, G., Gamstorp, I., and Tryding, N., Effect of Phenytoin on the tryptophan load test, *Acta Paediat. Scand.*, 57: 115-120, 1968.

247. Melchior, J. C. and Svensmark, O., A case of Phenytoin hypersensitivity, *Acta Paediat. Scand.*, 52: 138-140, 1963.

248. Mercer, E. N. and Osborne, J. A., The current status of diphenylhydantoin in heart disease, *Ann. Intern. Med.*, 67: 1084-1107, 1967.

249. Mercer, E. N., Ziegler, W. G., Wickland, G. F., and Dower, G. E., The effect of diphenylhydantoin upon beating of heart cells grown *in vitro*, *J. Pharm. Exp. Ther.*, 155: 267-270, 1967.

250. Merritt, H. H. and Putnam, T. J., A new series of anticonvulsant drugs tested by experiments on animals, *Arch. Neurol. Psychiat.*, 39: 1003-1015, 1938.

251. Mertens, H. G. and Zschocke, S., Neuromyotonia, *Klin. Wschr.*, 17: 917-925, 1965.

252. Michels, J. G., Wright, G. C., and Gever, G., Synthesis and pharmacological activity of a series of 2-substituted pyridazinones, *J. Med. Chem.*, 9: 612-615, 1966.

253. Middleton, J. W. and Hejtmancik, M. R., Severe leukopenia due to diphenylhydantoin sodium: case report, *Texas State J. Med.*, 46: 520-521, 1950.

254. Millichap. J. G. and Boldrey, E. E., Studies in hyperkinetic behavior: II. Laboratory and clinical evaluations of drug treatments, *Neurology*, 17: 467-472, 1967.

255. Mixter, C. G., Moran, J. M., and Austen, W. G., Cardiac and peripheral vascular effects of diphenylhydantoin sodium, *Amer. J. Cardiol.*, 17: 332-338, 1966.

256. Moore, M. T., Pulmonary changes in hydantoin therapy, *JAMA*, 171: 1328-1333, 1959.

257. Morrell, F., Bradley, W., and Ptashne, M., Effect of diphenylhydantoin on peripheral nerve, *Neurology*, 8: 140-144, 1958.

258. Morrell, F., Bradley, W., and Ptashne, M., Effect of drugs on discharge characteristics of chronic epileptogenic lesions, *Neurology*, 9: 492-498, 1959.

259. Morris, J. V., Fischer, E., and Bergin, J. T., Rare complication of Phenytoin sodium treatment, *Brit. Med. J.*, 2: 1529, 1956.

260. Mosey, L. and Tyler, M. D., The effect of diphenylhydantoin sodium (Dilantin), procaine hydrochloride, procaine amide hydrochloride, and quinidine hydrochloride upon ouabain-induced ventricular tachycardia in unanesthetized dogs, *Circulation*, 10: 65-70, 1954.

261. Mull, J. D. and Mullinax, F., Diphenylhydantoin allergy: clinical and immunological studies, *Arthritis Rheum.*, 9: 525-526, 1966.

262. Munsat, T. L., Therapy of myotonia: a double-blind evaluation of diphenylhydantoin, procainamide, and placebo, *Neurology*, 17: 359-367, 1967.

263. Naiman, J. G. and Williams, H. L., Effects of diphenylhydantoin on the duration of respiratory activity during anoxia, *J. Pharm. Exp. Ther.*, 145: 34-41, 1964.

264. Nakamura, K. and Kurebe, M., Differential effects of antiepileptics on hippocampal and pallidal afterdischarges in cats, *Jap. J. Pharmacol.*, 12: 180-190, 1962.

265. Nakamura, K. and Masuda, Y., Effects of 5,5-diphenylhydantoin and 3-ethoxycarbonyl-5,5-diphenylhydantoin (P-6127) on the dermal and gingival tissues of experimental animals, *Arch. Int. Pharmacodyn.*, 162: 255-264, 1966.

266. Nakamura, K., Masuda, Y., and Nakatsuji, K., Tissue distribution and metabolic fate of 3-ethoxycarbonyl-5,5-diphenylhydantoin (P-6127) and 5,5-diphenylhydantoin in rats, *Arch. Int. Pharmacodyn.*, 165: 103-111, 1967.

267. Nakamura, K., Masuda, Y., Nakatsuji, K., and Hiroka, T., Comparative studies on the distribution and metabolic fate of diphenylhydantoin and 3-ethoxycarbonyl-diphenylhydantoin (P-6127) after chronic administrations to dogs and cats, *Naunyn-Schmiedeberg Arch. Pharm.*, 254: 406-417, 1966.

268. Natelson, S., Walker, A. A., and Pincus, J. B., Chlordiazepoxide and diphenylhydantoin as antagonists to ACTH effect on serum calcium and citrate levels, *Proc. Soc. Exp. Biol. Med.*, 122: 689-692, 1966.

269. Noach, E. L., Woodbury, D. M., and Goodman, L. S., Studies on the absorption, distribution, fate and excretion of 4-C^{14}-labeled diphenylhydantoin, *J. Pharm. Exp. Ther.*, 122: 301-314, 1958.

270. Norris, F. H., Jr., Colella, J., and McFarlin, D., Effect of diphenylhydantoin on neuromuscular synapse, *Neurology*, 14: 869-876, 1964.

271. Oberst, B. B., Preventive care of infants and children. VI. School adjustment problems and their relationship to guided growth, *J. Lancet*, 86: 331-334, 1966.

272. Olesen, O. V., Determination of phenobarbital and Phenytoin in serum by ultraviolet spectrophotometry, *Scand. J. Clin. Lab. Invest.*, 20: 63-69, 1967.

273. Olesen, O. V., Disulfiramum (Antabuse) as inhibitor of Phenytoin metabolism, *Acta Pharmacol. Toxicol.*, 24: 317-322, 1966.

274. Olesen, O. V., Determination of 5-(p-hydroxyphenyl)-5-phenylhydantoin (HPPH) in urine by thin layer chromatography, *Acta Pharmacol. Toxicol.*, 26: 222-228, 1968.

275. Olesen, O. V., A simplified method for extracting Phenytoin from serum, and a more sensitive staining reaction for quantitative determination by thin layer chromatography, *Acta Pharmacol. Toxicol.*, 25: 123-126, 1967.

276. Oppenheimer, J. H., Fisher, L. V., Nelson, K. M., and Jailer, J. W., Depression of the serum protein-bound iodine level by diphenylhydantoin, *J. Clin. Endoc. Metab.*, 21: 252-262, 1961.

277. Orth, D. N., Almeida, H., Walsh, F. B., and Honda, M., Ophthalmoplegia resulting from diphenylhydantoin and primidone intoxication, *JAMA*, 201: 485-487, 1967.

278. Parrow, A., Use of anticonvulsive drugs in the treatment of recurrent cardiac arrhythmias, *Acta Med. Scand.*, 180: 413-419, 1966.

279. Patil, K. P., Chitre, R. G., and Sheth, U. K., Anti-folic acid activity of anti-epileptic drugs: Part I. Studies with bacterial cultures, *Indian J. Med. Sci.*, 20: 614-622, 1966.

280. Pennington, G. W. and Smyth, D., Identification reac-

tions of the hydantoin group of drugs, *Arch. Int. Pharmacodyn.*, 152: 285-297, 1964.

281. Penny, J. L., Megaloblastic anemia during anticonvulsant drug therapy, *Arch. Intern. Med.*, 111: 744-749, 1963.

282. Peters, H. A., Eichman, P. L., Price, J. M., Kozelka, F. L., and Reese, H. H., Abnormal copper and tryptophan metabolism and chelation therapy in anti-convulsant drug intolerance, *Dis. Nerv. Syst.*, 27: 97-106, 1966.

283. Petty, C. S., Muelling, R. J., and Sindell, H. W., Accidental, fatal poisoning with diphenylhydantoin (Dilantin), *J. Forensic Sci.*, 2: 279-286, 1957.

284. Petty, W. C. and Karler, R., The influence of aging on the activity of anti-convulsant drugs, *J. Pharm. Exp. Ther.*, 150: 443-448, 1965.

285. Pincus, J. H. and Giarman, N. J., The effect of diphenylhydantoin on sodium-, potassium-, magnesium-stimulated adenosine triphosphatase activity of rat brain, *Biochem. Pharmacol.*, 16: 600-603, 1967.

286. Pincus, J. H. and Glaser, G. H., The syndrome of minimal brain damage in childhood. *New Eng. J. Med.*, 275: 27-35, 1966.

287. Putnam, T. J. and Hood, O. E., Project Illinois: a study of therapy in juvenile behavior problems, *Western Med.*, 231-233, July, 1964.

288. Raines, A. and Levitt, B., The failure of diphenylhydantoin to influence the β-adrenergic receptor of the heart, *Arch. Int. Pharmacodyn.*, 172: 435-441, 1968.

289. Raines, A. and Standaert, F. G., Pre- and postjunctional effects of diphenylhydantoin at the cat soleus neuromuscular junction, *J. Pharm. Exp. Ther.*, 153: 361-366, 1966.

290. Ramirez, E., The use of diphenylhydantoin in the modification of acting-out behavior of post-detoxification addict patients, *Personal communication.* 1967.

291. Rand, B. O., Kelly, W. A., and Ward, A. A., Jr., Electrophysiological studies of the action of intravenous diphenylhydantoin (Dilantin), *Neurology*, 16: 1022-1032, 1966.

292. Rantakallio, P. and Furuhjelm, U., Diphenylhydantoin sensitivity: a case with exfoliative dermatitis and atypical lymphocytes in the peripheral blood, *Ann. Paediat. Fenn.*, 8: 146-151, 1962.

293. Rawson, M. D. and Pincus, J. H., The effect of diphenylhydantoin on sodium, potassium, magnesium-activated adenosine triphosphatase in microsomal fractions of rat and guinea pig brain and on whole homogenates of human brain, *Biochem. Pharmacol.*, 17: 573-579, 1968.

294. Recant, L. and Hartroft, W. S., Lymphoma or drug reaction occurring during hydantoin therapy for epilepsy, *Amer. J. Med.*, 321: 286-297, 1962.

295. Reichelderfer, T. E., Pearson, P. H., and Livingston, S., Thrombocytopenic purpura occurring in association with paradione (paramethadione) and Dilantin sodium (Phenytoin sodium) therapy, *J. Pediat.*, 43: 43-46, 1953.

296. Remmer, H., Estabrook, R. W., Schenkman, J., and Greim, H., Reaction of drugs with microsomal liver hydroxylase: its influence on drug action, *Naunyn-Schmiedeberg Arch. Pharm.*, 259: 98-116, 1968.

297. Resnick, O., The psychoactive properties of diphenylhydantoin: experiences with prisoners and juvenile delinquents, *Int. J. Neuropsychiat.* 3: S30-S48, 1967.

298. Livingston, S., Treatment of epilepsy with diphenylhydantoin sodium (Dilantin sodium), *Post-grad. Med.*, 20: 584-590, 1956.

299. Reynolds, E. H., Effects of folic acid on the mental state and fit-frequency of drug-treated epileptic patients, *Lancet*, 1: 1086-1088, 1967.

300. Reynolds, E. H., Mental effects of anticonvulsants, and folic acid metabolism, *Brain*, 91: 197-214, 1968.

301. Rhind, E. G. and Varadi, S., Megaloblastic anemia due to Phenytoin sodium, *Lancet*, 2: 921, 1954.

302. Rinne, U. K., Effect of diphenylhydantoin treatment on the release of corticotrophin in epileptic patients, *Confin. Neurol.*, 27: 431-440, 1966.

303. Rinne, U. K., Site of the inhibiting action of diphenylhydantoin on the release of corticotrophin in epileptic patients, *Med. Pharmacol. Exp.*, 17: 409-416, 1967.

304. Roberts, H. J., On the etiology, rational treatment and prevention of multiple sclerosis, *Southern Med. J.*, 59: 940-950, 1966.

305. Robinow, M., Diphenylhydantoin hypersensitivity: treatment with 6-mercaptopurine, *Amer. J. Dis. Child.*, 106: 553-557, 1963.

306. Robinson, D. S., MacDonald, M. G., and Hobin, F. P., Sodium diphenylhydantoin reaction with evidence of circulating antibodies, *JAMA*, 192: 171-172, 1965.

307. Robinson, L. J., The gingival changes produced by Dilantin sodium, *Dis. Nerv. Syst.*, 3: 88-94, 1942.

308. Rosati, R. A., Alexander, J. A., Schaal, S. F., and Wallace, A. G., Influence of diphenylhydantoin on electrophysiological properties of the canine heart, *Circ. Res.*, 21: 757-765, 1967.

309. Roseman, E., Dilantin toxicity: a clinical and electroencephalographic study, *Neurology*, 11: 912-921, 1961.

310. Rosen, M., Lisak, R., and Rubin, I. L., Diphenylhydantoin in cardiac arrhythmias, *Amer. J. Cardiol.*, 20: 674-678, 1967.

311. Rosenberg, P. and Bartels, E., Drug effects on the spontaneous electrical activity of the squid giant axon, *J. Pharm. Exp. Ther.*, 155: 532-544, 1967.

312. Rosenfeld, S., Swiller, A. I., Shenoy, Y. M. V., and Morrison, A. N., Syndrome simulating lymphosarcoma induced by diphenylhydantoin sodium, *JAMA*, 176: 491-493, 1961.

313. Ross, A. T. and Jackson, V., Dilantin sodium: its influence on conduct and psychometric ratings of institutionalized epileptics, *Ann. Intern. Med.*, 14: 770-773, 1940.

314. Rossi, A. O., Psychoneurologically impaired child: community mental health clinic approach, *New York J. Med.*, 67: 902-912, 1967.

315. Rowntree, L. G. and Waggoner, R. W., Prevention of migraine attacks by Dilantin sodium, *Dis. Nerv. Syst.*, 11: 148, 1950.

316. Rudzik, A. D. and Mennear, J. H., Antagonism of anticonvulsants by adrenergic blocking agents, *Proc. Soc. Exp. Biol. Med.*, 122: 278-280, 1966.

317. Rushton, J. G., Medical treatment of trigeminal neuralgia with a note on the results of alcohol injection, *Med. Clin. N. Amer.*, 52: 797-800, 1968.

318. Ruthen, G. C., Antiarrhythmic drugs: Part IV. Diphenylhydantoin in cardiac arrhythmias, *Amer. Heart J.*, 70: 275-278, 1965.

319. Ryan, G. M. S. and Forshaw, J. W. B., Megaloblastic anemia due to Phenytoin sodium, *Brit. Med. J.*, 2: 242-243, 1955.

320. Sack, L. P., The effects of sodium Dilantin on stuttering behavior, *Univ. of Calif., L. A. Doctoral thesis*, 1968.

321. Said, D. M., Fraga, J. R., and Reichelderfer, T. E., Hyperglycemia associated with diphenylhydantoin (Dilantin) intoxication, *Med. Ann. D.C.*, 37: 170-172, 1968.

322. Saltzstein, S. L. and Ackerman, L. V., Lymphadenopathy induced by anti-convulsant drugs and mimicking clinically and pathologically malignant lymphomas, *Cancer*, 12: 164-182, 1959.

323. Sanbar, S. S., Conway, F. J., Zweifler, A. J., and Smet, G., Diabetogenic effect of Dilantin (diphenylhydantoin), *Diabetes*, 16: 533, 1967.

324. Sandberg, D. H., Resnick, G. L., and Bacallao, C. Z., Measurement of serum diphenylhydantoin by gas-liquid chromatography, *Anal. Chem.*, 40: 736-738, 1968.

325. Sasyniuk, B. I. and Dresel, P. E., The effect of diphenylhydantoin on conduction in isolated, blood-perfused dog hearts, *J. Pharm. Exp. Ther.*, 161: 191-196, 1968.

326. Schaaf, M. and Payne, C. A., Effect of diphenylhydantoin and phenobarbital on overt and latent tetany, *New Eng. J. Med.*, 274: 1228-1233, 1966.

327. Scherlag, B. J., Helfant, R. H., and Damato, A. N., The

contrasting effects of diphenylhydantoin and procaine amide on A-V conduction in the digitalis-intoxicated and the normal heart, *Amer. Heart J.*, 75: 200-205, 1968.

328. Scherlag, B. J., Helfant, R. H., and Damato, A. N., The relationship between the ionic, inotropic and electrophysiological effects of digitalis, *Circulation*, 36: 230, 1967.

329. Schneider, E., Treatment of dysrhythmic migraine and other forms of cephalalgia with a new combinative preparation (Sanredo), *Schweiz. Med. Wschr.*, 37: 1340-1343, 1963.

330. Schön, A., Treatment with diphenylhydantoin in essential trigeminal neuralgia and in facial spasm, *Gior. Psichiat. Neuropat.*, 92: 1011-1020, 1964.

331. Schönhärl, E., Pharmacotherapeutic experiences in speech and vocal disturbances, *Med. Exp.*, 2: 179-183, 1960.

332. Schulte, C. J. A., and Good, T. A., Acute intoxication due to methsuximide and diphenylhydantoin, *J. Pediat.*, 68: 635-637, 1966.

333. Schwab, R. S., Timberlake, W. H., and Abbott, J. A., Control of side effects of anticonvulsant drugs, *Med. Clin. N. Amer.*, Boston Number, 1139-1150, 1954.

334. Serrate, J. P., Contribution to the treatment of chorea minor by diphenylhydantoin, *Gac. Mèd. Espan.*, 21: 160-161, 1947.

335. Shafer, W. G., The effect of Dilantin sodium on liver DNA and restitution, *J. Oral Ther. Pharm.*, 2: 319-323, 1966.

336. Shafer, W. G., Response of radiated human gingival fibroblast-like cells to Dilantin sodium in tissue culture, *J. Dent. Res.*, 44: 671-677, 1965.

337. Shafer, W. G., Beatty, R. E., and Davis, W. B., Effect of Dilantin sodium on tensile strength of healing wounds, *Proc. Soc. Exp. Biol.*, 98: 348-350, 1958.

338. Shapera, W., Dilantin therapy in certain nervous disorders, *Pittsburgh Med. Bull.*, 29: 732-736, 1940.

339. Shapiro, M., Acceleration of gingival wound healing in non-epileptic patients receiving diphenylhydantoin sodium, *Exp. Med. Surg.*, 16: 41-53, 1958.

340. Shulman, A. and Laycock, G. M., Action of central nervous system stimulant and depressant drugs in the intact animal: Part 3. Dual action of 5-ethyl-5-(1,3-dimethylbutyl) barbiturate, Dilantin and β-methyl-β-n-propylglutarimide, *Europ. J. Pharmacol.*, 2: 17-25, 1967.

341. Shulman, M. H., The use of Dilantin sodium in bronchial asthma: a preliminary report, *New Eng. J. Med.*, 226: 260-264, 1942.

342. Siegel, S. and Berkowitz, J., Diphenylhydantoin (Dilantin) hypersensitivity with infectious mononucleosis-like syndrome and jaundice, *J. Allergy*, 32: 447-451, 1961.

343. Sklans, S., Taylor, R. G., and Shklar, G., Effect of diphenylhydantoin sodium on healing of experimentally produced fractures in rabbit mandibles, *J. Oral Surg.*, 25: 310-319, 1967.

344. Simpson, G. M., Kunz, E., and Slafta, J., Use of sodium diphenylhydantoin in treatment of leg ulcers, *New York J. Med.*, 65: 886-888, 1965.

345. Simpson, W., Severe megaloblastic anemia induced by Phenytoin sodium, *Oral Surg.*, 22: 302-305, 1966.

346. Smith, I. M., Lindell, S. S., Hazard, E. C., and Rabinovich, S., Chemical treatments of staphylococcal infections in mice, *Nature*, 211: 720-722, 1966.

347. Snyder, C. H., Syndrome of gingival hyperplasia, hirsutism, and convulsions: Dilantin intoxication without Dilantin, *J. Pediat.*, 67: 499-502, 1965.

348. Solomon, H. M. and Schrogie, J. J., The effect of phenylramidol on the metabolism of diphenylhydantoin, *Clin. Pharm. Ther.*, 8: 554-556, 1967.

349. Sparberg, M., Diagnostically confusing complications of diphenylhydantoin therapy: a review, *Ann. Intern. Med.*, 59: 914-930, 1963.

350. Standish, S. M. and Clark, P. G., The effect of Dilantin sodium on connective tissue generation in polyvinyl sponge implants, *Transplantation Bull.*, 29: 439-445, 1962.

351. Stevens, H., Paroxysmal choreo-athetosis: a form of reflex epilepsy, *Arch. Neurol.*, 14: 415-420, 1966.

352. Stille, G., On the question of the action of diphenylhydantoin in states of pain: a neurophysiological analysis, *Nervenarzt*, 31: 109-112, 1960.

353. Swan, H. and Sawyer, D. C., Prevention of ventricular fibrillation during experimental hypothermia: failure of sodium diphenylhydantoin, *Arch. Surg.*, 95: 23-26, 1967.

354. Swerdlow, B., Acute brain syndrome associated with sodium diphenylhydantoin intoxication, *Amer. J. Psychiat.*, 122: 100-101, 1965.

355. Tec, L., Efficacy of diphenylhydantoin in childhood psychiatric disorders, *Amer. J. Psychiat.*, 124: 156-157, 1968.

356. Theopold, W., On the use of hydantoin derivatives in chorea minor, *Zschr. Kinderh.*, 69: 305-310, 1951.

357. Tichner, J. B. and Enselberg, C. D., Suicidal Dilantin (sodium diphenylhydantoin) poisoning, *New Eng. J. Med.*, 245: 723-725, 1951.

358. Toman, J. E. P., Neuropharmacologic considerations in psychic seizures, *Neurology*, 1: 444-460, 1951.

359. Toman, J. E. P., Drugs effective in convulsive disorders, *The Pharmacological Basis of Therapeutics*, 3rd Ed., 215-224, Goodman, L. S., Gilman, A., Eds., Macmillan, New York, 1965.

360. Tompsett, S. L., Note on the detection of hexoestrol, stilboestrol, dienoestrol and the p-hydroxy metabolites of phenobarbitone and Phenytoin in urine, *J. Pharm. Pharmacol.*, 16: 207-208, 1964.

361. Triedman, H. M., Fishman, R. A., and Yahr, M. D., Determination of plasma and cerebrospinal fluid levels of Dilantin in the human, *Trans. Amer. Neurol. Assn.*, 85: 166-170, 1960.

362. Turner, W. J., Anticonvulsive agents in the treatment of aggression, *Proc. Symp. Aggressive Behavior, Milan, May 1968*, 353–362, S. Garattini and E. B. Sigg, Eds., *Excerpta Medica*, Amsterdam, 1969.

363. Turner, W. J., Therapeutic use of diphenylhydantoin in neuroses, *Int. J. Neuropsychiat.*, 3: 94-105, 1967.

364. Turner, W. J., The usefulness of diphenylhydantoin in treatment of non-epileptic emotional disorders, *Int. J. Neuropsychiat.*, 3: suppl. 2, S8-S20, 1967.

365. Tuttle, R. S., and Preston, J. B., The effects of diphenylhydantoin (Dilantin) on segmental and suprasegmental facilitation and inhibition of segmental motoneurons in the cat, *J. Pharm. Exp. Ther.*, 141: 84-91, 1963.

366. Ungar, B. and Cowling, D. C., Megaloblastic anemia associated with anticonvulsant drug therapy, *Med. J. Aust.*, 2: 461-462, 1960.

367. Unger, A. H. and Sklaroff, H. J., Fatalities following intravenous use of sodium diphenylhydantoin for cardiac arrhythmias: report of two cases, *JAMA*, 200: 335-336, 1967.

368. van Wyk, J. J. and Hoffmann, C. R., Periarteritis nodosa: a case of fatal exfoliative dermatitis resulting from "Dilantin sodium" sensitization, *Arch. Intern. Med.*, 81: 605-611, 1948.

369. Vasko, J. S., Elkins, R. C., Fogarty, T. J., and Morrow, A. G., Effects of diphenylhydantoin on cardiac performance and peripheral vascular resistance, *Surg. Forum*, 17: 189-190, 1966.

370. Vastola, E. F. and Rosen, A., Suppression by anticonvulsants of focal electrical seizures in the neocortex, *Electroenceph. Clin. Neurophysiol.*, 12: 327-332, 1960.

371. Vernadakis, A. and Woodbury, D. M., Effects of cortisol and diphenylhydantoin on spinal cord convulsions in developing rats, *J. Pharm. Exp. Ther.*, 144: 316-320, 1964.

372. Vincent, M. C. and Blake, M. I., A note on the analysis of diphenylhydantoin sodium by an ion exchange procedure, *Drug Standards*, 26: 206-207, 1958.

373. Walker, C. F. and Kirkpatrick, B. B., Dilantin treatment for behavior problem children with abnormal electroencephalograms, *Amer. J. Psychiat.*, 103: 484-492, 1947.

374. Wallace, J., Biggs, J., and Dahl, E. V., Determination of diphenylhydantoin by ultraviolet spectrophotometry, *Anal. Chem.*, 37: 410-413, 1965.

375. Walsh, P. J. F., Prophylaxis in alcoholics in the withdrawal period, *Amer. J. Psychiat.*, 119: 262-263, 1962.

376. Weintraub, R. M., Pechet, L., and Alexander, B., Rapid diagnosis of drug-induced thrombocytopenic purpura, *JAMA*, 180: 528-532, 1962.

377. Werk, E. E., Jr., MacGee, J., and Sholiton, L. J., Effect of diphenylhydantoin on cortisol metabolism in man, *J. Clin. Invest.*, 43: 1824-1835, 1964.

378. Werk, E. E., Jr., Thrasher, K., Choi, Y., and Sholiton, L. J., Failure of metyrapone to inhibit 11-hydroxylation of 11-deoxycortisol during drug therapy, *J. Clin. Endoc. Metab.*, 27: 1358-1360, 1967.

379. Westerink, D., Chromatographic separation and microdetermination of phenobarbital, methylphenobarbital, butobarbital and Phenytoin, *Pharm. Weekbl.*, 97: 849-856, 1962.

380. Weidemann, D. H., New viewpoints on migraine therapy, *Med. Mschr.*, 20: 28-30, 1966.

381. Wilske, K. R., Shalit, I. E., Willkens, R. F., and Decker, J. L., Findings suggestive of systemic lupus erythematosus in subjects on chronic anticonvulsant therapy, *Arthritis Rheum.*, 8: 260-266, 1965.

382. Wilson, D. R., Electroencephalographic studies in diabetes mellitus, *Canad. Med. Assn., J.*, 65: 462-465, 1951.

383. Wilhoit, W. M. C., The broader treatment of acute alcoholism and delirium tremens, *J. Florida Med. Assn.*, 52: 254-255, 1965.

384. Winiker-Blanck, E., On the diphenylhydantoin therapy of trigeminal neuralgia, *Deutsch Stomat.*, 5: 321-322, 1955.

385. Ichikawa, J., Kimura, E., Terui, H., Wada, T., Sakurada, T., and Sakurada, S., Biochemical studies on antiepileptic drugs. I. Effect on glucose metabolism in guinea pig brain slices, *Seishin Shinkeigaku Zasshi*, 69: 1089-1100, 1967.

386. Wolnisty, C., Polyneuritis of pregnancy effectively managed with Dilantin: report of a case, *Obstet. Gynec.*, 23: 802-803, 1964.

387. Woodbury, D. M., Effect of diphenylhydantoin on electrolytes and radiosodium turnover in brain and other tissues of normal, hyponatremic and postictal rats, *J. Pharm. Exp. Ther.*, 115: 74-95, 1955.

388. Woodbury, D. M., Effect of diphenylhydantoin on pentylene tetrazol-induced seizures in developing rats, *Pharmacologist*, 8: 176, 1966.

389. Woodbury, D. M. and Esplin, D. W., Neuropharmacology and neurochemistry of anticonvulsant drugs, *Proc. Assn. Res. Nerv. Ment. Dis.*, 37: 24-57, 1959.

390. Yunis, A. A., Arimura, G. K., Lutcher, C. L., and Blasquez, J., Reversible erythroid aplasia induced by Dilantin: mechanism of action of Dilantin, *J. Lab. Clin. Med.*, 64: 1021, 1964.

391. Yunis, A. A., Arimura, G. K., Lutcher, C. L., Blasquez, J., and Halloran, M., Biochemical lesion in Dilantin-induced erythroid aplasia, *Blood*, 30: 587-600, 1967.

392. Zeft, H. J., Whalen, R. E., Ratliff, N. B., Jr., Davenport, R. D., Jr., and McIntosh, H. D., Diphenylhydantoin therapy in experimental myocardial infarction, *J. Pharm. Exp. Ther.*, 162: 80-84, 1968.

393. de Zeeuw, R. A. and Feitsma, M. T., Separation and identification of some barbiturates, bromoureides, Phenytoin and glutethimide by means of two-dimensional thin-layer chromatography, *Pharm. Weekbl.*, 101: 957-976, 1966.

394. Zetler, G., The harmine tremor and its antagonists, *Arch. Exper. Path. U. Pharmakol.*, 231: 34-54, 1957.

395. Zimmerman, F. T., Explosive behavior anomalies in children on an epileptic basis, *New York J. Med.*, 56: 2537-2543, 1956.

396. Zipes, D. P. and Orgain, E. S., Refractory paroxysmal ventricular tachycardia, *Ann. Intern. Med.*, 67: 1251-1257, 1967.

397. Zung, W. W. K., Effect of diphenylhydantoin on the sleep-dream cycle: an EEG study in normal adults, *Personal Communication*, 1967.

398. Agarwal, S. P. and Blake, M. I., Determination of the pKa' value for 5,5-diphenylhydantoin, *J. Pharm. Sci.*, 57: 1434-1435, 1968.

399. Alvarez, W. C., Why patients avoid telling what is wrong, *Mod. Med.*, 53-54, Nov. 18, 1968.

400. Rosenblum, I. and Stein, A. A., Preferential distribution of diphenylhydantoin in primary human brain tumors, *Biochem. Pharmacol.*, 12: 1453-1454, 1963.

401. Sayar, B. and Polvan, O., Epilepsy and bronchial asthma, *Lancet*, 1: 1038, 1968.

402. Nayler, W. G., McInnes, I., Swann, J. B., Race, D., Carson, V., and Lowe, T. E., Some effects of diphenylhydantoin and propranolol on the cardiovascular system, *Amer. Heart J.*, 75: 83-96, 1968.

403. Lüllman, H. and Weber, R., Inhibition of cardiac glycoside-induced arrhythmia by Phenytoin, *Naunyn-Schmiedeberg Arch. Pharm.*, 259: 182-183, 1968.

404. Hilmi, K. I. and Regan, T. J., Relative effectiveness of antiarrhythmic drugs in treatment of digitalis-induced ventricular tachycardia, *Amer. Heart J.*, 76: 365-369, 1968.

405. Mierzwiak, D. S., Mitchell, J. H., and Shapiro, W., The effect of diphenylhydantoin (Dilantin) and quinidine on left ventricular function in dogs, *Amer. Heart J.*, 74: 780-791, 1967.

406. Mierzwiak, D. S., Shapiro, W., McNalley, M. C., and Mitchell, J. H., Cardiac effects of diphenylhydantoin (Dilantin) in man, *Amer. J. Cardiol.*, 21: 20-22, 1968.

407. Wehrmacher, W. H., Dilantin in the management of cardiac arrhythmias, *Curr. Med. Dig.*, 36: 45-49, 1969.

408. Shine, K. I., Kastor, J. A., and Yurchak, P. M., Multifocal atrial tachycardia: clinical and electrocardiographic features in 32 patients, *New Eng. J. Med.*, 279: 344-349, 1968.

409. Seuffert, G. W., Helfant, R. H., Dana, J. F., and Urbach, K. F., Use of diphenylhydantoin in prevention and treatment of cardiac arrhythmias during general anesthesia. *Anesth. Analg.*, 47: 334-339, 1968.

410. Scherf, D., Blumenfeld, S., Taner, D., and Yildiz, M., The effect of diphenylhydantoin (Dilantin) sodium on atrial flutter and fibrillation provoked by focal application of aconitine or delphinine, *Amer. Heart J.*, 60: 936-947, 1960.

411. Carlson, E. E., Viral myocarditis, *Minn. Med.*, 51: 829-836, 1968.

412. Lawrie, D. M., Higgins, M. R., Godman, M. J., Oliver, M. F., Julian, D. G., and Donald, K. W., Ventricular fibrillation complicating acute myocardial infarction, *Lancet*, 2: 523-528, 1968.

413. Blachly, P. H., Diphenylhydantoin and arrhythmias, *JAMA*, 202: 173, 1967.

414. Editor, Hypertension in a young man, *JAMA*, 143: 939, 1954.

415. Conn, R. D., Newer drugs in the treatment of cardiac arrhythmia, *Med. Clin. N. Amer.*, 51: 1223-1240, 1967.

416. Criscitiello, M. G., Therapy of atrioventricular block, *New Eng. J. Med.*, 279: 808-810, 1968.

417. Schattenberg, T. T., Electrocardiographic diagnosis of left atrial myxoma, *Mayo Clin. Proc.*, 43: 620-627, 1968.

418. Bashour, F. A., Edmondson, R. E., Gupta, D. N., and Prati, R., Treatment of digitalis toxicity by diphenylhydantoin (Dilantin), *Dis. Chest*, 53: 263-270, 1968.

419. Chen, G., Bohner, B., and Bratton, A. C., Jr., The influence of certain central depressants on fighting behavior of mice, *Arch. Int. Pharmacodyn.*, 142: 30-34, 1963.

420. Editor, Childhood migraine, *New Eng. J. Med.*, 276: 56-57, 1967.

421. Ginabreda, J. M. S., Treatment of chorea with diphenylhydantoin sodium, *Rev. Espan. Pediat.*, 266-272, Mar.-Apr., 1945.

422. Roberts, H. J., Migraine and related vascular headaches due to diabetogenic hyperinsulinism, *Headache*, 7: 41-62, 1967.

423. Gribetz, D., Mizrachi, A., and London, R. B., Neonatal hypocalcemia, Correspondence, *New Eng. J. Med.*, 279: 327, 1968.

424. O'Malley, B. W. and Kohler, P. O., Hypoparathyroidism, *Postgrad. Med.*, 44: 182-186, 1968.

425. Werk, E. E., Sholiton, L. J., and Olinger, C. P., Enzyme inducer, *New Eng. J. Med.*, 276: 877, 1967.

426. Gilbert, J. C., Ortiz, W. R., and Millichap, J. G., The effects of anticonvulsant drugs on the permeability of brain cells to sugars, *Proc. Inst. Med. Chicago*, 25: May, 1965.

427. Werk, E. E., Jr., Sholiton, L. J., and Olinger, C. P., Amelioration of non-tumorous Cushing's syndrome by diphenylhydantoin, *Proc. 2nd Int. Cong. Hormonal Steroids, Excerpta Medica, No. 111*, Milan, 1966.

428. Bodkin, L. G., Pruritus ani, *Amer. Prac.*, 2: 580-581, 1948.

429. Roberts, H. J., The syndrome of narcolepsy and diabetogenic ("functional") hyperinsulinism, with special reference to obesity, diabetes, idiopathic edema, cerebral dysrhythmias and multiple sclerosis (200 patients), *J. Amer. Geriat. Soc.*, 12: 926-976, 1964.

430. Fabrykant, M., Pseudohypoglycemic reactions in insulin-treated diabetics: etiology, laboratory aids and therapy, *J. Amer. Geriat. Soc.*, 12: 221-238, 1964.

431. Ellenberg, M., Treatment of diabetic neuropathy with diphenylhydantoin, *New York J. Med.*, 68: 2653-2655, 1968.

432. Jonas, A. D., *Ictal and subictal neurosis*, C. C. Thomas, Springfield, Ill., 1965.

433. Kong, Y., Chen, J. T. T., Zeft, H. J., Whalen, R. E., and McIntosh, H. D., Natural history of experimental coronary occlusion in pigs: a serial cineangeographic study, *Amer. Heart J.*, 77: 45-54, 1969.

434. Klinefelter, H. F., Greene, C. A., Pauli, L. L. and Livingston, S., Precordial pain in an epileptic relieved by Dilantin, *Johns Hopkins Med. J.*, 124: 25-27, 1969.

435. Bjorge, I., Presthus, J., and Stoa, K. F., A spectrophotometric study on 5,5-diphenylhydantoin, *Norsk Farmaceutisk Selskap*, 19: 17-22, 1957.

436. Koster, R., Mechanism of chlorcyclizine block of diphenylhydantoin in mice, *Pharmacologist*, 6: 187, 1964.

437. Svensmark, O. and Kristensen, P., Determination of diphenylhydantoin and phenobarbital in small amounts of serum, *J. Lab. Clin. Med.*, 61: 501-507, 1963.

438. Wallace, J. E. and Dahl, E. V., New laboratory method for determining Dilantin, *Air Force Systems Command Research and Technology Briefs*, 3: 18-21, Sept., 1965.

439. Panalaks, T., A method for evaluation of physiological availability of diphenylhydantoin by urinary analysis, *Clin. Chim. Acta*, 8: 968-970, 1963.

440. Loeser, E. W., Jr., Studies on the metabolism of diphenylhydantoin (Dilantin), *Neurology*, 11: 424-429, 1961.

441. Schiller, P. J. and Buchthal, F., Diphenylhydantoin and phenobarbital in serum in patients with epilepsy, *Danish Med. Bull.*, 5: 161-163, 1958.

442. Burns, J. J. and Conney, A. H., Enzyme stimulation and inhibition in the metabolism of drugs, *Proc. Roy. Soc. Med.*, 58: 955-960, 1965.

443. Butler, T. C., The metabolic conversion of 5,5-diphenylhydantoin to 5-(p-hydroxyphenyl)-5-phenylhydantoin, *J. Pharm. Exp. Ther.*, 119: 1-11, 1957.

444. Maynert, E. W., The metabolic fate of diphenylhydantoin in the dog, rat and man, *J. Pharm. Exp. Ther.*, 130: 275-284, 1960.

445. Chang, T., Baukema, J., Dill, W. A., Buchanan, R. A., Goulet, J. R., and Glazko, A. J., Metabolic disposition of diphenylhydantoin (DPH) in human subjects following intravenous administration, *Clin. Res.*, 16: 464, 1968.

446. Svensmark, O., Schiller, P. J., and Buchthal, F., 5,5-diphenylhydantoin (Dilantin) blood levels after oral or intravenous dosage in man, *Acta Pharmacol. (Kobenhavn)*, 16: 331-346, 1960.

447. Toman, J. E. P. and Taylor, J. D., Mechanism of action and metabolism of anticonvulsants, *Epilepsia*, Third Series, 1: 31-48, 1952.

448. Rudzik, A. D. and Mennear, J. H., The mechanism of action of anticonvulsants. I. Diphenylhydantoin, *Life Sci.*, 4: 2373-2382, 1965.

449. Morpurgo, C., Aggressive behavior induced by large doses of 2-(2,6-dichlorphenylamino)-2-imidazoline hydrochloride (ST-155) in mice, *Europ. J. Pharmacol.*, 3: 374-377, 1968.

450. Sholiton, L. J., Werk, E. E., and MacGee, J., The effect of diphenylhydantoin *in vitro* on the metabolism of testosterone by rat liver slices, *Acta Endocr.*, 56: 490-498, 1967.

451. Sholiton, L., Werk, E. E., Jr., and MacGee, J., The *in vitro* effect of 5,5'-diphenylhydantoin on the catabolism of cortisol by rat liver, *Metabolism*, 13: 1382-1392, 1964.

452. Kutt, H., Verebely, K., and McDowell, F., Inhibition of diphenylhydantoin metabolism in rat liver microsomes by antituberculosis drugs, *Neurology*, 17: 318-319, 1967.

453. Kutt, H., Verebely, K., and McDowell, F., Inhibition of diphenylhydantoin metabolism in rats and in rat liver microsomes by antitubercular drugs, *Neurology*, 18: 706-710, 1968.

454. Verster, F. de B., Garoutte, J., Ichinosa, H., and Guerrero-Figueroa, R., Mode of action of diphenylhydantoin, *Fed. Proc.*, 24: 390, 1965.

455. Elliott, K. A. C. and van Gelder, N. M., The state of factor I in rat brain: the effects of metabolic conditions and drugs, *J. Physiol.*, 153: 423-432, 1960.

456. Shohl, J., Effects of oral administration of Dilantin sodium on abnormal behavior in the rat, *J. Comp. Psychol.*, 37: 243-250, 1944.

457. Weissman, A., Effect of anticonvulsant drugs on electroconvulsive shock-induced retrograde amnesia, *Arch. Int. Pharmacodyn.*, 154: 122-130, 1965.

458. Toman, J. E. P., The neuropharmacology of antiepileptics, *Electroenceph. Clin. Neurophysiol.*, 1: 33-44, 1949.

459. Ensor, C. R., Bohner, B., and Chen, G., Anticonvulsant effect of Dilantin sodium by intravenous administration in mice, *Proc. Soc. Exp. Med. Biol.*, 100: 133-135, 1959.

460. Hofmann, W. W., Koenig, G., Shumway, N. E., and Hanbery, J. W., Observations of the depressant effects of parenterally administered Dilantin on the cardiovascular system and cerebral cortex, *Stanford Med. Bull.*, 17: 193-197, 1959.

461. Riehl, J. and McIntyre, H. B., A quantitative study of the acute effects of diphenylhydantoin on the electroencephalogram of epileptic patients: Theoretical considerations for its use in the treatment of status epilepticus, *Neurology*, 18: 1107-1112, 1968.

462. Schallek, W. and Kuehn, A., Effects of trimethadione, diphenylhydantoin and chlordiazepoxide on after-discharges in brain of cat, *Proc. Soc. Exp. Biol. Med.*, 112: 813-816, 1963.

463. Chen, G. and Ensor, C. R., Antagonism studies on reserpine and certain CNS depressants, *Proc. Soc. Exp. Biol. Med.*, 87: 602-608, 1954.

464. Lu, F. C., Mazurkiewicz, I. M., Grewal, R. S., Allmark, M. G., and Boivin, P., The effect of sodium fluoride on responses to various central nervous system agents in rats, *Toxic. Appl. Pharmacol.*, 3: 31-38, 1961.

465. Druckman, R. and Moore, F. J., Effects of sodium diphenylhydantoinate upon isolated small intestine of the rabbit, *Proc. Soc. Exp. Biol. Med.*, 90: 173-176, 1955.

466. Van Harreveld, A. and Feigen, G. A., Effect of some drugs on the polarization state of spinal cord elements, *Amer. J. Physiol.*, 160: 451-461, 1950.

467. Raines, A. and Standaert, F. G., An effect of diphenylhydantoin on post-tetanic hyperpolarization of intramedullary nerve terminals, *J. Pharm. Exp. Ther.*, 156: 591-597, 1967.

468. Raines, A., Diphenylhydantoin suppression of post-tetanic hyperpolarization in nerve terminals of dorsal root fibers, *Pharmacologist*, 7: 142, 1965.

469. Brumlik, J. and Moretti, L., The effect of diphenylhydantoin on nerve conduction velocity, *Neurology*, 16: 1217-1218, 1966.

470. Hopf, H. C., Effect of diphenylhydantoin on peripheral nerves in man, *Electroenceph. Clin. Neurophysiol.*, 25: 411, 1968.

471. Orozco, A. and Sabelli, H. C., Effect of antiepileptic

drugs on calcium-induced hyperexcitability in earthworm ventral cords, *Pharmacologist*, 10: 161, 1968.

472. Korey, S. R., Effect of Dilantin and Mesantoin on the giant axon of the squid, *Proc. Soc. Exp. Biol. Med.*, 76: 297-299, 1951.

473. Kivalo, E., Tyrkkö, J., and Marjanen, P., The response to diphenylhydantoin of the neurosecretory substance in the mouse, *Ann. Med. Intern. Fenn.*, 47: 169-173, 1958.

474. Buchthal, F., Svensmark, O., and Schiller, P. J., Clinical and electroencephalographic correlations with serum levels of diphenylhydantoin, *Arch. Neurol.*, 2: 624-630, 1960.

475. Cohn, R., A neuropathological study of a case of petit mal epilepsy, *Electroenceph. Clin. Neurophysiol.*, 24: 282, 1968.

476. Haury, V. G. and Drake, M. E., The effect of intravenous injections of sodium diphenylhydantoinate (Dilantin) on respiration, blood pressure, and the vagus nerve, *J. Pharm. Exp. Ther.*, 68: 36-40, 1940.

477. Hrbek, J., Komenda, S., Dostalova, K., Siroka, A., Beran, I., and Szarowski, E., The acute effect of some drugs on the higher nervous activity in man. VII. Pyridoxine and diphenylhydantoin, *Acta Univ. Palacki Olomuc.*, *Fac. Med.*, 47: 625-638, 1967.

478. Takahashi, M., Effects of antiepileptic drugs on end plate region. Facilitation of acetazolamide, *Hirosaki Med. J.*, 19: 597, 1967.

479. Van Harreveld, A., Foster, R. J., and Fasman, G. D., Effect of diphenylhydantoin on ether and pentobarbital narcosis, *Amer. J. Physiol.*, 166: 718-722, 1951.

480. Toman, J. E. P., Neuropharmacology of diphenylhydantoin, *Int. J. Neuropsychiat.*, 3: S57-S62, 1967.

481. Woodbury, D. M., Effects of chronic administration of anticonvulsant drugs, alone and in combination with desoxycorticosterone, on electroshock seizure threshold and tissue electrolytes, *J. Pharm. Exp. Ther.*, 105: 46-57, 1952.

482. Oliver, J. T. and Troop, R. C., Plasma corticosterone levels in stressed rats following the administration of pentobarbital, morphine and diphenylhydantoin, *Steroids*, 1: 670-677, 1963.

483. Woodbury, D. M., Timiras, P. S., and Vernadakis, A., Modification of adrenocortical function by centrally acting drugs and the influence of such modification on the central response to these drugs, *Hormones, Brain Function, and Behavior*, 38-50, H. Hoagland, Ed., Academic Press, New York, 1957.

484. Staple, P. H., The effects of continued administration of 5:5-diphenylhydantoin (Dilantin) sodium on the adrenal glands in mice, *J. Roy. Micr. Soc.*, 74: 10-21, 1954.

485. Quinn, D. L., Influence of diphenylhydantoin on spontaneous release of ovulating hormone in the adult rat, *Proc. Soc. Exp. Biol. Med.*, 119: 982-985, 1965.

486. Christy, N. P. and Hofmann, A. D., The apparent lack of effect of diphenylhydantoin (Dilantin) upon adrenal cortical response to ACTH in man, *Clin. Res.*, 6: 258-259, 1958.

487. Takahashi, Y., Kipnis, D. M., and Daughaday, W. H., Growth hormone secretion during sleep, *J. Clin. Invest.*, 47: 2079-2090, 1968.

488. Levy, R. P. and Marshall, J. S., Short-term drug effects on thyroid function tests, *Arch. Intern. Med.*, 114: 413-416, 1964.

489. Zaninovich, A. A., Farach, H., Ezrin, C., and Volpé, R., Lack of significant binding of L-triiodothyronine by thyroxine binding globulin *in vivo* as demonstrated by acute disappearance of 131-I-labeled triiodothyronine, *J. Clin. Invest.*, 45: 1290-1301, 1966.

490. Oppenheimer, J. H. and Tavernetti, R. R., Studies on the thyroxin-diphenylhydantoin interaction: effect of 5,5′-diphenylhydantoin on the displacement of L-thyroxine from thyroxine-binding globulin (TBG), *Endocrinology*, 71: 496-504, 1962.

491. Oppenheimer, J. H. and Tavernetti, R. R., Displacement of thyroxine from human thyroxine-binding globulin by analogues of hydantoin. Steric aspects of the thyroxine binding site,

J. Clin. Invest., 41: 2213-2220, 1962.

492. Oppenheimer, J. H., Role of plasma proteins in the binding, distribution and metabolism of the thyroid hormones, *New Eng. J. Med.*, 278: 1153-1162, 1968.

493. Chin, W. and Schussler, G. C., Decreased serum free thyroxine concentration in patients treated with diphenylhydantoin, *J. Clin. Endocrinol.*, 28: 181-186, 1968.

494. Mendoza, D. M., Flock, E. V., Owen, C. A., Jr., and Paris, J., Effect of 5,5′-diphenylhydantoin on the metabolism of L-thyroxine-^{131}I in the rat. *Endocrinology*, 79: 106-118, 1966.

495. Merritt, H. H. and Foster, A., Vitamin C in epilepsy. Dilantin sodium not a cause of vitamin C deficiency, *Amer. J. Med. Sci.*, 200: 541-544, 1940.

496. Gupta, D. N., Unal, M. O., Bashour, F. A., and Webb, W. R., Effects of diphenylhydantoin (Dilantin) on peripheral and coronary circulation and myocardial contractility in the experimental animal, *Dis. Chest*, 51: 248-255, 1967.

497. Roberts, H. J., Spontaneous leg cramps and "restless legs" due to diabetogenic hyperinsulinism: observations on 131 patients, *J. Amer. Geriat. Soc.*, 13: 602-638, 1965.

498. Bhussry, B. R., and Rao, S., Effect of sodium diphenylhydantoinate on oral mucosa of rats, *Proc. Soc. Exp. Biol. Med.*, 113: 595-599, 1963.

499. Houck, J. C., The resorption of sodium Dilantin produced dermal collagen, *J. Clin. Invest.* 41: 179-184, 1962.

500. Houck, J. C., Dermal chemical response to analogues of Dilantin, *J. Invest. Derm.*, 40: 89-93, 1963.

501. Houck, J. C., Effect of cortisol and age upon the dermal chemical response to Dilantin, *J. Invest. Derm.*, 40: 125-126, 1963.

502. Houck, J. C. and Jacob, R. A., Connective tissue. VII. Factors inhibiting the dermal chemical response to cortisol, *Proc. Soc. Exp. Biol. Med.*, 113: 692-694, 1963.

503. Forscher, B. K. and Cecil, H. C., Biochemical studies on acute inflammation. II. The effect of Dilantin, *J. Dent. Res.*, 36: 927-931, 1957.

504. Kolbert, G. S., Oral diphenylhydantoin in corneal wound healing in the rabbit, *Amer. J. Ophthal.*, 66: 736-738, 1968.

505. Smith, D. L. and Robinson, W. A., The effect of diphenylhydantoin sodium on liver restitution in the rat following hepatectomy, *Proc. Soc. West. Pharmacol. Soc.*, 5: 9-12, 1962.

506. Shafer, W. G., Effect of Dilantin sodium analogues on cell proliferation in tissue culture, *Proc. Soc. Exp. Biol. Med.*, 106: 205-207, 1961.

507. Shafer, W. G., Effect of Dilantin sodium on various cell lines in tissue culture, *Proc. Soc. Exp. Biol. Med.*, 108: 694-696, 1961.

508. Shafer, W. G., Effect of Dilantin sodium on growth of human fibroblast-like cell cultures, *Proc. Soc. Exp. Biol. Med.*, 104: 198-201, 1960.

509. Chalmers, J. N. M. and Boheimer, K., Megaloblastic anaemia and anticonvulsant therapy, *Lancet*, 2: 920-921, 1954.

510. P'an, S. Y., Funderburk, W. H., and Finger, K. F., Anticonvulsant effect of nialamide and diphenylhydantoin, *Proc. Soc. Exp. Biol. Med.*, 108, 680-683, 1961.

511. Conn, R. D., Kennedy, J. W., and Blackmon, J. R., The hemodynamic effects of diphenylhydantoin, *Amer. Heart J.*, 73: 500-505, 1967.

512. Rowe, G. G., McKenna, D. H., Sialer, S., and Corliss, R. J., Systemic and coronary hemodynamic effects of diphenylhydantoin, *Amer. J. Med. Sci.*, 254: 534-541, 1967.

513. Hockman. C. H., Mauck, H. P., Jr., and Hoff, E. C., Experimental neurogenic arrhythmias, *Bull. N.Y. Acad. Med.*, 43: 1097-1105, 1967.

514. Raines, A., Levitt, B., and Standaert, F. G., Factors influencing diphenylhydantoin antagonism of ouabain-induced ventricular arrhythmia in the cat, *Pharmacologist*, 9: 237, 1967.

515. Roberts, J., Levitt, B., and Standaert, F. G., Autonomic nervous system and control of cardiac rhythm, *Nature*, 214: 912-913, 1967.

516. Stannard, M., Sloman, G., and Sangster, L., The haemodynamic effects of Phenytoin sodium (Dilantin) in acute myocardial infarction, *Med. J. Aust.*, 1: 335-337, 1968.

517. Lugo, V. and Sanabria, A., Treatment of extrasystole in chronic Chagasic cardiopathy with diphenylhydantoin, *Acta Medica Venezolana*, 148-151, Mar.-Apr., 1966.

518. Jensen, H. P., The treatment of trigeminal neuralgia with diphenylhydantoin, *Therapiewoche*, 5: 345, 1955.

519. Rosati, R. and Wallace, A. G., Electrophysiologic effects of diphenylhydantoin (Dilantin) on the heart of awake dogs, *Amer. J. Cardiol.*, 19: 147, 1967.

520. Bonnycastle, D. D. and Bradley, A. J., Diphenylhydantoin and the release of adrenocorticotropic hormone in the albino rat, *Endocrinology*, 66: 355-363, 1960.

521. Porter, I. H., The genetics of drug susceptibility, *Dis. Nerv. Syst.*, 27: 25-36, 1966.

522. Bhattacharya, S. S., Kishor, K., Saxena, P. N., and Bhargava, K. P., A neuropharmacological study of gamma-aminobutyric acid (GABA), *Arch. Int. Pharmacodyn.*, 150: 295-305, 1964.

523. de Ropp, R. S., and Snedeker, E. H., Effect of drugs on amino acid levels in brain: excitants and depressants, *Proc. Soc. Exp. Biol. Med.*, 106: 696-700, 1960.

524. Thomas, H. F. and Stone, C. P., Maze performance of albino rats under influence of Dilantin sodium while subjected to electroshock, *J. Psychol.*, 33: 127-132, 1952.

525. Blum, B., A differential action of diphenylhydantoin on the motor cortex of the cat, *Arch. Int. Pharmacodyn.*, 149: 45-55, 1964.

526. Bianchi, C., Anticonvulsant action of some antiepileptic drugs in mice pretreated with rauwolfia alkaloids, *Brit. J. Pharmacol.*, 11: 141-146, 1956.

527. Haward, L. R. C., A study of physiological responses of neurotic patients to diphenylhydantoin, *Int. J. Neuropsychiat.*, 3: S49-S56, 1967.

528. Gerber, N. and Arnold, K., The effect of diphenyl-piperazine compounds and other agents on diphenylhydantoin, zoxazolamine and hexobarbital metabolism, *J. Pharm. Exp. Ther.*, 164: 232-238, 1968.

529. Ariyoshi, V. T. and Remmer, H., The action of phenobarbital and diphenylhydantoin on various fat fractions of liver, *Naunyn-Schmiedeberg Arch. Pharm.*, 260: 90-91, 1968.

530. Pincus, J. H. and Rawson, M. D., Diphenylhydantoin and intracellular sodium concentration, *Neurology*, 19: 419-422, 1968.

531. Kemp, J. W. and Woodbury, D. M., Intracellular distribution of 4-C^{14} diphenylhydantoin (Dilantin) in rat brain, *Pharmacologist*, 4: 159, 1962.

532. Vernadakis, A. and Woodbury, D. M., Effects of diphenylhydantoin and adrenocortical steroids on free glutamic acid, glutamine, and gamma-aminobutyric acid concentrations of rat cerebral cortex, *Inhibitions of the nervous system and gamma-aminobutyric acid*, 242-248, Pergamon Press, Oxford, 1960.

533. Strauss, H. C., Bigger, J. T., Jr., Bassett, A. L., and Hoffman, B. F., Actions of diphenylhydantoin on the electrical properties of isolated rabbit and canine artia, *Circ. Res.*, 23: 463-477, 1968.

534. Ludmer, R. I. and Toman, J. E. P., Some drug effects on cardiac transmembranal potentials, *Fed. Proc.*, 27: 303, 1968.

535. Kimball, O. P. and Horan, T. N., The use of Dilantin in the treatment of epilepsy, *Ann. Intern. Med.*, 13: 787-793, 1939.

536. Janz, D. and Fuchs, U., Are anti-epileptic drugs harmful when given during pregnancy?, *German Med. Monthly*, 9: 20-22, 1964.

537. Andia, J., Westphal, M., Anthone, R., and Anthone, S., Severe, acute diphenylhydantoin intoxication treated with peritoneal lavage, *New York J. Med.*, 1861-1863, 1968.

538. Ayd, F. J., Jr., New uses for an old drug, *Intern. Drug Ther. Newsletter*, 2: 1-2, Jan., 1967.

539. Bakwin, R. M. and Bakwin, H., Psychologic aspects of pediatrics: epilepsy, *J. Pediat.*, 39: 766-784, 1951.

540. Bergman, H., Dilantin sodium in the control of a convulsive disorder during pregnancy, *Med. Rec.*, 155: 105-106, 1942.

541. Berlyne, N., Levene, M., and McGlashan, A., Megaloblastic anemia following anticonvulsants, *Brit. Med. J.*, 1: 1247-1248, 1955.

542. Benians, R. C. and Hunter, R. A., Megaloblastic anemia occurring during treatment of epilepsy with Phenytoin sodium, primidone and phenobarbitone, *J. Ment. Sci.*, 103: 606-609, 1957.

543. Braham, J., Pain in the face, *Brit. Med. J.*, 3: 316, 1968.

544. Burns, J. J., Cucinell, S. A., Koster, R., and Conney, A. H., Application of drug metabolism to drug toxicity studies, *Ann. N.Y. Acad. Sci.*, 123: 273-286, 1965.

545. Gray, W. D., Rauh, C. E. and Shanahan, R. W., The mechanism of the antagonistic action of reserpine on the anticonvulsant effect of inhibitors of carbonic anhydrase, *J. Pharm. Exp. Ther.*, 139: 350-360, 1963.

546. Eadie, M. J., Sutherland, J. M., and Tyrer, J. H., "Dilantin" overdosage, *Med. J. Aust.*, 2: 515, 1968.

547. Filkova, V., Hyperplastic gingivitis resulting from epilepsy treated with Phenytoin, *Deutsch Stomat.*, 18: 294-298, 1968.

548. Fitzpatrick, T. B., Diphenylhydantoin reaction, *Arch. Derm.*, 93: 766-767, 1966.

549. Hudgins, R. L. and Corbin, K. B., An uncommon seizure disorder: familial paroxysmal choreoathetosis, *Brain*, 89: 199-204, 1966.

550. Jonas, A. D., The emergence of epileptic equivalents in the era of tranquilizers, *Int. J. Neuropsychiat.*, 3: 40-45, 1967.

551. Kellaway, P., Crawley, J. W., and Kagawa, N., Paroxysmal pain and autonomic disturbances of cerebral origin: a specific electro-clinical syndrome, *Epilepsia*, 1: 466-483, 1959-1960.

552. Khoury, N. J., When alcoholics stop drinking, *Postgrad. Med.*, 43: 119-123, 1968.

553. Kutt, H., Haynes, J., and McDowell, F., Some causes of ineffectiveness of diphenylhydantoin, *Arch. Neurol.*, 14: 489-492, 1966.

554. Kutt, H., Winters, W., Scherman, R., and McDowell, F., Diphenylhydantoin and phenobarbital toxicity, *Arch. Neurol.*, 11: 649-656, 1964.

555. Kutt, H., Winters, W., Kokenge, R., and McDowell, F., Diphenylhydantoin metabolism, blood levels, and toxicity, *Arch. Neurol.*, 11: 642-648, 1964.

556. McCartan, W. and Carson, J., The use of sodium diphenylhydantoinate, *J. Ment. Sci.*, 85: 965-971, 1939.

557. Merritt, H. H. and Putnam, T. J., Sodium diphenylhydantoinate in the treatment of convulsive disorders, *JAMA*, 111: 1068-1073, 1938.

558. Nelson, D. A. and Ray, C. D., Respiratory arrest from seizure discharges in limbic system, *Arch. Neurol.*, 19: 199-207, 1968.

559. Olesen, O. V., The influence of disulfiram and calcium carbimide on the serum diphenylhydantoin, *Arch. Neurol.*, 16: 642-644, 1967.

560. Pasamanick, B., Anticonvulsant drug therapy of behavior problem children with abnormal electroencephalograms, *A.M.A. Arch. Neurol. Psychiat.*, 65: 752-766, 1951.

561. Pisciotta, A. V., Penalties of progress—Drug-induced hematologic disease, *Postgrad. Med.*, 43: 213-219, 1968.

562. Rail, L., "Dilantin" overdosage, *Med. J. Aust.*, 2: 339, 1968.

563. Rawson, M. D., Diphenylhydantoin intoxication and cerebrospinal fluid protein, *Neurology*, 18: 1009-1011, 1968.

564. Schubert, H. A. and Malooly, D. A., Convulsive equivalent states, *A.M.A. Arch. Intern. Med.*, 104: 585-588, 1959.

565. Tenckhoff, H., Sherrard, D. J., Hickman, R. O., and Ladda, R. L., Acute diphenylhydantoin intoxication, *Amer. J. Dis. Child.*, 116: 422-425, 1968.

566. Voigt, G. C., Death following intravenous sodium diphenylhydantoin (Dilantin), *Johns Hopkins Med. J.*, 123: 153-157, 1968.

567. Weaver, L. C., Swinyard, E. A., and Goodman, L. S.,

Anticonvulsant drug combinations: diphenylhydantoin combined with other antiepileptics, *J. Amer. Pharm. Assn.*, 47: 645-648, 1958.

568. Snyder, C. H., Syndrome of Dilantin intoxication without Dilantin, *Southern Med. J.*, 57: 1482, 1964.

569. Roseman, E. and Klein, L. J., Epilepsy—facts and fancy, *GP*, 35: 144-152, 1967.

570. Landy, P. J., Lucas, B. G., and Toakley, J. G., "Dilantin" overdosage, *Med. J. Aust.*, 2: 639-640, 1968.

571. Chafetz, M. F., Alcohol withdrawal and seizures, *JAMA*, 200: 195-196, 1967.

572. Editor, Cardiac arrhythmias and sodium diphenylhydantoin—an appraisal, *JAMA*, 201: 142-143, 1967.

573. Bonnycastle, D. D., Bonnycastle, M. F., and Anderson, E. G., The effect of a number of central depressant drugs upon brain 5-hydroxytryptamine levels in the rat, *J. Pharm. Exp. Ther.*, 135: 17-20, 1962.

574. Garrettson, L. K., Perel, J. M., and Dayton, P. G., Methylphenidate interaction with both anticonvulsants and ethyl biscoumacetate a new action of methylphenidate, *JAMA*, 207: 2053-2056, 1969.

575. Bonnycastle, D. D., Paasonen, M. K., and Giarman, N. J., Diphenylhydantoin and brain-levels of 5-hydroxytryptamine, *Nature*, 178: 990-991, 1956.

576. Lynk, S. M. and Amidon, E., Chemotherapy with delinquents, *Mich. Med.*, 762-766, Oct., 1965.

577. Gangloff, H. and Monnier, M., The action of anticonvulsant drugs tested by electrical stimulation of the cortex, diencephalon and rhinencephalon in the unanesthetized rabbit, *Electroenceph. Clin. Neurophysiol.*, 9: 43-58, 1957.

578. Riley, H. D., Jr., Harris, R. L., and Nunnery, A. W., The pediatric pharmacology unit of the Children's Memorial Hospital: studies in neonatal pharmacology, *Okla. State Med. Assn. J.*, 61: 400-410, 1968.

579. Fromm, G. H. and Landgren, S., Effect of diphenylhydantoin on single cells in the spinal trigeminal nucleus, *Neurology*, 13: 34-37, 1963.

580. Franz, D. N. and Esplin, D. W., Prevention by diphenylhydantoin of post-tetanic enhancement of action potentials in nonmyelinated nerve fibers, *Pharmacologist*, 7: 174, 1965.

581. Fink, G. B. and Swinyard, E. A., Modification of maximal audiogenic and electro-shock seizures in mice by psychopharmacologic drugs, *J. Pharm. Exp. Ther.*, 127: 318-324, 1959.

582. Esplin, D. W., Criteria for assessing effects of depressant drugs on spinal cord synaptic transmission, with examples of drug selectivity, *Arch. Int. Pharmacodyn.*, 143: 479-497, 1963.

583. Kong, Y., Heyman, A., Entman, M. L., and McIntosh, H. D., Glossopharyngeal neuralgia associated with bradycardia, syncope, and seizures, *Circulation*, 30: 109-113, 1964.

584. Fromm, G. H. and Killian, J. M., Effect of some anticonvulsant drugs on the spinal trigeminal nucleus, *Neurology*, 17: 275-280, 1967.

585. Haward, L. R. C., Drugs and concentration: cognitive effect of DPH, *Portsmouth J. Psychol.*, 1: 3-5, 1968.

586. Editor, Spasticity in multiple sclerosis, *Brit. Med. J.*, 3: 174, 1968.

587. Michael, M. I. and Williams, J. M., Migraine in children, *J. Pediat.*, 41: 18-24, 1952.

588. Muniz, F. J., Lynch, J., and Nusyowitz, M. L., Diphenylhydantoin (Dilantin) induced chromosomal abnormalities, *Clin. Res.*, 16: 310, 1968.

589. Perez del Cerro, M. and Snider, R. S., Studies on Dilantin intoxication. I. Ultrastructural analogies with the lipidoses, *Neurology*, 17: 452-466, 1967.

590. Russell, M. A. and Bousvaros, G., Fatal results from diphenylhydantoin administered intravenously, *JAMA*, 206: 2118-2119, 1969.

591. Schwartzman, J., McDonald, D. H., and Perillo, L., Sydenham's chorea, *Arch. Pediat.*, 65: 6-24, 1948.

592. Stein, E. and Kleinfeld, M., Effects of diphenylhydantoin on membrane potentials of Purkinje and ventricular muscle fibers in dog heart, *Bull. N.Y. Acad. Med.*, 45: 110, 1969.

593. Geever, E. F., Seifter, E. and Levenson, S. M., Toxicity of diphenylhydantoin and its effect on wound healing in young guinea pigs, *Toxic. Appl. Pharmacol.*, 11: 272-279, 1967.

594. Bashour, F. A., Petty, L. D., and Stephens, C. R., Value of Dilantin prophylaxis in epinephrine induced ventricular arrhythmias in the anesthetized dog, *Clin. Res.*, 17: 14, 1969.

595. Muniz, F., Houston, E., Schneider, R., and Nusyowitz, M., Chromosomal effects of diphenylhydantoins, *Clin. Res.*, 17: 28, 1969.

596. Nichols, R. E. and Walaszek, E. J., Antagonism of drug induced catatonia, *Fed. Proc.*, 24: 390, 1965.

597. Bigger, T. J., Jr., Schmidt, D. H., and Kutt, H., Relationship between the plasma level of diphenylhydantoin sodium and its cardiac antiarrhythmic effects, *Circulation*, 38: 363-374, 1968.

598. Gydesen, C. S. and Gydesen, F. R., Post micturition syndrome, *Rocky Mountain Med. J.*, 60: 35-36, 1963.

599. McNichol, R. W., Cirksena, W. J., Payne, J. T., and Glasgow, M. C., Management of withdrawal from alcohol (including delirium tremens), *Southern Med. J.*, 60: 7-12, 1967.

600. Pearce, K. I., Drug treatment of emotional disorders in general practice psychiatry, *J. Coll. Gen. Prac. Canad.*, 12: 28-32, 1965.

601. Moss-Herjanic, B., Prolonged unconsciousness following electroconvulsive therapy, *Amer. J. Psychiat.*, 124: 112-114, 1967.

602. Gordon, P. and Scheving, L. E., Covariant 24-hour rhythms for acquisition and retention of avoidance learning and brain protein synthesis in rats, *Fed. Proc.*, 27: 223, 1968.

603. Wilson, W. P. and Wolk, M., The treatment of delirium tremens, *N. Carolina Med. J.*, 26: 552-556, 1965.

604. Swinyard, E. A., Smith, D. L., and Goodman, L. S., Analgesic effects of clinically useful antiepileptics, *J. Amer. Pharm. Assn.*, 43: 212-214, 1954.

605. Ende, M., Diphenylhydantoin in tic douloureux and atypical facial pain, *Virginia Med. Monthly*, 84: 358-359, 1957.

606. Bird, A. V., Anticonvulsant drugs and congenital abnormalities, *Lancet*, 1: 311, 1969.

607. Gertenrich, R. L., Fry, A. E., and Hart, R. W., The effects of Mucoplex therapy and oral hygiene on Dilantin gingival hyperplasia, *Amer. J. Ment. Defic.*, 73: 896-902, 1969.

608. Hauser, H. M. and Brewer, E. J., Death?, *Electroenceph. Clin. Neurophysiol.*, 23: 293, 1967.

609. Sabih, K. and Sabih, K., Chromatographic method for determination of diphenylhydantoin blood level, *Anal. Chem.*, 41: 1452-1454, 1969.

610. Schwartz, R. S., and Costea, N., Autoimmune hemolytic anemia: clinical correlations and biological implications, *Sem. Hemat.*, 3: 2-26, 1966.

611. Reeve, H. S., Phenytoin in the treatment of trigeminal neuralgia, *Lancet*, 1: 404, 1961.

612. Babcock, J. R., Incidence of gingival hyperplasia associated with Dilantin therapy in a hospital population, *J. Amer. Dent. Assn.*, 71: 1447-1450, 1965.

613. Badenoch, J., The use of labelled vitamin B_{12} and gastric biopsy in the investigation of anemia, *Proc. Roy. Soc. Med.*, 47: 426-431, 1954.

614. Bailey, G., Rosenbaum, J. M., and Anderson, B., Toxic epidermal necrolysis, *JAMA*, 191: 979-982, 1965.

615. Bajoghli, M., Generalized lymphadenopathy and hepatosplenomegaly induced by diphenylhydantoin, *Pediatrics*, 28: 943-945, 1961.

616. Baldi, A., Suicide through poisoning with diphenylhydantoin, *Minerva Medicoleg.*, 74: 161-163, 1954.

617. Bernhardt, H., Fatal granulocytopenia following hydantoins—Mesantoin and Dilantin: report of a case, *J. Med. Assn. Alabama*, 19: 193-197, 1950.

618. Bihler, I., The sodium pump and regulation of sugar transport in skeletal muscle, *Pharmacologist*, 10: 198, 1968.

619. Billen, J. R., Griffin, J. W., and Waldron, C. A., Investi-

gations for pyronin bodies and fluorescent antibodies in 5,5-diphenylhydantoin gingival hyperplasia, *Oral Surg.*, 18: 773-782, 1964.

620. Bonard, E. C., Pseudocollagenosis or malignant pseudolymphoma, *Schweiz. Med. Wschr.*, 94: 57-59, 1964.

621. Burton, R. C., Symptomatology—organic or psychogenic?, *New York J. Med.*, 1304-1309, June 1, 1966.

622. Livingston, S., Seizures in a hypertensive patient, *JAMA*, 204: 412, 1968.

623. Livingston, S., Diphenylhydantoin in emotional disorders, *JAMA*, 204: 549, 1968.

624. Corday, E. and Vyden, J. K., Resuscitation after myocardial infarction, *JAMA*, 200: 781-784, 1967.

625. Cotten, M. S. and Lane, D. H., Massive strychnine poisoning: a successful treatment, *J. Mississippi Med. Assn.*, 7: 466-468, 1966.

626. Cucinell, S. A., Conney, A. H., Sansur, M., and Burns, J. J., Drug interactions in man. 1. Lowering effect of phenobarbital on plasma levels of bishydroxycoumarin (Dicumarol) and diphenylhydantoin (Dilantin), *Clin. Pharmacol. Ther.*, 6: 420-429, 1965.

627. Davis, R. K., Baer, P. N., and Palmer, J. H., A preliminary report on a new therapy for Dilantin gingival hyperplasia, *J. Periodont.*, 34: 17-22, 1963.

628. Ellis, F. A., Reactions to Nirvanol, Phenytoin sodium, and phenobarbital, *Southern Med. J.*, 36: 575-599, 1947.

629. Francis, L. E. and Melville, K. I., Effects of diphenylhydantoin on gingival histamine and serotonin, *J. Canad. Dent. Assn.*, 25: 608-620, 1959.

630. Fulop, M., Widrow, D. R., Colmers, R. A., and Epstein, E. J., Possible diphenylhydantoin-induced arrhythmia in hypothyroidism, *JAMA*, 196: 454-456, 1966.

631. Gabler, W. L., The effect of 5,5-diphenylhydantoin on the rat uterus and its fetuses, *Arch. Int. Pharmacodyn.*, 175: 141-152, 1968.

632. Gams, R. A., Neal, J. A., and Conrad, F. G., Hydantoin-induced pseudo-pseudolymphoma, *Ann. Intern. Med.*, 69: 557-568, 1968.

633. Gardner-Medwin, D. and Walton, J. N., Myokymia with impaired muscular relaxation, *Lancet*, 1: 127-130, 1969.

634. Gianni, E. and Bracchetti, A., Pathogenesis of gingival hypertrophy caused by diphenylhydantoin in experimental animals, *Minèrva Stomat.*, 17: 609-612, 1968.

635. Gibson, J. E. and Becker, B. A., Teratogenic effects of diphenylhydantoin in Swiss-Webster and A/J mice, *Proc. Soc. Exp. Biol. Med.*, 128: 905-909, 1968.

636. Girdwood, R. H., Folic acid, *Practitioner*, 199: 368-376, 1967.

637. Goldstein, L. J. and Verrastro, R., Meniere's disease twenty years later, *Eye, Ear, Nose & Throat Monthly*, 46: 746-752, 1967.

638. Hamfelt, A. and Wilmanns, W., Inhibition studies on folic acid metabolism with drugs suspected to act on the myeloproliferative system, *Clin. Chim. Acta*, 12: 144-154, 1965.

639. Hansen, J. M., Kristensen, M., and Skovsted, L., Sulthiame (Ospolot) as inhibitor of diphenylhydantoin metabolism, *Epilepsia*, 9: 17-22, 1968.

640. Hoffbrand, A. V. and Necheles, T. F., Studies on the mechanism of megaloblastic anemia due to anticonvulsants, *Abs. XII Cong. Int. Soc. Hematol.*, 92, New York, 1968.

641. Hoffbrand, A. V. and Necheles, T. F., Mechanism of folate deficiency in patients receiving Phenytoin, *Lancet*, 2: 528-530, 1968.

642. Hunninghake, D. B. and Azarnoff, D. L., Drug interactions with warfarin, *Arch. Intern. Med.*, 121: 349-352, 1968.

643. Hyman, G. A. and Sommers, S. C., The development of Hodgkin's disease and lymphoma during anticonvulsant therapy, *Blood*, 28: 417-427, 1966.

644. Jubiz, W., Meikle, W., West, C. D., and Tyler, F. H., Failure of dexamethasone suppression in patients on chronic diphenylhydantoin therapy, *Clin. Res.*, 17: 106, 1969.

645. Kemp, J. W. and Woodbury, D. M., The influence of diphenylhydantoin on cerebrospinal fluid electrolytes, *Pharmacologist*, 8: 199, 1966.

646. Kiørboe, E., Antabuse as a source of Phenytoin intoxication, *Ugeskr. Laeg.*, 128: 1531-1532, 1966.

647. Kokenge, R., Kutt, H., and McDowell, F., Neurological sequelae following Dilantin overdose in a patient and in experimental animals, *Neurology*, 15: 823-829, 1965.

648. Kruse, R., Rare, but dangerous, hydantoin side effects, *Mschr. Kinderheilk.*, 115: 289-290, 1967.

649. Malpas, J. S., Spray, G. H., and Witts, L. J., Serum folic-acid and vitamin-B_{12} levels in anticonvulsant therapy, *Brit. Med. J.*, 1: 955-957, 1966.

650. Martin. D. A., The therapeutic and toxic effects of tranquilizing drugs: medical aspects, *N. Carolina Med. J.*, 17: 396-401, 1956.

651. Kanzler, M., Malitz, S., and Higgins, J. C., How effective are antidepressants?, *JAMA*, 204: 34, 1968.

652. Merritt, H. H. and Putnam, T. J., Further experiences with the use of sodium diphenylhydantoinate in the treatment of convulsive disorders, *Amer. J. Psychiat.*, 96: 1023-1027, 1940.

653. O'Quinn, S. E., The use of the indirect basophil degranulation test in the investigation of drug allergy, *Southern Med. J.*, 58: 1147-1151, 1965.

654. Patil, K. P., Chitre, R. G., and Sheth, U. K., Anti-folic acid activity of antiepileptic drugs. Part 2—Experimental studies in rats, *Indian J. Med. Sci.*, 20: 623-627, 1966.

655. Plaa, G. L. and Hine, C. H., Hydantoin and barbiturate blood levels observed in epileptics, *Arch. Int. Pharmacodyn.*, 128: 375-382, 1960.

656. Ritchie, E. B. and Kolb, W., Reaction to sodium diphenylhydantoinate (Dilantin sodium) hemorrhagic erythema multiforme terminating fatally, *Arch. Derm. Syph.*, 46: 856-859, 1942.

657. Rosenberg, I. H., Godwin, H. A., Strieff, R. R., and Castle, W. B., Impairment of intestinal deconjugation of dietary folate: a possible explanation of megaloblastic anemia associated with Phenytoin therapy, *Lancet*, 2: 530-532, 1968.

658. Rümke, C. L., Increased susceptibility of mice to seizures after some anticonvulsant drugs, *Europ. J. Pharmacol.*, 1: 369-377, 1967.

659. Rummel, W., and Wellensiek, H. J., Premedication and nitrous oxide anesthesia, *Arch. Int. Pharmacodyn.*, 122: 339-349, 1959.

660. Sauter, E. K., Diphenylhydantoin toxicity in children, *Arch. Kinderheilk,*, 146: 64-70, 1953.

661. Scherf, D., Changes in the electrocardiogram after intravenous administration of Phenytoin sodium (Dilantin) in the acute experiment, *Bull. N.Y. Med. Coll.*, 6: 82-89, 1943.

662. Slavin, R. G. and Broun, G. O. Jr., Agranulocytosis after diphenylhydantoin and chlorothiazide therapy, *Arch. Intern. Med.*, 108: 940-944, 1961.

663. Snider, R. S. and del Cerro, M., Membranous cytoplasmic spirals in Dilantin intoxication, *Nature*, 212: 536-537, 1966.

664. Steinberg, S. H., Reaction to diphenylhydantoin sodium: report of a case simulating Rocky Mountain spotted fever and review of literature, *Med. Ann. D.C.*, 22: 600-603, 1953.

665. Svensmark, O. and Buchthal, F., Dosage of Phenytoin and phenobarbital in children, *Danish Med. Bull.*, 10: 234-235, 1963.

666. Svensmark, O. and Buchthal, F., Diphenylhydantoin and phenobarbital: serum levels in children, *Amer. J. Dis. Child.*, 108, 82-87, 1964.

667. Szymanski, F. J., and McGrae, J. D., Jr., Fibrous hyperplasia of the nose, possibly related to diphenylhydantoin sodium (Dilantin) therapy, *Arch. Derm.*, 88: 227-228, 1963.

668. Tanimukai, H., Tsukiyama, H., Yamamoto, M., and Yamada, R., A case with Hodgkin's disease-like syndrome induced by diphenylhydantoin, *Brain Nerve*, 15: 77-83, 1963.

669. Strean, L. P., Treatment of ulcers, *Chem. Abst. Biochem. Sec.*, 65: 11219c, 1966 (Merck & Co., Inc. Application for patent, Belg., May 12, 1965).

670. Block, J. D. and Moore, A. U., Hyperresponsive extinction behavior of protein-deprived pigs reduced by diphenylhydantoin *(in press)*.

671. Turner, P., Granulocytopenia after treatment with Phenytoin sodium, *Brit. Med. J.*, 1: 1790, 1960.

672. DaVanzo, J. P., Daugherty, M., Ruckart, R., and Kang, L., Pharmacological and biochemical studies in isolation-induced fighting mice, *Psychopharmacologia*, 9: 210-219, 1966.

673. Jonas, A. D., More experience with diphenylhydantoin, *Amer. J. Psychiatr.*, 124: 1139, 1968.

674. Vernadakis, A. and Woodbury, D. M., Effects of diphenylhydantoin on electroshock seizure thresholds in developing rats, *J. Pharm. Exp. Ther.*, 148: 144-150, 1965.

675. Waites, L. and Nicklas, T. O., Diphenylhydantoin sodium (Dilantin) intoxication in children, *J. Okla. Med. Assn.*, 54: 95-96, 1961.

676. Wallis, W., Kutt, H., and McDowell, F., Intravenous diphenylhydantoin in treatment of acute repetitive seizures, *Neurology*, 18: 513-525, 1968.

677. Watanabe, S., Hypersensitivity angiitis from diphenylhydantoin, *Acta Derm.*, (Kyoto), 59: 121-129, 1964.

678. Webster, J. M., Megaloblastic anemia due to Phenytoin sodium, *Lancet*, 2: 1017-1018, 1954.

679. Weintraub, M., Neonatal hypocalcemia, Correspondence, *New Eng. J. Med.*, 279: 327, 1968.

680. Welch, B. L., Symposium on aggressive behavior, *Bio-Science*, 18: 1061-1064, 1968.

681. Wilkinson, T., Megaloblastic anemia during antiepileptic therapy, *Med. J. Aust.*, 2: 894, 1959.

682. Levy, L. L. and Fenichel, G. M., Diphenylhydantoin activated seizures, *Neurology*, 15: 716-722, 1965.

683. Yen, H. C. Y., Silverman, A. J., and Salvatore, A., Iproniazid reinforcement of anticonvulsants, *Fed. Proc.*, 19: 181, 1960.

684. Holland, P. and Mauer, A. M., Drug-induced *in vitro* stimulation of peripheral lymphocytes, *Lancet*, 1: 1368-1369, 1964.

685. Helfant, R., Scherlag, B., and Damato, A. N., Protection from digitalis toxicity with prophylactic Dilantin: an electrophysiological-inotropic dissociation, *Clin. Res.*, 15: 206, 1967.

686. Johnson, J., Anticonvulsants and megaloblastic anemia, *J. Ment. Sci.*, 105: 819-820, 1959.

687. Keeran, M., Cardiac arrest following intravenous administration of diphenylhydantoin, *J. Okla. Med. Assn.*, 60: 334-335, 1967.

688. Klein, J. P., Diphenylhydantoin intoxication associated with hyperglycemia, *J. Pediat.*, 69: 463-465, 1966.

689. Klipstein, F. A., Folate deficiency secondary to disease of the intestinal tract, *Bull. N.Y. Acad. Med.*, 42: 638-653, 1966.

690. Krasznai, G. and Gyory, G., Hydantoin lymphadenopathy, *J. Path. Bact.*, 95: 314-317, 1968.

691. Levine, M. C., Lupus erythematosus and anticonvulsant drugs, *Pediatrics*, 33: 144-145, 1964.

692. Matthews, D. M. and Reynolds, E. H., Gastrointestinal function in anticonvulsant megaloblastic anemia, *Lancet*, 1: 210-211, 1966.

693. Jonas, A. D., The distinction between paroxysmal and non-paroxysmal migraine, *Headache*, 79-84, July, 1967.

694. Lucas, B. G., Dilantin overdosage, *Med. J. Aust.*, 2: 639-640, 1968.

695. Toakley, J. G., Dilantin overdosage, *Med. J. Aust.*, 2: 640, 1968.

696. Arushanyan, E. B. and Belozertsev, Y. A., Effects of diphenylhydantoin on different type of central inhibition of the knee-jerk reflex, *Farmakol. Tosik.*, 29: 12-17, 1966.

697. Haward, L. R. C., Differential modifications of verbal aggression by psychotropic drugs, *Proc. Symp. Aggressive Behavior, Milan, May, 1968*, 317-321, S. Garattini and E. B. Sigg, Eds., *Excerpta Medica*, New York, 1969.

698. Swinyard, E. A., Weaver, L. C., and Goodman, L. S., Effect of liver injury and nephrectomy on the anticonvulsant activity of clinically useful hydantoins, *J. Pharm. Exp. Ther.*, 104: 309-316, 1952.

699. Pincus, J. H., Grove, I., Marino, B. B., and Glaser, G. E., Studies on the mechanism of action of diphenylhydantoin, *Arch. Neurol.*, 22: 566-571, 1970.

700. Stephens, J. H. and Shaffer, J. W., A controlled study of the effects of diphenylhydantoin on anxiety, irritability, and anger in neurotic outpatients, *Psychopharmacologia*, 17: 169-181, 1970.

701. Davies, J. E., Edmundson, W. F., Carter, C. H., and Barquet, A., Effect of anticonvulsant drugs on dicophane (D.D.T.) residues in man, *Lancet*, 2: 7-9, 1969.

702. Doty, B. and Dalman, R., Diphenylhydantoin effects on avoidance conditioning as a function of age and problem difficulty, *Psychos. Sci.*, 14: 109-111, 1969.

703. Goodman, L. S. and Gilman, A., *The Pharmacological Basis of Therapeutics*, 2nd Ed., 181-188, Macmillan, New York, 1955.

704. Resnick, O. and Dreyfus, J. J., Jr., Worcester County Jail study: Beneficial effects of DPH on the nervous systems of nonepileptics (condensed), *Dreyfus Medical Foundation*, 1966.

705. Gottwald, W., An outline of the hydantoins, Synopsis der Hydantoine (German), *Fortschritte der Neurologie, Psychiatrie und ihrer Grenzgebiete*, 37: 573-648, 1969.

706. Baldwin, R. W., Behavior disorders in children, *Maryland Med. J.*, 18: 68-71, 1969.

707. Dreyfus, J. J. Jr., The beneficial effects of diphenylhydantoin on the nervous systems of nonepileptics—as experienced and observed in others by a layman. Presented at the Amer. College of Neuropsychopharmacology, Dec. 7, 1966, *Dreyfus Medical Foundation*, 1966.

708. Rosenblum, J. A. and Shafer, N., Effects of diphenylhydantoin (Dilantin) withdrawal on non-epileptics: preliminary report, *Curr. Ther. Res.*, 12: 31-33, 1970.

709. Haward, L. R. C., The organic integrity test as prognostic index in Phenytoin-facilitated autogenic training, *World J. of Psychosynthesis*, 1: 47-51, 1969.

710. Weintraub, M. I., Megahed, M. S., and Smith, B. H., Myotonic-like syndrome in multiple sclerosis, *New York J. Med.*, 70: 677-679, 1970.

711. Bianchine, J. R., Macaraeg, P. V. J., Jr., Lasagna, L., Azarnoff, D. L., Brunk, S. F., Hvidberg, E. F., and Owen, J. A., Jr., Drugs as etiologic factors in the Stevens-Johnson syndrome, *Amer. J. Med.*, 44: 390-405, 1968.

712. Council on Drugs, American Medical Association Drug Evaluations, *JAMA*, 204, 702-710, 1968.

713. Goldberg, J. and Kurland, A. A., Dilantin treatment of hospitalized cultural-familial retardates, *J. Nerv. Ment. Dis.*, 150: 133-137, 1970.

714. Pincus, J. H., Diphenylhydantoin and sodium influx, *Neurology*, 20: 393, 1970.

715. Silbermann, M., *Personal communication*, 1969.

716. Silverman, D., The electroencephalograph and therapy of criminal psychopaths, *Criminal Psychopathology*, 5: 439-457, 1944.

717. Forda, O. and McIlwain, H., Anticonvulsants on electrically stimulated metabolism of separated mammalian cerebral cortex, *Brit. J. Pharmacol.*, 8: 225-229, 1953.

718. Williams, J. and Stevens, H., Familial paroxysmal choreaathetosis, *Pediatrics*, 31: 656-659, 1963.

719. Capapas, L., Weiss, M. M., and Leight, L., The use of diphenylhydantoin sodium (Dilantin) in the treatment of cardiac arrhythmias, *J. Kentucky Med. Assn.*, 66: 970-975, 1968.

720. Helfant, R. H., Seuffert, G. W., Patton, R. D., Stein, E., and Damato, A. N., The clinical use of diphenylhydantoin (Dilantin) in the treatment and prevention of cardiac arrhythmias, *Amer. Heart J.*, 77: 315-323, 1969.

721. Gautam, H. P., Phenytoin in post-operative cardiac arrhythmias, *Brit. Heart J.*, 31: 641-644, 1969.

722. Delgado, J. M. R., Electrical stimulation of the brain, *Psychology Today*, 3: 49-53, 1970.

723. Rallison, M. L., Carlisle, J. W., Lee, R. E., Jr., Vernier, R. L., and Good, R. A., Lupus erythematosus and Stevens-Johnson syndrome, *Amer. J. Dis. Child.*, 101: 81-94, 1961.

724. Hess, W. R., Interdisciplinary discussion of selected problems with reference to "The Biology of Mind," *Perspect. Biol. Med.*, 13: 267-293, 1970.

725. Broad range of beneficial effects of diphenylhydantoin: one hundred letters, *Dreyfus Medical Foundation*, 1970.

726. Schmidt, R. P. and Wilder, B. J., *Epilepsy: A clinical textbook*, F. A. Davis Co., Phila., 150-153, 1968.

727. Vanasin, B., Bass, D. D., Mendeloff, A. I., and Schuster, M. M., Effect and site of action of diphenylhydantoin (DPH) on gastrointestinal smooth muscle, *Clin. Res.*, 18: 391, 1970.

728. Crane, P. and Swanson, P. D., Diphenylhydantoin and the cations and phosphates of electrically stimulated brain slices, *Neurology*, 20: 1119-1123, 1970.

729. Sokoloff, L., The action of drugs on the cerebral circulation, *Pharmacol. Rev.*, 11: 1-85, 1959.

730. Taylor, A. S., Behcet's syndrome treated with DPH, *Personal communication*, 1969.

731. Escueta, A. V. and Appel, S. H., The effects of electrically induced seizures on potassium transport within isolated nerve terminals, *Neurology*, 20: 392, 1970.

732. Barasch, K., Baras, I., and Galin, M. A., Early ambulation after cataract surgery, *Personal communication*, 1970.

733. Padis, N., Use of DPH to control low blood sugar, *Personal communication*, 1967.

734. Dreifus, L. S., Use of anti-arrhythmic agents other than digitalis, *J. Iowa Med. Soc.*, 60: 192-195, 1970.

735. Jensen, N. O. and Olesen, V. O., The clinical importance of folic acid in patients treated with anticonvulsant drugs, *Excerpta Medica*, 193: 260, 1969.

736. Anthony, J. J., Malignant lymphoma associated with hydantoin drugs, *Arch. Neurol.*, 22: 450-454, 1970.

737. Meadow, S. R., Congenital abnormalities and anticonvulsant drugs, *Proc. Roy. Soc. Med.*, 63: 12-13, 1970.

738. Eisenberg, H., Campbell, P. C., and Flannery, J. T., *Cancer in Connecticut. Incidence characteristics*, 1935-1962, Conn. State Dept. of Health, Hartford, Conn., 1967.

739. Hutchins, D. A. and Rogers, K. J., Physiological and drug-induced changes in the glycogen content of mouse brain, *Brit. J. Pharmacol.*, 39: 9-25, 1970.

740. Chen, G. and Bohner, B., A study of certain CNS depressants, *Arch. Int. Pharmacodyn.*, 125: 1-20, 1960.

741. Millichap, J. G., Egan, R. W., Hart, Z. H., and Sturgis, L. H., Auditory perceptual deficit correlated with EEG dysrhythmias response to diphenylhydantoin sodium, *Neurology*, 19: 870-872, 1969.

742. Covi, L., Derogatis, L. R., Uhlenhuth, E. H., and Kandel, A., Effect of diphenylhydantoin in violent prisoners, *Proc. 7th Cong. of the Int. College of Neuropsychopharmacol.*, Prague, 1970.

743. Cole, J. O., Psychopharmacology: The picture is not entirely rosy, *Amer. J. Psychiat.*, 127: 224-225, 1970.

744. Chamberlain, W., Use of diphenylhydantoin in surgery, *Personal communication*, 1970.

745. Eccles, J. C., The synapse, *Scientific Am.*, 212: 56-66, 1965.

746. Galin, M. A., Kwitko, M., and Restrepo, N., The use of diphenylhydantoin in the treatment of accommodative esotropia, *Proc. Int. Strabismological Assn., In Proc. Int. Ophthalmological Congress*, Mexico, 1969.

747. Jaffe, N. S., Use of diphenylhydantoin in ophthalmic surgery, *Personal communication*, 1966.

748. Wilson, P. *Medical News-Letter*, *Brit. Migraine Assn.*, Bournemouth, England, August, 1970.

749. Tedeschi, R. E., Tedeschi, D. H., Mucha, A., Cook, L., Mattis, P. A., and Fellows, E. J., Effects of various centrally acting drugs on fighting behavior of mice, *J. Pharmacol. and Exp. Therap.* 125: 28-34, 1959.

750. Alvarez, W. C., Enuresis, *Modern Medicine* (Editorial), 95-96, June, 1969.

DPH, 1975
(Ref. 751-1712)

751. Adamska-Dyniewska, H., Evaluation of myocardial contractility after hydantoinal and ouabain based polycardiographic methods, *Wiad. Lek.*, 23: 1749-1754, 1970.

752. Adamska-Dyniewska, H., Hydantoinal—New use of an old drug, *Wiad. Lek.*, 23: 1111-1115, 1970.

753. Adamska-Dyniewska, H., The effect of diphenylhydantoin sodium given with cardiac glycosides on the left ventricular systole dynamics, *Pol. Med. J.*, 9: 304-308, 1970.

754. Adamska-Dyniewska, H., The value of diphenylhydantoin for combating the rhythm and conduction disorders induced by cardiac glycosides, *Biul. Wojskowej. Akad. Medy.*, 14: 71-77, 1971.

755. Agarwal, S. P. and Blake, M. I., Differentiating spectrophotometric titration of phenobarbital-diphenylhydantoin combinations in nonaqueous medium, *Anal. Chem.*, 41: 1104-1106, 1969.

756. Alarcon-Segovia, D., Fishbein, E., Reyes, P. A., Dies, H., and Shwadsky, S., Antinuclear antibodies in patients on anticonvulsant therapy, *Clin. Exp. Immunol.*, 12: 39-47, 1972.

757. Alexander, E., Medical management of closed head injuries, *Clin. Neurosurg.*, 19: 240-250, 1972.

758. Alexander, E., Surgical management of head injuries in children in the acute phase, *Clin. Neurosurg.*, 19: 251-262, 1972.

759. Allen, C. D. and Klipstein, F. A., Brain folate concentration in folate-deficient rats receiving diphenylhydantoin, *Neurology*, 20: 403, 1970.

760. Allen, J. D., Kofi Ekue, J. M., Shanks, R. G., and Zaidi, S. A., The effect on experimental cardiac arrhythmias of a new anticonvulsant agent, Ko 1173 and its comparison with phenytoin and procainamide, *Brit. J. Pharmacol.*, 39: 183-184, 1970.

761. Alvarez, W. C., *Nerves in collision*, Pyramid House, New York, 1972.

762. American Medical Association Council on Drugs, *AMA drug evaluations*, 12-13 AMA, Chicago, 1971.

763. American Pharmaceutical Association, *Evaluations of drug interactions*, Washington, 1973.

764. Anderson, D. C., Davis, R. J., Dove, J. T., and Griggs, R. C., Cardiac conduction during treatment of myotonia, *Neurology*, 23: 390, 1973.

765. Anderson, R. J. and Raines, A., Suppression by Diphenylhydantoin of afferent discharges arising in muscle spindles of the triceps surae of the cat, *J. Pharmacol. Exp. Ther.*, 191: 290-299, 1974.

766. Anders, M. W. and Latorre, J. P., High-speed ion exchange chromatography of barbiturates, diphenylhydantoin, and their hydroxylated metabolites, *Anal. Chem.*, 42: 1430-1432, 1970.

767. Andreasen, B., Froland, A., Skovsted, L., Andersen, S. A., and Hauge, M., Diphenylhydantoin half-life in man and its inhibition by phenylbutazone: the role of genetic factors, *Acta Med. Scand.*, 193: 561-564, 1973.

768. Andreasen, P. B., Hansen, J. M., Skovsted, L., and Siersbaek-Nielsen, K., Folic acid and the half-life of diphenylhydantoin in man, *Acta Neurol. Scand.*, 47: 117-119, 1971.

769. Andreasen, P. B., Hansen, J. M., Skovsted, L., and Siersbaek-Nielsen, K., Folic acid and phenytoin metabolism, *Epilepsy Abstracts*, 4: 221, 1971.

770. Andreasen, P. B., Lyngbye, J., and Trolle, E., Tests for abnormalities in liver function during long-term diphenylhydantoin therapy in epileptic out-patients. *Acta Med. Scand.*, 194: 261-264, 1973.

771. Ariyoshi, T. and Takabatake, E., Effect of diphenylhydantoin on the drug metabolism and the fatty acid composition of phospholipids in hepatic microsomes, *Chem. Pharm. Bull.,* 20: 180-184, 1972.

772. Ariyoshi, T., Zange, M., and Remmer, H., Effects of diphenylhydantoin on the liver constituents and the microsomal drug metabolism enzyme systems in the partially hepatectomized rats, *J. Pharm. Soc. Jap.,* 94: 526-530, 1974.

773. Arky, R. A., Diphenylhydantoin and the beta cell, *New Eng. J. Med.,* 286: 371-372, 1972.

774. Arnold, K. and Gerber, N., The rate of decline of diphenylhydantoin in human plasma, *Clin. Pharmacol. Ther.,* 11: 121-134, 1970.

775. Arnold, K., Gerber, N., and Levy, G., Absorption and dissolution studies on sodium diphenylhydantoin capsules, *Canad. J. Pharm. Sci.,* 5: 89-92, 1970.

776. Asfeldt, V. H. and Buhl, J., Inhibitory effect of diphenylhydantoin on the feedback control of corticotrophin release, *Acta Endocrinol.,* 61: 551-560, 1969.

777. Atkinson, A. J., Jr., Clinical use of blood levels of cardiac drugs, *Mod. Conc. Cardiovasc. Dis.,* 42: 1-4, 1973.

778. Atkinson, A. J., Jr., Individualization of anticonvulsant therapy, *Med. Clin. N. Amer.,* 58: 1037-1050, 1974.

779. Atkinson, A. J., Jr., MacGee, J., Strong, J., Garteiz, D., and Gaffney, T. E., Identification of 5-metahydroxyphenyl-5-phenylhydantoin as a metabolite of diphenylhydantoin, *Biochem. Pharmacol.,* 19: 2483-2491, 1970.

780. Atkinson, A. J., Jr. and Davison, R., Diphenylhydantoin as an antiarrhythmic drug, *Ann. Rev. Med.,* 25: 99-113, 1974.

781. Ausman, J. I., New developments in anticonvulsant therapy, *Postgrad. Med.,* 48: 122-127, 1970.

782. Ayala, G. F. and Lin, S., Effect of diphenylhydantoin on an isolated neuron, *Fed. Proc.,* 30: Abstract 67, 1971.

783. Azarnoff, D. L., Clinical implications of drug metabolism—introduction, *Chem. Biol. Interactions,* 3: 241-242, 1971.

784. Azzaro, A. J. and Gutrecht, J. A., The effect of diphenylhydantoin (DPH) on the *in vitro* accumulation and catabolism of H^3-l-norepinephrine (H^3-NE) in cerebral cortex slices, *Neurology,* 23: 431, 1973.

785. Azzaro, A. J., Gutrecht, J. A., and Smith, D. J., Effect of diphenylhydantoin on the uptake and catabolism of L-(3H) norepinephrine *in vitro* in rat cerebral cortex tissue, *Biochem. Pharmacol.,* 22: 2719-2729, 1973.

786. Babb, R. R. and Eckman, P. B., Abdominal epilepsy, *JAMA,* 222: 65-66, 1972.

787. Bach-Y-Rita, G., Lion, J. R., Climent, C. E., and Ervin, F. R., Episodic dyscontrol: A study of 130 violent patients, *Amer. J. Psychiat.,* 127: 49-54, 1971.

788. Baggot, J. D. and Davis, L. E., Comparative study of plasma protein binding of diphenylhydantoin, *Comp. Gen. Pharmacol.,* 4: 399-404, 1973.

789. Baker, T., Okamoto, M., and Riker, W. F., Diphenylhydantoin (DPH) suppression of motor nerve terminal (MNT) excitation by acetylcholine (ACh), *Pharmacologist,* 13: 265, 1971.

790. Baldy-Moulinier, M., Cerebral blood flow and membrane ionic pump, *Europ. Neurol.,* 6: 107-113, 1971/72.

791. Ballek, R. E., Reidenberg, M. M., and Orr, L., Inhibition of diphenylhydantoin metabolism by chloramphenicol, *Lancet,* 150, 1973.

792. Baratieri, A., Gagliardi, V., and Simonetti, E., Further studies on effect of diphenylhydantoin sodium on oro facial tissues in offspring of female mice, *Epilepsy Abstracts,* 6: 91, 1973.

793. Barbedo, A. S., and Banks, T., Paroxysmal supraventricular tachycardia, *New Eng. J. Med.,* 288: 51, 1973.

794. Barlow, C. F., Diphenylhydantoin-2-C^{14} in cat brain, *J. Neuropath. Exp. Neurol.,* 22: 348-349, 1965.

795. Baro, W. Z., The non-convulsive convulsive disorder—its diagnosis and treatment, *Western Med.,* March, 1966.

796. Barsky, P., A clinical variant of tic convulsif, *J. Pediat.,* 71: 417-419, 1967.

797. Bartter, F. C. and Schwartz, W. B., The syndrome of inappropriate secretion of antidiuretic hormone, *Amer. J. Med.,* 42: 790-806, 1967.

798. Bashour, F. A., Coffman, G. K., and Ashby, E. A., Effect of diphenylhydantoin (Dilantin) on oxygen uptake by Sarcina lutea, *Clin. Res.,* 14: 439, 1966.

799. Baskin, S. I. and Dutta, S., Effects of antiarrhythmic drugs and ethacrynic acid on the accumulation of ouabain-H by the isolated guinea pig heart, *Fed. Proc.,* 29: 739, 1970.

800. Baskin, S. I. and Dutta, S., Relationships between prevention of ouabain (O) induced arrhythmia by diphenylhydantoin (DPH) and potassium (K) and their effects on ouabain accumulation and electrolyte composition in the heart, *Fed. Proc.,* 30: 394, 1971.

801. Baskin, S. I., Dutta, S., and Marks, B. H., The effects of diphenylhydantoin and potassium on the biological activity of ouabain in the guinea-pig heart, *Brit. J. Pharmacol.,* 47: 85-96, 1973.

802. Baskin, S. I., Melrose, B. L., Ferguson, R. K., Akera, T., and Brody, T. M., The effect of diphenylhydantoin on ouabain-induced arrhythmia and on the formation and dissociation of the ouabain-enzyme complex, *Personal Communication,* 1973.

803. Bassett, A. L., Bigger, J. T., and Hoffman, B. F., Effect of diphenylhydantoin on cat heart muscle, *Circulation,* 35 & 36: 61, 1967.

804. Bassett, A. L., Bigger, J. T., and Hoffman, B. F., Protective action of DPH on canine Purkinje fibers during hypoxia, *J. Pharmacol. Exp. Ther.,* 173: 336-343, 1970.

805. BasuRay, B. N., Dutta, S. N., and Pradhan, S. N., Central action of ouabain: effects of propranolol and diphenylhydantoin on ouabain-induced arrhythmias, *Fed. Proc.,* 30: Abstract 189, 1971.

806. Baugh, C. M. and Krumdieck, C. L., Effects of phenytoin on folic-acid conjugases in man, *Lancet,* 519-522, 1969.

807. Baughman, F. A. and Randinitis, E. J., Passage of diphenylhydantoin across the placenta, *JAMA,* 213: 466, 1970.

808. Baxter, M. G., Miller, A. A., and Webster, R. A., Some studies on the convulsant action of folic acid, *Brit. J. Pharmacol.,* 48: 350-351, 1973.

809. Baylis, E. M., Crowley, J. M., Preece, J. M., Sylvester, P. E., and Marks, V., Influence of folic acid on blood-phenytoin levels, *Lancet,* 1: 62-64, 1971.

810. Baylis, E. M., Fry, D. E., and Marks, V., Micro-determination of serum phenobarbitone and diphenylhydantoin by gas-liquid chromatography, *Clin. Chim. Acta,* 30: 93-103, 1970.

811. Bazin, S. and Delaunay, A., Effect of phenytoin on the maturation of collagen in normal skin and granulomatous tissue, *C. R. Acad. Sci. Ser. D.,* 275: 509-511, 1972.

812. Becker, B. and Podos, S. M., Diphenylhydantoin and its use in optic nerve disease, *Symposium on Ocular Therapy,* Vol. VI, I. H. Leopold, Ed., C. V. Mosby Co., St. Louis, 1973.

813. Becker, B., Stamper, R. L., Asseff, C., and Podos, S. M., Effect of diphenylhydantoin on glaucomatous field loss, *Trans. Amer. Acad. Ophthal. Otolaryng.,* 76: 412-422, 1972.

814. Beernink, D. H. and Miller, J. J., Anticonvulsant induced antinuclear antibodies and lupus like disease in children, *Epilepsy Abstracts,* 6: 210, 1973.

815. Bell, W. E. and McCormick, W. F., Striatopallidonigral degeneration, *Arch. Dis. Child.,* 46: 533-538, 1971.

816. Benaim, R., Chapelle, M., and Chiche, P., Action of diphenylhydantoin on atrioventricular and intraventricular conduction in humans, *Ann. Cardiol. Angeiol.,* 21: 379-388, 1972.

817. Bender, F., Modern drug therapy of arrhythmia, *Schweiz. Med. Wschr.,* 103: 272-276, 1973.

818. Bennett, W. M., Singer, I., and Coggins, C. H., Guide to drug usage in adult patients with impaired renal function, *JAMA,* 223: 991-997, 1973.

819. Berger, H., Fever: an unusual manifestation of epilepsy, *Postgrad. Med.,* 40: 479-481, 1966.

820. Bergouignan, M., Antiepileptic drugs in the treatment of

trigeminal neuralgia, *Presse Med.*, 78: 1832-1834, 1970.

821. Berlin, A., Agurell, S., Borga, O., Lund, L. and Sjoqvist, F., Micromethod for the determination of diphenylhydantoin in plasma and cerebrospinal fluid, *Scand. J. Clin. Invest.*, 29: 281-287, 1972.

822. Bernoulli, C., Diphenylhydantoin, *Schweiz. Med. Wschr.*, 100: 836, 1970.

823. Bernstein, J. D. and Johnson, S. L., Effects of diphenylhydantoin upon estrogen metabolism by liver microsomes of DDT-treated Japanese quail, *Bull. Environ. Contam. Toxicol.*, 10: 309-314, 1973.

824. Berry, D. J. and Grove, J., Emergency toxicological screening for drugs commonly taken in overdose, *J. Chromatogr.*, 80: 205-219, 1973.

825. Bhatt, G., Vijayan, N. and Dreyfus, P. M., Myotonia, *Calif. Med.*, 114: 16-22, 1971.

826. Bigger, J. T., Jr., Steiner, C., and Burris, J. O., The effects of diphenylhydantoin on atrioventricular conduction in man, *Clin. Res.*, 15: 196, 1967.

827. Bigger, J. T., Schmidt, D. H., and Kutt, H., A method for estimation of plasma diphenylhydantoin concentration, *Amer. Heart J.*, 77: 572-573, 1969.

828. Bigger, J. T., Weinberg, D. I., Kovalik, T. W., Harris, P. D., Cranefield, P. C., and Hoffman, B. F., Effects of diphenylhydantoin on excitability and automaticity in the canine heart, *Circ. Res.*, 26: 1-15, 1970.

829. Birket-Smith, E. and Krogh, E., Motor nerve conduction velocity during diphenylhydantoin intoxication, *Acta. Neurol. Scand.*, 47: 265-271, 1971.

830. Bissett, J. K., deSoyza, N. D. B., Kane, J. J., and Doherty, J. E., Case studies: effect of diphenylhydantoin on induced aberrant conduction, *J. Electrocardiol.*, 7: 65-69, 1974.

831. Bissett, J. K., deSoyza, N. D. B., Kane, J. J., and Murphy, M. L., Improved intraventricular conduction of premature beats after diphenylhydantoin, *Amer. J. Cardiol.*, 33: 493-497, 1974.

832. Bissett, J. K., Kane, J. J., deSoyza, N., and Doherty, J., Effect of diphenylhydantoin on bundle branch block in man, *Clin. Res.*, 21: 405, 1973.

833. Bissett, J. K., Kane, J., deSoyza, N., and Doherty, J., Improved intraventricular conduction after diphenylhydantoin, *Circulation*, 48: 146, 1973.

834. Bittar, E. E., Chen, S. S., Danielson, B. G., and Tong, E. Y., An investigation of the action of diphenylhydantoin on sodium efflux in barnacle muscle fibres, *Acta Physiol. Scand.*, 89: 30-38, 1973.

835. Bjerk, E. M. and Hornisher, J. J., Narcolepsy: a case report and a rebuttal, *Electroenceph. Clin. Neurophysiol.*, 10: 550-552, 1958.

836. Black, J. T., Garcia-Mullin, R., Good, E., and Brown, S., Muscle rigidity in a newborn due to continuous peripheral nerve hyperactivity, *Arch. Neurol.*, 27: 413-425, 1972.

837. Black, N. D., The value of diphenylhydantoinate (Dilantin) in psychoses with convulsive disorders, *Psychiatr. Quart.*, 13: 711-720, 1939.

838. Blum, M. R., McGilveray, I., Becker, C. E., and Riegelman, S., Clinical implications derived from pharmacokinetics of diphenylhydantoin (DPH), *Clin. Res.*, 19: 121, 1971.

839. Blum, M., Riegelman, S., and Becker, C. E., Altered protein binding of diphenylhydantoin in uremic plasma, *New Eng. J. Med.*, 286: 109, 1972.

840. Blumenkrantz, N. and Asboe-Hansen, G., Effect of diphenylhydantoin on connective tissue, *Acta Neurol. Scand.*, 50: 302-306, 1974.

841. Bochner, F., Hooper, W. D., Sutherland, J. M., Eadie, M. J., and Tyrer, J. H., The renal handling of diphenylhydantoin and 5-(P-Hydroxyphenyl)-5-phenylhydantoin, *Clin. Pharmacol. Ther.*, 14: 791-796, 1973.

842. Bochner, F., Hooper, W. D., Tyrer, J. H., and Eadie, M. J., Effect of a delayed-action phenytoin preparation on blood phenytoin concentration, *J. Neurol. Neurosurg. Psychiat.*, 35: 682-684, 1972.

843. Bochner, F., Hooper, W. D., Sutherland, J. M., Eadie, M. J., and Tyrer, J. H., Diphenylhydantoin concentrations in saliva, *Arch. Neurol.*, 31: 57-59, 1974.

844. Bochner, F., Hooper, W. D., Tyrer, J. H., and Eadie, M. J., Factors involved in an outbreak of phenytoin intoxication, *Epilepsy Abstracts*, 5: 245-246, 1971.

845. Bochner, F., Hooper, W., Tyrer, J., and Eadie, M., Clinical implications of certain aspects of diphenylhydantoin metabolism, *Proc. Aust. Assoc. Neurol.*, 9: 171-178, 1973.

846. Bogoch, S. and Dreyfus, J., The broad range of use of diphenylhydantoin, bibliography and review, *The Dreyfus Medical Foundation*, 1970.

847. Booker, H. E., Serum concentrations of free diphenylhydantoin and their relationship to clinical intoxication, *Epilepsia*, 14: 96-97, 1973.

848. Booker, H. E., Tormey, A., and Toussaint, J., Concurrent administration of phenobarbital and diphenylhydantoin: lack of an interference effect, *Neurology*, 21: 383-385, 1971.

849. Borga, O., Plasma protein binding of tricyclic antidepressants in man, *Psychopharm. Abs.*, 9: 500, 1970.

850. Borga, O., Garle, M., and Gutova, M., Identification of 5-(3, 4-dihydroxyphenyl)-5-phenylhydantoin as a metabolite of 5, 5-diphenylhydantoin (phenytoin) in rats and man, *Pharmacology*, 7: 129-137, 1972.

851. Borgstedt, A. D., Bryson, M. F., Young, L. W., and Forbes, G. B., Long-term administration of antiepileptic drugs and the development of rickets, *J. Pediat.*, 81: 9-15, 1972. (*cf.* Greenlaw, et al., *Clin. Res.*, 20: 56, 1972.)

852. Borofsky, L. G., Louis, S., and Kutt, H., Diphenylhydantoin in children, *Neurology*, 23: 967-972, 1973.

853. Borondy, P., Dill, W. A., Chang, T., Buchanan, R. A., and Glazko, A. J., Effect of protein binding on the distribution of 5, 5-diphenylhydantoin between plasma and red cells, *Ann. N.Y. Acad. Sci.*, 226: 82-87, 1973.

854. Bose, B. C., Gupta, S. S., and Sharma, S., Effect of anticonvulsant drugs on the acetylcholine content in rat tissues, *Arch. Int. Pharmacodyn.*, 67: 254-261, 1958.

855. Boshes, B. and Arieff, A. J., Clinical experience in the neurologic substance of pain, *Med. Clin. N. Amer.*, 52: 111-121, 1968.

856. Boston Collaborative Drug Surveillance Program, Diphenylhydantoin side effects and serum albumin levels, *Clin. Pharmacol. Ther.*, 14: 529-532, 1973.

857. Boudin, G., Pepin, B., Decroix, G., and Vernant, J. C., Diphenylhydantoin intoxication triggered by antituberculous treatment (2 cases), *Ann. Med. Intern.*, 122: 855-860, 1971.

858. Bouzarth, W. F., The ABC's of emergency care of serious head injuries in industry, *Industr. Med. Surg.*, 39: 25-29, 1970.

859. Bowe, J. C., Cornish, E. J., and Dawson, M., Evaluation of folic acid supplements in children taking phenytoin, *Develop. Med. Child Neurol.*, 13: 343-354, 1971.

860. Boyd, D. L. and Williams, J. F., The effect of diphenylhydantoin (Dilantin) on the positive inotropic action of ouabain, *Amer. J. Cardiol.*, 23: 712-718, 1969.

861. Boykin, M. E. and Hooshmand, H., CSF and serum folic acid and protein changes with diphenylhydantoin treatment: laboratory and clinical correlations, *Neurology*, 20: 403, 1970.

862. Boykin, M. E., *In vivo* and *in vitro* association of 5, 5-diphenylhydantoin with brain subfractions, *Neurology*, 4: 392-393, 1974.

863. Bozza, G. A., Normalization of intellectual development in the slightly brain-damaged, retarded child, *Paper presented at the 4th Italian National Congress on Child Neuropsychiatry*, Genoa, 1971.

864. Bray, P. F., Ely, R. S., and Kelley, V. C., Studies of 17-hydroxycorticosteroids VIII. Adrenocortical function in patients with convulsive disorders, *A.M.A. Arch. Neurol. Psychiat.*, 72: 583-590, 1954.

865. Bray, P. F., Ely, R. S., Zapata, G., and Kelley, V. C., Adrenocortical function in epilepsy I. The role of cortisol (hydrocortisone) in the mechanism and management of seizures, *Neurology*, 10: 842-846, 1960.

866. Bray, P. F., Kelley, V. C., Zapata, G., and Ely, R. S., Adrenocortical function in epilepsy II. The role of corticosterone in the mechanism and management of epilepsy, *Neurology*, 11: 246-250, 1961.

867. Brena, S. and Bonica, J. J., Nerve blocks for managing pain in the elderly, *Postgrad. Med.*, 47: 215-220, 1970.

868. Brennan, R. W., Dchejia, II., Kutt, H., Verebely, K., and McDowell, F., Diphenylhydantoin intoxication attendant to slow inactivation of isoniazid, *Neurology*, 20: 687-693, 1970.

869. Brien, J. F. and Inaba, T., Determination of low levels of 5,5-diphenylhydantoin in serum by gas liquid chromatography, *Epilepsy Abstracts*, 7: 198, 1974.

870. Bright, N. H., Effect of diphenylhydantoin on proline and hydroxyproline excretion in the rat, *Proc. Soc. Exp. Biol. Med.*, 120: 463-465, 1965.

871. Broddle, W. D., and Nelson, S. R., The effect of diphenylhydantoin on brain P-creatine, *Fed. Proc.*, 28: 1771, 1969.

872. Brodows, R. G. and Campbell, R. G., Control of refractory fasting hypoglycemia in a patient with suspected insulinoma with diphenylhydantoin, *J. Clin. Endocr.*, 38: 159-161, 1974.

873. Brown, G. L., and Wilson, W. P., Salicylate intoxication and the CNS with special reference to EEG findings, *Dis. Nerv. Syst.*, 32: 135-140, 1971.

874. Brown, J. M., Drug-associated lymphadenopathies with special reference to the Reed-Sternberg cell, *Med. J. Aust.*, 375-378, 1971.

875. Buchanan, R. A., and Allen, R. J., Diphenylhydantoin (Dilantin) and phenobarbital blood levels in epileptic children, *Neurology*, 21: 866-871, 1971.

876. Buchanan, R. A., Kinkel, A. W., Goulet, J. R., and Smith, T. C., The metabolism of diphenylhydantoin (Dilantin) following once-daily administration, *Neurology*, 22: 126-130, 1972.

877. Buchanan, R. A., Turner, J. L., Moyer, C. E., and Heffelfinger, J. C., Single daily dose of diphenylhydantoin in children, *J. Pediat.*, 83: 479-483, 1973.

878. Buchthal, F. and Lennox-Buchthal, M. A., Diphenylhydantoin, relation of anticonvulsant effect to concentration in serum, *Antiepileptic Drugs*, 193-209, Woodbury, D. M., Penry, J. K., and Schmidt, R. P., Eds., Raven Press, New York, 1972.

879. Buchthal, F. and Svensmark, O., Serum concentrations of diphenylhydantoin (phenytoin) and phenobarbital and their relation to therapeutic and toxic effects, *Psychiat. Neurol. Neurochir.*, 74: 117-136, 1971.

880. Burckhardt, D. and Sefidpar, M., Digitalis intoxication: contribution to diagnosis and therapy, *Schweiz. Rundschau. Med. (Praxis)*, 60: 1705-1711, 1971.

881. Buscaino, G. A., Labianca, O., Caruso, G., De Giacomo, P., and Ferrannini, E., Electromyographic and muscular histoenzymatic findings in a patient with continuous muscular activity syndrome ("Neuromyotonia"), *Acta Neurol. (Naples)*, 25: 206-224, 1970.

882. Calne, D. B., The drug treatment of epilepsy, *Epilepsy Abstracts*, 6: 177, 1973.

883. Cantor, F. K., Phenytoin treatment of thalamic pain. *Brit. Med. J.*, 4: 590-591, 1972.

884. Caracta, A. R., Damato, A. N., Josephson, M. E., Ricciutti, M. A., Gallagher, J. J., and Lau, S. H., Electrophysiologic properties of diphenylhydantoin, *Circulation*, 47: 1234-1241, 1973.

885. Carnay, L. and Grundfest, S., Excitable membrane stabilization by diphenylhydantoin and calcium, *Neuropharmacology*, 13: 1097-1108, 1974.

886. Caspary, W. F., Inhibition of intestinal calcium transport by diphenylhydantoin in rat duodenum, *Epilepsy Abstracts*, 6: 18, 1973.

887. Castleden, C. M., and Richens, A., Chronic phenytoin therapy and carbohydrate tolerance, *Lancet*, 966-967, 1973.

888. Chang, T. and Glazko, A. J., Diphenylhydantoin biotransformation, *Antiepileptic Drugs*, 149-162, Woodbury, D. M., Penry, J. K., and Schmidt, R. P., Eds., Raven Press, New York, 1972.

889. Chang, T., Okerholm, R. A., and Glazko, A. J., A 3-0-methylated catechol metabolite of diphenylhydantoin (Dilantin) in rat urine, *Res. Communications Chem. Path. Pharmacol.*, 4: 13-23, 1972.

890. Chang, T., Savory, A. and Glazko, A. J., A new metabolite of 5, 5-diphenylhydantoin (Dilantin), *Biochem. Biophys. Res. Commun.*, 38: 444-449, 1970.

891. Cheng, P. T. H. and Staple, P. H., Effect of a dorsal dermal surgical wound on the chemical response of rat abdominal skin to chronic administration of sodium diphenylhydantoin, *J. Dent. Res.*, 51: 131-143, 1972.

892. Cheng, T. O. and Damato, A. N., Dilantin in treatment and prevention of cardiac arrhythmias, *Amer. Heart J.*, 78: 285, 1969.

893. Chetchel, A. P., The influence of diphenine on the gum mucosa, *Epilepsy Abstracts*, 3: 203, 1970.

894. Chikhani, P., The use of "diphenylhydantoin sodium" in the treatment of periodontal disease, *Actualites Odontostomat.*, 98: 1-8, 1972.

895. Choi, Y. K. and Kee, C. S., Induction of steroid 6 beta-hydroxylase by administration of diphenylhydantoin, *Chem. Abstracts*, 74: 123576C, 1971.

896. Choi, Y., Thrasher, K., Werk, E. E., Sholiton, L. J., and Olinger, C., Effect of diphenylhydantoin on cortisol kinetics in humans, *J. Pharmacol. Exp. Ther.*, 176: 27-34, 1971.

897. Chokroverty, S. and Rubino, F. A., Motor nerve conduction study in patients on long term diphenylhydantoin therapy: correlation with clinical states and serum levels of diphenylhydantoin, folate and cyanocobalamine, *Epilepsy Abstracts*, 7: 111, 1974.

898. Choovivathanavanich, P., Wallace, E. M., and Scaglione, P. R., Pseudolymphoma induced by diphenylhydantoin, *J. Pediat.*, 76: 621-623, 1970.

899. Chou, C. C., Kuiper, D. H., and Hsieh, C. P., Effects of diphenylhydantoin on motility and compliance of the canine ileum and colon, *Gastroenterology*, 62: 734, 1972.

900. Chriskie, H. W., du Mesnil de Rochemont, W., Etzrodt, H., Grosser, K. D., Schulten, K. H., and Steinbruck, G., Influence of diphenylhydantoin and lidocaine on hemodynamics in patients with fixed-rate pacemakers, *Verh. Deutsch Ges. Inn. Med.*, 77: 960-963, 1971.

901. Christiansen, C., Rodbro, P., and Lund, M., Effect of vitamin D on bone mineral mass in normal subjects and in epileptic patients on anticonvulsants: a controlled therapeutic trial, *Brit. Med. J.*, 208-209, 1973. (*cf.* Christiansen, et al., *Brit. Med. J.*, 3: 738, 1972 and *Brit. Med. J.*, 4: 695, 1973.)

902. Christiansen, J. and Dam, M., Influence of phenobarbital and diphenylhydantoin on plasma carbamazepine levels in patients with epilepsy, *Epilepsy Abstracts*, 7: 137, 1974.

903. Christy, N. P. and Hofmann, A. D., Effects of diphenylhydantoin upon adrenal cortical function in man, *Neurology*, 9: 245-248, 1959.

904. Chrobok, F., Quantitative determination of phenytoin in biological material in the presence of phenobarbital and glutethimide, *Epilepsy Abstracts*, 5: 172, 1972.

905. Chung, E. K., The current status of digitalis therapy, *Modern Treatment*, 8: 643-714, 1971.

906. Clark, R. L., Kuhn, J. P., and Du Jovne, C. A., Absence of rickets after chronic dilantin administration: experimental radiological observations in rats, *Invest. Radiol.*, 6: 152-154, 1971.

907. Coburn, R. F., Enhancement by phenobarbital and diphenylhydantoin of carbon monoxide production in normal man, *New Eng. J. Med.*, 283: 512-515, 1970.

908. Cohen, H., Langendorf, R., and Pick, A., Intermittent parasystole—mechanism of protection, *Circulation*, 48: 761-774, 1973.

909. Cohen, M. S., Bower, R. H., Fidler, S. M., Johnsonbaugh, R. E., and Sode, J., Inhibition of insulin release by diphenylhydantoin and diazoxide in a patient with benign insulinoma, *Lancet*, 40-41, 1973.

910. Cole, P., Efficacy of oral diphenylhydantoin in reduction of premature ventricular contractions, *Clin. Pharmacol. Ther.*, 13: 137, 1972.

911. Collan, R., Boyd, W., and Hathaway, B., Effect of halothane on the liver of rats pretreated with diphenylhydantoin and norethindrone, *Scand. J. Clin. Lab. Invest.*, 25: 74, 1970.

912. Conn, H. L., Jr., Mechanisms of quinidine action. *Mechanisms and Therapy of Cardiac Arrhythmias*, 594-596, Dreifus, L. S. and Likoff, W., Eds., Grune and Stratton, New York, 1966.

913. Conners, C. K., Kramer, R., Rothschild, G. H., Schwartz, L., and Stone, A., Treatment of young delinquent boys with diphenylhydantoin sodium and methyphenidate, *Arch. Gen. Psychiat.*, 24: 156-160, 1971.

914. Conney, A. H. and Burns, J. J., Metabolic interactions among environmental chemicals and drugs, *Science*, 178: 576-586, 1972.

915. Conney, A. H., Jacobson, M., Schneidman, K., and Kuntzman, R., Induction of liver microsomal cortisol 6 β-hydroxylase by diphenylhydantoin or phenobarbital: an explanation for the increased excretion of 6-hydroxycortisol in humans treated with these drugs, *Life Sci.*, 4: 1091-1098, 1965.

916. Conard, G. J., Haavik, C. O., and Finger, K. F., Binding of 5,5-diphenylhydantoin and its major metabolite to human and rat plasma proteins, *J. Pharm. Sci.*, 60: 1642-1646, 1971.

917. Cooper, R. G., Greaves, M. S., and Owen, G., Gas liquid chromatographic isolation, identification, and quantitation of some barbiturates, glutethimide, and diphenylhydantoin in whole blood, *Epilepsy Abstracts*, 6: 184, 1973.

918. Costa, P. J., Glaser, G. H., and Bonnycastle, D. D., Effects of diphenylhydantoin (Dilantin) on adrenal cortical function, *A.M.A. Arch. Neurol. Psychiat.*, 74: 88-91, 1955.

919. Covi, L. and Uhlenhuth, E. H., Methodological problems in the psychopharmacological study of the dangerous anti-social personality, *Proc. Int. Symposium on Aggressive Behavior Biochem. Pharmacol. Psychol. Sociol.*, 326-335, May, 1969.

920. Covino, B. G., Wright, R., and Charleson, D. A., Effectiveness of several antifibrillary drugs in the hypothermic dog, *Amer. J. Physiol.*, 121: 54-58, 1955.

921. Cranmer, M. F., Effect of diphenylhydantoin on storage of DDT in the rat, *Toxic Appl. Pharmacol.*, 17: 315, 1970.

922. Critchley, E. M. R., Clark, D. B., and Wikler, A., An adult form of acanthocytosis, *Trans. Amer. Neurol. Assoc.*, 92: 132-137, 1967.

923. Cuan-Perez, M. C. and Ortiz, A., Comparative study of quinidine, propranolol and diphenylhydantoin for preventing recurrence in post-cardioversion auricular fibrillation, *Arch. Inst. Cardiol. Mex.*, 41: 278-284, 1971.

924. Cudworth, A. G. and Cunningham, J. L., The effect of diphenylhydantoin on insulin response, *Clin. Sci. Molec. Med.*, 46: 131-136, 1974.

925. Cummings, N. P., Rosenbloom, A. L., Kohler, W. C. and Wilder, B. J., Plasma glucose and insulin responses to oral glucose with chronic diphenylhydantoin therapy, *Pediatrics*, 51: 1091-1093, 1973.

926. Cunningham, J. L. and Price Evans, D. A., Urinary D-glucaric acid excretion and acetanilide pharmacokinetics before and during diphenylhydantoin administration, *Europ. J. Clin. Pharmacol.*, 7: 387-391, 1974.

927. Curtis, G. P., Experimental atrial fibrillation, *Univ. of Mich., Ann Arbor, Doctoral Thesis*, 1971.

928. Dack, S., Antiarrhythmic agents in the treatment of ventricular tachycardia, *Mechanisms and Therapy of Cardiac Arrhythmias*, 312-320, Dreifus, L. S. and Likoff, W., Eds., Grune and Stratton, New York, 1966.

929. Dalessio, D. J., Medical treatment of tic douloureux, *J. Chronic Dis.*, 19: 1043-1048, 1966.

930. Dalton, C. and Verebely, K., Hypotriglyceridemic activity of 5,5'-diphenyl-2-thiohydantoin (DPTH), *J. Pharmacol. Exp. Ther.*, 180: 484-491, 1971.

931. Daly, R. F. and Sajor, E. E., Inherited tic douloureux, *Neurology*, 23: 937-939, 1973.

932. Dam, M. and Christiansen, J., Evidence of drug action on serum level of carbamazepine, *Epilepsy Abstracts*, 7: 26, 1974.

933. Dam, M., Diphenylhydantoin, neurologic aspects of toxicity, *Antiepileptic Drugs*, 227-235, Woodbury, D. M., Penry, J. K., and Schmidt, R. P. Eds., Raven Press, New York, 1972.

934. Dam, M., The density and ultrastructure of the Purkinje cells following diphenylhydantoin treatment in animals and man, *Acta Neurol. Scand.*, 48: 1-65, 1972.

935. Damato, A. N., Berkowitz, W. D., Patton, R. D., and Lau, S. H., The effect of diphenylhydantoin on atrioventricular and intraventricular conduction in man, *Amer. Heart J.*, 79: 51-56, 1970.

936. Damato, A. N., Diphenylhydantoin: pharmacological and clinical use, *Progr. Cardiovasc. Dis.*, 12: 1-15, 1969.

937. Danckwardt-Lilliestrom, G., Grevsten, S., and Olerud, S., Investigation of effect of various agents on periosteal bone formation, *Upsala J. Med. Sci.*, 77: 125-128, 1972.

938. Daniel, R., Psychiatric drug use and abuse in the aged, *Geriatrics*, 144-156, January, 1970.

939. Daniels, C., Stein, A. A., and Moss, G., The shock lung syndrome: anemia as a predisposing factor, *Surg. Forum*, 24: 1, 1973.

940. Danielson, B. G., Bittar, E. E., Chen, S. S. and Tong, E. Y., Diphenylhydantoin as a blocking agent of the proton-sensitive component of Na efflux in barnacle muscle fibers, *Life Sci.*, 10: 721-726, 1971.

941. Danzig, R., Treatment of arrhythmias associated with acute myocardial infarction, *Nebraska Med. J.*, 56: 474-475, 1971.

942. Daube, J. R., and Peters, H. A., Hereditary essential myoclonus, *Arch. Neurol.*, 15: 587-594, 1966.

943. Davies, J. E., Edmundson, W. F., Maceo, A., Irvin, G. L., Cassady, J., and Barquet, A., Reduction of pesticide residues in human adipose tissue with diphenylhydantoin, *Food Cosmet. Toxic.*, 9: 413-423, 1971.

944. Davies, J. E., Pharmacological depletion of adipose pesticide residues, *Clin. Res.*, 19: 27, 1971.

945. Davies, R. O., Diphenylhydantoin in angina pectoris, *Chest*, 66: 421-422, 1974.

946. Davis, J. N., Diphenylhydantoin for hiccups, *Lancet*, 1: 997, 1974.

947. Dawson, K. P., and Jamieson, A., Value of blood phenytoin estimation in management of childhood epilepsy, *Arch. Dis. Child.*, 46: 386-388, 1971.

948. Dawson, K. P., Severe cutaneous reactions to phenytoin, *Arch. Dis. Child.*, 48: 239-240, 1973.

949. Day, H. W., Control and treatment of arrhythmias, *Cardiovascular Therapy, The Art and The Science*, 289-291, Russek, H. I., and Zohman, B. L., Eds., The Williams & Wilkins Co., Baltimore, 1971.

950. DeCastro, J. H. X., Acosta, M. L., Sica, R. E. P., and Guerico, N., Sensory and motor nerve conduction velocity in long-term diphenylhydantoin therapy, *Arq. Neuropsiquiat.*, 30: 215-220, 1972.

951. DeLuca, K., Masotti, R. E., and Partington, M. W., Altered calcium metabolism due to anticonvulsant drugs, *Develop. Med. Child Neurol.*, 14: 318-321, 1972.

952. Delaire, J., Moutet, H., and Talmant, J. C., Facial peripheric hemispasm and Paget's disease of bone, *Rev. Stomat. (Paris)*, 73: 601-612, 1972.

953. Delgado, J. M. R. and Mihailovic, L., Use of intracerebral

electrodes to evaluate drugs that act on the central nervous system, *Ann. N.Y. Acad. Sci.*, 64: 644-666, 1956.

954. Delgado, J. M. R., Mora, F. and Sanguinetti, A. M., Reduction by diphenylhydantoin of after-discharges in the amygdala of stimulated rhesus monkey, *Personal Communication*, 1973.

955. Den Hertog, A., The effect of diphenylhydantoin on the electronic component of the sodium pump in mammalian non-myelinated nerve fibers, *Europ. J. Pharmacol.*, 19: 94-97, 1972.

956. Dent, E., Richens, A., Rowe, D. J. F., and Stamp, T. C. B., Osteomalacia with long-term anticonvulsant therapy in epilepsy, *Brit. Med. J.*, 4: 69-72, 1970.

957. Desjacques, P., Study of the diffusion of phenytoin through the cellophane membrane of the artificial kidney used on a patient suffering from uremia and epilepsy, *Epilepsy Abstracts*, 5: 220, 1972.

958. De Sousa, R. C. and Grosso, A., Effects of diphenylhydantoin on transport processes in frog skin (Rana ridibunda), *Epilepsy Abstracts*, 7: 111, 1974.

959. deWolff, F. A., Drug effects on intestinal epithelium, *Doctoral Thesis*, 1973.

960. Dhar, G. J., Peirach, C. A., Ahamed, P. N., and Howard, R. B., Diphenylhydantoin induced hepatic necrosis, *Postgrad. Med.*, 56: 128-129, 1974.

961. Diamond, B. and Yaryura-Tobias, J. A., The use of diphenylhydantoin in non-epileptic psychotics, *V World Congress of Psychiatry*, 1971.

962. Diamond, W. D. and Buchanan, R. A., A clinical study of the effect of phenobarbital on diphenylhydantoin plasma levels, *J. Clin. Pharmacol.*, 306-311, 1970.

963. Diederich, K. W., Herzog, S. and Tielsen, I., Diphenylhydantoin: A comparative study on normal cats and animals intoxicated with digitalis glycosides, *Basic Research in Cardiology*, 69: 289-308, 1974.

964. Dill, R. E., Adrenal cortical response in rats treated with diphenylhydantoin sodium, *Anat. Rec.*, 148: 366, 1964.

965. Dill, W. A., Baukema, J., Chang, T., and Glazko, A. J., Colorimetric assay of 5,5-diphenylhydantoin (Dilantin) and 5 (p hydroxyphenyl) 5 phenylhydantoin, *Epilepsy Abstracts*, 4: 262, 1971.

966. Dill, W. A., Chucot, L., Chang, T., and Glazko, A. J., Simplified benzophenone procedure for determination of diphenylhydantoin in plasma, *Clin. Chem.*, 17: 1200-1201, 1971.

967. Dilman, V. M., Elivbaeva, G. V., Vishnevskii, A. S., Tsyrilina, E. V., and Bulovskaia, L. N., Justification of the use of diphenine (diphenylhydantoin) in oncologic practice, *Vop. Onkol.*, 17: 70-72, 1971.

968. Doe, W. F., Hoffbrand, A. V., Reed, P. I., and Scott, J. M., Jejunal pH and folic acid, *Brit. Med. J.*, 699-700, 1971.

969. Doherty, J. E., Digitalis glycosides. Pharmacokinetics and their clinical implications, *Ann. Intern. Med.*, 79: 229-238, 1973.

970. Domino, E. F. and Olds, M. E., Effects of d-amphetamine, scopolamine, chlordiazepoxide and diphenylhydantoin on self-stimulation behavior and brain acetylcholine, *Psychopharmacologia (Berlin)*, 23: 1-16, 1972.

971. Domzal, T., Effect of diphenylhydantoin on clinical manifestations and excretion of 5-hydroxyindoleacetic acid in Parkinson's disease, *Neurol. Neurochir. Pol.*, 6: 357-360, 1972.

972. Dreifus, L. S. and Watanabe, Y., Current status of diphenylhydantoin, *Amer. Heart J.*, 80: 709-713, 1970.

973. Dreifus, L. S., de Azevedo, I. M., and Watanabe, Y., Electrolyte and antiarrhythmic drug interaction, *Amer. Heart J.*, 88: 95-107, 1974.

974. Dreifus, L. S., Management of intractable atrial arrhythmias, *Mechanisms and Therapy of Cardiac Arrhythmias*, 205-210, Dreifus, L. S. and Likoff, W., Eds., Grune and Stratton, New York, 1966.

975. Dreifus, L. S., Use of quinidine, procainamide and diphenylhydantoin, *Cardiovascular Therapy, The Art and The Science*, 109-112, Russek, H. I. and Zohman, B. L., Eds., The Williams & Wilkins Co., Baltimore, 1971.

976. Dreifuss, F. E. and Sato, S., Anticonvulsant drugs in clinical practice, *Drug Therapy*, 2: 9-22, 1972.

977. Dreifuss, F. E., Diphenylhydantoin and visceral atony, *Drug Therapy*, 3: 101-102, 1973.

978. Dressler, W. E., Rossi, G. V., and Orzechowski, R. F., Effect of several anticonvulsant drugs and procainamide against ouabain-induced cardiac arrhythmias in rabbits, *J. Pharm. Sci.*, 61: 133-134, 1972.

979. Driessen, O. and Emonds, A., Simultaneous determination of antiepileptic drugs in small samples of blood plasma by gas chromatography. Column technology and extraction procedure. *Epilepsy Abstracts*, 7: 203-204, 1974.

980. Dronamraju, K. R., Epilepsy and cleft lip and palate, *Lancet*, 876-877, 1970.

981. Dry, J. and Pradalier, A., Phenytoin intoxication during treatment combined with disulfiram, *Therapie*, 28: 799-802, 1973.

982. Ducker, T. B., Blaylock, R. L. D., and Perot, P. L., Jr., Emergency care of patients with cerebral injuries, *Postgrad. Med.*, 55: 102-110, 1974.

983. Dudley, W. H. C., Jr., and Williams, J. G., Electroconvulsive therapy in delirium tremens, *Dig. Neurol. Psychiat.*, Series XL: 333, 1972.

984. Dujovne, C. A., Clark, R., and Lasagna, L., Calcium and CNS symptoms, *New Eng. J. Med.*, 281: 271-272, July, 1969.

985. Eadie, M. J., Tyrer, J. H., and Hooper, W. D., Aspects of diphenylhydantoin metabolism, *Proc. Aust. Assoc. Neurol.*, 7: 7-13, 1970.

986. Eastham, R. D. and Jancar, J., Macrocytosis associated with anticonvulsant therapy, *Epilepsia*, 11: 275-280, 1970.

987. Eddy, J. D. and Singh, S. P., Treatment of cardiac arrhythmias with phenytoin, *Brit. Med. J.*, 4: 270-273, 1969.

988. Editor, A guide to selection of a systemic antibacterial agent, *Drugs*, 4: 132-145, 1972.

989. Editor, Anticonvulsant drugs and hypocalcaemia, *Brit. Med. J.*, 4: 351, 1973.

990. Editor, Anticonvulsants or antiepileptics, *Behavioral Neuropsychiatry*, 3: 14-16, 1971.

991. Editor, Diphenylhydantoin for digitalis toxicity, *Postgrad. Med.*, 45: 244-245, 169.

992. Editor, For tic douloureux, lasting relief, *Medical World News*, 14: 66-67, 1973.

993. Editor, Monitoring drug therapy, *Lancet*, 668, 1974.

994. Editor, Phenytoin and carbamazepine combined, *Brit. Med. J.*, 1: 113, 1974.

995. Editor, Some important interactions with anticonvulsant drugs, *J. International Res. Communication*, 2: 5-7, 1974.

996. Editor, Treatment of trigeminal neuralgia, *Brit. Med. J.*, 2: 583-584, 1972.

997. Editors, Panel discussion: hormones and fetal metabolism, *Clin. Pharmacol. Ther.*, 14: 742-747, 1973.

998. Edmundson, W. F., Davies, J. E., Maceo, A., and Morgade, A., Drug and environmental effects on DDT residues in human blood, *Southern Med. J.*, 63: 1440-1441, 1970.

999. Edmundson, W. F., Frazier, D. E., and Maceo, A., Sequential biochemical tests in persons taking pH phenytoin, *Indust. Med.*, 41: 7-11, 1972.

1000. Ehrnebo, M., Agurell, S., Jalling, B., and Boreus, L. O., Age differences in drug binding by plasma proteins: studies on human fetuses, neonates and adults, *Europ. J. Clin. Pharmacol.*, 3: 189-193, 1971.

1001. Eipe, J., Drugs affecting therapy with anticoagulants, *Med. Clin. N. Amer.*, 56: 255-262, 1972.

1002. Eisen, A. A., Woods, J. F., and Sherwin, A. L., Peripheral nerve function in long-term therapy with diphenylhydantoin, *Neurology*, 24: 411-417, 1974.

1003. Eling, T. E., Harbison, R. D., Becker, B. A., and Fouts, J. R., Diphenylhydantoin effect on neonatal and adult rat hepatic drug metabolism, *J. Pharmacol. Exp. Ther.*, 171: 127-134, 1970.

1004. Eling, T. E., Harbison, R. D., Becker, B. A., and Fouts, J. R., Kinetic changes in microsomal drug metabolism with age and diphenylhydantoin treatment, *Europ. J. Pharmacol.*, 11: 101-108, 1970.

1005. Ellenberger, C., Burde, R. M., and Keltner, J. L., Acute optic neuropathy, *Arch. Ophthal.*, 91: 435-438, 1974.

1006. Elliott, T. H. and Natarajan, P. N., Infrared studies of hydantoin and its derivatives, *J. Pharm. Pharmacol.*, 19: 209-216, 1966.

1007. Ellis, J. G. and Dimond, E. G., Newer concepts of digitalis, *Amer. J. Cardiol.*, 17: 759-767, 1966.

1008. Elshove, J. and Van Eck, J. H. M., Congenital malformations, cleft lip and palate in particular, in children of epileptic women, *Ned. Tijdschr. Geneesk.*, 115: 1371-1375, 1971. (*cf.* Elshove, *Lancet*, 1074, 1969.)

1009. Elwood, J. C., Richert, D. A., and Westerfeld, W. W., A comparison of hypolipidemic drugs in the prevention of an orotic acid fatty liver, *Biochem. Pharmacol.*, 21: 1127-1134, 1972.

1010. Erdey, L., Kaplar, L., Takacs, J. and Dessouky, Y. M., Determination of hydantoins in pharmaceutical preparations by gas chromatography, *J. Chromatogr.*, 45: 63-67, 1969.

1011. Erickson, J. D. and Oakley, G. P., Seizure disorder in mothers of children with orofacial clefts: a case control study, *J. Pediat.*, 84: 244-246, 1974.

1012. Escueta, A. V. and Appel, S. H., Brain synapses—an *in vitro* model for the study of seizures, *Arch. Intern. Med.*, 129: 333-344, 1972.

1013. Escueta, A. V. and Appel, S. H., The effects of electroshock seizures on potassium transport within synaptosomes from rat brain, *Epilepsy Abstracts*, 5: 205, 1972.

1014. Escueta, A. V. and Appel, S. H., Diphenylhydantoin and potassium transport in isolated nerve terminals, *J. Clin. Invest.*, 50: 1977-1984, 1971.

1015. Esposito-Avella, M. and Mennear, J. H., Studies on the protective effect of diphenylhydantoin against alloxan diabetes in mice, *Proc. Soc. Exp. Biol. Med.*, 142: 82-85, 1973.

1016. Evans, D. E. and Gillis, R. A., Effect of diphenylhydantoin (DPH) on centrally induced vagal arrhythmias, *Pharmacologist*, 13: Abstract 188, 1971.

1017. Evenson, M. A., Jones, P., and Darcey, B., Simultaneous measurement of diphenylhydantoin and primidone in serum by gas-liquid chromatography, *Clin. Chem.*, 16: 107-110, 1970.

1018. Fariss, B. L. and Lutcher, C. L., Diphenylhydantoin-induced hyperglycemia and impaired insulin release—effect of dosage, *Diabetes*, 20: 177-181, 1971.

1019. FDA, Anticonvulsant linked with birth defect risk, *FDA Drug Bulletin*, July, 1974.

1020. Fedrick, J., Epilepsy and pregnancy: a report from the Oxford record linkage study, *Brit. Med. J.*, 2: 442-448, 1973.

1021. Ferrari, M. and Furlanut, M., Effects of diphenylhydantoin on smooth muscle, *Arch. Int. Pharmacodyn.*, 203: 101-106, 1973.

1022. Ferry, D. G., Owen, D., and McQueen, E. G., The effect of phenytoin on the binding of pesticides to serum proteins, *Proc. Univ. Otago Med. School*, 50: 8-9, 1972.

1023. Fertziger, A. P. and Dunham, P. B., Diphenylhydantoin stimulation of potassium influx in isolated lobster axons, *Epilepsy Abstracts*, 5: 61, 1972.

1024. Fertziger, A. P., Brain extracellular space: some considerations on the role it plays in brain function, *Cond. Reflex*, 8: 224-232, 1973.

1025. Fertziger, A. P., Liuzzi, S. E., and Dunham, P. B., Diphenylhydantoin (Dilantin): stimulation of potassium influx in lobster axons, *Brain Res.*, 33: 592-596, 1971.

1026. Fertziger, A. P., Lynch, J. J., and Stein, E. A., Modification of the morphine withdrawal syndrome in rats, *Brain Res.*, 78: 331-334, 1974.

1027. Fertziger, A. P., Stein, E. A., and Lynch, J. J., Suppression of morphine-induced mania in cats, *Psychopharmacologia*, 36: 185-187, 1974.

1028. Festoff, B. W. and Appel, S. H., The effect of diphenylhydantoin on synaptosome metabolism, *Neurology*, 19: 300, 1969.

1029. Fica, V., Panaitescu, G., Matrescu, F., and Popescu, E.. Indications and limitations of anti-arrhythmic drugs, *Med. Intern.*, 23: 523-536, 1971.

1030. Fincham, R. W., Schottelius, D. D., and Sahs, A. L., The influence of diphenylhydantoin on primidone metabolism, *Arch. Neurol.*, 30: 259-262, 1974.

1031. Finkle, B. S., Foltz, R. L., and Taylor, D. M., A comprehensive GC-MS reference data system for toxicological and biomedical purposes, *J. Chromatogr. Sci.*, 12: 304-328, 1974.

1032. Fish, B., The "one child, one drug" myth of stimulants in hyperkinesis, *Arch. Gen. Psychiat.*, 25: 193-203, 1971.

1033. Fisher, D. and DiMino, J. M., Case presentation of an alternative therapeutic approach for the borderline psychotic heroin addict: diphenylhydantoin, *Br. J. Addict.*, 70: 51-55, 1975.

1034. Fisher, D. D. and Ungerleider, J. T., Grand mal seizures following ingestion of LSD, *Calif. Med.*, 106: 210-211, 1967.

1035. Formby, B., The *in vivo* and *in vitro* effect of diphenylhydantoin and phenobarbitone on K$^+$-activated phosphohydrolase and (NA$^+$,K$^+$)-activated ATPase in particulate membrane fractions from rat brain, *J. Pharm. Pharmacol.*, 22: 81-85, 1970.

1036. Fouts, J. R. and Kutt, H., Diphenylhydantoin, some studies on the biotransformation and interactions with some other drugs and chemicals, *Antiepileptic Drugs*, 163-168, Woodbury, D. M., Penry, J. K., and Schmidt, R. P., Eds., Raven Press, New York, 1972.

1037. Freiwald, M. J., Prevention of complications of Herpes Zoster ophthalmicus with special reference to steroid therapy, *Eye, Ear, Nose and Throat Monthly*, 46: 444-450, 1967.

1038. Frenkel, E. P., McCall, M. S. and Sheehan, R. G., Cerebrospinal fluid folate, and vitamin B^{12} in anticonvulsant-induced megaloblastosis, *J. Lab. Clin. Med.*, 81: 105-115, 1973.

1039. Friedlander, W. J., Epilepsy—1973, *The Clinical Neurology Information Center*, The University of Nebraska Medical Center, 1-45, 1974.

1040. Friedman, A. P., An overview of chronic recurring headache, *Wisconsin Med. J.*, 71: 110-116, 1972.

1041. Friedman, A. P., Treatment of vascular headache, *International Encyclopedia of Pharmacology and Therapeutics*, Section 33, Vol. I: 225-251. Carpi, A., Ed., Pergamon Press, New York, 1972.

1042. Fromm, G. H., Pharmacological consideration of anticonvulsants, *Epilepsy Abstracts*, 2: 194, 1969.

1043. Frost, J. B., Mesoridazine and chlorpromazine in the treatment of alcohol withdrawal syndrome, *Canad. Psychiat. Assoc. J.*, 18: 385-387, 1973.

1044. Gabler, W. L. and Hubbard, G. L., The metabolism of 5,5-diphenylhydantoin (DPH) in nonpregnant and pregnant Rhesus monkeys, *Arch. Int. Pharmacodyn.*, 203: 72-91, 1973.

1045. Gabreels, F. J. M., The influence of phenytoin on the Purkinje cell of the rat, *Epilepsy Abstracts*, 4:131-132, 1971.

1046. Gallagher, B. B., Baumel, I. P., Mattison, R. H., and Woodbury, S. G., Primidone, diphenylhydantoin and phenobarbital: aspects of acute and chronic toxicity, *Neurology*, 23: 145-149, 1973.

1047. Gamstorp, I., Meeuwisse, G., and Tryding, N., Tryptophan loading test in convulsive disorders, *Acta Paediat. Scand.*, 55: 656-657, 1966.

1048. Gardner-Medwin, D., Why should we measure serum levels of anticonvulsant drugs in epilepsy? *Clinical Electroencephalography*, 4: 132-134, 1973.

1049. Gardner, C. R. and Webster, R. A., The effect of some anticonvulsant drugs on leptazol and bicuculline induced acetylcholine efflux from rat cerebral cortex, *Brit. J. Pharmacol.*, 47: 652P, 1973.

1050. Garrettson, L. K. and Curley, A., Dieldrin—studies in a poisoned child, *Arch. Environ. Health*, 19: 814-822, 1969.

1051. Garrettson, L. K., Pharmacology of anticonvulsants, *Pediat. Clin. N. Amer.*, 19: 179-191, 1972.

1052. Gattenlohner, W. and Schneider, K. W., The effect of diphenylhydantoin on hemodynamics, *Munchen Med. Wschr.*, 11: 2561-2566, 1969.

1053. Gauchel, F. D., Lehr, H. J., Gauchel, G., and von Harnack, G. A., Diphenylhydantoin in children, *Deutsch Med. Wschr.*, 98: 1391-1396, 1973.

1054. Gauchel, G., Gauchel, F. D., and Birkofer, L., A micromethod for the determination of phenytoin in blood by high speed liquid chromatography, *Epilepsy Abstracts*, 6: 210, 1973.

1055. Gavrilescu, S., Pop, T., and Goia, E., On a case of supraventricular paroxysmal tachycardia resistant to treatment. Transitory conversion into atrial fibrillation by rapid atrial electric stimulation, *Med. Intern (Bucur)*, 24: 1393-1400, 1972.

1056. Gebauer, D., Prevention and therapy of cardiac rhythm disorders. Experiences with a diphenylhydantoin-meprobamate preparation (Cusitan), *Munchen Med. Wschr.*, 113: 436-440, 1971.

1057. Gegick, C. G., Danowski, T. S., Khurana, R. C., Vidalon, C., Nolan, S., Stephan, T., Chae, S., and Wingard, L., Hyperostosis frontalis interna and hyperphosphatasemia, *Ann. Intern. Med.*, 79: 71-75, 1973.

1058. Gehres, L. D., Randall, C. L., Riccio, D. C., and Vardaris, R. M., Attenuation of hypothermic retrograde amnesia produced by pharmacologic blockage of brain seizures, *Physiol. Behav.*, 10: 1011-1017, 1973.

1059. Gerber, N., Lynn, R., and Oates, J., Acute intoxication with 5,5-diphenylhydantoin associated with impairment of biotransformation, *Ann. Intern. Med.*, 77: 765-771, 1972.

1060. Gerber, N., Seibert, R. A., and Thompson, R. M., Identification of a catechol glucuronide metabolite of 5,5-diphenylhydantoin (DPH) in rat bile by gas chromatography (GC) and mass spectrometry (MS), *Epilepsy Abstracts*, 7: 80, 1974.

1061. Gerber, N., Weller, W. L., Lynn, R., Rangno, R. E., Sweetman, B. J., and Bush, M. T., Study of dose-dependent metabolism of 5,5-diphenylhydantoin in the rat using new methodology for isolation and quantitation of metabolites *in vivo* and *in vitro*, *J. Pharmacol. Exp. Ther.*, 178: 567-579, 1971.

1062. Gerich, J. E., Charles, M. A., Levin, S. R., Forsham, P. H., and Grodsky, G. M., *In vitro* inhibition of pancreatic glucagon secretion by diphenylhydantoin, *J. Clin. Endocr.*, 35: 823-824, 1972.

1063. Gerlings, E. D., and Gilmore, J. P., Some cardiac effects of diphenylhydantoin, *Acta Physiol. Pharmacol. Neerl.*, 15: 461-408, 1909.

1064. German, J., Kowal, A., and Ehlers, K. H., Trimethadione and human teratogenesis, *Teratology*, 3: 349-362, 1970.

1065. Gerson, C. D., Hepner, G. W., Brown, N., Cohen, N., Herbert, V., and Janowitz, H. D., Inhibition by diphenylhydantoin of folic absorption in man, *Gastroenterology*, 63: 246-251, 1972.

1066. Gerz, H. O., Dilantin against "painful touching" (dysthesia), *Physician's Drug Manual*, 3: 144, 1972.

1067. Gettes, L. S., The electrophysiologic effects of antiarrhythmic drugs, *Amer. J. Cardiol.*, 28: 526-535, 1971.

1068. Gharib, H. and Munoz, J. M., Endocrine manifestations of diphenylhydantoin therapy, *Metabolism*, 23: 515-524, 1974.

1069. Gianelly, R. E. and Harrison, D. C., Drugs used in the treatment of cardiac arrhythmias, *Disease-A-Month*, 25-32, January 1969.

1070. Gibson, K. and Harris, P., Diphenylhydantoin and human myocardial microsomal (Na^+,K^+)-ATPase, *Biochem. Biophys. Res. Commun.*, 35: 75-78, 1969.

1071. Gilbert, J. C., Gray, P., and Heaton, G. M., Anticonvulsant drugs and brain glucose, *Biochem. Pharmacol.*, 20: 240-243, 1971.

1072. Gillis, R. A. and Raines, A., A comparison of the cardiovascular effects of diphenylthiohydantoin and diphenylhydantoin, *Europ. J. Pharmacol.*, 23: 13-18, 1973.

1073. Gimenez-Roldan, S. and Esteban, A., Orbicularis oculi "myotonia" in hypothyroid myopathy, *Europ. Neurol.*, 9: 44-55, 1973.

1074. Ginwalla, T. M. S., Gomes, B. C., and Nayak, R. P., Management of gingival hyperplasia in patients receiving Dilantin therapy, *J. Indian Dent. Assn.*, 39: 124-126, 1967.

1075. Glaser, G. H., Diphenylhydantoin, toxicity, *Antiepileptic Drugs*, 219-226, Woodbury, D. M., Penry, J. K., and Schmidt, R. P. Eds., Raven Press, New York, 1972. (*cf.* Adeloye, et al., *Ghana Med. J.*, 10: 56, 1971, Bosso and Chudzik, *Drug Intel. & Clin. Pharma.*, 7: 336, 1973, Greenberg, et al., *Epilepsy Abstracts*, 4: 151, 1971 and Watts, *Pediatrics*, 30: 592, 1962.)

1076. Glazko, A. J. and Chang, T., Diphenylhydantoin, absorption, distribution and excretion, *Antiepileptic Drugs*, 127-136, Woodbury, D. M., Penry, J. K., and Schmidt, R. P., Eds., Raven Press, New York, 1972.

1077. Glazko, A. J., Diphenylhydantoin, chemistry and methods for determination, *Antiepileptic Drugs*, 103-112, Woodbury, D. M., Penry, J. K., and Schmidt, R. P., Eds., Raven Press, New York, 1972.

1078. Glazko, A. J., Diphenylhydantoin, *Epilepsy Abstracts*, 6: 184, 1973.

1079. Godfraind, T., Lesne, M., and Pousti, A., The action of diphenylhydantoin upon drug binding, ionic effects and inotropic action of ouabain, *Arch. Int. Pharmacodyn.*, 191: 66-73, 1971.

1080. Goebel, R. W., Sodium diphenylhydantoin association with oral healing, *J. Oral Surg.*, 30: 191-195, 1972.

1081. Goldberg, M. A., and Todoroff, T., Binding of diphenylhydantoin to brain protein, *Epilepsy Abstracts*, 7: 112, 1974.

1082. Goldberg, M. A. and Todoroff, T., Diphenylhydantoin binding to brain fractions, *Neurology*, 22: 410, 1972.

1083. Goldberg, M. E. and Ciofalo, V. B., Effect of diphenylhydantoin sodium and chlordiazepoxide alone and in combination on punishment behavior, *Psychopharmacologia (Berlin)*, 14: 233-239, 1969.

1084. Goldstein, F. J., Continuing education via pharmatapes: Digitalis I. A basic pharmacological review, *Amer. J. Pharm.*, 145: 135-141, 1973.

1085. Goldstein, R. E., Penzotti, S. C., Kuehl, K. S., Prindle, K. H., Hall, C. A., Titus, E. O., and Epstein, S. E., Correlation of antiarrhythmic effects of diphenylhydantoin with digoxin-induced changes in myocardial contractility, sodium-potassium adenosine triphosphatase activity, and potassium efflux, *Circ. Res.*, 33: 175-182, 1973.

1086. Gordon, E., Respiratory control after acute head injury, *Lancet*, 483, 1973.

1087. Gordon, P., Aging: a search for drug-modifiable degeneracy in the polyribosomes of brain, *Proc. 8th Int. Cong. Geront.*, 1: 4pp., 1969.

1088. Gordon, P., Callaghan, O., and Doty, B., Diphenylhydantoin effects on nucleic acid biochemistry learning and neoplasm, *Pharmacologist*, 10: 169, 1968.

1089. Gordon, P., Molecular approaches to the drug enhancement of deteriorated functioning in the aged, *Advances Geront. Res.*, 3: 199-248, 1971.

1090. Gordon, P., Rational chemotherapy for aging, *Postgrad. Med.*, 40: 152-155, 1970.

1091. Gordon, P., Tobin, S. S., Doty, B., and Nash, M., Drug effects on behavior in aged animals and man: diphenylhydantoin and procainamide, *J. Geront.*, 23: 434-444, 1968.

1092. Gossel, T. A. and Mennear, J. H., Inhibition of alloxan-induced diabetes by diphenylhydantoin sodium, *Pharmacologist*, 13: 238, 1971.

1093. Gossel, T. A., On the mechanism of diphenylhydantoin protection against alloxan-induced diabetes mellitus in mice, *Dissertation Abstracts*, 33: 2729B, 1972.

1094. Gottschalk, L. A., Covi, L., Uliana, R., and Bates, D. E., Effects of diphenylhydantoin on anxiety and hostility in institutionalized prisoners, *Compr. Psychiat.*, 14: 503-511, 1973.

1095. Goudie, J. H. and Burnett, D., A gas chromatographic

method for the simultaneous determination of phenobarbitone, primidone and phenytoin in serum using a nitrogen detector, *Epilepsy Abstracts*, 6: 187, 1973.

1096. Grant, R. H. E. and Stores, O. P. R., Folic acid in folate-deficient patients with epilepsy, *Brit. Med. J.*, 4: 644-648, 1970.

1097. Green, R. S. and Rau, J. H., Treatment of compulsive eating disturbances with anticonvulsant medication, *Amer. J. Psychiat.*, 131: 428-432, 1974.

1098. Greenbaum, D. S., Ferguson, R. K., Kater, L. A., Kuiper, D. H., and Rosen, L. W., A controlled therapeutic study of the irritable-bowel syndrome, *New Eng. J. Med.*, 288: 13-16, 1973.

1099. Greenberg, C. and Papper, E. M., The indications for gasserian ganglion block for trigeminal neuralgia, *Anesthesiology*, 31: 566-573, 1969.

1100. Greenberg, I. M., Cerebral dysfunction in general psychiatric office practice, *Dis. Nerv. Syst.*, 33: 637-644, 1972.

1101. Greengard, O. and McIlwain, H., Anticonvulsants and the metabolism of separated mammalian cerebral tissues, *Biochem. J.*, 61: 61-68, 1955.

1102. Grob, P. J. and Herold, G. E., Immunological abnormalities and hydantoins, *Brit. Med. J.*, 2: 561-563, 1972.

1103. Gruener, R. P. and Stern, L. Z., Diphenylhydantoin reverses membrane effects in steroid myopathy, *Nature New Bio.*, 235: 54-55, 1972.

1104. Gudmundson, C. and Lidgren, L., Does diphenylhydantoin accelerate healing of fractures in mice, *Acta Orthop. Scand.*, 44: 640-649, 1973.

1105. Guzek, J. W., Russell, J. T., and Thorn, N. A., Inhibition by diphenylhydantoin of vasopressin release from isolated rat neurohypophyses, *Acta Pharmacol. et Toxicol.*, 34: 1-4, 1974.

1106. Haan, D., *Diagnosis and therapy of cardiac arrhythmia and acute heart disease*, Medizinisch Literarische Verlagsgesellschaft mbH, Uelzen, Germany, 1973.

1107. Haddad, R. I., Positive EEG spike activity in sleep, *JAMA*, 229: 1282, 1974.

1108. Hadfield, M. G. and Boykin, M. E., Effect of diphenylhydantoin administered *in vivo* on 3H-1-norepinephrine uptake in synaptosomes, *Res. Commun. Chem. Pathol. Pharmacol.*, 7: 209-212, 1974.

1109. Hadfield, M. G., Uptake and binding of catecholamines —effect of diphenylhydantoin and a new mechanism of action, *Arch. Neurol.*, 26: 78-84, 1972.

1110. Haft, J. I., Ricciutti, M. A. and Damato, A. N., Effects of IV diphenylhydantoin (DPH) on coronary blood flow and oxygen utilization of the heart, *Clinical Research*, 15: 204, 1967.

1111. Hagen, H., Treatment of cardiac arrhythmias with diphenylhydantoin, *Deutsch Med. Wschr.*, 96: 380-384, 1971.

1112. Haghshenass, M. and Rao, D. B., Serum folate levels during anticonvulsant therapy with diphenylhydantoin, *J. Amer. Geriat. Soc.*, 21: 275-277, 1973.

1113. Hahn, T. J., Hendin, B. A., Scharp, C. R., and Haddad, J. G., Jr., Effect of chronic anticonvulsant therapy on serum 25-hydroxycalciferol levels in adults, *New Eng. J. Med.*, 287: 900-909, 1972.

1114. Haiat, R., Chapelle, M., Benaim, R., Witchitz, S., and Chiche, P., Disappearance of an intraventricular conduction disorder under diphenylhydantoin, *Sem. Hop. Paris*, 47: 2957-2964, 1971.

1115. Hall, W. B., Prevention of Dilantin hyperplasia: a preliminary report, *Bull. Acad. Gen. Dent.*, 20-25, 1969.

1116. Hallaq, I. Y. and Harris, J. D., The syndrome of post-herpetic neuralgia: complication and an approach to therapy, *J. Amer. Osteopath. Assoc.*, 68: 1265-1267, 1969.

1117. Halpern, L. M. and Julien, R. M., Augmentation of cerebellar Purkinje cell discharge rate after diphenylhydantoin, *Epilepsy Abstracts*, 5: 236-237, 1972.

1118. Hancock, J. C. and Bevilacqua, A. R., Temporal lobe dysrhythmia and impulsive or suicidal behavior, *Southern Med. J.*, 64: 1189-1193, 1971.

1119. Handley, A. J., Phenytoin tolerance tests, *Brit. Med. J.*, 3: 203-204, 1970.

1120. Hansen, H. W. and Wagener, H. H., Sodium diphenylhydantoin for the treatment of cardiac arrhythmias, *Munchen Med. Wschr.*, 111: 417-421, 1969.

1121. Hansen, H. W. and Wagener, H. H., Diphenylhydantoin in the treatment of heart failure, *Deutsch. Med. Wschr.*, 96: 1866-1873, 1971.

1122. Hansen, H. W. and Wagener, H. H., Experimental studies on the influence of diphenylhydantoin glycoside effects on the heart, *Herz Kreislauf Zeitschrift Fur Kardiologie und Angiologie in Klinik und Praxis*, 6: 69-72, 1974.

1123. Hansen, H. W., Marquort, B., and Pelz, W., Indications for phenytoin in cardiac arrhythmias, *Deutsch. Med. Wschr.*, 99: 638-642, 1974.

1124. Hansen, J. M., Siersbaek-Nielsen, K. and Skovsted, L., Effect of diphenylhydantoin on the metabolism of carbamazepine-induced acceleration of dicoumarol in man, *Acta Med. Scand.*, 189: 15-19, 1971.

1125. Hansen, J. M., Skovsted, L., Lauridsen, U. B., Kirkegaard, C., and Siersbaek-Nielsen, K., The effect of diphenylhydantoin on thyroid function, *J. Clin. Endocrinol. Metab.*, 39: 785-786, 1974.

1126. Hansotia, P. and Keran, E., Dilantin binding by red blood cells of normal subjects, *Neurology*, 24: 575-578, 1974.

1127. Hansten, P. D., Diphenylhydantoin drug interactions, *Hosp. Formulary Manage.*, 4: 28-29, 1969.

1128. Haque, N., Thrasher, K., Werk, E. E., Jr., Knowles, H. C., Jr., and Sholiton, L. J., Studies on dexamethasone metabolism in man: effect of diphenylhydantoin, *J. Clin. Endocr.*, 34: 44-50, 1972.

1129. Harbison, R. D. and Becker, B. A., Effect of phenobarbital and SKF 525A pretreatment on diphenylhydantoin teratogenicity in mice, *J. Pharmacol. Exp. Ther.*, 175: 283-288, 1970.

1130. Harbison, R. D., Eling, T. E., and Becker, B. A., Effects of diphenylhydantoin on neonatal rat liver drug metabolizing enzymes, *Fed. Proc.*, 28(2): 1969.

1131. Harris, M., Jenkins, M. V. and Wills, M. R., Phenytoin inhibition of parathyroid hormone induced bone resorption *in vitro*, *Brit. J. Pharmac.*, 50: 405-408, 1974.

1132. Harrison, D. C., Kerber, R. E., and Alderman, E. L., Pharmacodynamics and clinical use of cardiovascular drugs after cardiac surgery, *Amer. J. Cardiol.*, 26: 385-393, 1970.

1133. Hart, B. L., Feline behavior, *Feline Practice*, 3: 8-10, 1973.

1134. Hartshorn, E. A., Interactions of cardiac drugs, *Drug Intell. Clin. Pharm.*, 4: 272-275, 1970.

1135. Hartshorn, E. A., Pyrazolone derivatives (antipyrine, aminopyrine, phenylbutazone, oxyphenbutazone), *Drug Intelligence Clinical Pharmacy*, 6: 6-10, 1972.

1136. Hasbani, M., Pincus, J. H. and Lee, S. H., Diphenylhydantoin and calcium movement in lobster nerves, *Arch. Neurol.*, 31: 250-254, 1974.

1137. Hatch, R. C. and Fischer, R., Cocaine elicited behavior and toxicity in dogs pretreated with synaptic blocking agents, morphine, or diphenylhydantoin, *Epilepsy Abstracts*, 6: 209, 1973.

1138. Hattwick, M. A. W., Weis, T. T., Stechschulte, C. J., Baer, G. M., and Gregg, M. B., Recovery from rabies: a case report, *Ann. Intern. Med.*, 76: 931-942, 1972.

1139. Haward, L. R. C., Effects of sodium diphenylhydantoinate and pemoline upon concentration: a comparative study, *Drugs and Cerebral Function*, 103-120, Smith, W. L., Ed., Charles C Thomas, 1970.

1140. Haward, L. R. C., Effects of DPH (sodium diphenylhydantoinate) upon concentration in pilots, *Rev. Med. Aeronautique Spatiale*, 12: 372-374, 1973.

1141. Haward, L. R. C., The effect of phenytoin-aided autogenic training on stress threshold, *Int. Congress for Psychosomatic Med. and Hypnosis*, Kyoto, Japan, July 12-14, 1967.

1142. Haward, L. R. C., Effects of sodium diphenylhydantoin upon concentration, *Bulletin Brit. Psychol. Soc.*, 22: 50, 1969.

1143. Hedger, R. W., The conservative management of acute

oliguric renal failure, *Med. Clin. N. Amer.*, 55: 121-135, 1971.

1144. Heinemann, U. and Lux, H. D., Effects of diphenylhydantoin on extracellular (K+) in cat cortex, *Electroenceph. Clin. Neurophysiol.*, 34: 735, 1973.

1145. Helfant, R., Scherlag, B., and Damato, A., The interaction of procaine amide and diphenylhydantoin on cardiac conductivity and automaticity, *Clin. Res.*, 15: 206, 1967.

1146. Hendricks, G. L., Jr., Barnes, W. T., and Hood, H. L., Seven-year "cure" of lung cancer with metastasis to the brain, *JAMA*, 220: 127, 1972.

1147. Hepner, G. W., Aledort, L. M., Gerson, C. D., Cohen, N., Herbert, V., and Janowitz, H. D., Inhibition of intestinal ATPase by diphenylhydantoin and acetazolamide, *Clin. Res.*, 18: 382, 1970.

1148. Herbinger, W., Result report of a control by an apparatus of 208 myocardial infarct patients in an intensive care station, *Wien. Med. Wschr.*, 121: 518-522, 1971.

1149. Hermansen, K., Antifibrillatory effect of some beta-adrenergic receptor blocking agents determined by a new test procedure in mice, *Acta Pharmacologica*, 28: 17-27, 1969.

1150. Hinkhouse, A., Craniocerebral trauma, *Amer. J. Nurs.*, 73: 1719-1722, 1973.

1151. Hobson, J. D. and Zettner, A., Digoxin serum half-life following suicidal digoxin poisoning, *JAMA*, 223: 147-149, 1973.

1152. Hodgson, E. R. and Reese, H. H., Clinical experiences with dilantin in epilepsies, *Wis. Med. J.*, 38: 968-971, 1939.

1153. Hoefer, P. F. A., Cohen, S. M., and Greeley, D. McL., Paroxysmal abdominal pain—a form of epilepsy in children, *JAMA*, 147: 1-6, 1951.

1154. Hofeldt, F. D., Dippe, S. E., Levin, S. R., Karam, J. H., Blum, M. R., and Forsham, P. H., Effects of diphenylhydantoin upon glucose-induced insulin secretion in three patients with insulinoma, *Diabetes*, 23: 192-198, 1974.

1155. Hogg, P. S., Three cases of 'restless legs' or 'Ekbom's syndrome' as seen in general practice, *Practitioner*, 209: 82-83, 1972.

1156. Holcomb, R., Lynn, R., Harvey, B., Sweetman, B. J., and Gerber, N., Intoxication with 5,5-diphenylhydantoin (Dilantin), *J. Pediat.*, 80: 627-632, 1972.

1157. Holdaway, P. A., Effects of amino-glutethimide and diphenylhydantoin sodium on the rat adrenal cortex, *Proc. Indiana Acad. Sci.*, 77: 427-433, 1968.

1158. Hommes, O. R. and Obbens, E. A., The epileptogenic action of Na-folate in the rat, *J. Neurol. Sci.*, 16: 271-281, 1972.

1159. Honda, Y., Podos, S. M., and Becker, B., The effect of diphenylhydantoin on the electroretinogram of rabbits. I. Effect of concentration, *Invest. Ophthal.*, 12: 567-572, 1973.

1160. Honda, Y., Podos, S. M., and Becker, B., The effect of diphenylhydantoin on the electroretinogram of rabbits. II. Effects of hypoxia and potassium, *Invest. Ophthal.*, 12: 573-578, 1973.

1161. Hooper, W. D., Sutherland, J. M., Bochner, F. et al., The effect of certain drugs on the plasma protein binding of phenytoin, *Epilepsy Abstracts*, 7: 112, 1974.

1162. Hopf, H. C. and Kauer, H., Effect of phenytoin on the excitable cell membrane, *Epilepsy Abstracts*, 4: 89, 1971.

1163. Houben, P. F. M., Hommes, O. R., and Knaven, P. J. H., Anticonvulsant drugs and folic acid in young mentally retarded epileptic patients, *Epilepsia*, 12: 235-247, 1971.

1164. Houck, J. C., Cheng, R. F., and Waters, M. D., Diphenylhydantoin, effects on connective tissue and wound repair, *Antiepileptic Drugs*, 267-273, Woodbury, D. M., Penry, J. K., and Schmidt, R. P., Eds., Raven Press, New York, 1972.

1165. Houck, J. C., Cheng, R. F., and Waters, M. D., The effect of Dilantin upon fibroblast proliferation, *Proc. Soc. Exp. Biol. Med.*, 139: 969-981, 1972.

1166. Houghton, G. W. and Richens, A., Inhibition of phenytoin metabolism by sulthiame in epileptic patients, *Brit. J. Clin. Pharmacol.*, 1: 59-66, 1974.

1167. Houghton, G. W. and Richens, A., Rate of elimination

of tracer doses of phenytoin at different steady state serum phenytoin concentrations in epileptic patients, *Brit. J. Clin. Pharmacol.*, 1: 155-161, 1974.

1168. Houghton, G. W., Latham, A. N., and Richens, A., Difference in the central actions of phenytoin and phenobarbitone in man, measured by critical flicker fusion threshold, *Europ. J. Clin. Pharmacol.*, 6: 57-60, 1973.

1169. Huessy, H. R., Study of the prevalence and therapy of the choreatiform syndrome or hyperkinesis in rural Vermont, *Acta Paedopsychiat.*, 34: 130-135, 1967.

1170. Huffman, D. H. and Azarnoff, D. L., The use of digitalis, *Ration. Drug Ther.*, 8: 1-7, 1974.

1171. Hughes, R. C. and Matthews, W. B., Pseudo-myotonia and myokymia, *J. Neurol. Neurosurg. Psychiat.*, 32: 11-14, 1969.

1172. Huisman, J. W., Van Heycop Ten Ham, M. W., and Van Zijl, C. H. W., Influence of ethylphenacemide on serum levels of other anti-epileptic drugs, *Epilepsia*, 11: 207-215, 1970.

1173. Humphries, J. O., New methods for the prevention and treatment of ventricular arrhythmias, *Maryland Med. J.*, 17: 75-76, 1968.

1174. Hunninghake, D. B., Drug interactions, *Postgrad. Med.*, 47: 71-75, 1970.

1175. Hunter, J., Maxwell, J. D., Stewart, D. A., Parsons, V., and Williams, R., Altered calcium metabolism in epileptic children on anticonvulsants, *Brit. Med. J.*, 202-204, 1971. (*cf.* Hahn, et al., *Clin. Res.*, 21: 626, 1973 and Herman and Pippenger, *Neurology*, 23: 437, 1973.)

1176. Iber, F. L., Prevention of alcohol withdrawal seizures, *JAMA*, 221: 608, 1972.

1177. Ide, C. H. and Webb, R. W., Penetrating transorbital injury with cerebrospinal orbitorrhea, *Amer. J. Ophthal.*, 71: 1037-1039, 1971.

1178. Idestrom, C. M., Schalling, D., Carlquist, U., and Sjoqvist, F., Acute effects of diphenylhydantoin in relation to plasma levels, *Psychol. Med.*, 2: 111-120, 1972.

1179. Imabayashi, K. and Matsumura, S., Four cases of idiopathic renal hematuria with abnormal electroencephalogram, *Jap. J. Clin. Urol.*, 27: 139-144, 1973.

1180. Inaba, T. and Brien, J. F., Determination of the major urinary metabolite of diphenylhydantoin by high-performance liquid chromatography, *J. Chromatogr.*, 80: 161-165, 1973.

1181. Iosub, S., Bingol, N., and Wasserman, E., The pregnant epileptic and her offspring, *Pediat. Res.*, 7: 420, 1973.

1182. Isaacs, H. and Frere, G., Syndrome of continuous muscle fibre activity. Histochemical, nerve terminal and end-plate study of two cases, *South African Medical Journal*, 18: 1601 7, 1974.

1183. Isaacs, H., Continuous muscle fibre activity in an Indian male with additional evidence of terminal motor fiber abnormality, *J. Neurol. Neurosurg. Psychiat.*, 30: 126-133, 1967.

1184. Janz, D. and Schmidt, D., Comparison of spectrophotometric and gas liquid chromatographic measurements of serum diphenylhydantoin concentrations in epileptic outpatients, *Epilepsy Abstracts*, 7: 268, 1974.

1185. Janz, D. and Schmidt, D., Anti-epileptic drugs and failure of oral contraceptives, *Lancet*, 1113, 1974.

1186. Jenkins, D. and Spector, R. G., The actions of folate and phenytoin on the rat heart *in vivo* and *in vitro*, *Biochem. Pharmacol.*, 22: 1813-1816, 1973.

1187. Jensen, O. N. and Olesen, O. V., Subnormal serum folate due to anticonvulsive therapy, *Arch. Neurol.*, 22: 181-182, 1970.

1188. Jensen, R. A. and Katzung, B. G., Electrophysiological actions of diphenylhydantoin on rabbit atria: dependence on stimulation frequency, potassium and sodium, *Circ. Res.*, 26: 17-27, 1970.

1189. Jonas, A. D., Diphenylhydantoin and the treatment of anxiety, *Amer. J. Psychiat.*, 126: 163, 1969.

1190. Jones, G. L. and Kemp, J. W., Characteristics of the hydrogen bonding interactions of diphenylhydantoin with nucleic acids and their components, *Fed. Proc.*, 31: 570, 1972.

1191. Jovanovic, T., Experiences in the treatment of psychoses occurring concomitantly with epilepsy, *Neuropsihiatrija*, 20: 173-183, 1972.

1192. Joynt, R. J. and Green, D., Tonic seizures as a manifestation of multiple sclerosis, *Arch. Neurol.*, 6: 293-299, 1962.

1193. Jubiz, W. and Rallison, M. L., Diphenylhydantoin treatment of glycogen storage diseases, *Arch. Intern. Med.*, 134: 418-421, 1974.

1194. Jubiz, W., Levinson, R. A., Meikle, A. W., West, C. D., and Tyler, F. H., Absorption and conjugation of metyrapone during diphenylhydantoin therapy: mechanism of the abnormal response to oral metyrapone, *Endocrinology*, 86: 328-331, 1970.

1195. Jubiz, W., Meikle, A. W., Levinson, R. A., Mizutani, S., West, C. D., and Tyler, F. H., Effect of diphenylhydantoin on the metabolism of dexamethasone, *New Eng. J. Med.*, 283: 11-14, 1970.

1196. Julien, R. M. and Halpern, L. M., Cerebellar action of diphenylhydantoin on penicillin-induced cerebral cortical epileptic foci, *Fed. Proc.*, 29: Abstract 784, 1970.

1197. Julien, R. M. and Halpern, L. M., Stabilization of excitable membrane by chronic administration of diphenylhydantoin, *J. Pharmacol. Exp. Ther.*, 175: 206-212, 1970.

1198. Julien, R. M. and Halpern, L. M., Diphenylhydantoin: evidence for a central action, *Life Sci.*, 10: 575-582, 1971.

1199. Julien, R. M. and Halpern, L. M., Effects of diphenylhydantoin and other antiepileptic drugs on epileptiform activity and Purkinje cell discharge rates, *Epilepsy Abstracts*, 5: 236, 1972.

1200. Jung, S. S., Chen, K. M., and Brody, J. A., Paroxysmal choreoathetosis: report of Chinese cases, *Neurology*, 23: 749-755, 1973.

1201. Jus, K., Jus, A., Gautier, J., Villeneuve, A., Pires, P., Pineau, R., and Villeneuve, R., Studies on the action of certain pharmacological agents on tardive dyskinesia and on the rabbit syndrome, *Int. J. Clin. Pharmacol.*, 9: 138-145, 1974.

1202. Kalman, P., Nanassy, A., and Csapo, G., Diphenylhydantoin treatment of atrial tachycardia with heart block, *Z. Kardiologie*, 62: 75-79, 1972.

1203. Kanzawa, F., Hoshi, A., and Kuretani, K., Relationship between antitumor activity and chemical structure in psychotropic agents, *Gann*, 61: 529-534, 1970.

1204. Kaplan, R., Blume, S., Rosenberg, S., Pitrelli, J., and Turner, W. J., Phenytoin, metronidazole and multivitamins in the treatment of alcoholism, *Quart. J. Stud. Alcohol.*, 33: 97-104, 1972.

1205. Kasai, S. and Yoshizumi, T., Effect of diphenylhydantoin sodium on the proliferation of cultured cells *in vitro*, *Bull. Tokyo Dent. Coll.*, 12: 223-234, 1971.

1206. Kater, R. M. H., Roggin, G., Tobon, F., Zeive, P., and Iber, F. L., Increased rate of clearance of drugs from the circulation of alcoholics, *Amer. J. Med. Sci.*, 258: 35-39, 1969.

1207. Kater, R. M. H., Tobon, F., Zeive, P. D., Roggin, G. M., and Iber, F. L., Heavy drinking accelerates drugs' breakdown in liver, *JAMA*, 206: 1709, 1968.

1208. Kato, R., Chiesara, E., and Vassanelli, P., Increased activity of microsomal strychnine-metabolizing enzyme induced by phenobarbital and other drugs, *Biochem. Pharmacol.*, 11: 913-922, 1962.

1209. Kaufmann, G. and Hauser, K., Experience with diphenylhydantoin (antisacer) in the treatment of cardiac arrhythmias, *Schweiz. Med. Wschr.*, 98: 1223-1226, 1968.

1210. Kaufmann, G. and Weber-Eggenberger, S., Hemodynamic changes due to diphenylhydantoin in digitalized cardiac patients, *Schweiz. Med. Wschr.*, 100: 2164-2168, 1970.

1211. Kazamatsuri, H., Elevated serum alkaline phosphatase levels in epilepsy during diphenylhydantoin therapy, *New Eng. J. Med.*, 283: 1411-1412, 1970.

1212. Kazamatsuri, H., Elevated serum alkaline phosphatase levels in the epileptic patients with diphenylhydantoin, *Folia Psychiat. Neurol. Jap.*, 24: 181-189, 1970.

1213. Keltner, J. L., Becker, B., Gay, A. J., and Podos, S. M., Effect of diphenylhydantoin in ischemic optic neuritis, *Trans. Amer. Ophthal. Soc.*, 70: 113-130, 1972.

1214. Kemp, G. L., Treatment of ventricular ectopic rhythms with diphenylhydantoin, *J. Amer. Geriat. Soc.*, 20: 265-267, 1972.

1215. Kemp, J. W. and Woodbury, D. M., Subcellular distribution of 4-^{14}C-diphenylhydantoin in rat brain, *J. Pharmacol. Exp. Ther.*, 177: 342-349, 1971.

1216. Kennedy, C., Anderson, W., and Sokoloff, L., Cerebral blood flow in epileptic children during the interseizure period, *Neurology*, 8: 100-105, 1958.

1217. Kennedy, C., Grave, G. D., Jehle, J. W., and Kupferberg, H. J., The effect of diphenylhydantoin on local cerebral blood flow, *Neurology*, 22: 451-452, 1972.

1218. Kessler, K. M., Individualization of dosage of antiarrhythmic drugs, *Medical Clinics of North America*, 58: 1019-26, 1974.

1219. Ketel, W. B. and Hughes, J. R., Toxic encephalopathy with seizures secondary to ingestion of composition C-4, *Neurology*, 22: 871-876, 1972.

1220. Kizer, J. S., Vargas-Cordon, M., Brendel, K., and Bressler, R., The *in vitro* inhibition of insulin secretion by diphenylhydantoin, *J. Clin. Invest.*, 49: 1942-1948, 1970.

1221. Kleinfeld, M. and Stein, E., Effects of diphenylhydantoin on action potentials of canine Purkinje and ventricular fibers, *Circulation*, 38: 116, 1968.

1222. Knopp, R. H., Sheinin, J. C., and Freinkel, N., Diphenylhydantoin and an insulin-secreting islet adenoma, *Arch. Intern. Med.*, 130: 904-908, 1972.

1223. Kobayashi, I., Yamashita, Y., and Yamazaki, H., Onset of systemic lupus erythematosus during the long-term administration of diphenylhydantoin, *Nippon Naika Gakkai Zasshi*, 60: 851-854, 1971.

1224. Koch-Weser, J., Antiarrhythmic prophylaxis in ambulatory patients with coronary heart disease, *Arch. Intern. Med.*, 129: 763-772, 1972.

1225. Koch, A., Higgins, R., Sande, M., Tierney, J., and Tulin, R., Enhancement of renal Na$^+$ transport by Dilantin, *Physiologist*, 5: 168, 1962.

1226. Koch, H. U., Kraft, D., Von Herrath, D., and Schaefer, K., Influence of diphenylhydantoin and phenobarbital on intestinal calcium transport in the rat, *Epilepsy Abstracts*, 6: 109, 1973.

1227. Kootstra, A. and Woodhouse, S. P., The effect of diphenylhydantoin on the Na$^+$-K$^+$-stimulated ouabain-inhibited ATPase, *Proceedings of the University of Otago Medical School*, 52: 6-7, 1974.

1228. Koppe, J. G., Bosman, W., Oppers, V. M., Spaans, F., and Kloosterman, G. J., Epilepsy and congenital anomalies, *Ned. T. Geneesk.*, 117: 220-224, 1973. (*cf.* Loughnan, et al., *Lancet*, 70, 1973.)

1229. Kormendy, C. G. and Bender, A. D., Experimental modification of the chemistry and biology of the aging process, *J. Pharm. Sci.*, 60: 167-180, 1971.

1230. Koski, C. L., Rifenberick, D. H., and Max, S. R., Energy metabolism in steroid atrophy, *Neurology*, 4: 352, 1974.

1231. Kostov, K. G., Tachev, A. M. and Nastev, G. T., The problem of pseudomyotonia (Isaac's syndrome), *Zh. Neuropatol. Psikhiatr. Korsakov*, 73: 825-829, 1973.

1232. Krasner, J., Drug-protein interaction, *Pediat. Clin. N. Amer.*, 19: 51-63, 1972.

1233. Krasner, J., Giacoia, G. P., and Yaffe, S. J., Drug protein binding in the newborn infant, *Pediat. Res.*, 7: 317, 1973.

1234. Krell, R. D. and Goldberg, A. M., Effect of diphenylhydantoin and ethanol feeding on the synthesis of rat liver folates from exogenous pteroylglutamate (^{3}H), *Epilepsy Abstracts*, 7: 195, 1974.

1235. Krikler, D. M., A fresh look at cardiac arrhythmias, *Lancet*, 1034-1037, 1974.

1236. Krsiak, M. and Steinberg, H., Psychopharmacological aspects of aggression: a review of the literature and some new experiments, *J. Psychosom. Res.*, 13: 243-252, 1969.

1237. Kruger, G., Effect of Dilantin in mice. 1. Changes in lymphoreticular tissue after acute exposure, *Virshows Arch.* (Path. Anat.), 349: 297-311, 1970. (*cf.* Juhasz, et al., *Acta Morphol. Acad. Sci. Hung.*, 18: 147, 1970.)

1238. Krupin, T., Podos, S. M., and Becker, B., Effect of diphenylhydantoin on dexamethasone suppression of plasma cortisol in primary open-angle glaucoma, *Amer. J. Ophthal.*, 71: 997-1002, 1971.

1239. Kuiper, J. J., Lymphocytic thyroiditis possibly induced by diphenylhydantoin, *JAMA*, 210: 2370-2372, 1969.

1240. Kuntzman, R. and Southern, A. L., The effects of CNS active drugs on the metabolism of steroids in man, *Adv. Biochem. Psychopharmacol.*, 1: 205-217, 1969.

1241. Kupferberg, H. J., Quantitative estimation of diphenylhydantoin, primidone and phenobarbital in plasma by gas-liquid chromatography, *Clin. Chim. Acta*, 29: 283-288, 1970.

1242. Kuroiwa, Y. and Araki, S., Lhermitte's sign and reflex tonic spasm in demyelinating diseases with special reference to their localizing value, *Kyushu J. Med. Sci.*, 14: 29-38, 1963.

1243. Kuroiwa, Y. and Shibasaki, H., Painful tonic seizures in multiple sclerosis—treatment with diphenylhydantoin and carbamazepine, *Folia. Psychiat. Neurol. Jap.*, 22: 107-119, 1968.

1244. Kutt, H. and Fouts, J. R., Diphenylhydantoin metabolism by rat liver microsomes and some of the effects of drug or chemical pretreatment on diphenylhydantoin metabolism by rat liver microsomal preparations, *J. Pharmacol. Exp. Ther.*, 176: 11-26, 1970.

1245. Kutt, H. and Penry, J. K., Usefulness of blood levels of antiepileptic drugs, *Arch. Neurol.*, 31: 283-288, 1974.

1246. Kutt, H. and Verebely, K., Metabolism of diphenylhydantoin by rat liver microsomes, *Biochem. Pharmacol.*, 19: 675-686, 1970.

1247. Kutt, H., Biochemical and genetic factors regulating Dilantin metabolism in man, *Ann. N.Y. Acad. Sci.*, 179: 704-722, 1971.

1248. Kutt, H., Diphenylhydantoin interactions with other drugs in man, *Antiepileptic Drugs*, 169-180, Woodbury, D. M., Penry, J. K., and Schmidt, R. P., Eds., Raven Press, New York, 1972. (*cf.* Evans, et al., *Lancet*, 517, 1970.)

1249. Kutt, H., Diphenylhydantoin relation of plasma levels to clinical control, *Antiepileptic Drugs*, 211-218, Woodbury, D. M., Penry, J. K., and Schmidt, R. P., Eds., Raven Press, New York, 1972.

1250. Kutt, H., Haynes, J., Verebely, K. and McDowell, F., The effect of phenobarbital on plasma diphenylhydantoin level and metabolism in man and rat liver microsomes, *Epilepsy Abstracts*, 3: 4, 1970.

1251. Kutt, H., Waters, L., and Fouts, J. R., Diphenylhydantoin-induced difference spectra with rat-liver microsomes, *Chem. Biol. Interactions*, 2: 195-202, 1970.

1252. Kutt, H., Waters, L., and Fouts, J. R., The effects of some stimulators (inducers) of hepatic microsomal drug-metabolizing enzyme activity on substrate-induced difference spectra in rat liver microsomes, *J. Pharmacol. Exp. Ther.*, 179: 101-113, 1971.

1253. Kwalick, D. S., Anticonvulsants and DDT residues, *JAMA*, 215: 120-121, 1971.

1254. Kyosola, K., Abdominal epilepsy, *Ann. Chir. Gyanaec. Fenn.*, 62: 101-103, 1973.

1255. Lamprecht, F., Epilepsy and schizophrenia: a neurochemical bridge, *Epilepsy Abstracts*, 7: 190, 1974.

1256. Landolt, A. M., Treatment of acute post-operative inappropriate antidiuretic hormone secretion with diphenylhydantoin, *Acta Endocr.*, 76: 625-628, 1974.

1257. Larsen, P. R., Atkinson, A. J., Wellman, H. N., and Goldsmith, R. E., Effect of diphenylhydantoin on thyroxine metabolism in man, *J. Clin. Invest.*, 49: 1266-1279, 1970.

1258. Lascelles, P. T., Kocen, R. S., and Reynolds, E. H., The distribution of plasma phenytoin levels in epileptic patients,

J. Neurol. Neurosurg. Psychiat., 33: 501-505, 1970.

1259. Lasser, R. P., Management of arrhythmia, *New York J. Med.*, 73: 1775-1777, 1973.

1260. Latham, A. N., Millbank, L., Richens, A., and Rowe, D. J. F., Liver enzyme induction by anticonvulsant drugs, and its relationship to disturbed calcium and folic acid metabolism, *J. Clin. Pharmacol.*, 13: 337-342, 1973.

1261. Lawrence. T., Antiarrhythmic drugs, *Topics on Medicinal Chemistry*, 3:360-363, Wiley-Interscience, New York, 1970.

1262. Lee, S. I. and Bass, N. H., Microassay of diphenylhydantoin: blood and regional brain concentrations in rats during acute intoxication, *Neurology*, 20: 115-124, 1970.

1263. Lefebvre, E. B., Haining, R. G., and Labbe, R. F., Coarse facies, calvarial thickening and hyperphosphatasia associated with long-term anticonvulsant therapy, *New Eng. J. Med.*, 286: 1301-1302, 1972. (*cf.* Falcone and Davidson, *Lancet*, 2: 1112, 1973, Griscom, *New Eng. J. Med.*, 287: 722, 1972, Lefebvre, et al., Nellhaus and Poskanzer, *ibid.*)

1264. Lesbre, J. P., Cathala, B., Salvador, M., Florio, R. Lescure, F., and Meriel, P., Diphenylhydantoin and digitalis toxicity, *Arch. Mal. Coeur.*, 62: 412-437, 1969.

1265. Lesne, M., Sturbois, X. and Wilmotte, L., Modifications by diphenylhydantoin of the pharmacokinetic of digitoxin in the rat, *J. Pharmacol.*, 5: 75-86, 1974.

1266. Letteri, J. M., Mellk, H., Louis, S., Kutt, H., Durante, P., and Glazko, A., Diphenylhydantoin metabolism in uremia, *New Eng. J. Med.*, 285: 648-652, 1971.

1267. LeVan, H., Gordon, P., and Stefani, S., Enhancement of radioresistance in mice treated with diphenylhydantoin, *J. Pharm. Sci.*, 59: 1178-1179, 1970.

1268. LeVan, H., Gordon, P., and Stefani, S., Effect of diphenylhydantoin on survival and morphology of Ehrlich ascites tumor mice, *Oncology*, 26: 25-32, 1972.

1269. Levin, S. R., Booker, J., Smith, D. F., and Grodsky, G. M., Inhibition of insulin secretion by diphenylhydantoin in the isolated perfused pancreas, *J. Clin. Endocr.*, 300: 400-401, 1970.

1270. Levin, S. R., Charles, M. A., O'Connor, M., and Grodsky, G. M., Use of diphenylhydantoin and diazoxide to investigate insulin secretory mechanisms, *Presented at the 8th Congress of International Diabetes Federation*, Brussels, Belgium, 1973.

1271. Levin, S. R., Charles, M. A., O'Connor, M., Hagura, R., Smith, D., and Grodsky, G. M., Comparative effects of diphenylhydantoin (DPH) and diazoxide (DZ) upon biphasic insulin secretion from the isolated, perfused rat pancreas, with computerized correlation of biologic responses. *Presented at the 8th Congress of International Diabetes Federation*, Brussels, Belgium, 1973.

1272. Levin, S. R., Grodsky, G., Hagura, R., Smith, D., Licko, V., and Forsham, P., Comparison of effects of diphenylhydantoin and diazoxide on insulin secretion in the isolated perfused rat pancreas, using computerized correlation of experimental data, *Clin. Res.*, 19: 375, 1971.

1273. Levin, S. R., Grodsky, G. M., Hagura, R., and Smith, D., Comparison of the inhibitory effects of diphenylhydantoin and diazoxide upon insulin secretion from the isolated perfused pancreas, *Diabetes*, 21: 856-862, 1972. (*cf.* Goldberg, *Diabetes*, 18: 101, 1969.)

1274. Levin, S. R., Reed, J. W., Ching, K. N., Davis, J. W., and Blum, R., Inhibition of insulin secretion after diphenylhydantoin (DPH) in diabetes and in obesity, *Clin. Res.*, 20: 178, 1972.

1275. Levin, S. R., Reed, J. W., Ching, K. N., Davis, J. W., Blum, M. R., and Forsham, P. H., Diphenylhydantion: its use in detecting early insulin secretory defects in patients with mild glucose intolerance, *Diabetes*, 22: 194-201, 1973.

1276. Levine, M. C., Reactions to anticonvulsants, *New Eng. J. Med.*, 286: 1217, 1972.

1277. Levitt, B., Raines, A., Sohn, Y. J., Standaert, F. G., and Hirshfeld, J. W., The nervous system as a site of action for digitalis and antiarrhythmic drugs, *Mt. Sinai Med. J.*, 37: 227-240, 1970.

1278. Levitt, M., Nixon, P. F., Pincus, J. H., and Bertino, J. R., Transport characteristics of folates in cerebrospinal fluid; a study utilizing doubly labeled 5-methyltetrahydrofolate and 5-formyl-tetrahydrofolate, *J. Clin. Invest.*, 50: 1301-1308, 1971.

1279. Levo, Y., The protective effect of hydantoin treatment on carcinogenesis, *Naunyn-Schmiedeberg's Arch. Pharmacol.*, 285: 29-30, 1974.

1280. Levy, J. A., Wittig, E. O., Ferraz, E. C. F., Scleroderma associated with continuous electro-muscular activity, *Arq. Neuro-Psiquiat.*, 23: 283-287, 1965.

1281. Levy, R. H., and Smith, G. H., Dosage regimens of antiarrhythmics, Part 1: Pharmacokinetic properties, *Amer. J. Hosp. Pharm.*, 30: 398-404, 1973.

1282. Lew, G. M., Increased hypothalamic norepinephrine in genetically hypertensive rats following administration of diphenylhydantoin, *Proc. Soc. Exp. Biol. Med.*, 148: 30-32, 1975.

1283. Lewin, E. and Bleck, V., The effect of diphenylhydantoin administration on sodium-potassium-activated ATPase in cortex, *Neurology*, 21: 647-651, 1971.

1284. Lewin, E. and Bleck, V., The effect of diphenylhydantoin administration on cortex potassium-activated phosphatase, *Neurology*, 21: 417-418, 1971.

1285. Lewin, E., Charles, G., and McCrimmon, A., Discharging cortical lesions produced by freezing—the effect of anticonvulsants on sodium-potassium-activated ATPase, sodium, and potassium in cortex, *Neurology*, 19: 565-569, 1969.

1286. Lien, E. J., and Gudauskas, G. A., Structure side-effect sorting of drugs—I: Extrapyramidal syndrome, *J. Pharm. Sci.*, 62: 645-647, 1973.

1287. Lifshitz, F. and Maclaren, N. K., Vitamin D-dependent rickets in institutionalized, mentally retarded children receiving long-term anticonvulsant therapy, *J. Pediat.*, 83: 612-620, 1973.

1288. Lightfoot, R. W., Jr., and Christian, C. L., Serum protein binding of thyroxine and diphenylhydantoin, *J. Clin. Endocr.*, 26: 305-308, 1966.

1289. Linde, L. M., Turner, S. W., and Awa, S., Present status and treatment of paroxysmal supraventricular tachycardia, *Pediatrics*, 50: 127-130, 1972.

1290. Lipicky, R. J., Gilbert, D. L., and Stillman, I. M., The effects of diphenylhydantoin on voltage-dependent currents of the squid axon, *Fed. Proc.*, 30: Abstract 65, 1971.

1291. Lipicky, R. J., Gilbert, D. L., and Stillman, I. M., Diphenylhydantoin inhibition of sodium conductance in squid giant axon, *Proc. Nat. Acad. Sci.*, 69: 1758-1760, 1972.

1292. Lisak, R. P., Lebeau, J., Tucker, S. H, and Rowland, L. P., Hyperkalemic periodic paralysis and cardiac arrhythmia, *Neurology*, 22: 810-815, 1972.

1293. Livingston, S., Abdominal pain as a manifestation of epilepsy (abdominal epilepsy) in children. *J. Pediat.*, 38: 687-695, 1951.

1294. Livingston, S. and Livingston, H. L., Diphenylhydantoin gingival hyperplasia, *Amer. J. Dis. Child.*, 117: 265-270, 1969.

1295. Livingston, S. and Pauli, L. L., Diphenylhydantoin and blood dyscrasias, *JAMA*, 320: 211-212, 1974.

1296. Livingston, S., Berman, W., and Pauli, L. L., Anticonvulsant drugs and vitamin D metabolism, *JAMA*, 224: 1634-1635, 1973.

1297. Livingston, S., Berman, W., and Pauli, L. L., Anticonvulsant drugs and vitamin D metabolism, *JAMA*, 226: 787, 1973.

1298. Livingston, S., Berman, W., and Pauli, L. L., Maternal epilepsy and abnormalities of the fetus and newborn, *Lancet*, 2: 1265, 1973.

1299. Lockman, L. A., Hunninghake, D. B., Krivit, W., and Desnick, R. J., Relief of pain of Fabry's disease by diphenylhydantoin, *Neurology*, 23: 871-875, 1973.

1300. Lockman, L. A., Krivit, W., and Desnick, R. J., Relief of the painful crises of Fabry's disease by diphenylhydantoin, *Neurology*, 21: 423, 1971.

1301. Loeser, J. D., Neuralgia, *Postgrad. Med.*, 53: 207-210, 1973.

1302. Lohrenz, J. G., Levy, L., and Davis, J. F., Schizophrenia or epilepsy? A problem in differential diagnosis, *Compr. Psychiat.*, 3: 54-62, 1962.

1303. Longshaw, R. N., Inhibition of hepatic drug metabolism, *Drug Intelligence and Clinical Pharmacy*, 7: 263-270, 1973.

1304. Looker, A. and Conners, C. K., Diphenylhydantoin in children with severe temper tantrums, *Arch. Gen. Psychiat.*, 23: 80-89, 1970.

1305. Loong, S. C. and Ong, Y. Y., Paroxysmal kinesigenic choreoathetosis, *J. Neurol. Neurosurg. Psychiat.*, 36: 921-924, 1973.

1306. Lotti, V. J., Torchiana, M. L., and Porter, C. C., Investigations on the action and mechanism of action of diphenylhydantoin as an antagonist of tetrabenazine and reserpine, *Arch. Int. Pharmacodyn.*, 203: 107-116, 1973.

1307. Lotto, A., Sanna, G. P., Bossi, M., and Lomanto, B., New therapeutic aspects of ventricular arrhythmias, *Cardiol. Prat.*, 22: 1-15, 1971.

1308. Louis, S., Kutt, H. and McDowell, F., Modification of experimental seizures and anticonvulsant efficacy by peripheral stimulation, *Neurology*, 21: 329-336, 1971.

1309. Lovell, R. R. H., Mitchell. M. E., Prineas, R. J., Sloman, J. G., Vajda, F. J., Pitt, A., Habersberger, P., Rosenbaum, M., Nestel, P. J., Goodman, H. T., and Sowry, G. S. C., Phenytoin after recovery from myocardial infarction—controlled trial in 568 patients, *Lancet*, 1055-1057, 1971.

1310. Lowe, C. R., Congenital malformations among infants born to epileptic women, *Lancet*, 9-10, 1973. (*cf.* Marsh and Fraser, *Teratology*, 7: A-23, 1973.)

1311. Lown, B., Temte, J. V. and Arter, W. J., Ventricular tachyarrhythmias—clinical aspects, *Circulation*, 47: 1364-1381, 1973.

1312. Lucchesi, B. R., The pharmacology and clinical uses of antiarrhythmic drugs, *U. Michigan Med. Cent. J.*, 37: 61-73, 1971.

1313. Ludtke, A. H., Autenrieth, G., and Dankert, D., On the effects of diphenylhydantoin, potassium-magnesium-asparaginate, insulin and female sex hormones on the hypothermic fibrillation threshold of the guinea-pig heart, *Arzneimittelforschung*, 20: 1554-1557, 1970.

1314. Lund, L., Berlin, A., and Lunde, K. M., Plasma protein binding of diphenylhydantoin in patients with epilepsy, *Clin. Pharmacol. Ther.*, 13: 196-200, 1972.

1315. Lunde, K. M., Plasma protein binding of diphenylhydantoin in man, *Acta Pharmacol.*, 29: 152-155, 1971.

1316. Lunde, K. M., Rane, A., Yaffe, S. J., Lund, L., and Sjoqvist, F., Plasma protein binding of diphenylhydantoin in man, *Clin. Pharmacol. Ther.*, 11: 846-855, 1970.

1317. Lund, L., Lunde, P. K., Rane, A., Borga, O. and Sjoqvist, F., Plasma protein binding, plasma concentrations, and effects of diphenylhydantoin in man, *Ann. N.Y. Acad. Sci.*, 179: 723-728, 1972.

1318. Lussier-Lazaroff, J. and Fletcher, B. D., Rickets and anticonvulsant therapy in children: a roentgenologic investigation, *J. Canad. Assn. Radiol.*, 22: 144-147, 1971.

1319. Lutz, E. G., Add vitamins to DPH, urges doctor, *National Spokesman*, 6: 7, 1973.

1320. Lutz, E. G., On vitamins and anticonvulsants, *Medical World News*, 3, 1973.

1321. Mace, J., and Schneider, S., Diphenylhydantoin and rickets, *Lancet*, 1119, 1973.

1322. MacGee, J., The rapid determination of diphenylhydantoin in blood plasma by gas-liquid chromatography, *Med. Res. Lab., V.A. Hosp. and Dept. Bio. Chem. and Exp. Med.*, Cincinnati, Ohio, 1970.

1323. MacKinney, A. A. and Booker, H. E., Diphenylhydantoin effects on human lymphocytes *in vitro* and *in vivo*, *Arch. Intern. Med.*, 129: 988-992, 1972.

1324. MacKinney, A. A. and Vyas, R., Diphenylhydantoin-induced inhibition of nucleic acid synthesis in cultured human lymphocytes, *Proc. Soc. Exp. Biol. Med.*, 141: 89-92, 1972.

1325. Mackinney, A. A. and Vyas, R., The assay of diphenylhydantoin effects on growing human lymphocytes, *J. Pharmacol. Exp. Ther.*, 186: 37-43, 1973.

1326. Maclaren, N. and Lifshitz, F., Vitamin D-dependency rickets in institutionalized, mentally retarded children on long term anticonvulsant therapy. II. The response to 25-hydroxycholecalciferol and to vitamin D, *Pediat. Res.*, 7: 914-922, 1973.

1327. Madsen, S. N., Hansen, J. M. and Deckert, T., Intravenous glucose tolerance during treatment with phenytoin, *Acta Neurol. Scand.*, 50: 257-260, 1974.

1328. Maletzky, B. M. and Klotter, J., Episodic dyscontrol: A controlled replication, *Dis. Nerv. Syst.*, 35: 175-179, 1974.

1329. Maletzky, B. M., Treatable violence, *Med. Times*, 100: 74-79, 1972.

1330. Malherbe, C., Burrill, K. C., Levin, S. R., Karam, J. H., and Forsham, P. H., Effect of diphenylhydantoin on insulin secretion in man, *New Eng. J. Med.*, 286: 339-342, 1972.

1331. Markkanen, T., Himanen, P., Pajula, R. L., and Molnar, G., Binding of folic acid to serum proteins, *Acta Haemat.*, 50: 284-292, 1973.

1332. Markkanen, T., Peltola, O., Himanen, P. and Riekkinen, P., Metabolites of diphenylhydantoin in human plasma inhibits the pentose phosphate pathway of leukocytes, *Pharmacology*, 6: 216-222, 1971.

1333. Martin, C. M., Reliability in product performance in an innovative environment, The Economics of Drug Innovation, 63-82, Cooper, J. D., Ed., *The Proceedings of the First Seminar of Economics of Pharmaceutical Innovation*, 1969.

1334. Martin, W. and Rickers, J., Cholestatic hepatosis induced by diphenylhydantoin. Case report and review of literature, *Wien. Klin. Wschr.*, 84: 41-45, 1972.

1335. Mason, D. T., Amsterdam, E. A., Massumi, R. A., and Zelis, R., Recent advances in antiarrhythmic drugs. clinical pharmacology and therapeutics, *The Acute Cardiac Emergency—Diagnosis and Management*, 95-123, Eliot, R. S., Ed., Futura Publishing, Mount Kisco, New York, 1972.

1336. Mason, D. T., DeMaria, A. N., Amsterdam, E. A., Zelis, R., and Massumi, R. A., Antiarrhythmic agents. II: Therapeutic consideration, *Drugs*, 5: 292-317, 1973.

1337. Mason, D. T., DeMaria, A. N., Amsterdam, E. A., Zelis, R., and Massumi, R. A., Antiarrhythmic agents. I: Mechanisms of action and clinical pharmacology, *Drugs*, 5: 261-291, 1973.

1338. Mason, D. T., Spann, J. F. Jr., Zelis, R., and Amsterdam, E. A., Evolving concepts in the clinical pharmacology and therapeutic uses of the antiarrhythmic drugs, *Cardiovascular Therapy, The Art and the Science*, 122-137, Russek, H. I. and Zohman, B. L., Eds., The Williams & Wilkins Co, Baltimore, 1971.

1339. Mathur, K. S., Wahal, P. K., Seth, H. C. and Hazra, D. K., Diphenylhydantoin sodium in cardiac arrhythmias, *J. Indian Med. Assoc.*, 57: 256-258, 1971.

1340. Matsuzaki, M. and Killam, K. F., Alterations in conditional behavioral and electrographic responses to interrupted visual stimuli following repeated doses of diphenylhydantoin, *Fed. Proc.*, 30: Abstract 483, 1971.

1341. Mattes, L. M., Spritzer, R. C., Nevins, M. A., Weisenseel, A. C., Donoso, E., and Friedburg, C. K., The cardiovascular effects of diphenylhydantoin in patients with cardiac pacemakers, *Circulation*, 37-38 (Suppl. 6): 135, 1968.

1342. Matthews, W. B., Tonic seizures in disseminated sclerosis, *Brain*, 81: 193-206, 1958.

1343. Matthews, W. D. and Connor, J. D., Effects of diphenylhydantoin on interhippocampal evoked responses, *Pharmacologist*, 16: 228, 1974.

1344. Mattson, R. H., Gallagher, B. B., Reynolds, E. H., and Glass, D., Folate therapy in epilepsy, *Arch. Neurol.*, 29: 78-81, 1973.

1345. McAllister, R. G., Jr., The possible role of antiarrhythmic drugs in the prevention of sudden death, *Heart and Lung*, 2: 857-861, 1973.

1346. McCabe, B. F., Chronic burning tongue syndrome, *Ann.*

Otol. Rhinol. Laryngol., 83: 264, 1974.

1347. McCabe, W. S., and Habovick, J. A., Thorazine as an epileptogenic agent, *Amer. J. Psychiat.*, 120: 595-597, 1963.

1348. McIlvanie, S. K., Phenytoin and depression of immunological function, *Lancet*, 323, February, 1972.

1349. McQueen, E. G., Owen, D., and Ferry, D. G., Effect of phenytoin and other drugs in reducing serum DDT levels, *New Zeal. Med. J.*, 75: 208-211, 1972.

1350. Meadow, S. R., Anticonvulsant drugs and congenital abnormalities, *Lancet*, 2: 1296, 1968.

1351. Meikle, W., Jubiz, W., West, C. D., and Tyler, F. H., Effect of diphenylhydantoin (Dilantin) on the metyrapone test demonstrated by a new assay for plasma metyrapone, *Clin. Res.*, 17: 107, 1969.

1352. Melikian, V., Eddy, J. D., and Paton, A., The stimulant effect of drugs on indocyanine green clearance by the liver, *Gut*, 13: 755-758, 1972.

1353. Mendelson, J. H., Biologic concomitants of alcoholism, *New Eng. J. Med.*, 283: 24-32, 1970.

1354. Mennear, J. H. and Gossel, T. A., Inhibitory effect of diphenylhydantoin on the diabetogenic action of alloxan in the mouse, *Diabetes*, 21: 80-83, 1972.

1355. Mennear, J. H., and Gossel, T. A., Interactions between diphenylhydantoin and tolbutamide in mice, *Toxic. Appl. Pharmacol.*, 24: 309-316, 1973.

1356. Meyer, J. G., The teratological effects of anticonvulsants and the effects on pregnancy and birth, *Europ. Neurol.* 10: 179-190, 1973.

1357. Meyer, J. S., Binns, P. M., Ericsson, A. D., and Vulpe, M., Sphenopalatine ganglionectomy for cluster headache, *Arch. Otolaryng.*, 92: 475-484, 1970.

1358. Michell, A. R., The effect of diphenylhydantoin on sodium appetite in rats, *J. Physiol.*, 237: 53-55, 1973.

1359. Mick, B. A., Diphenylhydantoin and intermittent edema, *JAMA*, 225: 1533, 1973.

1360. Miley, C. E. and Forster, F. M., Paroxysmal signs and symptoms in multiple sclerosis, *Neurology*, 24: 458-461, 1974.

1361. Millichap, J. G., Clinical efficacy and usage of anticonvulsants, *Chemical Modulation of Brain Function*, 199-205, Sabelli, H. C., Ed., Raven Press, New York, 1973.

1362. Millichap, J. G., Drugs in management of minimal brain dysfunction, *Ann. N.Y. Acad. Sci.*, 205: 321-334, 1973.

1363. Millichap, J. G., Efficacy, therapeutic regimens of drugs to control hyperkinesis in children with minimal brain dysfunction reported from trials, *Drug Res. Rep.*, 15: S5-S11, 1972.

1364. Mirkin, B. L. and Wright, F., Drug interactions: effect of methylphenidate on the disposition of diphenylhydantoin in man, *Neurology*, 21: 1123-1128, 1971.

1365. Mirkin, B. L., Diphenylhydantoin: placental transport, fetal localization, neonatal metabolism, and possible teratogenic effects, *J. Pediat.*, 78: 329-337, 1971.

1366. Mirkin, B. L., Maternal and fetal distribution of drugs in pregnancy, *Clin. Pharmacol. Ther.*, 14: 643-647, 1973.

1367. Mirkin, B. L., Placental transfer and neonatal elimination of diphenylhydantoin, *Amer. J. Obstet. Gynec.*, 109: 930-933, 1971.

1368. Mittler, J. C. and Glick, S. M., Radioimmunoassayable oxytocin release from isolated neural lobes: responses to ions and drugs, *Abstracts Fourth Int. Cong. Endocr.*, 47, June, 1972.

1369. Mladinich, E. K., Diphenylhydantoin in the Wallenberg syndrome, *JAMA*, 230: 372-373, 1974.

1370. Monson, R. R., Rosenberg, L., Hartz, S. C., Shapiro, S., Heinonen, O. P., and Slone, D., Diphenylhydantoin and selected congenital malformations, *New Eng. J. Med.*, 289: 1050-1052, 1973.

1371. Morgan, R. J., Scleroderma: treatment with diphenylhydantoin, *Cutis*, 8: 278-282, 1971.

1372. Moss, A. J. and Patton, R. D., Diphenylhydantoin, comparison of antiarrhythmic agents, and management of refractory arrhythmias, *Antiarrhythmic Agents*, 52-58, 101-115, Charles C Thomas, Springfield, Ill., 1973.

1373. Moss, G. and Stein, A. A., Cerebral etiology of the shock lung syndrome: protective effect of diphenylhydantoin, *Personal Communication*, 1972.

1374. Moss, G., Shock, cerebral hypoxia and pulmonary vascular control: the centri-neurogenic etiology of the "respiratory distress syndrome", *Bull. N.Y. Acad. Med.*, 49: 689, 1973.

1375. Mountain, K. R., Hirsh, J., and Gallus, A. S., Neonatal coagulation defect due to anticonvulsant drug treatment in pregnancy, *Lancet*, 1: 265-268, 1970. (*cf.* Davies, *Lancet*, 1: 413, 1970.)

1376. Mouravieff-Lesuisse, F. and Giurgea, C., Influence of electro-convulsive shock on the fixation of an experience at spinal level, *Arch. Int. Pharmacodyn.*, 183: 410-411, 1970.

1377. Nabwangu, J. F., Head injury, *E. Afr. Med. J.*, 49: 624-629, 1972.

1378. Narisawa, K., Honda, Y., and Arakawa, T., Effect of diphenylhydantoin administration on single carbon metabolism in folate deficient rats, *Tohoku, J. Exp. Med.*, 110: 359-365, 1973.

1379. Nasello, A. G., Montini, E. E., and Astrada, C. A., Effect of veratrine, tetraethylammonium and diphenylhydantoin on potassium release by rat hippocampus, *Pharmacology*, 7: 89-95, 1972.

1380. Negri, S., An atypical case of Steinert's disease (myotonia dystrophica) in infancy, *Confin. Neurol.*, 33: 323-333, 1971.

1381. Neville, B. G. R., The origin of infantile spasms: evidence from a case of hydranencephaly, *Epilepsy Abstracts*, 6: 179, 1973.

1382. Newtown, R., Amitriptyline and imipramine poisoning in children, *Brit. Med. J.*, 2: 176, 1974.

1383. Nielsen, T. and Cotman, C., The binding of diphenylhydantoin to brain and subcellular fractions, *Europ. J. Pharmacol.*, 14: 344-350, 1971.

1384. Niswander, J. D. and Wertelecki, W., Congenital malformation among offspring of epileptic women, *Lancet*, 1062, May, 1973.

1385. Noach, E. L., VanRees, H. and DeWolff, F. A., Effects of Diphenylhydantoin (DPH) on absorptive processes in the rat jejunum, *Archives Internationales de Pharmacodynamie et de Therapie*, 206: 392-393, 1973.

1386. Norris, J. W. and Pratt, R. F., A controlled study of folic acid in epilepsy, *Neurology*, 21: 659-664, 1971.

1387. Nuki, K. and Cooper, S. H., The role of inflammation in the pathogenesis of gingival enlargement during the administration of diphenylhydantoin sodium in cats, *J. Periodont. Res.*, 7: 102-110, 1972.

1388. O'Leary, J. A., Feldman, M., and Switzer, H. E., Phenobarbital-Dilantin treatment of the intrauterine patient, *J. Reprod. Med.*, 5: 81-83, 1970.

1389. O'Malley, W. E., Denckla, M. B., and O'Doherty, D. S., Oral absorption of diphenylhydantoin as measured by gas liquid chromatography, *Epilepsy Abstracts*, 3: 230, 1970.

1390. O'Reilly, M. V. and MacDonald, R. T., Efficacy of phenytoin in the management of ventricular arrhythmias induced by hypokalaemia, *Brit. Heart J.*, 35: 631-634, 1973.

1391. Oates, R. K. and Tonge, R. E., Phenytoin and the pseudolymphoma syndrome, *Med. J. Aust.*, 371-373, 1971.

1392. Obbens, E. A., Experimental epilepsy induced by folate derivatives, *Epilepsy Abstracts*, 6: 221-222, 1973.

1393. Odar-Cederlof, I. and Borga, O., Kinetics of diphenylhydantoin in uraemic patients: consequences of decreased plasma protein binding, *Europ. J. Clin. Pharmacol.*, 7: 31-37, 1974.

1394. Oge, V., Drug therapy in alcoholism, *Ill. Med. J.*, 139: 606-610, 1971.

1395. Olds, M. E., Comparative effects of amphetamine, scopolamine, chlordiazepoxide, and diphenylhydantoin on operant and extinction behavior with brain stimulation and food reward, *Neuropharmacology*, 9: 519-532, 1970.

1396. Osorio, C., Jackson, D. J., Gartside, J. M., and Goolden, A. W. G., Effect of carbon dioxide and diphenylhydantoin on the partition of triiodothyronine labelled with iodine-131 between the red cells and plasma proteins, *Nature*, 196: 275-276, 1962.

1397. Overall, J. E., Brown, D., Williams, J. D., and Neill, L. T., Drug treatment of anxiety and depression in detoxified alcoholic patients, *Arch. Gen. Psychiat.*, 29: 218-221, 1973.

1398. Pakszys, W. and Domzal, T., Ceruloplasmin stimulation test, *Epilepsy Abstracts*, 7: 107, 1974.

1399. Pakszys, W., Phenytoin, *Epilepsy Abstracts*, 6: 236, 1973.

1400. Parisi, A. F. and Raines, A., Diphenylhydantoin suppression of repetitive activity generated in nerve endings, *Fed. Proc.*, Abstract 22: 390, 1963.

1401. Pashayan, H., Pruzansky, D., and Pruzansky, S., Are anticonvulsants teratogenic?, *Lancet*, 702-703, 1971.

1402. Patton, R. D., and Helfant, R. H., Atrial flutter with one-to-one conduction, *Dis. Chest*, 55: 250-251, 1969.

1403. Payen, J., A study of changes in the gum during treatment with diphenylhydantoin sodium, *Rev. Odonto-Stomatol.*, 19: 47-53, 1972.

1404. Pelkonen, R. and Taskinen, M. R., Effect of diphenylhydantoin on plasma-insulin in insulinoma, *Lancet*, 604-605, 1973.

1405. Pento, J. T., Glick, S. M., and Kagan, A., Diphenylhydantoin inhibition of glucagon- and calcium-stimulated calcitonin release, *Fed. Proc.*, Abstract 31: 251, 1972.

1406. Pento, J. T., Glick, S. M., and Kagan, A., Diphenylhydantoin inhibition of calcitonin secretion in the pig. *Endocrinology*, 92: 330-333, 1973.

1407. Penttila, O., Neuvonen, P. J., Aho, K. and Lehtovaara, R., Interaction between doxycycline and some antiepileptic drugs, *Brit. Med. J.*, 2: 470-472, 1974.

1408. Persijn, G. G. and Van Zeben, W., Generalized lymphadenopathy caused by phenytoin in a six-year-old child, *Epilepsy Abstracts*, 6: 236, 1973.

1409. Peter, J. B., A $(Na^+ + K^+)$ ATPase of sarcolemma from skeletal muscle, *Biochem. Biophys. Res. Commun.*, 40: 1362-1367, 1970.

1410. Peters, B. H. and Samaan, N. A., Hyperglycemia with relative hypoinsulinemia in diphenylhydantoin toxicity, *New Eng. J. Med.*, 281: 91-92, 1969.

1411. Petroski, D. and Patel, A. N., Diphenylhydantoin for intractable hiccups, *Lancet*, 1: 739, 1974.

1412. Pezcon, J. D., and Grant, W. M., Sedatives, stimulants, and intraocular pressure in glaucoma, *Arch. Ophthal.*, 72: 177-188, 1964.

1413. Pezzimenti, J. F. and Hahn, A. L., Anicteric hepatitis induced by diphenylhydantoin, *Arch. Intern. Med.*, 125: 118-120, 1970.

1414. Phillips, J. R. and Eldridge. F. L., Respiratory myoclonus (Leeuwenhoek's disease), *New Eng. J. Med.*, 289: 1390-1395. 1973.

1415. Pinto, A., Simopoulos, A. M., Uhlenhuth, E. H. and De Rosa, E. R., Responses of chronic schizophrenic females to a combination of diphenylhydantoin and neuroleptics: a double-blind study, *Comprehensive Psychiatry*, 16(6): 529-536, 1975.

1416. Pincus, J. H. and Lee, S. H., Diphenylhydantoin and norepinephrine release, *Neurology*, 22: 410, 1972.

1417. Pincus, J. H., and Lee, S. H., Diphenylhydantoin and calcium in relation to norepinephrine release from brain slices, *Arch. Neurol.*, 29: 239-244, 1973.

1418. Pincus, J. H., Diphenylhydantoin and ion flux in lobster nerve, *Arch. Neurol.*, 26: 4-10, 1972.

1419. Pincus, J. H., Grove, I., Marino. B. B. and Glaser, G. E., Studies on the mechanism of action of diphenylhydantoin, *Presented at the International Soc. Neurochem.*, September, 1969.

1420. Pinkhas, J., Ben-Bassat, M., and DeVries, A., Death in anticonvulsant-induced megaloblastic anemia, *JAMA*, 224: 246, 1973.

1421. Podos, S. M., Becker, B., Beaty, C., and Cooper, D. G., Diphenylhydantoin and cortisol metabolism in glaucoma, *Amer*

J. Ophthal., 74: 498 500, 1972.

1422. Podos, S. M., Glaucoma, *Invest. Ophthal.*, 12: 3-4, 1973.

1423. Poley, J. R., and Bhatia, M., Recurrent abdominal pain: recurrent controversy, *Pediatrics*, 52: 144-145, 1973.

1424. Pollen, R. H., Cat-scratch encephalitis, *Neurology*, 18: 1031-1033, 1968.

1425. Porciello, P. I. and Zanini, S., Diphenylhydantoin: antiarrhythmic drug, *Fracastoro*, 64: 114-135, 1971.

1426. Porciello, P. I., Zanini, S., and Poppi, A., Comparative considerations on two modern antiarrhythmic drugs: lidocaine and diphenylhydantoin, *G. Ital. Cardiol.* 2: 579-583, 1972.

1427. Poschel, B. P. H., A simple and specific screen for benzodiazepine-like drugs, *Psychoparmacologia*, 19: 193-198, 1971.

1428. Postlethwaite, R. J. and Price, D. A., Amitriptyline and imipramine poisoning in children, *Brit. Med. J.*, 2: 504, 1974.

1429. Preston, T. A., Yates, J. D., and Brymer, J. F., Three therapeutic approaches in tachycardia, *Geriatrics*, 28: 110-116, 1973.

1430. Price, D. A. and Postlethwaite, J. R., Amitriptyline and imipramine poisoning in children, *Brit. Med. J.*, 1: 575, 1974.

1431. Pryles, C. V., Livingston, S. and Ford, F. R., Familial paroxysmal choreoathetosis of Mount and Reback, *Pediatrics*, 9: 44-47, 1952.

1432. Puri, P. S., The effect of diphenylhydantoin sodium (Dilantin) on myocardial contractility and hemodynamics, *Amer. Heart J.*, 82: 62-68, 1971.

1433. Puro, D. G. and Woodward, D. J., Effects of diphenylhydantoin on activity of rat cerebellar Purkinje cells, *Neuropharmacology*, 12: 433-440, 1973.

1434. Quiret, J. C., Bens, J. L., Duboisset, M., Lesbre, P. and Bernasconi, P., Diphenylhydantoin injectable in cardiology, *Arch. Mal. Coeur.*, 67: 87-96, 1974.

1435. Raines, A. and Standaert, F. G., Effects of anticonvulsant drugs on nerve terminals, *Epilepsia*, 10: 211-227, 1969.

1436. Raines, A., Levitt, B., Standaert, F. G. and Sohn, Y. J., The influence of sympathetic nervous activity on the antiarrhythmic efficacy of diphenylhydantoin, *Europ. J. Pharmacol.*, 11: 293-297, 1970.

1437. Raines, A., Sohn, Y. J., and Levitt, B., Spinal excitatory and depressant effects of sodium diphenylthiohydantoinate, *J. Pharmacol. Exp. Ther.*, 177: 350-359, 1971.

1438. Raines, A., Effects of diphenylhydantoin on post-tetanic alterations in the terminals of dorsal root fibers and motor nerves, *Georgetown University Doctoral Thesis*, June, 1965.

1439. Ralston, A. J., Snaith, R. P., and Hinley, J. B., Effects of folic acid on fit-frequency and behaviour in epileptics on anticonvulsants, *Lancet* 1: 867-868, 1970.

1440. Ramdohr, Von B., Schuren, K. P., Dennert, J., Macha, H.-N. and Schroder, A., Influence of diphenylhydantoin on hemodynamics in recent myocardial infarct., *Verhandlungen der Deutschen Gesellschaft fur Kreislaufforschung*, 35: 444-50, 1969.

1441. Rane, A., Garle, M., Borga, O., Sjoqvist, F., Plasma disappearance of transplacentally transferred diphenylhydantoin in the newborn studied with mass fragmentography, *Clin. Pharmacol. Ther.* 15: 39-45, 1974.

1442. Rane, A., Lunde, P. K. M., Jalling, B., et al., Plasma protein binding of diphenylhydantoin in normal and hyperbilirubinemic infants, *Epilepsy Abstracts*, 4: 223, 1971.

1443. Rane, A., Urinary excretion of diphenylhydantoin metabolites in newborn infants, *J. Pediat.*, 85: 543-545, 1974.

1444. Raskin, N. H., Levinson, S. A., Pickett, J. B., Hoffman, P. M., and Fields, H. L., Postsympathectomy neuralgia, *Amer. J. Surg.*, 128: 75-78, 1974.

1445. Raskovic, J., Phenomenological aspects of the psychotic epileptic state in terms of therapeutic argument, *Neuropsihialrya*, 20: 161-166, 1972.

1446. Ray, A. K., and Rao, D. B., Calcium metabolism in elderly epileptic patients during anticonvulsant therapy, *Epilepsy Abstracts*, 7: 210, 1974.

1447. Raz, S., Zeigler, M., and Caine, M., The effect of diphenylhydantoin on the urethra, *Invest. Urol.*, 10: 293-294, 1973.

1448. Reidenberg, M. M., Odar-Cederlof, I., Von Bahr, C., Borga, O., and Sjoqvist, F., Protein binding of diphenylhydantoin and desmethylimipramine in plasma from patients with poor renal function, *New Eng. J. Med.*, 285: 264-267, 1971.

1449. Reimann, H. A., Abdominal epilepsy and migraine, *JAMA*, 224: 128, 1973.

1450. Reimann, R., Lemmel, W., and Theisen, K., Efficacy and risks of diphenylhydantoin in cardiac arrhythmias, *Munchen Med. Wschr.*, 113: 893-899, 1971.

1451. Reizenstein, P. and Lund, L., Effect of anticonvulsive drugs on folate absorption and the cerebrospinal folate pump, *Epilepsy Abstracts*, 7: 86, 1974.

1452. Remmer, H., Induction of drug metabolizing enzyme system in the liver, *Eur. J. Clin. Pharmacol.*, 5: 116-136, 1972.

1453. Resnekov, L., Drug therapy before and after the electroversion of cardiac dysrhythmias, *Progr. Cardiovasc. Dis.*, 16: 531-538, 1974.

1454. Rettura, G., Stamford, W. and Seifter, E., Reversal of cardiac calcification by diphenylhydantoin, *Paper presented at N.E. Regional Meeting of the American Chemical Society*, Oct. 1973.

1455. Reynolds, E. H., Anticonvulsant drugs, folic acid metabolism and schizophrenia-like psychoses in epilepsy, *Psychische Storungen bei Epilepsie*, H. Penin, Ed., F. K. Schattauer Verlag, Stuttgart-New York, 1973.

1456. Reynolds, E. H., Anticonvulsant drugs, folic acid metabolism, fit frequency and psychiatric illness, *Psychiat. Neurol. Neurochir.*, 74: 167-174, 1971.

1457. Reynolds, E. H., Anticonvulsants, folic acid and epilepsy, *Lancet*, 1376-1378, June, 1973.

1458. Reynolds, E. H., Chanarin, I., Milner, G. and Matthews, D. M., Anticonvulsant therapy, folic acid and vitamin B[12] metabolism and mental symptoms, *Epilepsia*, 7: 261-270, 1966.

1459. Reynolds, E. H., Mattson, R., and Gallagher, B., Relationships between serum and cerebrospinal fluid anticonvulsant drug and folic acid concentrations in epileptic patients, *Neurology*, 22: 841-844, 1972.

1460. Reynolds, E. H., Streiff, R. R., Wilder, B. J., and Hammer, R. H., Diphenylhydantoin hematologic aspects of toxicity, *Antiepileptic Drugs*, 247-266, Woodbury, D. M., Penry, J. K., and Schmidt, R. P., Eds., Raven Press, New York, 1972. (cf. Bottomley, et al., *J. Mich. Dent. Ass.*, 53: 256, 1971 and Kolodzieczak and Prazanowski, *Epilepsy Abstracts*, 5: 149, 1972.)

1461. Reynolds, J. W. and Mirkin, B. L., Urinary corticosteroid and diphenylhydantoin metabolite patterns in neonates exposed to anticonvulsant drugs in utero, *JAMA*, 227. 577, 1974.

1462. Rhee, R. S., Margolin, M., and Pellock, J., Palatal myoclonus and diphenylhydantoin therapy, *New Eng. J. Med.*, 290: 1088-1089, 1974.

1463. Richens, A. and Houghton, G. W., Phenytoin intoxication caused by sulthiame, *Lancet*, 1442-1443, 1973.

1464. Richens, A. and Rowe, D. J. F., Disturbance of calcium metabolism by anticonvulsant drugs, *Brit. Med. J.*, 4: 73-76, 1970.

1465. Richens, A. and Rowe. D. J. F., Anticonvulsant hypocalcemia, *Epilepsy Abstracts*, 5: 224, 1972.

1466. Riddell, D. and Leonard, B. E., Some properties of a coma producing material obtained from mammalian brain, *Neuropharmacology*, 9: 283-299, 1970.

1467. Riehl, J. L. and McIntyre, H. B., Acute effects of Dilantin on the EEG of epileptic patients: a quantitative study, *Electroenceph. Clin. Neurophysiol.*, 28: 94, 1970.

1468. Rifkind, A. B., Gillette, P. N., Song, C. S., and Kappas, A., Drug stimulation of δ-Aminolevulinic acid synthetase and cytochrome P-450 *in vivo* in chick embryo liver, *J. Pharmacol. Exp. Ther.*, 185: 214-225, 1973.

1469. Riker, W. F., The pharmacology of the neostigmine-like facilitatory drug effect at the mammalian neuromuscular junction, *Jap. J. Pharmacol.*, 22: 1, 1972.

1470. Rish, B. L. and Caveness, W. F., Relation of prophylactic medication to the occurrence of early seizures following craniocerebral trauma, *J. Neurosurg.*, 38: 155-158, 1973.

1471. Rizzo, M., Morselli, P. L. and Garattini, S., Further observations on the interactions between phenobarbital and diphenylhydantoin during chronic treatment in the rat, *Biochem. Pharmacol.*, 21: 449-454, 1972.

1472. Robbins, M. M., Aplastic anemia secondary to anticonvulsants, *Amer. J. Dis. Child.*, 104: 64-74, 1962.

1473. Roberts, E., An hypothesis suggesting that there is a defect in the GABA system in schizophrenia, *Neurosciences Research Program Bulletin*, 10: 468-482, 1972.

1474. Roberts, J., The effect of diphenylhydantoin on the response to accelerator nerve stimulation, *Proc. Soc. Exp. Biol. Med.*, 134: 274-280, 1970.

1475. Robineaux, R., Lorans, G., and Beaure D'Augeres, C., Action of diphenylhydantoin on the growth and respiration of cell in culture, *Rev. Europ. Etudes Clin. Biol.*, 15: 1066-1071, 1970.

1475. Robineaux, R., Lorans, G., and Beaure D'Augeres, C., Action of diphenylhydantoin on the growth and respiration of cell in culture, *Rev. Europ. Etudes Clin. Biol.*, 15: 1066-1071, 1970.

1476. Rockliff, B. W., and Davis, E. H., Controlled sequential trials of carbamazepine in trigeminal neuralgia, *Arch. Neurol.*, 15: 129-136, 1966.

1478. Roman, I. C. and Caratzali, A., Effects of anticonvulsant drugs on chromosomes, *Brit. Med. J.*, 234, 1971.

1479. Romero, E., Maranon, A. and Bobillo, E. R., Antithyroid action of hydantoin derivatives, *Rev. Iber. Endocr.*, 101: 363-375, 1970.

1480. Rose, L. I., Williams, G. H., Jagger, P. I., Lauler, D. P., and Thorn, G. W., The paradoxical dexamethasone response phenomenon, *Metabolism*, 18: 369-375, 1969.

1481. Rosenthal, J. E. and Cohen, L. S., Therapeutic predicament—the unresponsive PVC, *Geriatrics*, 28: 88-92, 1973.

1482. Ross, G. S., A technique to study pain in monkeys; effect of drugs and anatomic lesions, *Henry Ford Hosp. Symposium on Pain*, Chap. 8, 100-101, Knighton, R. S. and Dumke, P. R., Eds., Little, Brown and Co., Boston, 1966.

1483. Ross, G. S., Effect of diphenylhydantoin on experimental pain in the monkey, *Neurology*, 15: 275, 1965.

1484. Ross, L. M., Diphenylhydantoin (DPH) induced cleft palate, *Teratology*, 7: A-26, June, 1973.

1485. Rovin, S., Sabes, W. R., Eversole, L. R., and Gordon, H. A., Dilantin as a caries retarder, *J. Dent. Res.*, 52: 267, 1973.

1486. Rubins, S., Lozano, J., Carrasco, H., Lang, T. W., and Corday, E., Tachyarrhythmias: Differential diagnosis and therapy after acute myocardial infarction, *Geriatrics*, 27: 123-133, 1972.

1487. Rudner, E. J., Diphenylhydantoin therapy, *Arch. Derm.*, 102: 561, 1970.

1488. Rumack, B. H., Wolfe, R. R. and Gilfrich, H., Phenytoin (diphenylhydantoin) treatment of massive digoxin overdose, *Brit. Heart J.*, 36: 405-408, 1974.

1489. Rundle, A. T. and Sudell, B., Leucine aminopeptidase isoenzyme changes after treatment with anticonvulsant drugs, *Clin. Chim. Acta*, 44: 377-384, 1973.

1490. Rushton, J. G., Medical treatment of trigeminal neuralgia, *Med. Clin. N. Amer.*, 52: 797-800, 1968.

1491. Ruskin, H. M., Theraputic Dilantin levels, *New Eng. J. Med.*, 284: 792, 1971.

1492. Rutkowski, M. M., Cohen, S. N., and Doyle, E. F., Drug therapy of heart disease in pediatric patients. II. The treatment of congestive heart failure in infants and children with digitalis preparations, *Amer. Heart J.*, 86: 270-275, 1973.

1493. Rutkowski, M. M., Doyle, E. F. and Cohen, S. N., Drug therapy of heart disease in pediatric patients III. The therapeutic challenge of supraventricular tachyarrhythmias in infants and children, *Amer. Heart J.*, 86: 562-568, 1973.

1494. Rutledge, R., Sohn, Y. J., and Sardinas, A., Interaction of diphenylhydantoin and succinylcholine at the neuromuscular junction, *Pharmacologist*, 13: 265, 1971.

1495. Saad, S. F., El Masry, A. M., and Scott, P. M., Influence of certain anticonvulsants on the concentration of 8-aminobutyric acid in the cerebral hemispheres of mice, *Communications in Behav. Biol.*, 9: February, 1972.

1496. Sabih, K. and Sabih, K., Combined GLC and high-resolution mass spectroscopic analysis of diphenylhydantoin, *J. Pharm. Sci.*, 60: 1216-1220, 1971.

1497. Sampliner, R., Diphenylhydantoin control of alcohol withdrawal seizures, *JAMA*, 230: 1430-1432, 1974.

1498. Sampson, D., Harasymiv, I. and Hensley, W. J., Gas chromatographic assay of underivatized 5,5-diphenylhydantoin (Dilantin) in plasma extracts, *Clin. Chem.*, 17: 382-385, 1971.

1499. Sano, T., Suzuki, F., Sato, S., and Iida, Y., Mode of action of new anti-arrhythmic agents, *Jap. Heart J.*, 9: 161-168, 1968.

1500. Sataline, L., Cardiac standstill simulating epileptic seizures, *JAMA*, 225: 747, 1973.

1501. Satoyoshi, E. and Yamada, K., Recurrent muscle spasms of central origin. A report of two cases, *Arch. Neurol.*, 16: 254-264, 1967.

1502. Satoyoshi, E., Recurrent muscle spasms of central origin, *Trans. Amer. Neurol. Assoc.*, 92: 153-157, 1967.

1503. Saunders, B. A. and Jenkins, L. C., Cardiac arrhythmias of central nervous system origin: possible mechanism and suppression, *Canad. Anaesth. Soc. J.*, 20: 617-628, 1973.

1504. Savini, E. C., Poitevin, R. and Poitevin, J., New treatment of periodontolysis, *Rev. Franc. Odontostomat.*, 19: 55-61, 1972.

1505. Schade, G. H. and Gofman, H., Abdominal epilepsy in childhood, *Pediatrics*, 25: 151-154, 1960.

1506. Scherlag, B. J. and Helfant, R. H., Effect of diphenylhydantoin on acetyl strophanthidin, *Amer. Heart J.*, 81(4): 577-579, 1971.

1507. Scherlag, B. J., Helfant, R. H., Ricciutti, M. A., Damato, A. N., Dissociation of the effects of digitalis on myocardial potassium flux and contractility, *Am. J. Physiology*, 215: 1288-1291, 1968.

1508. Schick, D. and Scheuer, J., Current concepts of therapy with digitalis glycosides, Part II., *Amer. Heart J.*, 87: 391-396, 1974.

1509. Schimmel, R. J., and Graham, D., Inhibition by diphenylhydantoin of the diabetogenic action of streptozotocin, *Horm. Metab. Res.*, 6: 475-477, 1974.

1510. Schoor, W. P., Effect of anticonvulsant drugs on insecticide residues, *Lancet*, 520-521, 1970.

1511. Schreiber, M. M. and McGregor, J. G., Pseudolymphoma syndrome, *Arch. Derm.*, 97: 297-300, 1968.

1512. Schulten, H. K., Etzrodt, H., du Mesnil de Rochemont, W., Chriske, H. W., Grosser, K. D. and Steinbruck, G., Clinical and electrophysiological observations in DPH therapy of arrhythmia, *Verh. Deutsch Ges. Inn. Med.*, 77: 952-956, 1971.

1513. Schussler, G. C., Diazepam competes for thyroxine binding sites, *Chem. Abstracts*, 75: 74395C, 1971.

1514. Schussler, G. C., Similarity of diazepam to diphenylhydantoin, *JAMA*, 218: 1832, 1971.

1515. Schwender, C. F., Antiarrhythmic agents, *Annual Reports in Medicinal Chemistry, 1970*, 80-87, Cain, C. K., Ed., Academic Press, New York, 1971.

1516. Scientific Review Subpanel on Antiarrhythmia Agents, Quinidine-reserpine, Evaluations of Drug Interactions, *American Pharmaceutical Association*, Washington, D.C., 130-131, 1973.

1517. Scientific Review Subpanel on Anticonvulsants, Diphenylhydantoin-Isoniazid, Evaluations of Drug Interactions, *American Pharmaceutical Association*, Washington, D.C., 51-52, 1973.

1518. Scientific Review Subpanel on Anticonvulsants, Diphenylhydantoin-phenobarbital, Evaluations of Drug Interactions, *American Pharmaceutical Association*, Washington, D.C., 54-56, 1973.

1519. Scientific Review Subpanel on Antidiabetic Agents, Insulin-diphenylhydantoin, Evaluation of Drug Interaction, *American Pharmaceutical Association*, Washington, D.C., 90-91, 1973.

1520. Scientific Review Subpanel on Anticonvulsants, Diphenylhydantoin-methylphenidate, Evaluations of Drug Interactions, *American Pharmaceutical Association*, Washington, D.C. 53-54, 1973.

1521. Scientific Review Subpanel on Steroids, Dexamethasone-diphenylhydantoin, Evaluations of Drug Interactions, *American Pharmaceutical Association*, Washington, D.C., 32-34, 1973.

1522. Scientific Review Subpanel on Anticonvulsants, Anticonvulsant therapy, Evaluations of Drug Interactions, *American Pharmaceutical Association*, Washington, D.C., 252-256, 1973.

1523. Scott, M., Peale, A. R., and Croissant, P. D., Intracranial midline anterior fossa ossifying fibroma invading orbits, paranasal sinuses, and right maxillary antrum, *J. Neurosurg.*, 34: 827-831, 1971.

1524. Seeman, P., Chau-Wong, M., and Moyyen, S., The membrane binding of morphine, diphenylhydantoin, and tetrahydrocannabinol, *Canad. J. Physiol. Pharmacol.*, 50: 1193-1200, 1972.

1525. Selye, H. and Szabo, S., Protection by various steroids against gold nephropathy, *J. Europ. Toxicol.*, 6: 512-516, 1972.

1526. Selye, H. and Tuchweber, B., Effect of various steroids upon the toxicity of bile acids, *Int. Symp. Hepatotoxicity*, 63, 1973.

1527. Selye, H., Szabo, S., and Kourounakis, P., Effect of various steroids and nonsteroidal microsomal enzyme inducers upon propoxyphene intoxication, *Neuroendocrinology*, 9: 316-319, 1972.

1528. Selye, H., Szabo, S. and Kourounakis, P., Protection against phenylisothicyanate by various steroids, phenobarbitone and diphenylhydantoin, *J. Pharm. Pharmacol.*, 24: 333-334, 1972.

1529. Selye, H., Szabo, S., and Kourounakis, P., Protection by catatoxic steroids, phenobarbital and diphenylhydantoin against methaqualone intoxication, *Steroids Lipids Res.*, 3: 156-159, 1972.

1530. Selye, H., Szabo, S., and Mecs, I., Protection by catatoxic steroids against the paralysis caused by combined treatment with thyroxine and methylphenidate, *Neuropharmacology*, 11: 693-696, 1972.

1531. Selye, H., Hormones and resistance, *J. Pharm. Sci.*, 60: 1-28, 1971.

1532. Selye, H., Prevention by catatoxic steroids of lithocholic acid-induced biliary concrements in the rat, *Proc. Soc. Exp. Biol. Med.*, 141: 555-558, 1972.

1533. Selye, H., Protection by glucocorticoids against allopurinol nephropathy, *Acta Endocr.*, 69: 347-354, 1972.

1534. Serrano, E. E., Roe, D. B., Hammer, R. H.,, and Wilder, B. J., Plasma diphenylhydantoin values after oral and intramuscular administration of diphenylhydantoin, *Neurology*, 23: 311-317, 1973.

1535. Shah, J. R., Vora, G., Karkhanis, A. V., and Talwalkar, C. V., The effect of diphenylhydantoin on ventilation tests in airway obstruction, *Indian J. Chest. Dis.*, 12: 10-14, 1970.

1536. Shalsha, K. G., The function of newer antiarrhythmic drugs under special consideration of beta blocking adrenergic agents, *Proc. Virchow Med Soc. (N.Y.)*. 27: 201-211, 1969.

1537. Shemano, I., Orzechowski, R., Goldstein, S., and Beiler, J. M., Effects of 3,5-diethylhydantoin on resistance to asphyxia in rats, *Toxic. Appl. Pharmacol.* 25: 250-258, 1973.

1538. Sher, S. P., Drug enzyme induction and drug interactions: literature tabulation, *Toxic. Appl. Pharmacol.*, 18: 780-834, 1971.

1539. Sherwin, A. L., Eisen, A. A. and Sokolowski, C. D., Anticonvulsant drugs in human epileptogenic brain, *Presented at the annual meeting of the American Neurological Association and the Canadian Congress of Neurological Sciences*, Montreal, 1973.

1540. Sherwin, I., Suppressant effects of diphenylhydantoin on the cortical epileptogenic focus, *Neurology*, 23: 274-281, 1973.

1541. Shibasaki, H. and Kuroiwa, Y., Painful tonic seizure in multiple sclerosis, *Arch. Neurol.*, 30: 47-51, 1974.

1542. Shinohara, Y., Ventricular fibrillation threshold (VFRT) in experimental coronary occlusion: comparative studies on the effect of G-I-K solution and some new antiarrhythmic agents, *Jap. Circ. J.*, 32: 1269-1281. 1968.

1543. Shoeman, D. W., Benjamin, D. M., and Azarnoff, D. L., The alteration of plasma proteins in uremia as reflected in the ability to bind diphenylhydantoin, *Ann. N. Y. Acad. Sci.*, 226: 127-130, 1973.

1544. Shoeman, D. W., Kauffman, R. E., Azarnoff, D. L., and Boulos, B. M., Placental transfer of diphenylhydantoin as determined at constant drug concentrations in the maternal blood, *Pharmacologist*, 13: 195, 1971.

1545. Shoeman, D. W., Kauffman, R. E., Azarnoff, D. L., and Boulos, B. M., Placental transfer of diphenylhydantoin in the goat, *Biochem. Pharmacol.*, 21: 1237-1244, 1972.

1546. Sholiton, L. J., Werk, E. E. and MacGee, J., The effect of diphenylhydantoin *in vitro* on the formation of the polar metabolites of testosterone by rat liver, *Acta Endocr.*, 62: 360-366, 1969.

1547. Siegel, G. H. and Goodwin, B. B., Sodium-potassium-activated adenosine triphosphatase of brain microsomes: modification of sodium inhibition by diphenylhydantoins, *J. Clin. Invest.*, 51: 1161-1169, 1972.

1548. Siegel, G. J. and Goodwin, B. B., Effects of 5,5-diphenlhydantoin (DPH) and 5-p-hydroxyphenyl-5-phenylhydantoin (HPPH) on brain Na-K-ATPase, *Neurology*, 21: 417, 1971.

1549. Sigwald, J., Raverdy, P., Fardeau, M., Gremy, F., Mace de Lepinay, A., Bouttier, D., and Danic, Mme., Pseudomyotonia, *Rev. Neurol.*, 115: 1003-1014, 1966.

1550. Simon, G. E., Jatlow, P. I., Seligson, H. T., and Seligson, D., Measurement of 5,5-diphenylhydantoin in blood using thin layer chromatography, *Epilepsy Abstracts*, 4: 136, 1971.

1551. Simopoulos, A. M., Pinto, A., Uhlenhuth, E. H., McGee, J. J., and DeRosa, E. R., Diphenylhydantoin (DPH) effectiveness in the treatment of chronic schizophrenics, *Arch. Gen. Psychiat.*, 30: 106-112, 1974.

1552. Simpson, J. F., Use of diphenylhydantoin, *Ann. Intern. Med.*, 78: 305-306, 1973.

1553. Singh, B. N. and Hauswirth, O., Comparative mechanisms of action of antiarrhythmic drugs, *Amer. Heart J.*, 87: 367-382, 1974.

1554. Singh, B. N. and Vaughan Williams, E. M., Effect of altering potassium concentration on the action of lidocaine and diphenylhydantoin on rabbit atrial and ventricular muscle, *Circ. Res.*, 29: 286-295, 1971.

1555. Singh, B. N., Explanation for the discrepancy in reported cardiac electrophysiological actions of diphenylhydantoin and lignocaine, *Brit. J. Pharmacol.*, 41: 385-386, 1971.

1556. Singh, H. P., Hebert, M. A., and Gualt, M. H., Effect of some drugs on clinical laboratory values as determined by technicon SMA 12/60, *Clin. Chem.*, 18: 137-144, 1972.

1557. Singh, N., Sinha, J. N., Rastogi, S. K., Dua, P. R., and Kohli, R. P., An experimental investigation on the antiarrhythmic activity of antiepileptic agents, *Jap. J. Pharmacol.* 21: 755-761, 1971.

1558. Sisca, T. S., An unusual dual hypersensitivity reaction induced by diphenylhydantoin, *Amer. J. Hosp. Pharm.*, 30: 446-449, 1973.

1559. Skrotsky, Y. A., Complications due to antiepileptic therapy in children and adolescents, *Epilepsy Abstracts*, 7: 138-139, 1974.

1560. Slosberg, P. S., Medical therapy for the cerebrovascular insufficiencies; eight years' experience, *Mt. Sinai Med. J.*, 37: 692-698, 1970.

1561. Smith, J. S., Brierley, . and Brandon, S., Akinetic mutism with recovery after repeated carbon monoxide poisoning, *Psychol. Med.*, 1: 172-177, 1971.

1562. Smith, T. W. and Haber, E., Digitalis, *New Eng. J. Med.*, 289: 1125-1129, 1973.

1563. Smith, T. W., Digitalis glycosides, *New Eng. J. Med.*, 288: 942-946, 1973.

1564. Smith, W. L. and Lowrey, J. B., The effects of diphenylhydantoin on cognitive functions in man, *Drugs, Development, and Cerebral Function*, Smith, W. L., Ed., Charles C Thomas, 344-351, 1972.

1565. Smith, W. L. and Lowrey, J. B., Effects of diphenylhydantoin on mental abilities in the elderly, *J. Amer. Geriat. Soc.*, 23: 207-211, 1975.

1566. Snider, R. S. and del Cerro, M., Diphenylhydantoin, proliferating membranes in cerebellum resulting from intoxication, *Antiepileptic Drugs*, 237-245, Woodbury, D. M., Penry, J. K., and Schmidt, R. P. Eds., Raven Press, New York, 1972.

1567. Sohn, R. S. and Ferrendelli, J. A., Inhibition of Ca^{++} uptake in rat brain synaptosomes by diphenylhydantoin, *Neurology*, 23: 443, 1973.

1568. Solomon, G. E., Hilgartner, M. W., and Kutt, H., Coagulation defects caused by diphenylhydantoin, *Neurology*, 22: 1165-1171, 1972.

1569. Solomon, P. and Kleeman, S. T., Medical aspects of violence, *Calif. Med.*, 114: 19-24, 1971.

1570. Solow, E. B. and Green, J. B., The simultaneous determination of multiple anticonvulsant drug levels by gas-liquid chromatography, *Neurology*, 22: 540-550, 1972.

1571. Solow, E. B., Metaxas, J. M. and Summers, T. R., Antiepileptic drugs. A current assessment of simultaneous determination of multiple drug therapy by gas liquid chromatography on column methylation, *J. Chromatographic Sci.*, 12: 256-260, 1974.

1572. Sorrell, T. C., Forbes, I. J., Burness, F. R., and Rischbieth, R. H. C., Depression of immunological function in patients treated with phenytoin sodium (sodium diphenylhydantoin), *Lancet*, 1233-1235, 1971.

1573. Sotaniemi, E. A., Arvela, P., Hakkarainen, H. K., and Huhti, E., The clinical significance of microsomal enzyme induction in the therapy of epileptic patients, *Ann. Clin. Res.*, 2: 223-227, 1970.

1574. Sotaniemi, E. A., Hakkarainen, H. K., Puranen, J. A. and Lahti, R. O., Radiologic bone changes and hypocalcemia with anticonvulsant therapy in epilepsy, *Ann. Intern. Med.*, 77(3): 389-394, 1972.

1575. South, J., Teratogenic effect of anticonvulsants, *Lancet*, 2: 1154, 1972.

1576. Spector, R. G., Effects of formyl tetrahydrofolic acid and noradrenaline on the oxygen consumption of rat brain synaptosome-mitrochondrial preparations, *Brit. J. Pharmacol.*, 44: 279-285, 1972.

1577. Spector, R. G., Influence of folic acid on excitable tissues, *Nature New Biol.*, 240: 247-249, 1972.

1578. Spector, R. G., The influence of anticonvulsant drugs on formyl tetrahydrofolic acid stimulation of rat brain respiration *in vitro*, *Epilepsy Abstracts*, 6: 110, 1973.

1579. Speidel, B. D. and Meadow, S. R., Maternal epilepsy and abnormalities of the fetus and newborn, *Lancet*, 839-843, October, 1972.

1580. Sperelakis, N. and Henn, F. A., Effect of diphenylhydantoin on membrane potentials and Na-K-ATPase of cultured chick heart cells, *Amer. J. Physiol.*, 218: 1224-1227, 1970.

1581. Spina, A., Pyridinolcarbamate in the therapy of hemicrania syndromes, *Acta Neurol.*, 27: 610-617, 1972.

1582. Spray, G. H. and Burns, D. G., Folate deficiency and anticonvulsant drugs, *Brit. Med. J.*, 2: 167-168, April, 1972.

1583. Stambaugh, J. E. and Tucker, D., Effect of diphenylhydantoin on glucose tolerance in patients with hypoglycemia, *Diabetes*, 23: 679-683, 1974.

1584. Stamp, T. C. B., Effects of long-term anticonvulsant therapy on calcium and vitamin D metabolism, *Proc. Roy. Soc. Med.*, 67: 64-68, 1974.

1585. Stamp, T. C. B., Round, J. M., Rowe, D. J. F., and Haddad, J. G., Plasma levels and therapeutic effect of 25-hydroxycholecalciferol in epileptic patients taking anticonvulsant drugs, *Brit. Med. J.*, 4: 9-12, 1972.

1586. Staples, R. E., Teratology, *Antiepileptic Drugs*, 55-62, Woodbury, D. M., Penry, J. K., and Schmidt, R. P. Eds., Raven Press, New York, 1972. (*cf.* Kuenssberg and Knox, *Lancet*, 198, 1973, Millar and Nevin, *Lancet*, 328, 1973 and Stenchever and Jarvis, *Amer. J. Obstet. Gynec.*, 109: 961, 1971.)

1587. Starreveld-Zimmerman, A. A. E., Van Der Kolk, W. J., Meinardi, H., and Elshove, J., Are anticonvulsants teratogenic?, *Lancet*, 48-49, July, 1973.

1588. Staunton, C., Stein, A. A., and Moss, G., The cerebral etiology of the respiratory distress syndrome (RDS): universal response, with prevention by unilateral pulmonary denervation, *Surg. Forum*, 24: 1973.

1589. Stavchansky, S. A., Lubawy, W. C. and Kostenbauder, H. B., Increase of hexobarbital sleeping time and inhibition of drug metabolism by the major metabolite of DPH, *Life Sci.*, 14: 1535-1539, 1974.

1590. Stazi, C. and Marasa, G., Arrhythmias due to digitalis and their treatment, *Ann. Med. Nav.* (Roma), 77: 51-80, 1972.

1591. Stein, A. A. and Moss, G., Cerebral etiology of the respiratory distress syndrome: diphenylhydantoin (DPH) prophylaxis, *Surg. Forum*, 24: 433-435, 1973.

1592. Stephens, J. H. and Shaffer, J. W., A controlled replication of the effectiveness of diphenylhydantoin in reducing irritability and anxiety in selected neurotic outpatients, *J. Clin. Pharmacol.*, 13: 351-356, 1973.

1593. Stephens, J. H., Shaffer, J. W., and Brown, C. C., A controlled comparison of the effects of diphenylhydantoin and placebo on mood and psychomotor functioning in normal volunteers, *J. Clin. Pharmacol.*, 14: 543-551, 1974.

1594. Stern, L. Z., Gruener, R., and Amundsen, P., Diphenylhydantoin for steroid-induced muscle weakness, *JAMA*, 223: 1287-1288, 1973.

1595. Stevens, H., Nine neuropathies, *Med. Ann.*, 37: 89-97, 1968.

1596. Stevens, M. W. and Harbison, R. D., Placental transfer of diphenylhydantoin: effects of species, gestational age, and route of administration, *Teratology*, 9: 317-326, 1974.

1597. Stevenson, M. M. and Gilbert, E. F., Anticonvulsants and hemorrhagic diseases of the newborn infant, *J. Pediat.*, 516, 1970.

1598. Stone, N., Klein, M. D., and Lown, B., Diphenylhydantoin in the prevention of recurring ventricular tachycardia, *Circulation*, 43: 420-427, 1971.

1599. Stowell, A., Physiologic mechanisms and treatment of histaminic or petrosal neuralgia, *Headache*, 9: 187-194, 1970.

1600. Strauss, H., Rahm, W. E., and Barrera, S. E., Studies on a group of children with psychiatric disorders. I. Electroencephalographic studies, *Psychosom. Med.*, 2: 34-42, 1940.

1601. Strittmatter, W. J. and Somjen, G. G., Depression of sustained evoked potentials and glial depolarization in the spinal cord by barbiturates and by diphenylhydantoin, *Brain Res.*, 55: 333-342, 1973.

1602. Su, P. C. and Feldman, D. S., Motor nerve terminal and muscle membrane stabilization by diphenylhydantoin administration, *Arch. Neurol.*, 28: 376-379, 1973.

1603. Swaiman, K. F. and Stright, P. L., The effects of anticonvulsants on *in vitro* protein synthesis in immature brain, *Brain Res.*, 58: 515-518, 1973.

1604. Swann, W. P., Effects of Dilantin on the repair of gingival wounds, *Indiana University School of Dentistry Thesis*, 1966.

1605. Sweet, W. H. and Wepsic, J. G., Relation of fiber size in trigeminal posterior root to conduction of impulses for pain and touch; production of analgesia without anesthesia in the effective treatment of trigeminal neuralgia, *Trans. Amer. Neurol. Assoc.*, 95: 134-139, 1970.

1606. Tabachnick, M., Hao, Y. L., and Korcek, L., Effect of oleate, diphenylhydantoin and heparin on the binding of 125 I-thyroxine to purified thyroxine-binding globulin, *J. Clin. Endocr.*, 36: 392-394, 1973.

1607. Taitz, L. S., Mental retardation elevated alkaline phosphatase, convulsive disorder and thickening of calvarium, *Epi-*

lepsy Abstracts, 6: 228, 1973. (*cf.* Kattan, *Amer. J. Roentgen.,* 110: 102, 1970.)

1608. Tappaz, M. and Pacheco, H., Effects of convulsant and anticonvulsant drugs on uptake of 14,-C GABA by rat brain slices, *J. Pharmacol.* (Paris), 4: 295-306, 1973.

1609. Tashima, C. K. and De Los Santos, R., Lymphoma and anticonvulsive therapy, *JAMA,* 228: 286-287, 1974.

1610. Tassinari, C. A. and Fine, R. D., Paroxysmal choreoathetosis, *Proc. Aust. Assoc. Neurol.,* 6: 71-75, 1969.

1611. Taylor, C. R., Double-blind crossover study of diphenylhydantoin in angina pectoris, *Chest,* 66: 422-427, 1974.

1612. Taylor, J. D., Krahn, P. M. and Higgins, T. N., Serum copper levels and diphenylhydantoin, *Amer. J. Clin. Path.,* 61: 577-578, 1974.

1613. Tenser, R. B. and Corbett, J. J., Myokymia and facial contraction in brain stem glioma, *Arch. Neurol.,* 30: 425-427, 1974.

1614. Thompson, C. E., Diphenylhydantoin for myotonia congenita, *New Eng. J. Med.,* 286: 893, 1972.

1615. Thurkow, I., Wesseling, H., and Meijer, D. K. F., Estimation of phenytoin in body fluids in the presence of sulphonyl urea compounds, *Clin. Chim. Acta,* 37: 509-513, 1972.

1616. Thurlow, H. J. and Girvin, J. P., Use of anti-epileptic medication in treating "flashbacks" from hallucinogenic drugs, *Canad. Med. Assoc. J.,* 105: 947-948, 1971.

1617. Tigelaar, R. E., Rapport, R. L., Inman, J. K., and Kupferberg, H. J., A radioimmunoassay for diphenylhydantoin, *Epilepsy Abstracts,* 6: 113, 1973.

1618. Tisman, G., Herbert, V., Go, L. T., and Brenner, L., *In vitro* demonstration of immunosuppression without bone marrow suppression by alcohol and bleomycin, *Clin. Res.,* 19: 730, 1971.

1619. Tobin, T., Dirdjosudjono, S., and Baskin, S. I., Pharmacokinetics and distribution of diphenylhydantoin in kittens, *Amer. J. Vet. Res.,* 34: 951-954, 1973.

1620. Tolman, K. G., Jubiz, W., DeLuca, H. F. and Freston, J. W., Rickets associated with anticonvulsant medications, *Clin. Res.,* 20: 414, 1972.

1621. Toman, J. E. P. and Sabelli, H. C., Comparative neuronal mechanisms, *Epilepsia,* 10: 179-192, 1969.

1622. Torretti, J., Hendler, E., Weinstein, E., Longnecker, R. E., and Epstein, F. H., Functional significance of Na-K-ATPase in the kidney: effects of ouabain inhibition, *Amer. J. Physiol.,* 222: 1398-1405, 1972.

1623. Tovi, D., The use of antifibrinolytic drugs to prevent early recurrent aneurysmal subarachnoid haemorrhage, *Acta Neurol. Scand.,* 49: 163-175, 1973.

1624. Treasure, T. and Toseland, P. A., Hyperglycaemia due to phenytoin toxicity, *Arch. Dis. Child.,* 46: 563-564, 1971.

1625. Tuchweber, B., Szabo, S., Kovacs, K., and Garg, B. D., Hormonal and nonhormonal factors influencing pyrrolizidine alkaloid hepatotoxicity, *Int. Symp. Hepatotoxicity,* 89, 1973.

1626. Turner, W. J., Dilantin effect on emotionally disturbed children, *Drugs and Cerebral Function,* 99-102, Smith, W. L., Ed., Charles C Thomas, 1970.

1627. Tyler, F. H., West, C. D., Jubiz, W., and Meikle, A. W., Dilantin and metyrapone: a clinically significant example of enzyme induction, *Trans. Amer. Clin. Climat. Assoc.,* 81: 213-219, 1970.

1628. Tyrer, J. H., Eadie, M. J., and Sutherland, J. M., Investigation of an outbreak of anticonvulsant intoxication, *Proc. Aust. Assoc. Neurol.,* 7: 15-18, 1970.

1629. Tyrer, J. H., Eadie, M. J., and Hooper, W. D., Further observations on an outbreak of diphenylhydantoin intoxication, *Proc. Aust. Assoc. Neurol.,* 8: 37-41, 1971.

1630. Uhlenhuth, E. H., Stephens, J. H., Dim, B. H., and Covi, L., Diphenylhydantoin and phenobarbital in the relief of psychoneurotic symptoms: a controlled comparison, *Psychopharmacologia* (Berlin), 27: 67-84, 1972.

1631. Uono, M., Treatment of myotonic dystrophy, *Naika,* 25: 664-668, 1970.

1632. Vaisrub, S., Diphenylhydantoin and insulin-secreting tumors, *JAMA,* 223: 553-554, 1973.

1633. Vaisrub, S., Diphenylhydantoin and early diabetes, *JAMA,* 226: 191, 1973.

1634. Vajda, F. J. E., Prineas, R. J., and Lovell, R. R. H., Interaction between phenytoin and the benzodiazepines, *Epilepsy Abstracts,* 4: 263, 1971.

1635. Vajda, F. J. E., Prineas, R. J., Lovell, R. R. H., and Sloman, J. G., The possible effect of long-term high plasma levels of phenytoin on mortality after acute myocardial infarction, *Europ. J. Clin. Pharmacol.,* 5: 138-144, 1973.

1636. van der Kleijn, E., Rijntjes, N. V. M., Guelen, P. J. M., and Wijffels, C. C. G., Systemic and brain distribution of diphenylhydantoin in the squirrel monkey, *Antiepileptic Drugs,* 124, Woodbury, D. M., Penry, J. K., and Schmidt, R. P., Eds., Raven Press, New York, 1972.

1637. Van Der Velde, C. D., Toxicity of lithium carbonate in elderly patients, *Amer. J. Psychiat.,* 127: 1075-1077, 1971.

1638. van Dijk, L., Pharmacotherapy of cardiac arrhythmias in acute myocardial infarction, *Folia Med. Neerl.,* 14: 225-236, 1971.

1639. Van Meter, J. C., Buckmaster, H. S., and Shelley, L. L., Concurrent assay of phenobarbital and diphenylhydantoin in plasma by vapor-phase chromatography, *Clin. Chem.,* 16: 135-138, 1970.

1640. Van Rees, H. and Noach, E. L., The intestinal absorption of diphenylhydantoin from a suspension in rats, *Epilepsy Abstracts,* 7: 197, 1974.

1641. Van Rees, H., DeWolff, F. A., Noach, E. L., The influence of diphenylhydantoin on intestinal glucose absorption in the rat, *European J. Pharmacology,* 28: 310-315, 1974.

1642. Van Rees, H., Woodbury, D. M. and Noach, E. L., Effects of ouabain and diphenylhydantoin on electrolyte and water shifts during intestinal absorption in the rat, *Arch. Int. Pharmacodyn.,* 182: 437, 1969.

1643. Van Riezen, H. and Delver, A., The effect of a number of drugs with different pharmacological properties upon reserpine induced hypothermia in mice, *Arzneimittelforschung.,* 21: 1562-1566, 1971.

1644. Vanasin, B., Bass, D. D., Mendeloff, A. I., and Schuster, M. M., Alteration of electrical and motor activity of human and dog rectum by diphenylhydantoin, *Amer. J. Dig. Dis.,* 18: 403-410, 1973.

1645. Vander Ark, C. R. and Reynolds, E. W., Jr., Cellular basis and clinical evaluation of antiarrhythmic therapy, *Med. Clin. N. Amer.,* 53: 1297-1308, 1969.

1646. Vaughan Williams, E. M., The development of new antidysrhythmic drugs, *Schweiz. Med. Wschr.,* 103: 262-271, 1973.

1647. Vedso, S., Rud, C., and Place, J. F., Determination of phenytoin in serum in the presence of barbiturates sulthiame and ethosuximid by thin-layer chromatography, *Scand. J. Clin. Lab. Invest.,* 23: 175-180, 1969.

1648. Verebel, K., Kutt, H., Sohn, Y. J., Levitt, B., and Raines, A., Uptake and distribution of diphenylthiohydantoin (DPTH), *Europ. J. Pharmacol.,* 10: 106-110, 1970.

1649. Villareale, M., Gould, L. V., Wasserman, R. H., Barr, A., Chiroff, R. T., and Bergstrom, W. H., Diphenylhydantoin: effects on calcium metabolism in the chick, *Science,* 183: 671-673, 1974.

1650. Viukari, N. M. A. and Tammisto, P., Central effects of diphenylhydantoin (Dilantin) in epileptic oligophrenics during phenobarbital-primidone withdrawal, sodium bicarbonate, and ammonium chloride administration, *Behav. Neuropsychiatr.,* 1: 13-16, 1969.

1651. Viukari, N. M. A., Diphenylhydantoin as an anticonvulsant: evaluation of treatment in forty mentally subnormal epileptics, *Epilepsy Abstracts,* 3: 150, 1970.

1652. Vulliamy, D., Unwanted effects of anticonvulsant drugs, *Dev. Med. Child. Neurol.,* 13: 107-109, 1971.

1653. Walker, W. J., Treatment of heart failure, *JAMA*, 228: 1276-1278, 1974.

1654. Wallace, J. E., Microdetermination of diphenylhydantoin in biological specimens by ultraviolet spectrophotometry, *Anal. Chem.*, 40: 978-980, 1968.

1655. Wallace, J. E., Simultaneous spectrophotometric determination of diphenylhydantoin and phenobarbital in biologic specimens, *Clin. Chem.*, 15: 323-330, 1969.

1656. Wallace, J. E., Spectrophotometric determination of diphenylhydantoin, *J. Forensic Sci. Soc.*, 11: 552-559, 1966.

1657. Wallis, W. E. and Plum, F., Continuous fasciculations, myokymia and muscle contraction due to peripheral nerve disease, *Trans. Assoc. Amer. Physicians*, 82: 286-292, 1969.

1658. Wallis, W. E., Van Poznak, A., and Plum, F., Generalized muscular stiffness, fasciculations, and myokymia of peripheral nerve origin, *Arch. Neurol.*, 22: 430-439, 1970.

1659. Walsh, G. O., Masland, W., and Goldensohn, E. S., Relationship between paroxysmal atrial tachycardia and paroxysmal cerebral discharges, *Bull. Los Angeles Neurol. Soc.*, 37: 28-35, 1972.

1660. Ware, E., The chemistry of the hydantoins, *Chem. Rev.*, 46: 403-470, 1950.

1661. Watanabe, Y., A-V conduction disturbance: its pathophysiology and pharmacology, *Singapore Med. J.*, 14(3): 249, 1973.

1662. Watson, E. L. and Woodbury, D. M., Effect of diphenylhydantoin on active sodium transport in frog skin, *J. Pharmacol. Exp. Ther.*, 180: 767-776, 1972.

1663. Watson, E. L. and Woodbury, D. M., The effect of diphenylhydantoin and ouabain, alone and in combination, on the electrocardiogram and on cellular electrolytes of guinea-pig heart and skeletal muscle, *Arch. Int. Pharmacodyn.*, 201: 389-399, 1973.

1664. Watson, E. L. and Woodbury, D. M., Effects of diphenylhydantoin on electrolyte transport in various tissues, *Chemical Modulation of Brain Function*, 187-198, Sabelli, H. C., Ed., Raven Press, New York, 1973.

1665. Watson, J. D. and Spellacy, W. N., Neonatal effects of maternal treatment with the anticonvulsant drug diphenylhydantoin, *Obstet. Gynec.*, 37: 881-885, 1971.

1666. Watson, M., Gabica, J., and Benson, W. W., Serum organochlorine pesticides in mentally retarded patients on differing drug regimens, *Clin. Pharmacol. Ther.*, 13: 186-192, 1972.

1667. Watson, P., Brainwave to save life, *London Times*, 1973.

1668. Wax, S. D., Webb, W. R., and Ecker, R. R., Myocardium stabilization by diphenylhydantoin, *Surg. Forum*, 20: 164-166, 1969.

1669. Weber-Eggenberger, S. and Kaufmann, G., Studies on absorption, elimination and antiarrhythmic serum concentrations of diphenylhydantoin (antisacer) in digitalized heart patients, *Z. Kreislaufforsch.*, 60: 420-432, 1971.

1670. Weckman, N. and Lehtovaara, R., Serum and cerebrospinal fluid folate values in epileptics on anticonvulsant treatment, *Scand. J. Clin. Lab. Invest.*, Supp. 101, 120-121, 1968.

1671. Weckman, N. and Lehtovaara, R., Folic acid and anticonvulsants, *Lancet*, 1: 207-208, 1969.

1672. Weinreich, D. and Clark, L. D., Anticonvulsant drugs and self-stimulation rates in rats, *Arch. Int. Pharmacodyn.*, 185: 269-273, 1970.

1673. Weisse, A. B., Moschos, C. B., Passannante, A. J., and Regan, T. J., Comparative effectiveness of procaine amide, lidocaine, and diphenylhydantoin in treating ventricular arrhythmias during acute myocardial infarction, *Circulation*, 38: VI205, 1968.

1674. Weiss, C. F., Yaffe, S. J., Cann, H. M., Gold, A. P., Kenny, F. M., Riley, H. D., Schafer, I., Stern, L., and Shirkey, H. C., An evaluation of the pharmacologic approaches to learning impediments, *Pediatrics*, 46: 142-144, 1970.

1675. Weisse, A. B., Moschos, C. B., Passannante, A. J., Khan, M. I., and Regan, T. J., Relative effectiveness of three anti-arrhythmic agents in the treatment of ventricular arrhythmias in experimental acute myocardial ischemia, *Amer. Heart J.*, 81: 503-510, 1971.

1676. Welch, L. K., Appenzeller, O., and Bicknell, J. M., Peripheral neuropathy with myokymia, sustained muscular contraction, and continuous motor unit activity, *Neurology*, 22: 161-169, 1972.

1677. Wepsic, J. G., Tic douloureux: etiology, refined treatment, *New Eng. J. Med.*, 288: 680-681, 1973.

1678. Werk, E. E., Choi, Y., Sholiton, L., Olinger, C., and Haque, N., Interference in the effect of dexamethasone by diphenylhydantoin, *New Eng. J. Med.*, 281: 32-34, 1969.

1679. Werk, E. E., Thrasher, K., Sholiton, L. J., Olinger, C., and Choi, Y., Cortisol production in epileptic patients treated with diphenylhydantoin, *Clin. Pharmacol. Ther.*, 12: 698-703, 1971.

1680. Wesseling, H. and Thurkow, I., Effect of sulphonylureas (tolazamide, tolbutamide and chlorpropamide) on the metabolism of diphenylhydantoin in the rat, *Biochem. Pharmacol.*, 22: 3033-3040, 1973.

1681. Westmoreland, B. and Bass, N. H., Chronic diphenylhydantoin intoxication in the albino rat during pregnancy, *Neurology*, 20: 411, 1970.

1682. Whelton, A., Snyder, D. S., and Walker, W. G., Acute toxic drug ingestions at the Johns Hopkins Hospital 1963 through 1970, *Johns Hopkins Med. J.*, 132: 157-167, 1973.

1683. White, C. W., Jr., Megirian, R., and Swiss, E. D., The effects of diphenylhydantoin sodium, glucose and β-diethylaminoethyl diphenylpropylacetate hydrochloride on cyclopropane-epinephrine arrhythmias in the dog, *Circ. Res.*, 3: 290-292, 1955.

1684. Wilder, B. J., Buchanan, R. A., and Serrano, E. E., Correlation of acute diphenylhydantoin intoxication with plasma levels and metabolite excretion, *Neurology*, 23: 1329-1332, 1973.

1685. Wilder, B. J., Serrano, E. E. and Ramsay, R. E., Plasma diphenylhydantoin levels after loading and maintenance doses, *Clin. Pharmacol. Ther.*, 14: 797-801, 1973.

1686. Wilder, B. J., Streiff, R. R., and Hammer, R. H., Diphenylhydantoin, absorption, distribution, and excretion: clinical studies, *Antiepileptic Drugs*, 137-148, Woodbury, D. M., Penry, J. K., and Schmidt, R. P., Eds., Raven Press, New York, 1972.

1687. Wilensky, A. J. and Lowden, J. A., Interaction of diphenylhydantoin 4¹⁴C with subcellular fractions of rat brain, *Epilepsy Abstracts*, 5: 194, 1972.

1688. Wilensky, A. J. and Lowden, J. A., The inhibitory effect of diphenylhydantoin on microsomal ATPases, *Life Sci.*, 11: 319-327, 1972.

1689. Wilensky, A. J. and Lowden, J. A., Inadequate serum levels after intramuscular administration of diphenylhydantoin, *Neurology*, 23: 318-324, 1973.

1690. Wilkinson, H. A., Epileptic pain—an uncommon manifestation with localizing value, *Neurology*, 23: 518-520, 1973.

1691. Wilson, J. T. and Wilkinson, G. R., Delivery of anticonvulsant drug therapy in epileptic patients assessed by plasma level analyses, *Neurology*, 24: 614-623, 1974.

1692. Winter, B., Bilateral carotid body resection for asthma and emphysema, *Int. Surg.*, 57: 458-466, 1972.

1693. Wolff, J., Standaert, M. E., and Rall, J. E., Thyroxine displacement from serum proteins and depression of serum protein-bound iodine by certain drugs, *J. Clin. Invest.*, 40: 1373-1377, 1961.

1694. Wood, R. A., Sinoatrial arrest: an interaction between phenytoin and lignocaine, *Brit. Med. J.*, 1: 645, 1971.

1695. Woodbury, D. M. and Kemp, J. W., Some possible mechanisms of action of anti-epileptic drugs, *Pharmakopsychiatr.*, 3: 201-226, 1970.

1696. Woodbury, D. M. and Kemp, J. W., Pharmacology and mechanisms of action of diphenylhydantoin, *Psychiat. Neurol. Neurochir.*, 74: 91-115, 1971.

1697. Woodbury, D. M. and Swinyard, E. A., Diphenylhydantoin, absorption, distribution, and excretion, *Antiepileptic Drugs,* 113-123, Woodbury, D. M., Penry, J. K., and Schmidt, R. P., Eds., Raven Press, New York, 1972.

1698. Woodbury, D. M., Koch, A., and Vernadakis, A., Relation between excitability and metabolism in brain as elucidated by anticonvulsant drugs, *Neurology,* 8: 113-116, 1958.

1699. Woodbury, D. M., Mechanisms of action of anticonvulsants, *Epilepsy Abstracts,* 3: 248, 1970.

1700. Woodbury, D. M., Penry, J. K. and Schmidt, R. P., Eds., *Antiepileptic Drugs,* Raven Press, New York, 1972.

1701. Yalaz, K. and Baytok, V., Mirror movement, *Turk. J. Pediat.,* 12: 85-88, 1970.

1702. Yanagihara, T. and Hamberger, A., Effect of diphenylhydantoin on protein metabolism in the central nervous system—study of subcellular fractions, *Exp. Neurol,* 31: 87-99, 1971.

1703. Yanagihara, T. and Hamberger, A., Effect of diphenylhydantoin on protein metabolism in neuron and neuroglial fractions of central nervous tissue, *Exp. Neurol,* 32: 152-162, 1971.

1704. Yanagihara, T., Distribution of diphenylhydantoin in the neuronal and glial fractions, *Antiepileptic Drugs,* 125-126, Woodbury, D. M., Penry, J. K., and Schmidt, R. P., Eds., Raven Press, New York, 1972.

1705. Yang, C. P., Persistent ventricular tachycardia. The use of diphenylhydantoin, *J. Kansas Med. Soc.,* 74: 418-421, 1973.

1706. Yaryura-Tobias, J. A. and Neziroglu, F., Violent behaviour, brain dysrhythmia and glucose dysfunction: a new syndrome, *Amer. J. Psychiat.,* 130: 825, 1973.

1707. Yasky, J., Moretti, O., Carosella, C., Phenytoin treatment of cardiac arrhythmias induced by digitalis, *Revista Argentina de Cardiologia,* 41: 53-61, 1973.

1708. Yoshida, T. and Arakawa, T., Serum histidine clearance in children with diphenylhydantoin administration, *Tohoku J. Exp. Med.,* 112: 257-259, 1974.

1709. Yoshimasu, F., Kurland, L. T., and Elveback, L. R., Tic douloureux in Rochester, Minnesota, 1945-1969, *Neurology,* 22: 952-956, 1972.

1710. Zanini, S. and Rossi, R., Ventricular parasystole: effective treatment with diphenylhydantoin, *G. Ital. Cardiol.,* 2: 575-578, 1972.

1711. Zeft, H. J., Rembert, J. C., Curry, C. L., and Greenfield, J. C., Effects of diphenylhydantoin on coronary and systemic haemodynamics in awake dogs, *Cardiovasc. Res.,* 7: 331-335, 1973.

1712. Zeft, H. J., Whalen, R. E., Morris, J. J., Jr., Rummo, N. J., and McIntoch, H. D., Prophylaxis versus treatment of acetylstrophanthidin intoxication, *Amer. Heart J.,* 77: 237-245, 1969.

Recent Work
(Ref. 1713-2140)

1713. Affrime, M. and Reidenberg, M. M., The protein binding of some drugs in plasma from patients with alcoholic liver disease, *Europ. J. Clin. Pharmacol.,* 8: 267–9, 1975.

1714. Agapova, E. N. and Mikhalev, I. D., Effectiveness of the use of diphenine in insuloma, *Ter. Arkh.,* 49(9): 124–5, 1977.

1715. Agnew, D. C. and Goldberg, V. D., A brief trial of phenytoin therapy for thalamic pain, *Bulletin Los Angeles Neurol. Soc.,* 41(1): 9–12, 1976.

1716. Aickin, C. C., Deisz, R. A. and Lux, H. D., The effect of diphenylhydantoin and picrotoxin on post-synaptic inhibition, *J. Physiol.,* 284: 125–6, 1978.

1717. Aldrete, J. A. and Franatovic, Y., Postponement of operations—its prevention in patients found to be mildly hypertensive, *Arch. Surg.,* 115: 1204–6, 1980.

1718. Aldrete, J. A., Romo-Salas, F., Jankovsky, L. and Franatovic, Y., Effect of pretreatment with thiopental and phenytoin

on postischemic brain damage in rabbits, *Critical Care Medicine,* 7(10): 466–70, 1979.

1719. Aldrete, J. A., Romo-Salas, F., Mazzia, V. D. B. and Tan, S., Diphenylhydantoin for reversal of neurological injury after cardiac arrest, *Rev. Bras. Anest.,* 30(4): 263–7, 1980.

1720. Ali, I. I. and Dutta, S., Distribution of C^{14}-diphenylhydantoin (DPH) in relation to its antidysrhythmic effect in dogs, *Fed. Proc.* 36: 1012, 1977.

1721. Allen, M. A., Wrenn, J. M., Putney, J. W. and Borzelleca, J. F., A study of the mechanism of transport of diphenylhydantoin in the rat submaxillary gland *in vitro, J. Pharmacol. Exp. Ther.,* 197(2): 408–13, 1976.

1722. Anderson, R. J. and Raines, A., Suppression of decerebrate rigidity by phenytoin and chlorpromazine, *Neurol.,* 26: 858–62, 1976.

1723. Appenzeller, O., Feldman, R. G. and Friedman, A. P., Migraine, headache, and related conditions, *Arch. Neurol.,* 36: 784–805, 1979.

1724. Apton, R., Dilantin and its relation to caries incidence, *Dent. Hyg.,* 51: 349–51, 1977.

1725. Arnaout, M. A. and Salti, I., Phenytoin in benign insulinoma, *Lancet,* 861, 1976.

1726. Arnsdorf, M. F. and Mehlman, D. J., Observations on the effects of selected antiarrhythmic drugs on mammalian cardiac Purkinje fibers with two levels of steady-state potential: Influences of lidocaine, phenytoin, propranolol, disopyramide and procainamide on repolarization, action potential shape and conduction, *J. Pharmacol. Exp. Ther.,* 207(3): 983–91, 1978.

1727. Artru, A. A. and Michenfelder, J. D., Cerebral potassium release reduced by diphenylhydantoin: mechanism of cerebral protection, *Ann. Neurol.,* 6(2): 151, 1979.

1728. Artru, A. A. and Michenfelder, J. D., Cerebral protective, metabolic, and vascular effects of phenytoin, *Stroke,* 11(4): 377–82, 1980.

1729. Asboe-Hansen, G., Treatment of generalized scleroderma: updated results, *Acta Derm. Venereol.,* 59(5): 465–7, 1979.

1730. Ayala, G. F. and Johnston, D., Phenytoin: electrophysiological studies in simple neuronal systems, *Antiepileptic Drugs: Mechanisms of Action,* 339–51, Glaser, G. H., Penry, J. K. and Woodbury, D. M., Eds., Raven Press, New York, 1980.

1731. Ayala, G. F. and Johnston, D., The influences of phenytoin on the fundamental electrical properties of simple neural systems, *Epilepsia,* 18(3): 299–307, 1977.

1732. Ayala, G. F., Johnson, D., Lin, S., and Dichter, H. N., The mechanism of action of diphenylhydantoin on invertebrate neurons: II. Effects on synaptic mechanisms, *Brain Res.,* 121: 250–70, 1977.

1733. Ayala, G. F., Lin, S. and Johnston, D., The mechanism of action of diphenylhydantoin on invertebrate neurons: I. Effects on basic membrane properties, *Brain Res.,* 121: 245–58, 1977.

1734. Baselt, R. C. and Cravey, R. H., A compendium of therapeutic and toxic concentrations of toxicologically significant drugs in human biofluids, *J. Anal. Toxicol.,* 1: 81–103, 1977.

1735. Baskin, S. I., Leibman, A. J., DeWitt, W. S., Orr, P. L., Tarzy, N. T., Levy, P., Krusz, J. C., Dhopesh, V. P. and Schraeder, P. L., Mechanism of the anticonvulsant action of phenytoin: regulation of central nervous system taurine levels, *Neurology,* 28(4): 331–2, 1978.

1736. Baskin, S. I. and Melrose, B. L., The effect of diphenylhydantoin on the formation and dissociation of the cardiac glycoside—(Na$^+$ + K$^+$)-ATPase complex, *Clin. Res.,* 23: 172A, April 1975.

1737. Baratz, R. and Mesulam, M. M., Adult-onset stuttering treated with anticonvulsants, *Arch. Neurol.,* 38: 132, 1981.

1738. Bauer, E. A., Cooper, T. W., Tucker, D. R. and Esterly, N. B., Phenytoin therapy of recessive dystrophic epidermolysis bullosa: clinical trial and proposed mechanism of action on collagenase, *New Eng. J. Med.,* 303(14): 776–81, 1980.

1739. Bayer, R., Kaufmann, R. and Gudjons, M., The effects of diphenylhydantoin on mechanical and electrical properties of isolated cat myocardium, *Naunyn-Schmied. Arch. Pharmacol.*, 298: 273–82, 1977.

1740. Bechtel, P., Delafin, C. and Bechtel, Y., Induction of hepatic cytochrome P-450 and b5 in mice by phenytoin during chronic hypoxia, *C. R. Soc. Biol. (Paris)*, 170(2): 325–30, 1976.

1741. Beckner, T. F. and Idsvoog, P., Drug use and distribution in a pain rehabilitation center, *Am. J. Hosp. Pharm.*, 32: 285–9, 1975.

1742. Benowitz, N. L., Rosenberg, J. and Becker, C. E., Cardiopulmonary catastrophes in drug-overdosed patients, *Med. Clin. North Am.*, 63(10): 267–96, 1979.

1743. Berger, M. and Berchtold, P., Side effects of antiepileptic agents, *Dtsch. Med. Wschr.*, 100: 2552, 1975.

1744. Berger, M., Berchtold, P., Cuppers, H. J., Wiegelmann, W., Drost, H., Sailer, R., Borchard, F. and Zimmermann, H., Suppressibility of serum insulin in patients with insulinoma by somatostatin, diazoxide and diphenylhydantoin, *Presented at 4th International Danube Symposium on Diabetes Mellitus, Dubrovnik*, 1975.

1745. Bianchi, C. P., Cell calcium and malignant hyperthermia, *International Symposium on Malignant Hyperthermia*, 147–51, Gordon, R. A., Britt, B. A. and Kalow, W., Eds., Charles C Thomas, Illinois, 1973.

1746. Bianchi, C., Beani, L. and Bertelli, A., Effects of some antiepileptic drugs on brain acetylcholine, *Epilepsy Abstracts*, 8(9): 231, 1975.

1747. Biberdorf, R. I. and Spurbeck, G. H., Phenytoin in IV fluids: results endorsed, *Drug Intell. Clin. Pharm.*, 12: 300–1, 1978.

1748. Bigger, J. T., Antiarrhythmic drugs in ischemic heart disease, *Hosp. Pract.*, 7: 69–80, 1972.

1749. Bigger, J. T., Heissenbuttel, R. H. and Lovejoy, W. P., Management of cardiac problems in the intensive care unit, *Med. Clin. N. Am.*, 55: 1183–1205, 1971.

1750. Bihler, I. and Sawh, P. C., Effects of Diphenylhydantoin on the transport of Na⁺ and K⁺ and the regulation of sugar transport in muscle *in vitro, Biochim. Biophys. Acta*, 249: 240–51, 1971.

1751. Binnion, P. F. and DasGupta, R. Tritiated digoxin metabolism after prior treatment with propranolol or diphenylhydantoin sodium, *Int. J. Clin. Pharmacol.*, 12: 96–101, 1975.

1752. Biryukov, V. B., The treatment of patients with different forms of myotonia with diphenine and novocainamide, *Zh. Nevropatol, Psikhiatr.*, 76: 1333–5, 1976.

1753. Boller, F., Wright, D. G., Cavalieri, R. and Mitsumoto, H., Paroxysmal "nightmares," *Neurology*, 25: 1026–28, 1975.

1754. Boon, W. H., Benign myoclonus in infants and children, *J. Singapore Paediat. Soc.*, 20(2): 60–8, 1978.

1755. Bowdle, T. A., Neal, G. D., Levy, R. H. and Heimbach, D. M., Phenytoin pharmacokinetics in burned rats and plasma protein binding of phenytoin in burned patients, *J. Pharmacol. Exp. Ther.*, 213(1): 97–9, 1980.

1756. Bricaire, H., Luton, J. P., Wechsler, B., Messing, B. and Halaby, G., Inappropriate secretion of insulin by an islet cell adenoma. Trial treatment with diphenylhydantoin, *Ann. Med. Intern.*, 127(5): 403–7, 1976.

1757. British Medical Journal, Editor, Treatment of tinnitus, *Br. Med. J.*, 1445–6, 1979.

1758. Broser, F., Ditzen, G. and Friedrich, K., Complementary electro-physiological findings in a case of neuromyotonia, *Nervenarzt*, 46: 100–4, 1975.

1759. Buda, F. B. and Joyce, R. P., Successful treatment of atypical migraine of childhood with anticonvulsants, *Mil. Med.*, 144(8): 521–3, 1979.

1760. Bustamante, L., Lueders, H., Pippenger, C. and Goldensohn, E. S., The effects of phenytoin on the penicillin-induced spike focus, *Electroencephalogr. Clin. Neurophysiol.*, 48: 90–7, 1980.

1761. Caillard, C., Menu, A., Plotkine, M. and Rossignol, P., Do anticonvulsant drugs exert protective effect against hypoxia?, *Life Sci.*, 16: 1607–12, 1975.

1762. Callaghan, N., Feely, M., O'Callaghan, M., Duggan, B., McGarry, J., Cramer, B., Wheelan, J. and Seldrup, J., The effects of toxic and non-toxic serum phenytoin levels on carbohydrate tolerance and insulin levels, *Acta Neurol. Scand.*, 56: 563–71, 1977.

1763. Caplan, L. R., Weiner, H., Weintraub, R. M. and Austen, W. G., "Migrainous" neurologic dysfunction in patients with prosthetic cardiac valves, *Headache*, 16: 218–21, 1976.

1764. Carney, J. M., Rosecrans, J. A. and Vasko, M. R., Barbitone-induced tolerance to the effects of sedative hypnotics and related compounds on operant behavior in the rat, *Br. J. Pharmac.*, 65: 183–92, 1979.

1765. Carson, I. W., Lyons, S. M. and Shanks, R. G., Antiarrhythmic drugs, *Br. J. Anaesth.*, 51: 659–70, 1979.

1766. Celis, G. R., Kula, R. W., Somasundaram, M., Sher, J. H. and Schutta, H. S., Myokymia of segmental spinal cord origin, *Ann. Neurol.*, 8(1): 95, 1980.

1767. Chadda, V. S. and Mathur, M. S., Double blind study of the effects of diphenylhydantoin sodium on diabetic neuropathy, *J. Assoc. Phys. Ind.*, 26: 403–6, 1978.

1768. Chai, C. Y., Lee, T. M. and Wang, S. C., Effects of diphenylhydantoin on cardiac arrhythmias induced by carotid occlusion in the cat, *Arch. Int. Pharmacodyn.*, 219: 180–92, 1976.

1769. Chalfie, M. and Perlman, R. L., Inhibition of catecholamine synthesis and tyrosine 3-monooxygenase activation in pheochromocytoma cells by diphenylhydantoin, *Neurochem.*, 29: 757–9, 1977.

1770. Chapa-Alvarez, J. R., Francisco-Mendiola, J., Espejo-Plascencia, I. and Rodriguez-Noriega, E., Results obtained in the treatment of burns with sodium diphenylhydantoin, *(In press)*, (1981).

1771. Chapman, J. H., Schrank, J. P. and Crampton, R. S., Idiopathic ventricular tachycardia—an intracardiac electrical hemodynamic and angiographic assessment of six patients, *Am. J. Med.*, 59: 470–80, 1975.

1772. Cisson, C. M., Entrikin, R. K. and Wilson, B. W., Actions of phenytoin on acetylcholinesterase (ACHE), creatine kinase (CK) and protein of cultured chick embryo muscle, *Fed. Proc.*, 36: 498, March, 1977.

1773. Clemmesen, J., Incidence of neoplasms in a population on anti-convulsant drugs, *Anti-convulsant Drugs and Enzyme Induction, Study Group 9 of the Institute for Research into Mental and Multiple Handicap*, 123–30, Richens, A. and Woodford, F. P., Eds., Associated Scientific Publication, Amsterdam, 1976.

1774. Cloyd, J. C., Bosch, D. E. and Sawchuk, R. J., Concentration-time profile of phenytoin after admixture with small volumes of intravenous fluids, *Am. J. Hosp. Pharm.*, 35: 45–8, 1978.

1775. Cobbs, B. W. and Kings, S. B., Ventricular buckling: A factor in the abnormal ventriculogran and peculiar hemodynamics associated with mitral valve prolapse, *Am. Heart J.*, 93(6): 741–58, 1977.

1776. Cochran, P. T., Linnebur, A. C., Wright, W. and Matsumoto, S., Electrophysiologic studies in patients with long Q-T syndrome, *Clin. Res.*, 25(2): 88A, Feb. 1977.

1777. Cohan, S. L., Anderson, R. J. and Raines, A., Diphenylhydantoin and chlorpromazine in the treatment of spasticity, *Neurology*, 367, April, 1976.

1778. Cohan, S. L., Raines, A., Panagakos, J. and Armitage, P., Phenytoin and chlorpromazine in the treatment of spasticity, *Arch. Neurol.*, 37: 360–4, 1980.

1779. Cohen, L. S., Diphenylhydantoin sodium (Dilantin), *Current Cardiovascular Topics, Vol. I., Drugs in Cardiology, Part I*, 49–79, Donoso, E., Ed., Stratton Intercontinental Medical Book Corp., New York, 1975.

1780. Connors, B. W., Pentobarbital and diphenylhydantoin effects on the excitability and GABA sensitivity of rat dorsal root ganglion cells, *Society for Neuroscience, 9th Annual Meeting*, Nov. 2–6, 1979.

1781. Cookson, S. L. and Mann, J. D., Reversal and prevention of acute morphine induced catalepsy by phenytoin in naive rats, *Neurosci. Abstr.*, 4: 488, 1978.

1782. Cordone, G., Iester, A., Venzano, V. and Minetti, C., A case of Thomsen's disease associated with hypoparathyroidism, *Minerva Pediatrica.*, 30: 1629–34, 1979.

1783. Corr, P. B. and Gillis, R. A., Beneficial cardiac rhythm effects produced by diphenylhydantoin in experimental myocardial infarction, *Fed. Proc.*, 35: 222, 1976.

1784. Cotler, H. M. and Christensen, H. D., Tissue distribution of diphenylhydantoin, *Fed. Proc.*, 35: 664, 1976.

1785. Counsell, R. E., Ranada, V. V., Kline, W., Hong, B. H. and Buswink, A. A., Potential organ or tumor imaging agents XV: radioiodinated phenytoin derivatives, *J. of Pharmac. Sci.*, 65(2): 285–7, 1976.

1786. Crampton, R. S., Another link between the left stellate ganglion and the long Q-T syndrome, *Am. Heart J.*, 96(1): 130–2, 1978.

1787. Cudworth, A. G. and Barber, H. E., The effect of hydrocortisone phosphate, methylprednisolone and phenytoin on pancreatic insulin release and hepatic glutathione-insulin transhydrogenase activity in the rat, *Eur. J. Pharmacol.*, 31: 23–8, 1975.

1788. Cullen, J. P., Aldrete, J. A., Jankovsky, L. and Romo-Salas, F., Protective action of phenytoin in cerebral ischemia, *Anesth. Analg.*, 58: 165–9, 1979.

1789. Dadkar, M. K., Gupte, R. D. and Dohadwalla, A. M., Effect of diphenylhydantoin on blood pressure of spontaneously hypertensive rats, *Med. Biol.*, 57: 398–401, 1979.

1790. Dalessio, D. J., Medical treatment of trigeminal neuralgia, *Clin. Neurosurg.*, 24: 579–83, 1976.

1791. Das, D., Ayromlooi, J., Tobias, M., Desiderio, D. and Steinberg, H., Effect of Dilantin (D) on hypoxic fetal rabbit lung, *Pediatr. Res.*, 14: 640, 1980.

1792. Data, J. L., Wilkinson, G. R. and Nies, A. S., Interaction of quinidine with anticonvulsant drugs, *New Eng. J. Med.*, 294(13): 699–702, 1976.

1793. Dawson, G. W., Brown, H. W. and Clark, B. G., Serum phenytoin after ethosuximide, *Neurology*, 4(6): 583–4, 1978.

1794. Deisz, R. A. and Lux, H. D., Diphenylhydantoin prolongs post-synaptic inhibition and iontophoretic GABA action in the crayfish stretch receptor, *Neuroscience Letters*, 5: 199–203, 1977.

1795. Deisz, R. A. and Lux, H. D., Postsynaptic inhibition of the crayfish stretch receptor: prolongation by diphenylhydantoin, *Pflugers Arch. Ges. Physiol.*, Suppl. 368: R33, 1977.

1796. Dekeban, A. S. and Lehman, E. J. B., Effects of different dosages of anticonvulsant drugs on mental performance in patients with chronic epilepsy, *Acta Neurol. Scand.*, 52: 319–30, 1975.

1797. de la Torre, R., Murgia-Suarez, J. J. and Aldrete, J. A., Comparison of phenytoin and conventional drug therapy in the treatment of mild hypertension, *Clin. Ther.*, 3(4): 117–24, 1980.

1798. Delgado-Escueta, A. V. and Horan, M. P., Phenytoin: biochemical membrane studies, *Antiepileptic Drugs: Mechanisms of Action*, 377–98, Glaser, G. H., Penry, J. K. and Woodbury, D. M., Eds., Raven Press, New York, 1980.

1799. DeLorenzo, R. J., Phenytoin: calcium- and calmodulin-dependent protein phosphorylation and neurotransmitter release, *Antiepileptic Drugs: Mechanisms of Action*, 399–414, Glaser, G. H., Penry, J. K. and Woodbury, D. M., Eds., Raven Press, New York, 1980.

1800. DeLorenzo, R. J. and Freedman, S. D., Phenytoin inhibition of neurotransmitter release and protein phosphorylation, *Neurology*, 28(4): 367–68, 1978.

1801. DesRosiers, M., Grave, G. D., Kupferberg, H. J. and Kennedy, C., Effects of diphenylhydantoin on local cerebral blood flow, *Pharmacology and Anesthesia*, 339–42, Springer-Verlag, New York, 1975.

1802. Deupree, J. D. and Weaver, J. A., Inhibition of rat brain phosphodiesterases and adenylate cyclase by phenytoin, *Fed. Proc.* 38(3): 754, March, 1979.

1803. De Weer, P., Phenytoin: blockage of resting sodium channels, *Antiepileptic Drugs: Mechanisms of Action*, 353–61, Glaser, G. H., Penry, J. K. and Woodbury, D. M., Eds., Raven Press, New York, 1980.

1804. Dhatt, M. S., Akhtar, M., Reddy, C. P., Gomes, J. A. C., Lau, S. H., Caracta, A. R. and Damato, A. N., Modification and abolition of re-entry within the His-Purkinje system in man by diphenylhydantoin, *Circulation*, 56(5): 720–26, 1977.

1805. Dhatt, M. S., Gomes, J. A. C., Reddy, C. P., Akhtar, M., Caracta, A. R., Lau, S. H. and Damato, A. N., Effects of phenytoin on refractoriness and conduction in the human heart, *J. Cardiovasc. Surg.*, 1: 3–18, 1979.

1806. Dilman, V. M. and Anisimov, V. N., Effect of treatment with phenformin, diphenylhydantoin or L-dopa on life span and tumour incidence in C3H/Sn mice, *Gerontology*, 26: 241–6, 1980.

1807. Dilman, V. M., Bershtein, L. M., Tsyrlina, E. V., Bobrov, Y. F., Kovaleva, I. G., Vasileva, I. A. and Kryloya, N. V., The correction of endocrinous metabolic disturbances in oncological patients. The effect of biguanides (phenformin and adebit), miskleron, and diphenine, *Vopr. Onkol.*, 21(11): 33–9, 1975.

1808. Dodrill, C. B., Effects of sulthiame upon intellectual, neuropsychological, and social functioning abilities among adult epileptics: comparison with diphenylhydantoin, *Epilepsia*, 16: 617–26, 1975.

1809. Drazin, B., Ayalon, D., Hoerer, E., Oberman, Z., Harell, A., Ravid, R. and Laurian, L., Effect of diphenylhydantoin on patterns of insulin secretion in obese subjects, *Acta Diabetol. Lat.*, 14: 51–61, Jan/Apr 1977.

1810. Dreifus, L. S. and Morganroth, J., Antiarrhythmic agents and their use in therapy, *Pharmacol. Ther.*, 9: 75–106, 1980.

1811. Dretchen, K. L., Standaert, F. G. and Raines, A., Effects of phenytoin on the cyclic nucleotide system in the motor nerve terminal, *Epilepsia*, 18(3): 337–48, 1977.

1812. Duckrow, R. B. and Tabu, A., The effect of diphenylhydantoin on self mutilation in rats produced by unilateral multiple dorsal rhizotomy, *Epilepsy Abstracts*, 11(1): 27, 1977.

1813. Duperrat, B., Puissant, A., Saurat, J. H., Delanoe, J., Doyard, P. A. and Grunfels, J. P., Fabry's disease neonatal angiokeratomas. Effect of diphenylhydantoin on acute pain episodes, *Ann. Derm. Syph.* (Paris), 102(4): 392–3, 1975.

1814. Eadie, M. J., The management of vertigo, *Med. J. Aust.*, 135–6, July 26, 1975.

1815. Ehring, G. R. and Hondeghem, L. M., Rate, rhythm and voltage dependent effects of phenytoin: a test of a model of the mechanisms of action of antiarrhythmic drugs, *Proc. West. Pharmacol. Soc.*, 21: 63–5, 1978.

1816. Ehrnebo, M. and Odar-Cederlof, I., Binding of amobarbital, pentobarbital and diphenylhydantoin to blood cells and plasma proteins in healthy volunteers and uraemic patients, *Europ. J. Clin. Pharmacol.*, 8: 445–53, 1975.

1817. Eisenberg, M., Stevens, L. H. and Schofield, P. J., Epidermolysis bullosa—new therapeutic approaches, *Aust. J. Derm.*, 19: 1–8, 1978.

1818. Elfstrom, J., Plasma protein binding of phenytoin after cholecystectomy and neurosurgical operations, *Acta Neurol. Scand.*, 55: 455–64, 1977.

1819. Ellenberg, M., Unremitting painful diabetic neuropathy, *JAMA*, 237(18): 1986, 1977.

1820. Elliott, P. N. C., Jenner, P., Chadwick, D., Reynolds, E. and Marsden, C. D., The effect of diphenylhydantoin on central catecholamine containing neuronal systems, *J. Pharm. Pharmac.*, 29: 41–3, 1977.

1821. Ellis, J. M. and Lee, S. I., Acute prolonged confusion in later life as an ictal state, *Epilepsia*, 19: 119–28, 1978.

1822. El-Sherif, N. and Lazzara, R., Re-entrant ventricular arrhythmias in the late myocardial infarction period, 5. Mechanism of action of diphenylhydantoin, *Circulation*, 57(3): 465–73, 1978.

1823. Entrikin, R. K., Patterson, G. T., Weidoff, P. M. and Wilson, B. W., Righting ability and skeletal muscle properties of phenytoin-treated dystrophic chickens, *Exp. Neurol.*, 61: 650–63, 1978.

1824. Entrikin, R. K., Swanson, K. L., Weidoff, P. M., Patterson, G. T. and Wilson, B. W., Avian muscular dystrophy: functional and bio-chemical improvement with diphenylhydantoin. *Science*, 195: 873–5, 1977.

1825. Esparza-Ahumada, S., Chapa-Alvarez, R., Andrade-Perez, J. S. and Rodriguez-Noriega, E., The improvement of chronic vascular leg ulcers while on treatment with diphenylhydantoin sodium, *(In press)*, (1981).

1826. Eviatar, L. and Eviatar, A., Vertigo in children: differential diagnosis and treatment, *Pediatrics*, 59: 833–8, 1977.

1827. Faugier-Grimaud, S., Action of anticonvulsants on pentylenetetrazol-induced epileptiform activity on invertebrate neurones (Helix aspersa), *Epilepsy Abstracts*, 12(11): 489, 1979.

1828. Ferrendelli, J. A., Phenytoin: cyclic nucleotide regulation in the brain, *Antiepileptic Drugs: Mechanisms of Action*, 429–33, Glaser, G. H., Penry, J. K. and Woodbury, D. M., Eds., Raven Press, New York, 1980.

1829. Ferrendelli, J. A. and Kinscherf, D. A., Inhibitory effects of anticonvulsant drugs on cyclic nucleotide accumulation in brain, *Ann. Neurol.*, 5: 533–8, 1979.

1830. Ferrendelli, J. A. and Kinscherf, D. A., Phenytoin: effects on calcium flux and cyclic nucleotides, *Epilepsia*, 18(3): 331–6, 1977.

1831. Ferrendelli, J. A. and Kinscherf, D. A., Similar effects of phenytoin and tetrodotoxin on cyclic nucleotide regulation in depolarized brain tissue, *J. Pharm. Exp. Ther.*, 207(3): 787–93, 1978.

1832. Fincham, R. W. and Schottelius, D. D., Decreased phenytoin levels in antineoplastic therapy, *Ther. Drug Monitoring*, 1: 277–83, 1979.

1833. Finelli, P. F., Phenytoin and methadone tolerance, *New Eng. J. Med.*, 294(4): 227, 1976.

1834. Fisher, J. D., Cohen, H. L., Mehra, R., Altschuler, H., Escher, D. J. W. and Furman, S., Cardiac pacing and pacemakers II. Serial electro-physiologic-pharmacologic testing for control of recurrent tachyarrhythmias, *Am. Heart J.*, 93(5): 658–68, 1977.

1835. Fleming, K., Japanese encephalitis in an Australian soldier returned from Vietnam, *Med. J. Aust.*, 2: 19–23, 1975.

1836. Friis, M. L., Epilepsy among parents of children with facial clefts, *Epilepsia*, 20: 69–76, 1979.

1837. Fromm, G. H., Glass, J. D., Chattha, A. S. and Martinez, A. J., Effect of anticonvulsant drugs on inhibitory and excitatory pathways, *Epilepsia*, 22: 65–73, 1981.

1838. Fromm, G. H., Glass, J. D., Chattha, A. S. and Terrence, C. F., Role of inhibitory mechanisms in trigeminal neuralgia, *Neurology*, 30: 417, 1980.

1839. Fry, B. and Ciarlone, A. E., Phenytoin increases norepinephrine (NE) and serotonin (5-HT) in mouse cerebellum, *Pharmacologist*, 21(3): 183, 1979.

1840. Frymoyer, J. W., Fracture healing in rats treated with diphenylhydantoin (Dilantin), *J. Trauma*, 16(5): 368–70, 1976.

1841. Fukuyama, Y., Ochiai, Y., Hayakawa, T. and Miyagawa, F., Overnight sleep EEG and cerebrospinal fluid monoamines in seizures induced by movement, *Neuropadiatrie*, 10(2): 138–49, 1979.

1842. Furman, R. E. and Barchi, R. L., The pathophysiology of myotonia produced by aromatic carboxylic acids, *Ann. Neurol.*, 4(4): 357–65, 1978.

1843. Gage, P. W., Lonergan, M. and Torda, T. A., Presynaptic and postsynaptic depressant effects of phenytoin sodium at the neuromuscular junction, *Br. J. Pharmac.*, 69: 119–21, 1980.

1844. Gage, P. W. and Spence, I., The origin of the muscle fasciculation caused by funnel-web spider venom, *Epilepsy Abstracts*, 11(9): 364, 1978.

1845. Gallaghan, J. T., Kinetic inhibition studies of microsomal phenytoin (DPH), *Fed. Proc.*, 35(3): 408, 1976.

1846. Gangji, D., Schwade, J. G. and Strong, J. M., Phenytoin-misonidazole: possible metabolic interaction, *Cancer Treat. Rep.*, 64(1): 155–6, 1980.

1847. Garson, A., Kugler, J. D., Gillette, P. C., Simonelli, A. and McNamara, D. G., Control of late postoperative ventricular arrhythmias with phenytoin in young patients, *Am. J. Cardiol.*, 46(2): 290–4, 1980.

1848. Gautray, J. P., Jolivet, A., Goldenberg, F., Tajchner, G., and Eberhard, A., Clinical investigation of the menstrual cycle. II Neuroendocrine investigation and therapy of the inadequate luteal phase, *Fertility and Sterility*, 29(3): 275–281, 1978.

1849. Gelehrter, T. D., Enzyme induction (second of three parts), *New Eng. J. Med.*, 294(11): 589–95, 1976.

1850. Gibberd, F. B. and Webley, M., Studies in man of phenytoin absorption and its implication, *Epilepsy Abstracts*, 9(2): 78, 1976.

1851. Gibbs, M. E. and Ng, K. T., Diphenylhydantoin facilitation of labile, protein-independent memory, *Brain Research Bulletin*, 1: 203–8, 1976.

1852. Gibbs, M. E. and Ng, K. T., Psychobiology of memory: towards a model of memory formation, *Biobehavioral Reviews*, 1: 113–36, 1977.

1853. Gilbert, J. C., Diseases of the cardiovascular system—drugs affecting the cardiovascular system: pharmacological basis of treatment, *Br. Med. J.*, 31–3, 1976.

1854. Gilbert, J. C. and Wyllie, M. G., Effects of anticonvulsant and convulsant drugs on the ATPase activities of synaptosomes and their components, *Br. J. Pharmac.*, 56: 49–57, 1976.

1855. Gilbert, J. C. and Wyllie, M. G., The relationship between nerve terminal adenosine triphosphatases and neurotransmitter release: as determined by the use of antidepressant and other CNS-active drugs, *Br. J. Pharmac.*, 69: 215–25, 1980.

1856. Gill, M. A., Miscia, V. F. and Gourley, D. R., The treatment of common cardiac arrhythmias, *J. Amer. Pharm. Assn.*, NS16(1): 20–9, Jan. 1976.

1857. Gillette, P. C. and Garson, A., Electrophysiologic and pharmacologic characteristics of automatic ectopic atrial tachycardia, *Circulation*, 56: 571–5, 1977.

1858. Glaser, G. H., Penry, J. K. and Woodbury, D. M., Eds., *Antiepileptic Drugs: Mechanisms of Action*, Raven Press, New York, 1980.

1859. Goldberg, M. A., Phenytoin: binding, *Antiepileptic Drugs: Mechanisms of Action*, 323–37, Glaser, G. H., Penry, J. K. and Woodbury, D. M., Eds., Raven Press, New York, 1980.

1860. Goldberg, M. A., Phenytoin, phospholipids and calcium, *Neurology*, 27: 827–33, 1977.

1861. Goldberg, M. A. and Crandall, P. H., Human brain binding of phenytoin, *Neurology*, 28: 881–5, 1978.

1862. Goldberg, M. A. and Todoroff, T., Phenytoin binding to brain phospholipids, *Neurology*, 26: 386, 1976.

1863. Goldberg, M. A., Todoroff, T. and Crandall, P., Phenytoin binding to human brain, *Neurology*, 27(4): 374, 1977.

1864. Goldman, E., Aldrete, J. A. and Sherrill, D., Phenytoin brain protection in acute reversible hypoxia, *7th World Congress of Anaesthesiologists*, Hamburg, 215–6, Sept. 1980.

1865. Goldsmith, S. and From, A. H. L., Arsenic-induced atypical ventricular tachycardia, *New Eng. J. Med.*, 303(19): 1096–8, 1980.

1866. Goodenough, D. J., Fariello, R. G., Annis, B. L. and Chun, R. W. M., Familial and acquired paroxysmal dyskinesias, *Arch. Neurol.*, 35: 827–31, 1978.

1867. Goultschin, J. and Shoshan, S., Inhibition of collagen breakdown by diphenylhydantoin, *Biochim. Biophys. Acta*, 631: 188–91, 1980.

1868. Grafova, V. N., Danilova, E. I. and Kryzhanovskii, G. N., Analgesic effects of antiepileptic drugs in a pain syndrome of spinal origin, *Bull. Exp. Biol. Med.*, 88(8): 837–40, 1979.

1869. Green, R. S. and Rau, J. H., The use of diphenylhydantoin in compulsive eating disorders; further studies, *Anorexia*

Nervosa, 377–82, Vigersky, R. A., Ed., Raven Press, New York, 1977.

1870. Greenblatt. D. J.. Allen. M. D.. Koch-Weser, J. and Shader, R. I., Accidental poisoning with psychotropic drugs in children, *Am. J. Dis. Child*, 130: 507–11, 1976.

1871. Greenblatt, D. J. and Shader, R. I., Intravenous phenytoin, *New Eng. J. Med.*, 1078, 1976.

1872. Griggs, R. C., Moxley, R. T., Riggs, J. E. and Engel, W. K., Effects of acetazolamide on myotonia, *Ann. Neurol.*, 3: 531–7, 1978.

1873. Gustafson, A., Svensson, S. E. and Ugander, L., Cardiac arrhythmias in chloral hydrate poisoning, *Acta Med. Scand.*, 201: 227–30, 1977.

1874. Hadfield, M. G. and Rigby, W. F. C., Dopamine: Adaptive uptake changes in striatal synaptosomes after 30 seconds of intense fighting, *Biochem. Pharmacol.*, 25: 2752–4, 1976.

1875. Hadfield, M. G. and Weber, N. E., Effect of fighting and diphenylhydantoin on the uptake of 3H-1-norepinephrine *in vitro* in synaptosomes isolated from retired male breeding mice. *Biochem. Pharmacol.*, 24: 1538–40, 1975.

1876. Haffner, Z. and Hovarth, E., Pseudomyotonia (Isaacs-syndroma), *Orvosi Hetilap*, 116(49): 2895–7, 1975.

1877. Hahn, T. J., Dibartelo, T. F. and Halstead, L. R., Comparative effects of diphenylhydantoin (DPH) and ouabain (Ou) ^{45}Ca release from cultured fetal rat forelimb rudiments, *Clin. Res.*, 26(5): 681A, 1978.

1878. Hahn, T. J., Scharp, C. R., Richardson, C. A., Halstead, L. R., Kahn, A. J. and Teitelbaum, S. L., Interaction of diphenylhydantoin (phenytoin) and phenobarbital with hormonal mediation of fetal rat bone resorption *in vitro*, *J. Clin. Invest.*, 62: 406–14, 1978.

1879. Hamed, M. A., Abdel-Aal, H. M., Abdel-Aziz, T. M., Nassar, S. K., Sweify, S. M., Atta, S. M., El-Awady, S. M., El-Aref, M., El-Garf, A. R., A trial of diphenylhydantoin in periodic disease (familial Mediterranean fever) in Egyptian children, *J. Egypt. Med. Assoc.*, 58(¾): 205–15, 1975.

1880. Hamer, J., Diseases of the cardiovascular system—cardiac failure, *Br. Med. J.*, 220–4, 1976.

1881. Hansotia, P., Mazza, J. J. and Gatlin, P., Diphenylhydantoin and fragility of erythrocytes in normal subjects and in patients with hereditary spherocytic anemia. *Amer. J. Clin. Path.*, 64(1): 75–9, 1975.

1882. Hanstom, L. and Jones, I. L., The effect of diphenylhydantoin upon degradation of sulphated macromolecules in cat palatal mucosa *in vitro*, *Med. Biol.*, 57: 177–81, 1979.

1883. Hardie, R. A. and Savin, J. A., Drug-induced skin diseases, *Br. Med. J.*, 935–7, 1979.

1884. Haruda, F., Phenytoin hypersensitivity, *Neurology*, 29: 1480–5, 1979.

1885. Harvey, S. C., The effects of ouabain and phenytoin on myocardial noradrenaline, *Arch. Int. Pharmacodyn.*, 213(2): 222–34, 1975.

1886. Hatangdi, V. S., Boas, R. A. and Richards, E. G., Postherpetic neuralgia: management with antiepileptic and tricyclic drugs, *Advances in Pain Research and Therapy*, Vol. 1, 583–587, Bonica, J. J. and Albe-Fessard, D., Eds., Raven Press, New York, 1976.

1887. Haward, L. R. C., Augmentation of autogenic training by sodium diphenylhydantoinate, *World J. Psychosynthesis*, 8: 26–29, 1976.

1888. Haward, L. R. C., Impairment of flying efficiency in anancastic pilots, *Aviation, Space & Environmental Medicine*, 156–161, 1977.

1889. Heesen, H. and Lahrtz, H., Treatment of severe digitalis intoxication in suicidal attempt, *Med. Klin.*, 70: 812–6, 1975.

1890. Hegarty, B. A., Treatment of severe self-imposed overdose of phencyclidine hydrochloride, *Bulletin Sinai Hosp.*, Detroit, 23(3): 147–51, 1975.

1891. Heinonen, O. P., Slone, D. and Shapiro, S., Birth defects and drugs in pregnancy, *Lancet* (Review) 1086, 1977.

1892. Helfant, R. H., Effectiveness of diphenylhydantoin as an antihypertensive, *Personal Communication*, 1975.

1893. Henry, D. A., Bell, G. D. and Glithero, P., Plasma high-density lipoproteins, *New Eng. J. Med.*, 300(14): 798, 1979.

1894. Herishanu, Y., Eylath, U. and Ilan, R., 'In vitro' studies on the fate of diphenylhydantoin in uremia, *Neurosci. Lett.*, 2: 97–101, 1976.

1895. Herishanu, Y., Eylath, U. and Ilan, R., Effects of calcium content of diet on absorption of diphenylhydantoin, *Israel J. Med. Sci.*, 12(12): 1453–6, 1976.

1896. Hertz, L., Drug-induced alterations of ion distribution at the cellular level of the central nervous system, *Pharmacol. Rev.*, 29(1): 35–65, 1977.

1897. Herzberg, G. R., Challberg, M. D., Hess, B. C. and Howland, J. L., Elevated potassium efflux from dystrophic diaphragm: influence of diphenylhydantoin and lithium, *Biochem. Biophys. Res. Commun.*, 63(4): 858–63, 1975.

1898. Heyma, P., Larkins, R. G., Perry-Keene, D., Peter, C. T., Ross, D. and Sloman, J. G., Thyroid hormone levels and protein binding in patients on long-term diphenylhydantoin treatment, *Clin. Endocrin.*, 6: 369–76, 1977.

1899. Homan, R. W., Vasko, M. R. and Blaw, M., Phenytoin plasma concentrations in paroxysmal kinesigenic choreoathetosis, *Neurology*, 30: 673–76, 1980.

1900. Hondeghem, L. M., Effects of lidocaine, phenytoin and quinidine on the ischemic canine myocardium, *J. Electrocardiol.*, 9(3): 203–9, 1976.

1901. Hondeghem, L. M., Effects of quinidine, lidocaine and phenytoin on the excitability of the ischemic rabbit heart, *Proc. West. Pharmacol. Soc.*, 19: 320–22, 1976.

1902. Hufnagl, H. D. and Sen, S., Phenytoin infusions in medical intensive care, *Fortschr. Med.*, 96: 415–24, 1978.

1903. Hulce, V. D., The action of chlorpromazine and phenytoin on muscle rigidity due to cerebellar lesions, *Society for Neuroscience*, III: 372, 7th Annual Meeting, Nov. 7–10, 1977.

1904. Ifabumuyi, O. I. and Jeffries, J. J., Treatment of drug-induced psychosis with diphenylhydantoin, *Can. Psychiatr. Assoc. J.*, 21: 565–9, 1976.

1905. Ionasescu, V., Ionasescu, R., Witte, D., Feld, R., Cancilla, P., Kaeding, L., Kraus, L. and Stern, L., Altered protein synthesis and creatine kinase in breast muscle cell cultures from dystrophic chick embryos, *J. Neurol. Sci.*, 46: 157–68, 1980.

1906. Ionasescu, V., Stern, L. Z., Ionasescu, R. and Rubenstein, P., Stimulatory effects of drugs for protein synthesis on muscle cell cultures in Duchenne dystrophy, *Ann. Neurol.* 5: 107–10, 1979.

1907. Irani, P. F., Purohit, A. V., and Wadia, N. H., The syndrome of continuous muscle fiber activity, *Acta Neurol. Scand.*, 55: 273–88, 1977.

1908. Ishibashi, F., Hamasaki, A., Shibata, Y., Naitoh, Y. and Kawate, R., Protection against alloxan inhibition of insulin release by glucose, cytochalasin B and diphenylhydantoin, *Hiroshima J. Med. Sci.*, 25(4): 199–202, 1976.

1909. Itil, T. M. and Seaman, P., Drug treatment of human aggression, *Prog. Neuro-Psychopharmacol.*, 2: 659–69, 1978.

1910. Jackson, D. L., Satya-Murti, S., Davis, L. and Drachman, D. B., Isaacs syndrome with laryngeal involvement: an unusual presentation of myokymia, *Neurology*, 29: 1612–5, 1979.

1911. JAMA, Questions and Answers, Recurrent transient motor aphasia in 39-year-old woman, *JAMA*, 238(23): 2541–2, 1977.

1912. JAMA, Questions and Answers, Anticonvulsant therapy and athletic performance, *JAMA*, 240(1): 59–60, 1978.

1913. Jannetta, P. J., Glossopharyngeal neuralgia, *JAMA*, 239(20): 2173, 1978.

1914. Jennett, W. B., *An Introduction to Neurosurgery*, 109, C. V. Mosby, St. Louis, 1970.

1915. Johanson, C. E. and Smith, Q. R., Phenytoin-induced stimulation of the Na-K pump in the choroid plexus cerebrospinal fluid system, *Society for Neuroscience*, III: 316, 7th Annual

Meeting, Nov. 7–10, 1977.

1916. Johnson, R. N., Englander, R. N., Quint, S. R., Hanna, G. R., Control of excitability and threshold in the thalamocortical motor system of the cat by cerebellar stimulation, *Epilepsy Abstracts*, 9(9): 277, 1976.

1917. Johnston, D. and Ayala, G. F., Diphenylhydantoin: action of a common anticonvulsant on bursting pacemaker cells in aplysia, *Science*, 189: 1009–11, 1975.

1918. Jonas, A. D., When a subclinical psychomotor seizure poses as a neurosis, *Medical Bulletin of the U.S. Army, Europe*, 32(5): 174–76, 1975.

1919. Kamio, M. and Sugita, T., Syncopal attacks with loss of consciousness and abnormal EEG in childhood, *Epilepsy Abstracts*, 10(6): 180, 1977.

1920. Kannan, K., Dash, R. J. and Rastogi, G. K., Evaluation of treatment of painful diabetic neuropathy with diphenylhydantoin, *J. Diabetic Assoc. India*, 18: 199–202, 1978.

1921. Karmazyn, M., Horrobin, D. F., Morgan, R. O., Manku, M. S., Ally, A. I. and Karmali, R. A., Diphenylhydantoin: a prostaglandin antagonist in the rat mesenteric vasculature, *IRCS Medical Science*, 5: 332, 1977.

1922. Kerstein, M. D., and Firestone, L., The role of Dilantin (DPH) in the prevention of the pulmonary lesions associated with CNS hypoxia, *Clin. Res.*, 25(3): 419A, April, 1977.

1923. Keith, D. A., Side effects of diphenylhydantoin: a review, *J. Oral Surg.*, 36: 206–10, 1978.

1924. Kinscherf, D. A. and Ferrendelli, J. A., Tetrodotoxin-like effect of phenytoin on cyclic nucleotide regulation in brain, *Fed. Proc.*, 37(3): 341, 1978.

1925. Kloppel, G., Functional pathomorphology of the pancreatic β cell system—Ultrastructural and calcium-cytochemical studies on insulin biosynthesis and secretion, *Veroeff Pathol.*, 108: 54–8, 1977.

1926. Koch, M. M., Lorenzini, I., Freddara, U., Jezequel, A. M. and Orlandi, F., Type 2 Crigler-Najjar syndrome. Quantitation of ultrastructural data and evolution under therapy with phenytoin, *Gastroenterol. Clin. Biol.*, 2: 831–42, 1978.

1927. Koch-Weser, J., The serum level approach to individualization of drug dosage, *Eur. J. Clin. Pharmacol.*, 9: 1–8, 1975.

1928. Koch-Weser, J. and Sellers, E. M., Binding of drugs to serum albumin (First of two parts), *New Eng. J. Med.*, 294(6): 311–9, 1976.

1929. Koch-Weser, J. and Sellers, E. M., Binding of drugs to serum albumin (Second of two parts), *New Eng. J. Med.*, 294(10): 526–31, 1976.

1930. Komatsu, K. and Sato, M., A comparison between ouabain treated and genetically dystrophic mice with reference to the effect of phenytoin on the membrane potential of their skeletal muscles, *Yakugaku Zasshi*, 99(8): 855–8, 1979.

1931. Kontani, H., Kudo, Y. and Fukuda, H., Effect of drugs affecting sodium permeability on the muscle spindle of the frog, *Folia Pharmacol. Japan*, 72: 325–30, 1978.

1932. Korczyn, A. D., Shavit, S. and Schlosberg, I., The chick as a model for malignant hyperpyrexia, *Eur. J. Pharmacol.*, 61: 187–9, 1980.

1933. Kornblith, P. L., Hartnett, L. C., Anderson, L. P., and Quindlen, E. A., Growth-inhibitory effect of diphenylhydantoin on murine astrocytomas, *Neurosurgery*, 5(2): 259–63, 1979.

1934. Kornblith, P. L., Callahan, L. V. and Caswell, P. A., Growth-inhibitory effects of diphenylhydantoin on human brain tumor cells in culture, *Neurosurgery*, 2(2): 122–7, 1978.

1935. Kornblith, P. L., Caswell, P. A., Bogoch, S., Callahan, L. V. and Dreyfus, J., Effects of diphenylhydantoin on cultured human glial cells, *In Vitro*, 324, April, 1976.

1936. Kramer, M. S., Menstrual epileptoid psychosis in an adolescent girl, *Amer. J. Dis. Child.*, 131: 316–7, 1977.

1937. Krumdieck, C. L., Fukushima, K., Fukushima, T., Shiota, T. and Butterworth, C. E., A long-term study of the excretion of folate and pterins in a human subject after ingestion of ¹⁴C folic acid, with observations on the effect of diphenylhydantoin administration, *Am. J. Clin. Nutr.*, 31: 88–93, 1978.

1938. Kupferberg, H. J., Lust, W. D., Yonekawa, W., Passonneau, J. V. and Penry, J. K., Effect of phenytoin (Diphenylhydantoin) on electrically-induced changes in the brain levels of cyclic nucleotides and GABA, *Fed. Proc.*, 35: 583, March, 1976.

1939. Kurihara, T., Tawara, S., Araki, S., Okamoto, S. and Shirabe, T., The therapeutic effects of diphenylhydantoin for myotonia and electron microscopic studies of Thomsen's disease, *Clin. Neurol. (Tokyo)*, 16: 661–8, 1976.

1940. Kutt, H. and Solomon, G. E., Phenytoin: relevant side effects, *Antiepileptic Drugs: Mechanisms of Action*, 435–45, Glaser, G. H., Penry, J. K. and Woodbury, D. M., Eds., Raven Press, New York, 1980.

1941. Lala, V. R., Juan, C. S., and AvRuskin, T. W., Effect of diphenylhydantoin (DPH) on arginine-induced glucagon (IRC) secretion in juvenile diabetes mellitus (JDM), *Pediatr. Res.*, 11: 517, April 1977.

1942. LaManna, J., Lothman, E., Rosenthal, M., Somjen, G. and Younts, W., Phenytoin, electric, ionic and metabolic responses in cortex and spinal cord, *Epilepsia*, 18(3): 317–29, 1977.

1943. Lance, J. W., Burke, D. and Pollard, J., Hyperexcitability of motor and sensory neurons in neuromyotonia, *Ann. Neurol.*, 5: 523–32, 1979.

1944. Lancet, Editor, Liquid-protein diets and ventricular tachycardia, *Lancet*, 976, 1978.

1945. Lancet, Editor, Tinnitus, *Lancet*, 1124, 1979.

1946. Lappas, D. G., Powell, W. M. J. and Daggett, W. M., Cardiac dysfunction in the perioperative period, *Anesthesiology*, 47: 117–37, 1977.

1947. Laxer, K. D., Robertson, L. T., Julien, R. M. and Dow, R. S., Phenytoin: relationship between cerebellar function and epileptic discharges, *Antiepileptic Drugs: Mechanisms of Action*, 415–27, Glaser, G. H., Penry, J. K. and Woodbury, D. M., Eds., Raven Press, New York, 1980.

1948. Lechin, F. and van der Dijs, B., Effects of diphenylhydantoin (DPH) on distal colon motility, *Acta Gastroenterol. Latinoam*, 9(3): 145–52, 1979.

1949. Lee, Y. T., Lee, T. K. and Tsai, H. C., Glossopharyngeal neuralgia as the cause of cardiac syncope, *J. Formosan Med. Assoc.*, 74: 103–7, 1975.

1950. Leon-Sotomayor, L., A new technique in the treatment of thromboembolic stroke, *Angiology*, 31(11): 729–43, 1980.

1951. Levin, S. R., Charles, M. A., O'Connor, M., Grodsky, G. M., Use of diphenylhydantoin and diazoxide to investigate insulin secretory mechanisms, *Amer. J. Physiol.*, 229(1): 49–54, July, 1975.

1952. Levin, S. R., Driessen, J. and Kasson, B., Adenosinetriphosphatases of pancreatic islets: comparison with those of kidney, *Endocr. Soc. Program*, 59: 75 (Abstract 38), 1977.

1953. Levin, S. R., Kasson, B. G. and Driessen, J. F., Adenosine triphosphatases of rat pancreatic islets—comparison with those of rat kidney, *J. Clin. Invest.*, 62: 692–701, 1978.

1954. Levinson, S., Canalis, R. F. and Kaplan, H. J., Laryngeal spasm complicating pseudomyotonia, *Arch. Otolaryngol.*, 102: 185–7, 1976.

1955. Levo, Y., Markowitz, O. and Trainin, N., Hydantoin immunosuppression and carcinogenesis, *Clin. Exp. Immun.*, 19: 521–7, March 1975.

1956. Levy, R. H., Phenytoin: biopharmacology, *Antiepileptic Drugs: Mechanisms of Action*, 315–21, Glaser, G. H., Penry, J. K. and Woodbury, D. M., Eds., Raven Press, New York, 1980.

1957. Lewin, E., Effects of phenytoin on the release of ¹⁴C-Adenine derivatives, *Epilepsia*, 18(3): 349–55, 1977.

1958. Lewin, E. and Bleck, V., Cyclic AMP accumulation in cerebral cortical slices: effect of carbamazepine, phenobarbital and phenytoin, *Epilepsia*, 18(2): 237–42, 1977.

1959. Lewis, D. V., Zbiez, K. I. and Wilson, W. A., Diphenylhydantoin depresses firing in the aplysia giant neuron by blocking a slow inward current, *Soc. for Neuroscience*, 251, 9th

Annual Meeting, Nov. 2–6, 1979.

1960. Lewis, J. S., Gilbert, B. and Garry, P. J., Glutathione reductase activity coefficients of children on anticonvulsant drugs and their normal siblings, *Fed. Proc.,* 37 (Abstract 2412): 671, March 1978.

1961. Linden, V., Brevik, J. I., and Hansen, T., Phenytoin, phenobarbitone and serum cholesterol, *Scand. J. Soc. Med.,* 5: 123–5, 1977.

1962. Livingston, S., Phenytoin and serum cholesterol, *Epilepsy Abstracts,* 9(10): 329, 1976.

1963. Loeser, J. D., The management of tic douloureux, *Pain,* 3: 155–62, 1977.

1964. Loeser, J. D., What to do about tic douloureux, *JAMA,* 239(12): 1153–5, 1978.

1965. Loh, C. K., Katz, A. M. and Pierce, E. C., Interactions of diphenylhydantoin and cardiac glycosides on atrial potassium, *Am. J. Physiol.,* 230(4): 965–69, 1976.

1966. Lown, B., Temte, J. V., Reich, P., Gaughan, C., Regestein, Q. and Hai, H., Basis for recurring ventricular fibrillation in the absence of coronary heart disease and its management, *New Eng. J. Med.,* 294(12): 623–29, 1976.

1967. Lublin, F. D., Tsairis, P., Streletz, L. J., Chambers, R. A., Riker, W. F., Van Poznak, A. and Duckett, S. W., Myokymia and impaired muscular relaxation with continuous motor unit activity, *J. Neurol. Neurosurg. Psychiatry,* 42: 557–62, 1979.

1968. Luoma, P. V., Myllyla, V. V., Sotaniemi, E. A. and Hokkanen, T. E. J., Plasma HDL cholesterol in epileptics with elevated triglyceride and cholesterol, *Acta Neurol. Scand.,* 60: 56–63, 1979.

1969. Lust, W. D., Kupferberg, H. J., Yonekawa, W. D., Penry, J. K., Passonneau, J. V. and Wheaton, A. B., Changes in brain metabolites induced by convulsants or electroshock: Effects of anticonvulsant agents, *Molec. Pharmacol.,* 14: 347–56, 1978.

1970. Lutschg, J., Jerusalem, F., Ludin, H. P., Vassella, F. and Mumenthaler, M., The syndrome of 'continuous muscle fiber activity,' *Arch. Neurol,* 35: 198–205, 1978.

1971. Maisov, N. I., Tolmacheva, N. S. and Raevsky, K. S., Liberation of ^{3}H-gamma-aminobutyric acid (^{3}H-GABA) from isolated nerve endings of the rat's brain under the effect of psychotropic substances, *Farmakol. Toksik.,* 39: 517–20, 1976.

1972. Matthews, E. C., Blount, A. W. and Townsend, J. I., Q-T prolongation and ventricular arrhythmias, with and without deafness, in the same family, *Am. J. Cardiol.,* 29: 702–11, 1972.

1973. Matthews, E. K. and Sakamoto, Y., Pancreatic islet cells: electrogenic and electrodiffusional control of membrane potential, *J. Physiol.,* 246: 439–57, 1975.

1974. Matthews, W. D. and Connor, J. D., Actions of iontophoretic phenytoin and medazepam on hippocampal neurons, *J. Pharmacol. Exp. Ther.,* 201(3): 613–21, 1977.

1975. Matthews, W. D. and Connor, J. D., Effects of diphenylhydantoin and diazepam on hippocampal evoked responses, *Neuropharmacol.,* 15: 181–6, 1976.

1976. Medical Letter on Drugs and Therapeutics, Treatment of cardiac arrhythmias, 20(26): 113–20, 1978.

1977. Medical World News, Editor, New clues to averting liquid-protein deaths, *Medical World News,* 61, 1978.

1978. Melacini, P., Furlanut, M., Ferrari, M. and Volta, S. D., Effects of quinidine and diphenylhydantoin on membrane resistance in smooth muscle, *Arch. Int. Pharmacodyn.,* 213(1): 17–21, 1975.

1979. Melding, P. S. and Goodey, R. J., The treatment of tinnitus with oral anticonvulsants, *J. Laryng.,* 93: 111–22, 1979.

1980. Melikian, A. P., Straughn, A. B., Slywka, G. W. A., Whyatt, P. L. and Meyer, M. C., Bioavailability of 11 phenytoin products, *J. Pharmacokinet. Biopharm.,* 5(2): 133–46, 1977.

1981. Mentzer, R. M., Alegre, C. and Nolan, S. P., Effects of diphenylhydantoin (Dilantin) on the pulmonary circulation, *Surgical Forum,* 26: 217–9, 1975.

1982. Merck Manual of Diagnosis and Therapy, 13th Edition,

Merck Sharp & Dohme Research Laboratories, Rahway, New Jersey, 1977.

1983. Mesulam, M. M., Dissociative states with abnormal temporal lobe EEG-multiple personality and the illusion of possession, *Arch. Neurol.,* 38: 176–81, 1981.

1984. Migdal, S. D., Slick, G. L. and McDonald, F. D., Diphenylhydantoin (DPH) renal vasodilator, *Clin. Res.,* 25(3): 273A, 1977.

1985. Migdal, S. D., Slick, G. L., Abu-Hamdan, D. and McDonald, F. D., Phenytoin, renal function and renin release, *J. Pharmacol. Exp. Ther.,* 215(2): 304–8, 1980.

1986. Migdal, S. D., Slick, G. L. and McDonald, F. D., Phenytoin (DPH) renal function and renin secretion (RSR), *Clin. Res.,* 26(3): 471, 1978.

1987. Millichap, J. G., Recurrent headaches in 100 children, *Child's Brain,* 4: 95–105, 1978.

1988. Mohan, K. J., Salo, M. W. and Nagaswami, S., A case of limbic system dysfunction with hypersexuality and fugue state, *Dis. Nerv. Syst.,* 36: 621–4, 1975.

1989. Moore, S. J., Digitalis toxicity and treatment with phenytoin: neurologic mechanism of action, *Heart & Lung,* 6(6): 1035–40, 1977.

1990. Morgan, P. H. and Mathison, I. W., Arrhythmias and antiarrhythmic drugs: mechanism of action and structure-activity relations, *J. Pharm. Sci.,* 65: 467–81, 1976.

1991. Moss, G., The role of the central nervous system in shock: the centroneurogenic etiology of the respiratory distress syndrome, *Critical Care Medicine,* 2(4): 181–5, 1974.

1992. Mueller, D. and Leuschner, U., Clinical and neurophysiological findings in blood-level controlled diphenylhydantoin application—considerations on the therapy of myotonic dystrophy, *Psychiatr. Neurol. Med. Psychol.,* 32(8): 464–8, 1980.

1993. Muller, N. R., Tsyrlina, E. V., Ostroumova, M. N. and Shemerovskaya, T. G., The effect of diphenine on the growth and metastasis of experimental malignant tumors, *Vopr. Onkol.,* 21(7): 86–90, 1975.

1994. Neldner, H. K., Treatment of localized linear scleroderma with phenytoin, *Cutis,* 22: 569–72, 1978.

1995. Nelson, E. W., Cerda, J. J., Wilder, B. J. and Streiff, R. R., Effect of diphenylhydantoin on the bioavailability of citris folate, *Am. J. Clin. Nutr.,* 31: 82–7, 1978.

1996. Neuman, R. S. and Frank, G. B., Effects of diphenylhydantoin and phenobarbital on voltage-clamped myelinated nerve, *Can. J. Physiol. Pharmacol.,* 55(1): 42–8, 1977.

1997. Neuvonen, P. J., Penttila, O., Lehtovaara, R. and Aho, K., Effect of antiepileptic drugs on the elimination of various tetracycline derivatives, *Europ. J. Clin. Pharmacol.,* 9: 147–54, 1975.

1998. Nevsimal, O., Suta, M. and Tuhacek, M., The stiffman syndrome, *Cesk. Neurol.,* 30(2): 133–8, 1967.

1999. Newell, I. M., Trigeminal neuralgia: induced remission without surgery, and observations on its aetiology, *Med. J. Aust.,* 1: 605–7, 1976.

2000. Newsom, J. A., Withdrawal seizures in an in-patient alcoholism program, *Currents in Alcoholism,* vol. 6, 11–14, Galanter, M., Ed., Grune and Stratton, New York, 1979.

2001. Nies, A. S., Cardiovascular disorders, I. Alteration of arterial pressure and regional blood flow, *Clinical Pharmacology, Basic Principles in Therapeutics,* K. L. Melmon and H. F. Morrelli, Eds., Macmillan, New York, 1972.

2002. Nikkila, E. A., Kaste, M., Ehnholm, C. and Viikari, J., Elevation of high-density lipoprotein in epileptic patients treated with phenytoin, *Acta Med. Scand,* 204: 517–20, 1978.

2003. Nishida, T., The effects of diphenylhydantoin sodium on the *in vivo* electroretinogram of rabbits, *Epilepsy Abstracts,* 9(2): 47, 1976.

2004. Nishikaze, O., Furuya, E. and Takase, T., Diphenylhydantoin inhibits the production of lipid peroxide in carrageenin induced inflammation in rats, *IRCS Med. Sci.,* 8: 552, 1980.

2005. Ochiai, Y., Hayakawa, T., Fukuyama, Y. and Miragawa,

F., Analysis of overnight sleep EEG and cerebrospinal fluid monoamine metabolites in seizures induced by movement, *Epilepsy Abstracts*, 11(8): 297, 1978.

2006. O'Donnell, J. M., Kovacs, T. and Szabo, B., Influence of the membrane stabilizer diphenylhydantoin on potassium and sodium movements in skeletal muscle, *Pflugers Arch*, 358: 275–88, 1975.

2007. Oettinger, L., Interaction of methylphenidate and diphenylhydantoin, *Drug Therapy*, 5: 107–8, 1975.

2008. Opie, L. H., Drugs and the heart—IV antiarrhythmic agents, *Lancet*, 861–8, 1980.

2009. Otto, G., Ludewig, R. and Kotzschke, H. J., Specific action of local phenytoin application on periodontal disease, *Stomatol. DDR*, 27: 262–8, 1977.

2010. Ozawa, H., Komatsu, K. and Sato, M., Reversal by phenytoin (diphenylhydantoin) of the resting membrane potential of skeletal muscle from genetically dystrophic mice, *J. Pharm. Soc. Japan*, 98(3): 386–9, 1978.

2011. Pace, C. S. and Livingston, E., Ionic basis of phenytoin sodium inhibition of insulin secretion in pancreatic islets, *Diabetes*, 28: 1077–82, 1979.

2012. Palmer, G. C., Jones, D. J., Medina, M. A., Palmer, S. J. and Stavinoha, W. B., Anticonvulsants: action on central adenylate cyclase systems, *Pharmacologist*, 20: 231, 1978.

2013. Palmer, G. C., Jones, D. J., Medina, M. A. and Stavinoha, W. B., Anticonvulsant drug actions on *in vitro* and *in vivo* levels of cyclic AMP in the mouse brain, *Epilepsia*, 20: 95–104, 1979.

2014. Pedley, T. A. and Guilleminault, C., Episodic nocturnal wanderings responsive to anticonvulsant drug therapy, *Ann. Neurol,*, 2(1): 30–5, 1977.

2015. Pelkonen, R., Fogelholm, R. and Nikkila, E. A., Increase in serum cholesterol during phenytoin treatment, *Br. Med. J.*, 85, 1975.

2016. Pendefunda, G., Oprisan, C., Ciobanu, M. and Cozma, V., Clinico-electromyographic considerations on a case of neuromyotonia, *Rev. Roum. Med. (Neurol. Psychiatr.)*, 13(4): 237–45, 1975.

2017. Pento, J. T., Diphenylhydantoin inhibitions of pentagastrin-stimulated calcitonin secretion in the pig, *Horm. Metab. Res.*, 8: 399–401, 1976.

2018. Peppercorn, M. A., Herzog, A. G., Dichter, M. A. and Mayman, C. I., Abdominal epilepsy—a cause of abdominal pain in adults, *JAMA*, 240(22): 2450–51, 1978.

2019. Peraino, C., Fry, R. J. M., Staffeldt, E. and Christopher, J. P., Comparative enhancing effects of phenobarbital, amobarbital, diphenylhydantoin, and dichlorodiphenyltrichloroethane on 2-acetylaminofluorene-induced hepatic tumorigenesis in the rat, *Cancer Res.*, 35: 2884–90, Oct. 1975.

2020. Perucca, E. and Richens, A., Water intoxication produced by carbamazepine and its reversal by phenytoin, *Br. J. Clin. Pharmacol.*, 9: 302–4P, 1980.

2021. Perry, J. G., McKinney, L. and DeWeer, P., The cellular mode of action of the anti-epileptic drug 5,5-diphenylhydantoin, *Nature*, 272: 271–3, 1978.

2022. Petrack, B., Czernik, A. J., Itterly, W., Ansell, J. and Chertock, H., On the suppression of insulin and glucagon released by diphenylhydantoin, *Diabetes*, 25, Suppl. 1: 380, 1976.

2023. Pincus, J. H., Yaari, Y. and Argov, Z., Phenytoin: electrophysiological effects at the neuromuscular junction, *Antiepileptic Drugs: Mechanisms of Action*, 363–76, Glaser, G. H., Penry, J. K. and Woodbury, D. M., Eds., Raven Press, New York, 1980.

2024. Pollen, D. A., Responses of single neurons to electrical stimulation of the surface of the visual cortex, *Brain Behav. Evol.*, 14: 67–86, 1977.

2025. Porras, C., Barboza, J. J., Fuenzalida, E., Adaros, H. L., de Diaz, A. M. O. and Furst, J., Recovery from rabies in man, *Ann. Int. Med.*, 85: 44–48, 1976.

2026. Prchal, V. and Smythies, J. R., Temporal-lobe epilepsy presenting as fugue state, *Lancet*, 1034, 1977.

2027. Pull, I. and McIlwain, H., Centrally-acting drugs and related compounds examined for action on output of adenine derivatives from superfused tissues of the brain, *Biochem. Pharmacol.*, 25: 293–7, 1976.

2028. Pulsinelli, W. A. and Rottenberg, D. A., Painful tic convulsif, *J. Neurol. Neurosurg. and Psychiat.*, 40(2): 192–5, 1977.

2029. Racy, A., Osborn, M. A., Vern, B. A. and Molinari, G. F., Epileptic aphasia, *Arch. Neurol.*, 37: 419–22, 1980.

2030. Raines, A., Phenytoin revisited, *Epilepsia*, 18(3): 297–8, 1977.

2031. Raines, A., Cohan, S. L., Panagakos, J. and Armitage, P., Utility of chlorpromazine (CPZ) and phenytoin (PH) in spasticity, *Pharmacologist*, 21(3): 183, 1979.

2032. Raines, A. and Niner, J. M., Blockade of a sympathetic nervous system reflex by diphenylhydantoin, *Neuropharmacology*, 14: 61–66, 1975.

2033. Ramsay, R. E., Wilder, B. J., Willmore, L. J. and Perchalski, R. J., Central nervous system penetration of anticonvulsant drugs, *Abstract of Amer. Epilepsy Soc. Ann. Meeting*, 1976.

2034. Rapport, R. L. and Ojemann, G. A., Prophylactically administered phenytoin, *Arch. Neurol.*, 32(8): 539–48, 1975.

2035. Rapport, R. L. and Penry, J. K., A survey of attitudes toward the pharmacological prophylaxis of posttraumatic epilepsy, *J. Neurosurg.*, 38: 159–166, 1973.

2036. Raskin, N. H. and Fishman, R. A., Neurologic disorders in renal failure, *New England Journal of Medicine*, 294(3): 143–8, 1976.

2037. Rau, J. H. and Green, R. S., Compulsive eating: a neuropsychologic approach to certain eating disorders, *Compr. Psychiat.*, 16: 223–31, 1975.

2038. Rau, J. H. and Green, R. S., Soft neurological correlates of compulsive eaters, *J. Nerv. Ment. Dis.*, 166(6): 435–7, 1978.

2039. Ravindran, M., Focal cerebral dysrhythmia—presenting as headache: report of a case, *Clin. Electroencephalogr.*, 9(1): 29–31, 1978.

2040. Reeback, J., Benton, S., Swash, M. and Schwartz, M. S., Penicillamine-induced neuromyotonia, *Br. Med. J.*, 1464–5, 1979.

2041. Reidenberg, M. M., Drug metabolism in uremia, *Clin. Nephrol.*, 4(3): 83–5, 1975.

2042. Reith, H., Availability of phenytoin infusion concentrate, *Drug Intell. Clin. Pharm*, 13(12): 783, 1979.

2043. Reynolds, E. H., Chronic antiepileptic toxicity: a review, *Epilepsia*, 16: 319–52, 1975.

2044. Reynolds, F., Ziroyanis, P. M., Jones, N. F. and Smith, S. E., Salivary phenytoin concentrations in epilepsy and in chronic renal failure, *Lancet*, 384–6, 1976.

2045. Richelson, E. and Tuttle, J. B., Diphenylhydantoin inhibits ionic excitation of mouse neuroblastoma cells, *Brain Res.*, 99: 209–12, 1975.

2046. Riddle, T. G., Mandel, L. J., Goldner, M. M., Dilantin-calcium interaction and active Na transport in frog skin, *Europ. J. Pharmacol.*, 33: 189–92, 1975.

2047. Riley, T. L. and Massey, E. W., The syndrome of aphasia, headaches, and left temporal spikes, *Headache*, 20(2): 90–2, 1978.

2048. Roberts, J. and Goldberg, P. B., Changes in responsiveness of the heart to drugs during aging, *Fed. Proc.*, 38(5): 1927–32, 1979.

2049. Robertson, S., Gibbs, M. E. and Ng, K. T., Sodium pump activity, amino acid transport and long-term memory, *Brain Res. Bull.*, 3(1): 53–8, 1978.

2050. Rogers, H. J., Haslam, R. A., Longstreth, J. and Lietman, P. S., Phenytoin intoxication during concurrent diazepam therapy, *J. Neurol. Neurosurg. Psychiatry*, 40: 890–5, 1977.

2051. Rootwelt, K., Ganes, T. and Johannessen, S. I., Effect of carbamazepine, phenytoin and phenobarbitone on serum levels of thyroid hormones and thyrotropin in humans, *Scand. J. Clin. Lab. Invest.*, 38: 731–6, 1978.

2052. Rose, J. Q., Choi, H. K., Schentag, J. J., Krinkel, W. R.

and Jusko, W. J., Intoxication caused by interaction of chloramphenicol and phenytoin, *JAMA*, 237(24): 2630–1, 1977.

2053. Rose, M. and Johnson, I., Reinterpretation of the haematological effects of anticonvulsant treatment, *Lancet*, 1349–50, 1978.

2054. Rosen, M., Danilo, P., Alonso, M. and Pippenger, C., Effects of diphenylhydantoin on the electrophysiologic properties of blood-superfused Purkinje fibers, *Fed. Proc.*, 34: 755 (Abstr. 3154), March 1975.

2055. Rosen, M. R., Danilo, P., Alonso, M. and Pippenger, C. E., Effects of therapeutic concentrations of diphenylhydantoin on transmembrane potentials of normal and depressed Purkinje fibers, *J. Pharmacol. Exp. Ther.*, 197(3): 594–604, 1976.

2056. Rosenblatt, S., Schaeffer, D. and Rosenthal, J. S., Effects of diphenylhydantoin on child-abusing parents, *Curr. Ther. Res.*, 19(3): 332–6, 1976.

2057. Roses, A. D., Butterfield, D. A., Appel, S. H. and Chestnut, D. B., Phenytoin and membrane fluidity in myotonic dystrophy, *Arch. Neurol.*, 32 (8): 535–38, 1975.

2058. Rotmensch, H. H., Graff, E., Ayzenberg, O., Amir, C. and Laniado, S., Self-poisoning with digitalis glycosides—successful treatment of three cases, *Israel J. Med. Sci.*, 13: 1109–13, 1977.

2059. Rowell, F. J. and Paxton, J. W., Conformational and chemical requirements for antibody recognition of diphenylhydantoin derivatives, *Immunochem.*, 13: 891–4, 1976.

2060. Runge, M. and Rehpenning, W., Behaviour of salivary electrolytes potassium and calcium in digitalized patients after administration of diphenylhydantoin, *Arzneim-Forsch*, 24(10): 1696–9, 1974.

2061. Ruskin, J. N., Garan, H., Silver, T. S. and Powell, W. J., CNS-mediated effect of phenytoin in delaying the onset of digoxin-induced ventricular arrhythmias, *Clin. Res.*, 26(3): 267, April 1975.

2062. Saad, S. F., Osman, O. H., Mustafa, A. and Hussein, K. J., Possible involvement of gamma-aminobutyric acid in morphine abstinence in rats, *IRCS Med. Sci.*, 5(7): 317, 1977.

2063. Sabai, Y., Kobayashi, K. and Iwata, M., Effects of an anabolic steroid and vitamin B complex upon myopathy induced by corticosteroids, *European J. Pharmacol.*, 52: 353–9, 1978.

2064. Sansom, L. N., O'Reilly, W. J., Wiseman, C. W., et al., Plasma phenytoin levels produced by various phenytoin preparations, *Epilepsy Abstracts*, 97: 249, 1976.

2065. Sastry, B. S. R. and Phillis, J. W., Antagonism of glutamate and acetylcholine excitation of rat cerebral cortical neurones by diphenylhydantoin, *Gen. Pharmac.*, 7: 411–13, 1976.

2066. Sawaya, M. C. B., Horton, R. W. and Meldrum, B. S., Effects of anticonvulsant drugs on the cerebral enzymes metabolizing GABA, *Epilepsia*, 16: 649–55, 1975.

2067. Schlosser, W., Franco, S. and Sigg, E. B., Differential attenuation of somatovisceral and viscerosomatic reflexes by diazepam, phenobarbital and diphenylhydantoin, *Neuropharmacol.*, 14: 525–31, 1975.

2068. Schmitz, I., Janzik, H. H. and Mayer, K., The personality structure and sexual behavior of patients with epilepsy on long-term therapy with diphenylhydantoin, *Epilepsia*, 16: 412–3, 1975.

2069. Schneider, R. R., Bahler, A., Pincus, J. and Stimmel, B., Asymptomatic idiopathic syndrome of prolonged Q-T interval in a 45-year-old woman, *Chest*, 71: 210–3, 1977.

2070. Schwartz, P. A., Rhodes, C. T. and Cooper, J. W., Solubility and ionization characteristics of phenytoin, *J. Pharm. Sci.*, 66(7): 994–7, 1977.

2071. Schwartz, P. J., Periti, M. and Malliani, A., The long Q-T syndrome, *Am. Heart J.*, 89(3): 378–90, 1975.

2072. Schwarz, J. R. and Vogel, W., Diphenylhydantoin: excitability reducing action in single myelinated nerve fibres, *European J. Pharmacol.*, 44: 241–9, 1977.

2073. Selzer, M. E., The action of phenytoin on a composite electrical-chemical synapse in the lamprey spinal cord, *Ann. Neurol.*, 3(3): 202–6, 1978.

2074. Selzer, M. E., The effect of phenytoin on the action potential of a vertebrate spinal neuron, *Brain Research*, 171: 511–21, 1979.

2075. Selzer, M. E., Phenytoin blocks post-tetanic potentiation at a vertebrate CNS synapse, *Trans. Am. Neurological Assoc.*, 102: 118–20, 1977.

2076. Shah, U. H., Jindal, M. N. and Patel, V. K., Beta-adrenoceptor blockade with diphenylhydantoin (DPH), *Arzneim-Forsch*, 27: 2316–8, 1977.

2077. Shealy, C. N., Drug use in a pain rehabilitation center, *Am. J. Hosp. Pharm.*, 32: 1083, 1975.

2078. Sherwin, A. L., Harvey, C. D., Leppik, I. E. and Gonda, A., Correlation between red cell and free plasma phenytoin levels in renal disease, *Neurol.*, 26: 874–8, 1976.

2079. Sheth, K. J. and Bernhard, G. C., The arthropathy of Fabry disease, *Arthritis Rheum.*, 22(7): 781–3, 1979.

2080. Shintomi, K., Effects of psychotropic drugs on methamphetamine-induced behavioral excitation in grouped mice, *Europ. J. Pharmacol.*, 31: 195–206, 1975.

2081. Silverman, H., Atwood, H. L. and Bloom, J. W., Phenytoin application in murine muscular dystrophy; behavioral improvement with no change in the abnormal intracellular Na : K ratio in skeletal muscles, *Exp. Neurol.*, 62: 618–27, 1978.

2082. Singh, B. N., Gaarder, T. D., Kanegae, T., Goldstein, M., Montgomerie, J. Z. and Mills, H., Liquid protein diets and *torsade de pointes*, *JAMA*, 240(2): 115–9, 1978.

2083. Sirohiya, M. K., Bhatnagar, H. N. S., Shah, D. R. and Narang, N. K., Phenytoin sodium in cardiac arrhythmias, *J. Indian Med. Assoc.*, 64(12): 329–34, 1975.

2084. Smith, I. M. and Burmeister, L. F., Biochemically assisted antibiotic treatment of lethal murine staphylococcus aureus septic shock, *Am. J. Clin. Nutr.*, 30: 1364–8, 1977.

2085. Sneer, A., Colev, V., Dughir, E. and Sneer, I., The protective effect of diphenylhydantoin on the diabetogenic action of alloxan, *Epilepsy Abstracts*, 12(9): 421, 1979.

2086. Snider, S. R. and Snider, R. S., Phenytoin and cerebellar lesions: similar effects on cerebellar catecholamine metabolism, *Arch. Neurol.*, 34: 162–7, 1977.

2087. Sohn, R. S. and Ferrendelli, J. A., Anticonvulsant drug mechanisms, phenytoin, phenobarbital, and ethosuximide and calcium flux in isolated presynaptic endings, *Arch. Neurol.*, 33: 626–9, 1976.

2088. Somerman, M. J., Au, W. Y. W. and Rifkin, B. R., Phenytoin inhibition of bone resorption in organ culture, *J. Dent. Res.*, 56 (Special Issue B) Abstr. 579, 1977.

2089. Sordillo, P., Sagransky, D. M., Mercado, R. and Michelis, M. F., Carbamazepine-induced syndrome of inappropriate antidiuretic hormone secretion—reversal by concomitant phenytoin therapy, *Arch. Intern. Med.*, 138: 299–301, 1978.

2090. Starkova, N. T., Marova, E. I., Lemesheva, S. N., Goncharova, V. N., Atamanova, T. M. and Sedykh, L. P., The effect of diphenin on functional condition of the adrenal cortex in patients with Itsenko-Cushing disease, *Problemy Endokrinologii*, 18: 35–8, Nov/Dec, 1972.

2091. Stavchansky, S. A., Tilbury, R. S., McDonald, J. M., Ting, C. T. and Kostenbauder, H. B., *In vivo* distribution of carbon-11 phenytoin and its major metabolite, and their use in scintigraphic imaging, *J. Nucl. Med.*, 19(8): 936–41, 1978.

2092. St. Louis, E. L., McLoughlin, M. J. and Wortzman, G., Chronic damage to medium and large arteries following irradiation, *J. Canad. Assoc. Radiol.*, 25: 94–104, 1974.

2093. Study, R. E., Phenytoin inhibition of cyclic guanosine 3':5'-monophosphate (cGMP) accumulation in neuroblastoma cells by calcium channel blockade, *J. Pharmacol. Exp. Ther.*, 215(3): 575–81, 1980.

2094. Suratt, P. M., Crampton, R. S. and Carpenter, M. A., Benign familial biventricular dysrhythmias with syncope limited to late childhood, adolescence and early youth, *Circulation*, 48 (Suppl. IV): 222, 1973.

2095. Swann, W. P., Swenson, H. M. and Shafer, W. G., Effects of Dilantin on the repair of gingival wounds, *J. Periodont.*, 46(5): 302–5, 1975.

2096. Swanson, J. W. and Vick, N. A., Basilar artery migraine, *Neurology*, 28: 782–6, 1978.

2097. Swerdlow, M., The treatment of 'shooting' pain, *Postgrad. Med. J.*, 56: 159–61, 1980.

2098. Swanson, P. D. and Crane, P. O., Diphenylhydantoin and movement of radioactive sodium into electrically stimulated cerebral slices. *Biochem. Pharmacol.*, 21: 2899–905, 1972.

2099. Swift, T. R., Gross, J. A., Ward, L. C. and Flicek, B. O., Electrophysiologic study of patients receiving anticonvulsant drugs, *Neurology*, 29: 581, 1979.

2100. Szyper, M. S. and Mann, J. D., Anorexia nervosa as an interictal symptom of partial complex seizures, *Neurology*, 28(4): 335, 1978.

2101. Tanay, A., Yust, I., Peresecenschi, G., Abramov, A. L. and Avriam, A., Long-term treatment of the syndrome of inappropriate antidiuretic hormone secretion with phenytoin, *Ann. Intern. Med.*, 90: 50–2, 1979.

2102. Taylor, P. H., Gray, K., Bicknell, P. G. and Rees, J. R., Glossopharyngeal neuralgia with syncope, *J. Laryngol. Otol.*, 91: 859–68, 1977.

2103. Thampi, N. S., Mader, M. M. and Earley, R. J., Effect of diphenylhydantoin on levels of cyclic AMP and cyclic GMP in rat brain synaptasomes, *Pharmacologist*, 16: Abstr. 551, Fall, 1974.

2104. Tuttle, J. B., Intracellular recordings from a clonal, tissue-cultured neuron: bioelectric differentiation of anti-metabolite survivors and the action of diphenylhydantoin, *Dissertation Abstracts International*, Section B,38: 91B–92B, 1977.

2105. Tuttle, J. B. and Richelson, E., Phenytoin action on the excitable membrane of mouse neuroblastoma, *J. Pharmacol. Exp. Ther.*, 2(3): 632–7, 1979.

2106. Tyler, G. S., McNeely, H. E. and Dick, M. L., Vascular headache treatment update, *Arizona Med.*, 36: 117–8, 1979.

2107. Vernillo, A. T. and Schwartz, N. B., Collagen and proteoglycan synthesis in 5,5 diphenylhydantoin (Dilantin) treated chondrocytes, *J. Cell. Biol.*, 83(pt. 2): 116a, 1979.

2108. Vincent, T. S., When to use Dilantin in alcoholism, *Resident and Staff Physician*, 22: 50–1, 1976.

2109. von Albert, H. H., Treatment of acute trigeminal neuralgia with intravenous infusions of phenytoin, *Munch. Med. Wsch.*, 120(15): 529–30, 1978.

2110. Wadell, M. C. and Chambers, D. A., Effect of diphenylhydantoin on the cell cycle of a serum free mouse symphocyte system, *Fed. Proc.*, 35(3): 749, March, 1976.

2111. Waller, D. A., Paroxysmal kinesigenic choreoathetosis or hysteria? *Am. J. Psychiat.*, 134(12): 1439–40, 1977.

2112. Walson, P., Trinca, C. and Bressler, R., New uses for phenytoin, *JAMA*, 233(13): 1385–9, 1975.

2113. Walton, J. N., Muscular dystrophies and their management, *Br. Med. J.*, 3(671): 639–42, 1969.

2114. Wasserman, T. H., Phillips, T. L., Van Raalte, G., Urtasun, R., Partington, J., Koziol, D., Schwade, J. G., Gangji, D. and Strong, J. M., The neurotoxicity of misonidazole: potential modifying role by phenytoin sodium and dexamethasone, *Br. J. Radiol.*, 53: 172–3, 1980.

2115. Weinberger, J., Nicklas, W. J. and Berl, S., Mechanism of action of anticonvulsants, *Neurology* 26: 162–166, 1976.

2116. Weiss, T. and Levitz, L., Diphenylhydantoin treatment of bulimia, *Am. J. Psychiatry*, 133(9): 1093, 1976.

2117. Wermuth, B. M., Davis, L. K., Hollister, L. E. and Stunkard, A. J., Phenytoin treatment of the binge-eating syndrome, *Am. J. Psychiat.*, 134(11): 1249–53, 1977.

2118. Wilson, J. T., Huff, J. G. and Kilroy, A. W., Brief clinical and laboratory observations, *J. Pediatr.*, 95(1): 135–8, 1979.

2119. White, R. A. S. and Workman, P., Phenytoin sodium-induced alterations in the pharmacokinetics of misonidazole in the dog, *Cancer Treat. Rep.*, 64: 360–1, 1980.

2120. Wit, A. L., Rosen, M. R. and Hoffman, B. F., Electrophysiology and pharmacology of cardiac arrhythmias, VIII. Cardiac effects of diphenylhydantoin Part A., *Am. Heart J.*, 90(3): 265–72, 1975.

2121. Wit, A. L., Rosen, M. R. and Hoffman, B. F., Electrophysiology and pharmacology of cardiac arrhythmias. VIII. Cardiac effects of diphenylhydantoin Part B., *Am. Heart J.*, 90(3): 397–404, 1975.

2122. Wohns, R. N. W. and Wyler, A. R., Prophylactic phenytoin in severe head injuries, *J. Neurosurg.*, 51: 507–8, 1979.

2123. Wolfe, G. W. and Schnell, R. C., Protection against alloxan-induced alterations in hepatic drug metabolism and plasma glucose levels in the male rat, *Toxicol. App. Pharmacol.*, 48(Pt 2): A69, 1979.

2124. Wolter, M. and Brauer, D., Neuromyotonia syndrome, *Fortschr. Neurol. Psychiat.*, 45: 98–105, 1977.

2125. Woo, E. and Greenblatt, D. J., Choosing the right phenytoin dosage, *Drug Therapy (Hospital Edition)*, 2: 35–41, Oct. 1977.

2126. Woodbury, D. M., Phenytoin: introduction and history, *Antiepileptic Drugs: Mechanisms of Action*, 305–13, Glaser, G. H., Penry, J. K. and Woodbury, D. M., Eds., Raven Press, New York, 1980.

2127. Woodbury, D. M., Phenytoin: Proposed mechanisms of anticonvulsant action, *Antiepileptic Drugs: Mechanisms of Action*, 447–71, Glaser, G. H., Penry, J. K. and Woodbury, D. M., Eds., Raven Press, New York, 1980.

2128. Workman, P., Effects of pretreatment with phenobarbitone and phenytoin on the pharmacokinetics and toxicity of misonidazole in mice, *Br. J. Cancer*, 40: 335–53, 1979.

2129. Workman, P., Bleehen, N. M. and Wiltshire, C. R., Phenytoin shortens the half-life of the hypoxic cell radiosensitizer misonidazole in man: implications for possible reduced toxicity, *Br. J. Cancer*, 41: 302–4, 1980.

2130. Yaari, Y., Pincus, J. H. and Argov, Z., Inhibition of synaptic transmission by phenytoin, *Arch. Neurol.*, 33: 391, 1976.

2131. Yaari, Y., Rahamemoff, H. and Pincus, J. H., Action of diphenylhydantoin at the frog neuromuscular junction, *Israel J. Med. Sci.*, 12(2): 171–2, 1976.

2132. York, G. K., Gabor, A. J. and Dreyfus, P. M., Paroxysmal genital pain: an unusual manifestation of epilepsy, *Neurology*, 29: 516–9, 1979.

2133. Yeh, J. Z., Quandt, F. N. and Kirsch, G. E., Comparative studies of phenytoin action on ionic channels in excitable membranes, *Fed. Proc.*, 40(3): 240, 1981.

2134. Young, B., Rapp, R., Brooks, W. H., Madauss, W. and Norton, J. A., Posttraumatic epilepsy prophylaxis, *Epilepsia*, 20: 671–81, 1979.

2135. Young, R. F., Facial pain, *The Practitioner*, 219: 731–7, 1977.

2136. Younglove, R. H., Newman, R. L. and Wall, L. A., Medical management of the unstable bladder, *J. Reprod. Med.*, 24: 215–8, 1980.

2137. Zenteno Vacheron, J. S., Carrasco Zanini, J. and Ramos Ramirez, R., Paroxysmal dystonic choreoathetosis. A form of reflex epilepsy (two sporadic cases), *Epilepsy Abstracts*, 10(3): 84, 1977.

2138. Zhiping, Q., Chuanzhen, L., Iiyun, Y., Hanbai, C. and Yue, D., Limb-pain epilepsy—report of 9 cases, *Chin. Med. J.*, 93(4): 265–8, 1980.

2139. Ziegler, B., Hahn, H. J., Ziegler, M. and Fiedler, H., Successful cultivation of isolated islets of Langerhans without attachment: relationship between glucose- and theophylline-induced insulin release and insulin content in rat islets after cultivation, *Endocrinologie*, 69(1): 103–11, 1977.

2140. Zweibel, P. C., Insulinoma: review of seven cases at the Mount Sinai Hospital in light of the current literature, *Mount Sinai J. Med.*, 43(5): 637–56, 1976.

INDEX TO CLINICAL AND BASIC SCIENCE INFORMATION

Page numbers that appear in *italics* refer to laboratory information—
all other page numbers refer to clinical information.